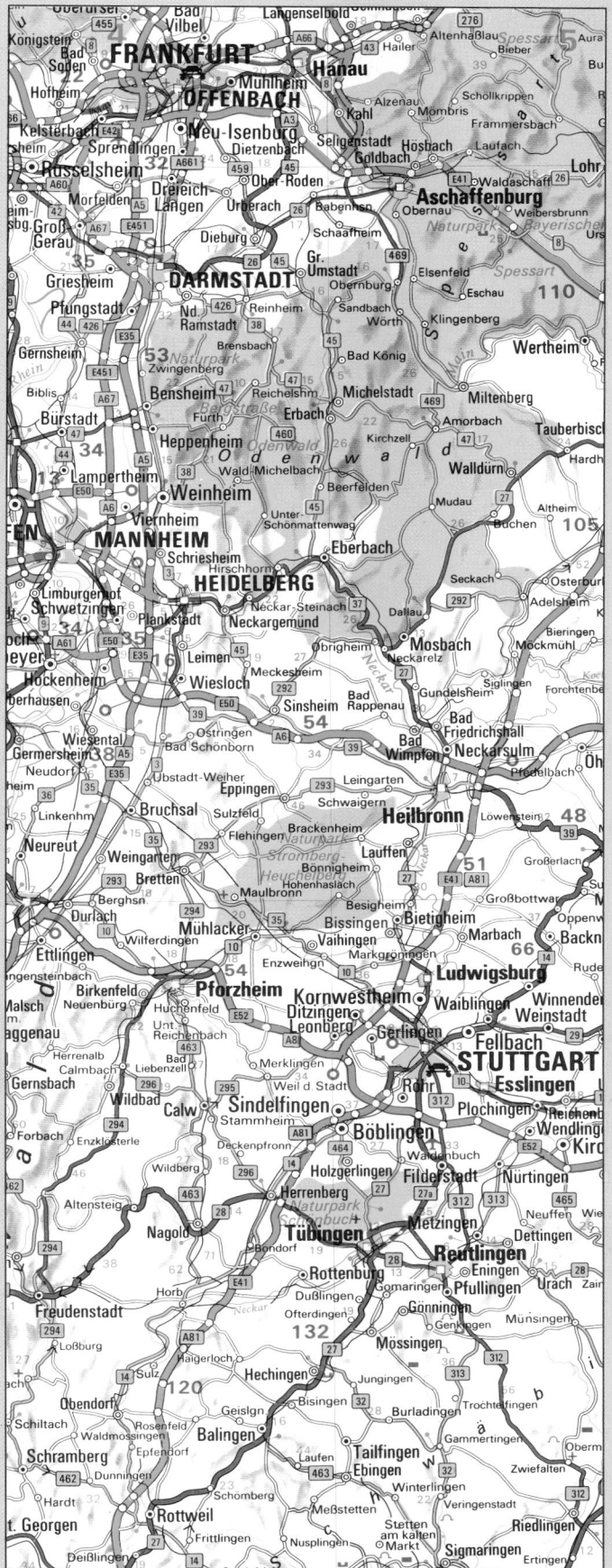

Map scales

Road maps: *16 miles to 1 inch, 1: 1 000 000*

Road maps of Eastern Europe: *63 miles to 1 inch, 1: 4 000 000*

Route planner: *71 miles to 1 inch, 1: 4 500 000*

50p.

NK
REF

MOTORING ATLAS
Europe

GW00697427

Contents

First published in 1991 by

George Philip Ltd
an imprint of Reed Books
Michelin House, 81 Fulham Road, London SW3 6RB
and Auckland and Melbourne

Sixth edition 1997
First impression 1997

Suffolk County Council
Libraries & Heritage
WITHDRAWN
FS   02.98

...vate study, research, criticism or
...988, no part of this publication may be
...for by any means, electronic, electrical,
...e, without prior written permission.

...was correct at the time of going to
...equences.

...ence of the existence of a right of way.
...on of the Controller of

Cartography by Philip's

Copyright © 1997 George Philip Ltd.

Printed and bound in Spain by Cayfosa

30127 05045594 3

Road map symbols

	Motorway with Junction		International Boundary
	Motorway Under Construction		Inter-entity Boundary (as agreed in the 1995 Dayton Peace Accord)
	Principal Trunk Highway		Ski Lift/Funicular
	Other Main Highway		Car Ferry
	Road Under Construction		Motorail
	Other Important Road		Major Airport
	Other Road		Castle
	Unsurfaced Road		Monastery/Cathedral
E25	European Road Number		Ancient Monument
411	National Road Number		Cave
	Toll Road		Other Place of Interest
	Steep Hill (arrow points downhill)		Beach
96	Distances (in kms)		Ski Resort
	Mountain Pass		National Park

Country index

Key to road map pages

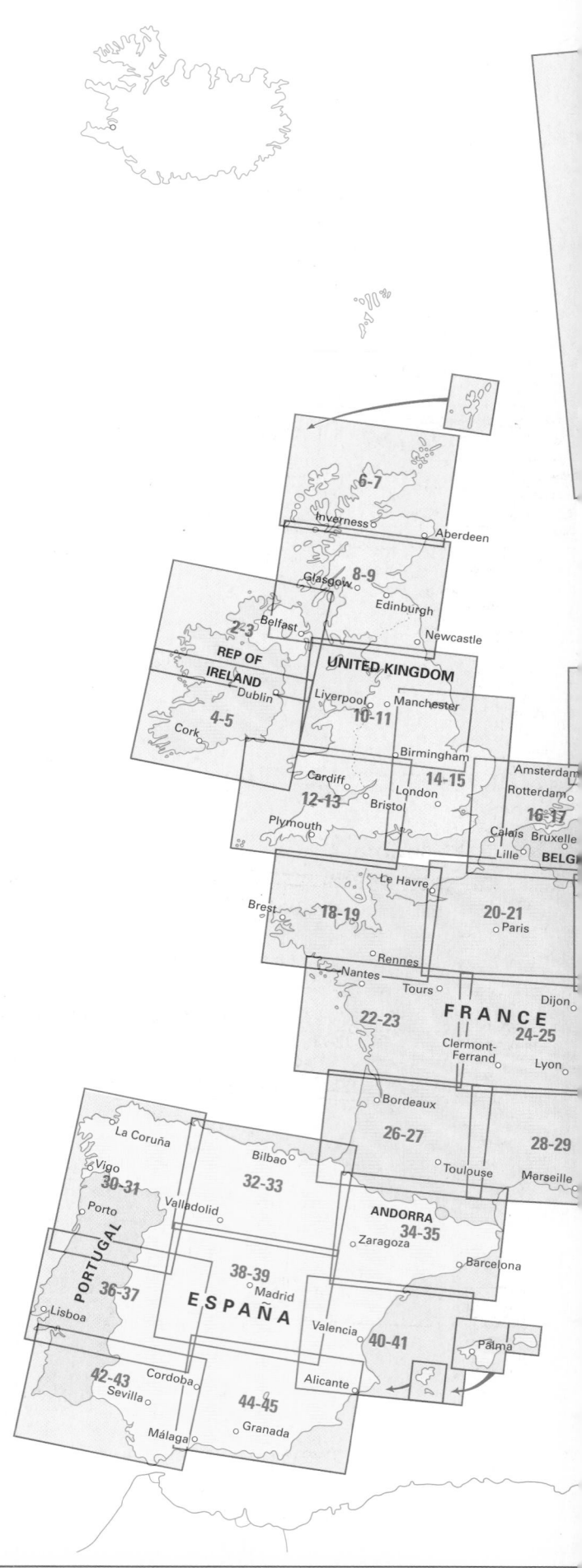

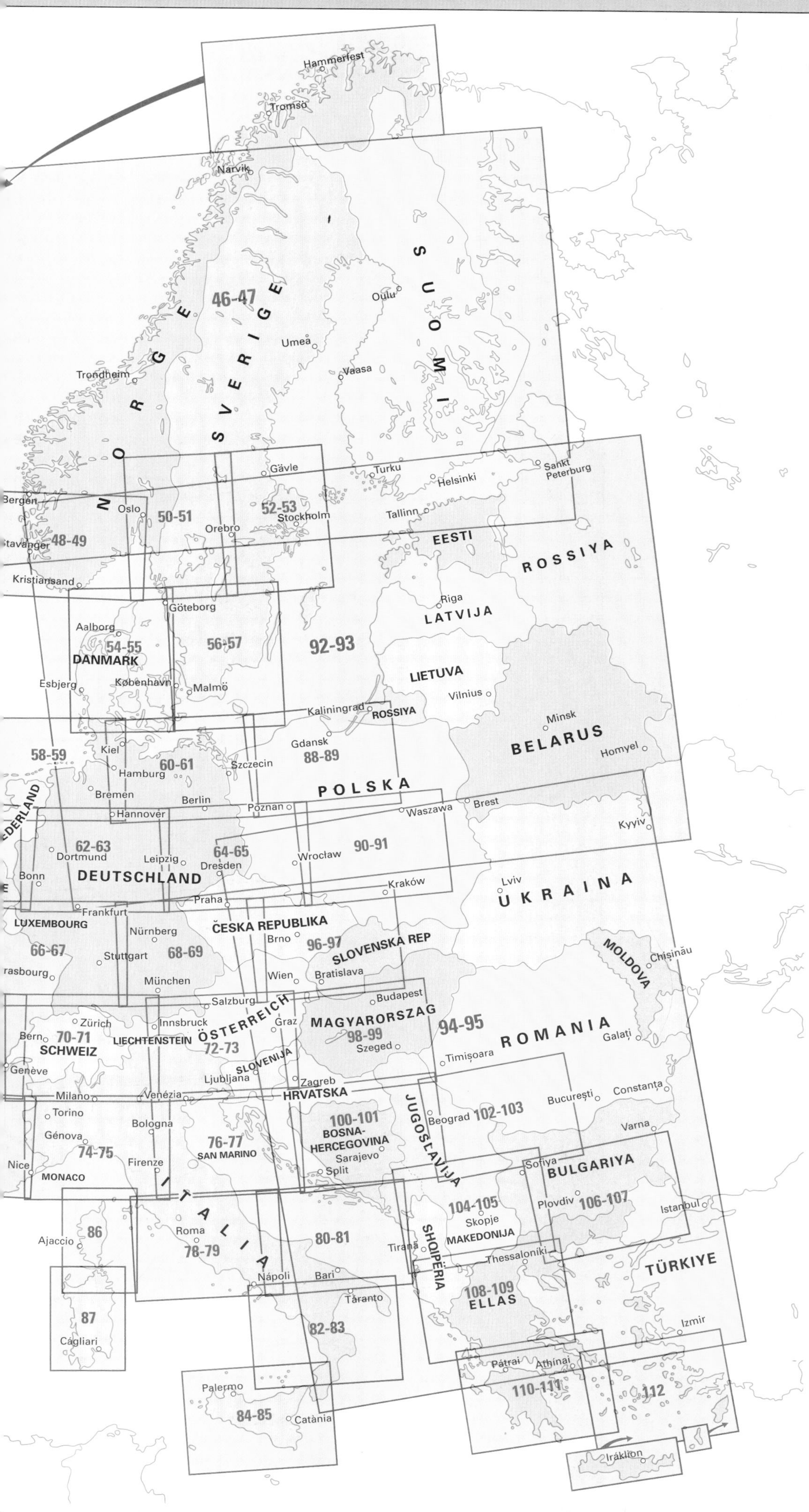
Hammerfest
Tromsø
Narvik
46-47
NORGE
SVERIGE
SUOMI
Oulu
Umeå
Vaasa
Trondheim
Gävle
Turku
Helsinki
Sankt Peterburg
Bergen
Oslo
50-51
52-53
Stockholm
Tallinn
Orebro
Stavanger
48-49
EESTI
ROSSIYA
Kristiansand
Riga
LATVIJA
Göteborg
Aalborg
54-55
DANMARK
56-57
92-93
LIETUVA
Esbjerg
København
Malmö
Vilnius
Kaliningrad
ROSSIYA
Minsk
BELARUS
Gdansk
88-89
58-59
Kiel
60-61
Hamburg
Szczecin
Homyel
Bremen
Berlin
POLSKA
Hannover
Poznan
Waszawa
Brest
Kyyiv
62-63
Dortmund
Leipzig
Dresden
64-65
Wrocław
90-91
Bonn
DEUTSCHLAND
Kraków
Lviv
UKRAINA
Frankfurt
Praha
LUXEMBOURG
Nürnberg
ČESKA REPUBLIKA
Brno
96-97
SLOVENSKA REP
MOLDOVA
Chişinău
66-67
Stuttgart
68-69
Wien
Bratislava
München
Salzburg
Budapest
Zürich
Innsbruck
ÖSTERREICH
Graz
MAGYARORSZAG
94-95
Bern
70-71
SCHWEIZ
LIECHTENSTEIN
72-73
98-99
Szeged
ROMANIA
Galaţi
Genève
SLOVENIJA
Ljubljana
Timişoara
Zagreb
Milano
Venézia
HRVATSKA
Bucureşti
Constanţa
Torino
Bologna
100-101
BOSNA-HERCEGOVINA
JUGOSLAVIJA
Beograd
102-103
Varna
Génova
76-77
SAN MARINO
Sarajevo
74-75
Firenze
Split
Sofiya
BULGARIYA
Nice
MONACO
104-105
Skopje
MAKEDONIJA
Plovdiv
106-107
Istanbul
Ajaccio
86
ITALIA
Roma
78-79
80-81
Tirana
SHQIPËRIA
Thessaloniki
TÜRKIYE
Nápoli
Bari
Taranto
108-109
ELLAS
87
Cágliari
82-83
Izmir
Pátrai
Athínai
Palermo
84-85
Catania
110-111
112
Iráklion

City plans

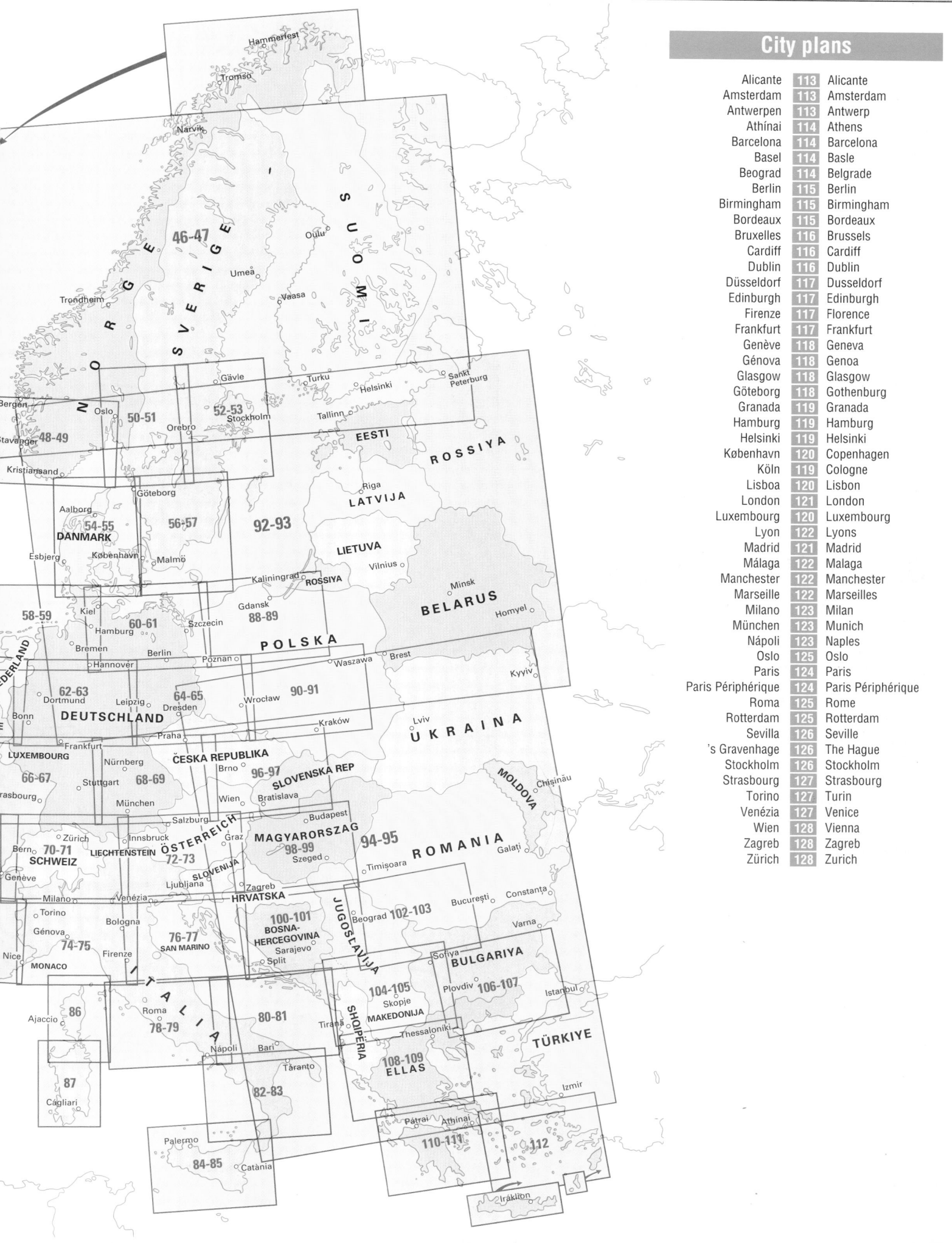

IV DISTANCE TABLE

* By ferry

Kilometres

	Amsterdam	Athínai	Barcelona	Basel	Beograd	Berlin	Bordeaux	Brindisi	Bruxelles	Bucuresti	Budapest	Calais	Cherbourg	Dover	Edinburgh	Frankfurt	Genève	Genova	Gibraltar	Hamburg	Helsinki	Istanbul	København	Köln
Amsterdam		1840	940	457	1130	406	686	1305	123	1403	887	229	465	229*	683*	275	565	769	1571	279	975*	1722	473	160
Athínai	2945		1995	1561	710	1507	2019	132*	1809	761	956	1937	2036	1937*	2391*	1561	1572	1431	2734	1699	1574*	714	1738*	1677
Barcelona	1505	3192		649	1285	1164	375	1225	812	1641	1241	788	775	788*	1238*	815	468	559	734	1105	1451*	1856	1297*	854
Basel	732	2499	1039		855	538	574	848	334	1181	665	449	531	449*	903*	206	163	311	1387	509	829*	1447	715*	320
Beograd	1809	1136	2056	1369		797	1310	362*	1099	388	246	1227	1327	1227*	1681*	854	862	712	2015	989	871*	591	1028*	970
Berlin	650	2412	1863	861	1276		1018	1218	477	1066	551	587	819	587*	1060*	343	695	753	1903	178	295*	1389	231*	353
Bordeaux	1099	3231	601	919	2095	1630		1283	564	1698	1275	518	405	518*	966*	726	440	639	879	909	1307*	1889	1102*	664
Brindisi	2089	542*	1990	1357	580*	1950	2053		1176	1415	1008	1289	1365	1289*	1740*	1047	839	676	1958	1317	1353*	679*	1510*	1162
Bruxelles	197	2895	1308	535	1759	764	902	1894		1354	843	133	339	133*	584*	237	441	643	1439	349	769*	1680	542*	123
Bucuresti	2245	1219	2644	1890	622	1707	2717	2280	2181		512	1489	1645	1489*	1940*	1120	1243	1103	2388	1250	1139*	428	1289*	1231
Budapest	1420	1530	1999	1065	394	882	2041	1624	1358	852		976	1132	976*	1427*	608	832	693	1968	738	626*	832	777*	719
Calais	367	3100	1269	719	1964	956	830	2076	215	2398	1573		280	*	450*	357	491	736	1394	471	888*	1807	664*	242
Cherbourg	744	3259	1249	850	2122	1311	648	2199	547	2649	1824	452		142*	447*	577	529	774	1281	690	1380*	1905	881*	462
Dover	367*	3150*	1269*	719*	1964*	956*	830*	2076*	215*	2398*	1573*	*	228*		450	357*	491*	736*	1394*	471*	888*	1807*	664*	242*
Edinburgh	1093*	3826*	1995*	1445*	2690*	1696*	1556*	2802*	941*	3124*	2299*	726*	720*	726		732	942*	1187*	1845*	922*	767*	2270*	1115*	617*
Frankfurt	441	2499	1313	330	1367	550	1170	1687	383	1804	979	575	930	575*	1301*		372	514	1550	301	992*	1436	493*	114
Genève	905	2516	754	262	1380	1123	709	1352	710	2002	1340	791	852	791*	1517*	599		245	1202	642	1333*	1437	834*	432
Genova	1231	2291	901	499	1140	1206	1030	1089	1036	1777	1116	1186	1247	1186*	1912*	829	395		1294	785	1476*	1301	977*	629
Gibraltar	2515	4375	1183	2220	3224	3046	1416	3153	2318	3846	3170	2246	2064	2246*	2972*	2496	1937	2084		1788	2480*	2590	1981*	1548
Hamburg	447	2719	1780	815	1583	286	1465	2122	563	2014	1189	760	1120	760*	1486	485	1034	1264	2880		691*	1571	192*	250
Helsinki	1560*	2539*	2338*	1336*	1403*	475*	2105*	2180*	1239*	1834*	1009*	1431*	2223*	1431*	1236*	1598*	2147*	2377*	3994*	1113*		1459*	498*	950*
Istanbul	2756	1145	2990	2316	947	2223	3042	1094*	2706	690	1341	2911	3069	2911*	3657*	2314	2315	2095	4171	2530	2350*		1610*	1551
København	757*	2782*	2090*	1145*	1646*	370*	1775*	2432*	873*	2077*	1252*	1070*	1420*	1070*	479*	795*	1344*	1574*	3191*	310*	803*	2593*		443*
Köln	256	2684	1376	512	1553	566	1070	1872	198	1983	1158	390	745*	390*	1116*	180	696	1014	2493	404	1517*	2499	714*	
Lisboa	2331	4460	1268	2158	3295	2869	1239	3213	3141	3917	3222	2069	1887	2069*	2795*	2400	2022	2169	659	2700	3817*	4342	3014*	2339
London	480*	3200*	1387*	837*	2064*	1074*	948*	2194*	333*	2591*	1766*	118*	112*	118	608	693*	909*	1304*	2364*	878*	1991*	3107*	1188*	508*
Luxembourg	406	2661	1190	326	1525	749	930	1683	209	2052	1227	424	693	424*	1150*	240	510	825	2349	590	1703*	2472	900*	186
Madrid	1790	3809	617	1617	2640	2364	698	2601	1600	3262	2622	1528	1346	1528*	2254*	1930	1371	1518	718	2160	3276*	3589	2473*	1798
Marseille	1210	2683	509	680	1532	1541	652	1481	1030	2154	1505	1063	1124	1063*	1789*	1023	423	392	1692	1412	2525*	2479	1722*	1006
Milano	1085	2182	1038	353	1046	1060	1049	1004	890	1668	992	1072	1195	1072*	1798*	683	348	146	2230	1118	1535*	1993	1428*	868
München	839	2106	1340	393	970	594	1295	1370	789	1497	672	994	1152	994*	1720*	398	586	589	2523	765	1069*	1907	969*	580
Napoli	1908	930*	1602	1176	1503*	1719	1720	388	1715	2125*	1470	1887	1948	1887*	2613*	1506	1096	701	2785	1941	2194*	2451*	2200*	1691
Narvik	2827*	4852*	4160*	3215*	3716*	2440*	3845*	4502*	2943*	4147*	3322*	3140*	3550*	3140*	2178*	2866*	3414*	3644*	5261*	2360*	1289	4569*	2070*	2784*
Nürnberg	670	2270	1471	432	1134	429	1324	1525	616	1565	740	810	1123	810*	1412*	233	694	735	2631	600	904*	2081	799*	415
Oslo	1347*	3372*	2680*	1735*	2236*	960*	2365*	3022*	1463*	2667*	1842*	1660*	2070*	1660*	729*	1385*	1934*	2164*	3781*	900*	697*	3089*	590*	1304*
Paris	510	2917	988	504	1780	1051	582	1850	320	2307	1482	281	342	281*	1007*	591	510	905	1998	899	2012*	2727	1209*	495
Porto	2120	4384	1192	1947	3052	2661	1028	3027	1927	3674	3034	1858	1676	1858*	2584*	2201	1737	1938	979	2490	3603*	3990	2800*	2105
Praha	950	2067	1750	712	931	345	1604	1708	888	1362	537	1097	1403	1090*	1816*	512	974	977	2911	652	770*	1878	715*	690
Roma	1691	1140*	1385	959	1290*	1502	1513	590	1520	1904	1263	1678	1731	1678*	2404*	1289	879	484	2564	1683	1977*	2237*	1993*	1474
Sevilla	2347	4223	1031	2060	3087	2894	1248	2995	2150	3709	3010	2078	1896	2078*	2804*	2344	1785	1932	258	2713	3826*	4034	3023*	2318
Sofiya	2206	828	2453	1766	397	1673	2492	2047	2156	391	790	2361	2519	2361*	3087*	1764	1775	1537	3621	1980	1800*	550	2043*	1949
Stockholm	1393*	3418*	2726*	1780*	2282*	1006*	2411*	2960*	1509*	2713*	1888*	1673*	2056*	1706*	1069*	1431*	1980*	2210*	3827*	946*	167*	3185*	590*	1350*
Strasbourg	631	2461	1130	134	1325	768	998	1523	434	1858	1027	639	798	639*	1365*	219	394	665	2313	704	1817*	2276	1014*	378
Thessaloniki	2410	509	2683	1996	677	1903	2722	458*	2386	710	1021	2591	2749	2591*	3317*	1994	2007	1782	3851	2210	2030*	636	2273*	2179
Valencia	1851	3545	353	1392	2390	2216	824	2313	1661	3012	2360	1654	1472	1645*	2380*	1666	1107	1254	830	2133	2691*	3337	2443*	1720
Venezia	1324	1914	1258	621	778	1079	1316	890	1158	1400	739	1340	1468	1340*	2066*	883	616	377	2460	1250	1253*	1725	1449*	1065
Warszawa	1256	2128	2366	1328	1042	606	2220	2140	1350	1473	648	1542	1969	1542*	2268*	1136	1590	1593	3527	886	361*	1989	956*	1152
Wien	1168	1772	1856	823	633	640	1733	1472	1114	1067	242	1308	1582	1308*	2034*	731	1016	965	3042	947	1088*	1583	1010*	916

Amsterdam Athínai Barcelona Basel Beograd Berlin Bordeaux Brindisi Bruxelles Bucuresti Budapest Calais Cherbourg Dover Edinburgh Frankfurt Genève Genova Gibraltar Hamburg Helsinki Istanbul København Köln

Distances in these tables are based upon Main Routes as far as possible and are not necessarily the shortest distances between any two towns.

Miles

	Lisboa	London	Luxembourg	Madrid	Marseille	Milano	München	Napoli	Narvik	Nürnberg	Oslo	Paris	Porto	Praha	Roma	Sevilla	Sofiya	Stockholm	Strasbourg	Thessaloniki	Valencia	Venezia	Warszawa	Wien
Amsterdam	1447	298*	252	1111	751	673	521	1184	1755*	416	836	316	1316	590	1050	1457	1370	865*	391	1496	1149	822	780	725
Athínai	2769	1987*	1652	2365	1666	1355	1307	577	3013*	1409	2094*	1811	2722	1283	707*	2622	514	2122*	1528	316	2201	1188	1352	1100
Barcelona	787	861*	739	383	316	644	832	994	2583*	913	1664*	613	740	1086	860	640	1523	1692*	701	1666	219	781	1469	1152
Basel	1340	519*	202	1004	422	219	244	730	1996*	268	1077*	313	1209	442	595	1279	1096	1105*	83	1239	864	385	824	511
Beograd	1921	1281*	947	1639	951	649	602	939*	2307*	704	1388*	1105	1895	578	628*	1917	246	1417*	822	389	1484	483	647	395
Berlin	1781	667*	465	1468	957	658	369	1067	1515*	267	596*	653	1652	214	932	1797	1038	624*	477	1181	1376	670	376	397
Bordeaux	769	588*	577	434	405	651	804	1075	2387*	822	1468*	361	638	996	939	775	1547	1497*	620	1690	511	817	1378	1076
Brindisi	1995	1362*	1045	1615	919	623	850	240	2795*	970	1876*	1148	1879	1058	366	1859	1271	1838*	945	284*	1436	552	1328	914
Bruxelles	1329	206*	129	993	639	552	490	1086	1827*	382	908*	198	1195	551	943	1335	1339	937*	269	1481	1031	719	838	691
Bucuresti	2432	1609*	1274	2025	1337	1035	929	1319	2575*	971	1656*	1432	2281	845	1182	2303	243	1684*	1150	440	1870	869	914	662
Budapest	2001	1096*	763	1628	934	616	417	912	2062*	459	1143*	920	1884	333	784	1869	490	1172*	637	634	1465	459	402	150
Calais	1284	73*	263	948	660	665	617	1171	1949*	503	1030*	174	1153	676	1042	1290	1466	1059*	396	1609	1027	832	957	812
Cherbourg	1171	69*	430	835	698	742	715	1209	2204*	697	1285*	212	1040	871	1080	1177	1564	1276*	495	1707	914	911	1222	988
Dover	1284	73	263*	948*	660*	665*	617*	1171*	1949*	503*	1030*	174*	1153*	676*	1042*	1290*	1466	1059*	396*	1609*	1027*	832*	957*	812*
Edinburgh	1735*	377	714*	1399*	1110*	1116*	1068*	1622*	1134	876*	452*	625*	1604*	1127*	1492*	1741*	1917*	663*	847*	2059*	1478*	1282*	1408*	1271*
Frankfurt	1490	430*	149	1198	635	424	247	935	1779*	144	860*	367	1366	317	800	1455	1095	888*	136	1238	1034	548	705	454
Genève	1255	564*	316	851	263	216	364	680	2120*	431	1201*	316	1078	605	542	1108	1102	1229*	244	1246	687	382	987	631
Genova	1346	809*	512	942	243	91	366	435	2262*	456	1343*	562	1203	606	300	1199	954	1372*	413	1106	778	234	989	599
Gibraltar	409	1468*	1458	445	1050	1384	1566	1729	3257*	1633	2348*	1240	607	1807	1604	160	2248	2376*	1438	2391	515	1517	2190	1889
Hamburg	1676	545*	366	1341	876	694	475	1205	1477*	372	558*	558	1546	404	1045	1684	1229	587*	437	1372	1324	776	550	588
Helsinki	2370*	1236*	1037*	2034*	1570*	953*	663*	1362*	800	561*	432*	1249*	2237*	478*	1277*	2375*	1117*	103*	1128*	1260*	1682*	778*	224*	675*
Istanbul	2696	1929*	1535	2228	1539	1237	1190	1522	2837*	1292	1918*	1693	2477	1166	1389*	2505	341	1975*	1413	395	2072	1071	1235	983
København	1871*	737*	558*	1535*	1069*	886*	601*	1366*	1285*	496*	366*	750*	1738*	444*	1237*	1877*	1268*	366*	629*	1411*	1517*	899*	598*	627*
Köln	1452	315*	115	1116	624	539	360	1050	1728*	257	809*	307	1307	428	915	1439	1210	838*	234	1353	1068	661	715	568
Lisboa		1358	1341	404	1103	1437	1580	1782	3157*	1608	2238*	1130	199	1782	1647	249	2301	2266*	1389	2431	622	1551	2161	1935
London	2187*		336*	1022*	734*	739*	679*	1250*	2023*	575*	1104*	247*	1227*	748*	1115*	1363*	1528	1132*	470*	1671*	1104*	905*	1043*	946*
Luxembourg	2160	542*		1010	510	421	344	925	1844*	294	925*	218	1215	467	798	1352	1193	953*	139	1336	958	588	835	616
Madrid	651	1646*	1628		699	1028	1248	1378	2821*	1272	1902*	794	357	1446	1243	341	1885	1930*	1084	2028	218	1176	1838	1535
Marseille	1777	1182*	822	1126		334	627	678	2354*	690	1435*	485	968	868	544	956	1197	1464*	499	1328	535	477	1251	840
Milano	2315	1190*	679	1655	538		293	511	2172*	391	1253*	532	1294	529	376	1290	896	1281*	322	1038	869	166	912	507
München	2545	1094*	555	2010	1011	473		698	1877*	103	968*	503	1452	241	570	1472	848	993*	220	991	1051	301	618	267
Napoli	2870	2013*	1490	2219	1093	823	1125		2652*	807	1732*	997	1638	934	135	1653	1179	1761*	820	530	1214	460	1317	822
Narvik	5084*	3258*	2970*	4543*	3792*	3498*	3039*	4270*		1850*	919	2036*	3024*	1729*	2523*	2553*	2553*	916	1915*	2697*	2802*	2185*	1879*	1853*
Nürnberg	2590	926*	473	2049	1112	630	165	1300	2980*		931	485	1460	174	673	1552	950	878*	202	1093	1132	403	556	309
Oslo	3604*	1778*	1490*	3063*	2312*	2018*	1559*	2790*	1480	1500*		1117*	2105*	810*	1604*	2243*	1634*	329*	996*	1777*	1883*	1351*	980*	1000*
Paris	1821	399*	351	1280	782	857	810	1606	3279*	781	1799*		999	658	862	1136	1351	1145*	283	1494	832	695	1041	770
Porto	320	1976*	1958	575	1560	2084	2340	2639	4870*	2352	3390*	1610		1634	1504	447	2141	2133*	1259	2284	575	1425	2017	1720
Praha	2870	1205*	753	2329	1399	853	388	1505	2785*	280	1305*	1061	2632		812	1727	824	838*	376	967	1306	506	382	183
Roma	2653	1796*	1285	2002	876	606	918	217	4063	1083	2583*	1389	2422	1309		1518	1047	1632*	678	1190	1079	325	1150	699
Sevilla	401	2196*	2178	550	1540	2078	2371	2663	5093*	2500*	3613*	1830	721	2781	2446		2163	2272*	1340	2306	421	1421	2109	1785
Sofiya	3706	2461*	1922	3037	1929	1443	1367	1900	4112*	1531	2632*	2177	3449	1328	1687	3484		1663*	1069	198	1717	711	893	641
Stockholm	3650*	1824*	1536*	3109*	2358*	2064*	1600*	2836*	1476	1415*	530	1845*	3436*	1351*	2629*	3659*	2679		1024*	1806*	1912*	1294*	1001*	1028*
Strasbourg	2237	757*	225	1747	805	519	355	1322	3084*	326	1604	455	2026	606	1093	2158	1722	1650*		1246	912	487	758	487
Thessaloniki	3916	2691*	2152	3267	2139	1673	1597	840*	4343*	1761	2863	2407	3679	1558	1917	3714	319	2909*	1952		1873	872	1012	784
Valencia	1002	1772*	1543	351	862	1400	1693	1955	4513*	1824	3033*	1341	926	2104	1738	678	2765	3079*	1470	3017		1012	1689	1374
Venezia	2498	1458*	947	1895	769	268	485	741	3519*	650	2039*	1120	2295	815	524	2289	1146	2085*	785	1405	1631		776	373
Warszawa	3480	1680*	1345	2960	2015	1469	996	2121	3026*	896	1506*	1677	3248	616	1853	3397	1439	1612	1222	1669	2720	1250		451
Wien	3100	1524*	993	2473	1353	818	430	1325	2985*	498	1600*	1240	2770	295	1126	2876	1033	1646*	785	1263	2213	602	727	

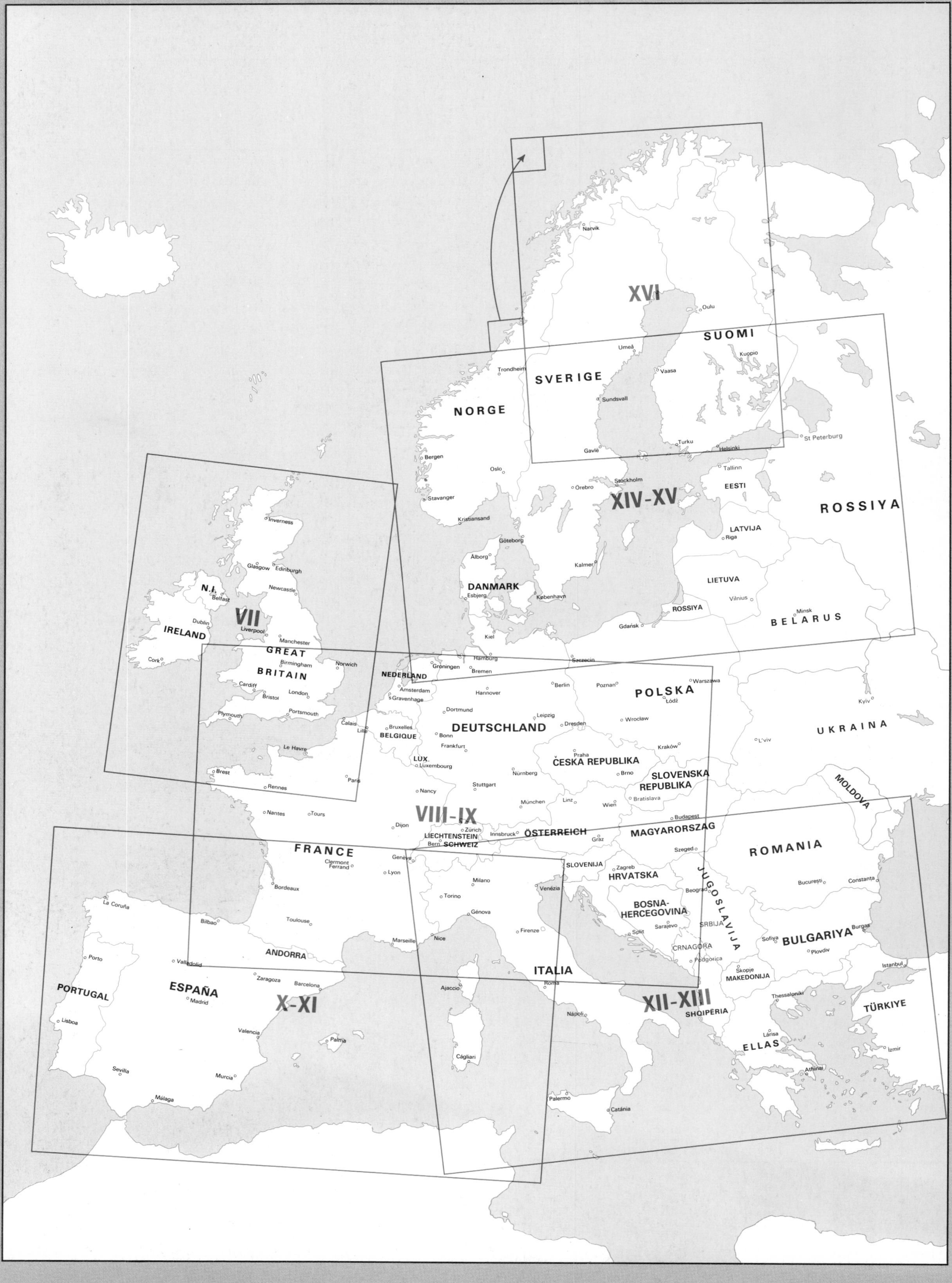
XVI
XIV-XV
VII
VIII-IX
X-XI
XII-XIII
NORGE
SVERIGE
SUOMI
ROSSIYA
EESTI
LATVIJA
LIETUVA
BELARUS
DANMARK
N.I.
IRELAND
GREAT BRITAIN
NEDERLAND
BELGIQUE
LUX.
DEUTSCHLAND
POLSKA
ČESKA REPUBLIKA
SLOVENSKA REPUBLIKA
UKRAINA
MOLDOVA
ÖSTERREICH
MAGYARORSZAG
ROMANIA
LIECHTENSTEIN
SCHWEIZ
FRANCE
SLOVENIJA
HRVATSKA
BOSNA-HERCEGOVINA
JUGOSLAVIJA
SRBIJA
CRNAGORA
BULGARIYA
MAKEDONIJA
SHQIPERIA
ELLAS
TÜRKIYE
ITALIA
ANDORRA
ESPAÑA
PORTUGAL
Narvik
Oulu
Umeå
Vaasa
Kuopio
Trondheim
Sundsvall
Turku
Helsinki
Gavle
St Peterburg
Bergen
Oslo
Tallinn
Stockholm
Örebro
Stavanger
Kristiansand
Riga
Göteborg
Ålborg
Kalmer
Esbjerg
København
Vilnius
Minsk
Gdańsk
Kiel
Hamburg
Szczecin
Groningen
Bremen
Inverness
Glasgow
Edinburgh
Newcastle
Belfast
Dublin
Liverpool
Manchester
Cork
Birmingham
Norwich
Cardiff
Bristol
London
Plymouth
Portsmouth
Amsterdam
s'Gravenhage
Hannover
Berlin
Poznań
Warszawa
Łódż
Kyiv
Dortmund
Leipzig
Dresden
Wrocław
Calais
Lille
Bruxelles
Bonn
Frankfurt
Luxembourg
Praha
Kraków
L'viv
Le Havre
Brest
Paris
Rennes
Nancy
Stuttgart
Nürnberg
Brno
München
Linz
Wien
Bratislava
Budapest
Nantes
Tours
Dijon
Zürich
Bern
Innsbruck
Graz
Szeged
Clermont Ferrand
Genève
Lyon
Milano
Torino
Venézia
Zagreb
Beograd
București
Constanța
Bordeaux
Génova
Toulouse
Firenze
Sarajevo
Split
Sofiya
Burgas
Plovdiv
Podgorica
Marseille
Nice
Skopje
Istanbul
La Coruña
Bilbao
Porto
Valladolid
Zaragoza
Barcelona
Roma
Ajaccio
Thessaloniki
Madrid
Lisboa
Valencia
Palma
Nápoli
Lárisa
İzmir
Cágliari
Athínai
Sevilla
Murcia
Málaga
Palermo
Catánia

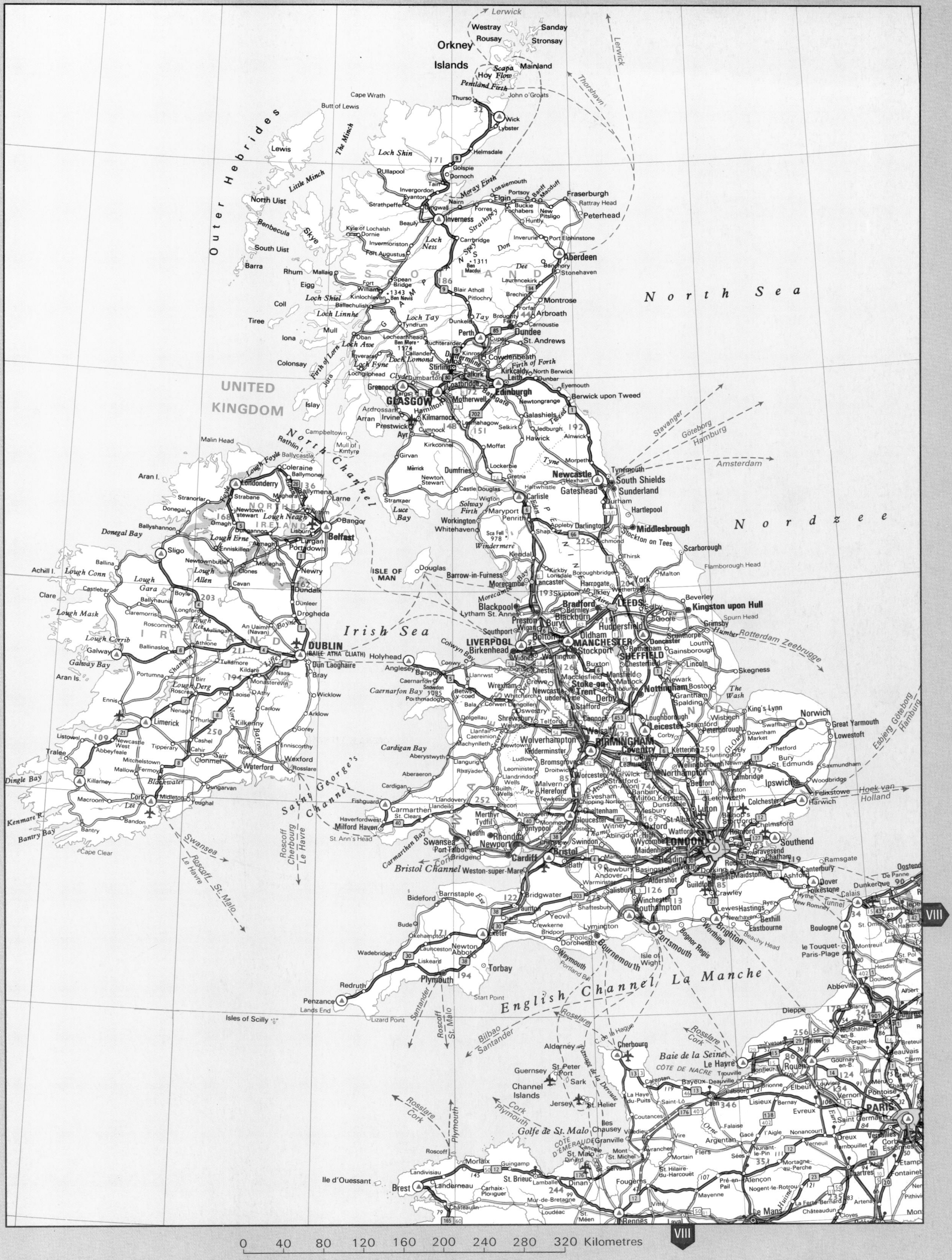

Lerwick
Westray
Sanday
Rousay
Stronsay
Orkney
Islands
Mainland
Hoy
Scapa Flow
Pentland Firth
Thurso
John o'Groats
Thorshavn
Cape Wrath
Butt of Lewis
Wick
Lybster
Outer Hebrides
Lewis
The Minch
Loch Shin
Helmsdale
Golspie
Dornoch
Ullapool
Little Minch
Invergordon
Tain
Moray Firth
Lossiemouth
Elgin
Portsoy
Banff
Macduff
Fraserburgh
Rattray Head
Peterhead
North Uist
Strathpeffer
Dingwall
Nairn
Forres
Buckie
Fochabers
New Pitsligo
Inverness
Benbecula
Beauly
Strathspey
Huntly
Port Elphinstone
Skye
Kyle of Lochalsh
Dornie
Loch Ness
Carrbridge
Don
Inverurie
Aberdeen
South Uist
Invermoriston
Fort Augustus
Barra
Rhum
Mallaig
SCOTLAND
GRAMPIANS
Ben Macdui
Dee
Banchory
Stonehaven
Eigg
Spean Bridge
Fort William
Ben Nevis
Laurencekirk
Loch Shiel
Kinlochleven
Ballachulish
Blair Atholl
Pitlochry
Brechin
Montrose
Coll
Loch Linnhe
North Sea
Forfar
Arbroath
Tiree
Loch Tay
Tyndrum
Dunkeld
Tay
Broughty Ferry
Carnoustie
Mull
Oban
Perth
Dundee
Iona
Lochearnhead
Ben More
Auchterarder
Cupar
St. Andrews
Loch Awe
Firth of Lorn
Inveraray
Callander
Kinross
Colonsay
Loch Fyne
Loch Lomond
Stirling
Dunfermline
Cowdenbeath
Firth of Forth
Jura
Lochgilphead
Alloa
Falkirk
Kirkcaldy
North Berwick
Clyde
Dumbarton
Coatbridge
Leith
Dunbar
UNITED
KINGDOM
Greenock
Largs
GLASGOW
Edinburgh
Eyemouth
Motherwell
Bathgate
Newtongrange
Berwick upon Tweed
Islay
Ardrossan
Hamilton
Kilmarnock
Galashiels
Tweed
Arran
Irvine
Prestwick
Lesmahagow
Selkirk
Jedburgh
Ayr
Cumnock
Hawick
Alnwick
Campbeltown
Mull of Kintyre
Stavanger
Göteborg
Hamburg
Malin Head
North Channel
Rathlin I.
Lough Foyle
Ballycastle
Girvan
Kirkconnel
Moffat
Tyne
Morpeth
Amsterdam
Coleraine
Ballymoney
Lockerbie
Tynemouth
Aran I.
Londonderry
Dumfries
Newcastle
South Shields
Newton Stewart
Gretna
Hexham
Gateshead
Sunderland
Ballymena
Larne
Castle Douglas
Haltwhistle
Carlisle
Durham
Stranorlar
Strabane
Stranraer
Wigton
Eden
Donegal
Newtownstewart
NORTHERN IRELAND
Lough Neagh
Antrim
Luce Bay
Solway Firth
Maryport
Penrith
Hartlepool
Bangor
Workington
Whitehaven
PENNINES
Appleby
Darlington
Middlesbrough
Nordzee
Omagh
Ballyshannon
Dungannon
Lisburn
Belfast
Stockton on Tees
Donegal Bay
Lough Erne
Armagh
Lurgan
Portadown
Shap
Sca Fell
Windermere
Richmond
Scarborough
Sligo
Enniskillen
Kendal
Ballina
Newtownbutler
Monaghan
Newry
Thirsk
Flamborough Head
Achill I.
Lough Conn
Clones
Lough Allen
ISLE OF MAN
Douglas
Barrow-in-Furness
Kirkby Lonsdale
Boroughbridge
Malton
Castlebar
Lough Gara
Cavan
Dundalk
Morecambe
Lancaster
Harrogate
York
Clare
Ballyhaunis
Boyle
Morecambe Bay
Skipton
Ilkley
Wetherby
Beverley
Longford
Dunleer
Blackpool
Bradford
LEEDS
Selby
Kingston upon Hull
Lough Mask
Claremorris
Drogheda
Lytham St. Annes
Preston
Burnley
Blackburn
Goole
Ouse
Spurn Head
IRELAND
Roscommon
Lough Ree
Mullingar
An Uaimh (Navan)
Boyne
Irish Sea
Southport
Wigan
Bury
Huddersfield
Scunthorpe
Grimsby
Humber
Rotterdam Zeebrugge
Lough Corrib
Athlone
Liverpool
Bolton
Oldham
Galway
Ballinasloe
DUBLIN
(BAILE ATHA CLIATH)
Birkenhead
MANCHESTER
Stockport
Doncaster
Louth
Galway Bay
Shannon
Tullamore
Kildare
Liffey
Dun Laoghaire
Holyhead
Colwyn Bay
Widnes
Warrington
Rotherham
SHEFFIELD
Gainsborough
Aran Is.
Portumna
Naas
Bray
Anglesey
Bangor
Conwy
Llanrwst
Denbigh
Chester
Buxton
Chesterfield
Mansfield
Lincoln
Skegness
Lough Derg
Roscrea
Birr
Monasterevin
Port Laoise
Athy
Caernarfon
Snowdon
Wrexham
Crewe
Matlock
Nottingham
Newark
Boston
Ennis
Nenagh
Wicklow
Caernarfon Bay
Porthmadog
Betws-y-coed
Whitchurch
Newcastle under Lyme
Stoke-on-Trent
Derby
Ashbourne
Grantham
The Wash
Spalding
Thurles
Carlow
Arklow
Bala
Corwen
Llangollen
Oswestry
Stafford
Loughborough
King's Lynn
Limerick
Kilkenny
Nore
Dolgellau
Shrewsbury
Welshpool
Telford
Cannock
Leicester
Stamford
Wisbech
Norwich
Great Yarmouth
Listowel
Newcastle West
Tipperary
Barrow
Gorey
Llanfair-Caereinion
Walsall
Peterborough
Swaffham
Lowestoft
Tralee
Abbeyfeale
Cashel
Cahir
Enniscorthy
Machynlleth
Wolverhampton
BIRMINGHAM
Coventry
Corby
Kettering
Downham Market
Thetford
Esbjerg Göteborg Hamburg
Suir
New Ross
Wexford
Cardigan Bay
Aberystwyth
Newtown
Kidderminster
Rugby
Wellingborough
Ely
Bury St. Edmunds
Saxmundham
Mitchelstown
Clonmel
Waterford
Rosslare
Llangurig
Ludlow
Bromsgrove
Droitwich
Leamington
Northampton
Newmarket
Cambridge
Ipswich
Woodbridge
Dingle Bay
Killarney
Mallow
Fermoy
Blackwater
Saint George's Channel
Rhayader
Leominster
Llandrindod Wells
Worcester
Warwick
Stratford-on-Avon
Bedford
Felixstowe
Hoek van Holland
Dungarvan
Aberaeron
Cardigan
Builth Wells
Wye
Malvern
Hereford
Evesham
Banbury
Milton Keynes
Letchworth
Royston
Colchester
Harwich
Macroom
Cork
Midleton
Youghal
Fishguard
Llandovery
Llandeilo
Brecon
Chipping Norton
Dunstable
Kenmare R.
Lee
Bandon
Carmarthen
St. Clears
Merthyr Tydfil
Abergavenny
Gloucester
Cheltenham
Aylesbury
St. Albans
Luton
Bishop's Stortford
Chelmsford
Bantry Bay
Bantry
Haverfordwest
Milford Haven
Pontypool
Witney
Oxford
High Wycombe
Watford
Romford
Southend
Cape Clear
St. Ann's Head
Carmarthen Bay
Swansea
Neath
Rhondda
Newport
Thames
Swindon
Maidenhead
LONDON
Gravesend
Chatham
Ramsgate
Swansea
Roscoff
Cherbourg
Le Havre
Port Talbot
Bridgend
Cardiff
Bristol
Reading
Rochester
Canterbury
Ostende
Roscoff St. Malo
Le Havre
Bristol Channel
Weston-super-Mare
Bath
Newbury
Basingstoke
Dorking
Reigate
Maidstone
Ashford
Dover
Folkestone
Dunkerque
Calais
Andover
Warminster
Aldershot
Guildford
Hythe
Crawley
Tunnel
Bideford
Barnstaple
Exe
Bridgwater
Salisbury
Winchester
Southampton
Lewes
Hastings
Newhaven
Bexhill
Eastbourne
New Romney
Boulogne
Taunton
Shaftesbury
Chard
Yeovil
Lymington
Worthing
Brighton
Beachy Head
St. Omer
Bude
Okehampton
Exeter
Crewkerne
Bridport
Poole
Dorchester
Bournemouth
Portsmouth
Bognor Regis
le Touquet-Paris-Plage
Montreuil
St. Pol
Wadebridge
Launceston
Newton Abbot
Weymouth
Portland Bill
Isle of Wight
Liskeard
Torbay
Hesdin
Doullens
Plymouth
Abbeville
Redruth
Start Point
English Channel
La Manche
Penzance
Lands End
Santander
Roscoff
St. Malo
Dieppe
Isles of Scilly
Lizard Point
Rosslare
Cork
C. de la Hague
Passage de la Déroute
Blangy
Bilbao
Santander
Neufchâtel-en-Bray
Forges-les-Eaux
Breteuil
Beauvais
Alderney
Cherbourg
Yvetot
Baie de la Seine
Le Havre
CÔTE DE NACRE
Trouville
Honfleur
Rouen
Gournay-en-B.
Guernsey
St. Peter Port
Sark
Channel Islands
Bayeux
Deauville
La Haye-du-Puits
Carentan
Cabourg
Brionne
Elbeuf
Pontoise
Jersey
St. Helier
Caen
Saint-Lô
Lisieux
Bernay
Vernon
Évreux
PARIS
Rosslare
Cork
Cork
Plymouth
Plymouth
Coutances
Orne
Falaise
Saint Germain
Eure
Îles Chausey
Villedieu
Vire
Argentan
Gacé
l'Aigle
Nonancourt
Dreux
Versailles
Golfe de St. Malo
CÔTE D'ÉMERAUDE
Granville
Mont St. Michel
Avranches
Flers
Mortain
Sées
Nonant-le-Pin
Verneuil
Rambouillet
Corbeil Essonnes
Roscoff
Morlaix
Guingamp
St. Malo
Dinard
Pontorson
St. Servan
St. Hilaire-du-Harcouët
Mortagne-au-Perche
Chartres
Étampes
Fontainebleau
Landivisiau
St. Brieuc
Lamballe
Dinan
Fougères
Pré-en-Pail
Alençon
Nogent-le-Rotrou
Ile d'Ouessant
Brest
Landerneau
Carhaix-Plouguer
Mur-de-Bretagne
Loudéac
Mayenne
Huisne
La Ferté-Bernard
Artenay
Pithiviers
Châteaulin
Vitré
Rennes
St. Méen
Laval
Le Mans
Château-du-Loir
Cloyes
Châteaudun
0
40
80
120
160
200
240
280
320 Kilometres

VIII
VIII

VII

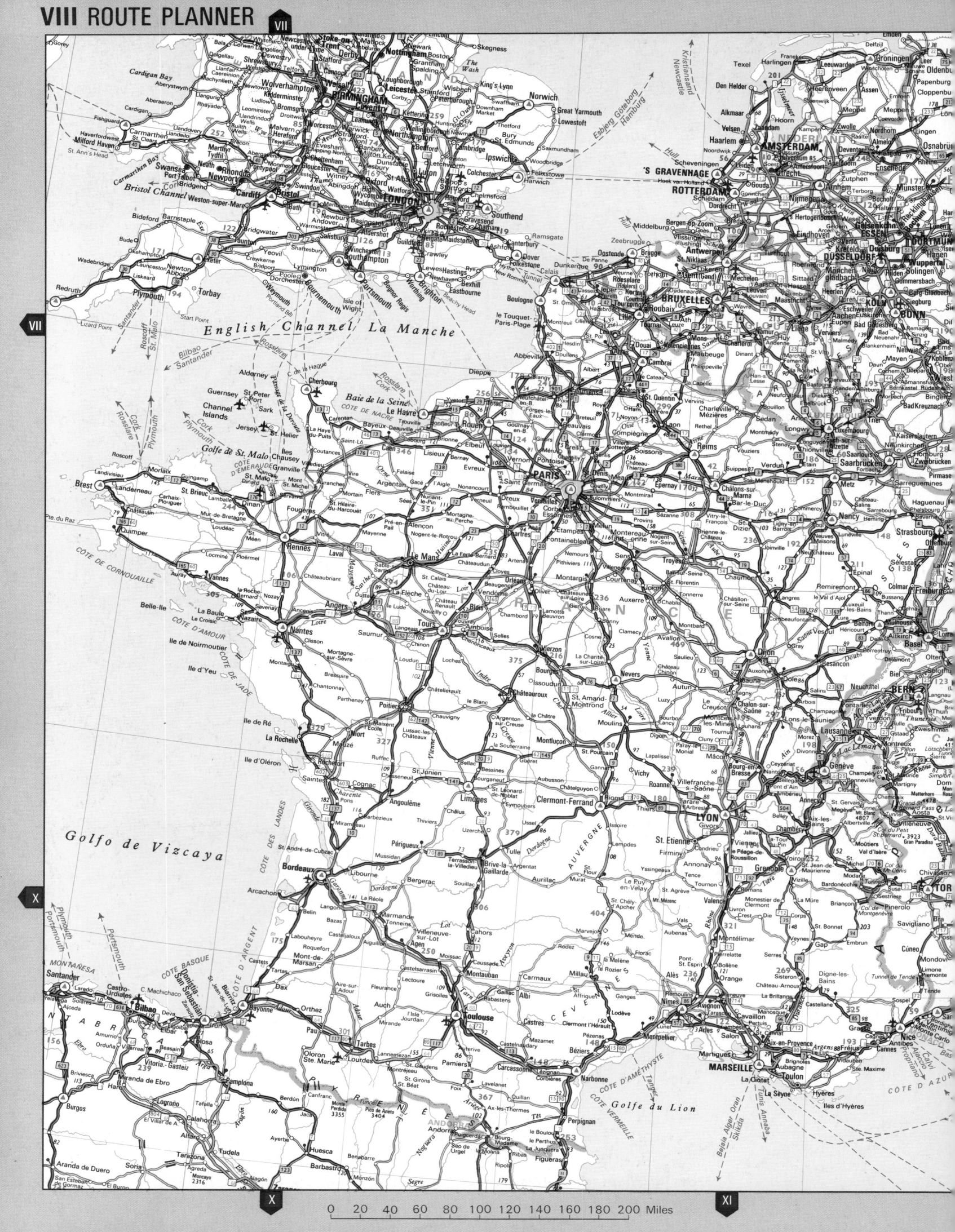
English Channel La Manche
Golfo de Vizcaya
Golfe du Lion
Cardigan Bay
Bristol Channel
Baie de la Seine
Golfe de St. Malo
Channel Islands
LONDON
BIRMINGHAM
PARIS
BRUXELLES
AMSTERDAM
ROTTERDAM
'S GRAVENHAGE
LYON
MARSEILLE
BORDEAUX
TOULOUSE
NANTES
RENNES
BREST
LILLE
REIMS
DIJON
STRASBOURG
KÖLN
BONN
DÜSSELDORF
ESSEN
LUXEMBOURG
BERN
GENÈVE
NICE
BILBAO
Santander
Pamplona
Burgos
Cherbourg
Le Havre
Rouen
Amiens
Orléans
Tours
Le Mans
Limoges
Clermont-Ferrand
Grenoble
Montpellier
Nîmes
Avignon
Toulon
Perpignan
Andorra
Bayonne
Biarritz
Pau
Lourdes
Poitiers
La Rochelle
Angers
Caen
Calais
Boulogne
Dunkerque
Dover
Folkestone
Portsmouth
Southampton
Plymouth
Exeter
Bristol
Cardiff
Swansea
Oxford
Cambridge
Norwich
Ipswich
Harwich
Antwerpen
Brugge
Oostende
Gent
Liège
Namur
Maastricht
Eindhoven
Utrecht
Arnhem
Metz
Nancy
Mulhouse
Basel
Besançon
Chambéry
Annecy
Lausanne
Valence
Saint-Étienne
Vichy
Nevers
Bourges
Châteauroux
Périgueux
Angoulême
Brive-la-Gaillarde
Cahors
Montauban
Carcassonne
Narbonne
Béziers
Albi
Rodez
Pyrénées
Cévennes
Auvergne
Vosges
Côte d'Azur
Côte Vermeille
Côte d'Améthyste
Côte d'Argent
Côte Basque
Côte des Landes
Côte de Jade
Côte d'Amour
Côte de Cornouaille
Côte d'Émeraude
Côte de Nacre
Nederland
Belgique
Andorra

X

0 20 40 60 80 100 120 140 160 180 200 Miles

X

XI

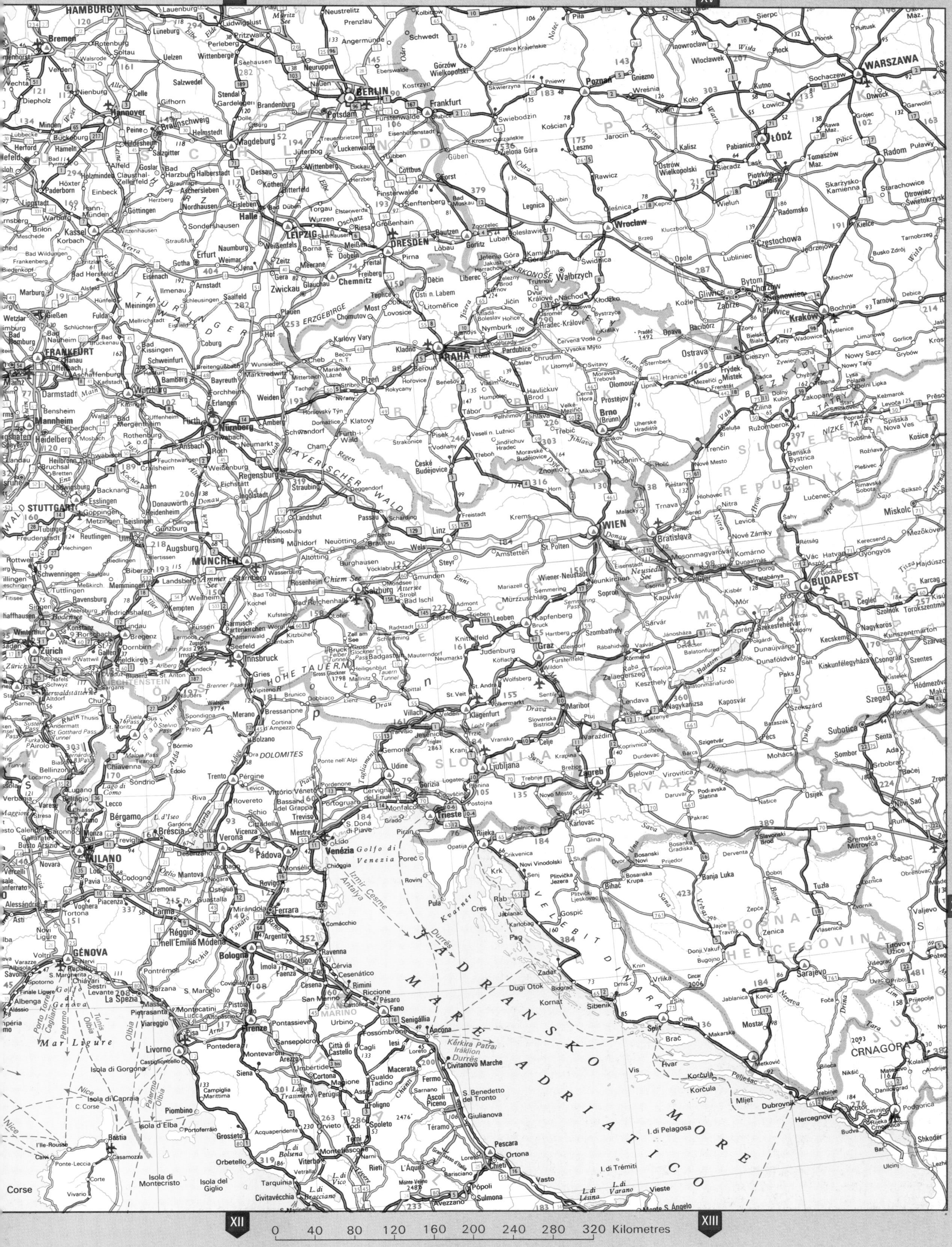
XIV
XV
XIII
XII
XIII
HAMBURG
Bremen
Hannover
Braunschweig
Magdeburg
BERLIN
Potsdam
Frankfurt
Poznań
WARSZAWA
Łódź
Radom
Wrocław
Częstochowa
Kraków
Katowice
LEIPZIG
Halle
DRESDEN
Chemnitz
Erfurt
Kassel
FRANKFURT
Mannheim
Würzburg
Nürnberg
Regensburg
STUTTGART
Augsburg
MÜNCHEN
Salzburg
Linz
WIEN
Bratislava
Brno
Ostrava
PRAHA
Plzeň
Győr
BUDAPEST
Miskolc
Košice
Zürich
Innsbruck
Graz
Maribor
Zagreb
Ljubljana
Trieste
Rijeka
Venézia
Verona
MILANO
Bologna
GÉNOVA
Firenze
Ancona
Pescara
Split
Sarajevo
Dubrovnik
Szeged
Osijek
Banja Luka
Podgorica
Corse
MARE ADRIATICO
JADRANSKO MORE
Mar Ligure
SLOVENIJA
HRVATSKA
BOSNA-HERCEGOVINA
CRNAGORA
MAGYARORSZÁG
SLOVENSKÁ REPUBLIKA
BAYERISCHER WALD
ERZGEBIRGE
HOHE TAUERN
DOLOMITES
0 40 80 120 160 200 240 280 320 Kilometres

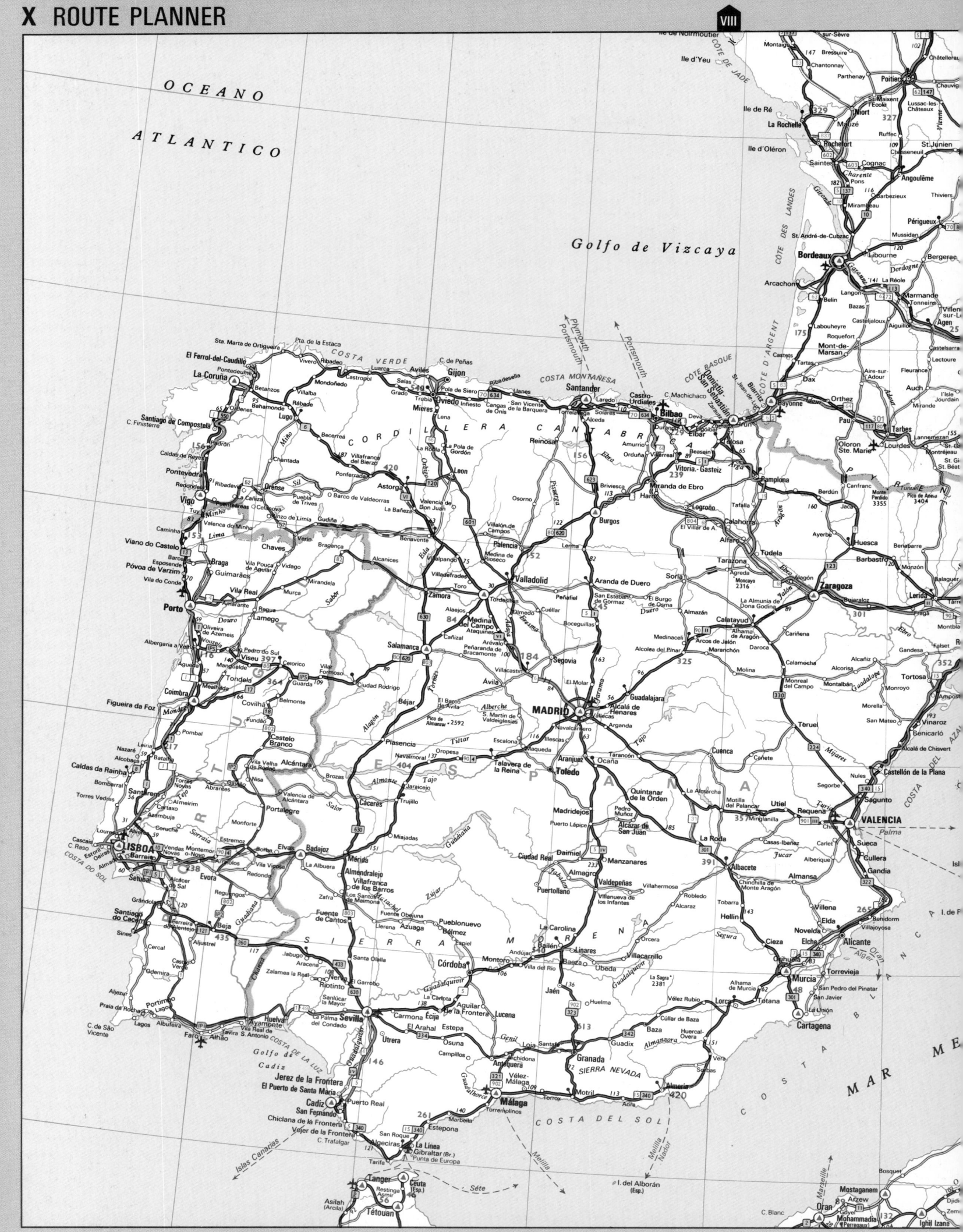
VIII
OCEANO
ATLANTICO
Golfo de Vizcaya
COSTA VERDE
COSTA MONTAÑESA
CÔTE BASQUE
CÔTE D'ARGENT
CÔTE DES LANDES
CÔTE DE JADE
CORDILLERA CANTABRICA
PORTUGAL
ESPAÑA
SIERRA MORENA
SIERRA NEVADA
COSTA DEL SOL
COSTA DE LA LUZ
COSTA DO SOL
COSTA BLANCA
COSTA DEL AZAHAR
MAR MEDITERRANEO
Golfo de Cadiz
PYRENEES
Plymouth
Portsmouth
Islas Canarias
Melilla
Sète
Marseille
Alger
Oran
Palma
Ile de Noirmoutier
Ile d'Yeu
Ile de Ré
Ile d'Oléron
La Rochelle
Rochefort
Niort
Poitiers
Angoulême
Cognac
Saintes
Bordeaux
Arcachon
Libourne
Périgueux
Bergerac
Agen
Mont-de-Marsan
Dax
Bayonne
Biarritz
Pau
Tarbes
Lourdes
Auch
El Ferrol-del-Caudillo
La Coruña
Santiago de Compostela
C. Finisterre
Lugo
Pontevedra
Vigo
Orense
Ponferrada
Astorga
Leon
Oviedo
Gijon
Avilés
Mieres
Santander
Bilbao
Donostia-San Sebastián
Vitoria-Gasteiz
Pamplona
Burgos
Palencia
Valladolid
Zamora
Salamanca
Logroño
Soria
Tudela
Huesca
Zaragoza
Lerida
Calatayud
Teruel
Tortosa
Castellón de la Plana
Sagunto
VALENCIA
Cuenca
Guadalajara
MADRID
Alcalá de Henares
Segovia
Ávila
Toledo
Aranjuez
Talavera de la Reina
Plasencia
Cáceres
Badajoz
Mérida
Ciudad Real
Albacete
Alicante
Murcia
Cartagena
Lorca
Almeria
Granada
Jaén
Córdoba
Sevilla
Huelva
Cadiz
Jerez de la Frontera
Málaga
Marbella
Algeciras
La Línea
Gibraltar (Br.)
Tarifa
Tanger
Ceuta (Esp.)
Tétouan
I. del Alborán (Esp.)
Viano do Castelo
Braga
Porto
Aveiro
Viseu
Coimbra
Figueira da Foz
Castelo Branco
Leiria
Nazaré
Santarém
LISBOA
Setúbal
Evora
Beja
Faro
Lagos
C. de São Vicente
Sagres
Portimão
Mostaganem
Arzew
0 20 40 60 80 100 120 140 160 180 200 Miles

MER MÉDITERRANÉE

MEDITERRANEO

0   40   80   120   160   200   240   280   320 Kilometres

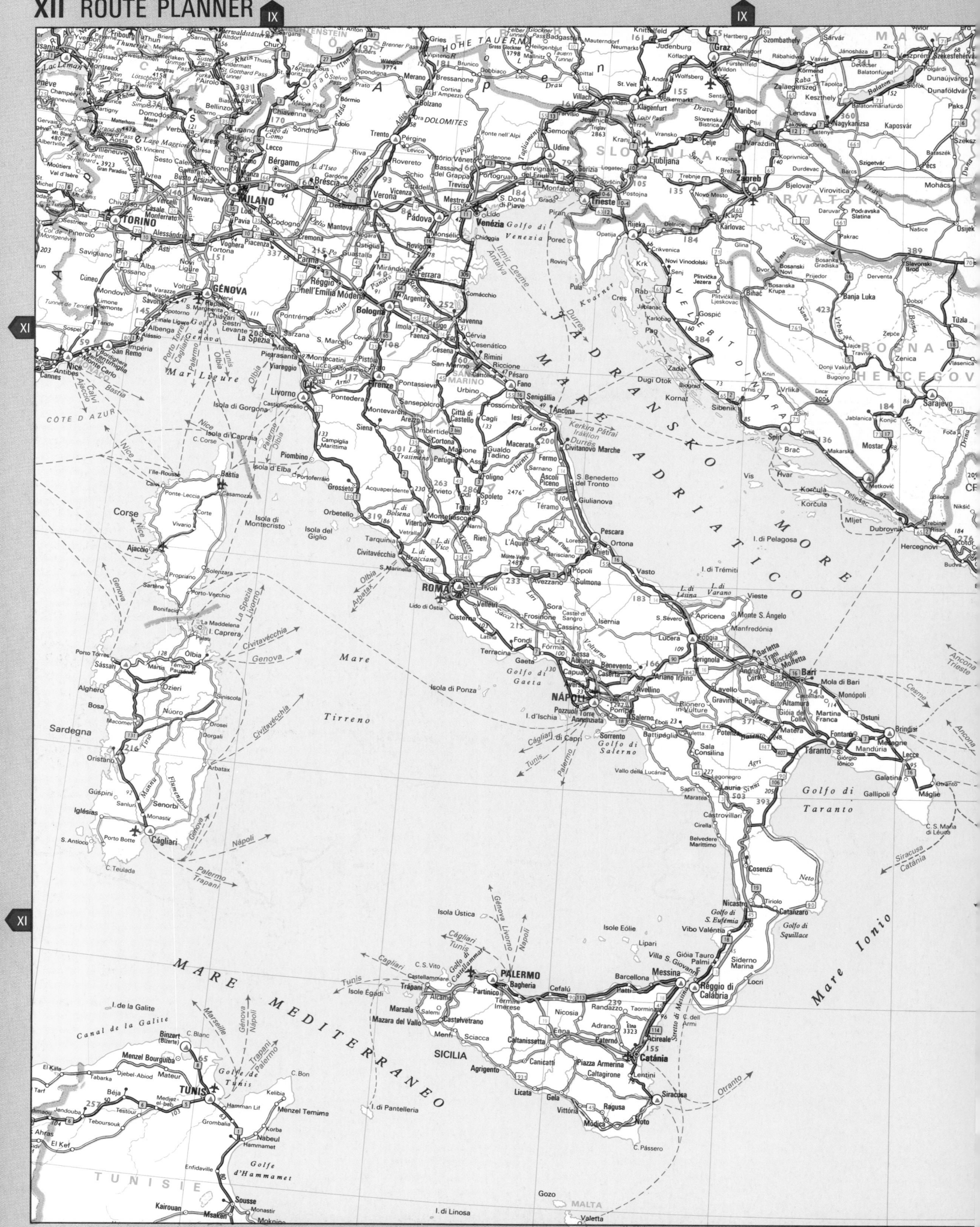
IX
IX
XI
XI
MAGYAR
HOHE TAUERN
Alpen
DOLOMITES
SLOVENIJA
HRVATSKA
BOSNA-HERCEGOV
Graz
Szombathely
Sárvár
Veszprém
Székesfehérvár
Klagenfurt
Villach
Maribor
Ljubljana
Zagreb
Rijeka
Trieste
Udine
Gorizia
Bolzano
Merano
Trento
Bressanone
Cortina d'Ampezzo
Lugano
Como
Bérgamo
Brescia
Verona
Vicenza
Pádova
Treviso
Mestre
Venézia
Golfo di Venezia
MILANO
TORINO
Alessándria
Novara
Pavia
Piacenza
Parma
Cremona
Mántova
Ferrara
Bologna
Módena
Rovigo
Ravenna
Rímini
Pésaro
Ancona
GÉNOVA
La Spezia
Pisa
Livorno
Lucca
Firenze
Siena
Arezzo
Perúgia
Assisi
Foligno
Spoleto
Terni
Viterbo
Civitavécchia
ROMA
Lido di Óstia
Latina
Fondi
Gaeta
Golfo di Gaeta
Pescara
Chieti
L'Áquila
Sulmona
Ortona
Vasto
Isernia
Foggia
Barletta
Bari
Mola di Bari
Monópoli
Brindisi
Lecce
Táranto
Matera
Potenza
Avellino
Benevento
Caserta
NÁPOLI
Salerno
Golfo di Salerno
Sorrento
I. di Capri
I. d'Ischia
Isola di Ponza
Cosenza
Catanzaro
Golfo di Squillace
Golfo di S. Eufémia
Vibo Valéntia
Reggio di Calábria
Messina
Stretto di Messina
PALERMO
Trápani
Marsala
Agrigento
Caltanissetta
Enna
Catánia
Etna 3323
Siracusa
Ragusa
C. Pássero
SICILIA
Isole Égadi
Isole Eólie
Isola Ústica
I. di Pantelleria
I. di Linosa
Gozo
MALTA
Valletta
Corse
Bastia
Ajaccio
Calvi
Bonifacio
Sardegna
Sássari
Olbia
Nùoro
Oristano
Cágliari
C. Teulada
Isola d'Elba
Isola di Capraia
Isola di Montecristo
Isola del Giglio
Mar Ligure
Mare Tirreno
MARE ADRIATICO
JADRANSKO MORE
Mare Ionio
Golfo di Taranto
MARE MEDITERRANEO
CÔTE D'AZUR
Nice
Monaco
San Remo
Cannes
Antibes
Genève
Lausanne
Montreux
Zagreb
Split
Zadar
Šibenik
Dubrovnik
Mostar
Sarajevo
Banja Luka
Bihać
TUNISIE
TUNIS
Bizerte
Menzel Bourguiba
Hammamet
Golfe d'Hammamet
Sousse
Kairouan
Canal de la Galite
I. de la Galite
0 20 40 60 80 100 120 140 160 180 200 Miles

Black Sea
Kara Deniz
Marmara Denizi
Aiyaion Pélagos
Thrakión Pélagos
Mirtóön Pélagos
Iónion Pélagos
Iónioi Nisoi
Dhodhekanisos
TRANSYLVANIAN ALPS
STARA PLANINA
RODOPI
PINDHOS
BULGARIYA
MAKEDONIJA
SHQIPËRIJA
ELLAS
TÜRKIYE
SRBIJA
JUGOSLAVIJA
ROMANIA
BUCURESTI
SOFIYA
BEOGRAD
ATHINAI
ISTANBUL
TIRANË
Thessaloníki
Skopje
Odessa
Constanta
Varna
Burgas
Plovdiv
Ruse
Craiova
Timişoara
Cluj
Braşov
Ploieşti
Galati
Braila
Izmir
Bursa
Edirne
Larisa
Pátrai
Kalamáta
Szeged
Novi Sad
Niš
Podgorica
0 40 80 120 160 200 240 280 320 Kilometres

XVI

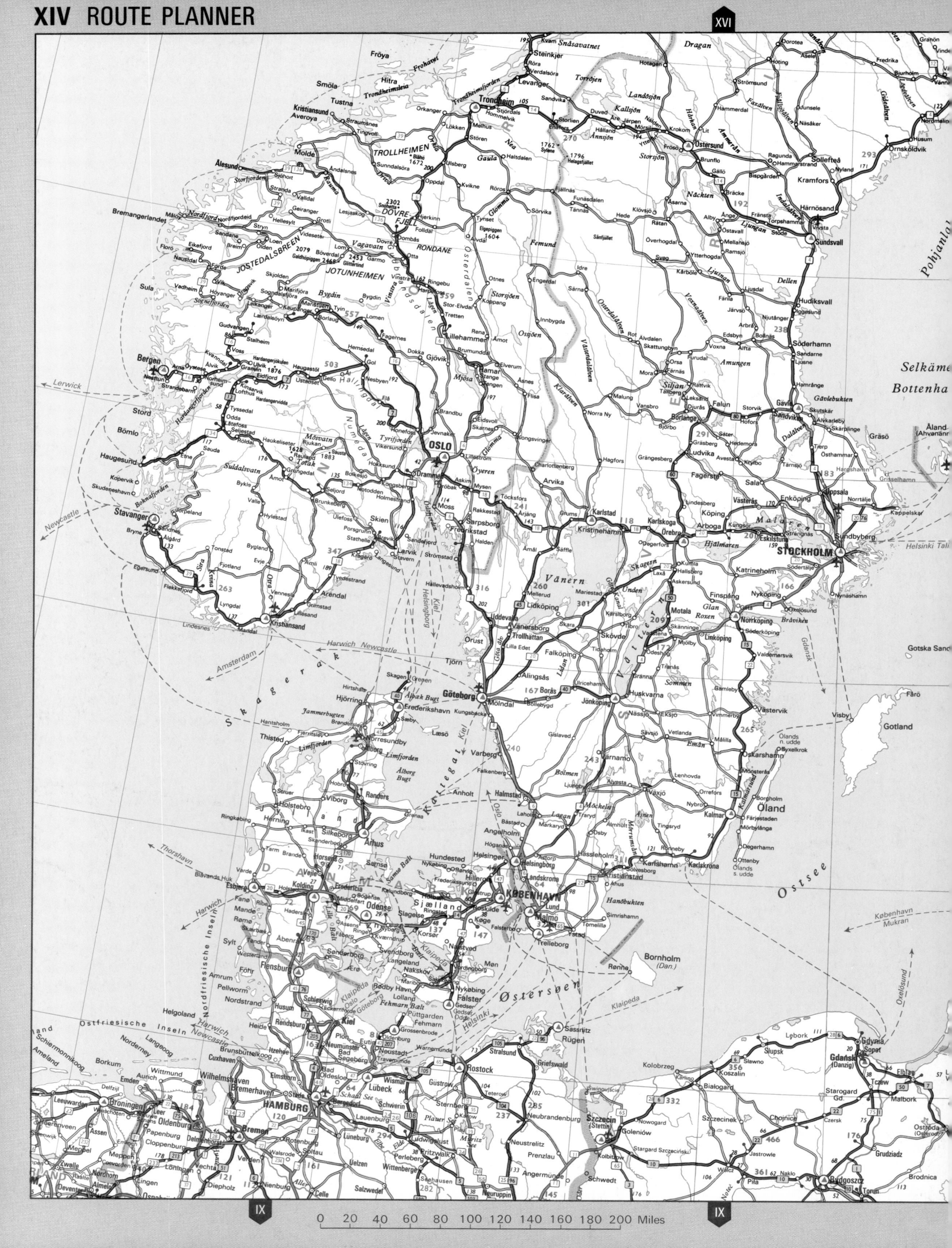
Fröya
Hitra
Smöla
Tustna
Kristiansund
Averoya
Trondheim
Steinkjer
Levanger
Östersund
Storsjön
Molde
TROLLHEIMEN
Ålesund
DOVRE-FJELL
RONDANE
JOSTEDALSBREEN
JOTUNHEIMEN
Bygdin
Lillehammer
Mjösa
Hamar
Gjövik
Bergen
Voss
Stord
Bömlo
Haugesund
Stavanger
OSLO
Drammen
Skien
Larvik
Arendal
Kristiansand
Lindesnes
Sundsvall
Härnösand
Kramfors
Hudiksvall
Söderhamn
Gävle
Falun
Siljan
Karlstad
Vänern
Vättern
Örebro
Västerås
Uppsala
STOCKHOLM
Norrköping
Linköping
Jönköping
Göteborg
Skagerrak
Kattegat
Hjörring
Frederikshavn
Ålborg
Randers
Århus
Esbjerg
Odense
Sjælland
KØBENHAVN
Helsingør
Helsingborg
Malmö
Lund
Ystad
Trelleborg
Kalmar
Öland
Gotland
Karlskrona
Bornholm
Rönne
Östersöen
Ostsee
Flensburg
Kiel
Lübeck
HAMBURG
Bremen
Bremerhaven
Wilhelmshaven
Groningen
Oldenburg
Rostock
Stralsund
Rügen
Szczecin (Stettin)
Koszalin
Słupsk
Gdańsk (Danzig)
Gdynia
Bydgoszcz
Neubrandenburg
Selkämeri
Bottenhavet
Pohjanlahti
Åland
Ostfriesische Inseln
Nordfriesische Inseln

0 20 40 60 80 100 120 140 160 180 200 Miles

IX IX

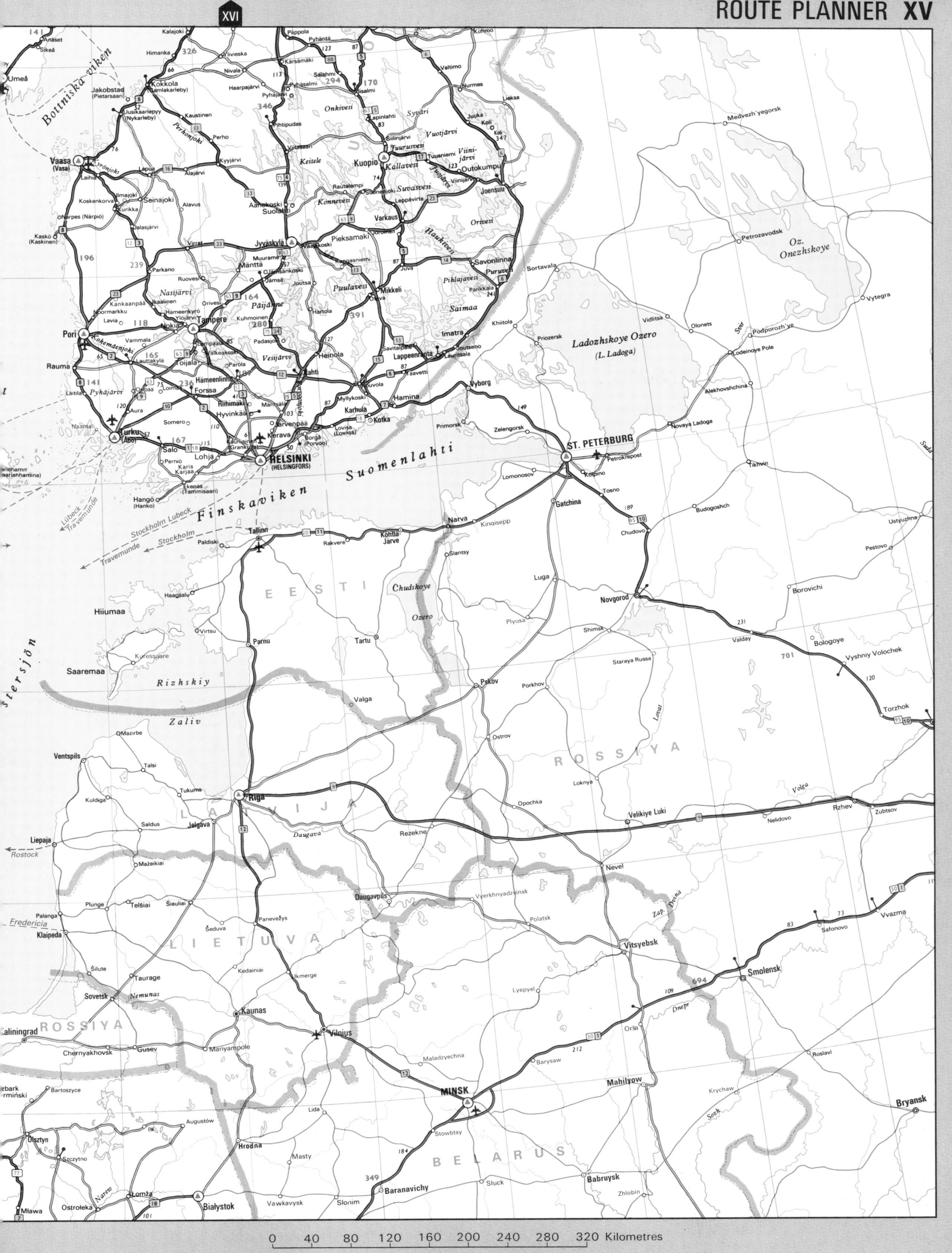
XVI
Bottniska viken
Umeå
Kalajoki
Pyhäntä
Kuhmo
Himanka
Ylivieska
Nivala
Kärsämäki
Salahmi
Valtimo
Nurmes
Kokkola
Gamlakarleby
Jakobstad
(Pietarsaari)
Haarpajärvi
Pyhäjärvi
Pyhäsalmi
Iisalmi
Lieksa
Onkivesi
Syväri
Jusikaarlepyy
(Nykarleby)
Kaustinen
Pihtipudas
Lapinlahti
Juuka
Koli
Perhonjoki
Perho
Vuotjärvi
Siilinjärvi
Juurusvesi
Tuusniemi
Viini-järvi
Viitasaari
Keitele
Kuopio
Kallavesi
Outokumpu
Vaasa
(Vasa)
Laihia
Lapua
Alajärvi
Kyyjärvi
Rautalampi
Suonenjoki
Suvasvesi
Viinijärvi
Joensuu
Ilmajoki
Seinäjoki
Koskenkorva
Kurikka
Alavus
Äänekoski
Suolahti
Konnevesi
Leppävirta
Närpes (Närpiö)
Jalasjärvi
Varkaus
Joroinen
Orivesi
Kaskö
(Kaskinen)
Virrat
Jyväskylä
Vaajakoski
Pieksamaki
Haukivesi
Muurame
Jämsänkoski
Jämsä
Kangasniemi
Juva
Savonlinna
Puruvesi
Sortavala
Parkano
Ruovesi
Mänttä
Joutsa
Mikkeli
Pihlajavesi
Parikkala
Nasijärvi
Päijänne
Puulavesi
Saimaa
Kankaanpää
Ikaalinen
Orivesi
Otava
Noormarkku
Hameenkyrö
Ylöjärvi
Hartola
Kuhmoinen
Lavia
Nokia
Tampere
Imatra
Khiitola
Pori
Vammala
Padasjoki
Savitaipale
Joutseno
Lauritsala
Kokemäenjoki
Lempäälä
Valkeakoski
Vesijärvi
Heinola
Lappeenranta
Rauma
Lauttakylä
Toijala
Parola
Lahti
Taavetti
Hameenlinna
Kouvola
Vyborg
Laitila
Pyhäjärvi
Loimaa
Oripaa
Forssa
Riihimäki
Hyvinkää
Mäntsälä
Myllykoski
Hamina
Karhula
Kotka
Aura
Somero
Järvenpää
Kerava
Lovisa
(Loviisa)
Primorsk
Zelenogorsk
Naantali
Turku
(Åbo)
Salo
Lohja
Kauniainen
Grankulla
Borgå
(Porvoo)
HELSINKI
(HELSINGFORS)
Suomenlahti
Perniö
Karis
Karjaa
Hangö
(Hanko)
Ekenäs
(Tammisaari)
Finskaviken
Lübeck
Travemünde
Stockholm
Tallinn
Paldiski
Rakvere
Kohtla-Järve
Narva
Kingisepp
Slantsy
Haapsalu
Hiiumaa
EESTI
Chudskoye
Ozero
Virtsu
Parnu
Tartu
Kuressaare
Saaremaa
Rizhskiy
Zaliv
Valga
Medvezh'yegorsk
Petrozavodsk
Oz. Onezhskoye
Vytegra
Ladozhskoye Ozero
(L. Ladoga)
Priozersk
Vidlitsa
Olonets
Svir
Podporozh'ye
Lodeinoye Pole
Alekhovshchina
Novaya Ladoga
ST. PETERBURG
Petrokrepost
Lomonosov
Kolpino
Tikhvin
Tosno
Gatchina
Budogoshch
Chudovo
Ustyuzhna
Pestovo
Luga
Novgorod
Borovichi
Plyusa
Shimsk
Valday
Bologoye
Vyshniy Volochek
Staraya Russa
Pskov
Porkhov
Lovat
Torzhok
Ostrov
ROSSIYA
Loknya
Volga
Opochka
Velikiye Luki
Nelidovo
Rzhev
Zubtsov
Mazirbe
Ventspils
Talsi
Tukums
Riga
Kuldiga
LATVIJA
Saldus
Jelgava
Daugava
Rezekne
Liepaja
Rostock
Mažeikiai
Nevel
Plunge
Telšiai
Šiauliai
Daugavpils
Vyerkhnyadzvinsk
Palanga
Fredericia
Panevežys
Šeduva
Polatsk
Zap. Dvina
Vyazma
Safonovo
Klaipeda
LIETUVA
Vitsyebsk
Šilute
Taurage
Kedainiai
Ukmerge
Smolensk
Sovetsk
Nemunas
Kaunas
Lyepyel
Dnepr
Kaliningrad
ROSSIYA
Vilnius
Orša
Chernyakhovsk
Gusev
Mariyampole
Barysaw
Roslavl
Maladzyechna
Minsk
Mahilyow
Krychaw
Lidzbark
Warmiński
Bartoszyce
Bryansk
Augustów
Ełk
Lida
Sozh
Olsztyn
Stowbtsy
Hrodna
Szczytno
Masty
BELARUS
Narew
Łomża
Baranavichy
Sluck
Babruysk
Mława
Ostrołeka
Białystok
Vawkavysk
Slonim
Zhlobin
0 40 80 120 160 200 240 280 320 Kilometres

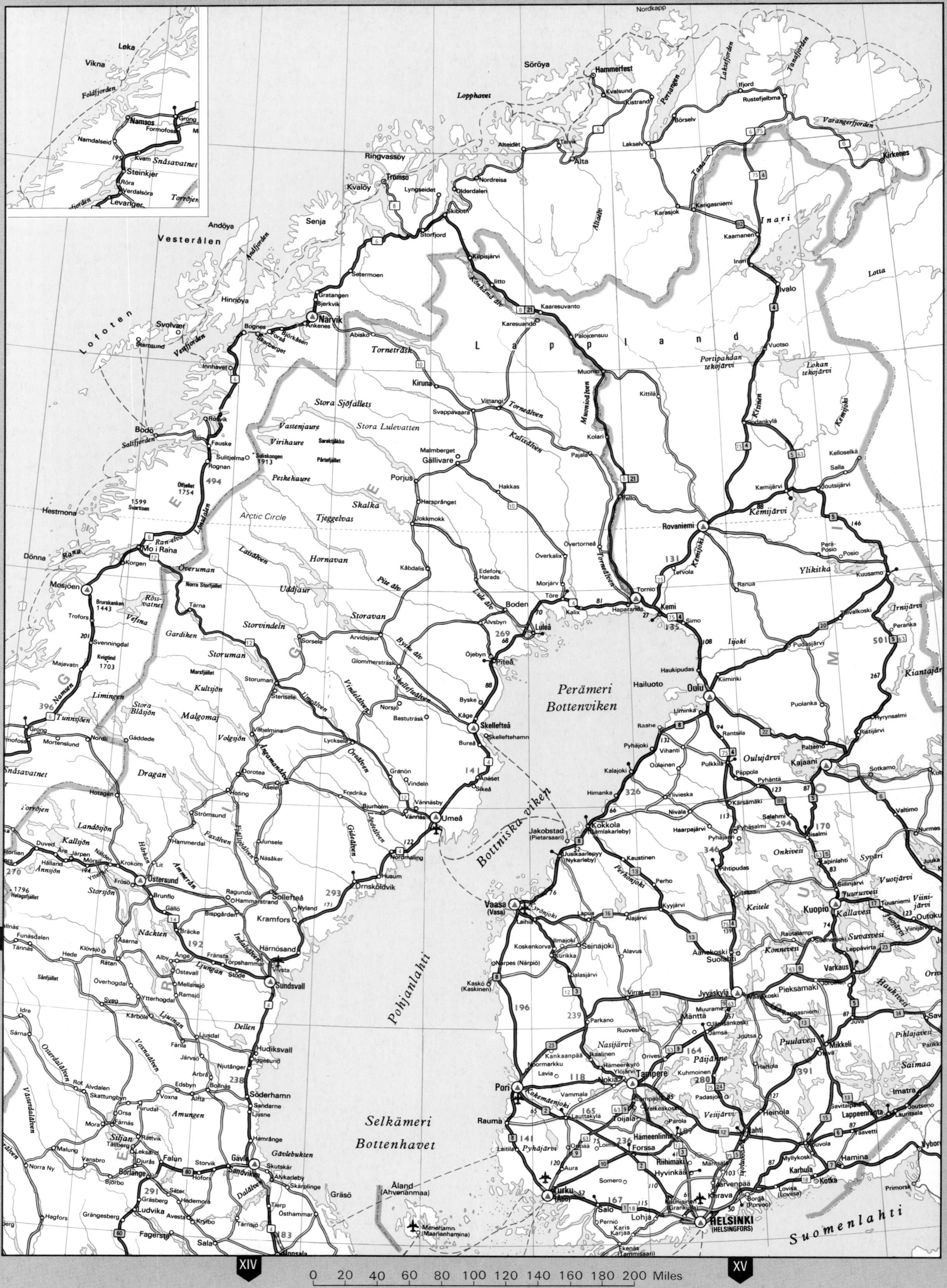
Nordkapp
Söröya
Hammerfest
Kvalsund
Kistrand
Porsangen
Laksefjorden
Tanafjorden
Ifjord
Rustefjelbma
Loppahavet
Alta
Talvik
Alteidet
Lakselv
Börselv
Varangerfjorden
Kirkenes
Ringvassöy
Tromsö
Kvalöy
Lyngseidet
Nordreisa
Olderdalen
Skibotn
Storfjord
Karasjok
Karigasniemi
Kaamanen
Inari
Ivalo
Lotta
Senja
Andöya
Vesterålen
Hinnöya
Lofoten
Svolvær
Setermoen
Gratangen
Bjerkvik
Narvik
Ankenes
Bognes
Kilpisjärvi
Kaaresuvanto
Karesuando
Palojœnsuu
Lapland
Abisko
Tornetråsk
Kiruna
Muonio
Kittilä
Vuotso
Portipahdan tekojärvi
Lokan tekojärvi
Stora Sjöfallets
Stora Lulevatten
Vittangi
Svappavaara
Malmberget
Gällivare
Porjus
Jokkmokk
Arctic Circle
Bodö
Fauske
Rognan
Sulitjelma
Mo i Rana
Mosjöen
Hestmona
Dönna
Kolari
Pajala
Pello
Sodankylä
Kemijärvi
Salla
Rovaniemi
Posio
Kuusamo
Ylikitka
Övertorneå
Boden
Luleå
Piteå
Haparanda
Tornio
Kemi
Simo
Arvidsjaur
Sorsele
Storuman
Stensele
Vilhelmina
Lycksele
Skellefteå
Umeå
Vännäs
Nordmaling
Örnsköldvik
Perämeri
Bottenviken
Hailuoto
Oulu
Kiiminki
Pudasjärvi
Taivalkoski
Raahe
Kajaani
Oulujärvi
Sotkamo
Kokkola (Gamlakarleby)
Jakobstad (Pietarsaari)
Bottniska viken
Östersund
Vaasa (Vasa)
Lapua
Seinäjoki
Kuopio
Kallavesi
Varkaus
Jyväskylä
Pohjanlahti
Sollefteå
Kramfors
Härnösand
Sundsvall
Hudiksvall
Söderhamn
Kaskö (Kaskinen)
Pori
Rauma
Tampere
Nokia
Hämeenlinna
Lahti
Mikkeli
Saimaa
Imatra
Lappeenranta
Kotka
Hamina
Selkämeri
Bottenhavet
Gävle
Sandviken
Falun
Borlänge
Ludvika
Siljan
Mora
Åland (Ahvenanmaa)
Maarianhamina
Turku (Åbo)
Salo
Lohja
Forssa
Riihimäki
Hyvinkää
Kerava
Järvenpää
HELSINKI (HELSINGFORS)
Porvoo
Suomenlahti
Ekenäs (Tammisaari)
Namsos
Steinkjer
Levanger
Vikna
Leka
0 20 40 60 80 100 120 140 160 180 200 Miles

XIV
XV

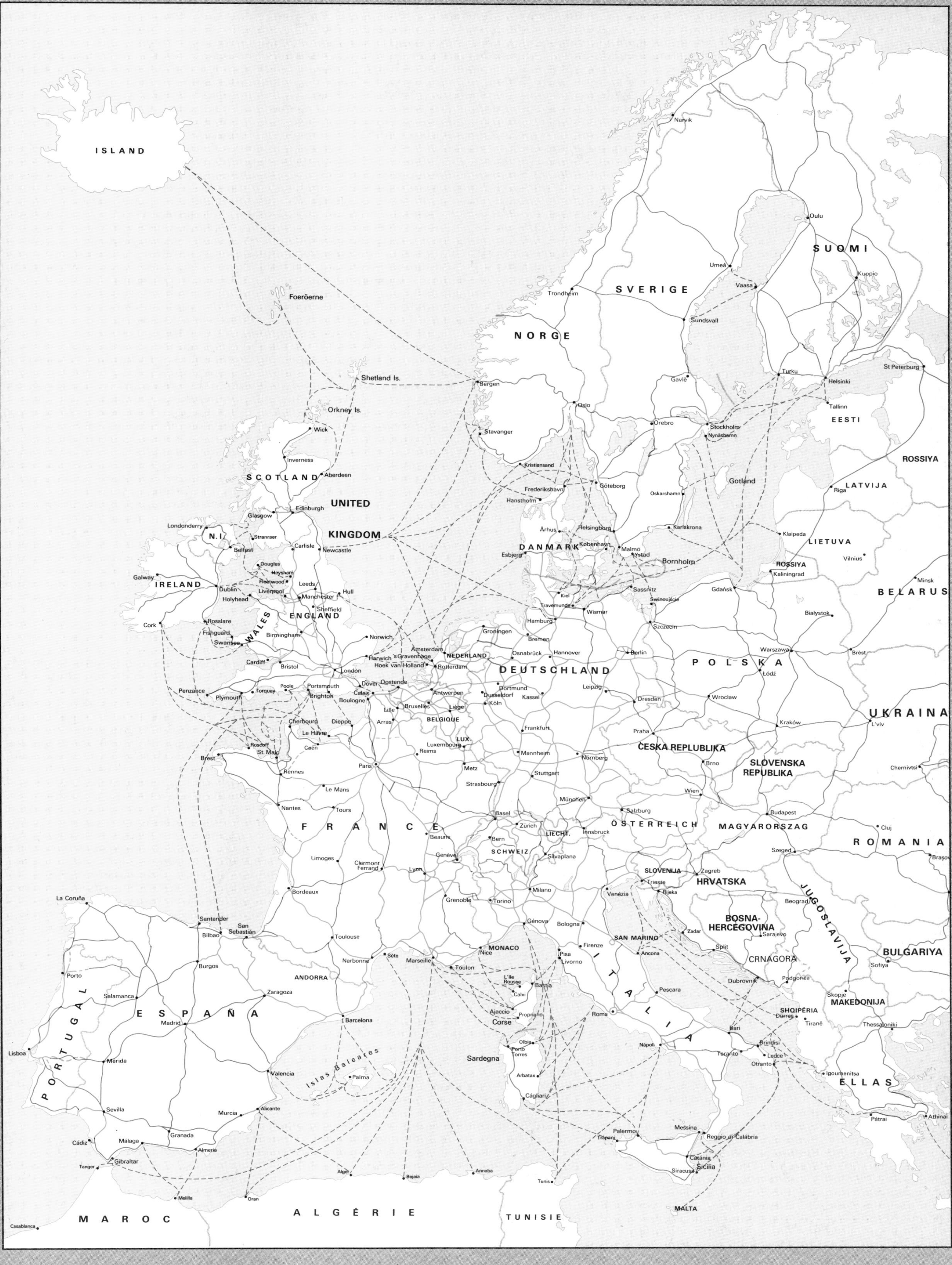
ISLAND
Foeröerne
Shetland Is.
Orkney Is.
Wick
Inverness
Aberdeen
SCOTLAND
UNITED
KINGDOM
Edinburgh
Glasgow
Londonderry
N.I.
Stranraer
Belfast
Carlisle
Newcastle
Douglas
Heysham
Fleetwood
Galway
IRELAND
Dublin
Liverpool
Leeds
Hull
Holyhead
Manchester
Sheffield
ENGLAND
Cork
Rosslare
Fishguard
Swansea
WALES
Birmingham
Norwich
Cardiff
Bristol
London
Harwich
Penzance
Plymouth
Torquay
Poole
Portsmouth
Brighton
Dover
Ostende
Calais
Boulogne
Cherbourg
Dieppe
Le Havre
Caen
Roscoff
St. Malo
Brest
Rennes
Le Mans
Nantes
Tours
Paris
Lille
Arras
FRANCE
Limoges
Clermont Ferrand
Bordeaux
Toulouse
Narbonne
Sète
Marseille
Toulon
Lyon
Grenoble
Genève
Beaune
Reims
Metz
Strasbourg
Luxembourg
LUX
Bruxelles
Liège
Antwerpen
BELGIQUE
Amsterdam
's Gravenhage
Hoek van Holland
Rotterdam
NEDERLAND
Groningen
Bremen
Hamburg
Osnabrück
Hannover
Dortmund
Düsseldorf
Köln
Kassel
DEUTSCHLAND
Frankfurt
Mannheim
Stuttgart
Nürnberg
München
Leipzig
Dresden
Berlin
Basel
Zürich
Bern
SCHWEIZ
LIECHT.
Silvaplana
Innsbruck
Salzburg
ÖSTERREICH
Wien
Praha
ČESKA REPUBLIKA
Brno
SLOVENSKA REPUBLIKA
Budapest
MAGYARORSZAG
Szeged
Cluj
ROMANIA
Braşov
Kiel
Travemünde
Wismar
Sassnitz
Swinoujście
Szczecin
Gdańsk
Kaliningrad
ROSSIYA
Białystok
Warszawa
Łódź
Wrocław
Kraków
POLSKA
Brest
Minsk
BELARUS
L'viv
UKRAINA
Chernivtsi
Vilnius
Klaipeda
LIETUVA
Riga
LATVIJA
Tallinn
EESTI
St Peterburg
ROSSIYA
Helsinki
Turku
SUOMI
Kuopio
Oulu
Vaasa
Umeå
Sundsvall
Gavle
Stockholm
Nynäsbamn
Örebro
Oskarshamn
Gotland
Karlskrona
Bornholm
Ystad
Malmö
København
Helsingborg
Göteborg
SVERIGE
Narvik
Trondheim
NORGE
Bergen
Stavanger
Kristiansand
Oslo
Frederikshavn
Hanstholm
Århus
Esbjerg
DANMARK
La Coruña
Santander
Bilbao
San Sebastián
Burgos
Porto
Salamanca
PORTUGAL
ESPAÑA
Madrid
Zaragoza
ANDORRA
Barcelona
Lisboa
Mérida
Valencia
Islas Baleares
Palma
Sevilla
Murcia
Alicante
Cádiz
Málaga
Granada
Almeria
Gibraltar
Tanger
Melilla
Oran
Alger
Bejaia
Annaba
Tunis
Casablanca
MAROC
ALGÉRIE
TUNISIE
MONACO
Nice
L'Ile Rousse
Bastia
Calvi
Ajaccio
Propriano
Corse
Olbia
Porto Torres
Sardegna
Arbatax
Cágliari
Torino
Milano
Génova
Bologna
Venézia
Trieste
Pisa
Livorno
Firenze
SAN MARINO
Ancona
ITALIA
Pescara
Roma
Nápoli
Bari
Brindisi
Taranto
Lecce
Otranto
Palermo
Trapani
Messina
Reggio di Calábria
Catánia
Sicilia
Siracusa
MALTA
SLOVENIJA
Zagreb
HRVATSKA
Rijeka
Zadar
Split
BOSNA-HERCEGOVINA
Sarajevo
CRNAGORA
Dubrovnik
Podgorica
Beograd
JUGOSLAVIJA
SHQIPËRIA
Durres
Tiranë
Skopje
MAKEDONIJA
BULGARIYA
Sofiya
Thessaloniki
Igoumenitsa
ELLAS
Pátrai
Athinai

1 2 3

A

B

C

Tory
Island

Inishbofin
Bloody
Foreland

Dun

Inishfree Bay

Bunbeg
Gweedore Errigal
752
Crolly
Slieve Snaght
683
Burtonport
Dunglow

Aran
Island

Derryv

Crohy Head

Gweebarra Bay
Lettermacaward
Dawros Head
Maas
Fintown
Loughros More
Bay
Glenties
Ardara
Blue Stag
67
Slievetooey
517
Glencolumbkille
Rossan Point
Malin More
56
Inver
Slieve League
601
De
Rathlin O'Birne
Island
Carrick
Killybegs
Mountpark
Carrigan Head
Dunkineely
Muckros
Head
McSwyne's Bay
Inver
Bay
Balli
St. John's
Point
23

Donegal Bay
Ballyshar
Bundoran
Belleek
Inishmurray
Cliffony
15
Kinlough
Lou
Me
35
Grange
Glenade
Roskeeragh Point
Truskmore
644
Benwee Head
Downpatrick
Head
Drumcliff
Manorhamilton
16
Erris Head
Broad
Haven
Belderg
Lenadoon
Point
Sligo Bay
26
Easky
Sligo
Gl
Mullet
Peninsula
Glenamoy
Ballycastle
Killala
Bay
Dromore
West
Dromard
Beltra
59
Ballysadare
Belmullet
Carrowmore
Lough
Killala
Inishcrone
59
The Ox Mountains
545
Collooney
Inishkea North
Bangor
Bellacorick
25
17
Inishkea South
59
Crossmolina
59
Ballina
Ballymote
43
Blacksod
Bay
Slieve Car
721
Lough
Con
May
Tubbercurry
Lough
Arrow
32
Saddle Head
Slieve More
672
Ballycroy
Nephin
806
Lough
Key
Achill Head
Dooagh Keel
32
Nephin Beg Range
Foxford
26
Callow
Charlestown
Boyle
4
Achill
Island
Dooega Head
Achill
40
58
Beltra
Beltra
Lough
Cullin
Swinford
Carracastle
Lough
Gara
4
90
Mullaranny
Newport
Castlebar
5
Bellavary
Tawnyinah
83
Ballaghaderreen
Clare
Island
Clew Bay
31
18
Balla
27
Swinford
17
Frenchpark
Bellanagare
42
Westport
60
60
Ballyhaunis
60
Castlerea
Tulsk
Stro
Louisburgh
C   O   N   N   N   A   U   G   H   61
Cregganbaun
59
Ballindine
Ballinlough
Ballymoe
Ballydooley
Ballye
Mweelrea
819
Partry Mountains
Lough
Mask
Cloonfad
Pollremon
Williamstown
60
Roscommon
Inishturk
Ballinrobe
84
Milltown
Dunmore
C
Inishbofin
Letterfrack
Leenaun
Cong
23
Kilmaine
83
Athleague
Ballye
Inishark
Moyard
Maum
Clonbur
Shrule
I   R   E
Mount Talbot
The Twelve
Pins 730
Maumturk Mts.
Tuam
Moylough
Newbridge
Ballygar
Clifden
59
35
Recess
Maam Cross
Headford
84
17
Barnaderg
63
Mount
Bellew
Bridge
Ballyforan
Thomas
Street
Brideswell
Slyne Head
Connemara
Oughterard
Lough
Corrib
Derryrush
Screeb
Rosscahill
43
Moyullen
Ballinasloe
Kilconnell
90
Glinsk
Kilkieran
59
26
Claregalway
Athenry
Aughrim
Costelloe
2
Moycullen
64
3
Kiltullagh
29
Gorumna
Island
Spiddle
Galway
6
Barna
Oranmore
6

0 5 10   20   30   40 Miles

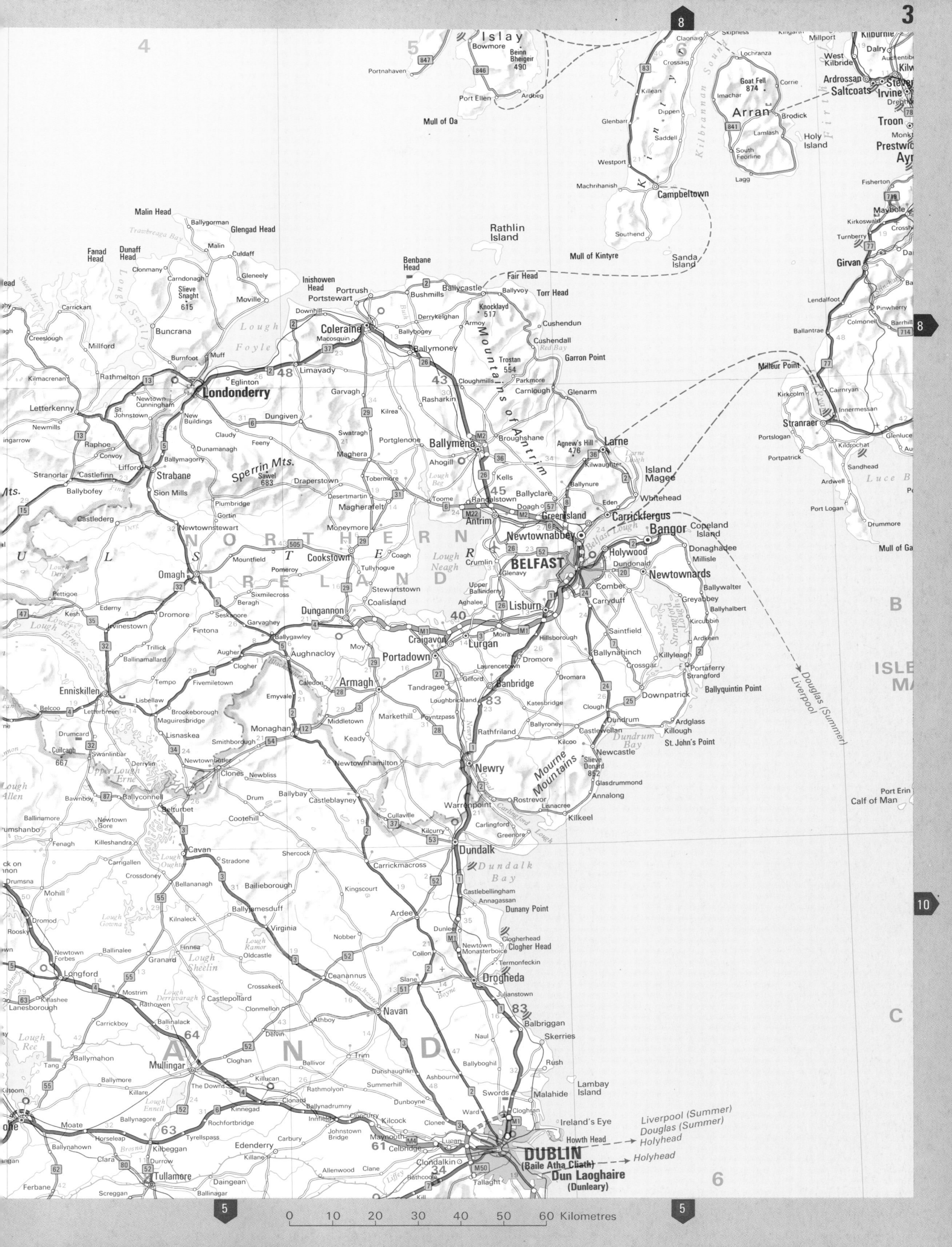
8
Islay
Bowmore
Beinn Bheigeir 490
Portnahaven
Port Ellen
Ardbeg
Mull of Oa
Claonaig
Skipness
Crossaig
Killean
Glenbarr
Dippen
Saddell
Westport
Machrihanish
Campbeltown
Southend
Sanda Island
Mull of Kintyre
Kilbrannan Sound
Lochranza
Goat Fell 874
Corrie
Imachar
Arran
Brodick
Lamlash
Holy Island
South Feorline
Lagg
Millport
West Kilbride
Ardrossan
Saltcoats
Irvine
Troon
Prestwick
Ayr
Dalry
Fisherton
Maybole
Kirkoswald
Turnberry
Girvan
Lendalfoot
Pinwherry
Colmonell
Barrhill
Ballantrae
Milleur Point
Kirkcolm
Cairnryan
Innermessan
Stranraer
Portslogan
Kildrochat
Portpatrick
Sandhead
Luce Bay
Ardwell
Port Logan
Drummore
Mull of Galloway
Glenluce
Malin Head
Ballygorman
Trawbreaga Bay
Glengad Head
Malin
Culdaff
Fanad Head
Dunaff Head
Clonmany
Carndonagh
Gleneely
Slieve Snaght 615
Moville
Carrickart
Creeslough
Milford
Buncrana
Lough Swilly
Lough Foyle
Burnfoot
Muff
Kilmacrenan
Rathmelton
Eglinton
Londonderry
Newtown Cunningham
Letterkenny
St. Johnstown
Newmills
Raphoe
Convoy
Lifford
Stranorlar
Castlefinn
Ballybofey
Strabane
Sion Mills
Castlederg
Newtownstewart
Omagh
Inishowen Head
Portrush
Portstewart
Downhill
Coleraine
Macosquin
Benbane Head
Bushmills
Ballycastle
Rathlin Island
Fair Head
Ballyvoy
Torr Head
Knocklayd 517
Derrykeighan
Armoy
Ballybogey
Ballymoney
Limavady
Dungiven
Claudy
Feeny
Dunamanagh
Ballymagorry
Sperrin Mts.
Sawel 683
Draperstown
Garvagh
Kilrea
Swatragh
Maghera
Portglenone
Ballymena
Rasharkin
Cloughmills
Mountains of Antrim
Trostan 554
Cushendun
Cushendall
Red Bay
Garron Point
Parkmore
Carnlough
Glenarm
Broughshane
Agnew's Hill 476
Larne
Larne Lough
Island Magee
Whitehead
Kells
Ahogill
Lough Beg
Tobermore
Desertmartin
Magherafelt
Moneymore
Toome
Randalstown
Antrim
Ballyclare
Doagh
Greenisland
Carrickfergus
Ballynure
Eden
Kilwaughter
Newtownabbey
Belfast Lough
Bangor
Copeland Island
Donaghadee
Millisle
Holywood
Dundonald
Newtownards
Comber
Ballywalter
Greyabbey
Ballyhalbert
Kircubbin
Strangford Lough
Ardkeen
Killyleagh
Portaferry
Strangford
Ballyquintin Point
Crossgar
Saintfield
Ballynahinch
Hillsborough
Carryduff
BELFAST
Crumlin
Glenavy
Lough Neagh
Upper Ballinderry
Aghalee
Lisburn
Moira
Lurgan
Craigavon
Portadown
NORTHERN IRELAND
Cookstown
Coagh
Mountfield
Pomeroy
Tullyhogue
Stewartstown
Coalisland
Dungannon
Sixmilecross
Beragh
Seskinore
Garvaghey
Dromore
Fintona
Ballygawley
Aughnacloy
Moy
Augher
Clogher
Ederny
Kesh
Pettigoe
Lower Lough Erne
Irvinestown
Trillick
Ballinamallard
Enniskillen
Tempo
Fivemiletown
Lisbellaw
Brookeborough
Maguiresbridge
Lisnaskea
Belcoo
Letterbreen
Drumcarn
Cuilcagh 667
Swanlinbar
Derrylin
Upper Lough Erne
Newtownbutler
Clones
Newbliss
Emyvale
Caledon
Armagh
Middletown
Keady
Monaghan
Smithborough
Tandragee
Gilford
Laurencetown
Banbridge
Loughbrickland
Poyntzpass
Markethill
Rathfriland
Ballyroney
Katesbridge
Dromara
Dromore
Downpatrick
Clough
Dundrum
Dundrum Bay
Castlewellan
Ardglass
Killough
St. John's Point
Kilcoo
Newcastle
Slieve Donard 852
Mourne Mountains
Glasdrummond
Annalong
Kilkeel
Lisnacree
Rostrevor
Warrenpoint
Newry
Newtownhamilton
Castleblayney
Ballybay
Drum
Ballyconnell
Bawnboy
Belturbet
Cootehill
Cullaville
Carlingford
Carlingford Lough
Greenore
Kilcurry
Dundalk
Dundalk Bay
Shercock
Carrickmacross
Cavan
Stradone
Killeshandra
Ballinamore
Newtown Gore
Fenagh
Carrigallen
Crossdoney
Bellananagh
Bailieborough
Kingscourt
Castlebellingham
Annagassan
Dunany Point
Ardee
Dunleer
Clogherhead
Clogher Head
Newtown Monasterboice
Termonfeckin
Drogheda
Julianstown
Mohill
Drumsna
Dromod
Roosky
Newtown Forbes
Longford
Ballinalee
Granard
Lough Gowna
Kilnaleck
Ballyjamesduff
Virginia
Lough Ramor
Oldcastle
Finnea
Lough Sheelin
Nobber
Collon
Slane
Ceanannus
Crossakeel
Castlepollard
Lough Derravaragh
Rathowen
Mostrim
Killashee
Lanesborough
Clonmellon
Athboy
Navan
Delvin
Ballinalack
Carrickboy
Lough Ree
Ballymahon
Tang
Mullingar
Cloghan
Ballivor
Trim
Naul
Balbriggan
Skerries
Ballyboghil
Rush
Lambay Island
Dunshaughlin
Ashbourne
Swords
Malahide
Ballymore
Killare
The Downs
Killucan
Rathmolyon
Summerhill
Dunboyne
Kilcock
Ward
Cloghran
Ireland's Eye
Howth Head
Lough Ennell
Kinnegad
Clonard
Ballynadrumny
Innfield
Clonee
Lucan
Moate
Ballynagore
Rochfortbridge
Tyrrellspass
Horseleap
Kilbeggan
Clara
Ballynahown
Durrow
Tullamore
Edenderry
Carbury
Johnstown Bridge
Maynooth
Celbridge
DUBLIN (Baile Atha Cliath)
Dun Laoghaire (Dunleary)
Clondalkin
Tallaght
Rathcoole
Killane
Allenwood
Clane
Daingean
Ballinagar
Screggan
Ferbane
Liverpool (Summer)
Douglas (Summer)
Holyhead
Port Erin
Calf of Man
ISLE OF MAN
10
0 10 20 30 40 50 60 Kilometres

4

2 2

1 Inishbofin
Inishark

3 Williamstown
Roscommon

I R E

Partry Mount Lough Mask Ballindine Athleague
819 Ballinrobe 60 Ballygar Mount Talbot
Moyard Letterfrack Leenaun 84 Milltown Dunmore Newbridge Moylough Thomas Street Ballinasloe Brideswell
Clifden The Twelve 730 Maum Clonbur Cong Kilmaine Tuam 83 Barnaderg Mount Bellew Bridge Ballyforan
59 Pins Maam Cross Shrule 23 63 Kilconnell Kiltullagh Newbridge Athenry Aughrim 90
Mannin Bay Recess Maumturk Mts Headford 84 17 Kilreekill Ballydavid Laurence
Slyne Head Connemara Oughterard Claregalway 64 Athenry Kilmor Carrig
Derryrush Screeb Rosscahill 43 Galway 6 Oranmore 6 Craughwell Ballinasloe
Glinsk Bertraghboy Bay Moycullen 59 Oranmore Loughrea 65
Kilkieran Costelloe Spiddle Barna Clarinbridge Kilcolgan Ardrahan 66 65 Killimor Portumna
Gorumna Island Inveran Burren Kinvarra Laban Petersewell 367 Abbey 52
Cashla Bay North Sound Galway Bay Ballyvaghan Gort Derrybrien Slieve Aughty Mts Borrisokane
Black Head Lisdoonvarna 55 Modreeny
Inishmore Inishmaan Ennistimon Crusheen Scarriff Whitegate 65
Aran Islands South Inisheer Sound Hags Head Liscannor Bay Inagh 18 Tulla Bodyke Tuamgraney Nenagh 72
Milltown 391 85 Ennis Killaloe Keeper Hill
Spanish Point Malbay Slievecallan Clarecastle Kilkishen Slieve Bernagh 694 Newport Uppercl
Mal Bay Quilty Darragh Newmarket 533 40 7
67 Doonbeg Lissycasey on Fergus Sixmilebridge Cratloe 37
Kilkee 68 18 Limerick
Kilrush New Kildimo Askeaton Patrickswell Cahercornish
Carrigaholt Shannon 69 Foynes Shanagolden Adare Croom 24 Pallas Green (New)
Loop Head Tarbert Glin Rathkeale 20 Bruff Herbertstown
Mouth Ballybunnion 21 Newcastle West Rockhill Hospital Emly Tipper
of The Kerry Head Listowel 108 Kilmallock Galtymore
Shannon 69 Ardagh Rath Luirc Ballylanders Mountain
Brandon Bay Kilkinlea Mullaghareirk (Charleville) 519 920 Galty Mour
Rough Abbeyfeale Mountains Newtown 20 Kildorrery Kilbeheny
Brandon Point Point 357 Dromcolliher Milford 73 Mitchelstown
Ballydavid Tralee Bay Tralee 21 M U N Buttevant S T E K.
Head Brandon 853 21 Castleisland Newmarket Kanturk Castletownroche 80
Mountain Stradbally 22 23 Farranfore 72 Mallow Ballyde
Sybil Point Murreagh 953 Mountain 86 Slieve Mish Castlemaine Ballydesmond Banteer Fermoy Blackt
Dingle 826 Mountains Miltown 24 Nagles Rathcormack Tallow
Great Blasket Anascaul 70 Castlemaine Rathmore Millstreet Mts. 429
Island Milltown Harbour 22 Killorglin Killarney Ballynamona Watergrasshill
Slea Head Dingle Bay Killorglin 72 21 The Paps Boggeragh 35
Inishvickillane Glenbeigh 70 Lough Muckross 696 650 Mts 645 Dungourney
Doulus Head Carrauntoohil Leane Mangerton 87 Blarney Midleton
Valencia 1041 Macgillycuddy's Mountain Derrynasaggart Mts Macroom Coachford CORK Carrigtwohill
Island Cahersiveen Reeks 71 840 Ballyvourney 22 Ballynac
Bray Head New Chapel Cross Kilgarvan Carran Crookstown Lee Ballincollig Passage Cobh
Kenmare Cleady 606 Ballingeary Ballinhassig West Cloyne
The Skelligs Templenoe St Finan's Knockboy Shehy Mts Nowen Ballineen Carrigaline
Bolus Head Bay Sneem 70 707 Shehy Enniskean Bandon Crosshaven
Hog's Waterville Parknasilla Glengarriff Mountain Hill Dunmanway Inishannon Belgooly
Scariff Head Lauragh Knockowen 547 Ballinascarthy Kinsale
Island Ardgroom Caha Mountains 661 Kealkill Drimoleague Ballinspittle Frower Point
Lamb's Kenmare River Glengarriff Clonakilty Old Head
Cod's Head Head Hungry Adrigole Bantry Dunmanus Bay Timoleague of Kinsale
Dursey Castletown Hill Curryglass Durrus Connonagh Seven Heads
Island Bearhaven 886 Bear Ballydehob Kilcoe Leap Ross Carbery Clonakilty Bay
Dursey Head Cahermore Island Schull Skibbereen Galley Head Toe Head
Crow Munvertary or Toormore Roaringwater Bay
Head Sheeps Head Goleen Sherkin
Mizen Head Island
Cape Clear Clear Island

1 2 3

0 5 10 20 30 40 Miles

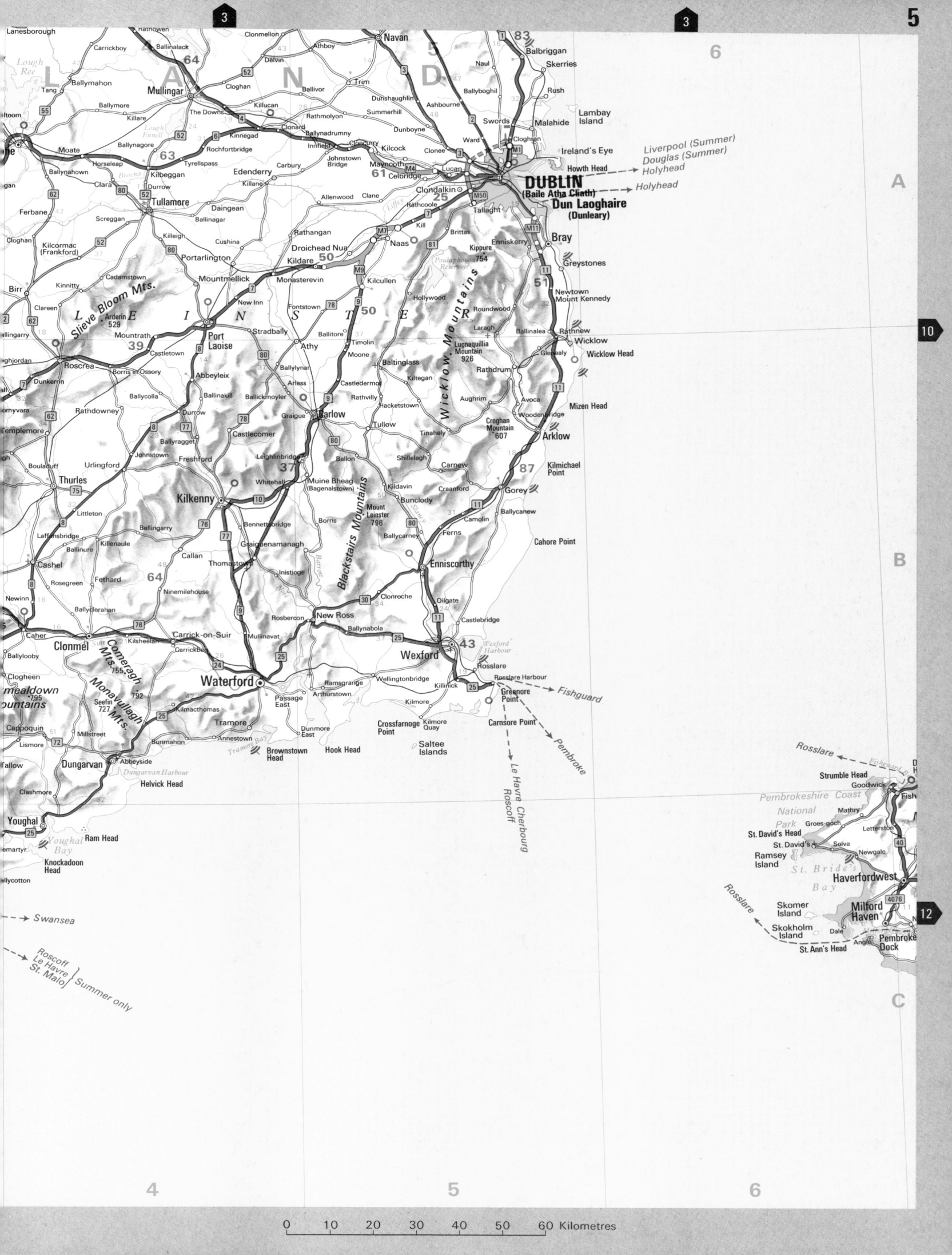
3
3
6
A
B
C
4
5
6
10
12
Lanesborough
Rathowen
Clonmellon
Navan
Athboy
Delvin
Carrickboy
Ballinalack
Lough Ree
Ballymahon
Tang
Mullingar
Cloghan
Trim
Ballivor
Dunshaughlin
Ashbourne
Ballyboghil
Naul
Balbriggan
Skerries
Rush
Lambay Island
Malahide
Swords
Ballymore
Killare
The Downs
Killucan
Rathmolyon
Summerhill
Dunboyne
Lough Ennell
Kinnegad
Clonard
Ballynadrumny
Ballynagore
Moate
Horseleap
Rochfortbridge
Tyrrellspass
Kilbeggan
Edenderry
Innfield
Clonee
Kilcock
Cloncurry
Johnstown Bridge
Carbury
Maynooth
Celbridge
Lucan
Ward
Cloghran
Ireland's Eye
Howth Head
Liverpool (Summer)
Douglas (Summer)
Holyhead
DUBLIN
(Baile Atha Cliath)
Dun Laoghaire
(Dunleary)
Holyhead
Clondalkin
Ballynahown
Clara
Durrow
Killane
Tullamore
Daingean
Allenwood
Clane
Rathcoole
Tallaght
Ferbane
Screggan
Ballinagar
Rathangan
Kill
Naas
Brittas
Enniskerry
Bray
Cloghan
Kilcormac
(Frankford)
Killeigh
Cushina
Droichead Nua
Kildare
Portarlington
Kippure 754
Poulaphouca Reservoir
Greystones
Birr
Kinnitty
Cadamstown
Mountmellick
Monasterevin
Kilcullen
Newtown Mount Kennedy
Slieve Bloom Mts.
Clareen
Arderin 529
New Inn
Fontstown
Hollywood
Roundwood
LEINSTER
Mountrath
Port Laoise
Stradbally
Ballitore
Timolin
Laragh
Ballinalea
Rathnew
Wicklow
Wicklow Mountains
Lugnaquillia Mountain 926
Glenealy
Wicklow Head
Castletown
Athy
Moone
Baltinglass
Roscrea
Dunkerrin
Borris in Ossory
Abbeyleix
Ballylynan
Arless
Kiltegan
Rathdrum
Castledermot
Ballinakill
Ballickmoyler
Ballycolla
Rathvilly
Aughrim
Avoca
Woodenbridge
Mizen Head
Templemore
Rathdowney
Durrow
Graigue
Carlow
Hacketstown
Tullow
Tinahely
Croghan Mountain 607
Arklow
Ballyragget
Castlecomer
Johnstown
Freshford
Leighlinbridge
Ballon
Shillelagh
Carnew
Kilmichael Point
Bouladuff
Urlingford
Thurles
Whitehall
Muine Bheag
(Bagenalstown)
Kildavin
Craanford
Gorey
Kilkenny
Bunclody
Mount Leinster 796
Blackstairs Mountains
Ballycanew
Littleton
Bennettsbridge
Borris
Camolin
Ferns
Ballycarney
Ballingarry
Laffansbridge
Killenaule
Ballinure
Graiguenamanagh
Cahore Point
Cashel
Callan
Thomastown
Enniscorthy
Rosegreen
Fethard
Inistioge
Ninemilehouse
Clonroche
Oilgate
Newinn
Ballyclerahan
Rosbercon
New Ross
Castlebridge
Caher
Clonmel
Kilsheelan
Carrick-on-Suir
Mullinavat
Ballynabola
Wexford
Wexford Harbour
Carrickbeg
Ballylooby
Comeragh Mts. 755
Waterford
Rosslare
Rosslare Harbour
Clogheen
Monavullagh Mts. 792
Ramsgrange
Wellingtonbridge
Killinick
Greenore Point
Fishguard
Knockmealdown Mountains 795
Seefin 727
Passage East
Arthurstown
Kilmore
Kilmacthomas
Tramore
Crossfarnoge Point
Kilmore Quay
Carnsore Point
Cappoquin
Millstreet
Dunmore East
Lismore
Bunmahon
Annestown
Tramore Bay
Brownstown Head
Hook Head
Saltee Islands
Pembroke
Le Havre Cherbourg Roscoff
Tallow
Dungarvan
Abbeyside
Dungarvan Harbour
Helvick Head
Clashmore
Youghal
Ram Head
Youghal Bay
Knockadoon Head
Ballycotton
Swansea
Roscoff
Le Havre
St. Malo
Summer only
Rosslare
Strumble Head
Goodwick
Fishguard Bay
Pembrokeshire Coast National Park
Mathry
Groes-goch
St. David's Head
St. David's
Solva
Letterston
Newgale
Ramsey Island
St. Bride's Bay
Haverfordwest
Rosslare
Skomer Island
Milford Haven
Skokholm Island
Dale
Angle
Pembroke Dock
St. Ann's Head

0 10 20 30 40 50 60 Kilometres

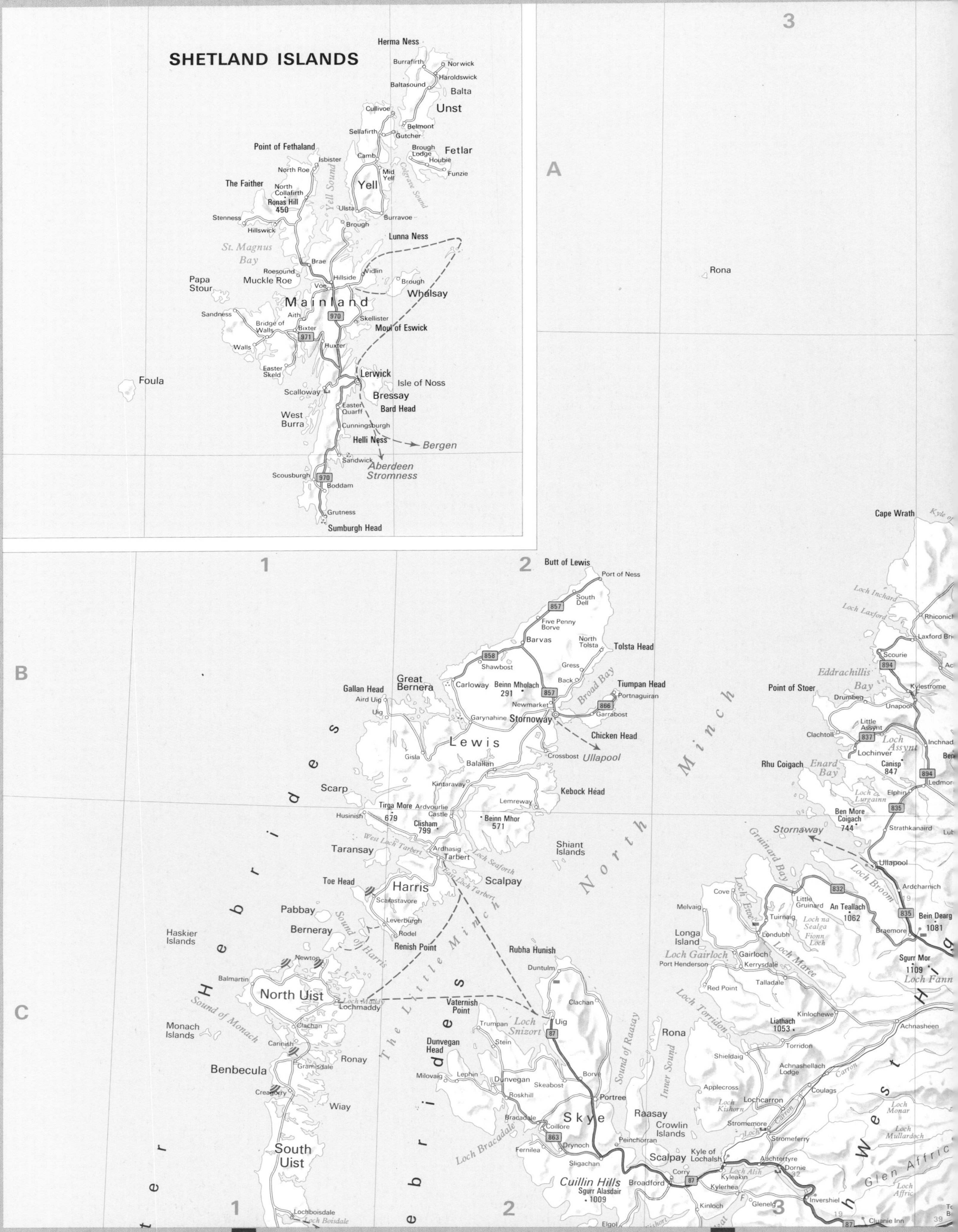

SHETLAND ISLANDS

Herma Ness
Burrafirth
Norwick
Haroldswick
Baltasound
Balta
Cullivoe
Unst
Belmont
Gutcher
Point of Fethaland
Sellafirth
Camb
Brough Lodge
Fetlar
Isbister
Mid Yell
Houbie
Funzie
North Roe
The Faither
North Collafirth
Yell
Ronas Hill 450
Ulsta
Stenness
Burravoe
Hillswick
Brough
Lunna Ness
St. Magnus Bay
Roesound
Brae
Vidlin
Papa Stour
Muckle Roe
Hillside
Brough
Voe
Whalsay
Sandness
Mainland
Aith
Skellister
Bridge of Walls
Bixter
Moul of Eswick
Walls
Huxter
Easter Skeld
Lerwick
Isle of Noss
Scalloway
Bressay
Easter Quarff
Bard Head
West Burra
Cunningsburgh
Helli Ness
Bergen
Sandwick
Aberdeen
Stromness
Scousburgh
Boddam
Grutness
Sumburgh Head

Foula

Rona

Cape Wrath
Kyle of
Loch Inchard
Loch Laxford
Rhiconich
Laxford Bri
Scourie
894
Eddrachillis Bay
Point of Stoer
Kylestrome
Drumbeg
Unapool
Little Assynt
Clachtoll
837
Loch Assynt
Inchnad
Lochinver
Rhu Coigach
Enard Bay
Canisp 847
894
Ben More Coigach 744
835
Elphin
Ledmore
Strathkanaird
Stornaway
Ullapool
Ardcharnich

Butt of Lewis
Port of Ness
857
South Dell
Five Penny Borve
Barvas
North Tolsta
Tolsta Head
858
Shawbost
Gress
Gallan Head
Great Bernera
Carloway
Beinn Mholach 291
Back
Tiumpan Head
Aird Uig
Newmarket
857
Broad Bay
Portnaguiran
Uig
Garynahine
866
Garrabost
Lewis
Stornoway
Gisla
Chicken Head
Balallan
Crossbost
Ullapool
Scarp
Kintaravay
Kebock Head
Tirga More
Ardvourlie Castle
Lemreway
Husinish
679
Beinn Mhor 571
Shiant Islands
Clisham 799
Taransay
West Loch Tarbert
Ardhasig
Tarbert
North Minch
Toe Head
Harris
Scalpay
Scaristavore
Pabbay
Loch Seaforth
Berneray
Leverburgh
Rodel
Renish Point
Rubha Hunish
Cove
Loch Ewe
Melvaig
Little Gruinard
An Teallach 1062
Bein Dearg 1081
832
Haskier Islands
Duntulm
Longa Island
Tuirnaig
Loch na Sealga
Fionn Loch
835
Braemore
Balmartin
Newton
Sound of Harris
Vaternish Point
Clachan
Londubh
Loch Gairloch
Gairloch
Port Henderson
Sgurr Mor 1109
Loch Fann
North Uist
Lochmaddy
Uig
Red Point
Kerrysdale
Talladale
Loch Maree
Monach Islands
Clachan
Trumpan
Loch Snizort
Stein
87
Dunvegan Head
Rona
Liathach 1053
Achnasheen
Carinish
Milovaig
Lephin
Loch Torridon
Kinlochewe
Benbecula
Gramisdale
Ronay
Dunvegan
Skeabost
Borve
Torridon
Achnashellach Lodge
Creagorry
Wiay
Roskhill
Portree
Raasay
Shieldaig
Bracadale
Sound of Raasay
Loch Kishorn
Lochcarron
Carron
Coulags
863
Coillore
Crowlin Islands
Stromeferry
Loch Monar
South Uist
Fernilea
Drynoch
Peinchorran
Stromemore
Loch Mullardoch
Skye
Sligachan
Scalpay
Kyle of Lochalsh
Auchtertyre
Corry
Dornie
Inner Sound
Lochboisdale
Loch Boisdale
Cuillin Hills
Sgurr Alasdair 1009
Broadford
Kyleakin
87
Kylerhea
Glenelg
Glen Affric
Invershiel
Elgol
Kinloch
Cluanie Inn
87

Outer Hebrides
Inner Hebrides
The Little Minch
Sound of Monach
North Minch
North West High

0 5 10   20   30   40 Miles

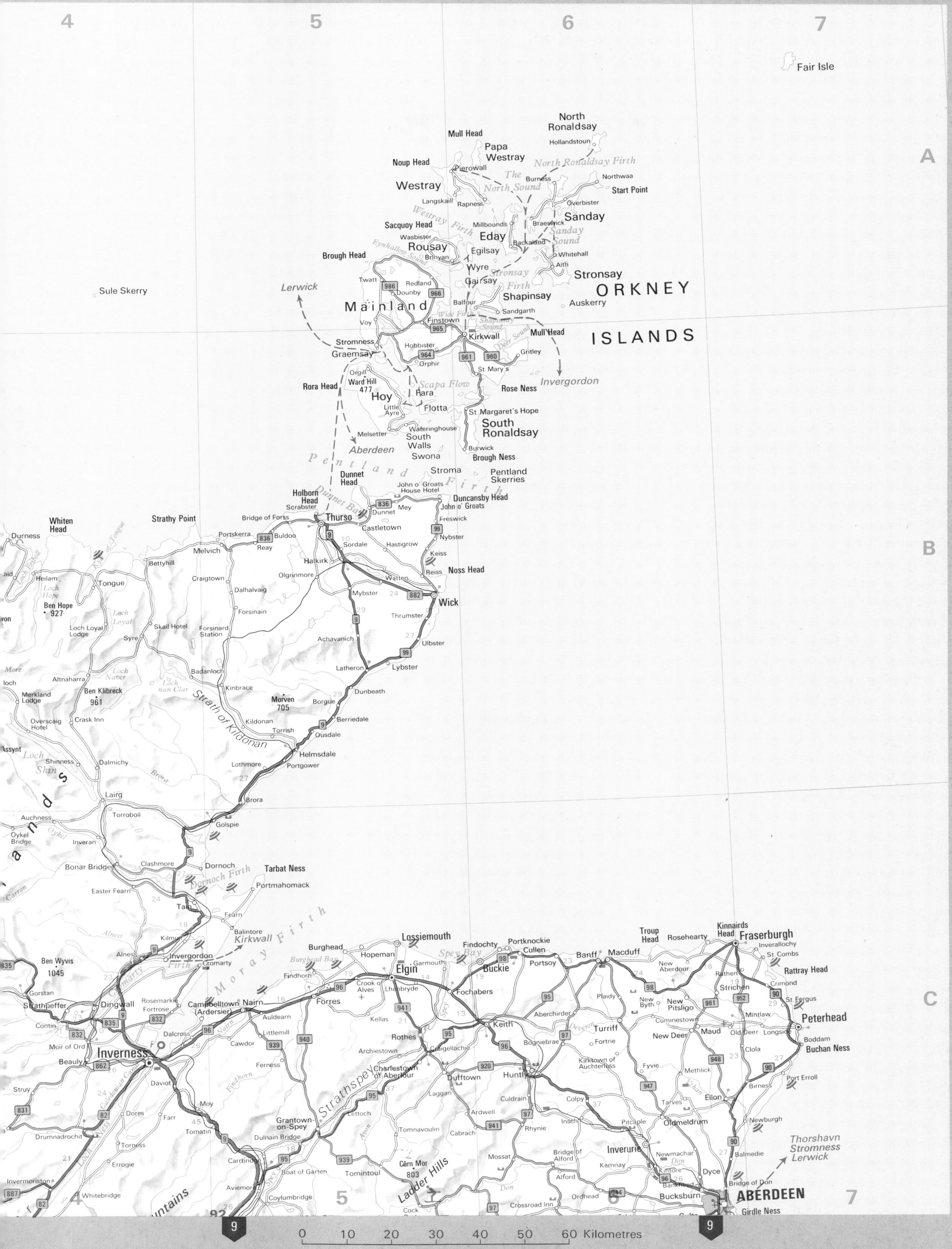

4   5   6   7

A

Fair Isle

North Ronaldsay
Hollandstoun

Mull Head
Papa
Westray
Noup Head
Pierowall
The
North Sound
Burness
Northwaa
Westray
Langskaill
Rapness
Start Point
Overbister

North Ronaldsay Firth

Sacquoy Head
Wasbister
Millbounds
Braeswick
Sanday
Brough Head
Rousay
Brinyan
Eday
Egilsay
Backaland
Sanday Sound
Whitehall
Aith

Twatt
Redland
Wyre
Gairsay
Stronsay Firth
Stronsay
ORKNEY

Lerwick
986
Dounby
966
Wide Firth
Shapinsay

Mainland
Voy
Finstown
965
Sandgarth
Auskerry
ISLANDS

Stromness
Hobbister
Kirkwall
Shapinsay Sound
Mull Head
Sule Skerry
Graemsay
964
Orphir
961
960
Gritley

Orgill
Ward Hill
477
St. Mary's
Rose Ness
Invergordon

Rora Head
Little
Ayre
Cara
Scapa Flow
St. Margaret's Hope
Hoy
Flotta

Melsetter
Waterinhouse
South
Walls
South
Ronaldsay

Aberdeen
Swona
Burwick
Dunnet
Head
Stroma
Brough Ness
Pentland
Skerries

Pentland Firth
Dunnet Bay
John o' Groats
House Hotel
Duncansby Head

Whiten
Head
Strathy Point
Bridge of Forss
Holborn
Head
Scrabster
836
Dunnet
Mey
John o' Groats
Freswick
836

Durness
Portskerra
836
Buldoo
Thurso
Castletown
9
99
Nybster
B

Heilam
Bettyhill
Melvich
Reay
Halkirk
10
Sordale
Hastigrow
Keiss
Tongue
Craigtown
Dalhalvaig
Olgrinmore
Watten
Reiss
Noss Head
Loch
Hope
Ben Hope
927
Loch Loyal
Lodge
Skail Hotel
Forsinain
Mybster
24
882
Wick

Syre
Forsinard
Station
9
Thrumster
Loch Loyal
Achavanich
27
Ulbster
More
loch
Altnaharra
Badanloch
Kinbrace
Latheron
99
Lybster

Merkland
Lodge
Ben Klibreck
961
Loch
nan Clar
Morven
705
Borgue
Dunbeath
Overscaig
Hotel
Crask Inn
Kildonan
Torrish
29
Berriedale
Assynt
Shinness
Dalmichy
Strath of Kildonan
Lothmore
Ousdale
9
Helmsdale
Loch
Shin
Lairg
Portgower
27
Brora

Auchness
Torroboll
Golspie
Oykel
Bridge
Inveran
9
Bonar Bridge
Clashmore
Dornoch
Tarbat Ness

Easter Fearn
Dornoch Firth
Portmahomack

Carron
24
Tain
Fearn
Kirkwall Firth
Balintore
Troup
Head
Rosehearty
Kinnaird's
Head
Fraserburgh
18
Kilmuir
Inverallochy

Alness
Burghead
Lossiemouth
Findochty
Portknockie
Cullen
St Combs
Ben Wyvis
1045
Invergordon
Cromarty
Moray Firth
Burghead Bay
Hopeman
Garmouth
Spey Bay
98
Portsoy
Banff
Macduff
New
Aberdour
Rathen
19
Rattray Head
435
Gorstan
Findhorn
Elgin
14
Buckie
95
Plaidy
98
Strichen
952
90
St Fergus
Strathpeffer
Rosemarkie
Fortrose
Dingwall
Forres
96
Crook of
Alves
Lhanbryde
Fochabers
Aberchirder
New
Byth
New
Pitsligo
981
Mintlaw
Peterhead
Contin
835
Campbelltown
(Ardersier)
16
Nairn
941
Kellas
Rothes
Keith
97
Cuminestown
Maud
Old Deer
Clola
Boddam
832
832
Auldearn
13
Craigellachie
96
Turriff
New Deer
948
23
Buchan Ness
Muir of Ord
96
Dalcross
Littlemill
Cawdor
939
940
Archiestown
Bogniebrae
Fortrie
Fyvie
Methlick
27
Port Erroll
Beauly
862
Ferness
Charlestown
of Aberlour
920
Huntly
Kirkton of
Auchterless
Tarves
Birness
90
Stru
831
Moy
Dufftown
Culdrain
Colpy
Inch
Pitcaple
Ellon
Newburgh
82
Dores
Farr
Laggan
Ardwell
97
Rhynie
Oldmeldrum
Thorshavn
Stromness
Lerwick
Inverness
Drumnadrochit
Tomatin
Grantown-
on-Spey
Cettock
Tomnavoulin
Cabrach
941
Bridge of
Alford
Mossat
Kemnay
Newmachar
Don
Balmedie
887
Errogie
Dulnain Bridge
18
Càirn Gorm
803
Ladder Hills
Alford
Insch
90
Inverurie
Dyce
82
Whitebridge
95
939
Boat of Garten
Tomintoul
Kintore
96
26
Bridge of Don
Invermoriston
Carrbridge
Aviemore
Coylumbridge
Cock
97
Ordhead
844
Bucksburn
ABERDEEN
Girdle Ness
Crossroad Inn
Cults

C

9   9

0   10   20   30   40   50   60 Kilometres

6

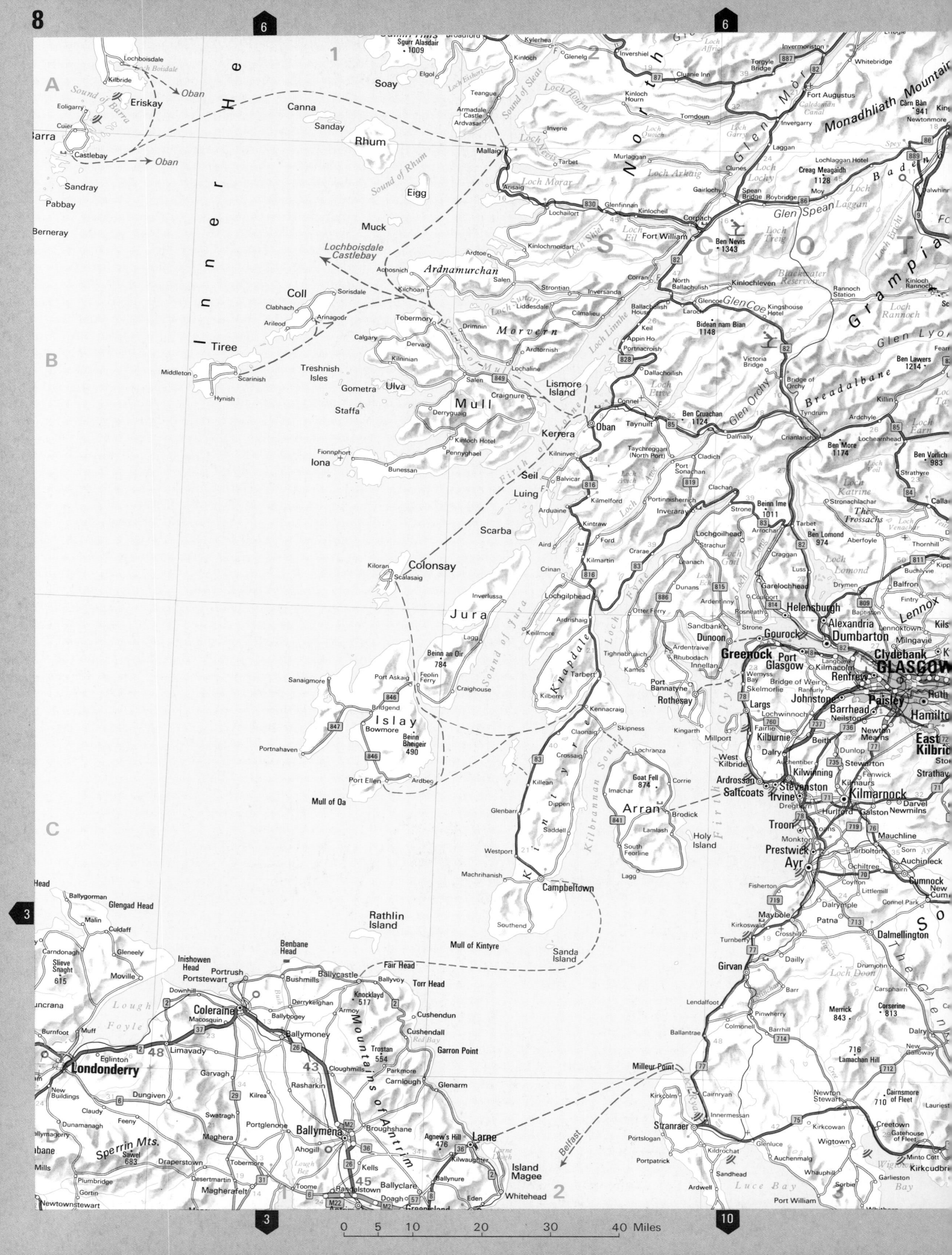

A
B
C
D
1
2
3
Inner Hebrides
North
SCOT
Grampian
Barra
Lochboisdale
Loch Boisdale
Kilbride
Sound of Barra
Eriskay
Eoligarry
Cuier
Castlebay
Oban
Sandray
Pabbay
Berneray
Sgurr Alasdair
1009
Soay
Elgol
Canna
Sanday
Rhum
Sound of Rhum
Eigg
Muck
Lochboisdale
Castlebay
Coll
Sorisdale
Clabhach
Arileod
Arinagour
Tiree
Middleton
Scarinish
Hynish
Kylerhea
Kinloch
Glenelg
Sound of Sleat
Loch Eishort
Teangue
Armadale Castle
Ardvasar
Loch Hourn
Inverie
Loch Nevis
Mallaig
Tarbet
Loch Morar
Arisaig
Lochailort
Glenfinnan
Kinlocheil
Corpach
Fort William
Ben Nevis
1343
Loch Eil
Loch Shiel
Kinlochmoidart
Ardtoe
Achosnich
Kilchoan
Ardnamurchan
Salen
Strontian
Inversanda
Corran
North Ballachulish
Kinlochleven
Blackwater Reservoir
Loch Sunart
Liddesdale
Cilmalieu
Ballachulish House
Glencoe
Glen Coe
Laroch
Kingshouse Hotel
Bidean nam Bian
1148
Tobermory
Drimnin
Morvern
Dervaig
Calgary
Kilninian
Sound of Mull
Ardtornish
Lochaline
Treshnish Isles
Gometra
Ulva
Salen
Mull
Craignure
Lismore Island
Staffa
Derryguaig
Kinloch Hotel
Pennyghael
Fionnphort
Iona
Bunessan
Oban
Kerrera
Kilninver
Firth of Lorne
Seil
Luing
Balvicar
Arduaine
Scarba
Aird
Kiloran
Colonsay
Scalasaig
Jura
Inverlussa
Lagg
Sound of Jura
Beinn an Oir
784
Feolin Ferry
Craighouse
Port Askaig
Sanaigmore
Bridgend
Islay
Bowmore
Beinn Bheigeir
490
Portnahaven
Port Ellen
Ardbeg
Mull of Oa
Crinan
Lochgilphead
Ardrishaig
Kilmartin
Kilmelford
Kintraw
Ford
Keillmore
Knapdale
Tarbert
Kilberry
Kennacraig
Claonaig
Skipness
Crossaig
Kintyre
Killean
Glenbarr
Westport
Machrihanish
Campbeltown
Southend
Mull of Kintyre
Sanda Island
Kilbrannan Sound
Lochranza
Goat Fell
874
Imachar
Corrie
Arran
Brodick
Lamlash
Holy Island
South Feorline
Lagg
Dippen
Saddell
Kilchoan
Invergarry
Inverlochy
Glen Spean
Spean Bridge
Roybridge
Laggan
Loch Laggan
Loch Treig
Taynuilt
Connel
Loch Etive
Ben Cruachan
1124
Dalmally
Glen Orchy
Bridge of Orchy
Victoria Bridge
Dallachoilish
Keil
Appin Ho
Portnacroish
Loch Linnhe
Taychreggan (North Port)
Port Sonachan
Cladich
Clachan
Loch Awe
Portinnisherrich
Inveraray
Strone
Cairndow
Lochgoilhead
Strachur
Loch Fyne
Cruachan
Otter Ferry
Tighnabruaich
Kames
Sandbank
Dunoon
Rothesay
Port Bannatyne
Kingarth
Millport
Gourock
Greenock
Port Glasgow
Helensburgh
Dumbarton
Alexandria
Balloch
Clydebank
GLASGOW
Renfrew
Paisley
Johnstone
Barrhead
Neilston
Hamilton
East Kilbride
Largs
Lochwinnoch
Fairlie
Kilburnie
Dalry
Beith
West Kilbride
Ardrossan
Saltcoats
Stevenston
Kilwinning
Irvine
Kilmarnock
Troon
Prestwick
Ayr
Monkton
Mauchline
Auchinleck
Cumnock
Maybole
Dalmellington
Girvan
Turnberry
Kirkoswald
Crosshill
Barr
Loch Doon
Merrick
843
Corserine
813
Ballantrae
Lendalfoot
Colmonell
Barrhill
Pinwherry
Glenluce
Cairnryan
Stranraer
Portpatrick
Portslogan
Kirkcolm
Loch Ryan
Milleur Point
Sandhead
Ardwell
Luce Bay
Port William
Wigtown
Newton Stewart
Creetown
Gatehouse of Fleet
Kirkcudbright
Wigtown Bay
Lamachan Hill
716
Cairnsmore of Fleet
710
New Galloway
Dalry
Carsphairn
Fort Augustus
Invermoriston
Whitebridge
Monadhliath Mountains
Carn Ban
941
Newtonmore
Laggan
Lochlaggan Hotel
Creag Meagaidh
1128
Moy
Glen Mor
Loch Lochy
Clunes
Gairlochy
Loch Arkaig
Murlaggan
Loch Quoich
Loch Garry
Tomdoun
Kinloch Hourn
Cluanie Inn
Torgyle Bridge
Inverarie
Loch Affric
Rannoch Station
Loch Rannoch
Kinloch Rannoch
Glen Lyon
Ben Lawers
1214
Breadalbane
Killin
Tyndrum
Crianlarich
Ben More
1174
Ardchyle
Lochearnhead
Loch Earn
Ben Vorlich
983
Strathyre
Loch Katrine
The Trossachs
Stronachlachar
Ben Lomond
974
Aberfoyle
Loch Lomond
Tarbet
Arrochar
Luss
Drymen
Balfron
Garelochhead
Coulport
Rosneath
Lennox
Milngavie
Beinn Ime
1011
Rathlin Island
Benbane Head
Fair Head
Ballycastle
Torr Head
Ballyvoy
Knocklayd
517
Cushendun
Cushendall
Red Bay
Trostan
554
Garron Point
Glenarm
Carnlough
Parkmore
Cloughmills
Mountains of Antrim
Agnew's Hill
476
Larne
Island Magee
Whitehead
Belfast
Ballymena
Broughshane
Ahogill
Kells
Ballyclare
Antrim
Randalstown
Toome
Portglenone
Rasharkin
Ballymoney
Ballybogey
Bushmills
Portrush
Portstewart
Coleraine
Macosquin
Derrykeighan
Armoy
Downhill
Inishowen Head
Lough Foyle
Limavady
Londonderry
Eglinton
Muff
Burnfoot
Buncrana
Moville
Glengad Head
Malin
Culdaff
Ballygorman
Carndonagh
Gleneely
Slieve Snaght
615
Garvagh
Kilrea
Dungiven
Claudy
Feeny
Dunamanagh
Swatragh
Maghera
Sperrin Mts.
Sawel
683
Draperstown
Tobermore
Magherafelt
Desertmartin
Plumbridge
Gortin
Newtownstewart
New Buildings
Lough Beg

3

3

10

0 5 10 20 30 40 Miles

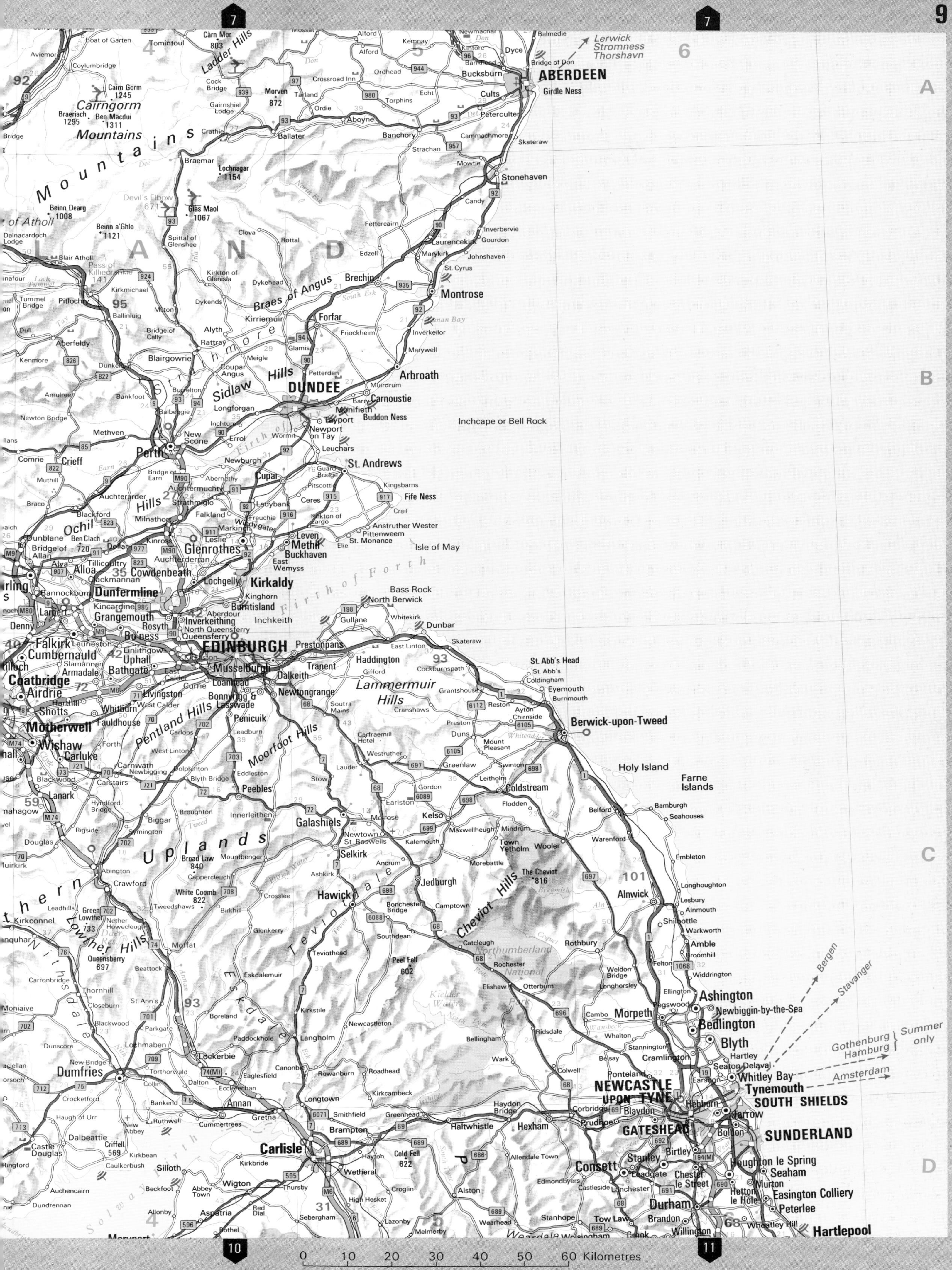
7
7
Tomintoul
Càrn Mor 803
Ladder Hills
Alford
Kemnay
Balmedie
Lerwick
Stromness
Thorshavn
Aviemore
Boat of Garten
Coylumbridge
Cairn Gorm 1245
Cairngorm Mountains
Braeriach 1295
Ben Macdui 1311
Cock Bridge
Gairnshiel Lodge
Morven 872
Crossroad Inn
Tarland
Ordie
Ordhead
Echt
Torphins
Aboyne
Ballater
Crathie
Banchory
Bucksburn
Cults
Peterculter
Dyce
Bridge of Don
ABERDEEN
Girdle Ness
Cammachmore
Skateraw
Strachan
Mowtie
Stonehaven
Braemar
Lochnagar 1154
Devil's Elbow 671
Glas Maol 1067
Beinn Dearg 1008
Beinn a'Ghlo 1121
Spittal of Glenshee
Dalnacardoch Lodge
Blair Atholl
Pass of Killiecrankie
Clova
Rottal
Fettercairn
Candy
Inverbervie
Gourdon
Laurencekirk
Marykirk
Johnshaven
Edzell
St. Cyrus
Kirkton of Glenisla
Dykehead
Kirkmichael
Pitlochry
Brechin
Montrose
Braes of Angus
Forfar
Kirriemuir
Dykends
Ballinluig
Aberfeldy
Bridge of Cally
Alyth
Rattray
Glamis
Friockheim
Inverkeilor
Marywell
Kenmore
Blairgowrie
Meigle
Coupar Angus
Dunkeld
Arbroath
Sidlaw Hills
DUNDEE
Carnoustie
Muirdrum
Petterden
Amulree
Bankfoot
Longforgan
Monifieth
Buddon Ness
Tayport
Newport on Tay
Inchcape or Bell Rock
Newton Bridge
Methven
New Scone
Errol
Wormit
Leuchars
Perth
Firth of Tay
Comrie
Crieff
Newburgh
St. Andrews
Muthill
Bridge of Earn
Auchtermuchty
Cupar
Kingsbarns
Fife Ness
Auchterarder
Strathmiglo
Ladybank
Ceres
Crail
Braco
Ochil Hills
Blackford
Milnathort
Falkland
Freuchie
Markinch
Kirkton of Largo
Anstruther Wester
Pittenweem
St. Monance
Elie
Isle of May
Dunblane
Ben Clach 720
Kinross
Glenrothes
Leslie
Leven
Methil
Buckhaven
East Wemyss
Bridge of Allan
Dollar
Tillicoultry
Alva
Alloa
Clackmannan
Cowdenbeath
Auchterderran
Lochgelly
Kirkaldy
Firth of Forth
Bannockburn
Dunfermline
Kinghorn
Burntisland
Bass Rock
North Berwick
Larbert
Kincardine
Grangemouth
Inverkeithing
Aberdour
Inchkeith
Gullane
Whitekirk
Dunbar
Denny
Falkirk
Bo'ness
Rosyth
North Queensferry
Queensferry
Cumbernauld
Laurieston
Linlithgow
EDINBURGH
Prestonpans
East Linton
Skateraw
Slamannan
Uphall
Bathgate
Armadale
Musselburgh
Tranent
Haddington
Gifford
Cockburnspath
St. Abb's Head
St. Abb's
Coldingham
Eyemouth
Burnmouth
Coatbridge
Airdrie
Livingston
Currie
Loanhead
Dalkeith
Newtongrange
Lammermuir Hills
Grantshouse
Reston
Ayton
Chirnside
Berwick-upon-Tweed
Harthill
Shotts
Whitburn
West Calder
Bonnyrigg & Lasswade
Soutra Mains
Cranshaws
Motherwell
Fauldhouse
Penicuik
Pentland Hills
Moorfoot Hills
Preston
Duns
Mount Pleasant
Wishaw
Carluke
Forth
Carlops
Leadburn
Carfraemill Hotel
Westruther
Greenlaw
Swinton
Holy Island
Farne Islands
West Linton
Carnwath
Newbigging
Dolphinton
Eddleston
Lauder
Leitholm
Coldstream
Blackwood
Carstairs
Blyth Bridge
Peebles
Stow
Gordon
Lanark
Earlston
Flodden
Bamburgh
Seahouses
Belford
Lesmahagow
Hyndford Bridge
Broughton
Innerleithen
Galashiels
Melrose
Kelso
Biggar
Newtown St. Boswells
Maxwellheugh
Mindrum
Town Yetholm
Wooler
Warenford
Rigside
Symington
Uplands
Selkirk
Kalemouth
Douglas
Broad Law 840
Mountbenger
Ancrum
Morebattle
Embleton
Abington
Cappercleuch
Ashkirk
The Cheviot 816
Crawford
Jedburgh
Hawick
101
Alnwick
Longhoughton
White Coomb 822
Crosslee
Teviotdale
Bonchester Bridge
Camptown
Cheviot Hills
Lesbury
Alnmouth
Leadhills
Tweedshaws
Birkhill
Shilbottle
Kirkconnel
Green Lowther 733
Nether Howecleugh
Lowther Hills
Glenkerry
Southdean
Catcleugh
Warkworth
Sanquhar
Moffat
Rothbury
Amble
Queensberry 697
Beattock
Teviothead
Peel Fell 602
Rochester
Northumberland National Park
Felton
Broomhill
Widdrington
Carronbridge
Eskdalemuir
Elishaw
Otterburn
Weldon Bridge
Longhorsley
Bergen
Stavanger
Thornhill
Closeburn
St Ann's
Kielder Water
Ellington
Ashington
Moniaive
Boreland
Kirkstile
Pegswood
Newbiggin-by-the-Sea
Blackwood
Parkgate
Eskdale
Cambo
Morpeth
Bedlington
Dunscore
Lochmaben
Newcastleton
Langholm
Paddockhole
Ridsdale
Bellingham
Whalton
Stannington
Blyth
Summer only
Gothenburg
Hamburg
Hartley
Seaton Delaval
Whitley Bay
Amsterdam
New Bridge
Torthorwald
Lockerbie
Eaglesfield
Canonbie
Roadhead
Wark
Belsay
Ponteland
Cramlington
Earsdon
Tynemouth
Dumfries
Dalton
Ecclefechan
Rowanburn
Colwell
NEWCASTLE UPON TYNE
SOUTH SHIELDS
Collin
Crocketford
Bankend
Annan
Longtown
Kirkcambeck
Haydon Bridge
Corbridge
Blaydon
Hebburn
Haugh of Urr
New Abbey
Ruthwell
Gretna
Smithfield
Greenhead
Haltwhistle
Hexham
Prudhoe
GATESHEAD
Jarrow
Boldon
SUNDERLAND
Cummertrees
Brampton
Dalbeattie
Criffell 569
Kirkbean
Carlisle
Cold Fell 622
Allendale Town
Consett
Stanley
Birtley
Castle Douglas
Caulkerbush
Silloth
Kirkbride
Hayton
Wetheral
Leadgate
Chester le Street
Houghton le Spring
Seaham
Murton
Edmondbyers
Ringford
Beckfoot
Abbey Town
Wigton
Thursby
Croglin
Alston
Castleside
Lanchester
Hetton le Hole
Easington Colliery
Auchencairn
Dundrennan
Solway Firth
Allonby
Aspatria
Red Dial
Sebergham
High Hesket
Durham
Peterlee
Stanhope
Tow Law
Brandon
Wearhead
Lazonby
Melmerby
Wolsingham
Willington
Crook
Wheatley Hill
Hartlepool
Maryport
Bothel
Weardale
10
11
0 10 20 30 40 50 60 Kilometres
A
B
C
D
4
5
6

8
9
3
5

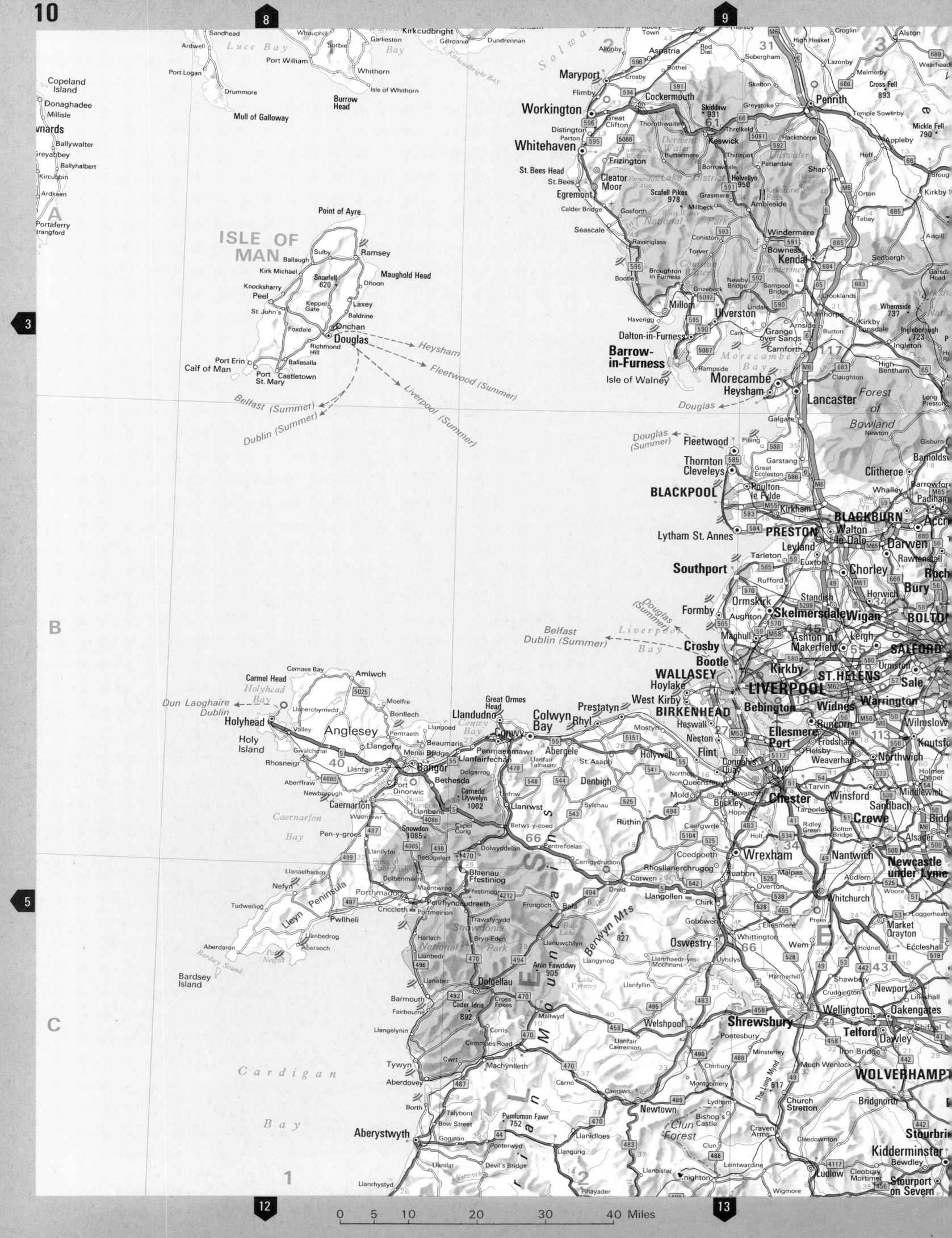

Sandhead
Ardwell
Luce Bay
Whauphill
Sorbie
Kirkcudbright
Garlieston
Wigtown Bay
Gillroanie
Dundrennan
Kirkcudbright Bay
Solway
Port William
Port Logan
Whithorn
Isle of Whithorn
Drummore
Burrow Head
Mull of Galloway
Copeland Island
Donaghadee
Millisle
Ballywalter
Greyabbey
Ballyhalbert
Kircubbin
Ardkeen
Portaferry
Strangford
A
B
C
ISLE OF MAN
Point of Ayre
Sulby
Ramsey
Ballaugh
Kirk Michael
Snaefell 620
Maughold Head
Dhoon
Knocksharry
Peel
Keppel Gate
Laxey
Baldrine
St. John's
Onchan
Foxdale
Douglas
Richmond Hill
Port Erin
Calf of Man
Ballasalla
Port St. Mary
Castletown
Heysham
Fleetwood (Summer)
Liverpool (Summer)
Belfast (Summer)
Dublin (Summer)
Allonby
Aspatria
Red Dial
Sebergham
High Hesket
Croglin
Alston
Maryport
Crosby
Bothel
Lazonby
Melmerby
Wearhead
Flimby
Cockermouth
Skelton
Cross Fell 893
Workington
Great Clifton
Skiddaw 931
Greystoke
Penrith
Temple Sowerby
Thornthwaite
Threlkeld
Mickle Fell 790
Distington
Parton
Whitehaven
Derwent Water
Keswick
Hackthorpe
Appleby
Ullswater
Frizington
Buttermere
Thirlspot
Patterdale
Hoff
St. Bees Head
St. Bees
Cleator Moor
Helvellyn 950
Shap
Lake District
Egremont
Scafell Pikes 978
Grasmere
Kirkstone Pass
Orton
Kirkby
Calder Bridge
Gosforth
Ambleside
Millbeck
National Park
Tebay
Seascale
Windermere
Ravenglass
Coniston
Bowness
Kendal
Aisgill
Torver
Sedbergh
Garsdale Head
Broughton in Furness
Coniston Water
Bootle
Newby Bridge
Sampool Bridge
Crooklands
Grizebeck
Millom
Lindale
Ulverston
Milnthorpe
Whernside 737
Haverigg
Arnside
Kirkby Lonsdale
Ingleborough 723
Dalton-in-Furness
Cark
Grange over Sands
Burton
Ingleton
Barrow-in-Furness
Carnforth
Morecambe Bay
High Bentham
Rampside
Claughton
Isle of Walney
Morecambe
Heysham
Lancaster
Forest of Bowland
Long Preston
Douglas
Galgate
Newton
Fleetwood
Pilling
Gisburn
Thornton Cleveleys
Garstang
Great Eccleston
Clitheroe
Barnoldswick
Poulton le Fylde
BLACKPOOL
Whalley
Barrowford
Padiham
Kirkham
BLACKBURN
Accrington
Lytham St. Annes
PRESTON
Walton le Dale
Darwen
Leyland
Rawtenstall
Tarleton
Euxton
Southport
Chorley
Rufford
Rochdale
Horwich
Bury
Ormskirk
Standish
Formby
Skelmersdale
Wigan
BOLTON
Aughton
Maghull
Ashton in Makerfield
Leigh
Liverpool Bay
Belfast
Dublin (Summer)
Douglas (Summer)
Crosby
SALFORD
Bootle
Urmston
WALLASEY
Kirkby
ST. HELENS
Hoylake
Sale
West Kirby
LIVERPOOL
BIRKENHEAD
Bebington
Widnes
Warrington
Heswall
Ellesmere Port
Runcorn
Wilmslow
Neston
Frodsham
Knutsford
Flint
Connah's Quay
Helsby
Weaverham
Northwich
Holmes Chapel
Tarvin
Middlewich
Chester
Winsford
Sandbach
Crewe
Alsager
Nantwich
Newcastle under Lyme
Audlem
Whitchurch
Market Drayton
Eccleshall
Newport
Wellington
Oakengates
Telford
Dawley
Shifnal
Iron Bridge
Much Wenlock
WOLVERHAMPTON
Bridgnorth
Stourbridge
Kidderminster
Bewdley
Stourport on Severn
Cleobury Mortimer
Ludlow
Cemaes Bay
Carmel Head
Amlwch
Holyhead Bay
Dun Laoghaire
Dublin
Moelfre
Llanerchymedd
Benllech
Holyhead
Valley
Anglesey
Llangoed
Pentraeth
Holy Island
Beaumaris
Llangefni
Menai Bridge
Rhosneigr
Gwalchmai
Llanfair P.G.
Bangor
Aberffraw
Newborough
Port Dinorwic
Bethesda
Caernarfon
Llanberis
Great Ormes Head
Llandudno
Conwy Bay
Conwy
Colwyn Bay
Rhyl
Prestatyn
Mostyn
Penmaenmawr
Llanfairfechan
Abergele
St. Asaph
Holywell
Denbigh
Mold
Queensferry
Hawarden
Buckley
Hope
Dolgarrog
Trefriw
Llanrwst
Carnedd Llywelyn 1062
Betws-y-coed
Snowdon 1085
Capel Curig
Caernarfon Bay
Pen-y-groes
Beddgelert
Dolwyddelan
Pentrefoelas
Cerrigydrudion
Ruthin
Caergwrle
Wrexham
Coedpoeth
Rhosllanerchrugog
Ruabon
Llanaelhaearn
Nefyn
Blaenau Ffestiniog
Maentwrog
Ffestiniog
Porthmadog
Penrhyndeudraeth
Criccieth
Portmeirion
Llangollen
Corwen
Druid
Chirk
Overton
Ellesmere
Whittington
Oswestry
Wem
Tudweiliog
Lleyn Peninsula
Pwllheli
Llanbedrog
Abersoch
Aberdaron
Bardsey Island
Bardsey Sound
Harlech
Trawsfynydd
Bryn-Eden
Snowdonia National Park
Frongoch
Bala
Bala Lake
Berwyn Mts
827
Llanuwchllyn
Aran Fawddwy 905
Llangynog
Llanrhaeadr-ym-Mochnant
Llanfyllin
Lake Vyrnwy
Llanbedr
Llanaber
Dolgellau
Barmouth
Fairbourne
Cader Idris 892
Cross Foxes
Mallwyd
Llangelynin
Corris
Cemmaes Road
Llanfair Caereinion
Welshpool
Shrewsbury
Pontesbury
Tywyn
Machynlleth
Aberdovey
Cardigan Bay
Carno
Caersws
Newtown
Montgomery
Chirbury
Bishop's Castle
Church Stretton
The Long Mynd 517
Borth
Talybont
Bow Street
Pumlumon Fawr 752
Aberystwyth
Goginan
Ponterwyd
Llanidloes
Llangurig
Clun
Clun Forest
Craven Arms
Leintwardine
Knighton
Llanbister
Devil's Bridge
Llanilar
Llanrhystyd
Rhayader
Wigmore
Cambrian Mountains
WALES
1
2
3

12
13

0 5 10 20 30 40 Miles

5 · 6

Lumbards · Castleside · le Street · Hetton · Murton · le Hole · Easington Colliery · Peterlee
Stanhope · Tow Law · Durham · Brandon · Wheatley Hill · Trimdon · Hartlepool
Wolsingham · Crook · Willington · Ferryhill · Coxhoe
Bishop Auckland · Spennymoor · Shildon · Sedgefield · Greatham · Redcar
West Auckland · Newton Aycliffe · Wolviston · Billingham · Marske by the Sea · Saltburn by the Sea
Staindrop · Gainford · Stockton on Tees · Middlesbrough · Loftus · Hinderwell · Whitby
Barnard Castle · Darlington · Yarm · Thornaby on Tees · Guisborough · High Hawsker
Bowes · Scotch Corner · Stokesley · Great Ayton · Sleights · Robin Hood's Bay
Keld · Reeth · Richmond · Catterick · Cleveland Hills · North Yorks Moors National Park · Eller Beck Bridge
Hawes · Aysgarth · Catterick Camp · Northallerton · Laskill · Saltergate · Cloughton
Leyburn · Bedale · Leeming Bar · Kirkby Moorside · Scalby · Scarborough
Middleham · Thornton-le-Dale · Seamer · Filey
Masham · Thirsk · Helmsley · Pickering · Snainton
Great Whernside 704 · Sowerby · Hovingham · Sherburn · Hunmanby · Reighton
Kettlewell · Ripon · Easingwold · Malton · Norton · Foxholes · Flamborough
Grassington · Boroughbridge · Stillington · Rudston · Flamborough Head
Threshfield · Pateley Bridge · Strensall · Sledmere · Bridlington
Summer Bridge · Knaresborough · Haxby · Barmby Moor · Fridaythorpe · Driffield · Bridlington Bay
Skipton · Harrogate · York · Huntington · Pocklington · Nafferton · Lissett
Addingham · Ilkley · Burley in Wharfedale · Wetherby · Stamford Bridge · Middleton on the Wolds · Skipsea
Silsden · Spofforth · Tadcaster · Market Weighton · Hornsea
Keighley · Bingley · Otley · Harewood · Collingham · Leven
Nelson · Shipley · Cawood · Sherburn in Elmet · Holme upon Spalding Moor · Beverley · Aldbrough
Colne · Pudsey · LEEDS · Selby · South Cave · Cottingham · KINGSTON UPON HULL · Roos
Burnley · BRADFORD · Rothwell · Castleford · Howden · Elloughton · Hessle · Preston · Withernsea
Halifax · Dewsbury · Pontefract · Goole · North Ferriby · New Holland · Keyingham · Patrington
Brighouse · Wakefield · Snaith · Rawcliffe · Winterton · Barton upon Humber · Barrow upon Humber · Easington
Littleborough · Hemsworth · Thorne · Crowle · Scunthorpe · Immingham Dock · Grimsby · Spurn Head
HUDDERSFIELD · South Kirkby · Adwick le Street · Hatfield · Broughton · Healing · Rotterdam Zeebrugge
OLDHAM · Holmfirth · Darton · Bentley · Belton · Barnetby le Wold · Cleethorpes · Humberston
Penistone · Barnsley · Goldthorpe · Doncaster · Epworth · Brigg · Laceby · Waltham
Ashton under Lyne · Stocksbridge · Grenoside · Mexborough · Misterton · Kirton in Lindsey · Hibaldstow · Caistor · North Somercotes · Saltfleet
MANCHESTER · Conisbrough · Rotherham · Bawtry · Beckingham · Lea · Caenby Corner · Market Rasen · Ludborough · Saltfleetby St. Clement
STOCKPORT · New Mills · Maltby · Tickhill · Gainsborough · Binbrook · Ludford Magna · Mablethorpe
SHEFFIELD · Blyth · Worksop · Faldingworth · Louth · Sutton-on-Sea
Hazel Grove · Hathersage · Whitwell · East Retford · Saxilby · Wragby · Scamblesby · Withern · Tothill
Whaley Bridge · Eckington · Saltergate · Tuxford · East Markham · Lincoln · Bardney · Horncastle · Alford · Hogsthorpe
Macclesfield · Chapel en le Frith · Dronfield · Staveley · Bolsover · North Hykeham · Bracebridge Heath · Nettleham · Ulceby Cross · Burgh le Marsh
Chesterfield · Warsop · Ollerton · Woodhall Spa · Partney · Spilsby
Buxton · Bakewell · Clay Cross · Mansfield · Mansfield Woodhouse · Waddington · Metheringham · Skegness
Youlgreave · Matlock · Sutton in Ashfield · Martin · Wainfleet All Saints
Congleton · Leek · Newhaven House · Cromford · Alfreton · Navenby · Coningsby · Billinghay · Sibsey
Wirksworth · Ripley · Hucknall · Southwell · Newark · Leadenham · Ruskington · Wrangle
STOKE-ON-TRENT · Belper · Eastwood · Arnold · Balderton · Caythorpe · Sleaford · Heckington · Bennington · Boston
Kingsley · Mayfield · Heanor · Carlton · Long Bennington · Honington · Swineshead · Kirton · The Wash · Hunstanton · Heacham
Cheadle · Ashbourne · Ilkeston · NOTTINGHAM · West Bridgford · Bottesford · Grantham · Donington · Sutterton · Brancaster · Wells next the Sea
Blythe Bridge · Upper Tean · Stapleford · Beeston · Denton · Folkingham · Gosberton · Holbeach · Burnham Market · Little Walsingham
Stone · Uttoxeter · Weston on Trent · Long Eaton · Kegworth · Waltham on the Wolds · Pinchbeck · Weston · King's Lynn · Docking · Dersingham · Fakenham
Rocester · Hatton · Castle Donington · Melbourne · Colsterworth · Spalding · Long Sutton · Sutton Bridge · Gayton · East Rudham
Abbot's Bromley · Tutbury · Shepshed · Loughborough · Corby Glen · Bourne · Deeping St. Nicholas · Tydd St. Giles · Terrington St. Clement · Castle Acre · Litcham
Stafford · Burton upon Trent · Swadlincote · Barrow upon Soar · Melton Mowbray · Cottesmore · Twenty · Deeping St. James · Crowland · Middleton · Bawdeswell
Rugeley · Ashby de la Zouch · Coalville · Sileby · Market Deeping · Thorney · Wisbech · Swaffham · Shipdham
Cannock · Lichfield · Measham · Mountsorrel · Syston · Oakham · Ketton · Stamford · Eye · Outwell · Hingham
WALSALL · Ibstock · Markfield · Anstey · LEICESTER · Billesdon · Duddington · Crowland · Downham Market · Scarning
WEST BROMWICH · Brownhills · Aldridge · Tamworth · Desford · Oadby · Uppingham · Wansford · Peterborough · March · Hilgay · Stoke Ferry · Watton
Sutton Coldfield · Polesworth · Atherstone · Earl Shilton · Wigston · Peterborough · Whittlesey · Methwold · Mundford
BIRMINGHAM · Nuneaton · Hinckley · Kibworth Beauchamp · Market Harborough · Corby · Yaxley · Wimblington · Southery · Breckland · Brandon
SOLIHULL · Coleshill · Bedworth · Lutterworth · Husbands Bosworth · Desborough · Oundle · Norman Cross · Doddington · Downham · Feltwell · Thetford
Halesowen · COVENTRY · Rugby · Rothwell · Kettering · Brigstock · Sawtry · Ramsey · Chatteris · Littleport · Lakenheath · Eleveden
Kenilworth · Dunchurch · Welford · Broughton · Trapston · Alconbury Hill · Warboys · Somersham · Ely · Mildenhall
Bromsgrove · Leamington · Wellingborough · Rushden · Huntingdon · St. Ives · Soham · Barton Mills · Bury
Northwich · Higham Ferrers · Godmanchester · Cottenham · Fordham

A · B · C

0 10 20 30 40 50 60 Kilometres

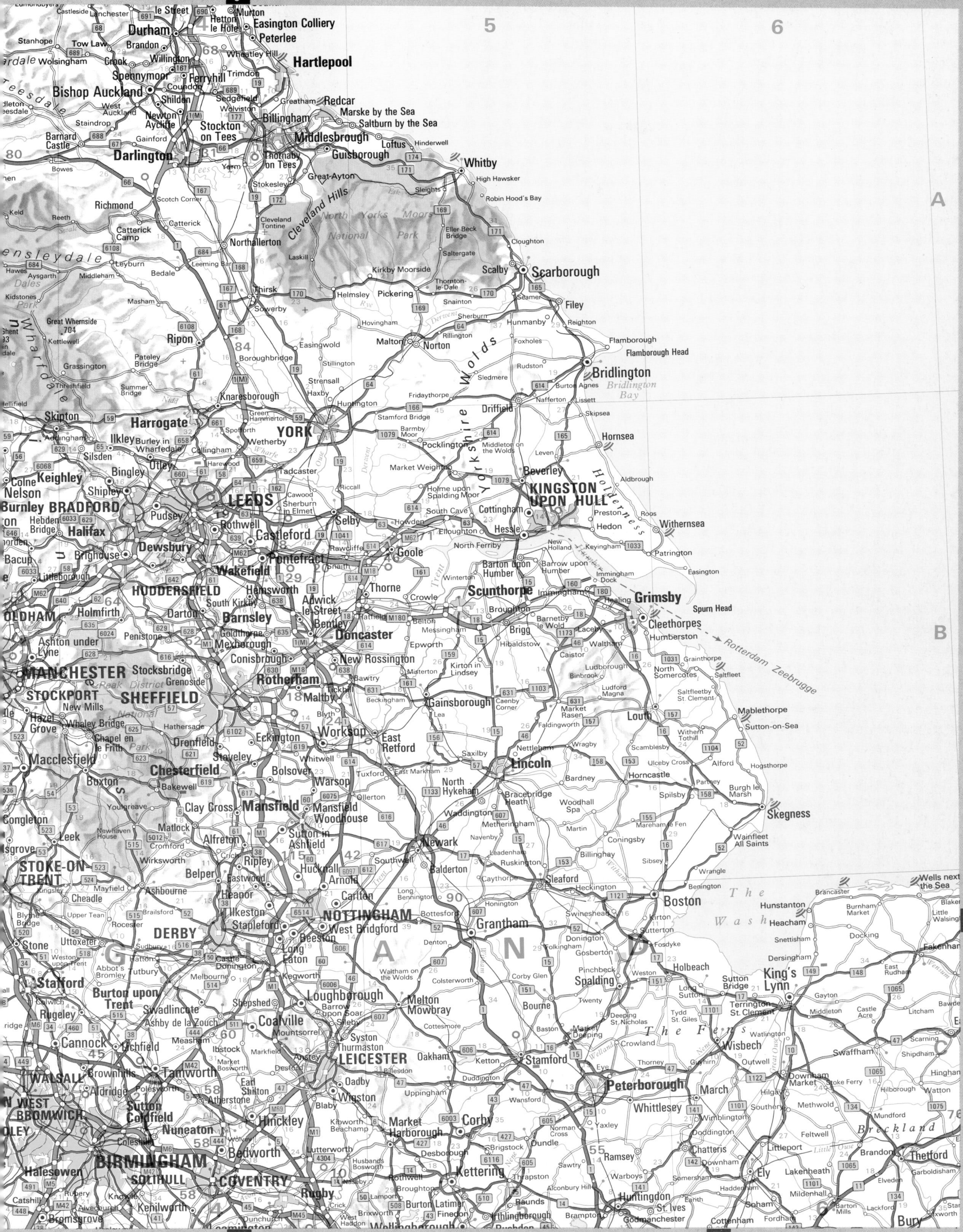

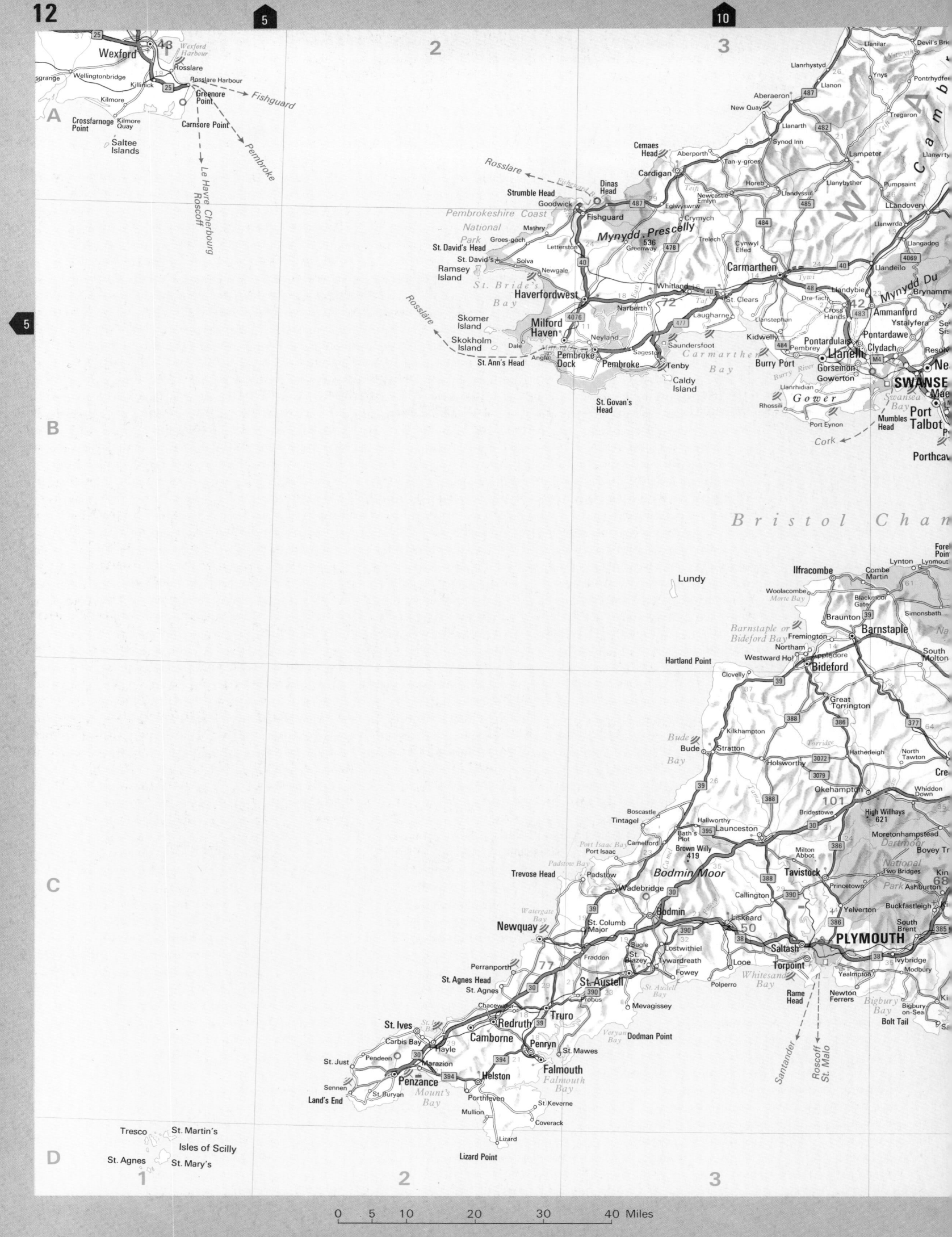

Scale:
0 5 10 20 30 40 Miles

B
D
Wexford
Wexford Harbour
Rosslare
Rosslare Harbour
Wellingtonbridge
Killinick
Kilmore
Greenore Point
Fishguard
Crossfarnoge Point
Kilmore Quay
Carnsore Point
Saltee Islands
Pembroke
Le Havre Cherbourg Roscoff
Rosslare
Llanilar
Devil's Bridge
Llanrhystyd
Llanon
Ynys
Pontrhydfendigaid
Aberaeron
New Quay
Llanarth
Tregaron
Synod Inn
Lampeter
Cemaes Head
Aberporth
Tan-y-groes
Cardigan
Horeb
Llanybyther
Pumpsaint
Dinas Head
Strumble Head
Goodwick
Fishguard
Newcastle Emlyn
Llandyssul
Eglwyswrw
Llandovery
Pembrokeshire Coast National Park
Mathry
Mynydd Prescelly
536
Greenway
Crymych
Trelech
Cynwyl Elfed
Llanwrda
Llangadog
Groes-goch
Letterston
St. David's Head
St. David's
Solva
Ramsey Island
Newgale
Carmarthen
Tywi
Llandeilo
St. Bride's Bay
Haverfordwest
Whitland
St. Clears
Llandybie
Mynydd Du
Brynamman
Narberth
Taf
Dre-fach
Cross Hands
Ammanford
Ystalyfera
Skomer Island
Milford Haven
Laugharne
Llanstephan
Neyland
Kidwelly
Pontardulais
Pontardawe
Skokholm Island
Dale
Saundersfoot
Pembrey
Clydach
Angle
Pembroke Dock
Sageston
Carmarthen Bay
Llanelli
St. Ann's Head
Pembroke
Tenby
Burry Port
Gorseinon
Caldy Island
Gowerton
SWANSEA
Llanrhidian
Gower
Swansea Bay
St. Govan's Head
Rhossili
Port Eynon
Mumbles Head
Port Talbot
Cork
Porthcawl
Bristol Channel
Lynton
Lynmouth
Foreland Point
Ilfracombe
Combe Martin
Lundy
Woolacombe
Morte Bay
Blackmoor Gate
Simonsbath
Braunton
Barnstaple or Bideford Bay
Fremington
Barnstaple
Northam
Appledore
South Molton
Westward Ho!
Bideford
Hartland Point
Clovelly
Great Torrington
Kilkhampton
Torridge
Bude
Bude Bay
Stratton
Hatherleigh
North Tawton
Holsworthy
Crediton
Okehampton
Whiddon Down
Boscastle
Tintagel
Bridestowe
High Willhays 621
Hallworthy
Bath's Plot
Launceston
Port Isaac Bay
Port Isaac
Camelford
Brown Willy 419
Milton Abbot
Moretonhampstead
Dartmoor
Bovey Tracey
Padstow Bay
Trevose Head
Padstow
Bodmin Moor
Tavistock
National Park
Two Bridges
Princetown
Ashburton
Wadebridge
Callington
Watergate Bay
Bodmin
Yelverton
Buckfastleigh
Newquay
St. Columb Major
Liskeard
South Brent
Bugle
Lostwithiel
Saltash
PLYMOUTH
Fraddon
St. Blazey
Tywardreath
Looe
Torpoint
Ivybridge
Perranporth
Fowey
Modbury
St. Agnes Head
St. Austell
Polperro
Whitsand Bay
Yealmpton
St. Agnes
Probus
St. Austell Bay
Rame Head
Newton Ferrers
Bigbury Bay
Chacewater
Mevagissey
Bigbury-on-Sea
Truro
Bolt Tail
St. Ives
St. Ives Bay
Redruth
Veryan Bay
Dodman Point
Carbis Bay
Hayle
Camborne
Penryn
St. Mawes
Santander
Roscoff St. Malo
St. Just
Pendeen
Marazion
Falmouth
Falmouth Bay
Sennen
Penzance
Helston
Mount's Bay
Land's End
St. Buryan
Porthleven
St. Keverne
Mullion
Coverack
Lizard
Lizard Point
Tresco
St. Martin's
Isles of Scilly
St. Agnes
St. Mary's

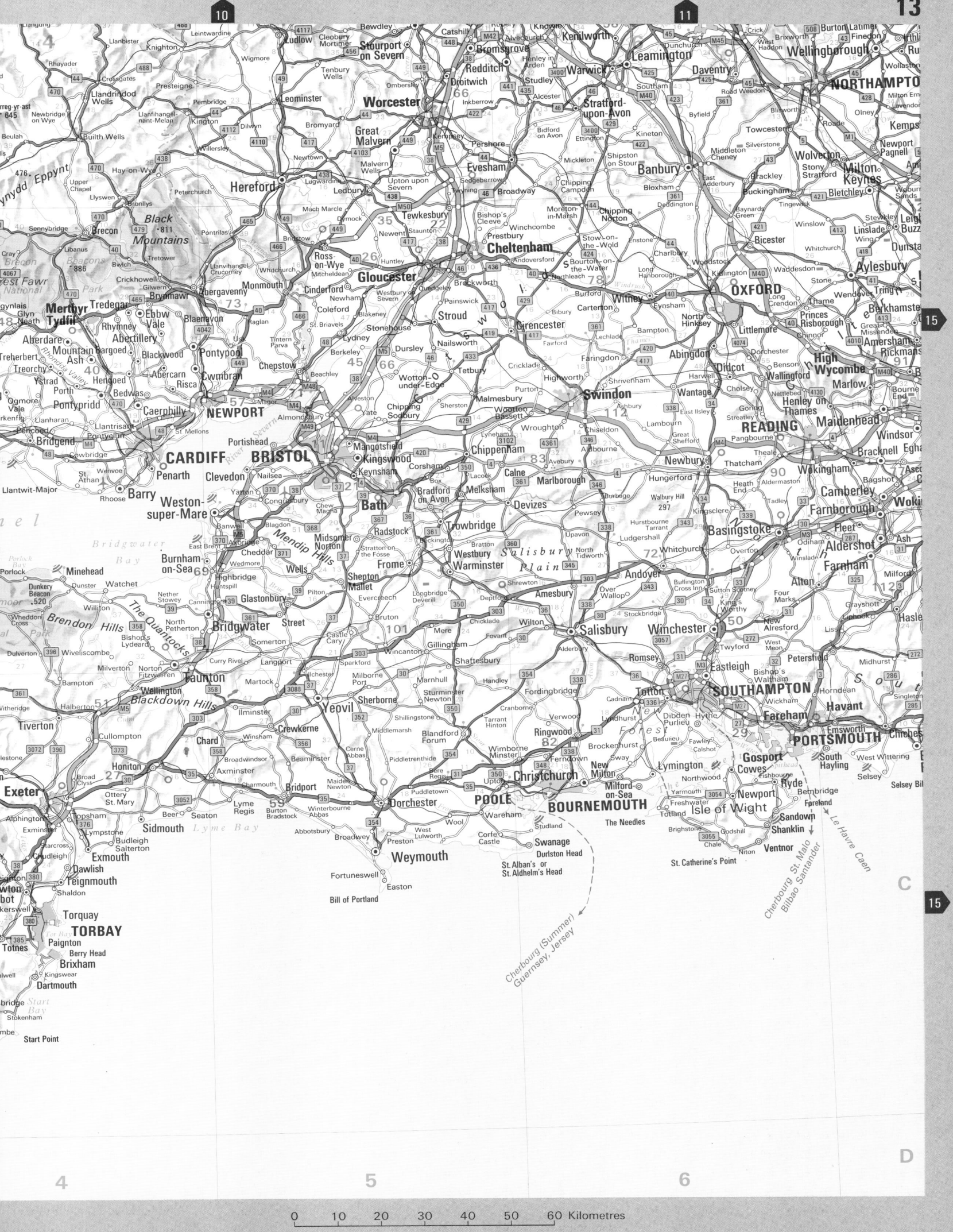
10
11
15
Ludlow
Kidderminster
Stourport on Severn
Bromsgrove
Redditch
Droitwich
Kenilworth
Leamington
Warwick
Daventry
Wellingborough
NORTHAMPTON
Worcester
Stratford-upon-Avon
Leominster
Great Malvern
Hereford
Evesham
Banbury
Milton Keynes
Ledbury
Tewkesbury
Cheltenham
Bicester
Aylesbury
Brecon
Black Mountains
Ross-on-Wye
Gloucester
Witney
OXFORD
Abergavenny
Monmouth
Merthyr Tydfil
Stroud
Cirencester
Pontypool
Cwmbran
Chepstow
Abingdon
Didcot
High Wycombe
Marlow
Swindon
Pontypridd
Caerphilly
NEWPORT
READING
Maidenhead
Windsor
Bridgend
CARDIFF
BRISTOL
Chippenham
Newbury
Penarth
Barry
Clevedon
Weston-super-Mare
Bath
Trowbridge
Devizes
Marlborough
Basingstoke
Camberley
Farnborough
Aldershot
Frome
Warminster
Salisbury Plain
Andover
Farnham
Burnham-on-Sea
Minehead
Wells
Shepton Mallet
Glastonbury
Bridgwater
Street
Salisbury
Winchester
Taunton
Yeovil
Sherborne
Shaftesbury
Romsey
Eastleigh
SOUTHAMPTON
Fareham
Havant
PORTSMOUTH
Tiverton
Honiton
Chard
Crewkerne
Blandford Forum
Ringwood
Christchurch
BOURNEMOUTH
POOLE
Exeter
Exmouth
Sidmouth
Bridport
Dorchester
Weymouth
Swanage
Lymington
Gosport
Cowes
Newport
Ryde
Isle of Wight
Sandown
Shanklin
Ventnor
Teignmouth
Torquay
TORBAY
Paignton
Brixham
Dartmouth
Start Point
Bill of Portland
St. Catherine's Point
The Needles
Lyme Bay
Bridgwater Bay
Cherbourg (Summer) Guernsey, Jersey
Cherbourg, St. Malo, Bilbao Santander
Le Havre Caen
4
5
6
C
D

0 10 20 30 40 50 60 Kilometres

A

B

4

3

Great Yarmouth

Lowestoft

Winterton-on-Sea
Ormesby St. Margaret
Caister-on-Sea

Kessingland
Wrentham
Southwold
Blythburgh
Walberswick

Waxham
Acle
Reedham
72
47
143
Beccles
146
Aldeburgh
Orford

Sea Palling
Mundesley
Bacton
Stalham
Hoveton
Wroxham
Blofield
Brundall
31
Loddon
146
Bungay
143
Halesworth
Laxfield
Saxmundham
Leiston

Overstrand
North Walsham
140
47
NORWICH
Hempnall
140
Harleston
Stradbroke
Earl Soham
Wickham Market
Melton
31

Cromer
Sheringham
148
143
Holt
Aylsham
Cawston
Saxthorpe
Reepham
Wymondham
45
Attleborough
111
Diss
Eye
Scole
Debenham
14
76

Cley next the Sea
Blakeney
Little Walsingham
Melton Constable
Guist
East Dereham
Hingham
Watton
East Harling
Kenninghall
Palgrave
1066
Stanton
143
Needham Market
Stowmarket
14
Monks Eleigh

Wells next the Sea
148
Burnham Market
Docking
148
Litcham
Scarning
Shipdham
1065
Hilborough
Mundford
16
Brandon
Garboldisham
Thetford
Elveden
Lackford
134
Barton Mills
St. Edmunds
Bury
Lavenham
134
Haverhill

Brancaster
Snettisham
Hunstanton
Heacham
Dersingham
Sedgeford
149
Gayton
Middleton
Castle Acre
Swaffham
Methwold
Feltwell
Mildenhall
1101
Lakenheath
Soham
142
Newmarket
Fordham
Linton
Glemsford

King's Lynn
21
Sutton Bridge
Terrington St. Clement
Watlington
Wisbech
1122
Southery
Downham Market
Stoke Ferry
10
Littleport
Ely
Cottenham
Waterbeach
CAMBRIDGE

Skegness
Mablethorpe
Sutton-on-Sea
Hogsthorpe
Burgh le Marsh
Wainfleet All Saints
Wrangle
Friskney
52
52

The Wash

Holbeach
151
Long Sutton
Tydd St. Giles
Wisbech
141
March
Chatteris
Somersham
St. Ives
Swavesey
Histon
Grantchester
Shelford
10

Boston
Kirton
Sutterton
Swineshead
Donington
Gosberton
Pinchbeck
52
Spalding
Crowland
Thorney
Whittlesey
PETERBOROUGH
24
Ramsey
141
Warboys
Huntingdon
St. Neots
428

Saltfleet
Grainthorpe
North Somercotes
Saltfleetby St. Clement
1104
Alford
Partney
158
Spilsby
Stickney
157
16

Wragby
Market Rasen
157
Ludford Magna
Binbrook
Caistor
1173
46
Brigg
18
Barnetby le Wold
180
160

Rotterdam Zeebrugge

Withernsea
Easington
Patrington
Spurn Head
Kilnsea
Keyingham
1033
Immingham Dock
Grimsby
Cleethorpes
Humberston
1031
Waltham

Louth
153
Horncastle
Scamblesby
Ludford
607
Bardney
Woodhall Spa
Martin
153
Sleaford

Hornsea
Aldbrough
Roos
Hedon
Preston
Holderness

KINGSTON UPON HULL
Hessle
Cottingham
Beverley
14
Barton upon Humber
New Holland
Barrow upon Humber
Scunthorpe
Broughton
Kirton in Lindsey
Messingham
15
Epworth
18

Skipsea
Leven
Middleton on the Wolds
Pocklington
Holme upon Spalding Moor
South Cave
Market Weighton
163
North Ferriby
614
Winterton
161
Crowle
Belton

YORK
Wetherby
Tadcaster
Cawood
Sherburn in Elmet
Selby
Goole
Thorne
Snaith
Rawcliffe
M62
M180
Doncaster
Askern
Bentley

Grantham
90
Colsterworth
Bottesford
Denton
52
607
Long Bennington
Melton Mowbray
Oakham
Uppingham
606
Corby
Market Harborough
427
Kettering
510
Wellingborough
Rushden
Kimbolton
Higham Ferrers
Raunds
Thrapston
Oundle
605
Brigstock
427
NORTHAMPTON
Wollaston
Olney
Newport

Newark
133
Balderton
Southwell
Caunton
Ollerton
East Markham
Tuxford
617
Retford
East Retford
Gainsborough
631
Blyth
Bawtry

Lincoln
Nettleham
46
Saxilby
Bracebridge Heath
607
Metheringham
Branston
Washingborough
North Hykeham
Waddington
Bassingham
Leadenham

Stamford
151
Bourne
Deeping St. Nicholas
Market Deeping
15
Ketton
Easton on the Hill
Wansford
Norman Cross
Stilton
Sawtry
14
Alconbury
Buckden
Grafham

LEICESTER
Syston
Thurmaston
Oadby
Wigston
Blaby
Kibworth
Billesdon
Great Glen
Husbands Bosworth
50
Lutterworth
Crick

SHEFFIELD
Stocksbridge
Grenoside
Chapeltown
Rotherham
Maltby
Worksop
Whitwell
Bolsover
Clowne
Eckington
Staveley
Clay Cross
Alfreton
Ripley
Belper
Heanor
Ilkeston
Eastwood
Hucknall
Arnold
Carlton
West Bridgford
NOTTINGHAM
Beeston
Long Eaton
Stapleford
Ruddington
Bingham

Chesterfield
Bakewell
619
Matlock
Wirksworth
Ashbourne
Belper
DERBY
Melbourne
Ashby de la Zouch
Swadlincote
444
Coalville
Ibstock
Market Bosworth
Earl Shilton
Hinckley
60
58
Burbage
Nuneaton
Bedworth
COVENTRY
Bulkington

LEEDS
Pudsey
Dewsbury
Wakefield
Pontefract
Castleford
Knottingley
BARNSLEY
Hemsworth
Cudworth
Royston
Wath upon Dearne
Mexborough
Conisbrough

HARROGATE
Ilkley
Burley in Wharfedale
Keighley
Shipley
Bingley
HUDDERSFIELD
Holmfirth

Penistone

HALIFAX

Kenilworth
Leamington
Warwick
Stratford-upon-Avon

BIRMINGHAM
SOLIHULL
Sutton Coldfield

Peak District National Park

Yorkshire

Holderness

N

A

G

L

A

N

D

The Fens

Breckland

Burton Latimer

Desborough
Rothwell

Silverstone
Towcester

Daventry
Rugby

DERBY

0   5   10   20   30   40 Miles

11

11   11

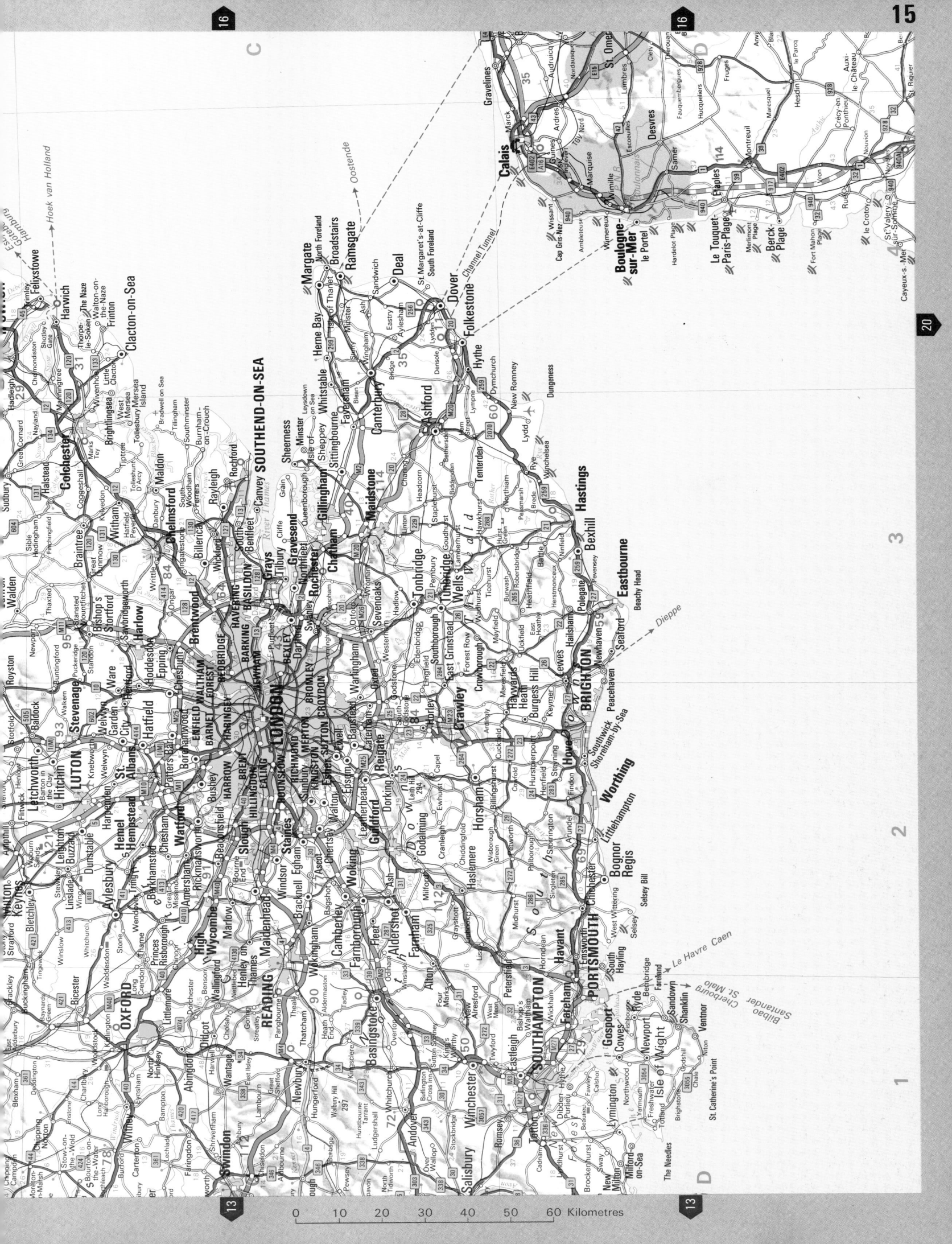

Scale bar:
0 10 20 30 40 50 60 Kilometres

16
16
13
13
D
D
LONDON
READING
OXFORD
LUTON
SOUTHAMPTON
PORTSMOUTH
BRIGHTON
SOUTHEND-ON-SEA
Swindon
Salisbury
Winchester
Basingstoke
Guildford
Woking
Crawley
Horsham
Worthing
Hove
Eastbourne
Hastings
Bexhill
Tunbridge Wells
Tonbridge
Maidstone
Chatham
Rochester
Gillingham
Canterbury
Ashford
Folkestone
Dover
Deal
Ramsgate
Margate
Broadstairs
Whitstable
Herne Bay
Chelmsford
Colchester
Harwich
Felixstowe
Clacton-on-Sea
Braintree
Harlow
Stevenage
Hitchin
Letchworth
Hatfield
St. Albans
Watford
Slough
Maidenhead
High Wycombe
Aylesbury
Bicester
Newbury
Andover
Chichester
Bognor Regis
Littlehampton
Havant
Fareham
Gosport
Isle of Wight
Newport
Ryde
Sandown
Shanklin
Ventnor
Cowes
Lymington
Calais
Boulogne-sur-Mer
Le Touquet-Paris-Plage
Étaples
Berck-Plage
Montreuil
Desvres
St. Omer
Gravelines
Hesdin
Channel Tunnel
Oostende
Hoek van Holland
Dieppe
Le Havre Caen
Bilbao Santander
Cherbourg St. Malo

A

1075 Wymondham
East Harling Hempnall Loddon 143
Attleborough
Thetford Kenninghall Diss Bungay Beccles 146 Lowestoft
Garboldisham Palgrave Harleston Stone Street Kessingland
143 Stanton Scole Brampton Wrentham
1066 Eye Stradbroke Southwold
Haughley Debenham Laxfield Peasenhall Blythburgh
Stowmarket Earl Soham Yoxford Halesworth
Needham Market Framlingham Leiston
St. Edmunds Lavenham Monks Eleigh Wickham Market Aldeburgh
Claydon Melton
Bramford IPSWICH Woodbridge Orford
Hadleigh Orford Ness
Great Cornard Nayland Chelmondiston Felixstowe
Wester Manningtree Harwich
Brightlingsea Wivenhoe Thorpe-le-Soken The Naze
West Mersea Little Clacton Walton-on-the-Naze Frinton
Tollesbury Mersea Island Clacton-on-Sea
Bradwell on Sea

B

Tillingham
Southminster
Burnham-on-Crouch

's G (Den
Harwich
Hull

Hoek van Holland

Esbjerg / Goteborg / Hamburg

Ouddo N5
Brouwershav Scho
Haamstede
Zierikzee Noord N255
Domburg Seroskerke Beveland N256
Westkapelle Walcheren Arnemuiden
Middelburg
Vlissingen Oost-en West-Souburg Gravenpolde
Zuid Beveland Wester

Knokke Breskens
Heist Zeebrugge Oostburg Sluis
Blankenberge Schoondijke IJzendijke N61 Zeeuws
Bredene Uitkerke N58 Aardenburg N253
Oostende Middelkerke Brugge St. Kruis Maldegem Adegem 49 Wachtebe
Ramsgate Stene St. Andries St. Michiels Eeklo Waarschoot
Nieuwpoort Oostkamp 52 Oedelem Evergem Sleidinge Oostakker
De Panne Bray Dunes Koekelare Torhout Beernem Zomergem Lovendegem GENT
Adinkerke Veurne Diksmuide Kortemark Wingene Deinze Drongen Melle
Malo-les-Bains Woumen Zarren Staden Lichtervelde Tielt Petegem Nevele Merelbeke
St. Pol-sur-Mer Dunkerque Merkem Roeselare Izegem Deinze Oosterzele
Gravelines Bergues Hondschoote Poelkapelle Ardooie Meulebeke Oudenaarde Nieuwerk
Bourbourg Oostvleteren Passendale Ingelmunster Waregem Zottegem
Watten Wormhoudt Elverdinge Vlamertinge Moorslede Harelbeke Eine
Poperinge Ieper Wevelgem Menen Kortrijk Nederbrakel Geraardsbergen
St. Omer Cassel Dadizele Wervik Lauwe Avelgem Berchem
Hazebrouck Bailleul Comines Mouscron Ronse
Armentières Ploegsteert Tourcoing Ath
Merville ROUBAIX Leuze
LILLE Frasnes-lez-Buissenal
Lillers Béthune La Bassée Seclin Tournai Chièvres
Bruay-en-Artois Carvin Cysoing Antoing Péruwelz
Noeux-les-Mines Orchies St. Amand-les-Eaux Condé-sur-l'Escaut
Lens Douai Somain Valenciennes
Hénin-Beaumont Denain
Arras Cambrai

C

Margate
Whitstable Herne Bay North Foreland
Faversham Isle of Thanet Broadstairs
Canterbury Minster Ramsgate
Sandwich Oostende
Ashford Deal
St. Margaret's-at-Cliffe South Foreland
Dover
Folkestone Channel Tunnel
Hythe Dungeness
New Romney

Calais Marck
Wissant Guines Ardres Audruicq
Cap Gris-Nez Watten
Boulogne-sur-Mer Marquise St. Omer Arques Bailleul
le Portel Wimereux Desvres Hazebrouck
Samer Lumbres
Le Touquet-Paris Plage Étaples Montreuil Béthune
Berck-Plage Hesdin St. Pol-sur-Ternoise Lens
Fort Mahon Plage Frévent Arras
le Crotoy Crécy-en-Ponthieu Auxi-le-Château Bapaume
Rue Doullens le Cateau
St. Valery-sur-Somme Abbeville Cambrai
Cayeux-s.-Mer St. Riquier Caudry
Ault Beauval
Mers-les-Bains Le Tréport

Strait of Dover

0 5 10 20 30 40 Miles

58
58

NEDERLAND
AMSTERDAM
HAARLEM
Zaandam
Castricum
Uitgeest
Beverwijk
Ijmuiden
Nat. Park De Kennemerduinen
Zandvoort
Heemstede
Hillegom
Noordwijkerhout
Noordwijk aan Zee
Katwijk aan Zee
Oegstgeest
LEIDEN
Wassenaar
Voorburg
'S-GRAVENHAGE
Delft
Schiedam
Maassluis
Vlaardingen
ROTTERDAM
Gouda
Dordrecht
Zwijndrecht
Sliedrecht
Gorinchem
Purmerend
Edam
Volendam
Monnickendam
Lelystad
Dronten
Harderwijk
Nunspeet
Elburg
Zwolle
Hattem
Kampen
Ommen
Raalte
Nijverdal
Rijssen
Wierden
Almelo
Oldenzaal
Hengelo
ENSCHEDE
Deventer
Apeldoorn
Vaassen
Epe
Twello
Zutphen
Lochem
Borculo
Haaksbergen
Eibergen
Groenlo
Winterswijk
Doetinchem
Doesburg
Dieren
Velp
ARNHEM
Ede
Wageningen
Rhenen
Veenendaal
Barneveld
Amersfoort
Nijkerk
Putten
Ermelo
Soest
Baarn
HILVERSUM
Bussum
Naarden
Huizen
Weesp
Amstelveen
Aalsmeer
Uithoorn
UTRECHT
Zeist
De Bilt
Woerden
Alphen a/d Rijn
Bodegraven
Culemborg
Leerdam
Tiel
Geldermalsen
Zaltbommel
NIJMEGEN
Wijchen
Oss
Emmerich
Kleve
Goch
Rees
Bocholt
Borken
Wesel
Xanten
's-Hertogenbosch
Waalwijk
Vught
Boxtel
Uden
Veghel
TILBURG
BREDA
Oosterhout
Roosendaal
Bergen op Zoom
EINDHOVEN
Helmond
Geldrop
Deurne
Venray
Venlo
Tegelen
Weert
Roermond
Sittard
Geleen
Heerlen
Kerkrade
Maastricht
Valkenburg
AACHEN
Eschweiler
Stolberg
Düren
KREFELD
DUISBURG
DÜSSELDORF
MÖNCHENGLADBACH
Neuss
Viersen
Moers
OBERHAUSEN
MÜLHEIM
Grevenbroich
Dormagen
Frechen
Hürth
Brühl
Erftstadt
Euskirchen
Zülpich
Rheinbach
Mechernich
Schleiden
Monschau
Eupen
Verviers
Spa
Malmedy
Stavelot
St. Vith
Vielsalm
Houffalize
Gerolstein
Prüm
Eifel
ANTWERPEN (ANVERS)
Mechelen
Lier
Turnhout
Herentals
Geel
Mol
Lommel
Hasselt
Genk
Diest
Aarschot
Leuven
Tienen
St. Truiden
Tongeren
Herstal
LIÈGE
Seraing
Huy
Namur
Gembloux
Wavre
BRUXELLES
Vilvoorde
Aalst
Halle
Nivelles
Charleroi
Binche
La Louvière
Dinant
Ciney
Marche-en-Famenne
Givet
Rochefort
Philippeville
Beaumont
Chimay
Avesnes
Maubeuge
St. Niklaas
Ninove

0 10 20 30 40 50 60 Kilometres

21
66
62
62

1   2   3

A

CHANNEL ISLANDS

Alderne

Poole

Guernsey   Herm
St Peter
Port   Sark

Golfe de St.

Plymouth

Rosslare
Cork

CÔTE DE GRANIT ROSE

Ploumanac'h   Plougrescant   Île de Bréhat
Trégastel   Perros-
788   Guirec   Pleubian   Pte. de l'Arcouest
Pleumeur-   Ploubazlanec
Bodou   786   Lézardrieux   Paimpol
Île de Batz   Primel-   Trébeurden   Tréguier   Plouézec
Trégastel   Lannion
Roscoff   767   La Roche   CÔTE D'EM
St.   Plougasnou   Derrien   Pontrieux   Plouha   Cap
St. Pol-de-Léon   Carantec   Effiam   St. Michel   Plouaret   Bégard   786   Ploubazlanec   St. Quay-
58   en-Grève   Plestin-   33   Portrieux   Sables-d'Or
CÔTE DU LÉON   les-Grèves   Louargat   Lanvollon   Binic   -les-Pins   St. C
Brignogan   Faou   786   Plouigneau   147   54   Guingamp   Pordic   Erquy   54
Kerlouan   Plouescat   36   Lanmeur   E50   12(81)   Châtelaudren   Pléneuf-   786   Matignon
Plouguerneau   Cléder   788   Morlaix   Belle-Isle-   52   E50   32   12   Les Rosaires   Val-André   43
Portsall   Lesneven   Plouzévédé   en-Terre   Mousteru   Plouagat   St. Brieuc   Yffiniac   768
Lannilis   Landivisiau   St Thégonnec   Plougonven   Plougonver   53   Bourbriac   168   Lamballe
Île d'Ouessant   Le Folgoet   770   Pleyber-   Lannéanou   787   Kérien   767   Quintin   168   Ploeuc-   12(81)
Plabennec   12(81)   712   Christ   21   Callac   sur-Lié   790   Moncontour   37
Lampaul   788   E50   764   Ploudiry   St   785   Poullaouen   37   764   St. Nicolas   Corlay   41   Plouguenast   Collinée   Broons
Goueshou   Sauveur   N.R.   du-Pélem   Uzel
St. Renan   Guipavas   Landerneau   Sizun   384   Armorique   Huelgoat   Maël-Carhaix   24   1   Plémet-   45
BREST   le Relecq-Kerhuon   B   27   Brasparts   Carhaix-   R   24   Mur-de-   la-Pierre   St N
789   Daoulas   E60   Plouguer   21   164   Rostrenen   Gourec   E   164   Bretagne   21   Merdrignac
Le Conquet   Plougastel-   165   18   Pont-   787   Plouaray   Glomel   769   Cléguérec   767   Loudéac   Ménéac
Pte. de St. Mathieu   Daoulas   Landévennec   de-Buis   Pleyben   36   Spézet   Châteauneuf-   Gourin   764   Noyal-   La Chèze
Camaret   791   Le   78   Châteaulin   du-Faou   Roudouallec   27   Guémené-   Pontivy   Rohan   La Trinité
887   Faou   785   Briec   27   Guiscriff   sur-Scorff   Plumieau   Porhoët
Crozon   P.N.R.   33   Locronan   Coray   31   Le Faouët   Kernascléden   Pontivy   764   Josselin
Morgat   d'Armorique   27   770   Scaër   767   Bubry   168   Moréac   24
Baie de   Plogoff   Pont-Croix   22   Quimper   782   Bannalec   Arzano   Plouay   768   767   Ploerme
Douarnenez   Pont-Croix   765   22   Rosporden   68   Plouay   Baud   166
Douarnenez   Pte. du Raz   Audierne   784   Plomelin   765   Fouesnant   26   Locminé   767
Plouhinec   Landudec   35   Plogastel   E60   165   Questembert
Plozévet   St. Germain   783   Concarneau   Pont-Aven   Quimperlé   15   Camors   28   St Jean   Sérent
Plonéour-   785   19   Bénodet   783   Trégunc   Riec-s-Bélon   26   Pont Scorff   Languidic   Brévelay   Maleste
Lanvern   Pont-l'Abbé   Beg-Meil   Nizon   Mélano   Camoël   38   31
St. Guénolé   Penmarch   Loctudy   Pont-   Clohars-   Hennebont   Landévant   Pluvigner   Grand-Champ   38
Guilvinec   Lesconil   Manech   Carnoët   Lanester   Ste Anne   39
Pte. de Penmarch   Le Pouldu   Ploemeur   Lorient   d'Auray   166   Questembert
CÔTE DE   Port-Louis   165   Elven   Roc
Larmor-Plage   Auray   Vannes
Iles de   Groix   781   13   165   20
CORNOUAILLE   768
Île de Groix

0   5   10   20   30   40 Miles

22

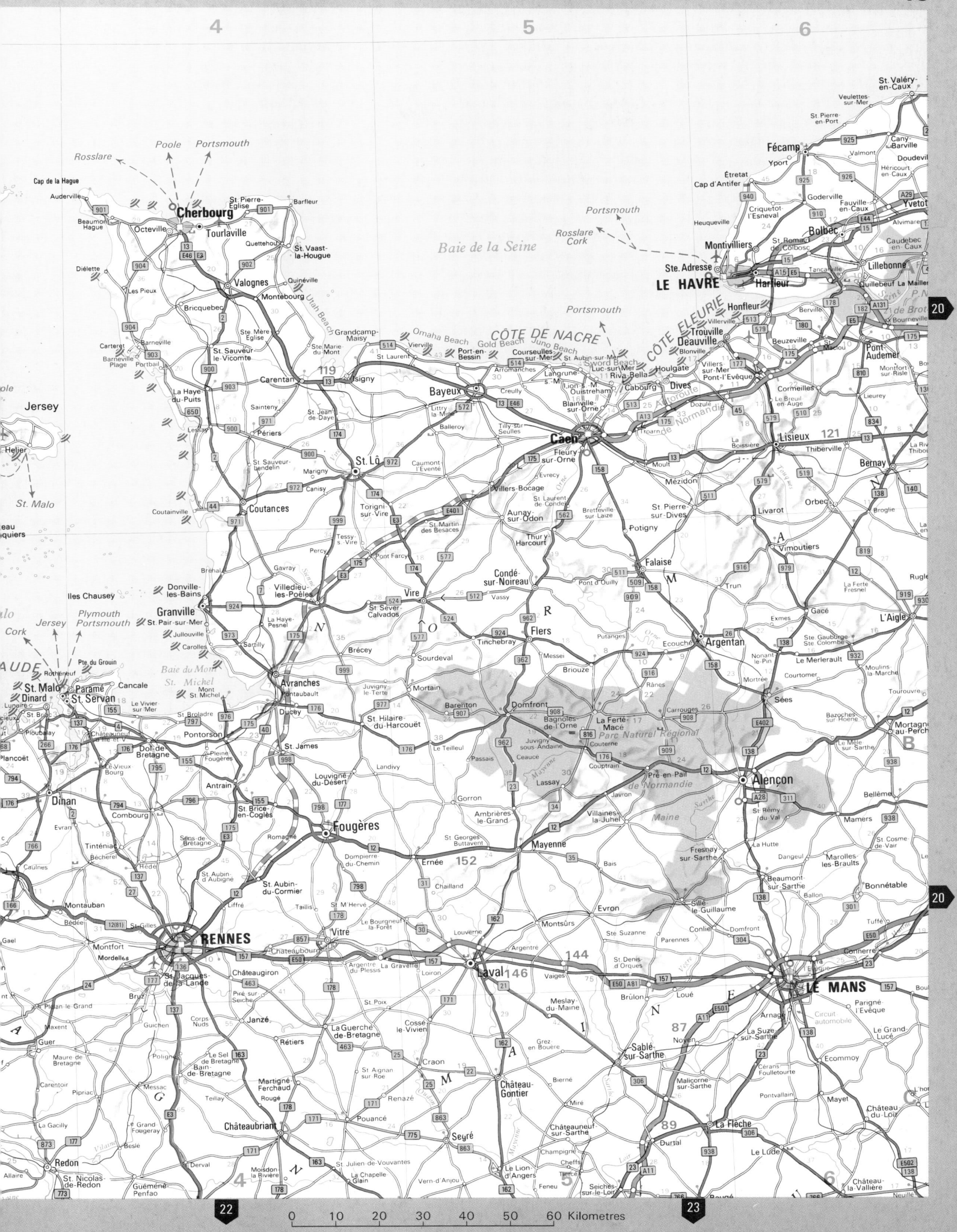

4
5
6
St. Valéry-en-Caux
Veulettes-sur-Mer
St. Pierre-en-Port
Fécamp
Yport
Étretat
Cap d'Antifer
Goderville
Fauville-en-Caux
Yvetot
Bolbec
Montivilliers
Lillebonne
Ste. Adresse
LE HAVRE
Harfleur
Honfleur
Trouville
Deauville
Pont-Audemer
Poole
Portsmouth
Rosslare
Cork
Cap de la Hague
Auderville
Cherbourg
Octeville
Tourlaville
Barfleur
St. Vaast-la-Hougue
Valognes
Montebourg
Baie de la Seine
Utah Beach
Omaha Beach
Gold Beach
Juno Beach
Sword Beach
CÔTE DE NACRE
CÔTE FLEURIE
Grandcamp-Maisy
Port-en-Bessin
Courseulles-sur-Mer
Ouistreham
Riva-Bella
Cabourg
Houlgate
Dives
Villers-sur-Mer
Pont-l'Evêque
Isigny
Carentan
Bayeux
Caen
Lisieux
Bernay
Jersey
St. Helier
St. Malo
Coutances
St. Lô
Villers-Bocage
Aunay-sur-Odon
Thury Harcourt
Falaise
Vimoutiers
Orbec
Livarot
Îles Chausey
Granville
Villedieu-les-Poêles
Vire
Condé-sur-Noireau
Flers
Argentan
Gacé
L'Aigle
Avranches
Mortain
Domfront
Bagnoles-de-l'Orne
La Ferté-Macé
Sées
Parc Naturel Régional de Normandie Maine
Alençon
Mortagne-au-Perche
Dinard
Dinan
Pontorson
Dol-de-Bretagne
Cancale
Fougères
Mayenne
Ernée
Pré-en-Pail
Mamers
Bellême
Combourg
Fresnay-sur-Sarthe
Beaumont-sur-Sarthe
Bonnétable
Evron
Sillé-le-Guillaume
RENNES
Vitré
Laval
LE MANS
Montfort
Bain-de-Bretagne
La Guerche-de-Bretagne
Craon
Sablé-sur-Sarthe
Château-Gontier
La Flèche
Châteaubriant
Redon
Segré
Le Lion-d'Angers
Le Lude
Château-la-Vallière
Château-du-Loir
0 10 20 30 40 50 60 Kilometres

20
20
22
23

16

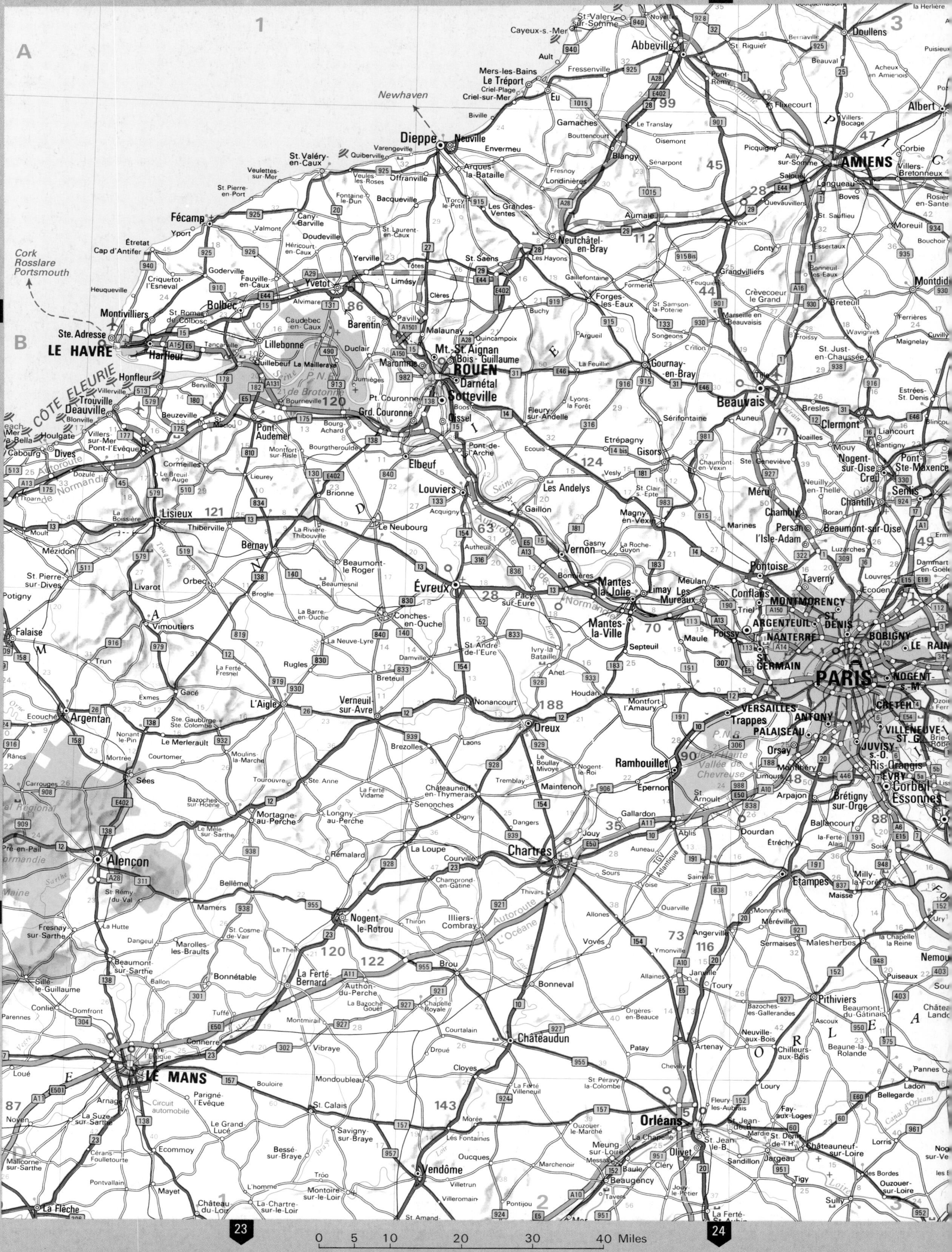

1

A

St-Valéry-sur-Somme · Noyelles · la Herlière · Doullens · 3

Cayeux-s.-Mer · Abbeville · St Riquier · Beauval · Acheux-en-Amiénois · Villers-Bocage

Ault · Mers-les-Bains · Le Tréport · Fressenville · Pont-Remy · Flixecourt · Albert

Criel-Plage · Criel-sur-Mer · Eu · Biville · Gamaches · Bouttencourt · Oisemont · Le Translay · Picquigny · Ailly-sur-Somme · AMIENS · 47 · Corbie · Villers-Bretonneux

Newhaven

DIEPPE · Neuville · Envermeu · Blangy · Sénarpont · Poix · Longueau · Boves · Rosières-en-Santerre

Varengeville · Quiberville · Arques-la-Bataille · Fresnoy · Londinières · Aumale · Conty · Essertaux · Moreuil · Montdidier

St-Valéry-en-Caux · Offranville · Veules-les-Roses · Neufchâtel-en-Bray · Les Hayons · Grandvilliers · Crèvecoeur-le-Grand · Bonneuil-les-Eaux · Breteuil

Veulettes-sur-Mer · St Pierre-en-Port · Fontaine-le-Dun · Bacqueville · St Saëns · Gaillefontaine · Formerie · Feuquières · Ferrières · Wavignies

Fécamp · Yport · Cany-Barville · Doudeville · St Laurent-en-Caux · Yerville · Tôtes · Forges-les-Eaux · Songeons · Crillon · Froissy · St Just-en-Chaussée

Étretat · Cap d'Antifer · Criquetot-l'Esneval · Goderville · Fauville-en-Caux · Limésy · Clères · Buchy · Marseille en Beauvaisis · Maignelay

Heuqueville · Montivilliers · Bolbec · St Romain-de-Colbosc · Caudebec-en-Caux · Barentin · Pavilly · Malaunay · Quincampoix · Argueil · Gournay-en-Bray · Beauvais · Clermont · Liancourt

Ste Adresse · LE HAVRE · Harfleur · Lillebonne · Duclair · Mt-St-Aignan · Bois-Guillaume · ROUEN · La Feuillie · Lyons-la-Forêt · Noailles · Mouy · Hantigny

Honfleur · Quillebeuf · La Mailleraye · Jumièges · Maromme · Darnétal · Sotteville · Pont-de-l'Arche · Gisors · Chaumont-en-Vexin · Méru · Chambly · Pont-Ste-Maxence · Creil · Senlis

CÔTE FLEURIE · Trouville · Deauville · Berville · Bourneville · Grd. Couronne · Oissel · Fleury-sur-Andelle · Étrépagny · Vesly · Ste Geneviève · Neuilly-en-Thelle · Chantilly

Blonville · Villerville · Beuzeville · Pont-Audemer · Bourg-Achard · Bourgtheroulde · Elbeuf · Les Andelys · Magny-en-Vexin · Marines · Persan · Beaumont-sur-Oise

Houlgate · Villers-sur-Mer · Pont-l'Évêque · Cormeilles · Le Breuil-en-Auge · Montfort-sur-Risle · Louviers · Gaillon · Gasny · La Roche-Guyon · Pontoise · l'Isle-Adam · Luzarches · Dammartin-en-Goële

Dives · Cabourg · Dozulé · Lisieux · Thiberville · Lieurey · Brionne · Le Neubourg · Acquigny · Magny-en-Vexin · Mantes-la-Jolie · Meulan · Conflans · MONTMORENCY · Louvres · Écouen

La Boissière · St Pierre-sur-Dives · Bernay · La Rivière-Thibouville · Beaumont-le-Roger · Autheuil · Vernon · Bonnières · Limay · Les Mureaux · Triel · ARGENTEUIL · ST DENIS · BOBIGNY

Mézidon · Livarot · Orbec · Broglie · Beaumesnil · ÉVREUX · Pacy-sur-Eure · Mantes-la-Ville · Maule · Poissy · ST GERMAIN · NANTERRE · LE RAINCY

Moult · Falaise · Vimoutiers · La Neuve-Lyre · Conches-en-Ouche · Damville · St André-de-l'Eure · Ivry-la-Bataille · Septeuil · PARIS · NOGENT-S.-M.

Potigny · Trun · La Ferté-Fresnel · Rugles · Breteuil · Nonancourt · Ahet · Houdan · VERSAILLES · ANTONY · CRÉTEIL

Écouché · Argentan · Gacé · L'Aigle · Verneuil-sur-Avre · Dreux · Montfort-l'Amaury · Trappes · PALAISEAU · VILLENEUVE-ST-G.

Rânes · Exmes · Ste Gauburge · Ste Colombe · Le Merlerault · Moulins-la-Marche · Brezolles · Laons · Nogent-le-Roi · Orsay · JUVISY-S.-O.

Carrouges · Courtomer · Mortrée · Sées · Tourouvre · Ste Anne · Le Boullay-Mivoye · Rambouillet · Épernon · Montlhéry · RIS-ORANGIS · ÉVRY · Corbeil-Essonnes

Pré-en-Pail · Bazoches-sur-Hoëne · Mortagne-au-Perche · La Ferté-Vidame · Maintenon · St Arnoult · Arpajon · Brétigny-sur-Orge · Ballancourt

Fresnay-sur-Sarthe · Alençon · Bellême · Longny-au-Perche · Senonches · Digny · Dangers · Gallardon · Dourdan · Étréchy · la Ferté-Alais

St Rémy-du-Val · La Loupe · Courville · Champrond-en-Gâtine · Jouy · CHARTRES · Ablis · Auneau · Sainville · Étampes · Milly-la-Forêt

La Hutte · Dangeul · Mamers · Rémalard · Thivars · Sours · Ouarville · Angerville · Maisse

Beaumont-sur-Sarthe · Marolles-les-Braults · Nogent-le-Rotrou · Thiron · Illiers-Combray · Voves · Ymonville · Sermaises · Malesherbes · Nemours

Sillé-le-Guillaume · St Cosme-de-Vair · Le Theil · Brou · Bonneval · Allaines · Janville · Toury · Puiseaux

Conlie · Bonnétable · La Ferté-Bernard · Authon-du-Perche · Chapelle-Royale · Patay · Orgères-en-Beauce · Pithiviers · Beaumont-du-Gâtinais

Domfront · Ballon · La Bazoche-Gouet · Courtalain · Châteaudun · Artenay · Neuville-aux-Bois · Ascoux · Chilleurs-aux-Bois · Beaune-la-Rolande · Bellegarde

Parennes · Tuffé · Montmirail · Vibraye · Cloyes · St Péravy-la-Colombe · Chevilly · Loury · Ladon

Loué · LE MANS · St Calais · Mondoubleau · Morée · La Ferté-Villeneuil · ORLÉANS · Fay-aux-Loges · Nogent-sur-Vernisson

Noyen · Arnage · La Suze-sur-Sarthe · Bouloire · St Calais · Savigny-sur-Braye · Ouzouer-le-Marché · La Chapelle · Meung-sur-Loire · Olivet · Châteauneuf-sur-Loire

Malicorne-sur-Sarthe · Ecommoy · Bessé-sur-Braye · Trôo · Ucques · Marchenoir · Baule · Cléry · Jargeau

Cérans Foulletourte · Le Grand-Lucé · VENDÔME · Villetrun · Beaugency · Jouy-le-Potier · Tigy

Pontvallain · Mayet · Montoire-sur-le-Loir · Villeromain · Pontijou · Sandillon · Ouzouer-sur-Loire

La Flèche · Château-du-Loir · La Chartre-sur-le-Loir · St Amand · Sully

Cork · Rosslare · Portsmouth

0 5 10 20 30 40 Miles

16 17

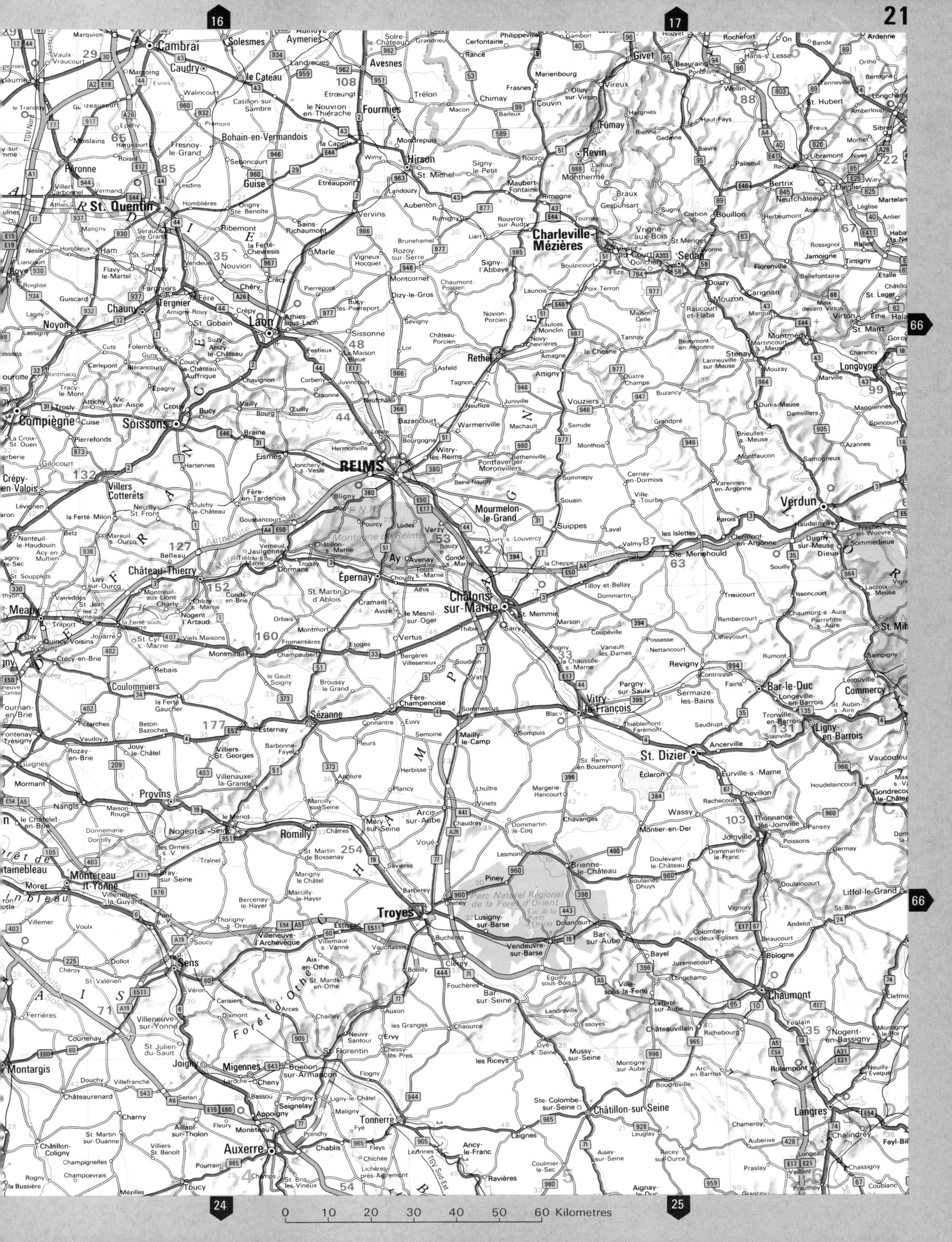
Cambrai
Solesmes
Aymeries
Caudry
le Cateau
Landrecies
Avesnes
Fourmies
Trélon
Chimay
Couvin
Givet
Vireux
Fumay
Revin
Philippeville
Marienbourg
Rochefort
Beauraing
Wellin
St. Hubert
Libramont
Neufchâteau
Bertrix
Bouillon
Florenville
Carignan
Virton
Montmédy
Longuyon
Marquion
Péronne
St. Quentin
Bohain-en-Vermandois
Guise
Hirson
la Capelle
Vervins
Ribemont
Marle
Nouvion
Ham
Nesle
Roye
Chauny
Tergnier
Noyon
Laon
St. Gobain
Sissonne
Rozoy-sur-Serre
Signy-l'Abbaye
Charleville-Mézières
Sedan
Rethel
Vouziers
le Chesne
Stenay
Dun-s-Meuse
Compiègne
Soissons
Pierrefonds
Villers Cotterêts
Crépy-en-Valois
Fismes
Braine
REIMS
Bazancourt
Warmeriville
Fère-en-Tardenois
Château-Thierry
Dormans
Épernay
Ay
Avize
Vertus
Mourmelon-le-Grand
Suippes
Châlons-sur-Marne
Ste. Menehould
Clermont-en-Argonne
Verdun
Meaux
la Ferté-sous-Jouarre
Coulommiers
Montmirail
Sézanne
Fère-Champenoise
Vitry-le-François
St. Dizier
Bar-le-Duc
Commercy
Ligny-en-Barrois
Provins
Nogent-s.-Seine
Romilly
Arcis-sur-Aube
Brienne-le-Château
Montier-en-Der
Joinville
Troyes
Piney
Parc Naturel Régional de la Forêt d'Orient
Vendeuvre-sur-Barse
Bar-sur-Aube
Chaumont
Montereau
Sens
Villeneuve-l'Archevêque
Bar-sur-Seine
Langres
Joigny
St. Florentin
Tonnerre
Chablis
Auxerre
Châtillon-sur-Seine
Montargis
Courtenay
Les Riceys
Laignes
Forêt d'Othe
Autoroute du Soleil
0 10 20 30 40 50 60 Kilometres

66
66
24 25

18

19

A

B

C

1

2

3

26

Carnoët
Le Pouldu
Ploëmeur
Lanester
Lorient
Larmor-Plage
Groix
Port-Louis
Ile de Groix

Landévant
Pluvigner
Grand-Champ
767
Ste Anne
d'Auray
165
166
Auray
768
781
Belz
13
Vannes
Questembert
165
Noyalo
41
165
Locmariaquer
Carnac
La
Trinité
St Pierre
Quiberon
780
Port
Navalo
34
Sarzeau
32
CÔTE SAUVAGE
Quiberon
Baie de
Quiberon
St Gildas
de-Rhuys
Ile de Houat

Elven
Arz
Rochefort
en-Terre
873
775
775
Allaire
Redon
St Nicolas-
de-Redon
20
Vilaine
Muzillac
La Roche
Bernard
Herbignac
774
P.N.R.
de Brière
St.
Joachim
773

La Gacilly
177
E3
Grand-
Fougeray
171
178
Besle
178
Châteaubriant
775
171
Rougé
Teillay
Perchaud
16
Pouancé
171
Renazé

G
3

Sauzon
Le Palais
Bangor
Locmaria
Belle Île
Ile de Hœdic

Piriac-sur-Mer
La Turballe
Guérande
Le Croisic
Le Pouliguen
La Baule
171
92
Pornichet
Montoir
Trignac
Mindin
St Marc
St
Brevin-
les-Pins
277
13
St Michel
Chef-Chef

Savenay
E60
165
171
Donges
Paimbœuf
Le Temple-
de-Bretagne
St Père-
en-Retz
48
Le Pellerin
St Etienne-
de-Montluc
Le Loroux-
Bottereau
723
Bouguenais
Bouaye
751

N
163
St Julien-de-Vouvantes
La Chapelle-
Glain
Vern-d'
Nozay
La Meilleraye-
de-Bretagne
Riaillé
St Mars
la-Jaille
Candé
Louroux-
Béconn
Ligné
Oudon
Varades
Ancenis
23
751
Liré
Champtoceaux
St Florent-
le-Vieil
St Pierre-
Montlimart
12
Montrevault
752

90

CÔTE D'AMOUR

St
Nazaire

722

NANTES
Vertou
149
178
137
Pont
St Martin
Lac de
Grand-
Lieu
St Philbert-
de-Grand-Lieu
262
Aigrefeuille-
s/Maine
Clisson
Montfaucon
Vallet
Gesté
Beaupréau

A11

A821
Orvault
Carquefou
St Julien-
de-Concelles
St Laurent-
des Autels
249
763

E

Ja

CÔTE D'AMOUR

Préfailles
Pornic
La Bernerie-
en-Retz
13
Arthon
758
Bourgneuf-
en-Retz
Baie de
Bourgneuf
Noirmoutier-
en-l'Ile
Ile de
Noirmoutier
La Guérinière
388
Barbâtre
La Barre-
de-Monts
22
Beauvoir-
sur-Mer
948
758
Bouin

751
60
St Philbert-
de-Grand-Lieu
117
Machecoul
13
La Garnache
Touvois
753
Legé
Palluau
Les Lucs-
sur-Boulogne
978
La Chaize-
le-Vicomte

937
A83
E3
La
Bruffière
Vieillevigne
Rocheservière
Montaigu
La Gaubretière
Chavagnes-
en-Paillers
24
St Fulgent
Les
Herbiers

Cholet
160
Mortagne-
sur-Sèvre
St Michel-
Mont-Mercure

CÔTE DE JADE

38
St Jean-
de-Monts
Ile d'Yeu
Port-Joinville
Sion-sur-l'Océan
St Hilaire-
de-Riez
St Gilles-Croix-
de-Vie
Beaulieu-
s/s la Roche
753
St Christophe-
du-Ligneron
948
Le Poiré-
sur-Vie
Aizenay
Belleville-
sur-Vie
937
La Ferrière
160
Les
Essarts
**La Roche-
sur-Yon**
948
949B
Bourg-sous-
la-Roche
Bournezeau
Chantonnay
949 Bis

147

49

O

P

St Martin-
de-Brem
160
La Mothe-
Achard
Aubigny
746
Lay
Ste Hermine
Les Sables-
d'Olonne
Olonne-s Mer
747
13
949
Talmont
Moutiers-
les-Mauxfaits
19
949
Mareuil-
sur-Lay
Ste Gemme-
la-Plaine
949
Nalliers
148
Longeville
Angles
Jard-s-Mer
14
Triaize
Luçon
Chaillé
les Marais
L'Aiguillon-
sur-Mer
746
St Michel-
en-l'Herm
32
La Tranche-
sur-Mer
Marans
137
E3
Nuaillé
Pe

Pertuis Breton
Ars-en-Ré
735
St Martin-
de-Ré
La Flotte
Nieul-
sur-Mer
11
Dompierre-s.-M
Ile de Ré
Rivedoux-
Plage
La
Pallice
Aytré
La Rochelle
Aigrefeuille-
d'Aunis
Ciré-
d'Aunis
Pertuis
d'Antioche
St Denis-
d'Oléron
Chatelaillon-
Plage
137
Ile d'Aix
E602
St Georges
St Pierre
734
La Cotinière
Fouras
Port-des-
Barques
Roc
Rochefort
St Trojan
Le Château
Ile d'Oléron
Bourcefranc
20
Marennes
733
Ronce-les-Bains
728
La Tremblade
39
14
Pte. de la Coubre
25
St Palais-
sur-Mer
Cad
S
A
Royan
St Geo
de-Dido
Pte. de Grave
Le Verdon-
sur-Mer
Soulac-s.-Mer
Gironde
215
Montalivet-
les-Bains
40
Vendays-
Montalivet
St Vivien-
de-Méd oc
Les

19
20

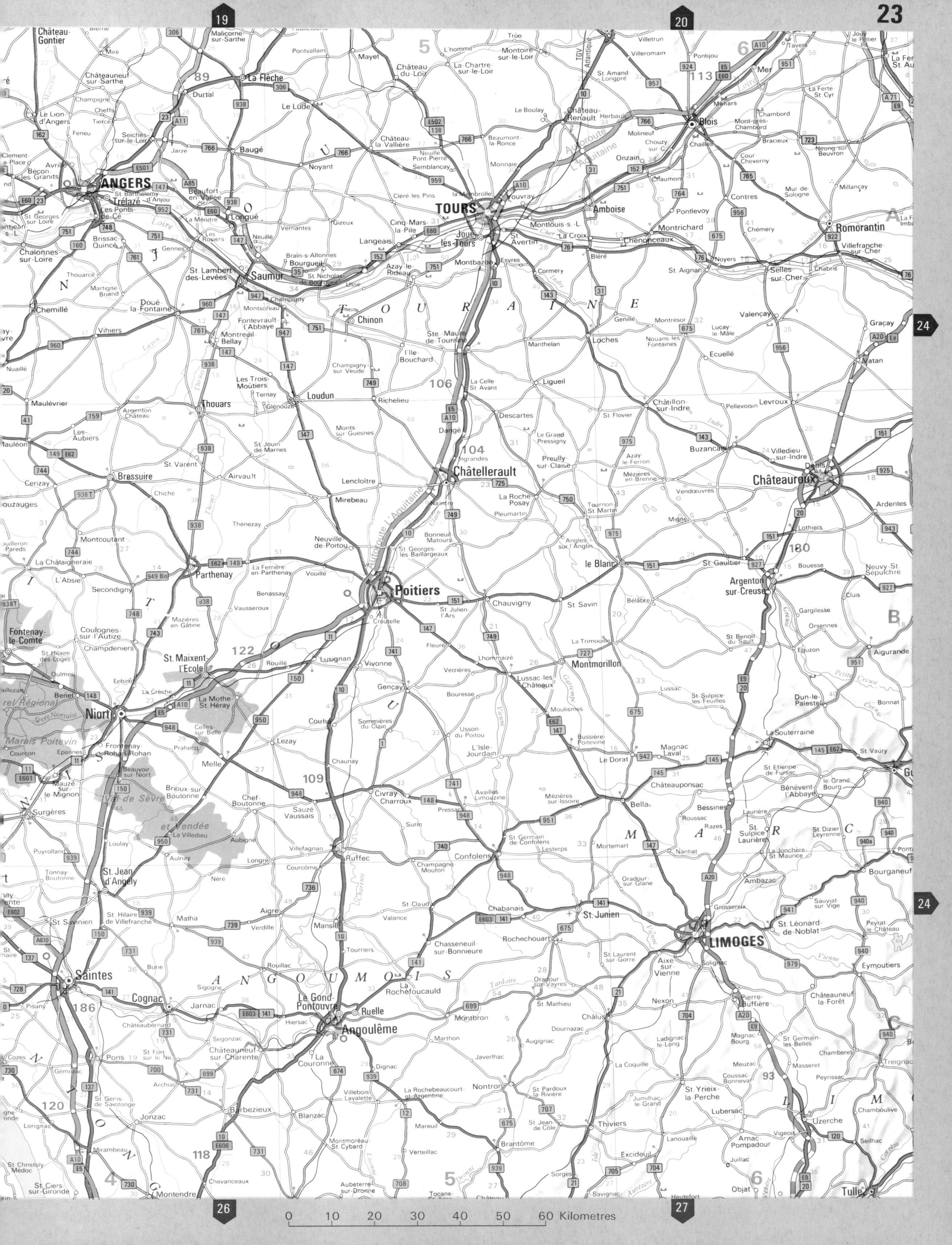
Château-Gontier
La Flèche
Durtal
Le Lude
Baugé
ANGERS
Trélazé
Saumur
Chemillé
Chinon
Loudun
Thouars
Bressuire
Parthenay
Fontenay-le-Comte
Niort
St. Maixent-l'Ecole
Poitiers
Châtellerault
Lusignan
Vivonne
Gençay
Couhé
Melle
Civray
Ruffec
Confolens
Chabanais
St. Junien
LIMOGES
St. Jean-d'Angély
Saintes
Cognac
Jarnac
Angoulême
La Rochefoucauld
Ruelle
Barbezieux
Jonzac
Pons
Brantôme
Nontron
Thiviers
St. Yrieix-la-Perche
Uzerche
Tulle
TOURS
Amboise
Blois
Loches
Romorantin
Valençay
Vatan
Châteauroux
Le Blanc
Argenton-sur-Creuse
Chauvigny
Montmorillon
Bellac
La Souterraine
Château-Renault
Ste. Maure-de-Touraine
Richelieu
Montrichard
Chenonceaux
Gracay
Buzançais
St. Savin
Eymoutiers
T O U R A I N E
A N G O U M O I S
L I M
M A R C H E

24
24

0 10 20 30 40 50 60 Kilometres

26
27

20 21 23

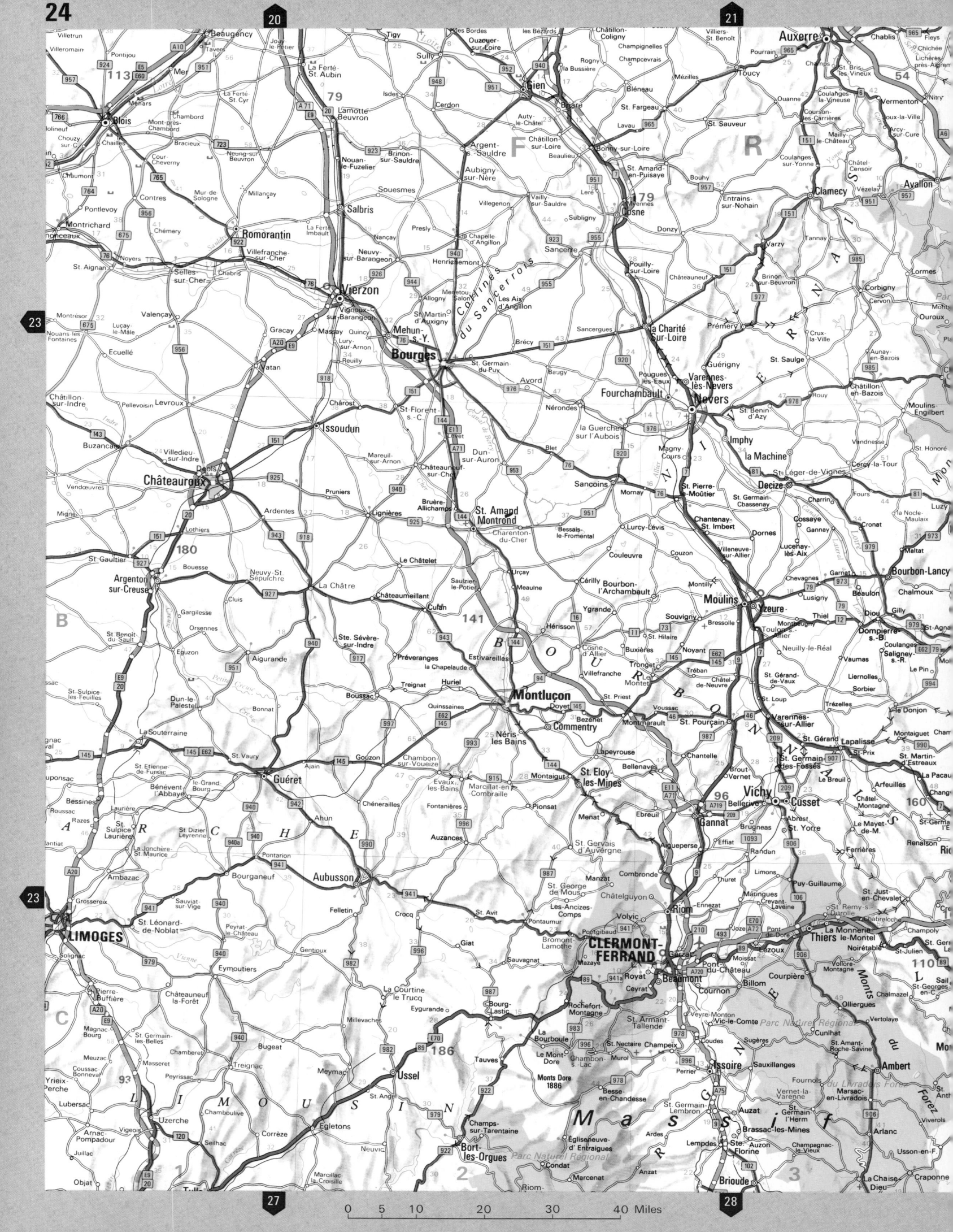

Beaugency
Villetrun
Villeromain
Pontijou
Tavers
Mer
Jouy-le-Potier
La Ferté-St. Aubin
Tigy
Sully
Les Bordes
Ouzouer-sur-Loire
les Bézards
Châtillon-Coligny
Villiers-St. Benoît
Auxerre
Chablis
Fleys
Chichée
Lichères-près-Aigremont
Champignelles
Rogny
La Bussière
Champcevrais
Pourrain
Toucy
St. Bris-les-Vineux
Champs
Gien
Briare
Bléneau
Mézilles
Ouanne
Coulanges-la-Vineuse
Vermenton
Nitry
Blois
Ménars
La Ferté-St. Cyr
Lamotte-Beuvron
Isdes
Cerdon
Chambord
Mont-près-Chambord
Chailles
Bracieux
Neung-sur-Beuvron
Nouan-le-Fuzelier
Brinon-sur-Sauldre
Argent-s.-Sauldre
Auty-le-Châtel
Châtillon-sur-Loire
Beaulieu
Bonny-sur-Loire
St. Fargeau
Lavau
St. Sauveur
Courson-les-Carrières
Mailly-le-Château
Joux-la-Ville
Arcy-sur-Cure
Coulanges-sur-Yonne
Châtel-Censoir
Chaumont
Cour-Cheverny
Mur-de-Sologne
Millançay
Contres
Pontlevoy
Montrichard
Chémery
Romorantin
Salbris
Souesmes
Aubigny-sur-Nère
Villegenon
Vailly-sur-Sauldre
Sublігny
Léré
St. Amand-en-Puisaye
Bouhy
Entrains-sur-Nohain
Clamecy
Vézelay
Avallon
Cosne
Myennes
Donzy
La Ferté-Imbault
Villefranche-sur-Cher
Noyers
St. Aignan
Selles-sur-Cher
Chabris
Nançay
Presly
La Chapelle-d'Angillon
Neuvy-sur-Barangeon
Henrichemont
Sancerre
Pouilly-sur-Loire
Châteauneuf
Varzy
Tannay
Brinon-sur-Beuvron
Corbigny
Cervon
Lormes
Vierzon
Vignoux-sur-Barangeon
Menetou-Salon
Allogny
St. Martin-d'Auxigny
Les Aix-d'Angillon
Collines du Sancerrois
Montrésor
Valençay
Luçay-le-Mâle
Nouans-les-Fontaines
Gracay
Massay
Quincy
Mehun-s.-Y.
Lury-sur-Arnon
Reuilly
Bourges
Brécy
Sancergues
La Charité-sur-Loire
Prémery
Crux-la-Ville
Aunay-en-Bazois
Ecuellé
Vatan
St. Germain-du-Puy
Avord
Baugy
Pougues-les-Eaux
Varennes-lès-Nevers
Guérigny
St. Saulge
Châtillon-en-Bazois
Châtillon-sur-Indre
Pellevoisin
Levroux
Chârost
St. Florent-s.-C.
Nérondes
Fourchambault
Nevers
Rouy
St. Benin-d'Azy
Moulins-Engilbert
Buzançais
Issoudun
Villedieu-sur-Indre
Mareuil-sur-Arnon
Levet
Dun-sur-Auron
la Guerche-sur-l'Aubois
Imphy
la Machine
Vandenesse
St. Honoré
Châteauroux
Déols
Vendœuvres
Châteauneuf-sur-Cher
Blet
Magny-Cours
St. Léger-de-Vignes
Cercy-la-Tour
Decize
Sancoins
Mornay
St. Pierre-le-Moûtier
St. Germain-Chassenay
Charrin
Fours
Luzy
Migné
Ardentes
Pruniers
Lignières
Bruère-Allichamps
St. Amand-Montrond
Charenton-du-Cher
Bessais-le-Fromental
Lurcy-Lévis
Chantenay-St. Imbert
Dornes
Cossaye
Gannay
La Nocle-Maulaix
Cronat
Lothiers
St. Gaultier
Argenton-sur-Creuse
Bouesse
Neuvy-St. Sépulchre
Le Châtelet
La Châtre
Châteaumeillant
Saulzier-le-Potier
Urçay
Meaulne
Couleuvre
Couzon
Villeneuve-sur-Allier
Lucenay-lès-Aix
Maltat
Bourbon-Lancy
Cérilly
Bourbon-l'Archambault
Montilly
Moulins
Yzeure
Chevagnes
Garnat
Beaulon
Chalmoux
Lusigny
Cluis
Gargilesse
Orsennes
Culan
Ygrande
Souvigny
Bressolle
Thiel
Diou
Gilly
Dompierre-s.-B.
St. Agnan
St. Benoît-du-Sault
Ste. Sévère-sur-Indre
Hérisson
Cosne-d'Allier
Buxières
St. Hilaire
Toulon-s.-Allier
Montbeugny
Neuilly-le-Réal
Coulanges
Saligney-s.-R.
Eguzon
Aigurande
Préveranges
La Chapelaude
Estivareilles
Villefranche
Tronget
Le Montet
Noyant
Tréban
Châtel-de-Neuvre
St. Gérand-de-Vaux
Vaumas
Liernolles
Le Pin
Sorbier
St. Sulpice-les-Feuilles
Dun-le-Palestel
Bonnat
Treignat
Huriel
Boussac
Montluçon
Quinssaines
St. Priest
Doyet
Bezenet
Commentry
Voussac
Montmarault
St. Pourçain
St. Loup
Varennes-sur-Allier
Trézelles
Le Donjon
La Souterraine
Néris-les-Bains
Lapeyrouse
Chantelle
St. Gérand
Lapalisse
Montaiguet
St. Etienne-de-Fursac
St. Vaury
Gouzon
Chambon-sur-Voueize
Bellenaves
St. Germain-des-Fossés
St. Prix
St. Martin-d'Estreaux
La Pacaudière
Uponsac
Bénévent-l'Abbaye
le-Grand-Bourg
Guéret
Ajain
Evaux-les-Bains
Marcillat-en-Combraille
Montaigut
St. Eloy-les-Mines
Brout-Vernet
Vichy
Bellerive
Cusset
Le Breuil
Arfeuilles
Bessines
Laurière
Chénérailles
Fontanières
Pionsat
Menat
Ebreuil
Gannat
Châtel-Montagne
Le Mayet-de-M.
Rousac
Razes
St. Sulpice-Laurière
St. Dizier-Leyrenne
Ahun
Auzances
Aigueperse
Abrest
St. Yorre
Brugheas
Effiat
Randan
Ferrières
Renaison
La Jonchère-St. Maurice
St. Gervais-d'Auvergne
Ambazac
Pontarion
Bourganeuf
Aubusson
Manzat
Combronde
Limons
Puy-Guillaume
Grossereix
Sauviat-sur-Vige
St. Léonard-de-Noblat
Peyrat-le-Château
Felletin
Crocq
St. Avit
St. George-de-Mous
Les Ancizes-Comps
Châtelguyon
Riom
Ennezat
Maringues
Crevant-Laveine
St. Just-en-Chevalet
St. Remy-s.-Durolle
Chabreloche
Limoges
Solignac
Gentioux
Giat
Pontaumur
Volvic
Pontgibaud
Bromont-Lamothe
Clermont-Ferrand
Gerzat
Joze
Pont-de-Dore
Thiers
La Monnerie-le-Montel
Noirétable
Champoly
St. Julien
Eymoutiers
Sauvagnat
Mazaye
Royat
Ceyrat
Beaumont
Pont-du-Château
Lezoux
Moissat
Vollore-Montagne
Courpière
Billom
Pierre-Buffière
Châteauneuf-la-Forêt
La Courtine-le Trucq
Eygurande
Bourg-Lastic
Rochefort-Montagne
Cournon
Monts du Forez
Chalmazel
St. Georges-en-C.
Magnac-Bourg
St. Germain-les-Belles
Millevaches
La Bourboule
St. Armant-Tallende
Veyre-Monton
Vic-le-Comte
Parc Naturel Régional
Cunlhat
Olliergues
Vertolaye
Chamberet
Bugeat
Le Mont-Dore
Chambon-s.-Lac
Murol
St. Nectaire
Champeix
Coudes
Sugères
St. Amant-Roche-Savine
Meuzac
Coussac-Bonneval
Masseret
Treignac
Peyrissac
Meymac
Ussel
Tauves
Monts Dore 1886
Perrier
Issoire
Sauxillanges
Ambert
Yrieix-Perche
Lubersac
Chamboulive
St. Angel
Besse-en-Chandesse
St. Germain-Lembron
Vernet-la-Varenne
Livradois Forez
Marsac-en-Livradois
Arnac-Pompadour
Vigeois
Uzerche
Seilhac
Corrèze
Egletons
Champs-sur-Tarentaine
Eglisneuve-d'Entraigues
Ardes
Lempdes
Auzat
St. Germain-l'Herm
Brassac-les-Mines
Ste. Florine
Champagnac-le-Vieux
Arlanc
Viverols
Juillac
Neuvic
Bort-les-Orgues
Condat
Marcenat
Anzat
Brioude
Usson-en-F.
La Chaise-Dieu
Craponne
Objat
Marcillac-la-Croisille
Riom-
Tulle
Massif Central
Limousin
Bourbonnais
Nivernais
Marche
Forez

27 28

0 5 10 20 30 40 Miles

21
66

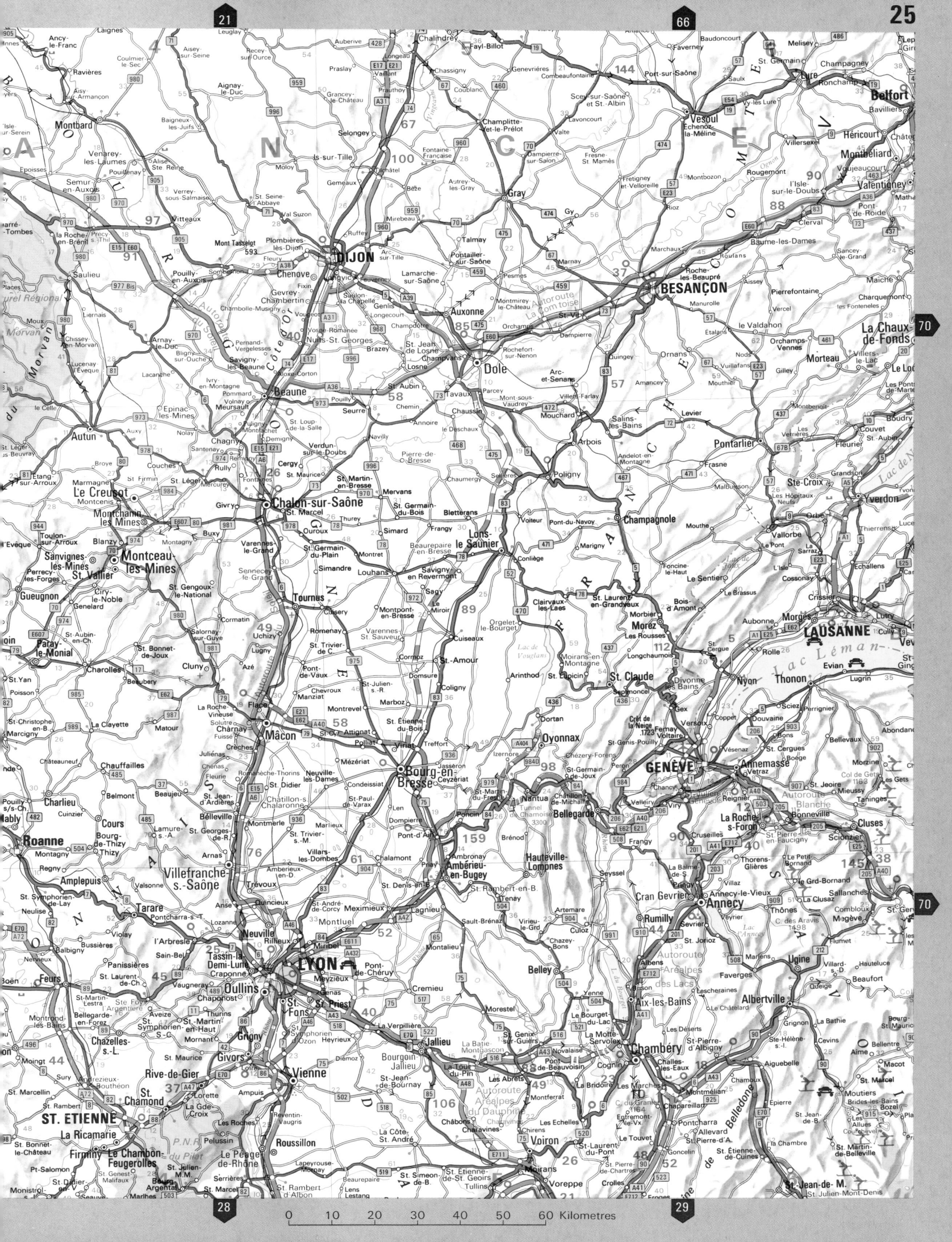

Laignes
Ancy-le-Franc
Ravières
Montbard
Venarey-les-Laumes
Alise Ste Reine
Semur-en-Auxois
Vitteaux
Saulieu
Pouilly-en-Auxois
Mont Tasselot 593
Plombières-lès-Dijon
DIJON
Chenove
Gevrey-Chambertin
Nuits-St. Georges
Savigny-les-Beaune
Beaune
Meursault
Autun
Epinac-les-Mines
Chagny
Le Creusot
Montceau-les-Mines
Chalon-sur-Saône
St. Marcel
Givry
Buxy
Gueugnon
Paray-le-Monial
Charolles
Cluny
Tournus
Uchizy
Mâcon
Roanne
Charlieu
Villefranche-s.-Saône
Tarare
Feurs
Neuville
Tassin-la-Demi-Lune
LYON
Oullins
St. Priest
Givors
Vienne
Rive-de-Gier
St. Chamond
ST. ETIENNE
La Ricamarie
Firminy
Le Chambon-Feugerolles
Roussillon
Pelussin
Le Péage-de-Rhône
Chalindrey
Fayl-Billot
Langres
Selongey
Is-sur-Tille
Mirebeau
Gray
Champlitte-et-le-Prélot
Auxonne
Dole
Tavaux
Seurre
Louhans
Lons-le-Saunier
Bourg-en-Bresse
Oyonnax
Nantua
Bellegarde
Ambérieu-en-Bugey
Belley
Hauteville-Lompnes
St. Claude
Morez
Les Rousses
Champagnole
Poligny
Arbois
Salins-les-Bains
Pontarlier
BESANÇON
Vesoul
Port-sur-Saône
Lure
Belfort
Héricourt
Montbéliard
Valentigney
Baume-les-Dames
Clerval
L'Isle-sur-le-Doubs
Maîche
La Chaux-de-Fonds
Morteau
Le Locle
Ste-Croix
Yverdon
Vallorbe
Orbe
LAUSANNE
Morges
Nyon
Thonon
Evian
Lac Léman
GENÈVE
Annemasse
Bonneville
La Roche-s-Foron
Cluses
Sallanches
Annecy
Rumilly
Aix-les-Bains
Chambéry
Albertville
Ugine
Faverges
Montmélian
Allevard
Voiron
Moirans
Voreppe
St.-Jean-de-M.
Moutiers
Bourgoin-Jallieu
La Tour-du-Pin
Les Abrets
Pont-de-Beauvoisin
Les Echelles
Meximieux
Montluel
Trévoux
Pont-de-Chéryu
Crémieu

0 10 20 30 40 50 60 Kilometres

70
70
28
29

1   2   3

118

A

BORDEAUX

CÔTE DES LANDES

Montalivet-les-Bains
Vendays-Montalivet
Lesparre-Médoc
Hourtin-Plage
Hourtin
Lacanau-Océan
Lacanau
Carcans-Plage
Lac d'Hourtin-Carcans
Étang de Lacanau

St Vivien de Médoc
Lorignac
Mirambeau
Jonzac
St Christoly Médoc
St Ciers-sur-Gironde
St Seurin-de-Cadourne
St Estèphe
Le Pouyalet
Pauillac
St Julien
Beychevelle
Blaye
Bourg
Montendre
Chevanceaux
Chalais
Montguyon
La Roche-Chalais
Coutras
Libourne
St Émilion

Margaux
Castelnau-de-Médoc
Blanquefort
St Médard-en-Jalles
Mérignac
Pessac
Gradignan
Villenave-d'Ornon

B

CÔTE D'ARGENT

Arcachon
Cap Ferret
Pyla-sur-Mer
La Teste
Gujan-Mestras
Biganos
Andernos-les-Bains
Arès
Lanton
Audenge
Cazaux
Sanguinet
Biscarrosse
Biscarrosse-Plage
Étang de Cazaux et de Sanguinet
Étang de Biscarrosse et de Parentis
Parentis-en-Born
Pontenx-les-Forges
Mimizan-Plage
Mimizan
Bias
Escsource
Contis-Plage
St-Julien-en-Born
Mézos
Lit-et-Mixe
Laharie

Parc Naturel Régional
des Landes de Gascogne

57
175

Marcheprime
Mios
Salles
Le Barp
Béliet
Belin
Le Muret
Mano
St Symphorien
Hostens
Belhade
Moustey
Liposthey
Pissos
Luxey
Sore
Trensacq
Commensacq
Labouheyre
Sabres
Labrit
Morcenx
Arengosse
Brocas
Garein
Ygos-St-Saturnin
Le Calen
Pujols

Villagrains
Cabanac-et-Villagrains
Illats
Preignac
Sauternes
Yquem
Langon
Villandraut
Bazas
Auros
Captieux
Beaulac
Grignols
Castelnau de Médoc

St Macaire
La Réole
Marm...
Créon
Rauzan
Targon
Branne
Sauveterre-de-Guyenne
Cadillac
Barsac
Pellegrue
Monségur
La Castillon la-Batail
Lerm-et-Musset
Casteljaloux
Allons

932
655
651
933
934

C

CÔTE BASQUE

Biarritz
Anglet
Bayonne
Boucau
Tarnos
Capbreton
Hossegor
Soorts
St Vincent-de-Tyrosse
Labenne
St Geours-de-Maremne
Soustons
Vieux-Boucau
Azur
Magescq
St-Paul
Dax
Pontonx
Castets
Léon
Rion-des-Landes
Tartas
Meilhan
Souprosse
Mugron
St Sever
Montfort-en-Chalosse
St Girons
St Girons-Plage
Souquet

Mont-de-Marsan
Villeneuve-de-Marsan
Roquefort
St Justin
Gabarret
Cazaubon
Estang
Mauvezin
Grenade-sur-l'Adour
Manciet
Le Houga
Nogaro
Aire-sur-l'Adour
Riscle
Geaune
Garlin
Lembeye
Vic-en-Bigorre

146

Peyrehorade
Orthez
Salies-de-Béarn
Sauveterre
Bidache
Hasparren
Cambo-les-Bains
Ustaritz
St-Jean-de-Luz
Guéthary
St Pée
Espelette
Ascain
Urrugne
Hendaye
Béhobie
Fuenterrabia
Irún
Pasajes
Renteria
Oyarzun
Hernani
Andoain

DONOSTIA-SAN SEBASTIÁN

Lequeitio
Ondárroa
Motrico
Zumaya
Guetaria
Zarauz
Orio
Aya
Usurbil
Lasarte
Eibar
Elgóibar
Placencia
Azcoitia
Azpeitia
Cestona
Deva
Vergara
Oñate
Zumárraga
Villafranca de Oria
Beasain
Ataun
Tolosa
Villabona
Alsasua
Idiazabal

27
65

Pau
Jurançon
Oloron-Ste-Marie
Mourenx Ville-Nouvelle
Lagor
Artix
Monein
Navarrenx
Mauléon Licharre
Tardets-Sorholus
St-Jean-Pied-de-Port
Arnéguy
Roncesvalles
Burguete
Puerto de Ibañeta
Tarbes
Lourdes
Argelès-Gazost
Pierrefitte-Nestalas
Eaux-Bonnes
Arrens
Laruns
Louvie-Juzon
Arudy
Asasp
Accous
Pic d'Anie 2504
Pic d'Orhy 2015

PYRÉNÉES

Elizondo
Errazu
Maya de Baztán
Sumbilla
Santesteban
Goizueta
Leiza
Lecumberri
Irurzun
Ostiz
Zubiri
Villava

0   5   10   20   30   40 Miles

23
24

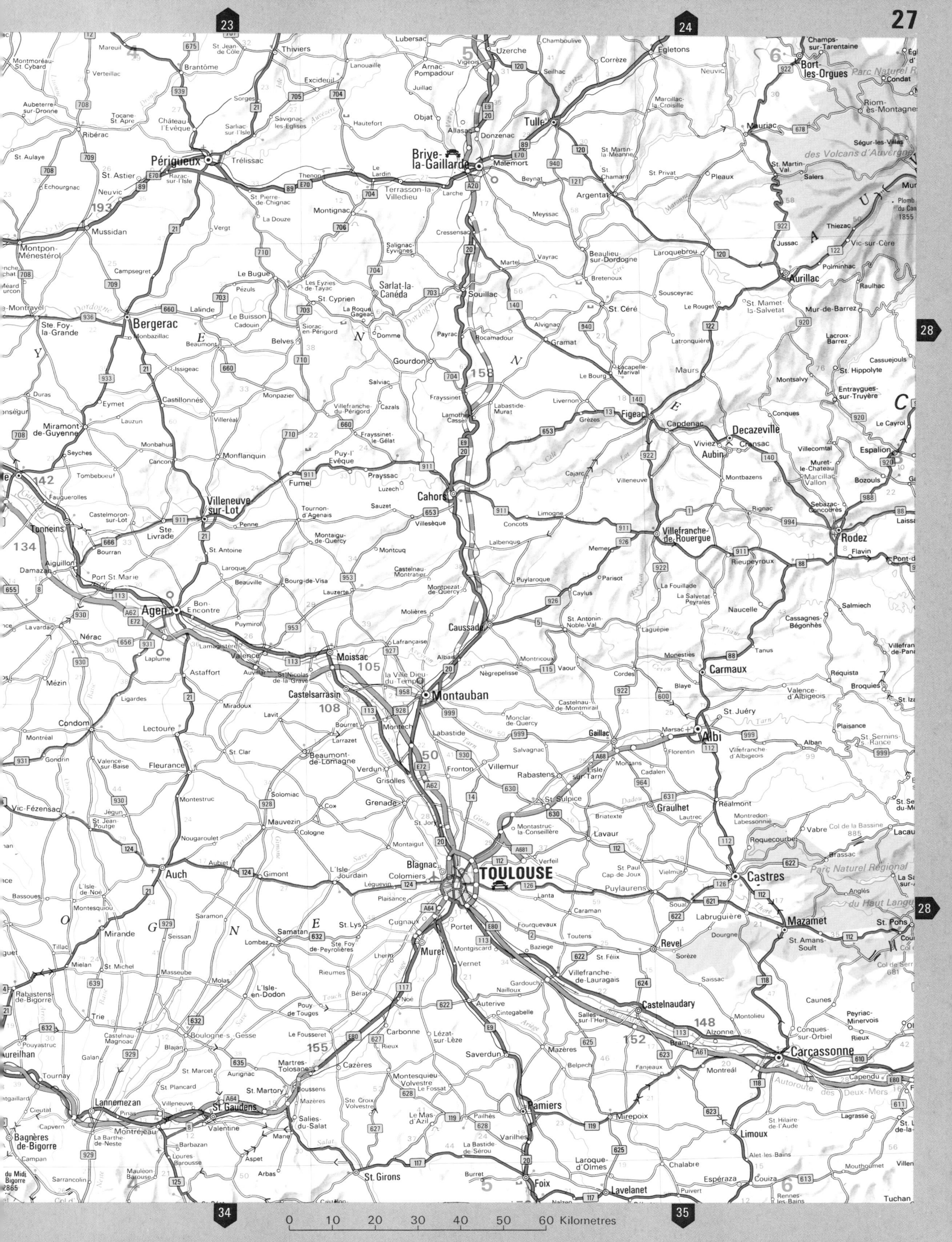
Montmoreau-St. Cybard
Mareuil
Verteillac
Aubeterre-sur-Dronne
Ribérac
Tocane-St. Apre
St. Aulaye
Périgueux
St. Astier
Razac-sur-l'Isle
Trélissac
Brantôme
St. Jean-de-Côle
Thiviers
Sorges
Château-l'Evêque
Sarliac-sur-l'Isle
Excideuil
Savignac-les-Eglises
Lanouaille
Hautefort
Lubersac
Arnac-Pompadour
Juillac
Objat
Vigeois
Uzerche
Allassac
Donzenac
Brive-la-Gaillarde
Malemort
Larche
Terrasson-la-Villedieu
Le Lardin
Thenon
St. Pierre-de-Chignac
Montignac
La Douze
Chamboulive
Corrèze
Seilhac
Egletons
Neuvic
Tulle
Marcillac-la-Croisille
St. Martin-la-Méanne
St. Chamant
Argentat
St. Privat
Pleaux
Beynat
Meyssac
Champs-sur-Tarentaine
Bort-les-Orgues
Parc Naturel Régional des Volcans d'Auvergne
Condat
Riom-ès-Montagnes
Mauriac
Ségur-les-Villas
St. Martin-Valmeroux
Salers
Thiezac
Plomb du Cantal 1855
Vic-sur-Cère
Jussac
Aurillac
Polminhac
Raulhac
Echourgnac
Neuvic
Mussidan
Montpon-Ménestérol
Vergt
Campsegret
Le Bugue
Pézuls
Les Eyzies-de-Tayac
St. Cyprien
Sarlat-la-Canéda
Salignac-Eyvignes
Cressensac
Souillac
Martel
Vayrac
Beaulieu-sur-Dordogne
Bretenoux
Laroquebrou
Sousceyrac
Le Rouget
St. Mamet-la-Salvetat
Mur-de-Barrez
St. Céré
Alvignac
Gramat
Rocamadour
Payrac
Lalinde
Le Buisson-Cadouin
La Roque-Gageac
Siorac-en-Périgord
Domme
Belves
Bergerac
Monbazillac
Beaumont
Ste. Foy-la-Grande
Issigeac
Gourdon
Salviac
Frayssinet
Lamothe-Cassel
Labastide-Murat
Livernon
Latronquière
Lacapelle-Marival
Maurs
Le Bourg
Figeac
Grèzes
Capdenac
Decazeville
Viviez
Aubin
Cransac
Lacroix-Barrez
Cassuejouls
St. Hippolyte
Montsalvy
Entraygues-sur-Truyère
Conques
Le Cayrol
Espalion
Villecomtal
Muret-le-Château
Marcillac-Vallon
Bozouls
Sebazac-Concourès
Rodez
Flavin
Duras
Eymet
Castillonnès
Monpazier
Villefranche-du-Périgord
Cazals
Miramont-de-Guyenne
Lauzun
Villeréal
Monbahus
Frayssinet-le-Gélat
Puy-l'Evêque
Seyches
Cancon
Monflanquin
Prayssac
Luzech
Fumel
Tombeboeuf
Cahors
Cajarc
Villeneuve
Montbazens
Rignac
Fauguerolles
Castelmoron-sur-Lot
Villeneuve-sur-Lot
Tournon-d'Agenais
Sauzet
Villesèque
Concots
Limogne
Villefranche-de-Rouergue
Tonneins
Ste. Livrade
Penne
Bourran
Aiguillon
Damazan
St. Antoine
Montaigu-de-Quercy
Montcuq
Lalbenque
Memer
Rieupeyroux
Parisot
Port St. Marie
Laroque
Beauville
Bourg-de-Visa
Castelnau-Montratier
Lauzerte
Montpezat-de-Quercy
Puylaroque
Caylus
La Fouillade
La Salvetat-Peyralès
Naucelle
Salmiech
Agen
Bon-Encontre
Puymirol
Molières
Caussade
St. Antonin-Noble-Val
Laguépie
Cassagnes-Bégonhès
Lavardac
Nérac
Lamagistère
Valence
Laplume
Mézin
Astaffort
Auvillar
St. Nicolas-de-la-Grave
Moissac
Lafrançaise
Albias
Montricoux
Nègrepelisse
Vaour
Cordes
Monestiés
Carmaux
Tanus
Réquista
Villefranche-de-Panat
Broquiès
St. Izaire
Ligardes
Castelsarrasin
la Ville Dieu-du-Temple
Montauban
Castelnau-de-Montmirail
Blaye
Valence-d'Albigeois
Condom
Lectoure
Miradoux
Lavit
Bourret
Larrazet
Montech
Labastide-St. Pierre
Monclar-de-Quercy
Gaillac
Marssac
Albi
St. Juéry
Plaisance
St. Sernin-s.-Rance
Montréal
Gondrin
Valence-sur-Baïse
Fleurance
St. Clar
Beaumont-de-Lomagne
Verdun
Grisolles
Fronton
Villemur
Salvagnac
Rabastens
Lisle-sur-Tarn
Montans
Cadalen
Florentin
Villefranche-d'Albigeois
Alban
Vic-Fézensac
Montestruc
Solomiac
Jégun
St. Jean-Poutge
Mauvezin
Cologne
Cox
Grenade
St. Jory
St. Sulpice
Graulhet
Briatexte
Réalmont
Montredon-Labessonnié
Vabre
Col de la Bassine 885
Lacaune
Nougaroulet
Montaigut
Montastruc-la-Conseillère
Lavaur
Lautrec
Roquecourbe
Brassac
Parc Naturel Régional du Haut Languedoc
Auch
Aubiet
Gimont
L'Isle-Jourdain
Blagnac
Colomiers
Léguevin
Toulouse
Verfeil
St. Paul-Cap-de-Joux
Vielmur
Castres
La Salvetat-sur-Agout
Bassoues
L'Isle-de-Noé
Montesquiou
Plaisance
Lanta
Puylaurens
Soual
Labruguière
Anglès
Mirande
Seissan
Saramon
Samatan
St. Lys
Cugnaux
Portet
Caraman
Fourquevaux
Mazamet
St. Pons
Dourgne
St. Amans-Soult
Tillac
Lombez
Ste. Foy-de-Peyrolières
Muret
Montgiscard
Baziège
Toulouse
Revel
Sorèze
St. Félix
Villefranche-de-Lauragais
Mielan
St. Michel
Masseube
Lherm
Rieumes
Vernet
Gardouch
Nailloux
Col de Serre 681
Rabastens-de-Bigorre
Trie
Molas
L'Isle-en-Dodon
Pouy-de-Touges
Bérat
Noé
Auterive
Cintegabelle
Castelnaudary
Saissac
Caunes
Peyriac-Minervois
Montolieu
Salles-sur-l'Hers
Alzonne
Conques-sur-Orbiel
Rieux
Castelnau-Magnoac
Boulogne-s.-Gesse
Le Fousseret
Carbonne
Rieux
Lézat-sur-Lèze
Saverdun
Mazères
Bram
Carcassonne
Pouyastruc
Galan
Blajan
Martres-Tolosane
Cazères
Belpech
Fanjeaux
Montréal
Tournay
St. Marcet
Aurignac
Montesquieu-Volvestre
Le Fossat
Capendu
Autoroute des Deux-Mers
St. Plancard
St. Martory
Boussens
Mazères
Ste. Croix-Volvestre
Pamiers
Mirepoix
Lagrasse
Lannemezan
Cieutat
Pinas
Villeneuve
St. Gaudens
Salies-du-Salat
Le Mas-d'Azil
Pailhès
Bagnères-de-Bigorre
Capvern
Montréjeau
Valentine
Mane
La Bastide-de-Sérou
Varilhes
Limoux
St. Hilaire-de-l'Aude
La Barthe-de-Neste
Barbazan
Loures-Barousse
Aspet
Arbas
Campan
Mauléon-Barousse
Sarrancolin
St. Girons
Burret
Foix
Laroque-d'Olmes
Chalabre
Alet-les-Bains
Mouthoumet
Espéraza
Couiza
Lavelanet
Puivert
Rennes-les-Bains
Tuchan
Pic du Midi de Bigorre 2865
Dordogne
Garonne

28
28
34
35

0 10 20 30 40 50 60 Kilometres

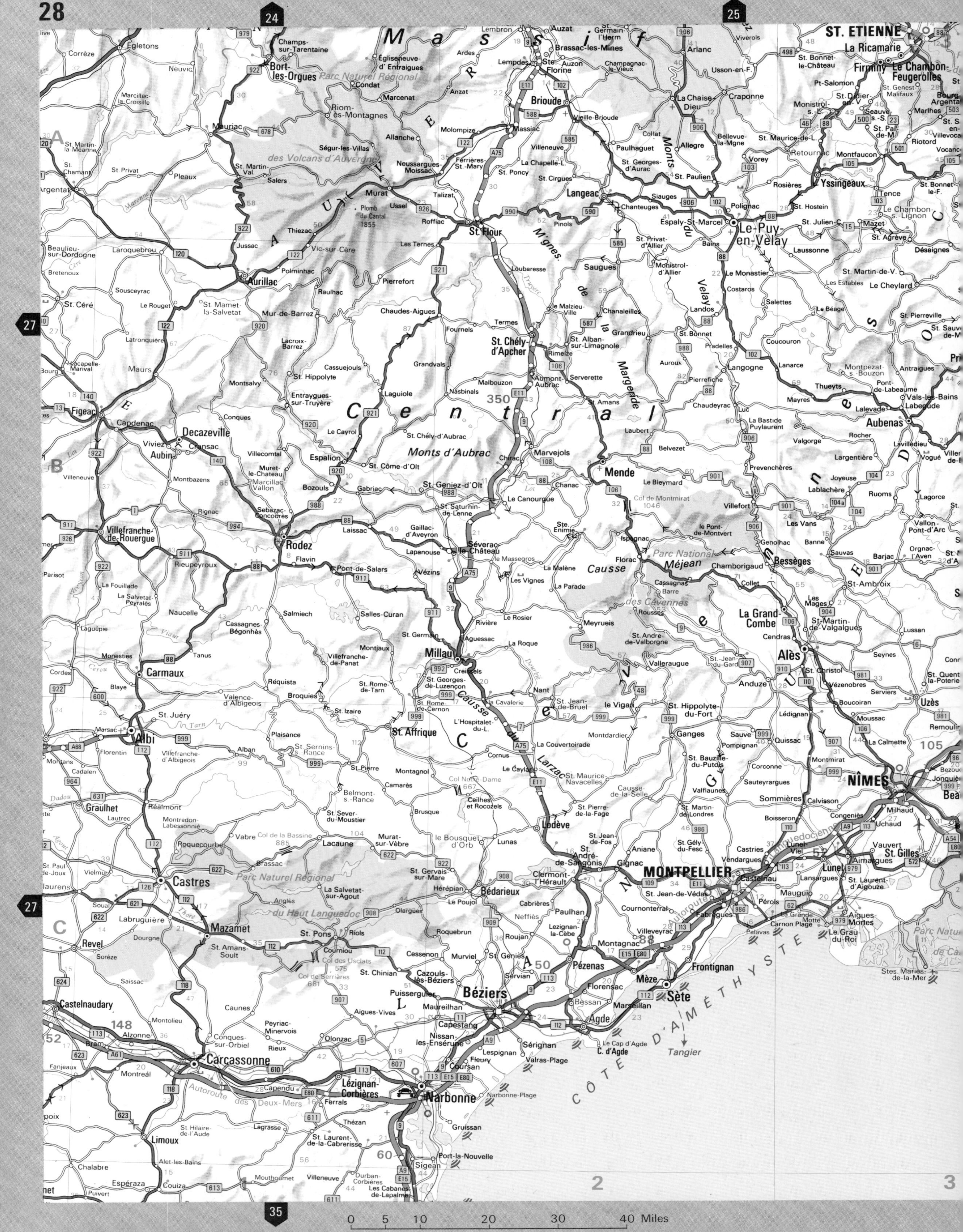
24
25
27
35
Massif Central
Parc Naturel Régional des Volcans d'Auvergne
Monts d'Aubrac
Causse Méjean
Parc National des Cévennes
Causse du Larzac
Parc Naturel Régional du Haut Languedoc
Autoroute des Deux-Mers
Autoroute Languedocienne
Côte d'Améthyste
Golfe du Lion
Tangier
ST. ETIENNE
La Ricamarie
Firminy
Le Chambon-Feugerolles
Egletons
Corrèze
Bort-les-Orgues
Mauriac
Riom-ès-Montagnes
Salers
Murat
Plomb du Cantal 1855
St. Flour
Aurillac
Brioude
Massiac
Langeac
Le-Puy-en-Velay
Yssingeaux
Aubenas
Figeac
Decazeville
Capdenac
Villefranche-de-Rouergue
Rodez
Espalion
Laguiole
St. Chély-d'Apcher
Marvejols
Mende
Séverac-le-Château
Millau
St. Affrique
Meyrueis
Florac
La Grand-Combe
Alès
Bessèges
Les Vans
Uzès
Nîmes
Carmaux
Albi
Castres
Mazamet
Revel
Castelnaudary
Carcassonne
Limoux
Lodève
Bédarieux
Clermont-l'Hérault
Pézenas
Béziers
Agde
Sète
Frontignan
MONTPELLIER
Lunel
Aigues-Mortes
St. Gilles
Sommières
Ganges
le Vigan
Narbonne
Lézignan-Corbières
Sigean
Port-la-Nouvelle
0 5 10 20 30 40 Miles

25
70
74
74

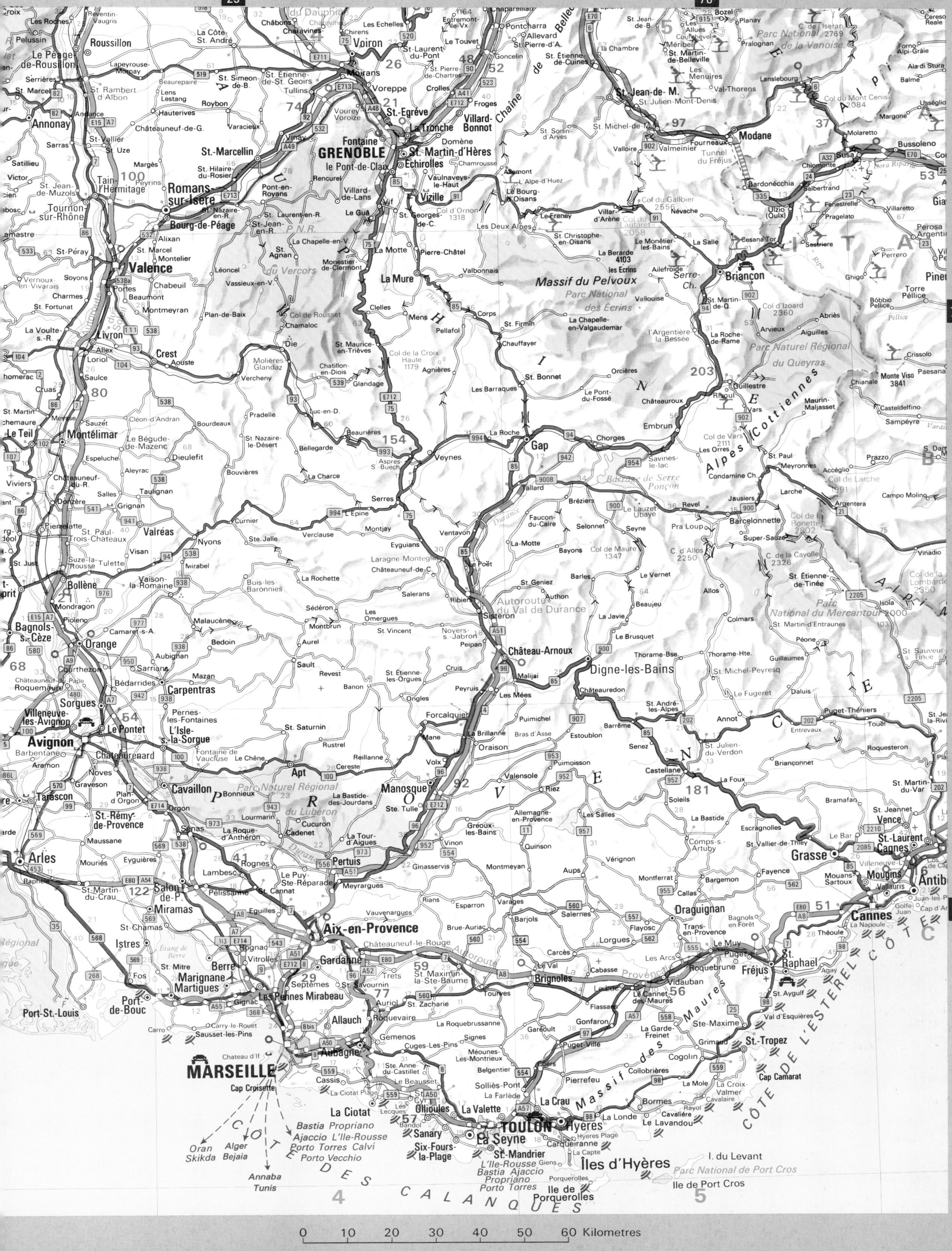
Les Roches
Pelussin
Roussillon
Le Péage-de-Roussillon
Serrières
St. Rambert d'Albon
Annonay
Hauterives
Châteauneuf-de-G.
St.-Vallier
Sarras
St. Uze
Satillieu
Victor
Tain-l'Hermitage
St. Jean-de-Muzols
Tournon-sur-Rhône
Romans-sur-Isère
Bourg-de-Péage
St.-Marcellin
St. Hilaire-du-Rosier
Pont-en-Royans
St.-Péray
Valence
Alixan
St. Marcel
Montelier
Chabeuil
Beaumont
Montmeyran
Soyons
Vernoux-en-Vivarais
Charmes
St. Fortunat
La Voulte-s.-R.
Livron
Allex
Loriol
Crest
Aouste
Saulce
Cruas
Montélimar
Le Teil
Sauzet
Viviers
Châteauneuf-du-R.
Donzère
Grignan
Taulignan
Valréas
Pierrelatte
St. Paul-Trois-Châteaux
Visan
Nyons
Suze-la-Rousse
Tulette
Bollène
Mondragon
Vaison-la-Romaine
Mirabel
Bagnols-s.-Cèze
Orange
Courthezon
Châteauneuf-du-Pape
Roquemaure
Sorgues
Carpentras
Bédarrides
Villeneuve-les-Avignon
Le Pontet
Avignon
Barbentane
Châteaurenard
L'Isle-s.-la-Sorgue
Pernes-les-Fontaines
Fontaine de Vaucluse
Cavaillon
Noves
Graveson
Tarascon
St.-Rémy-de-Provence
Maussane
Arles
Apt
Bonnieux
Lourmarin
Cadenet
La Roque-d'Anthéron
Pertuis
Rognes
Lambesc
Salon-de-P.
Miramas
Pélissanne
St.-Chamas
Istres
Berre
Fos
Marignane
Martigues
Port-de-Bouc
Port-St.-Louis
Vitrolles
Aix-en-Provence
Gardanne
Les Pennes Mirabeau
Allauch
Aubagne
Carry-le-Rouet
Sausset-les-Pins
Chateau d'If
MARSEILLE
Cap Croisette
Cassis
La Ciotat
Bandol
Sanary
Six-Fours-la-Plage
Ollioules
La Seyne
TOULON
La Valette
Hyères
St.-Mandrier
Carqueiranne
Iles d'Hyères
Ile de Porquerolles
Ile de Port Cros
I. du Levant
Parc National de Port Cros
Oran
Skikda
Alger
Bejaia
Annaba
Tunis
Bastia Propriano
Ajaccio L'Ile-Rousse
Porto Torres Calvi
Porto Vecchio
L'Ile-Rousse
Bastia Ajaccio
Propriano
Porto Torres
CÔTE DES CALANQUES
Voiron
Moirans
Voreppe
St.-Egrève
GRENOBLE
Fontaine
La Tronche
St.-Martin-d'Hères
Echirolles
Le Pont-de-Claix
Vizille
Villard-de-Lans
Pontcharra
Allevard
Villard-Bonnot
Domène
Chamrousse
Le Bourg-d'Oisans
L'Alpe-d'Huez
La Mure
Mens
Corps
Monestier-de-Clermont
Die
Chamaloc
Col de Rousset
Châtillon-en-Diois
Luc-en-D.
Veynes
Gap
Aspres-s-Buech
Serres
Laragne-Montéglin
Sisteron
Château-Arnoux
Digne-les-Bains
Manosque
Forcalquier
Oraison
Valensole
Riez
Gréoux-les-Bains
Massif du Pelvoux
Parc National des Écrins
Briançon
Embrun
Chorges
Savines-le-lac
Barrage de Serre Ponçon
Barcelonnette
Jausiers
Guillestre
Modane
St.-Jean-de-M.
Val-Thorens
Les Menuires
Méribel
Parc National de la Vanoise
Lanslebourg
Col du Mont Cenis 2084
Susa
Bardonécchia
Col du Galibier 2556
Col du Lautaret 2058
Parc Naturel Régional du Queyras
Monte Viso 3841
Alpes Cottiennes
Parc National du Mercantour
Col de la Bonette 2802
Col de Larche 1991
Castellane
St.-Julien-du-Verdon
Puget-Théniers
Entrevaux
Grasse
Vence
St.-Laurent
Cagnes
Antibes
Mougins
Vallauris
Cannes
La Napoule
Théoule
St. Raphaël
Fréjus
Draguignan
Brignoles
St. Maximin-la-Ste-Baume
Le Luc
Le Cannet-des-Maures
Vidauban
Ste-Maxime
St.-Tropez
Grimaud
Cogolin
Cap Camarat
Massif des Maures
Collobrières
Pierrefeu
Solliès-Pont
La Crau
Bormes
Le Lavandou
CÔTE DE L'ESTÉREL
CÔTE D'AZUR
0 10 20 30 40 50 60 Kilometres

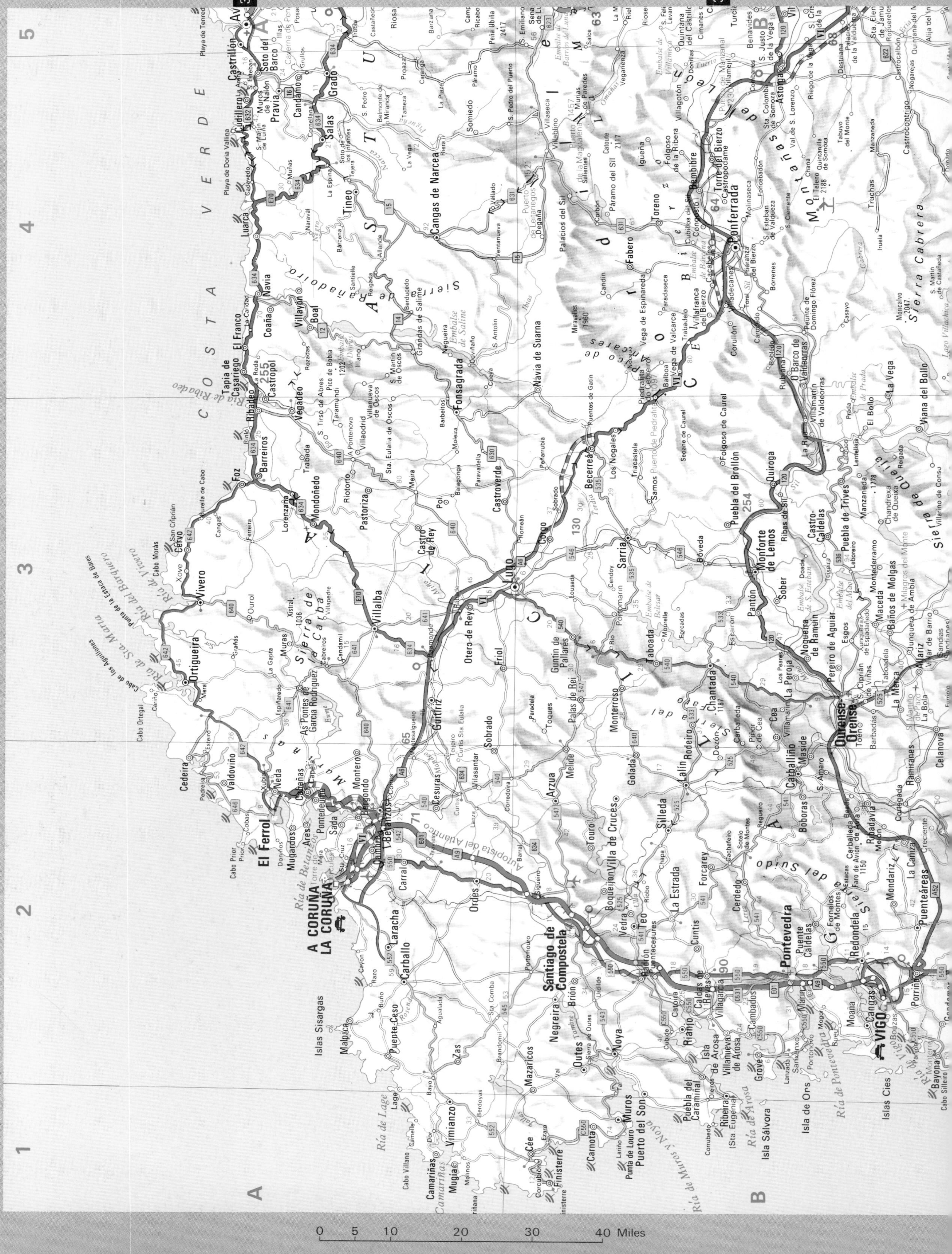

Map — Galicia / Asturias (Northwest Spain)

Grid references: **5 4 3 2 1** (left margin), **A** and **B** (right margin), route panel numbers **32 / 32**

Major places and labels (selection):

Coastal / western (A column):
A CORUÑA / LA CORUÑA, El Ferrol, Betanzos, Sada, Pontedeume, Cedeira, Cariño, Ortigueira, Vivero, Cervo, Foz, Ribadeo, Barreiros, Mondoñedo, Villalba, Carballo, Laracha, Malpica, Islas Sisargas, Camariñas, Mugía, Vimianzo, Zas, Negreira, Finisterre, Corcubión, Cée, Carnota, Muros, Puerto del Son, Noya, Outes, Mazaricos, SANTIAGO DE COMPOSTELA, Ordes, Teo, Padrón, Caldas de Reyes, Villagarcía, Villanueva de Arosa, Cambados, El Grove, Rianjo, Isla de Arosa, Puebla del Caramiñal, Ribeira, Sta Eugenia

Central / eastern (B column):
Castrillón, Avilés, Soto del Barco, Pravia, Grado, Salas, Tineo, Cangas de Narcea, Luarca, Navia, Coaña, Boal, Villayón, El Franco, Tapia de Casariego, Castropol, Vegadeo, Grandas de Salime, Fonsagrada, Navia de Suarna, Becerreá, Los Nogales, Piedrafita do Cebreiro, Vega de Valcarce, Villafranca del Bierzo, Cacabelos, PONFERRADA, Bembibre, Torre del Bierzo, Astorga, Benavides, Toreno, Fabero, LUGO, Castroverde, Sarria, Monforte de Lemos, Quiroga, Puebla del Brollón, O Barco de Valdeorras, Rubiana, La Rúa, Viana del Bollo, Puebla de Trives, Castro-Caldelas, Chantada, Taboada, Pantón, Sober, OURENSE / Orense, Carballiño, Maside, Boboras, Ribadavia, Celanova, Bande, PONTEVEDRA, Marín, Cangas, Moaña, Redondela, VIGO, Porriño, Puenteáreas, Mondariz, La Cañiza, Bayona, Islas Cíes

Physical features:
COSTA VERDE, ASTURIAS, Sierra de la Carba, Picos de Ancares, Montañas de León, Sierra Cabrera, Ría de Ribadeo, Ría de Betanzos, Ría de Vivero, Ría del Barquero, Ría de Sta Marta, Cabo Ortegal, Cabo Prior, Cabo de Sta Eulalia

Scale bar: **0 5 10 20 30 40 Miles**

0 10 20 30 40 50 60 Kilometres

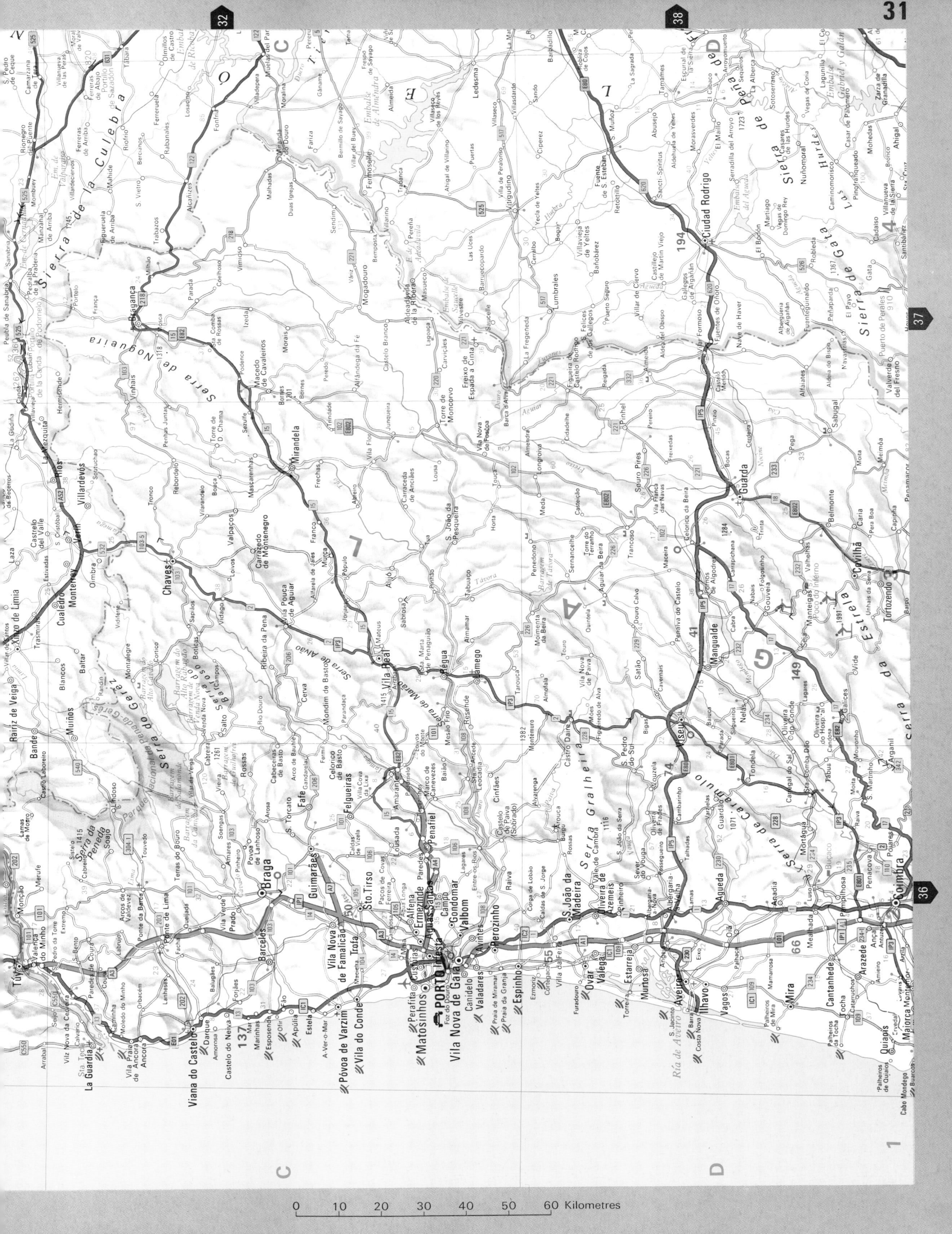
32
38
37
36
C
D
1
4
PORTO
Vila Nova de Gaia
Matosinhos
Braga
Guimarães
Viana do Castelo
Póvoa de Varzim
Vila do Conde
Barcelos
Vila Nova de Famalicão
Sto. Tirso
Espinho
Ovar
Aveiro
Ílhavo
Coimbra
Viseu
Guarda
Covilhã
Mangualde
Lamego
Régua
Vila Real
Chaves
Bragança
Mirandela
Macedo de Cavaleiros
Ciudad Rodrigo
Vitigudino
Ledesma
Tuy
Valença do Minho
Monção
La Guardia
Verín
Serra da Estrela
Serra de Caramulo
Serra Gralheira
Serra de Nogueira
Sierra de la Culebra
Sierra de Gata
Sierra de Peña de Francia
Serra do Gerez
Parque Nacional da Peneda-Gerês
Ría de Aveiro
Cabo Mondego

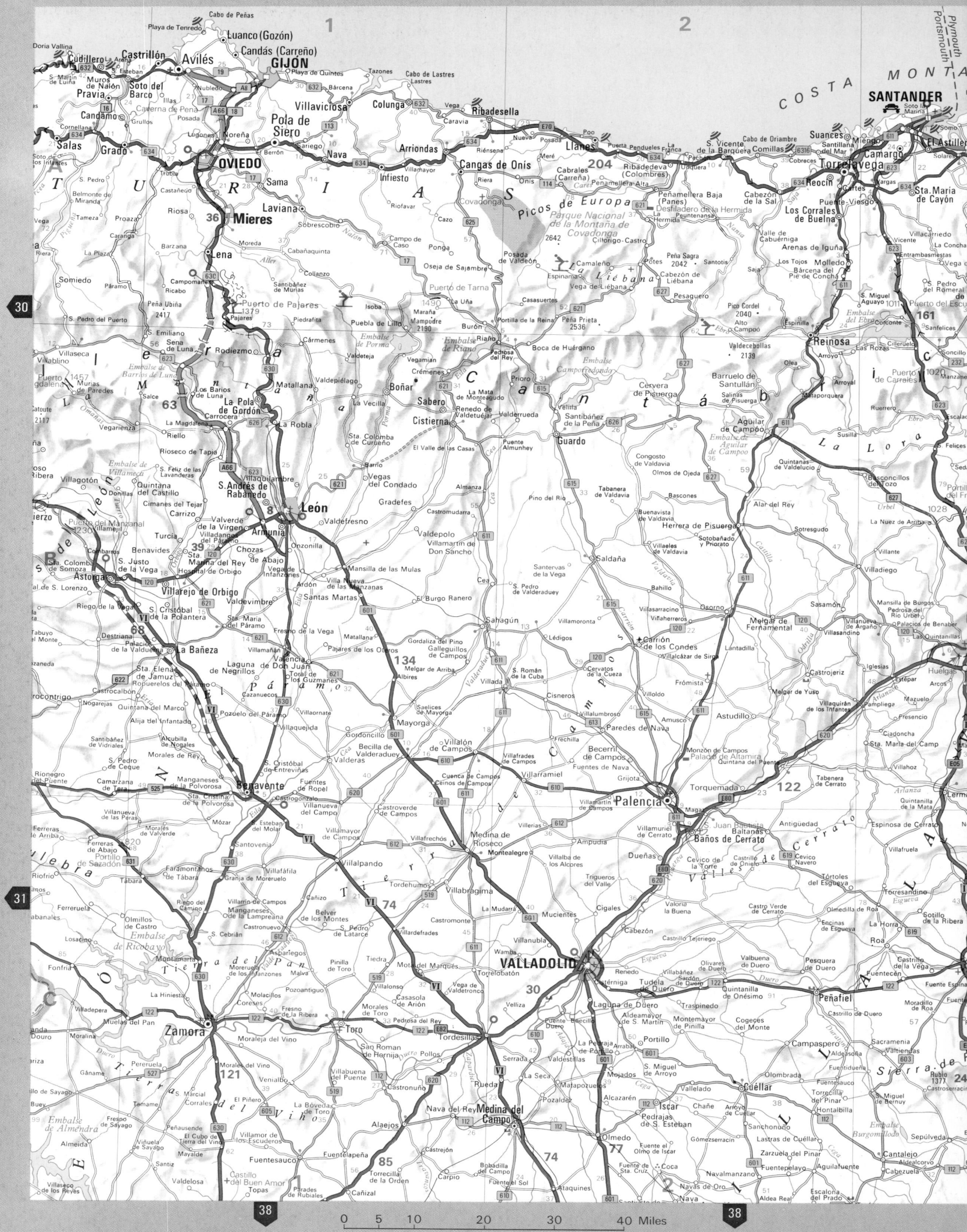
1
2
Cabo de Peñas
Playa de Tenredo
Luanco (Gozón)
Candás (Carreño)
GIJÓN
Avilés
Castrillón
Cudillero
Doria Vallina
Pravia
Soto del Barco
Muros de Nalón
Candamo
Salas
Grado
OVIEDO
Noreña
Lugones
Pola de Siero
Villaviciosa
Colunga
Tazones
Cabo de Lastres
Lastres
Ribadesella
Nava
Arriondas
Cangas de Onís
Infiesto
Llanes
Posada
Ribadedeva (Colombres)
Peñamellera Alta
Peñamellera Baja (Panes)
Desfiladero de la Hermida
Picos de Europa
Parque Nacional de la Montaña de Covadonga
Covadonga
COSTA
MONTA
SANTANDER
Plymouth — Portsmouth
Suances
S. Vicente de la Barquera
Cabo de Oriambre
Comillas
Santillana del Mar
Torrelavega
Camargo
El Astillero
Reocín
Cabezón de la Sal
Los Corrales de Buelna
Puente-Viesgo
Sta. María de Cayón
Sama
Laviana
Mieres
Riosa
Proaza
Lena
Campomanes
Somiedo
Puerto de Pajares
Pajares
Peña Ubiña
2417
Puerto de Tarna
Riaño
Embalse de Riaño
Embalse de Porma
Boca de Huérgano
Potes
Camaleño
Liébana
Vega de Liébana
Cabezón de Liébana
Peña Sagra
2042
Peña Prieta
2536
Pico Cordel
2040
Alto Campoo
Reinosa
Embalse del Ebro
Puerto del Escudo
Valdecebollas
2139
Barruelo de Santullán
Cervera de Pisuerga
Aguilar de Campoo
Embalse de Aguilar de Campoo
Guardo
Villablino
Murias de Paredes
Sena de Luna
Rodiezmo
Embalse de Barrios de Luna
Los Barrios de Luna
La Pola de Gordón
La Robla
La Magdalena
Boñar
Sabero
Cistierna
Crémenes
Vegamián
La Vecilla
Sta. Colomba de Curueño
Riello
Villagotón
Embalse de Villameca
Astorga
Puerto del Manzanal
León
Valverde de la Virgen
Armunia
S. Andrés de Rabanedo
Villaquilambre
Vegas del Condado
Gradefes
Valdepolo
Villamartín de Don Sancho
Almanza
Cea
Saldaña
Herrera de Pisuerga
Alar del Rey
Osorno
Melgar de Fernamental
Villadiego
Sasamón
Castrojeriz
Huelgas
Mansilla de las Mulas
Santas Martas
Villarejo de Orbigo
Hospital de Orbigo
La Bañeza
Sahagún
El Burgo Ranero
Carrión de los Condes
Frómista
Astudillo
Villada
Valencia de Don Juan
Laguna de Negrillos
Mayorga
Paredes de Nava
Becerril de Campos
Palencia
Grijota
Torquemada
Baños de Cerrato
Dueñas
Villalón de Campos
Villarramiel
Benavente
Villalpando
Medina de Rioseco
Montealegre
Castroverde de Campos
Villabrágima
Tordehumos
Cigales
La Mudarra
Mucientes
Villanubla
VALLADOLID
Cabezón
Tudela de Duero
Laguna de Duero
Peñafiel
Quintanilla de Onésimo
Roa
Zamora
Toro
Tordesillas
Simancas
Medina del Campo
Rueda
La Seca
Serrada
Portillo
Íscar
Cuéllar
Olmedo
Coca
Navas de Oro
Nava del Rey
Alaejos
Castronuño
Fuentesaúco
Fuentelapeña
Carpio
Ataquines
Fuente el Sol
Villaralbo
Tierra del Pan
Tierra del Vino
Tierra de Campos
Embalse de Ricobayo
Embalse de Almendra
Campaspero
Sacramenia
Cantalejo
Sepúlveda
Sierra de
Rubio
1377
Embalse de Burgomillodo
El Páramo
La Lora
Cantábrica
Cordillera
Asturias
Valles de Cerrato
Cerrato
E70
E80
E82
E05
A66
A8
VI
630
601
611
620
621
623
625
626
627
632
634
610
612
615
122
120
112
525
605
519
527
204
134
121
122
161
68
63
74
85
77
30
36
39

30

31

38

0 5 10 20 30 40 Miles

38

26

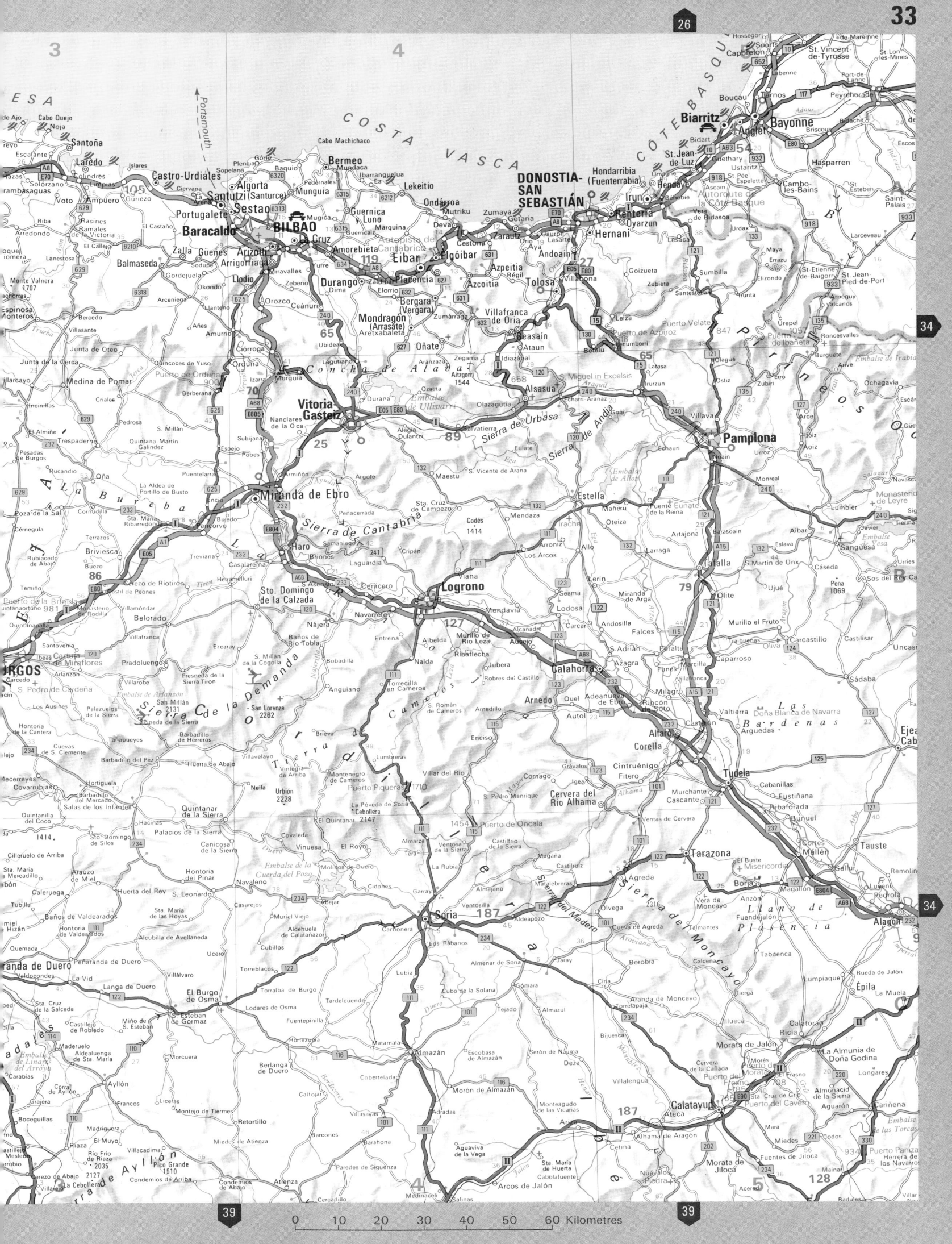

COSTA VASCA
CÔTE BASQUE
Portsmouth
Santoña
Laredo
Castro-Urdiales
Algorta
Santurtzi (Santurce)
Portugalete
Sestao
Baracaldo
BILBAO
Munguia
Bermeo
Mundaca
Cabo Machichaco
Guernica y Luno
Lekeitio
Ondárroa
Mutriku
Deva
Zumaya
Getaria
Zarautz
DONOSTIA-SAN SEBASTIÁN
Hondarribia (Fuenterrabia)
Irun
Renteria
Hernani
Hendaye
St. Jean de-Luz
Biarritz
Anglet
Bayonne
Capbreton
Hossegor
St. Vincent-de-Tyrosse
Peyrehorade
Hasparren
Cambo-les-Bains
St. Jean-Pied-de-Port
Roncesvalles
Balmaseda
Zalla
Güeñes
Arrigorriaga
Llodio
Amorebieta
Durango
Eibar
Elgóibar
Placencia
Bergara (Vergara)
Mondragón (Arrasate)
Oñate
Azpeitia
Azcoitia
Tolosa
Andoain
Villafranca de Oria
Beasaín
Alsasua
Leiza
Puerto Velate
Pamplona
Vitoria-Gasteiz
Concha de Alava
Embalse de Ullivarri
Sierra de Urbasa
Sierra de Andía
Medina de Pomar
Orduña
Miranda de Ebro
La Bureba
Sierra de Cantabria
Haro
Briviesca
Estella
Tafalla
Logrono
Sto. Domingo de la Calzada
Belorado
Nájera
Navarrete
Calahorra
Lodosa
Olite
Sangüesa
Pirineos
Las Bardenas
Arnedo
Alfaro
Corella
Tudela
Cervera del Río Alhama
Tarazona
Borja
Sierra del Moncayo
Llano de Plasencia
Alagón
Ejea
BURGOS
Sierra de la Demanda
San Millán 2131
San Lorenzo 2262
Sierra de Cameros
Tierra de Cameros
Puerto Piqueras 1710
Cebollera 2147
Puerto de Oncala
Soria
El Burgo de Osma
Aranda de Duero
Almazán
Medinaceli
Calatayud
Ateca
La Almunia de Doña Godina
Cariñena
Épila
Sierra de Ayllón
Ayllón
Atienza
Arcos de Jalón
Morata de Jiloca
Daroca

0 10 20 30 40 50 60 Kilometres

34
34
39
39

26
27
33

Pamplona
Lourdes
Bagnères-de-Bigorre
Lannemezan
St-Gaudens
Montréjeau
Tardets-Sorholus
Roncesvalles
Puerto de Ibañeta
Pirineos Occidentales
Parc National des Pyrénées
Pic d'Anie 2504
Pic du Midi d'Ossau 2885
Pic Balaitous ou Marmure 3144
Pic du Midi de Bigorre 2865
Col du Tourmalet 2114
Col d'Aspin 1489
Pic de Vignemale 3298
Pic Long 3194
Pic d'Arbizon 2831
Col du Somport 1631
Canfranc
Jaca
Sabiñánigo
Sierra de La Peña
Sierra de Guara 2077
Monte Perdido 3355
Parque Nacional del Valle de Ordesa
Pirineos Centrales
Pico de Aneto 3404
Maladeta
Mt. Bacanere 2194
Col de Peyresourde 1565
Bagnères-de-Luchon
Vielha
Tunel de Vielha
Benasque
Sobrarbe
Sierra Ferrera
Boltaña
Ainsa
Embalse Mediano
Embalse de el Grado
Huesca
Barbastro
Somontano
Monzón
Binéfar
Lleida-Lérida
Fraga
Ejea de los Caballeros
Las Bardenas
Tudela
Tafalla
Olite
Sangüesa
Tauste
Zuera
El Castellar
Llano de Plasencia
Alagón
ZARAGOZA
Épila
Sierra de Alcubierre
Autopista del Nordeste
Los Monegros
Mequinenza
Embalse de Mequinenza
Caspe
Ebro
Calatayud
La Almunia de Doña Godina
Cariñena
Belchite
Daroca
Calamocha
Monreal del Campo
Alcañiz
Andorra
Montalbán
Valderrobres
Gandesa
Mora de Ebro
Flix
Tortosa
Amposta
Balaguer
Sierra del Montsec
Llanos de Urgel
Puerto de Torre Miró 1250
San Just 1517
Sierra Palomera
ARAGÓN

40
40

0 5 10 20 30 40 Miles

27   28

5   6

Ste Croix
Volvestre   Le Mas
d'Azil   Pailhes   Mirepoix   St Hilaire
de-l'Aude   Lagrasse   St Laurent-
de-la-Cabrerisse   Gruissan
Mazeres
628   119   Varilhes   623   Thézar   29   9   Port-la-Nouvelle
Salat   627   626   La Bastide   Laroque-   Chalabre   Espéraza   Couiza   Villeneuve   Durbàn   Corbières   Sigean   E15   E90
St Girons   117   Burret   de-Sérou   d'Olmes   613   Rennes-   de-Lapalme   Leucate
    Foix   117   Lavelanet   Puivert   les-Bains   611   Autoroutes les Cabanes   60
Castillon   179   Nalzen   Quillan   117   St Paul-   la Catalane   de Fitou   Le Barcarès
en-Couserans   Saurat   E9   Tarascon-   Pic de   Axat   de-Fenouillet   A9   Salses   Le Barcarès
Pic de Montvalier   sur-Ariège   St Barthelemy   Usson-   Caudies-   Tuchan   Maury   Rivesaltes   St Laurent-
2839   Massat   2348   les-Bains   118   de-Fenouillèdes   611   614   Estagel   de-la-Salanque
    Aulus-les-Bains   Les Cabannes   613   Sournia   Millas   Perpignan   617   Canet-Plage
Pic de Montcalm   Vicdessos   Ax-les-Thermes   Agly   St Paul-   Thuir   612   9   114   Alenya
3141   El Serrat   118   Formiguères   Vinca   Boule   615   Fourques   Elne   Argelès
Ordino   2   Col de Puymorens   Prades   116   d'Amont   35   Céret   Port Vendres
ANDORRA   22   1915   Olette   Vernet-les-Bains   Amélie-les-   Le Boulou   Cap Béar
    Encamp   618   1579   Font-Romeu   Mt.Canigou   Bains-Palalda-   Perthus   Banyuls-s-Mer
la Vella   Port d'Envalira   Fontpédrouse   2785   Arles   La Junquera   Cerbère
Les Escaldes   2407   Mont-Louis   La Preste   115   Espolla   Port Bou
S. Julià   Col de la Perche   Ja-Preste   Massanet   Colera
de Lòria   Saillagouse   Prats-de-Mollo   de Cabrenys   Pont de Molins   Puerto de Llansá
145   Puigcerdá   Setcasas   Massanet   Albanà   Peralada   Selva de Mar
260   116   Bourg-Madame   Mollo   Camprodón   Sadernas   Figueras   83   Cabo Creus
Seo   S. Vicente   Caixans   Nuria   2913   Pont de Seguries   Cabanellas   Castellò   Rosas   Cadaqués
de Urgel   Montella   Belver   La Molina   Puigmal   Ribas de Freser   Pablo de Seguries   de Ampurias   260   Pedro Pescador
    La Cerdaña   Bellver   152   S. Juan de   Castellfullit   150   Ampurias   252   Golfo de Rosas
Novés   260   de Cerdaña   las Abadesas   153   de la Roca   150   La Escala
de Segre   Baga   La Pobla   Ripoll   150   Artigas   Besalú   Estartit
Orgañá   de Noch   de Lillet   172   Olot   Fluvià   Verges   Torroella
Embalse   Guardiola   S. Quirico de Besora   Bas   Sta. Pau   Bañolas   150   de Montgrí
de Oliana   de Berga   Palmerola   149   Mieras   II   E15   Colomés   La Bisbal
    Serchs   Borredá   Las Planas   S. Martin   E90   Verges   Pals
Berga   Llinás   Torelló   152   de Llemaná   141   Girona-   Tamariu
Gironella   S. Augustin   153   Sta Maria   Palafrugell   255   Gerona   Llafranch
Espunyola   de Llusanés   Manlleu de Corcó   Amer   Calella
Puigreig   S. Hipólito   Roda de Ter   253   Caldas   250   Palamós
Solsona   de Voltrega   Olost   Angles   de Malavella   S. Antonio   Playa de Aro
Navás   Vich   S. Hilario   253   de Calonge   S. Feliu
Cardona   Taradell   Sacalm   Sils   de Guixols
Balsareny   1411   Tona   152   Arbucias   Canyet
1410   Suria   Centelles   Sierra de Montseny   104   Blanes   Tossa de Mar
Artés   141   Viladrau   1704   Breda   Lloret de Mar
Sampedor   Moya   Montseny   S. Celoni   A7   Playa de Fanals
Calders   Estany   S. Feliu   Hostalric   Malgrat
Manresa   Callús   Castelltersol   de Codinas   La Garriga   Calella
S. Vicente   Navarcles   S. Lorenzo   Cardedeu   Canet de Mar
de Castellet   Savall   Granollers   A7   Arenys de Mar
1411   Castellbell   Caldas de   Argentona   Arenys
Tarrasa   Montbúy   1415   de Munt   Arenys de Mar
A18   Castellar   155   Mataró
del Vallés   Sabadell   A19   S. Juan de Vilasar
Olesa de   Sardanyola   Masnou   Premiá de Mar
Montserrat   Rubi   A7   Badalona
S. Cugat   A17   Barcelona
del Vallés   Hospitalet
Molins de Rei   S. Feliu
Sant Boi   Cornella
Prat de   San Baudillo
Llobregat

COSTA   DORADA   Mahón

COSTA   BRAVA
CÔTE VERMEILLE
A
MEDITERRÁNEO
B

Golfo
Mar
San Jorge   C

4   5   6

41   41

0   10   20   30   40   50   60 Kilometres

1

A

B

C

1

Ria de Aveiro · Aveiro · Ilhavo · Costa Nova · Barra · Eixo · Oiã · Lamas · Talhadas · Cambarinho · Penalva do Castelo · Viseu · IP5 · E80 · 41 · Mangualde · Fornos de Algodres · Carrapichana · Vagos · Oliveirinha · Agueda · Guardão · Baiuca · Parada · Silgueiros · Nelas · Cabra · Varzielas · Nabais · Folgosinho · Gouveia · 232 · Mira · Anadia · Tondela · Oliveira do Conde · Lagares · Seia · Manteigas · Poço do Inferno · Mealhada · Luso · Bucaco · Sta-Comba Dão · Tábua · Candosa · Vide · 1991 · Cantanhede · Palheiros da Tocha · Tocha · Pampilhosa · Penacova · Raiva · Moita · Mouronho · Galices · Covilhã · Catarruchos · Arazede · Ança · S. Martinho · Arganil · Tortozendo · Palheiros de Quiaios · Amieiro · Antuzede · Polares · 342 · Unhais da Serra · Quiaios · Ervedal · Lavaris · Arrifa · Coimbra · Barco · Cabo Mondego · Buarcos · Maiorca · Montemor-o-Velho · Ceirã · Semide · Góis · Silvares · Fundão · Figueira da Foz · Alfarelos · Valonga · Condeixa · Vila Seca · Portela · Orvalho · Vale de Prazeres · Lavos · Soure · Venda Nova · Miranda do Corvo · Penela · Espinhal · Pampilhosa · S. Miguel d'A · Rego da Leirosa · Outeiro · Marinha das Ondas · Lousã · Barragem Sta. Luzia · Serra da Guardunha · Louriçal · Alvares · Castanheira de Pêra · Foz do Giraldo · Almaceda · Mattos · Guia · Barroco · Alvorge · Pontão · Pedrógão Grande · Cabeço 1080 · Oleiros · Azenha de Cima · Cafede · Alcains · Pedrógão · Pombal · Ansião · Figueiró dos Vinhos · Isna · Sarzedas · Castelo Branco · Praia da Vieira · Vieira · Monte Redondo · Souto da Carpalhosa · Santiago de Litem · Abiul · Alvaiázere · Barqueiro · Sernache de Bonjardim · Figueiredo · Sobreira Formosa · Monte Real · Boa Vista · Memoria · Venda Nova · Cabaços · Sertã · Proença-a-Nova · Sarnadas · Marinha Grande · Albergaria dos Doze · Pereiro · Aguas Belas · S. Pedro de Muel · Azóia · Maceira · Caranguejeira · Rio de Couros · Beco · Leiria · Cardosos · Olival · Vila Nova de Ourém · Ferreira do Zêzere · Vila de Rei · Vila Velha de Ródão · Montalvão · Martingança · Batalha · Moita · Alviobeira · Amendoa · Maxieira · Cedilho · Nazaré · S. Jorge · Porto de Mós · Fátima · Vargas · Chão de Codes · Monforte · Valado · Aljubarrota · Mira · Tomar · Aldeia do Mato · B. de Pracana · B. de Fratel · Alcobaça · Mendiga · Asseiceira · Sardoal · Mação · Póvoa e Meadas · S. Martinho do Porto · Murteira · Alpedriz · Golegã · Torres Novas · Barragem do Bode · B. de Belver · Amieira · Nisa · Alfeizerão · Tornada · Turquel · Entroncamento · Sta. Margarida · Tramagal · Arez · 364 · Ilhas Farilhões · Praia · Foz do Arelho · Caldas da Rainha · Abrantes · Gavião · Tolosa · Apalhão · Castelo · Ilha Berlenga · Óbidos · Parceiros · Atalaia · 245 · 359 · Ilhas Estelas · Cabo Carvoeiro · Remédios · Baleal · Alcanede · Pernes · Golegã · Pinheiro Grande · Monte da Pedra · Vale do Peso · Peniche · Consolação · S. Bernardino · Rio Maior · Tremês · Chamusca · Portalegre · S. João da Ribeira · Ulme · Bemposta · Torre das Vargens · Crato · Areia Branca · Bombarral · Vermelha · Zambujeira · Azinhaga · Chouto · Ponte de Sor · Cabeço de Vide · Lourinha · Moita dos Ferreiros · Cadava · Cercal · Almoster · Santarém · Alpiarça · Mugem · Domingão · Vale de Açor · Galveias · Alter do Chão · Vimeiro · Campelos · Monte Junto · Vilar · Ereira · Almeirim · Rosquete · Assumar · Santa Cruz · Ramalhal · Maxial · Olhavo · Vila Verde · Cartaxo · Vale de Santarém · Vila Chã de Ourique · Benfica · Benavila · Fronteira · Torres Vedras · Carvoeira · Aveiras de Cima · Valada · Muge · Raposa · Aviz · Monforte · S. Pedro da Cadeira · Ota · Azambuja · Reguengo · Montargil · B. de Montargil · B. do Maranhão · Turcifal · Runal · Aldeia Gavinha · Gloria · Lamarosa · Monte Agraço · Dois Portos · Cadafais · Tejo · Sto. Amaro · Encarnação · Gradil · Sobral de Monte Agraço · Salvaterra de Magos · Erra · Couço · Móra · Pavia · Sto. Alexo · Ericeira · Sapataria · Alenquer · Benavente · Tapada · Coruche · Quinta Grande · Brotas · Orada · Foz do Lizandro · Mafra · Arruda dos Vinhos · Póvoa da Galega · Samora Correia · Sorraia · Santana do Mato · Casa Branca · Vieiros · Magoito · Alcainça · Malveira · Bucelas · Vila Franca de Xira · Alto · Cortiçadas · Barbacena · Azenhas do Mar · Lousa · Alverca · Póvoa de Sta Iria · Sto. Estêvão · Canha · Lavre · Ciborro · Sant'Ana · Estremoz · Praia Grande · Colares · Sintra · Odivelas · Loures · Sacavem · Alcochete · Taipadas · Santa Suzana · Gafanhoeira · Arraiolos · Évoramonte · Borba · Vila Viçosa · Adraga · Amadora · Moscavide · Montijo · Pegões Velhos · Atalho · Vendas Novas · Aldeia da Serra · Malveira da Serra · Cabo Raso · Deliras · Algés · LISBOA · Alhos Vedros · Rio Frio · Pegões-Estação · Cabrela · Montemor-o-Novo · S. Miguel de Machede · Redondo · Cascais · Estoril · Trafaria · Barreiro · Moita · Poceirão · S. Romão · Valeiro · S. Matias · Alandre · Costa do Sol · Almada · Seixal · Pinhal Novo · Maratêca · Sto. António da Charneca · Palmela · Aguas de Moura · S. Romão · Santiago do Escoural · Évora · Santiago Maior · Fernão Ferro · Vila Nogueira · Vila Fresca · Setúbal · Palma · S. Martinho · Montoito · Capelins · Alfarim · Santana · Praia de Tróia · S. Cristóvão · S. Braz do Reguedoura · S. Manços · Reguengos · Nossa Senhora do Cabo · Portinho da Arrábida · Sesimbra · Cabo de Espichel · Comporta · Vale de Reis · Barragem do Pego do Altar · Alcáçovas · Torre de Coelheiros · Monte do Trigo · Torrão · Baía de Setúbal · Torroal · Alcácer do Sal · Aguiar · João de Loura · Viana Alentejo · Vila Nova da Baronia · Oriola · Portel · Casa Branca · Porto de Rei · Torrão · Vila Ruiva · Alvito · Cuba · Grândola · Melides · Odivelas · Barragem de Vale de Gaio · Serra Mendro · Vera Cruz · Vidigueira · Alqueva

0 5 10 20 30 40 Miles

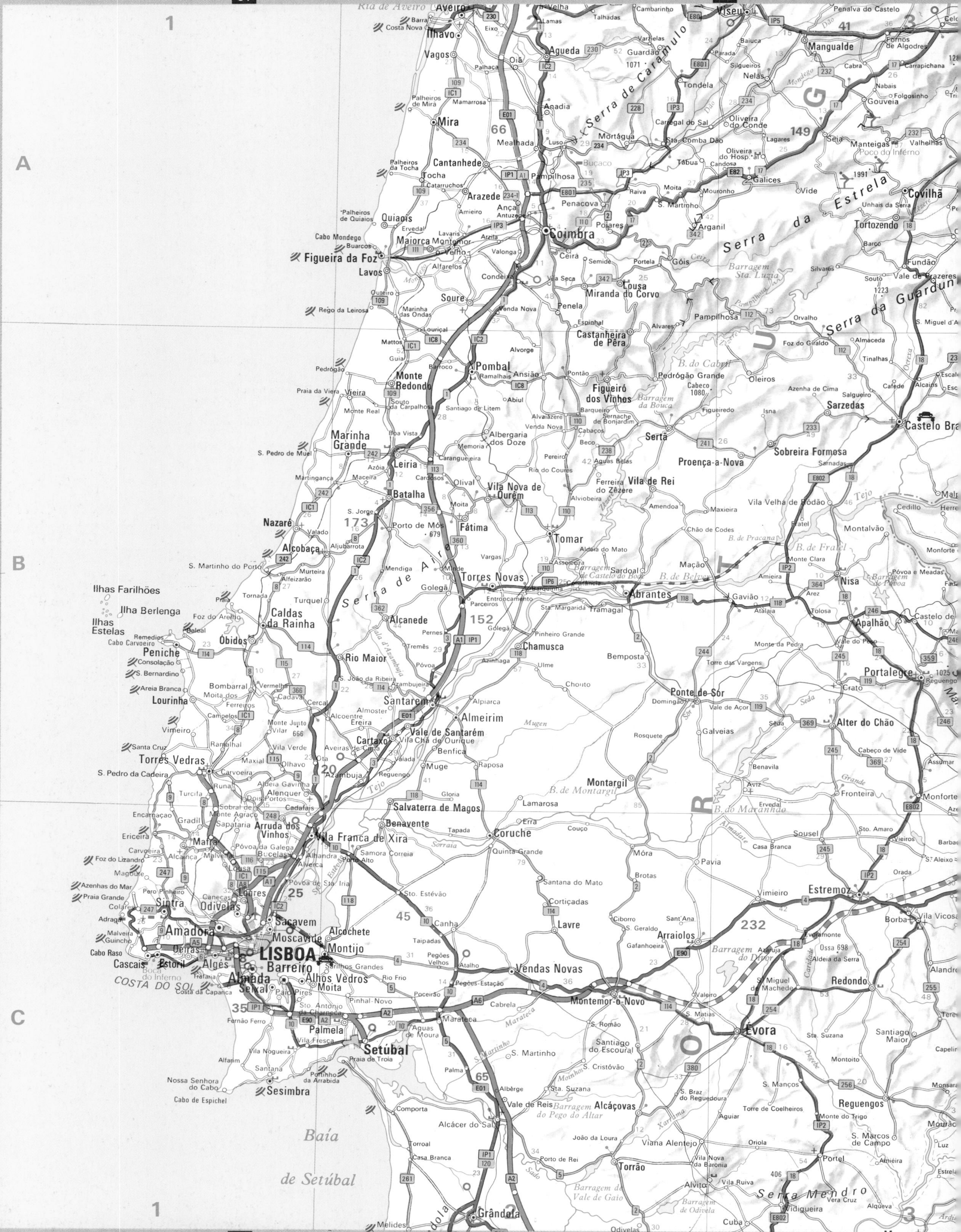

31
38

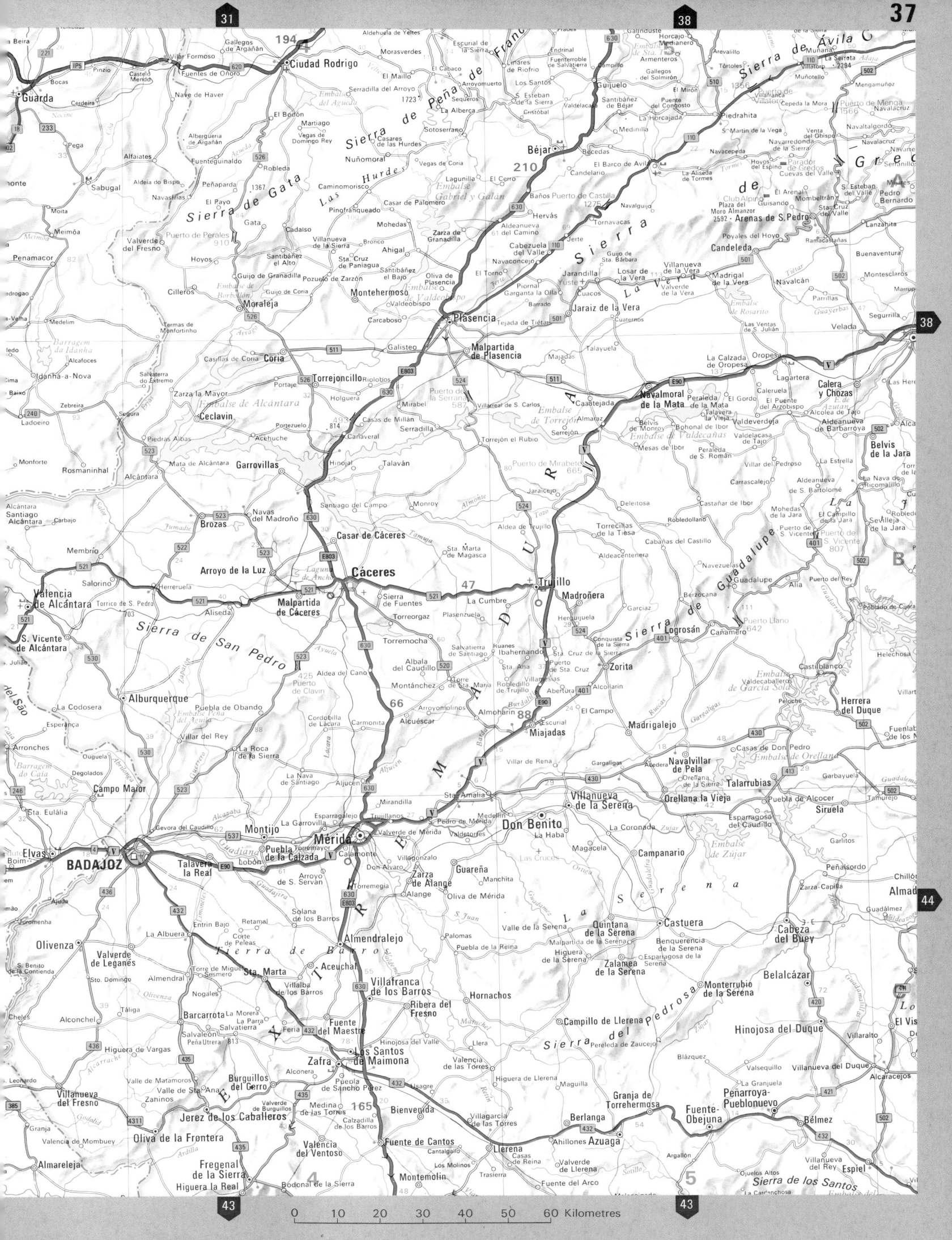
Guarda
Ciudad Rodrigo
Fuentes de Oñoro
Vilar Formoso
Gallegos de Argañán
Pinzio
Castelo Mendo
Bocas
Cerdeira
Nave de Haver
El Bodón
Martiago
Vegas de Domingo Rey
Albergueria de Argañán
Alfaiates
Pega
Fuenteguinaldo
Robleda
Sabugal
Aldeia do Bispo
Peñaparda
Navasfrías
El Payo
Sierra de Gata
Gata
Puerto de Perales 910
Valverde del Fresno
Moita
Meimoa
Penamacor
Hoyos
Cilleros
Moraleja
Guijo de Granadilla
Pozuelo de Zarzón
Montehermoso
Valdeobispo
Carcaboso
Plasencia
Galisteo
Coria
Casillas de Coria
Medelim
Termas de Monfortinho
Idanha-a-Nova
Alcafoces
Salvaterra do Extremo
Torrejoncillo
Riolobos
Portaje
Zarza la Mayor
Embalse de Alcántara
Ceclavin
Zebreira
Ladoeiro
Segura
Piedras Albas
Acehuche
Portezuelo
Monforte
Rosmaninhal
Alcántara
Mata de Alcántara
Garrovillas
Santiago de Alcántara
Carbajo
Brozas
Navas del Madroño
Membrío
Arroyo de la Luz
Valencia de Alcántara
Salorino
Herreruela
Aliseda
Malpartida de Cáceres
Cáceres
Casar de Cáceres
Sierra de San Pedro
S. Vicente de Alcántara
Alburquerque
La Codosera
Esperança
Puebla de Obando
Villar del Rey
Arronches
La Roca de la Sierra
Ouguela
Degolados
Campo Maior
La Nava de Santiago
Sta. Eulália
Montijo
Elvas
BADAJOZ
Talavera la Real
Lobón
Puebla de la Calzada
Mérida
Esparragalejo
La Garrovilla
Arroyo de S. Servan
Olivenza
Valverde de Leganés
S. Benito de la Contienda
Sto. Domingo
Almendral
La Albuera
Torre de Miguel Sesmero
Sta. Marta
Nogales
Táliga
Cheles
Alconchel
Barcarrota
Salvaleón
Higuera de Vargas
Villanueva del Fresno
Valle de Matamoros
Valle de Sta. Ana
Zahinos
Jerez de los Caballeros
Oliva de la Frontera
Valencia de Mombuey
Almareleja
Fregenal de la Sierra
Higuera la Real
Burguillos del Cerro
Zafra
Los Santos de Maimona
Fuente del Maestre
Feria
Villafranca de los Barros
Ribera del Fresno
Almendralejo
Aceuchal
Villalba de los Barros
Solana de los Barros
Tierra de Barros
Medina de las Torres
Calzadilla de los Barros
Puebla de Sancho Pérez
Bienvenida
Valencia del Ventoso
Fuente de Cantos
Bodonal de la Sierra
Montemolín
Llerena
Villagarcia de las Torres
Usagre
Hornachos
Valencia de las Torres
Higuera de Llerena
Maguilla
Berlanga
Azuaga
Ahillones
Valverde de Llerena
Fuente del Arco
Trasierra
Casas de Reina
Los Molinos
Cantalgallo
Granja de Torrehermosa
Fuente-Obejuna
Peñarroya-Pueblonuevo
Bélmez
Espiel
Villanueva del Rey
Sierra de los Santos
Argallón
Valsequillo
Villanueva del Duque
Alcaracejos
Hinojosa del Duque
Villaralto
Blázquez
Belalcázar
Monterrubio de la Serena
Sierra del Pedroso
Campillo de Llerena
Peraleda de Zaucejo
Cabeza del Buey
Castuera
Benquerencia de la Serena
Zalamea de la Serena
Higuera de la Serena
Quintana de la Serena
Malpartida de la Serena
Valle de la Serena
La Serena
Campanario
Magacela
Don Benito
Villanueva de la Serena
La Haba
La Coronada
Medellín
Guareña
Oliva de Mérida
Alange
Zarza de Alange
Villagonzalo
Don Álvaro
Valverde de Mérida
Trujillanos
Mirandilla
Aljucén
Carmonita
Cordobilla de Lácara
Alcuéscar
Arroyomolinos
Montánchez
Almoharín
Miajadas
Escurial
Villar de Rena
Sta. Amalia
Orellana la Vieja
Orellana de la Sierra
Navalvillar de Pela
Acedera
Talarrubias
Puebla de Alcocer
Siruela
Esparragosa del Caudillo
Garbayuela
Casas de Don Pedro
Embalse de Orellana
Herrera del Duque
Castilblanco
Peloche
Madrigalejo
El Campo
Alcollarín
Abertura
Zorita
Logrosán
Cañamero
Sierra de Guadalupe
Guadalupe
Alía
Puerto Llano 642
Berzocana
Navezuelas
Conquista de la Sierra
Herguijuela
Madroñera
Trujillo
La Cumbre
Sierra de Fuentes
Torreorgaz
Torremocha
Albalá del Caudillo
Aldea del Cano
Puerto de Clavin
Salvatierra de Santiago
Ruanes
Ibahernando
Robledillo de Trujillo
Plasenzuela
Sta. Marta de Magasca
Aldea de Trujillo
Jaraicejo
Torrecillas de la Tiesa
Deleitosa
Aldeacentenera
Cabañas del Castillo
Robledollano
Castañar de Ibor
Mohedas de la Jara
El Campillo de la Jara
Sevilleja de la Jara
Puerto de S. Vicente 807
Carrascalejo
Aldeanueva de S. Bartolomé
La Estrella
Villar del Pedroso
Belvis de la Jara
Peraleda de S. Román
Valdelacasa de Tajo
Mesas de Ibor
Bohonal de Ibor
Embalse de Valdecañas
Belvis de Monroy
Valdeverdeja
Aldeanueva de Barbarroya
El Puente del Arzobispo
Alcolea de Tajo
Calera y Chozas
Lagartera
Caleruela
Navalmoral de la Mata
Peraleda de la Mata
Talavera la Vieja
El Gordo
La Calzada de Oropesa
Oropesa
Velada
Las Ventas de S. Julián
Embalse de Rosarito
Navalcán
Parrillas
Segurrilla
Candeleda
Madrigal de la Vera
Villanueva de la Vera
Valverde de la Vera
Losar de la Vera
Jarandilla
Yuste
Cuacos
Jaraiz de la Vera
Cuartemos
Guijo de Sta. Bárbara
Sierra de la Vera
Talayuela
Majadas
Casatejada
Almaraz
Serrejón
Embalse de Torrejón
Puerto de Mirabete 665
Torrejón el Rubio
Villarreal de S. Carlos
Puerto de la Serrana 587
Mirabel
Serradilla
Casas de Millán
Cañaveral
Hinojal
Talaván
Santiago del Campo
Monroy
Malpartida de Plasencia
Tejada de Tiétar
Barrado
Piornal
Garganta la Olla
El Torno
Navaconcejo
Cabezuela del Valle
Jerte
Tornavacas
Aldeanueva del Camino
Hervás
Baños Puerto de Castilla 1275
Navalguijo
Béjar
Candelario
Becedas
El Barco de Ávila
La Aliseda de Tormes
Hoyos del Espino
Parador de Gredos
Cuevas del Valle
Club Alpino
Plaza del Moro Almanzor 2592
Guisando
Arenas de S. Pedro
El Arenal
Mombeltrán
Sta. Cruz del Valle
S. Esteban del Valle
Pedro Bernardo
Lanzahita
Ramacastañas
Poyales del Hoyo
Buenaventura
Montesclaros
Sierra de Gredos
Navacepeda
Navarredonda de la Sierra
Venta del Obispo
Navalacruz
Navaltalgordo
Puerto de Menga 1566
Cepeda la Mora
Villafranca de la Sierra
Puerto de Villatoro 1356
Piedrahita
S. Martín de la Vega
Sierra de Ávila
Muñana
La Serrota 2294
Muñotello
Mengamuñoz
Villatoro
Arevalillo
Tórtoles
Horcajo-Medianero
Armenteros
Gallegos del Solmirón
El Mirón
Puente del Congosto
La Horcajada
Medinilla
Santibáñez de Béjar
Valdelacasa
Guijuelo
Campillo
Fuenterroble de Salvatierra
Endrinal
Linares de Riofrío
Los Santos
S. Esteban de la Sierra
Cristóbal
La Alberca
Sequeros
Arroyomuerto
El Cabaco
Escurial de la Sierra
Morasverdes
Aldehuela de Yeltes
El Maíllo
Serradilla del Arroyo
Embalse del Agueda
Sierra de Peña de Francia
1723
Sotoserrano
Casares de las Hurdes
Nuñomoral
Vegas de Coria
Las Hurdes
Caminomorisco
Lagunilla
El Cerro
Embalse Gabriel y Galán
Casar de Palomero
Pinofranqueado
Mohedas
Cadalso
Villanueva de la Sierra
Bronco
Zarza de Granadilla
Ahigal
Santibáñez el Alto
Sta. Cruz de Paniagua
Santibáñez el Bajo
Oliva de Plasencia
Embalse de Valdeobispo
Embalse de Borbollón
Guijo de Coria
Holguera
Caminomorisco
Estremadura
0 10 20 30 40 50 60 Kilometres

38
44
43
43

32
32
31
37

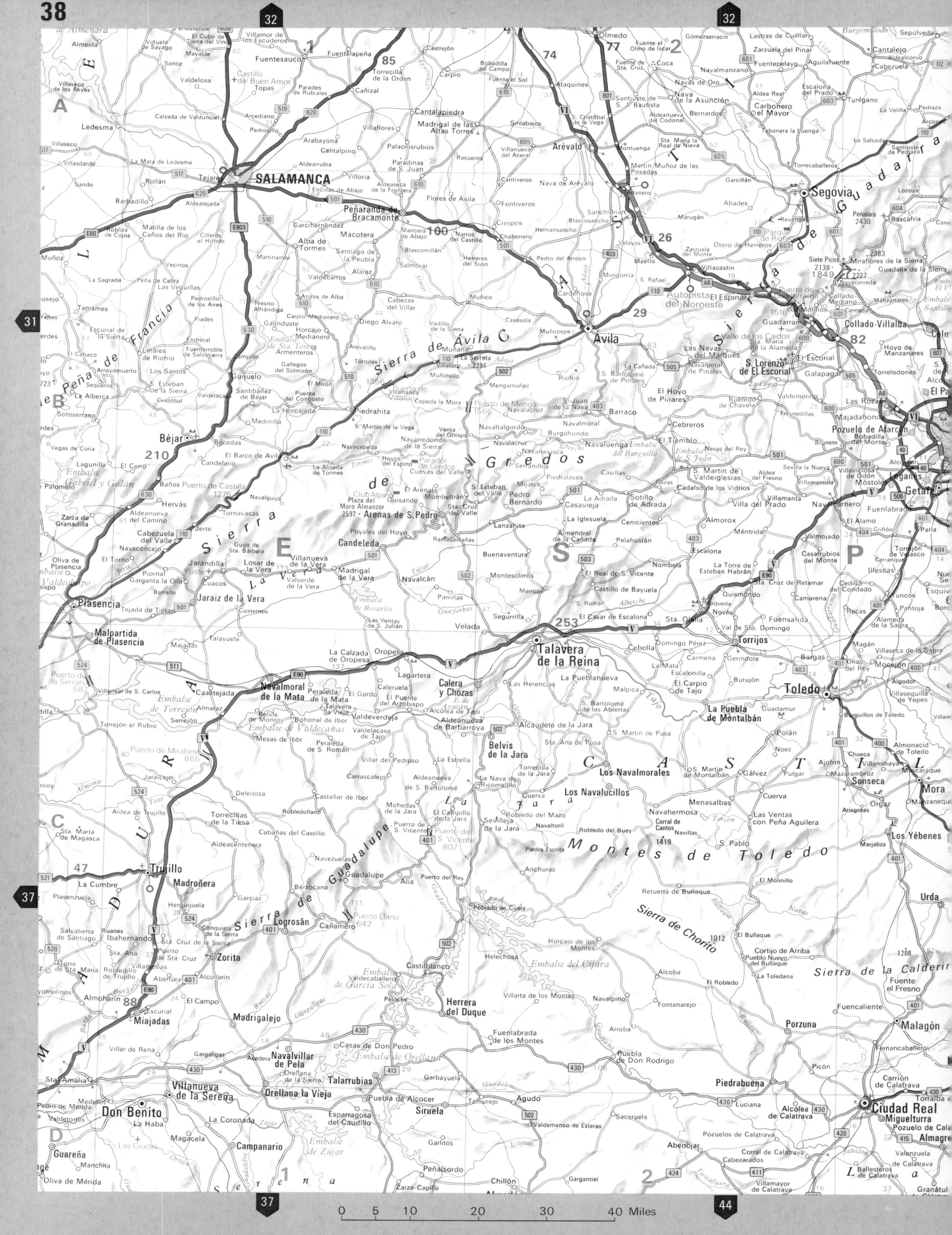
SALAMANCA
Olmedo
Coca
Cantalejo
Sepúlveda
Fuentesaúco
Fuentelapeña
Cantalapiedra
Madrigal de las Altas Torres
Arévalo
Ataquines
Navas de Oro
Nava de la Asunción
Turégano
Ledesma
Peñaranda de Bracamonte
Segovia
Alba de Tormes
Macotera
Martín Muñoz de las Posadas
Villacastín
El Espinar
Guadarrama
Collado-Villalba
Avila
Sierra de Ávila
S. Lorenzo de El Escorial
Galapagar
Las Rozas
Majadahonda
Pozuelo de Alarcón
Móstoles
Leganés
Getafe
Navalcarnero
Guijuelo
Béjar
Piedrahita
El Barco de Ávila
Sierra de Gredos
Arenas de S. Pedro
Candeleda
Mombeltrán
Cebreros
El Tiemblo
Navas del Marqués
Sotillo de Adrada
Cadalso de los Vidrios
Villa del Prado
Escalona
Plasencia
Malpartida de Plasencia
Jaraiz de la Vera
Navalmoral de la Mata
Oropesa
Talavera de la Reina
Torrijos
Toledo
Illescas
Calera y Chozas
La Puebla de Montalbán
Los Navalmorales
Los Navalucillos
Sonseca
Mora
Los Yébenes
Orgaz
Belvis de la Jara
Montes de Toledo
Sierra de Guadalupe
Guadalupe
Trujillo
Madroñera
Logrosán
Zorita
Miajadas
Madrigalejo
Herrera del Duque
Navalvillar de Pela
Orellana la Vieja
Talarrubias
Villanueva de la Serena
Don Benito
Campanario
Siruela
Puebla de Don Rodrigo
Piedrabuena
Porzuna
Malagón
Ciudad Real
Miguelturra
Almagro
Urda
Sierra de Chorito
Sierra de la Calderina
Embalse de Cíjara
Embalse de García Sola
Embalse de Orellana
Embalse de Zújar
Embalse de Valdecañas
Embalse de Torrejón
Embalse de Rosarito
Embalse Gabriel y Galán
Peña de Francia
Puerto de Miravete
Guareña
Alcolea de Calatrava
Agudo
Chillón
Peñalsordo
LEÓN
EXTREMADURA
CASTILLA
Autopista del Noroeste
0 5 10 20 30 40 Miles

37
44

33 33

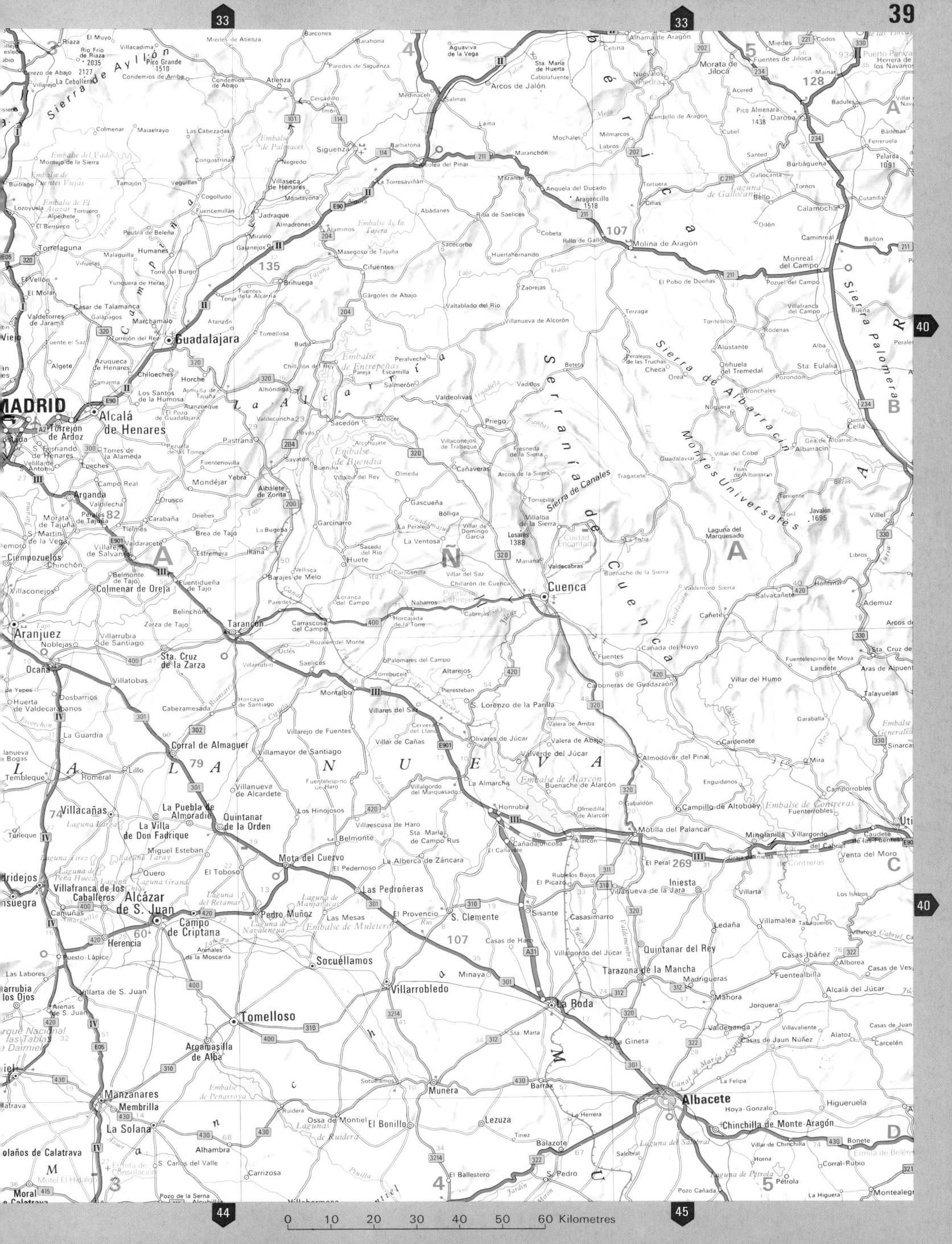
MADRID
Alcalá de Henares
Torrejón de Ardoz
Guadalajara
Sierra de Ayllón
Pico Grande 1510
Siguenza
Medinaceli
Arcos de Jalón
Alhama de Aragón
Molina de Aragón
Daroca
Calamocha
Monreal del Campo
Sierra Palomera
Sierra de Albarracín
Albarracín
Montes Universales
Serranía de Cuenca
Cuenca
Sierra de Canales
Tarancón
Aranjuez
Ocaña
Embalse de Entrepeñas
Embalse de Buendía
Sacedón
Huete
Brihuega
Cifuentes
Chinchón
Colmenar de Oreja
Arganda
La Alcarria
LA MANCHA
Corral de Almaguer
Quintanar de la Orden
Mota del Cuervo
Alcázar de S. Juan
Campo de Criptana
Pedro Muñoz
Las Pedroñeras
S. Clemente
Socuéllamos
Villarrobledo
Tomelloso
Argamasilla de Alba
Manzanares
Membrilla
La Solana
Villanueva de los Infantes
Munera
El Bonillo
Ossa de Montiel
Lezuza
Balazote
Albacete
Chinchilla de Monte-Aragón
La Roda
La Gineta
Tarazona de la Mancha
Quintanar del Rey
Madrigueras
Mahora
Motilla del Palancar
Iniesta
Minglanilla
Embalse de Alarcón
Embalse de Contreras
Belmonte
Villacañas
La Villa de Don Fadrique
Madridejos
Villafranca de los Caballeros
Herencia
Pastrana
Mondéjar
Villarejo de Salvanés
Landete
Cañete
Salvacañete
Teruel
Ademuz
Villar del Humo
Campillo de Altobuey
Casas-Ibáñez
Fuentealbilla
Alcalá del Júcar
Valdeganga
Hoya-Gonzalo
Higueruela
Bonete
Montealegre
Pétrola
Horna
Corral-Rubio

0 10 20 30 40 50 60 Kilometres

44 45 40 40

39

45

Sierra de Albarracín · Montes Universales · Serranía de Cuenca

Teruel · Cuenca · Albarracín · Sta. Eulalia · Cella

Mora de Rubielos · Sarrión · Manzanera · Sierra de Gúdar · El Maestrazgo

Morella · Castellón de la Plana · El Grao · Almazora · Burriana · Nules · Vall de Uxó · Sagunto · Grao de Sagunto

Segorbe · Vall de Uxó · Onda · Villarreal de los Infantes · Benicasim

Utiel · Requena · Venta del Moro · Buñol · Chiva · Cheste

Lliria · Bétera · Benaguacil · Ribarroja · Paterna · Manises · Burjasot · **VALENCIA**

Torrente · Catarroja · Picassent · Silla · Masanasa · Aldaya · Alaquás · Quart de Poblet

Albacete · Chinchilla de Monte-Aragón · Almansa · La Roda · Tarazona de la Mancha · Quintanar del Rey

Alzira · Carcaixent (Carcagente) · Sueca · Cullera · Algemesí · Tabernes de Valldigna · Gandía · Oliva

Xàtiva (Játiva) · Ontinyent · Alcoy · Cocentaina · Villena · Yecla · Caudete

Denia · Jávea · Benissa · Calpe · Altea · Benidorm · Villajoyosa · Jijona

Hellín · Jumilla · Cieza · Elda · Petrel · Monóvar · Novelda · Aspe

ALICANTE · ELX/ELCHE · Crevillente · Sta. Pola · S. Juan de Alicante · S. Vicente del Raspeig

Golfo de Valencia

COSTA DEL AZAHAR · COSTA BLANCA

0 5 10 20 30 40 Miles

A

B

Islas Columbretes

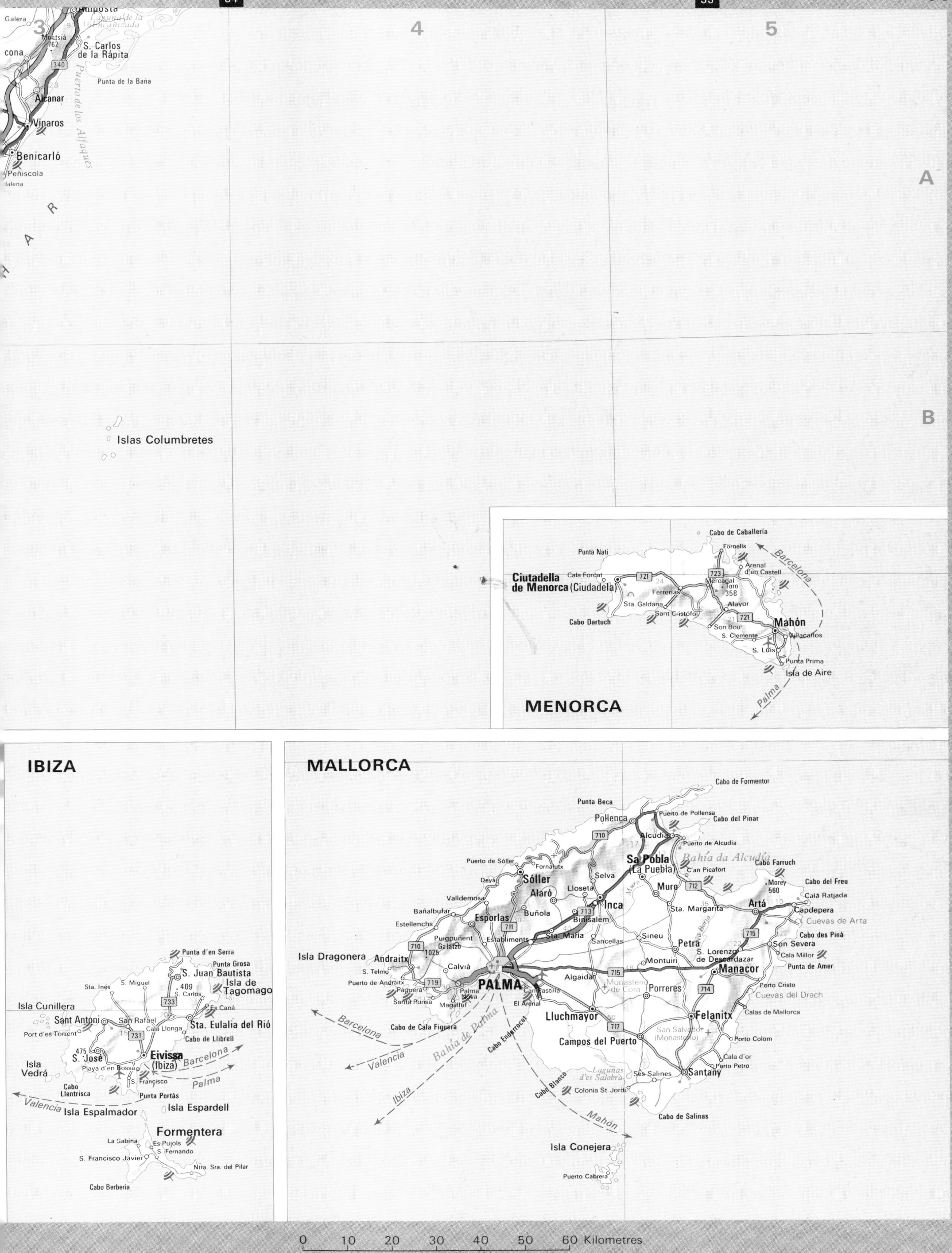

MENORCA

Cabo de Caballeria
Fornells
Punta Nati
Arenal d'en Castell
Cala Forcat
Ciutadella
de Menorca (Ciudadela)
721
24
723
Mercadal
Toro
358
Barcelona
Ferrerias
Alayor
Sta. Galdana
Sant Cristófol
Cabo Dartuch
721
721
Mahón
Son Bou
S. Clemente
Villacarlos
S. Luis
Punta Prima
Isla de Aire
Palma

IBIZA

Punta d'en Serra
Punta Grosa
S. Juan Bautista
Sta. Inés
S. Miguel
409
S. Carlos
Isla de
Tagomago
Isla Cunillera
733
Es Caná
Sant Antoni
San Rafael
Cala Llonga
Sta. Eulalia del Rió
Port d'es Tortent
731
Cabo de Llibrell
475
S. José
Barcelona
Eivissa
(Ibiza)
Isla
Vedrá
Playa d'en Bossa
S. Francisco
Palma
Cabo
Llentrisca
Punta Portás
Valencia
Isla Espalmador
Isla Espardell

Formentera
La Sabina
Es Pujols
S. Fernando
S. Francisco Javier
Ntra. Sra. del Pilar
Cabu Berberia

MALLORCA

Cabo de Formentor
Punta Beca
Pollenca
Puerto de Pollensa
Cabo del Pinar
710
Alcúdia
Puerto de Alcudia
Puerto de Sóller
Sa Pobla
(La Puebla)
C'an Picafort
Bahía da Alcudia
Fornalutx
Selva
Sóller
Deyá
Muro
Cabo Farruch
Morey
560
Cabo del Freu
Valldemosa
Alaró
712
Lloseta
Cala Ratjada
Inca
Sta. Margarita
Artá
Bañalbufar
Buñola
Capdepera
Estellenchs
713
715
Cuevas de Arta
Esporlas
Binisalem
Cabo des Piná
711
Sancellas
Son Severa
Puigpunent
Galatzó
Sta. Maria
Sineu
Petra
Cala Millor
Isla Dragonera
710
Establiments
S. Lorenzo
de Descardazar
Punta de Amer
Andraitx
1025
de Cora
S. Telmo
Montuiri
Manacor
Calviá
719
PALMA
715
Algaida
Monasterio
de Cora
Porto Cristo
Puerto de Andraitx
Paguera
San Castilla
Porreres
714
Cuevas del Drach
Santa Ponsa
Magallut
El Arenal
Calas de Mallorca
Barcelona
Cabo de Cala Figuera
Lluchmayor
717
Felanitx
Valencia
Bahía de Palma
San Salvador
(Monasterio)
Porto Colom
Ibiza
Cabo Enderrocat
Campos del Puerto
Porto Petro
Cala d'or
Cabo Blanco
Colonia St. Jordi
Ses Salines
Santany
Mahón
Lagunas
d'es Salobra
Cabo de Salinas

Isla Conejera

Puerto Cabrera

0   10   20   30   40   50   60 Kilometres

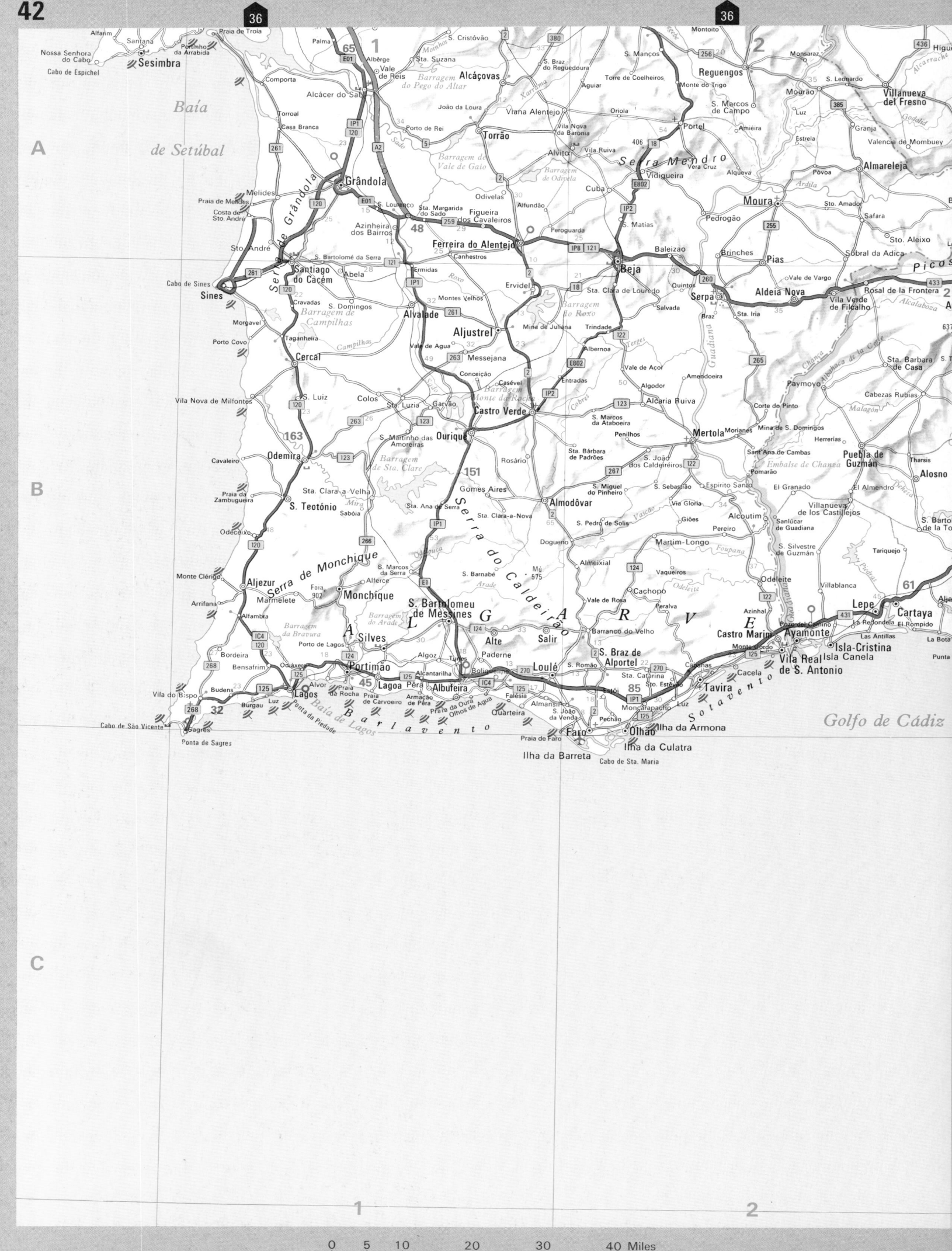

36   36

Nossa Senhora do Cabo
Cabo de Espichel
Santana
Alfarim
Portinho da Arrábida
Sesimbra

Praia de Tróia
Palma
Comporta
Alcácer do Sal
Torroal
Casa Branca

65
E01
Albérge
Vale de Réis
S. Cristóvão
Sta. Suzana
Alcáçovas

Baía de Setúbal

380
S. Manços
Montoito
Reguengos
2
Monsaraz
Alcarrache
436
Higue

João de Loura
Porto de Rei
S. Braz do Reguedoura
Aguiar
Torre de Coelheiros
Monte do Trigo
S. Marcos de Campo
Mourão
S. Leonardo
35
Luz
Villanueva del Fresno
Godah

IP1
120
A2

Viana Alentejo
Vila Nova da Baronia
Oriola
Portel
54
385
Granja
Estrela
Valencia de Mombuey

A

Torrão
Alvito
Vila Ruiva
406
18
Amieira
Vera Cruz
Alqueva
Povoa
Almareleja

Grândola
Melides
Praia de Mendes
Costa de Sto. André
Sto. André

261
120
E01
15

S. Lourenço
S. Margarida do Sado
Figueira dos Cavaleiros
48
259
29
Odivelas
Alfundão
Peroguarda
S. Matias
Cuba
E802
Vidigueira
Serra Mendro
Moura
Sto. Amador
Safara

Azinheira dos Bairros
IP2
Pedrogão
255
Ardila

261
121
S. Bartolomé da Serra
Abela
Ferreira do Alentejo
Canhestros
10
Ermidas
IP1
Beja
IP8
121
Baleizao
Brinches
Pias
Sobral da Adica
Sto. Aleixo
Picos
La

Santiago do Cacém
Cravadas
Cabo de Sines
Sines
120
S. Domingos
Montes Velhos
32
Ervidel
18
Sta. Clara de Loureido
21
260
Quintos
Salvada
Serpa
Braz
Sta. Iria
Vale de Vargo
35
Aldeia Nova
Rosal de la Frontera
433
Vila Verde de Ficalho
Alcaláboça
2
Ar

B

Barragem de Campilhas
Morgavel
Porto Covo
Taganheira
Cercal
Alvalade
261
Vale de Agua
263
Aljustrel
Messejana
Albernoa
Mina de Juliana
Trindade
122
Vale de Açor
E802
637
Sta. Barbara de Casa
S. Te

Vila Nova de Milfontes
120
S. Luiz
Colos
Sta. Luzia
Garvão
Conceição
263
123
Casével
Entradas
IP2
Algodor
Amendoeira
265
Corte de Pinto
Cabezas Rubias
Malagón
Alosno

163
Odemira
Cavaleiro
123
S. Martinho das Amoreiras
Ourique
Castro Verde
Rosário
50
Alcaria Ruiva
123
S. Marcos da Ataboeira
Penilhos
267
Mertola
Morianes
Mina de S. Domingos
Herrerias
Tharsis
Puebla de Guzmán

Barragem de Sta. Clare
151
Sta. Clara-a-Velha
S. Teotónio
Gomes Aires
Sta. Ana de Serra
Saboia
Sta. Clara-a-Nova
Almodôvar
S. Pedro de Solis
65
Dogueno
Sta. Bárbara de Padrões
S. João dos Caldeiréiros
Pomarão
122
Espirito Santo
El Granado
Embalse de Chanza
Villanueva de los Castillejos
S. Bartolo de la To

Odeceixe
120
266
IP1
3
S. Miguel do Pinheiro
S. Sebastião
Via Gloria
34
Alcoutim
Giões
Pereiro
Sanlúcar de Guadiana
S. Silvestre de Guzmán
Tariquejo

Monte Clérigo
Aljezur
Arrifana
Alfambra
Serra de Monchique
Foia 902
Marmelete
S. Marcos da Serra
Alferce
E1
S. Barnabé
Arade
Mú 575
Martim-Longo
124
Almeixial
Vaqueiros
Odeleite
Villablanca
Piedras
61

Monchique
S. Bartolomeu de Messines
Vale de Rosa
Barranco do Velho
Peralva
Cachopo
122
Azinhal
Odeleite
431
Lepe
45
Las Antillas
Cartaya
El Rompido

Barragem da Bravura
IC4
120
Barragem do Arade
S. Marcos da Serra
Silves
124
33
Alte
Salir
13
S. Braz de Alportel
270
Castro Marim
Ayamonte
Isla-Cristina
La Bota
Punta

Bordeira
268
Bensafrim
Odiáxere
Porto de Lagos
124
Algoz
Tunes
Paderne
Boliqueime
Loulé
S. Romão
Sta. Catarina
IP1
125
Vila Real de S. Antonio
Isla Canela

Vila do Bispo
Budens
125
Lagos
Alvor
Portimão
125
Alcantarilha
Albufeira
IC4
Almansil
S. João da Venda
85
Sto. Estêvão
Moncarapacho
Cabanas
Cacela
Tavira
Sotavento

Cabo de São Vicente
268
32
Sagres
Ponta de Sagres
Burgau
Luz
Ponta da Piedade
Baía de Lagos
Praia da Rocha
Lagoa
Péra
Praia de Carvoeiro
Armação de Péra
Praia da Oura
Praia dos Olhos de Água
Quarteira
Falésia
Barlavento
Faro
Praia de Faro
Pechão
Olhão
Ilha da Armona
Ilha da Culatra
Golfo de Cádiz

Ilha da Barreta
Cabo de Sta. Maria

C

1   2

0   5   10   20   30   40 Miles

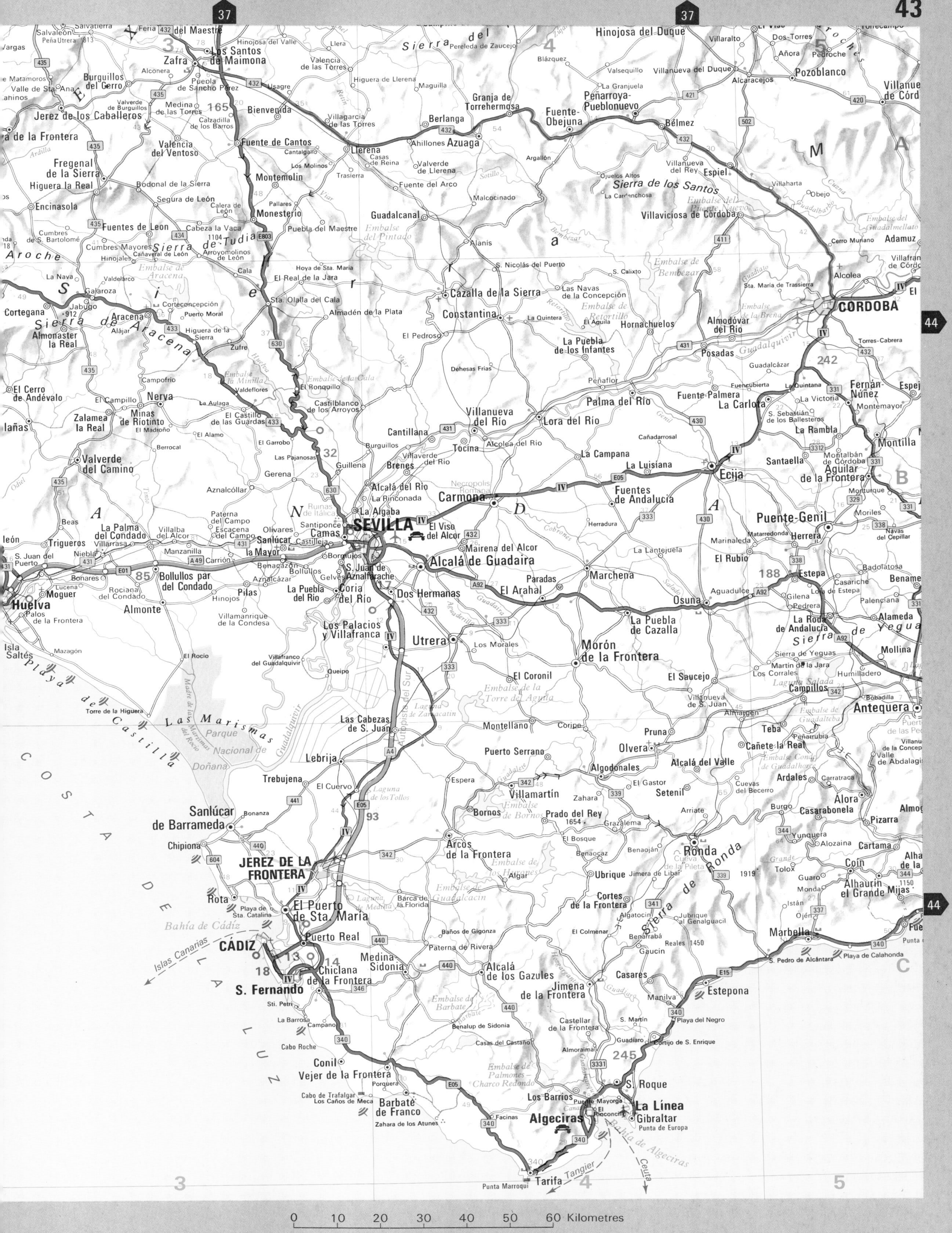
37
Hinojosa del Duque
Villanueva del Duque
Pozoblanco
Peñarroya-Pueblonuevo
Fuente-Obejuna
Bélmez
Espiel
Sierra de los Santos
Villaviciosa de Córdoba
Sierra del Pereleda de Zaucejo
Zafra
Los Santos de Maimona
Jerez de los Caballeros
Burguillos del Cerro
Fregenal de la Sierra
Higuera la Real
Encinasola
Fuentes de León
Fuente de Cantos
Llerena
Azuaga
Berlanga
Granja de Torrehermosa
Bienvenida
Valencia del Ventoso
Montemolín
Monesterio
Guadalcanal
Alanís
Sierra de Tudia
Aroche
Aracena
Sierra de Aracena
Cortegana
Almonaster la Real
Cala
Cazalla de la Sierra
Constantina
Hornachuelos
Almodóvar del Río
CÓRDOBA
Posadas
Palma del Río
La Carlota
Fernán-Núñez
Montilla
Aguilar de la Frontera
Puente-Genil
Lora del Río
Villanueva del Río
Cantillana
Nerva
Minas de Riotinto
Zalamea la Real
Valverde del Camino
Trigueros
La Palma del Condado
SEVILLA
Camas
Sanlúcar la Mayor
Carmona
Ecija
Fuentes de Andalucía
La Luisiana
La Campana
Alcalá de Guadaira
Dos Hermanas
Coria del Río
Marchena
El Arahal
Osuna
Estepa
Huelva
Moguer
Bollullos par del Condado
Almonte
Los Palacios y Villafranca
Utrera
Morón de la Frontera
La Puebla de Cazalla
El Saucejo
Campillos
Antequera
Las Marismas
Parque Nacional de Doñana
Playa de Castilla
COSTA DE LA LUZ
Lebrija
Las Cabezas de S. Juan
Olvera
Algodonales
Villamartín
Bornos
Arcos de la Frontera
Ronda
Sierra de Ronda
Ardales
Alora
Coín
Alhaurín el Grande
Marbella
Estepona
Sanlúcar de Barrameda
Chipiona
JEREZ DE LA FRONTERA
Rota
El Puerto de Sta. María
Puerto Real
CÁDIZ
Bahía de Cádiz
Islas Canarias
S. Fernando
Chiclana de la Frontera
Medina-Sidonia
Alcalá de los Gazules
Jimena de la Frontera
Conil
Vejer de la Frontera
Barbate de Franco
Cabo de Trafalgar
Algeciras
La Línea
Gibraltar
S. Roque
Tarifa
Punta Marroquí
Tangier
Ceuta
Bahía de Algeciras
44
0 10 20 30 40 50 60 Kilometres

Siruela · Samprejo · Luciana · Torralba de Calatrava · Membrilla · Emb

Garlitos · Caldillo · Valdemanco de Esteras · Sacaruela · Alcolea de Calatrava · Ciudad Real · La Solana

Peñalsordo · Zarza-Capilla · Chillón · Gargantiel · Fontanosas · Abenójar · Pozuelos de Calatrava · Miguelturra · 420 · Almagro · Bolaños de Calatrava · Alhambra · 68

Almadén · Guadálmez · Almadenejos · Tirteafuera · 411 · Villamayor de Calatrava · Valenzuela de Calatrava · Moral de Calatrava · Carrizosa

Cabeza del Buey · 420 · S. Eufemia · Guadalmez · Puerto del Montoro · Montoro · Almodóvar del Campo · Puertollano · Villanueva de S. Carlos · Sta. Cruz de Mudela · Valdepeñas · Villanueva de los Infantes

hojosa del Duque · El Viso · Dos-Torres · Torrecampo · Puerto de Niefla · Sierra Madrona · Solana del Pino · El Viso del Marqués · Almuradiel · Castellar · Cózar

Villaralto · Añora · Pedroche · Conquista · El Hoyo · Estrella 1300 · Aldeaquemada · Venta de los Santos

Villanueva del Duque · Alcaracejos · Pozoblanco · Villanueva de Córdoba · El Centenillo · Sta. Elena · La Carolina · Chiclana de Segura · Castellar de Santisteban

Belalcázar · Bélmez · Espiel · Villaharta · Cardeña · Baños de la Encina · Isabela · Vilches · Santisteban del Puerto · Navas de S. Juan · Iznatoraf · Villanueva del Arzobispo

Sierra de los Santos · Villaviciosa de Córdoba · Cerro Muriano · Adamuz · Marmolejo · Andújar · Villanueva de la Reina · Bailén · Guarromán · Linares · Baeza · Úbeda · Sabiote · Villacarrillo

CÓRDOBA · Alcolea · Villafranca de Córdoba · Pedro Abad · El Carpio · Villa del Río · Arjonilla · Lopera · Arjona · Higuera de Arjona · Mengíbar · Torreblascopedro · Begijar · Torreperogil · Chilluévar

Almodóvar del Río · Posadas · Guadalcázar · Bujalance · Cañete de las Torres · Porcuna · Higuera de Calatrava · Villadompardo · Fuerte del Rey · Jaén · Mancha Real · Jimena · Bedmar · Jódar · Quesada · La Iruela · Cazorla

Fuente-Palmera · La Carlota · Fernán-Núñez · Espejo · Castro del Río · Valenzuela · Santiago de Calatrava · Torredonjimeno · Martos · Torre del Campo · La Guardia de Jaén · Pegalajar · Larva · Huesa · Pozo Alcón

Luisiana · Écija · Santaella · Montalbán de Córdoba · Aguilar de la Frontera · Montilla · Doña Mencía · Nueva-Carteya · Baena · Alcaudete · Los Villares · Fuensanta de Martos · Cambil · Huelma · Cabra del Sto. Cristo

Puente-Genil · Herrera · La Rambla · Cabra · Luque · Zuheros · Fuente-Tójar · Valdepeñas de Jaén · Castillo de Locubín · Frailes · Montillana · Torre-Cardela · Pedro-Martínez · Gorafe

El Rubio · Estepa · Lucena · Carcabuey · Priego de Córdoba · Alcalá la Real · Almedinilla · Las Navas · Benalúa de las Villas · Moreda · Fonelas · Benalúa de Guadix

Osuna · Puebla Cazalla · La Roda de Andalucía · Mollina · Rute · Iznájar · Algarinejo · Montefrío · Íllora · Moclín · Deifontes · Iznalloz · Bogarre · Gor

Campillos · Archidona · Loja · Huétor-Tájar · Villanueva de Mesía · Pinos-Puente · Albolote · Maracena · GRANADA · Diezma · Purullena · Guadix

Antequera · Villanueva del Rosario · Sta. Cruz de Alhama · Santafé · Churriana · Armilla · Cenes · Jeres del Marquesado · Lacalahorra

Ronda · Teba · Cañete la Real · Ardales · Carratraca · Casarabonela · Pizarra · Almogía · Colmenar · Periana · Alhama de Granada · Agrón · Padul · Dúrcal · Pico Veleta 3392 · Mulhacén 3478 · Sierra Nevada

Alcalá del Valle · Setenil · Arriate · Álora · Alhaurín el Grande · Mijas · Churriana · MÁLAGA · Rincón de la Victoria · Vélez-Málaga · Torrox · Nerja · Almuñécar · Salobreña · Motril · Adra

Marbella · Fuengirola · Torremolinos · Benalmádena · Playa de Calahonda · COSTA DEL SOL

0 5 10 20 30 40 Miles

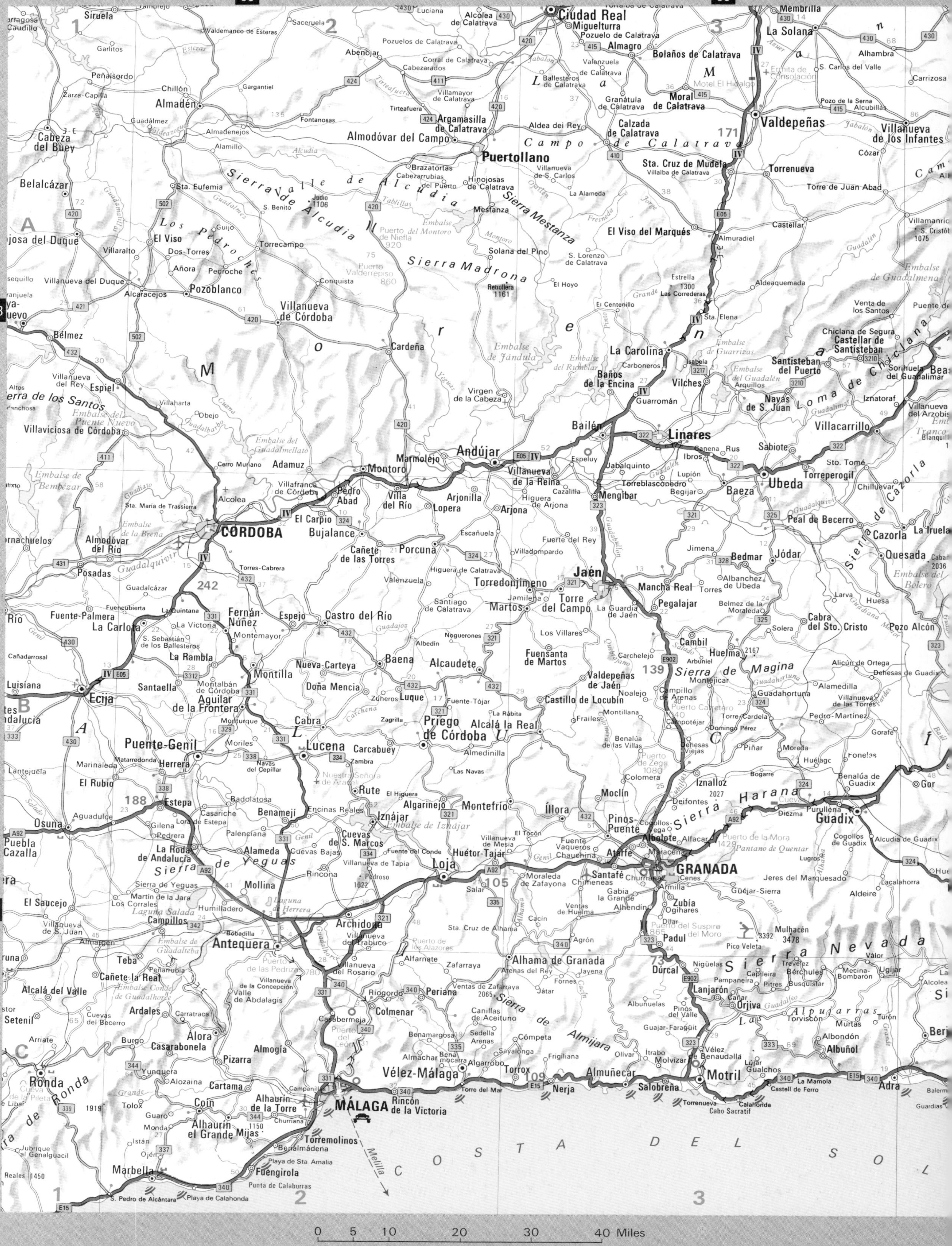

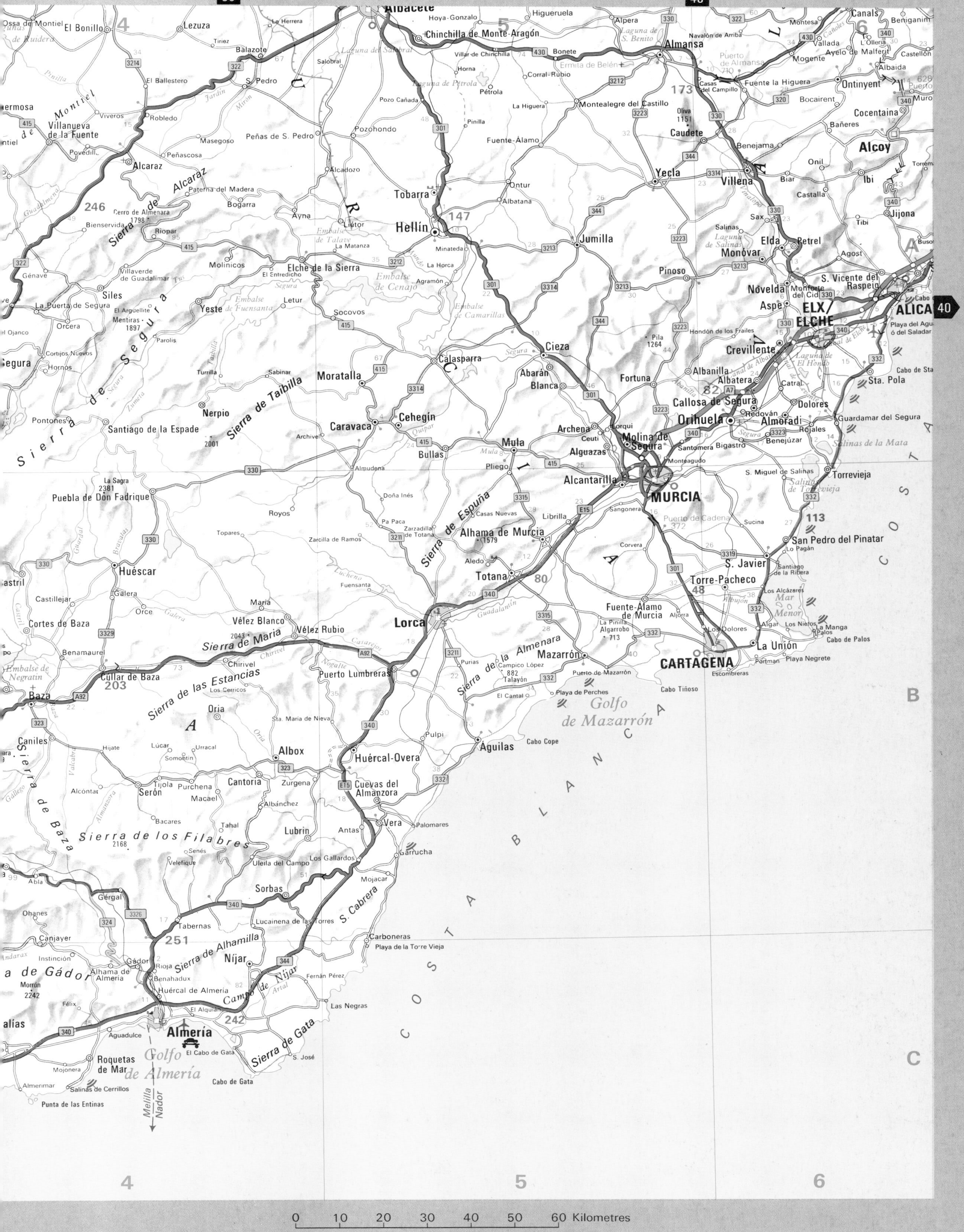
39
40
Albacete
Hoya-Gonzalo
Higueruela
Alpera
Chinchilla de Monte-Aragón
Almansa
Bonete
Ermita de Belén
Corral-Rubio
Pétrola
Laguna de Pétrola
Laguna del Salobral
Salobral
Pozo Cañada
Pinilla
La Higuera
Montealegre del Castillo
Caudete
Oliva
1151
Fuente-Álamo
Pozohondo
Peñas de S. Pedro
Alcadozo
Tobarra
Ontur
Albatana
Hellín
Minateda
La Horca
Agramón
Liétor
La Matanza
Ayna
Bogarra
Paterna del Madera
Sierra de Alcaraz
Alcaraz
Peñascosa
Masegoso
Robledo
Viveros
Villanueva de la Fuente
Povedilla
El Bonillo
Ossa de Montiel
Lezuza
Tiriez
Balazote
S. Pedro
El Ballestero
Riopar
Bienservida
Cerro de Almenara
1798
Molinicos
Villaverde de Guadalimar
Elche de la Sierra
El Entredicho
Embalse de Talave
Embalse de Cenajo
Embalse de Camarillas
Embalse de Fuensanta
Génave
Siles
Yeste
Letur
Socovos
La Puerta de Segura
Orcera
El Arguellite
Mentiras
1897
Parolis
Sierra de Segura
Hornos
Cortijos Nuevos
Pontones
Santiago de la Espade
Nerpio
Sierra de Taibilla
Turrilla
Sabinar
Moratalla
Calasparra
Cieza
Abarán
Blanca
Fortuna
Cehegín
Caravaca
Archivel
Bullas
Mula
Pliego
Archena
Ceuti
Lorquí
Alguazas
Molina de Segura
Alcantarilla
MURCIA
Santomera
Monteagudo
Orihuela
Callosa de Segura
Albatera
Albanilla
Crevillente
ELX/ELCHE
ALICANTE
Aspe
Novelda
Monforte del Cid
S. Vicente del Raspeig
Hondón de los Frailes
Pinoso
Pila
1264
Jumilla
Yecla
Villena
Sax
Elda
Petrel
Monóvar
Salinas
Laguna de Salinas
Agost
Benejama
Biar
Onil
Castalla
Ibi
Tibi
Jijona
Alcoy
Bañeres
Cocentaina
Bocairent
Ontinyent
Albaida
Fuente la Higuera
Mogente
Canals
Benigànim
Puerto de Almansa
Casas del Campillo
Montesa
Vallada
L'Ollería
Ayelo de Malferit
Navalón de Arriba
Laguna de S. Benito
Castellón
Muro
Redován
Dolores
Almoradí
Rojales
Benejúzar
Bigastro
Guardamar del Segura
Catral
Sta. Pola
Cabo de Santa Pola
Playa del Agua o del Salador
Laguna de El Hondo
Salinas de la Mata
Torrevieja
Salinas de Torrevieja
S. Miguel de Salinas
San Pedro del Pinatar
Lo Pagán
S. Javier
Santiago de la Ribera
Torre-Pacheco
Mar Menor
Los Alcázares
Los Nietos
La Manga
Palos
Cabo de Palos
La Unión
Portman
Playa Negrete
CARTAGENA
Escombreras
Cabo Tiñoso
Los Dolores
Fuente-Álamo de Murcia
Aljorra
La Pinilla
Algarrobo
713
Corvera
Sucina
Sangonera
Puerto de Cadena
372
Librilla
Alhama de Murcia
1579
Sierra de España
Casas Nuevas
Aledo
Totana
Sierra de la Almenara
Mazarrón
Puerto de Mazarrón
Campico López
882
Talayón
El Cantal
Playa de Perches
Golfo de Mazarrón
Cabo Cope
Aguilas
Purias
Lorca
Zarzadilla de Totana
Pa Paca
Doña Inés
Almudena
Royos
Topares
Zarcilla de Ramos
Fuensanta
La Sagra
2381
Puebla de Don Fadrique
Huéscar
Galera
Orce
Castillejar
Cortes de Baza
María
Vélez Blanco
Vélez Rubio
Sierra de María
2043
Chirivel
Benamaurel
Embalse de Negratín
Cúllar de Baza
Baza
Sierra de las Estancias
Los Cerricos
Puerto Lumbreras
Oria
Sta. María de Nieva
Caniles
Sierra de Baza
Hijate
Lúcar
Somontín
Urracal
Albox
Huércal-Overa
Pulpí
Cuevas del Almanzora
Zurgena
Cantoria
Purchena
Tíjola
Serón
Alcóntar
Macael
Albánchez
Bacares
Tahal
Lubrín
Antas
Vera
Palomares
Garrucha
Sierra de los Filabres
2168
Senés
Velefique
Uleila del Campo
Los Gallardos
Mojácar
Sorbas
Gérgal
Abla
Ohanes
Tabernas
Lucainena de las Torres
S. Cabrera
Carboneras
Playa de la Torre Vieja
Canjayer
Instinción
Sierra de Alhamilla
Níjar
Fernán Pérez
Gádor
Rioja
Alhama de Almería
Benahadux
Huércal de Almería
Campo de Níjar
Las Negras
El Alquián
Almería
Aguadulce
Roquetas de Mar
El Cabo de Gata
Sierra de Gata
S. José
Cabo de Gata
Golfo de Almería
Mojonera
Almerimar
Salinas de Cerrillos
Punta de las Entinas
Félix
Morrón
2242
Melilla Nador
COSTA BLANCA
MURCIA
A
B
C
4
5
6
0 10 20 30 40 50 60 Kilometres

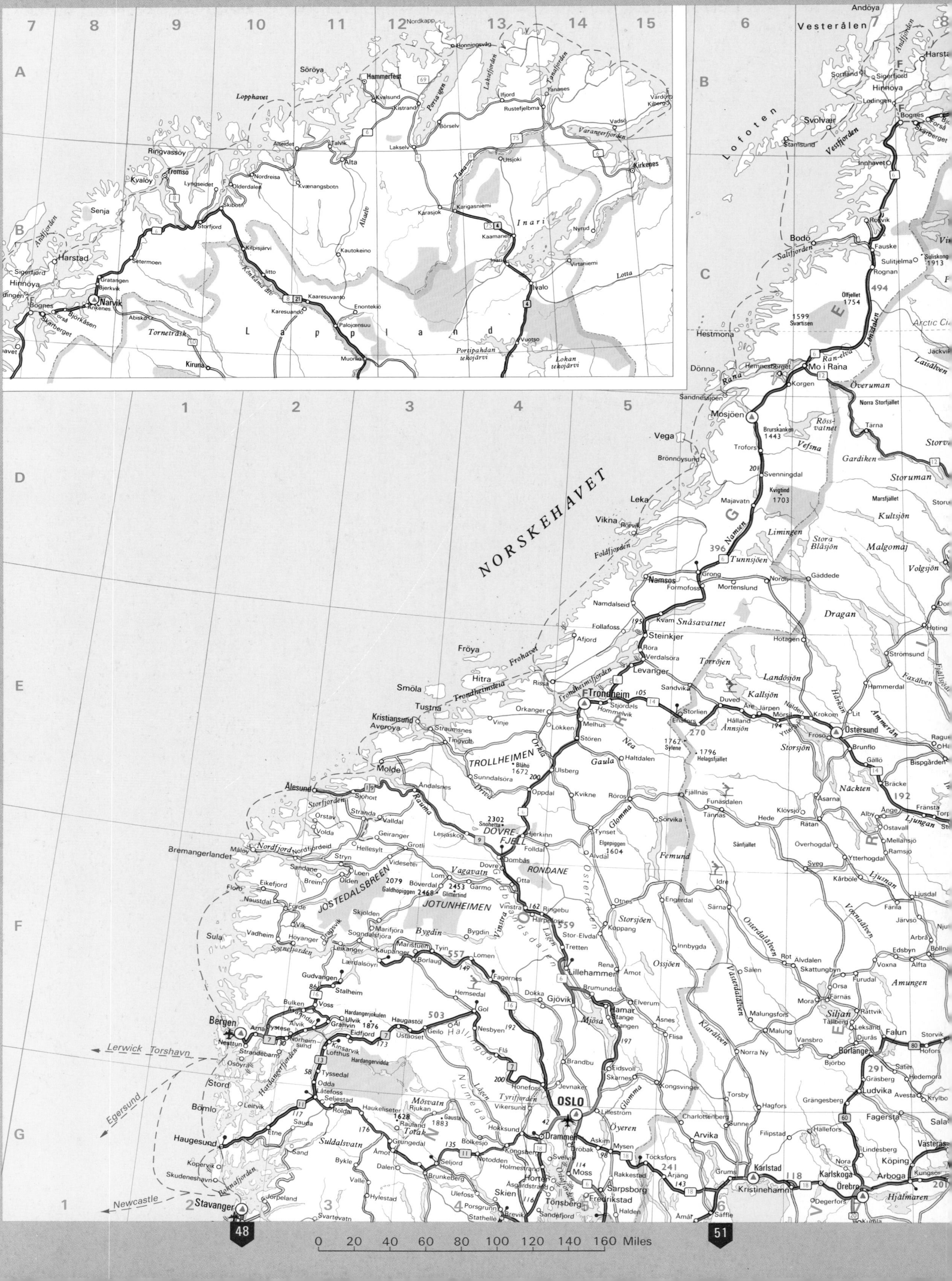

7 8 9 10 11 12 13 14 15 6 Vesterålen 8

A B

Andøya
Nordkapp
Söröya
Hammerfest
Honningsvåg
Sønland
Sigerfjord
Hinnøya
Harstad
F
Bognes
Skärberget
Lofoten
Svolvær
Stamsund
Vestfjorden
Innhavet
Kvalsund
Kistrand
Ifjord
Tananes
Rustefjelbma
Børselv
Vadsø
Vardø
Kiberg
Ringvassøy
Alteidet
Talvik
Lakselv
Utsjoki
Varangerfjorden
Tromsö
Kvaløy
Lyngseidet
Olderdalen
Väenangsbotn
Alta
Kirkenes
Nyrud
Skibotn
Karasjok
Inari
Lotta
Senja
Storfjord
Kilpisjärvi
Kautokeino
Kaamanen
Virtaniemi
Andfjorden
Harstad
Setermoen
Litto
Sigerfjord
Hinnöya
Gratangen
Bjerkvik
Kaaresuvanto
Ivalo
Saltfjorden
Bodö
Fauske
Sulitjelma
Rognan
Ölfjellet 1754
494
Arctic Circle
 dingen
Bognes
Narvik
Ankenes
Björkåsen
Abisko
Kaaresuando
Enontekio
Palojoensuu
Hestmona
1599
Svartisen
Dönna
Hemnesberget
Mo i Rana
Rana
Korgen
Överuman
Norra Storfjallet
Tärna
Tornetrask
Karesuando
Lapland
Muonio
Portipahdan tekojärvi
Lokan tekojärvi
Vuotso
Sandnessjöen
Mosjöen
Brurskanken 1443
Rössvatnet
Kiruna
Vega
Trofors
Vefsna
Gardiken
Storuman
Brönnöysund
Svenningdal
201
Kvigtind 1703
Marsfjallet
Leka
Majavatn
Limingen
Stora Blåsjön
Malgomaj
Vikna
Rørvik
Namsen
396
Tunnsjöen
Volgsjön
Foldfjorden
Grong
Nordli
Gäddede
Dragan
Namsos
Formofoss
Mortenslund
Heting
Namdalseid
Follafoss
195
Kvam Snåsavatnet
Hotagen
Strömsund
Fröya
Afjord
Steinkjer
Torröjen
Landösjön
Faxälven
Rissa
Røra
Verdalsora
Levanger
Sandvika
Kallsjön
Hammerdal
Hitra
Trondheimsleia
Smöla
Trondheim
Stjördals
105
Storlien
Duved
Åre Järpen
Krokom
Lit
Tustna
Orkanger
Melhus
Hommelvik
14
Enafors
Hålland
194
Ytterån
Östersund
Kristiansund
Averøya
Straumsnes
Vinje
Lökken
Stören
Nea
Gaula
1762 Sylene
270
Mörsil
Annsjön
Fröson
Brunflo
Averöya
Tingvoll
Melhus
1796 Helagsfjallet
Storsjön
Gällö
Bispgården
Molde
TROLLHEIMEN
Blåhö 1672
Ulsberg
Haltdalen
Fjällnäs
Funäsdalen
Hede
Rätan
Ange
192
Näcken
Bräcke
Ålesund
Sjöholt
Andalsnes
Oppdal
Kvikne
Röros
Glomma
Sörvika
Sånfjallet
Overhogdal
Sveg
Mellansjö
Ramsjo
Storfjorden
Stranda
Valldal
Orsta
2302 Snohetta
Hjerkinn
DOVRE FJELL
Folldal
Tynset
Elgepiggen 1604
Femund
Ytterhogdal
Kårböle
Ljusnan
Volda
Geiranger
Grotli
Lesjaskog
9
Dovre
Dombås
RONDANE
Alvdal
Idre
Särna
Ljusdal
Bremangerlandet
Nordfjord
Nordfjordeid
Stryn
Hellesylt
Videseth
Lom
Vagavatn
Garmo
Otta
Osterdalen
Engerdal
Färila
Järvsö
Målöy
Sandane
Breim
Loen
Olden
2079 Bøverdal 2453
Glittertind
Vinstra
Ringebu
Storsjöen
Koppang
Arbrå
JOSTEDALSBREEN
Galdhöpiggen 2468
JOTUNHEIMEN
162
Harpefoss
559
Stor-Elvdal
Innbygda
Rot Alvdalen
Edsbyn
Alfta
Floró
Eikefjord
Förde
Skjolden
Marifjöra
Bygdin
Bygdin
Rena
Lillehammer
Ossjöen
Sälen
Furudal
Amungen
Sula
Vadheim
Höyanger
Sogndalsfjöra
557
Lomen
149
Fagernes
Tretten
Åmot
VSäla
Skattungbyn
Mora
Farnäs
Sognefjorden
Leikanger
Lærdalsöyri
Borlaug
Hemsedal
Dokka
Gjövik
Brumunddal
Elverum
Malungsfors
Orsa
Siljan
Rättvik
Gudvangen
864 Stalheim
Voss
Haugastöl
503
Gol
16
Brandbu
Eidsvoll
Flisa
Mjösa
Hamar
Asnes
Leksand
Djurås
Falun
Bergen
Arna
Hardangerjökulen
Ulvik
Granvin
1876
Al
Nesbyen
192
Flå
Stange
Hallingdal
197
Elverum
Malung
Vansbro
Borlänge
Bulken
Norheim
Eidfjord
Geilo
Ustaoset
7
Honefoss
Jevnaker
Skarnes
Kongsvinger
Norra Ny
291
Säter
Hedemora
Nesttun
Osteröy
7 30
Finsarvik
Lofthus
173
Brandbu
200
Tyrifjorden
Vikersund
Eidsvoll
Glomma
Torsby
Hagfors
Grängesberg
Ludvika
Avesta
Strandebarm
Osöyra
13
Tyssedal
Odda
Hardangervidda
Mösvatn
Rjukan
Drammen
42
Öyeren
Askim
Mysen
Charlottenberg
Sunne
Filipstad
Nora
Köping
Stord
Leirvik
117
Lätefoss
Seljestad
Roldal
58
Hokksund
OSLO
Drammen
Svelvik
98
Tocksfors
Arvika
Hällefors
Fagersta
Bömlo
Etne
Sauda
176
1628 Rauland 1883
Totak
Gausta
Gvungedal
135
Bolkesjo
Notodden
Kongsberg
114 Moss
Rakkestad
Årjäng
241
Grums
Lindesberg
Köping
Sala
Haugesund
Sand
Bykle
Valle
Dalen
Brunkeberg
Seljord
Horten
Åsgardstrand
Skien
Holmestrand
Sandefjord
Sarpsborg
18
Kristinehamn
18
Örebro
Kopervik
Skudeneshavn
Jørpeland
Hylestad
Ulefoss
Porsgrunn
Tönsberg
Fredrikstad
Halden
Åmal
143
Karlstad
118
Karlskoga
Arboga
Kungsor
Stavanger
Svartevatn
Stathelle
Larvik
Åmal
Säffle
Hjälmaren
Vänern

Lerwick Torshavn
Egersund
Newcastle

NORSKEHAVET

48

51

0 20 40 60 80 100 120 140 160 Miles

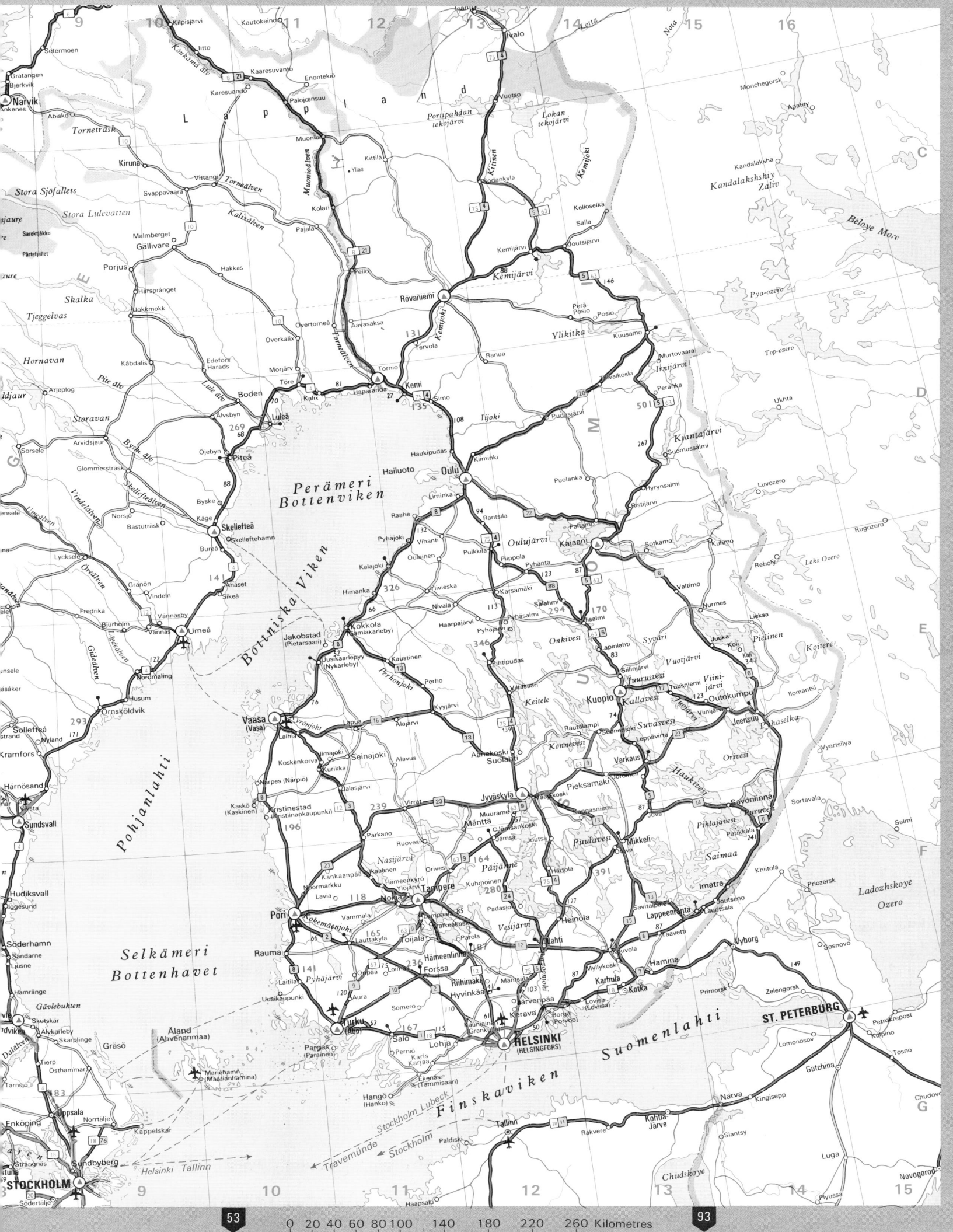

0 20 40 60 80 100   140   180   220   260 Kilometres

Lappland
Kilpisjärvi
Kautokeino
Inari
Ivalo
Karesuvanto
Enontekiö
Karesuando
Palojoensuu
Vuotso
Portipahdan tekojärvi
Lokan tekojärvi
Narvik
Abisko
Tornetrask
Kiruna
Muonio
Kittilä
Sodankylä
Kemijoki
Tornealven
Vittangi
Svappavaara
Stora Sjöfallets
Stora Lulevatten
Kolari
Kalixälven
Pajala
Gällivare
Malmberget
Porjus
Kelloselkä
Salla
Kemijärvi
Monchegorsk
Apatity
Kandalaksha
Kandalakshskiy Zaliv
Beloye More
Pello
Rovaniemi
Harsprånget
Jokkmokk
Skalka
Tjeggelvas
Posio
Pyа-ozero
Overtorneå
Aavasaksa
Tervola
Ylikitka
Kuusamo
Hornavan
Arvidsjaur
Arjeplog
Edefors Harads
Morjärv
Tornio
Kemi
Haparanda
Ranua
Murtovaara
Irnijärvi
Boden
Luleå
Kalix
Simo
Taivalkoski
Pudasjärvi
Iijoki
Ukhta
Storavan
Älvsbyn
Piteå
Sorsele
Haukipudas
Kiiminki
Kiantajärvi
Suomussalmi
Glommersträsk
Hailuoto
Oulu
Perämeri Bottenviken
Puolanka
Hyrynsalmi
Luvozero
Byske
Kåge
Skellefteå
Skellefteälven
Skellefteham
Bastuträsk
Liminka
Raahe
Rantsila
Ristijärvi
Paltamo
Kajaani
Oulujärvi
Sotkamo
Kuhmo
Rugozero
Pyhäjoki
Vihanti
Oulainen
Pulkkila
Piippola
Pyhäntä
Reboly
Leks Ozero
Lycksele
Burea
Kalajoki
Bottniska Viken
Himanka
Ylivieska
Kärsämäki
Vindeln
Ånäset
Sikeå
Valtimo
Nurmes
Salahmi
Iisalmi
Kokkola (Gamlakarleby)
Nivala
Haapajärvi
Pyhäsalmi
Lieksa
Vännäs
Umeå
Jakobstad (Pietarsaari)
Onkivesi
Syväri
Pielinen
Lapinlahti
Juuka
Koli
Uusikaarlepyy (Nykarleby)
Kaustinen
Pihtipudas
Kotterо
Nordmaling
Perho
Perhonjoki
Siilinjärvi
Vuotjärvi
Juurusvesi
Viinijärvi
Tuusniemi
Outokumpu
Keitele
Viitasaari
Kuopio
Kallavesi
Ilomantsi
Husum
Örnsköldvik
Kyyjärvi
Joensuu
Vaasa (Vasa)
Lapua
Alajärvi
Suonenjoki
Rautalampi
Suvasvesi
Pyhäselkä
Sollefteå
Nyland
Laihia
Kramfors
Ilmajoki
Seinäjoki
Alavus
Äänekoski
Suolahti
Konnevesi
Leppävirta
Varkaus
Orivesi
Vyartsilya
Koskenkorva
Kurikka
Härnösand
Närpes (Narpio)
Jalasjärvi
Pohjanlahti
Haukivesi
Pieksämäki
Joroinen
Kasko (Kaskinen)
Kristinestad (Kristiinankaupunki)
Jyväskylä
Virrat
Juva
Savonlinna
Sortavala
Sundsvall
Muurame
Jämsänkoski
Mänttä
Rantasalmi
Pihlajavesi
Puruvesi
Parikkala
Salmi
Parkano
Jämsä
Joutsa
Puulavesi
Mikkeli
Ruovesi
Näsijärvi
Kankaanpää
Ikaalinen
Orivesi
Päijänne
Hartola
Saimaa
Noormarkku
Hämeenkyrö
Ylöjärvi
Tampere
Kuhmoinen
Imatra
Khiitola
Priozersk
Ladozhskoye Ozero
Hudiksvall
Pori
Kokemäenjoki
Lavia
Nokia
Vammala
Padasjoki
Savitaipale
Lappeenranta
Joutseno
Lauritsala
Söderhamn
Sandarne
Ljusne
Rauma
Lauttakylä
Toijala
Lempäälä
Parola
Vesijärvi
Heinola
Lahti
Taavetti
Vyborg
Sosnovo
Selkämeri Bottenhavet
Hämeenlinna
Forssa
Kouvola
Myllykoski
Hamina
Hamrånge
Gävlebukten
Laitila
Pyhäjärvi
Loimaa
Oripää
Riihimäki
Hyvinkää
Mäntsälä
Karhula
Kotka
Primorsk
Zelenogorsk
Uusikaupunki
Aura
Somero
Järvenpää
Lovisa (Loviisa)
Skutskär
Älvkarleby
Åland (Ahvenanmaa)
Turku (Åbo)
Salo
Kerava
Borgå (Porvoo)
ST. PETERBURG
Petrokrepost
Kolpino
Skärplinge
Gräsö
Tierp
Östhammar
Lohja
Kauniainen (Grankulla)
HELSINKI (HELSINGFORS)
Suomenlahti
Lomonosov
Tosno
Pargas (Parainen)
Pernio
Karis (Karjaa)
Ekenäs (Tammisaari)
Mariehamn (Maarianhamina)
Gatchina
Tärnsjö
Hangö (Hanko)
Finskaviken
Narva
Kingisepp
Chudovo
Uppsala
Norrtälje
Enköping
Kappelskär
Stockholm Lübeck
Tallinn
Kohtla-Järve
Rakvere
Paldiski
Slantsy
Travemünde Stockholm
Strängnäs
Sundbyberg
Helsinki Tallinn
STOCKHOLM
Södertälje
Haapsalu
Chudskoye
Luga
Novgorod
Plyussa

1

2

3

4

A

B

C

BERGEN

Store
Sotra

Solsvik
Hetlevik
E16
Eidsvåg

Arna
Haus
Trengereid
E16

Øystese
Indre
Ålvik
Utne
Kinsarvik

Eidfjord
13

Hardangervidda
69 1250

Hardanger

Telavåg
Nestun
580
Haukeland
Espeland

Norheimsund
7
Tysse 129

Herand
Ullensvang
13

Lofthus

Viveli
Dyranut

Fana
E39
Syfteland
48

Strandebarm
49
Jondal
Eikelandsosen
Holdhus

Hardangervidda

Hallaskar

Hårteigen
1691

Florø
Torshavn

Osøyra
Fusa

Strandvik
Ølve
Løfallstrand
Kvinnherad

42

Litlos

Nasjonalpa

Lerwick

Krossfjorden

Huftarøy
Møkster
Selbjørn

Bjørnafjorden
Tysnes
Tysnesøy
Onarheim
49

Varaldsøy

Gjermundshamn
Hatlestrand

Folgefonn
59
Tyssedal
Odda

Song

Fitjar
Jektevik
49

Stord
51 Uskedal
48

Skare
13 E134
22

Litlabø
Leirvik

Husnes
Sunde
Sæbøvik

Åkra
E134
Fjæra
E134
13

Røldal

Haukelifjell
E134
Edland

Haukeligrend

Rubbestadneset
Bremnes

Halsnøy
Uåker
Skånevik
48

45
520
13

Nesflaten

Bjåen
9

Egersund Stavanger

Bømlo

Lykling
Mosterhamn
Valevåg

120

42
24

Espevær
Bømlo
Førde
Buavåg
Uttjoa

Etne
26
Saudasjøen
Sauda
520

Snønuten
1605

Hovden

79

Sveio
44
E39
Strand

Ølen
514
Sandeid

Sand
Suldal
13 27

Solheimsvik

F

Skjold
37
E134
Vikedal
Imsland
27

B

Setesdal

Haugesund
386
Førde

Vårenes
27
Ullatun

Visnes
Utvik
Fiskå
47

Nedstrand
Stranda
Jelsa
Erfjord
Vadla

Blåfjellhytta

Bykle

9

Vedavågen
Kopervik
E39

Tysvær

Vindsvik
Tøtlandsvik

Nilsebu

Rjuven

9

Åkrehamn
47
23

Ombo
Hjelmelandsvågen

 Årdal

*NJARDARHEIM
VEIDEMARK*
45
Øyuvsbu

Karmøy
Vestre
Bokn
Hesby
67

Hyles

Skudeneshavn

Bergen

Utstein
kloster
Finnøy
Rennesøy
Talgje
Fiskå
13

Lysebotn
Adneran

Fidjeland

Ystebøhamn
Mosterøy
Vikevåg

Tau
13

Jørpeland
Lysefjorden

Sinnes

45

Øvre Sirdal

Ljosland

Åkernes

Randaberg
Hundvåg

13

Oanes
Forsand
Espedal

105

Stavanger
Vaulen
510 16

Hommersåk
45
Helle
Dirdal

Newcastle

Sola
E39
Sandnes

Lauvvik
Oftedal

468

Øvre Sirdal

Ganddal
Figgjo

507
Kleppe
Ålgård
506

Bryne
Orre

JÆREN
Bue
36
Øvrebygd

Tonstad

Knaben

Netlandsnes
Aseral

455

Nærbø

Varhaug

Bjerkreim
42

Haughom

Kvinlog

Eiken

Grindheim
16

455

Vigrestad

Ogna

DALANE

Helleland
E39
Heskestad
61
Moi
240

103
42

Eiken

Sirevåg
Hellvik

44
42

Gyland
Sira

Bergen

Eigerøya
Egersund

Lundevatn
69

Søndal

Hauge
Åna-Sira
44

Loga
Flekkefjord
Kvinesdal
Øye
Hægebostad

43

64

Kvås
Konsmo
Laudal
455

Kirkehamn

Listafjorden

Herad
Lista
Vanse
Vestbygd
Farsund
Spind
39 43

Lyngdal
Rom
E39
Vigmostad
Holum
31
455

Øyslebø

Spangereid
Lindesnes

Hansholm

Mandal

N

O

0 5 10 20 30 40 Miles

46
46

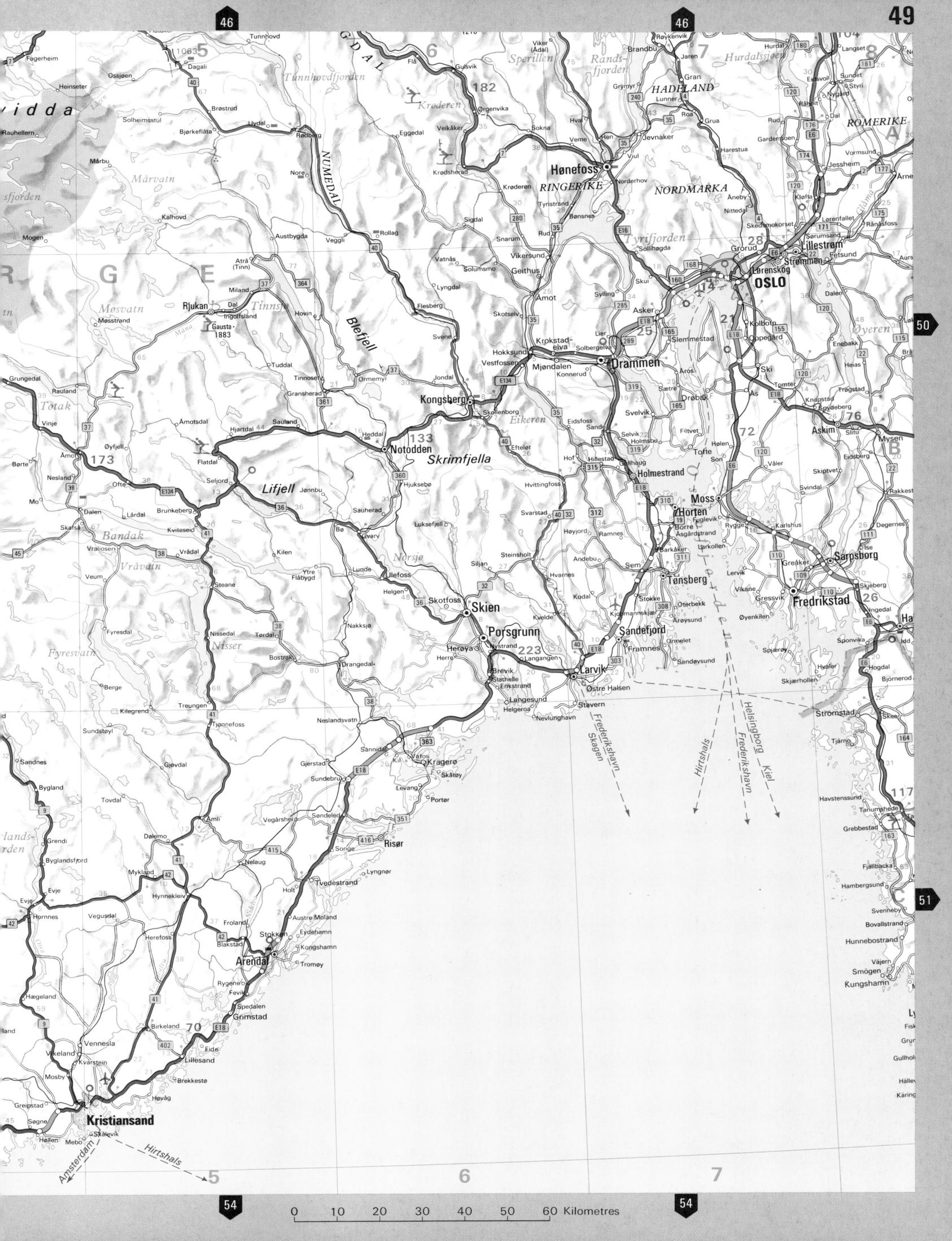
OSLO
Drammen
Hønefoss
RINGERIKE
NORDMARKA
HADELAND
ROMERIKE
Lillestrøm
Strømmen
Lørenskog
Asker
Kongsberg
Notodden
Skien
Porsgrunn
Larvik
Sandefjord
Tønsberg
Horten
Moss
Fredrikstad
Sarpsborg
Askim
Holmestrand
Kragerø
Risør
Tvedestrand
Arendal
Grimstad
Lillesand
Kristiansand
Rjukan
Gausta 1883
Blefjell
Skrimfjella
Lifjell
NUMEDAL
Tyrifjorden
Randsfjorden
Hurdalssjøen
Sperillen
Krøderen
Tinnsjø
Møsvatn
Totak
Bandak
Vråvatn
Nisser
Fyresvatn
Norsjø
Eikeren
Øyeren
Glomma
Mårvatn
Tunnhovdfjorden
Strömstad
Kungshamn
Smögen
Frederikshavn
Skagen
Hirtshals
Helsingborg
Kiel
Amsterdam
5
6
7
8
0 10 20 30 40 50 60 Kilometres

50
51
54
54

52 52

46

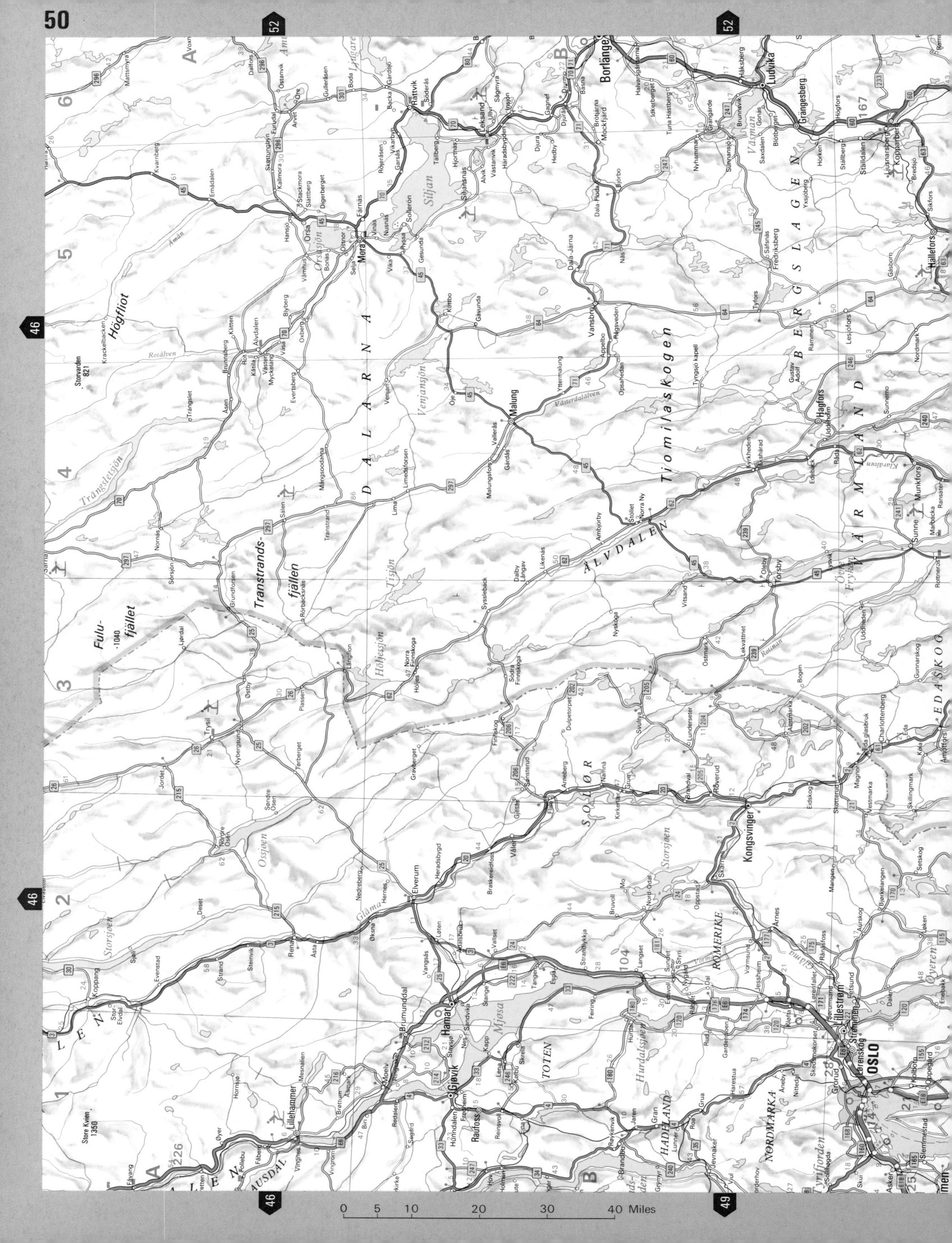

DALARNA
BERGSLAGEN
VÄRMLAND
Tiomilaskogen
ÄLVDALEN
SOLØR
ROMERIKE
TOTEN
HADELAND
NORDMARKA
Höglfliot
Transtrands-fjällen
Fulu-fjället
Siljan
Orsasjön
Venjansjön
Tisjön
Mjøsa
Storsjøen
Ossjøen
Väsman
Glåma
Västerdalälven
Klarälven
Trängsletsjön
Rotälven
Mora
Rättvik
Leksand
Borlänge
Ludvika
Grängesberg
Orsa
Älvdalen
Malung
Sälen
Vansbro
Hagfors
Munkfors
Sunne
Torsby
Stöllet
Kongsvinger
Elverum
Hamar
Gjøvik
Lillehammer
Lillestrøm
OSLO
Trysil
Rena
Koppang
Brumunddal
Raufoss
Jessheim
Hällefors
Kopparberg
Charlottenberg
Eda

46

46

46 49

0 5 10 20 30 40 Miles

53
53
56
54

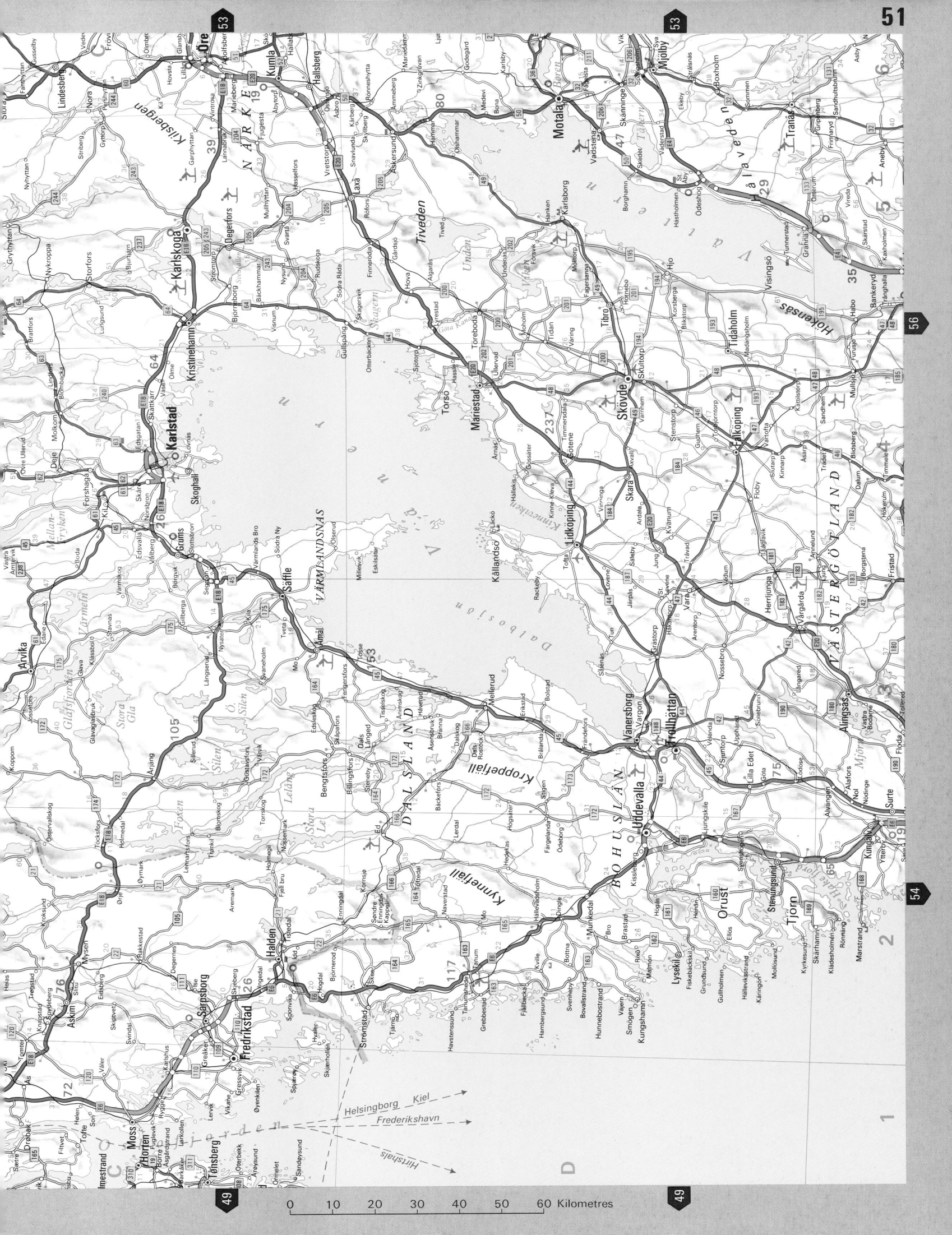

Örebro
Kumla
Hallsberg
Lindesberg
Nora
Kilsbergen
NÄRKE
Laxå
Askersund
Motala
Vadstena
Mjölby
Skänninge
Tranås
Gränna
Hjo
Tibro
Tidaholm
Vättern
Visingsö
Hökensås
Karlsborg
Tiveden
Unden
Degerfors
Karlskoga
Kristinehamn
Karlstad
Mariestad
Skövde
Falköping
Götene
Skara
Lidköping
Kållandsö
Vänern
Dalbosjön
VÄRMLANDSNÄS
Säffle
Grums
Kil
Arvika
Åmål
Mellerud
Vänersborg
Trollhättan
Uddevalla
Alingsås
Vårgårda
Herrljunga
VÄSTERGÖTLAND
DALSLAND
Bengtsfors
Dals Långed
Kroppefjäll
Kynnefjäll
BOHUSLÄN
Lysekil
Orust
Tjörn
Stenungsund
Kungälv
Marstrand
Strömstad
Tanumshede
Halden
Fredrikstad
Sarpsborg
Moss
Horten
Tønsberg
Askim
Mysen
Helsingborg Kiel
Frederikshavn
Hirtshals

49
49

0 10 20 30 40 50 60 Kilometres

47

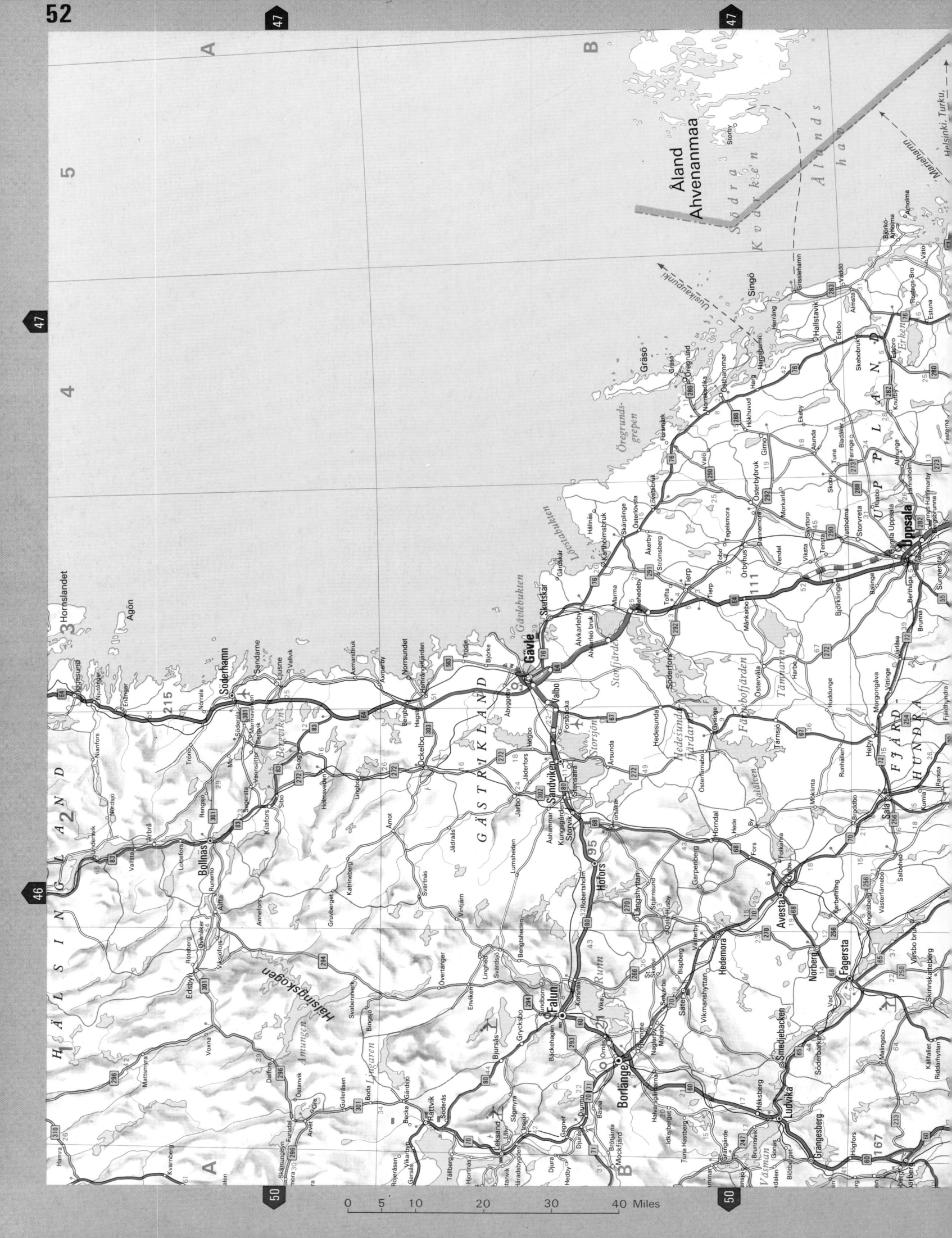
Åland
Ahvenanmaa
Södra Kvarken
Ålands hav
Mariehamn
Helsinki, Turku
Uusikaupunki
Storby
Singö
Gräsö
Öregrund
Östhammar
Öregrundsgrepen
Forsmark
Hallstavik
Grisslehamn
Norrtälje
Herräng
Hargshamn
Lövstabukten
Gävlebukten
Skutskär
Gävle
Älvkarleby
Tierp
Uppsala
Gamla Uppsala
Storvreta
Björklinge
Örbyhus
Dannemora
Österbybruk
Gimo
Alunda
Knutby
Edsbro
Enköping
Sala
Heby
Tärnsjö
Fjärdhundra
U P P L A N D
F J Ä R D - H U N D R A
Hedesunda
Hedesundafjärdarna
Färnebofjärden
Östervåla
Söderfors
Valbo
Sandviken
Storsjön
Ockelbo
Hofors
Storvik
Kungsgården
Torsåker
Jäderfors
Järbo
G Ä S T R I K L A N D
Söderhamn
Sandarne
Ljusne
Vallvik
Axmar bruk
Norrsundet
Hamrångefjärden
Bergby
Hornslandet
Agön
Iggesund
Enånger
Bollnäs
Arbrå
Undersvik
Alfta
Edsbyn
Voxna
Hälsingskogen
Amungen
H Ä L S I N G L A N D
Falun
Borlänge
Ludvika
Smedjebacken
Hedemora
Avesta
Fagersta
Norberg
Krylbo
Säter
Grängesberg
Rättvik
Leksand
Gagnef
Djurås
Runn
Långshyttan
Vikmanshyttan
Bjursås
Svärdsjö
Sundborn
Ornäs
Torsång
Hagfors
Horndal
Garpenberg
Skinnskatteberg
Virsbo bruk
Kvarnberg
Furudal
Ore
Orsa
Boda
Siljan
Amot
Hedby
Mockfjärd
Insjön
Tällberg
Häradsbygden
Vikarbyn
E4
Miles

0 5 10 20 30 40 Miles

50

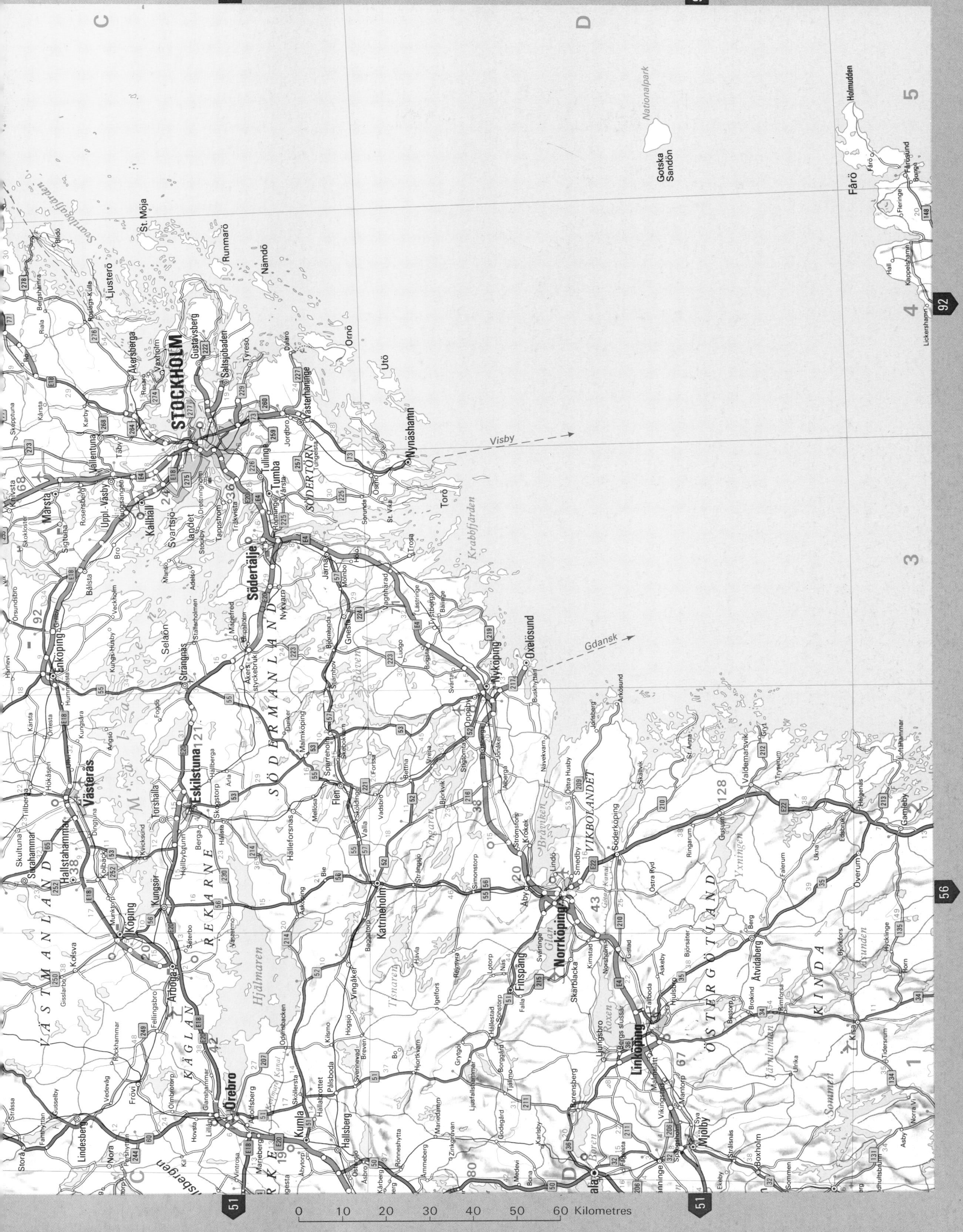
93
93
C
D
5
4
3
1
92
56
51
51
Holmudden
Fårö
Fårösund
Gotska Sandön
Nationalpark
Visby
Gdansk
STOCKHOLM
Södertälje
Nynäshamn
Nyköping
Oxelösund
Norrköping
Linköping
Eskilstuna
Västerås
Örebro
Katrineholm
Enköping
Märsta
Uppl.-Väsby
Vallentuna
Åkersberga
Gustavsberg
Saltsjöbaden
Västerhaninge
Tumba
Tullinge
Strängnäs
Flen
Finspång
Motala
Mjölby
Arboga
Köping
Kungsör
Hallstahammar
Surahammar
Sigtuna
Bålsta
Trosa
Gnesta
Vingåker
Hallsberg
Kumla
Lindesberg
Söderköping
Valdemarsvik
Åtvidaberg
Kisa
Norrtälje
Ljusterö
Runmarö
Nämdö
Ornö
Utö
Torö
St. Möja
SÖDERMANLAND
VÄSTMANLAND
ÖSTERGÖTLAND
VIKBOLANDET
KINDA
SÖDERTÖRN
Hjälmaren
Mälaren
Roxen
Glan
Bråviken
Krabbfjärden
0 10 20 30 40 50 60 Kilometres

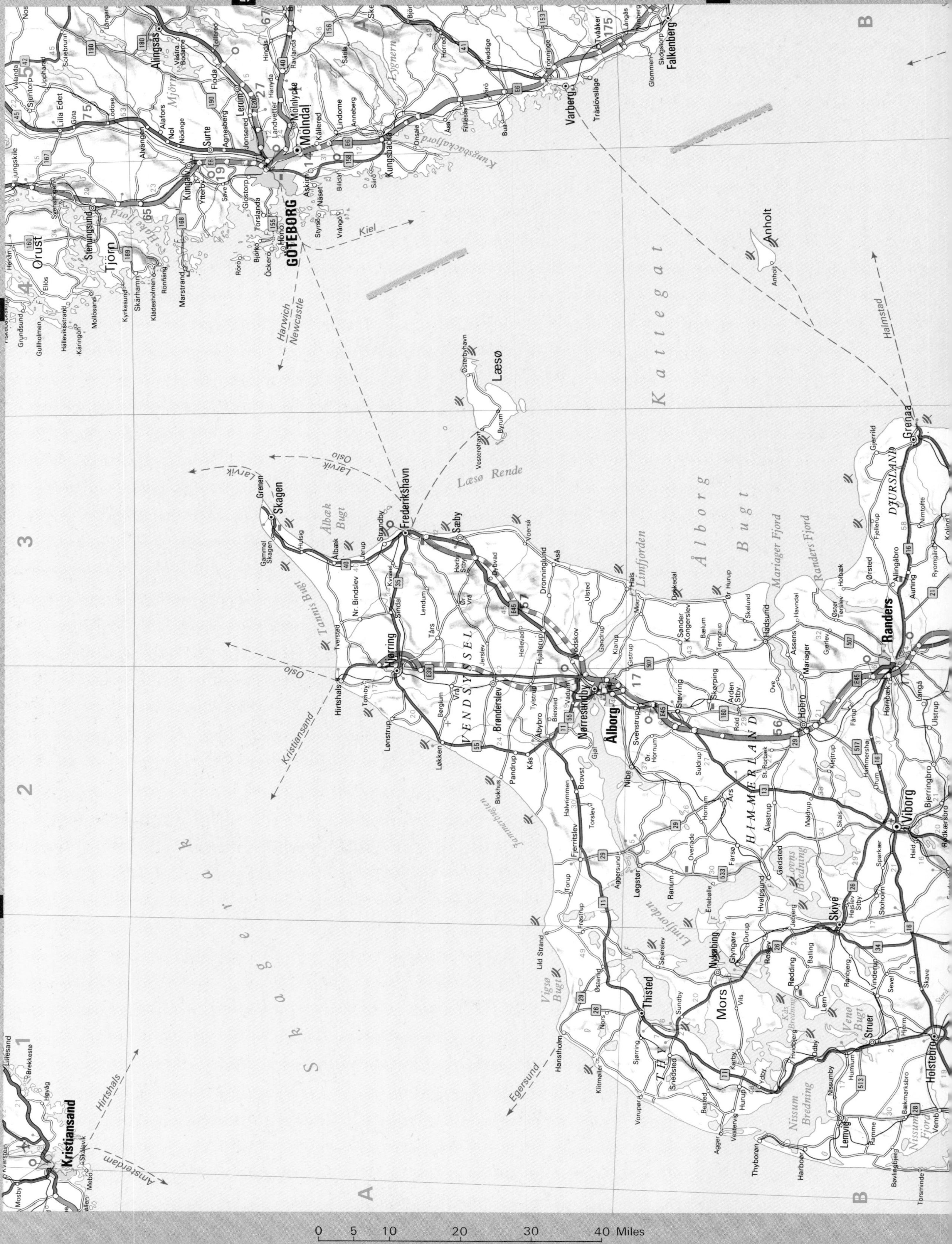
56
56
51
49
Skagerrak
Kattegat
Ålborg Bugt
Læsø Rende
Jammerbugten
Tannis Bugt
Ålbæk Bugt
Vigsø Bugt
Limfjorden
Mariager Fjord
Randers Fjord
VENDSYSSEL
HIMMERLAND
DJURSLAND
THY
Mors
Læsø
Anholt
Orust
Tjörn
GÖTEBORG
Mölndal
Kungsbacka
Alingsås
Kungälv
Varberg
Falkenberg
Skagen
Grenen
Frederikshavn
Sæby
Hjørring
Hirtshals
Brønderslev
Nørresundby
Ålborg
Hobro
Randers
Grenaa
Viborg
Skive
Thisted
Nykøbing
Struer
Holstebro
Lemvig
Thyborøn
Løkken
Kristiansand
Kiel
Larvik
Oslo
Harwich
Newcastle
Kristiansand
Halmstad
Egersund
Hirtshals
Amsterdam
A
B
1
2
3
4
5
0 5 10 20 30 40 Miles

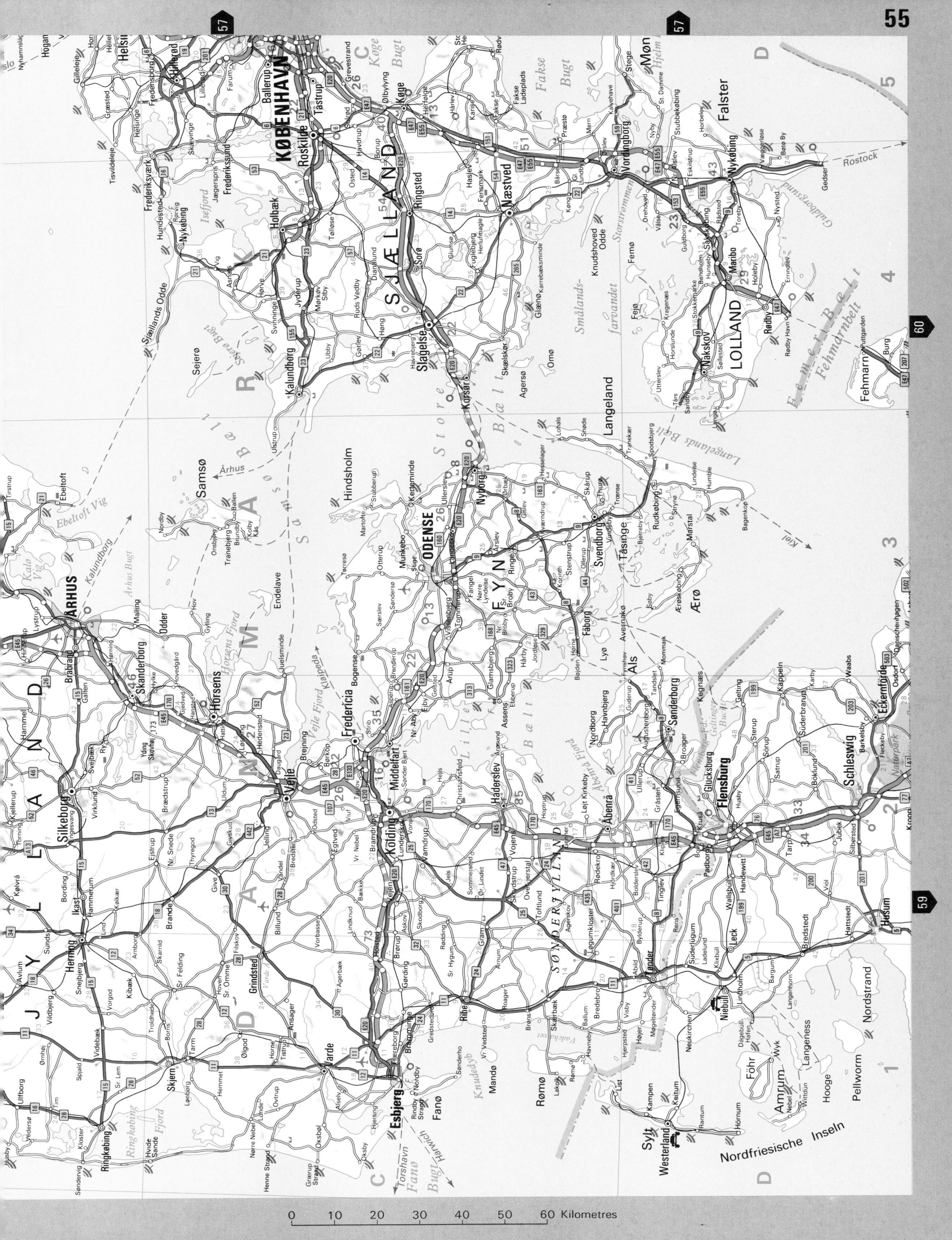
KØBENHAVN
SJÆLLAND
FYN
LOLLAND
Falster
Møn
Langeland
Ærø
Samsø
Fehmarn
JYLLAND
SØNDERJYLLAND
DANMARK
ÅRHUS
ODENSE
Roskilde
Helsingør
Hillerød
Køge
Holbæk
Kalundborg
Slagelse
Næstved
Vordingborg
Nykøbing
Nakskov
Rødby
Korsør
Nyborg
Svendborg
Fåborg
Middelfart
Fredericia
Vejle
Horsens
Skanderborg
Silkeborg
Herning
Ringkøbing
Skjern
Varde
Esbjerg
Fanø
Ribe
Kolding
Haderslev
Åbenrå
Sønderborg
Als
Tønder
Flensburg
Schleswig
Eckernförde
Husum
Niebüll
Westerland
Sylt
Föhr
Amrum
Pellworm
Nordfriesische Inseln
Rømø
Mandø
Nordstrand
Sjællands Odde
Store Bælt
Lille Bælt
Kattegat
Fehmarnbelt
Langelands Bælt
Smålandsfarvandet
Køge Bugt
Fakse Bugt
Århus Bugt
Ebeltoft Vig
Ringkøbing Fjord
Horsens Fjord
Vejle Fjord
Isefjord
Guldborgsund
Storstrømmen
Kalundborg
Århus
Kiel
Rostock
Torshavn
Harwich
Klaipeda

0 10 20 30 40 50 60 Kilometres

92

92

53

51

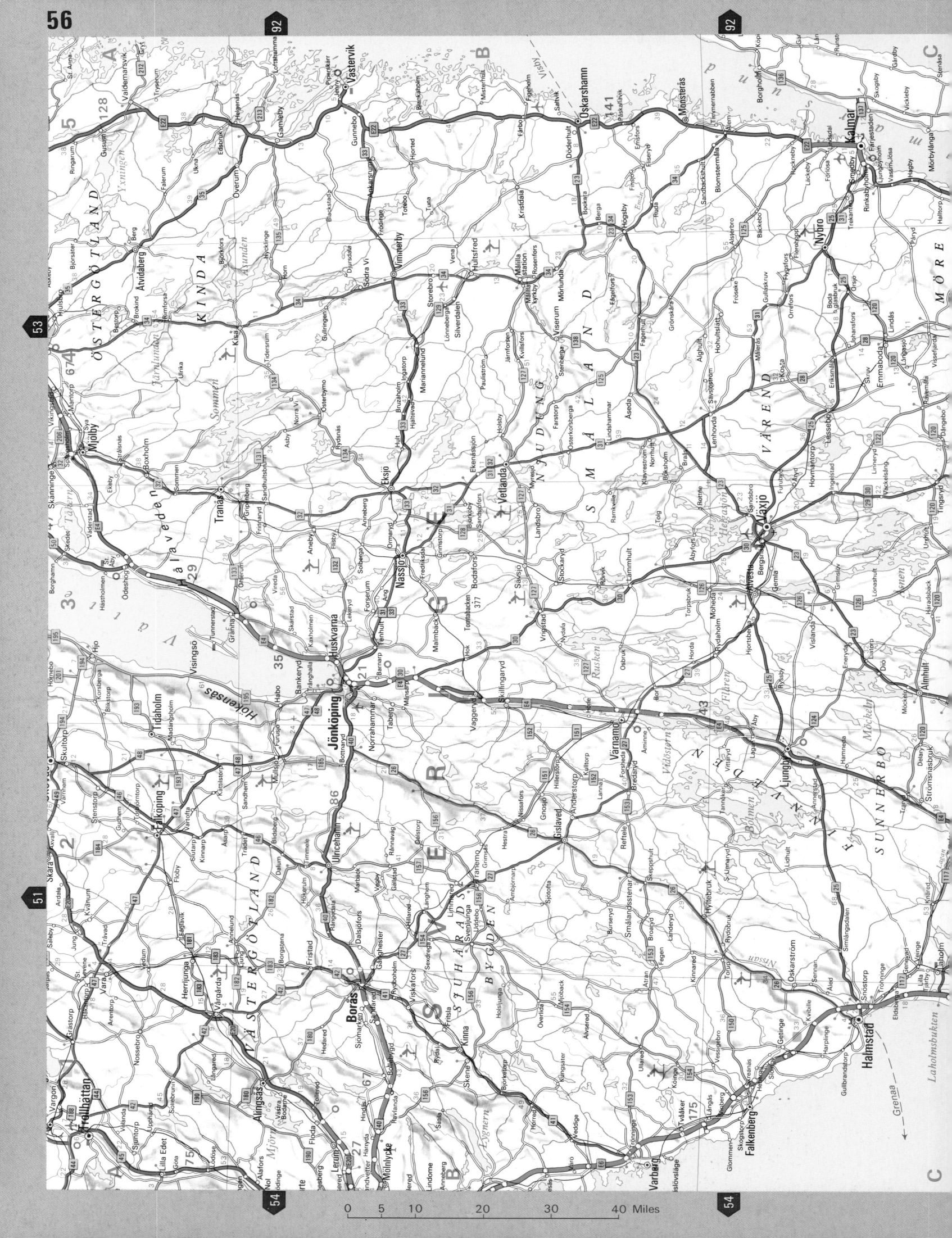
ÖSTERGÖTLAND
KINDA
SMÅLAND
NJUDUNG
VÄREND
MÖRE
SUNNERBO
VÄSTERGÖTLAND
SJUHÄRADSBYGDEN
Västervik
Oskarshamn
Mönsterås
Borgholm
Kalmar
Nybro
Vimmerby
Hultsfred
Åtvidaberg
Kisa
Mjölby
Tranås
Eksjö
Nässjö
Vetlanda
Växjö
Alvesta
Ljungby
Älmhult
Värnamo
Gislaved
Jönköping
Huskvarna
Gränna
Visingsö
Vättern
Skara
Falköping
Tidaholm
Ulricehamn
Borås
Alingsås
Trollhättan
Vårgårda
Herrljunga
Kinna
Skene
Falkenberg
Halmstad
Varberg
Laholm
Mölnlycke
Lerum
Laholmsbukten
Grenaa
Bolmen
Åsnen
Vidöstern

54

54

0 5 10 20 30 40 Miles

92
92
88
61
55
55
BORNHOLM
Rønne
Hasle
Allinge
Sandvig
Hammeren
Gudhjem
Svaneke
Årsdale
Nexø
Snogebæk
Dueodde
Pedersker
Akirkeby
Nyker
Klemensker
Rø
Tejn
Olsker
Ertholmene
Bornholmsgattet
Hanöbukten
Swinoujscie
Sassnitz
København
Mukran
Gdynia
Travemünde
Rostock
Rønne
Oslo
Øresund
Køge Bugt
Hjelm Bugt
Skälderviken
Hallandsås
GÖINGE
SKÅNE
KØBENHAVN
MALMÖ
Lund
Helsingborg
Helsingør
Landskrona
Trelleborg
Ystad
Simrishamn
Kristianstad
Hässleholm
Karlshamn
Karlskrona
Ronneby
Sölvesborg
Olofström
Ängelholm
Höganäs
Klippan
Perstorp
Eslöv
Höör
Hörby
Sjöbo
Tomelilla
Skurup
Svedala
Falsterbo
Skanör
Hillerød
Amager
Møn
Stege
Torekov
Båstad
Åhus

0 10 20 30 40 50 60 Kilometres

1   2   3

A

B

C

Nationalpark Niederså

Norderney
Juist
Juist
Memmert
Borkum
Norddeich
Norden
Hage
Nessmersiel
N70

Schiermonnikoog
Eemshaven
Pewsum   Loppersum
N70

Ameland
Nes
Warffum   Berum
Uithuizen
Uithuizermeeden
Emden

Terschelling
Hollum
Holwerd
Metslawier   Leens   Usquert   Spijk
N383
Baflo
Middelstum
N46

West
Terschelling
Oosterend
Ferwerd
Marrum
Dokkum
Murmerwoude
Kollum
Ee
Zoutkamp
Ulrum
N361
Winsum
Loppersum   N41
Delfzijl
Appingedam

Vlieland
Oost-
Vlieland
St. Annaparochie
St. Jacobiparochie
Berlikum
Steins
Zwaagwesteinde
Veenwouden
Buitenpost
Grijpskerk   43   Noordhorn
Zuidwolde   Ten
Boer
N362
Ditzum   Jemgum
Dollard

Sexbierum
Franeker
Leeuwarden
Hardegarijp
Nd
Bergum
Bergum
95   Grootegast
Surhuisterveen
GRONINGEN
Hoogkerk   Haren
Siddeburen
Schildwolde
Slochteren
Foxhol   Noordbroek   Midwolda
Nieuwolda
Finsterwolde
Nieuwe-
Schans
Bund

Harlingen
Texel
Den Burg
N31
Dronrijp
Warga   Garijp
Opende
18
Leek   Paterswolde
Eexta
Sappemeer
Muntendam
Hoogezand   147
Veendam   Wildervank
Winschoten
Bellingwolde
Oude-Pekela
Nieuwe-Pekela
Rhede
A31

Wommels
Witmarsum
Makkum
Bolsward
A7
Grouw
Drachten
59
Beetsterzwaag
Roden   26   Norg
N372
Zuidlaren
N34
Onstwedde
Stadskanaal
Heede
A31

36   Sneek
IJlst
Akkrum
Oldeboorn
Tijnje
Gorredijk
Haulerwijk
Oosterwolde
N33
Assen
Gieten   42
Musselkanaal
Walchum
Laten

Den Helder
43
Workum
Woudsend
N354
Joure
Heerenveen
Oldeberkoop
Noordwolde
N371
Beilen
Westerbork   28
Ter
Apel
Ter Apelkanaal
Emmer-
Compascuum
Haren

Hippolytushoef
N99
Breezand
Koudum
Balk
Oudehaske
St. Nicolaasga
Wolvega
Vledder
Diever
Smilde
Rolde
Nw. Buinen
N366
Nieuw-
Weerdinge
Emmer-
Erfscheidenveen
Emmer

N9   N249
Staveren
Oudemirdum
Lemmer
Rutten   56
Kuinre
38
Havelte   Ruinen
Borger
Odoorn
Emmen
Erica
Klazienaveen
Schoonebeek

Schagen
Medemblik
Andijk
IJsselmeer
Noordwolde
Dwingeloo
Ruinerwold
Hoogeveen
N34
Nieuw
Amsterdam
Zwartemeer
Ruhle

N245
Nwe Niedorp
N242
A7
Grootebroek
Enkhuizen
NOORDOOST-
POLDER
Steenwijk
N32
N333   N334
Meppel
N375
De
Wijk
Coevorden
Nw
Schoonebeek
N377

Nd. Scharwoude
Opmeer
32
Broek op Langendijk
Bergen
Heerhugowaard
Berkhout
57
Hoorn
Bovenkarspel
Emmeloord
Urk
Blokzijl
Marknesse
Zwartsluis
Staphorst
Zuidwolde
N48
Slagharen
N34
Ruhlertwist   70
Baw

Alkmaar
Egmond aan Zee
Heiloo
Limmen
Castricum
Uitgeest
Schermerhorn
N244
N247
Oosthuizen
N302
Nagele
Ens
Genemuiden
Hasselt
Balkbrug
Dedemsvaart
Hardenberg
Wilsum   40
Emlichheim
Hoogstede
Bathorn
403

Heemskerk
IJmuiden
Velsen
Krommenie
Wormerveer
Purmerend
Edam
Volendam
Monnikendam
Lelystad
OOSTELIJK-
FLEVOLAND
Dronten
IJsselmuiden
Kampen
N50
Zwolle
Ommen
Vroomshoop
Westerhaar
Neuenhaus
Wietmarschen
Lingen

HAARLEM
Zandvoort
Heemstede
Hillegom
Zaandam
AMSTERDAM
Koog a/d
Zaan
Landsmeer
A6
Biddinghuizen
Elburg
Oldebroek
Hattem
Heerde
Wijhe
Raalte
N35
Heino
Nijverdal
Wierden
Almelo
N349
Tubbergen
Ootmarsum
Denekamp
Nordhorn
Brandlecht

Noordwijkerhout
rdwijk aan Zee
Hoofddorp
Amstelveen
Muiden
Ouderkerk
Weesp
Naarden
Huizen
Bussum
Nunspeet
Harderwijk
60
Ermelo
Epe
Vaassen
Rijssen
N337
N48
Olst
Deventer
Borne
Oldenzaal
N342
Bentheim
Salzbe
A30

NEDERLAND

0   5   10   20   30   40 Miles

55
55
60
60

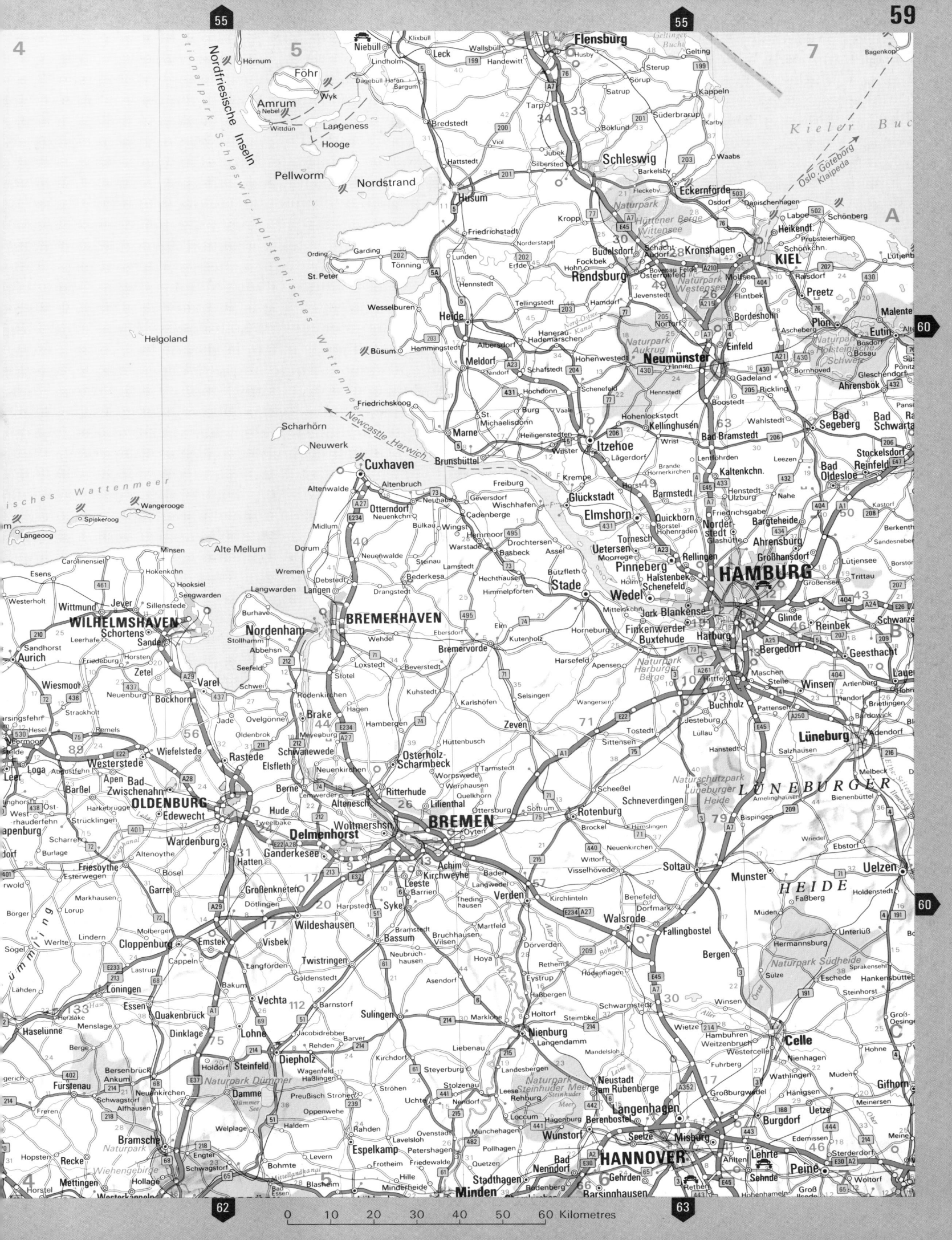
Flensburg
Niebüll
Leck
Husum
Föhr
Amrum
Wyk
Pellworm
Nordstrand
Nordfriesische Inseln
Schleswig-Holsteinisches Wattenmeer
Helgoland
Schleswig
Eckernförde
Kappeln
Kieler Bucht
KIEL
Rendsburg
Kronshagen
Preetz
Plön
Eutin
Malente
Neumünster
Heide
Büsum
Meldorf
Tönning
St. Peter
Marne
Brunsbüttel
Itzehoe
Bad Segeberg
Bad Bramstedt
Bad Oldesloe
Cuxhaven
Otterndorf
Glückstadt
Elmshorn
Pinneberg
Uetersen
Wedel
HAMBURG
Norderstedt
Ahrensburg
Reinbek
Geesthacht
Bergedorf
Harburg
Buxtehude
Stade
Bremervörde
BREMERHAVEN
Nordenham
WILHELMSHAVEN
Jever
Aurich
Varel
Wiesmoor
Westerstede
OLDENBURG
Bad Zwischenahn
Leer
Papenburg
Delmenhorst
BREMEN
Achim
Verden
Rotenburg
Zeven
Buchholz
Winsen
Lüneburg
LÜNEBURGER HEIDE
Soltau
Munster
Uelzen
Walsrode
Fallingbostel
Celle
Gifhorn
Cloppenburg
Wildeshausen
Vechta
Diepholz
Sulingen
Nienburg
Syke
Bassum
Neustadt am Rübenberge
Langenhagen
Burgdorf
HANNOVER
Lehrte
Sehnde
Peine
Wunstorf
Stadthagen
Minden
Espelkamp
Bramsche
Damme
Dümmer
Naturpark Lüneburger Heide
Naturpark Südheide
Steinhuder Meer
Helgoland
Scharhörn
Neuwerk
Wangerooge
Spiekeroog
Langeoog
Newcastle Harwich
Oslo, Göteborg Klaipeda

0 10 20 30 40 50 60 Kilometres

62
63

55 55

59

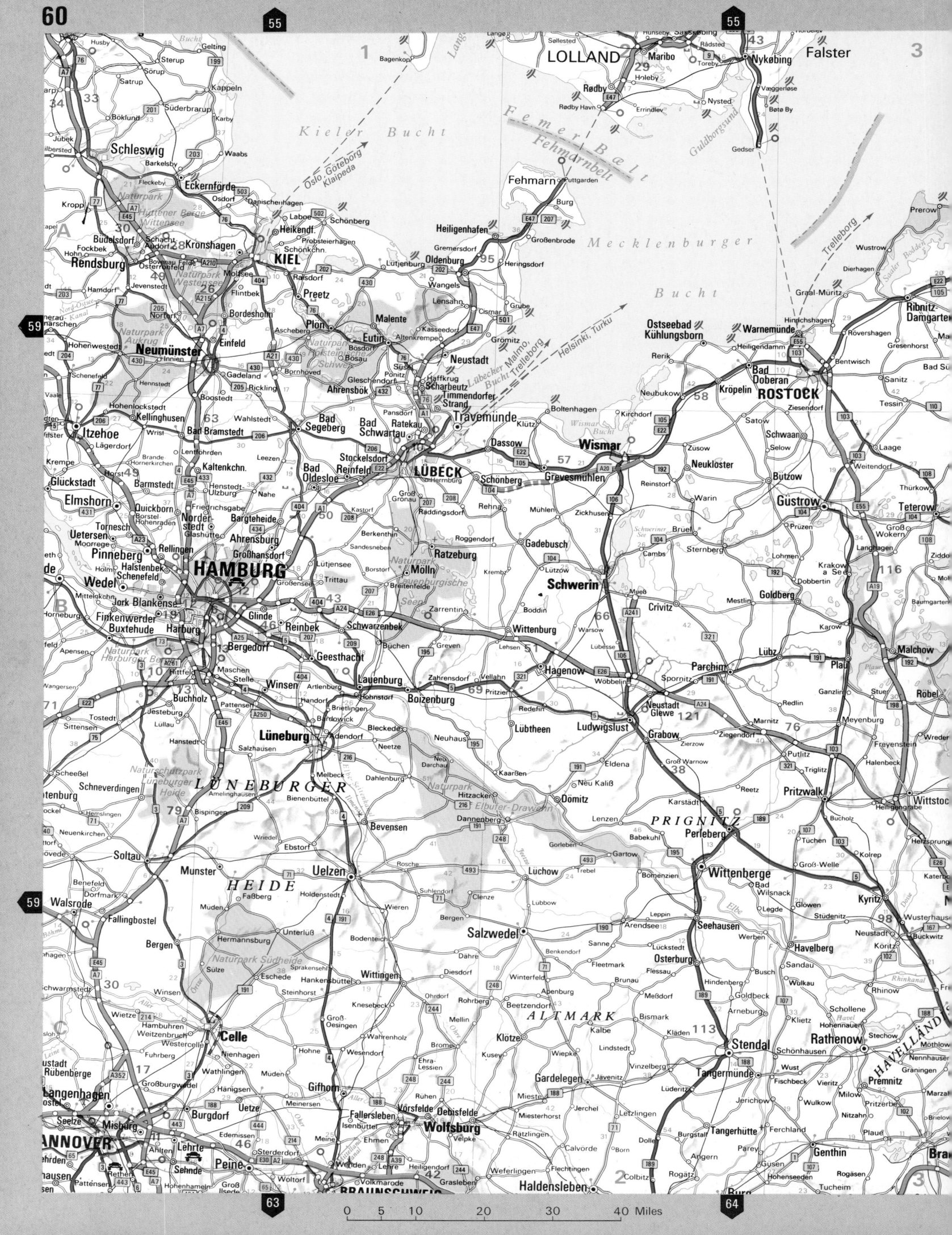

LOLLAND
Falster
Maribo
Nykøbing
Rødby
Gedser
Kieler Bucht
Femer Bælt
Fehmarnbelt
Fehmarn
Puttgarden
Burg
Heiligenhafen
Mecklenburger Bucht
Oslo, Göteborg, Klaipeda
Helsinki, Turku
Lübecker Malmö, Bucht Trelleborg
Trelleborg
Schleswig
Kappeln
Eckernförde
KIEL
Kronshagen
Rendsburg
Neumünster
Plön
Eutin
Malente
Preetz
Oldenburg
Neustadt
Grömitz
Ostseebad Kühlungsborn
Warnemünde
ROSTOCK
Bad Doberan
Ribnitz-Damgarten
Prerow
Travemünde
Bad Segeberg
Bad Schwartau
LÜBECK
Wismar
Grevesmühlen
Schönberg
Itzehoe
Bad Bramstedt
Kaltenkchn.
Bad Oldesloe
Glückstadt
Elmshorn
Pinneberg
Wedel
Norderstedt
Ahrensburg
HAMBURG
Ratzeburg
Mölln
Gadebusch
Schwerin
Bützow
Güstrow
Teterow
Sternberg
Goldberg
Buxtehude
Harburg
Bergedorf
Reinbek
Geesthacht
Schwarzenbek
Lauenburg
Boizenburg
Wittenburg
Hagenow
Ludwigslust
Parchim
Lübz
Plau
Malchow
Röbel
Winsen
Buchholz
Lüneburg
Grabow
Neustadt Glewe
Pritzwalk
Wittstock
Perleberg
Wittenberge
Kyritz
LÜNEBURGER HEIDE
PRIGNITZ
Soltau
Munster
Uelzen
Bevensen
Dömitz
Dannenberg
Lüchow
Salzwedel
Seehausen
Havelberg
Walsrode
Fallingbostel
Bergen
Celle
Wittingen
Osterburg
Stendal
Tangermünde
Rathenow
ALTMARK
HAVELLAND
Gifhorn
Gardelegen
Klötze
Wolfsburg
Fallersleben
Burgdorf
Lehrte
Peine
HANNOVER
Langenhagen
Haldensleben
Tangerhütte
Genthin
Premnitz
BRAUNSCHWEIG
Naturpark Lauenburgische Seen
Naturpark Südheide
Naturpark Elbufer-Drawehn

59

63 64

0 5 10 20 30 40 Miles

ØSTERSØEN

POLSKA

SZCZECIN (STETTIN)

BERLIN

POTSDAM

Frankfurt

Stralsund

Greifswald

Neubrandenburg

Neustrelitz

Gorzów Wielkopolski

Kołobrzeg

Stargard Szczeciński

0   10   20   30   40   50   60 Kilometres

58

59

17

Zwolle
Lingen
Nordhorn
Almelo
Oldenzaal
Deventer
Hengelo
ENSCHEDE
Gronau
Rheine
Bramsche
OSNABRÜCK
Minden
Lübbecke
Bad Oeynhausen
Herford
BIELEFELD
Detmold
Emsdetten
Greven
MÜNSTER
Warendorf
Gütersloh
Paderborn
Bocholt
Borken
Coesfeld
Dülmen
Haltern
Wesel
Ahlen
Lippstadt
Hamm
Soest
Marl
RECKLINGHAUSEN
Lünen
Gladbeck
BOTTROP
GELSENK
HERNE
DORTMUND
Unna
Moers
OBERHAUSEN
BOCHUM
ESSEN
DUISBURG
MÜLHEIM
Witten
KREFELD
HAGEN
Iserlohn
Arnsberg
Meschede
Brilon
Velbert
WUPPERTAL
Neheim Hüsten
DÜSSELDORF
MÖNCHENGLADBACH
Neuß
Rheydt
SOLINGEN
REMSCHEID
Lüdenscheid
Plettenberg
Korbach
Leverkusen
KÖLN
Bergisch Gladbach
Olpe
Siegen
Düren
Eschweiler
Stolberg
Euskirchen
BONN
Bad Godesberg
Siegburg
Marburg
Wetzlar
Gießen
Andernach
Neuwied
KOBLENZ
Limburg
Mayen
Boppard
WIESBADEN
FRANKFURT
OFFENBACH
Hanau
Bad Homburg
M Ü N S T E R L A N D
S A U E R L A N D
E i f e l
W e s t e r w a l d
Teutoburger Wald
Naturpark

17

66

67

0 5 10 20 30 40 Miles

59
60

HANNOVER
Langenhagen
Burgdorf
Gifhorn
Wolfsburg
Fallersleben
Vorsfelde
Gardelegen
Lüderitz
Genthin
Tangerhütte
Peine
Lehrte
Sehnde
Springe
Barsinghausen
Wunstorf
BRAUNSCHWEIG
Königslutter
Helmstedt
Haldensleben
Wolmirstedt
Burg
MAGDEBURG
Schönebeck
Zerbst
Wolfenbüttel
SALZGITTER
HILDESHEIM
Schöningen
Oschersleben
Wanzleben
Barby
Alfeld
Goslar
Seesen
Bad Harzburg
Wernigerode
Halberstadt
Quedlinburg
Aschersleben
Staßfurt
Bernburg
Köthen
Dessau
Holzminden
Einbeck
Northeim
Osterode
Clausthal-Zellerfeld
Blankenburg
Thale
Ballenstedt
Hettstedt
Eisleben
HALLE
Merseburg
Uslar
Herzberg
Bad Lauterberg
Braunlage
Harzgerode
Mansfeld
GÖTTINGEN
Duderstadt
Nordhausen
Sangerhausen
Querfurt
Münden
Witzenhausen
Heiligenstadt
Sondershausen
Bad Frankenhausen
Artern
Mücheln
Weissenfels
Naumburg
Zeitz
KASSEL
Eschwege
Mühlhausen
Bad Langensalza
Sömmerda
Apolda
Weimar
ERFURT
Jena
GERA
Eisenach
Gotha
Arnstadt
Bad Hersfeld
Fulda
Meiningen
Suhl
Ilmenau
Saalfeld
Rudolstadt
Zeulenroda
Plauen
Hof
Coburg
Sonneburg
Kronach
Kulmbach
Lichtenfels
Bad Kissingen
Schweinfurt
Hammelburg
Bad Brückenau
Bad Neustadt
Königshofen
Hildburghausen
Schleusingen
Münchberg
Selb
Wunsiedel
Harz
Hainleite
Finne
Thüringer Wald
Frankenwald
Naturpark Harz
Naturpark Hessische Rhön
Naturpark Bayerische Rhön
Naturpark Frankenwald
Naturpark Fichtelgebirge
Naturpark Haßberge
GRABFELD
Brocken 1153

0 10 20 30 40 50 60 Kilometres

64
64
67
68

60
61
63

Letzlingen
Tangerhütte
Ferchland
Genthin
Ketzin
POTSDAM
Teltow
Woltersdorf
Rüdersdorf
Erkner
Herzfelde
Heinersdorf
Podelzig
Brandenburg
Werder
Fürstenwalde
Frankfurt
Burg
Wolmirstedt
Michendorf
Blankenfelde
Ludwigsfelde
Rangsdorf
Königs Wusterhausen
Storkow
Bad Saarow-Pieskow
Müllrose
Brieskow-Finkenheerd
Barleben
MAGDEBURG
Ziesar
Beelitz
Zossen
Eisenhüttenstadt
Belzig
Brück
Beeskow
Gommern
Schönebeck
Treuenbrietzen
Luckenwalde
Baruth
Jüterbog
Lübben
Zerbst
Barby
Calbe
Roßlau
Wittenberg
Zahna
Dahme
Lübbenau
Aken
Dessau
Coswig
Luckau
Bernburg
Köthen
Oranienbaum
Kemberg
Jessen
Schweinitz
Herzberg
Calau
Cottbus
Gräfenhainichen
Raguhn
Jeßnitz
Wolfen
Bitterfeld
Bad Schmiedeberg
Bad Düben
Pretzsch
Finsterwalde
Doberlug-Kirchhain
Großräschen
Senftenberg
Welzow
Spremberg
Eisleben
HALLE
Landsberg
Delitzsch
Torgau
Falkenberg
Lauchhammer
Bad Liebenwerda
Elsterwerda
Schwarzheide
Lauta
Hoyerswerda
Merseburg
Schkeuditz
Eilenburg
Wurzen
Gröditz
Ruhland
Leuna
Bad Dürrenberg
Markranstädt
LEIPZIG
Brandis
Oschatz
Riesa
Strehla
Großenhain
Kamenz
Naunhof
Markkleeberg
Lützen
Weissenfels
Naumburg
Grimma
Leisnig
Meißen
Coswig
Radebeul
Radeberg
Bischofswerda
Bautzen
Hohenmölsen
Borna
Colditz
Döbeln
Roßwein
Nossen
Zeitz
Meuselwitz
Altenburg
Rochlitz
Geringswalde
Hartha
Waldheim
Mittweida
Freital
DRESDEN
Pirna
Heidenau
Sebnitz
Eisenberg
Hermsdorf
Schmölln
GERA
Ronneburg
Meerane
Glauchau
Limbach-Oberfrohna
Penig
Burgstädt
CHEMNITZ
Hainichen
Frankenberg
Freiberg
Flöha
Oederan
Dippoldiswalde
Glashütte
Bad Gottleuba
Königstein
Bad Schandau
Děčín
Crimmitschau
Werdau
Weida
Greiz
ZWICKAU
Lichtenstein
Hohenstein-Ernstthal
Stollberg
Zschopau
Olbernhau
Altenberg
Teplice
Ústí n. Labem
Zeulenroda
Reichenbach
Schneeberg
Aue
Annaberg-Buchholz
Marienberg
Most
Litvínov
Bílina
Litoměřice
Lovosice
Plauen
Auerbach
Falkenstein
Eibenstock
Johanngeorgenstadt
Chomutov
Kadaň
Louny
Roudnice n. Labem
Oelsnitz
Klingenthal
Hof
Rehau
Schwarzenbach
Selb
Aš
Münchberg
Marktredwitz
Wunsiedel
Cheb
Waldsassen
Karlovy Vary
Ostrov
Sokolov
Žatec
Slaný
Kladno
Kralupy n. Vltavou
PRAHA
Rakovník
Erzgebirge
Krušné hory
FLÄMING
SPREEWALD
LAUSITZ
CESKÁ REPUBLIKA

0 5 10 20 30 40 Miles

68
69

61
88

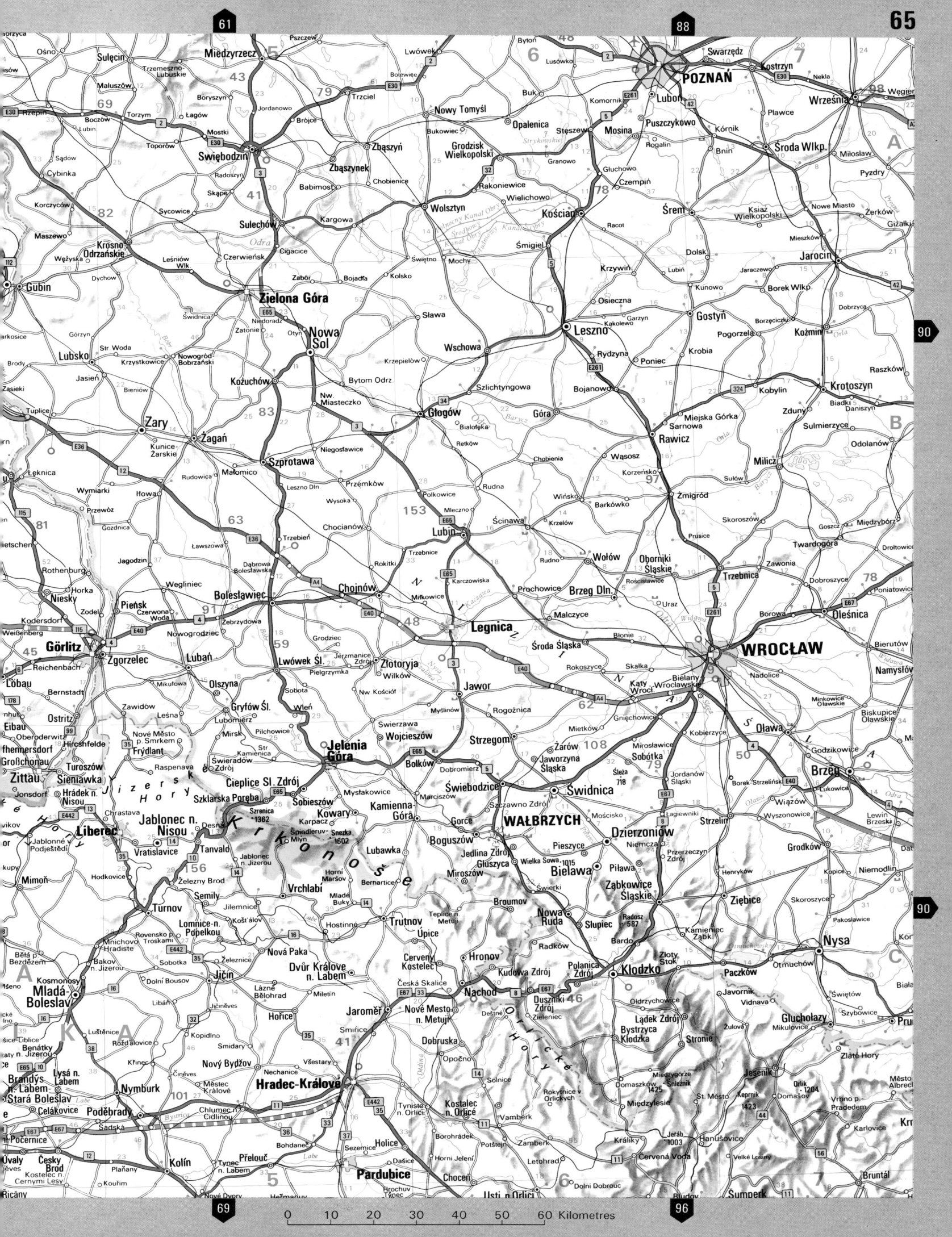
Międzyrzecz
Sulęcin
Ośno
Pszczew
Lwówek
Bytoń
Lusówko
POZNAŃ
Swarzędz
Kostrzyn
Nekla
Września
Trzemeszno-Lubuskie
Maluszów
Boryszyn
Torzym
Łagów
Trzciel
Nowy Tomyśl
Opalenica
Buk
Komorniki
Luboń
Puszczykowo
Mosina
Stęszew
Kórnik
Bnin
Środa Wlkp.
Miłosław
Pyzdry
Rzepin
Boczów
Lubin
Mostki
Toporów
Świebodzin
Zbąszyń
Zbąszynek
Grodzisk Wielkopolski
Rakoniewice
Wielichowo
Granowo
Głuchowo
Czempiń
Rogalin
Plawce
Cybinka
Sądów
Radoszyn
Skąpe
Babimost
Chobienice
Wolsztyn
Kościan
Śrem
Książ Wielkopolski
Nowe Miasto
Żerków
Gizałki
Korczyców
Sycowice
Sulechów
Kargowa
Śmigiel
Racot
Dolsk
Mieszków
Jarocin
Maszewo
Krosno Odrzańskie
Wężyska
Czerwieńsk
Cigacice
Odra
Leśniów Wlk.
Świętno
Mochy
Krzywiń
Lubiń
Jaraczewo
Gubin
Dychow
Zielona Góra
Zabór
Bojadła
Kolsko
Kunowo
Borek Wlkp.
Osieczna
Świdnica
Niedoradz
Zatonie
Otyń
Nowa Sól
Sława
Leszno
Kąkolewo
Garzyn
Gostyń
Dobrzyca
Borzęciczki
Koźmin
Górzyn
Lubsko
Str. Woda
Nowogród Bobrzański
Krzystkowice
Wschowa
Rydzyna
Pogorzela
Krobia
Poniec
Brody
Jasień
Kożuchów
Krzepielów
Bytom Odrz.
Szlichtyngowa
Bojanowo
Kobylin
Krotoszyn
Raszków
Tuplice
Bieniów
Nw. Miasteczko
Głogów
Góra
Rawicz
Miejska Górka
Sarnowa
Zduny
Biadki
Daniszyn
Żary
Żagań
Kunice-Żarskie
Szprotawa
Niegosławice
Białołęka
Retków
Wąsosz
Sulmierzyce
Odolanów
Milicz
Łęknica
Rudowica
Małomice
Przemków
Leszno Dln
Chobienia
Rudna
Wińsko
Barkówko
Korzeńsko
Żmigród
Sułów
Wymiarki
Iłowa
Przewóz
Gozdnica
Wysoka
Polkowice
Mleczno
Ścinawa
Krzelów
Skoroszów
Międzybórz
Chocianów
Lubin
Trzebień
Prusice
Goszcz
Twardogóra
Łazowa
Jagodzin
Rothenburg
Dąbrowa Bolesławska
Rokitki
Trzebnice
Rudno
Wołów
Oborniki Śląskie
Zawonia
Trzebnica
Dobroszyce
Drołtowice
Horka
Niesky
Węgliniec
Bolesławiec
Chojnów
Karczowiska
Miłkowice
Prochowice
Brzeg Dln.
Rościsławice
Uraz
Poniatowice
Oleśnica
Kodersdorf
Zodel
Pieńsk
Czerwona Woda
Żebrzydowa
Nowogrodziec
Malczyce
Borowa
Weißenberg
Görlitz
Zgorzelec
Lubań
Grodziec
Lwówek Śl.
Jerzmanice Zdrój
Złotoryja
Wilków
Pielgrzymka
Legnica
Środa Śląska
Błonie
Wrocław
Bierutów
Namysłów
Reichenbach
Löbau
Bernstadt
Mikułowa
Olszyna
Sobota
Nw. Kościół
Jawor
Rokoszyce
Skałka
Kąty Wrocł.
Bielany Wrocławskie
Nadolice
Minkowice Oławskie
Biskupice Oławskie
Zawidów
Leśna
Gryfów Śl.
Ostritz
Lubomierz
Wleń
Myślinów
Rogoźnica
Gniechowice
Świerzawa
Wojcieszów
Mietków
Kobierzyce
Oława
Eibau
Oberoderwitz
Hirschfelde
Nové Město p. Smrkem
Frýdlant
Mirsk
Pilchowice
Str. Kamienica
Świeradów Zdrój
Jelenia Góra
Bolków
Strzegom
Żarów
Jaworzyna Śląska
Mirosławice
Sobótka
Ślęża 718
Jordanów Śląski
Borek Strzeliński
Godzikowice
Brzeg
Łukowice
Seifhennersdorf
Großschönau
Zittau
Turoszów
Sieniawka
Jonsdorf
Hrádek n. Nisou
Raspenava
Jizerské Hory
Cieplice Śl. Zdrój
Szklarska Poręba
Mysłakowice
Sobieszów
Dobromierz
Świebodzice
Świdnica
Szczawno Zdrój
Marciszów
Wiązów
Lewin Brzeski
Chrastava
Jablonec n. Nisou
Liberec
Desná
Szrenica 1362
Krkonoše
Karpacz
Kowary
Kamienna Góra
Gorce
Wałbrzych
Mościsko
Łagiewniki
Strzelin
Wyszonowice
Jablonné v Podještědí
Vratislavice
Tanvald
Jablonec n. Jizerou
Špindlerův Mlýn
Sněžka 1602
Lubawka
Boguszów
Jedlina Zdrój
Głuszyca
Wielka Sowa 1015
Pieszyce
Dzierżoniów
Niemcza
Przerzeczyn Zdrój
Grodków
Bielawa
Piława
Mimoň
Hodkovice
Železný Brod
Horní Maršov
Bernartice
Mieroszów
Ząbkowice Śląskie
Henryków
Kopice
Niemodlin
Vrchlabí
Semily
Jilemnice
Mladé Buky
Broumov
Teplice n. Metují
Nowa Ruda
Słupiec
Radosz 587
Ziębice
Skoroszyce
Turnov
Lomnice n. Popelkou
Košťálov
Hostinné
Trutnov
Úpice
Kamieniec Ząbk.
Pakosławice
Nysa
Rovensko p. Troskami
Mnichovo Hradiště
Nová Paka
Radków
Bardo
Złoty Stok
Otmuchów
Paczków
Bělá p. Bezdězem
Bakov n. Jizerou
Sobotka
Železnice
Jičín
Dvůr Králové n. Labem
Červený Kostelec
Hronov
Kudowa Zdrój
Polanica Zdrój
Kłodzko
Kosmonosy
Dolní Bousov
Lázně Bělohrad
Miletín
Česká Skalice
Náchod
Duszniki Zdrój
Zieleniec
Mladá Boleslav
Libáň
Jičíněves
Hořice
Jaroměř
Nové Město n. Metují
Dešťné
Oldrzychowice
Lądek Zdrój
Javorník
Vidnava
Bystrzyca Kłodzka
Stronie
Głuchołazy
Mikulovice
Świętów
Szybowice
Luštěnice
Kopidlno
Rožďalovice
Smidary
Smiřice
Dobruška
Opočno
Orlické Hory
Žulová
Zlaté Hory
Benátky n. Jizerou
Kněžice
Nový Bydžov
Nechanice
Všestary
Hradec Králové
Solnice
Domaszków
Śnieżnik 1425
Międzygórze
Jeseník
Orlík 1204
Město Albrechtice
Brandýs n. Labem-Stará Boleslav
Lysá n. Labem
Činěves
Městec Králové
Nymburk
Chlumec n. Cidlinou
Týniště n. Orlicí
Kostelec n. Orlicí
Vamberk
Międzylesie
Keprník 1423
St. Město
Domašov
Vrbno p. Pradědem
Čelákovice
Poděbrady
Sadská
Bohdaneč
Holice
Sezemice
Borohrádek
Potštejn
Zamberk
Rokytnice v Orlických
Králiky
Jeřáb 1003
Hanušovice
Karlovice
Počernice
Úvaly
Český Brod
Kostelec n. Černými Lesy
Kolín
Týnec n. Labem
Přelouč
Plaňany
Kouřim
Pardubice
Dašice
Horní Jelení
Choceň
Letohrad
Červená Voda
Velké Losiny
Bruntál
Říčany
Nové Dvory
Hrochův Týnec
Ústí n. Orlicí
Dolní Dobrouc
Šumperk

90
90
69
96

0 10 20 30 40 50 60 Kilometres

17   62

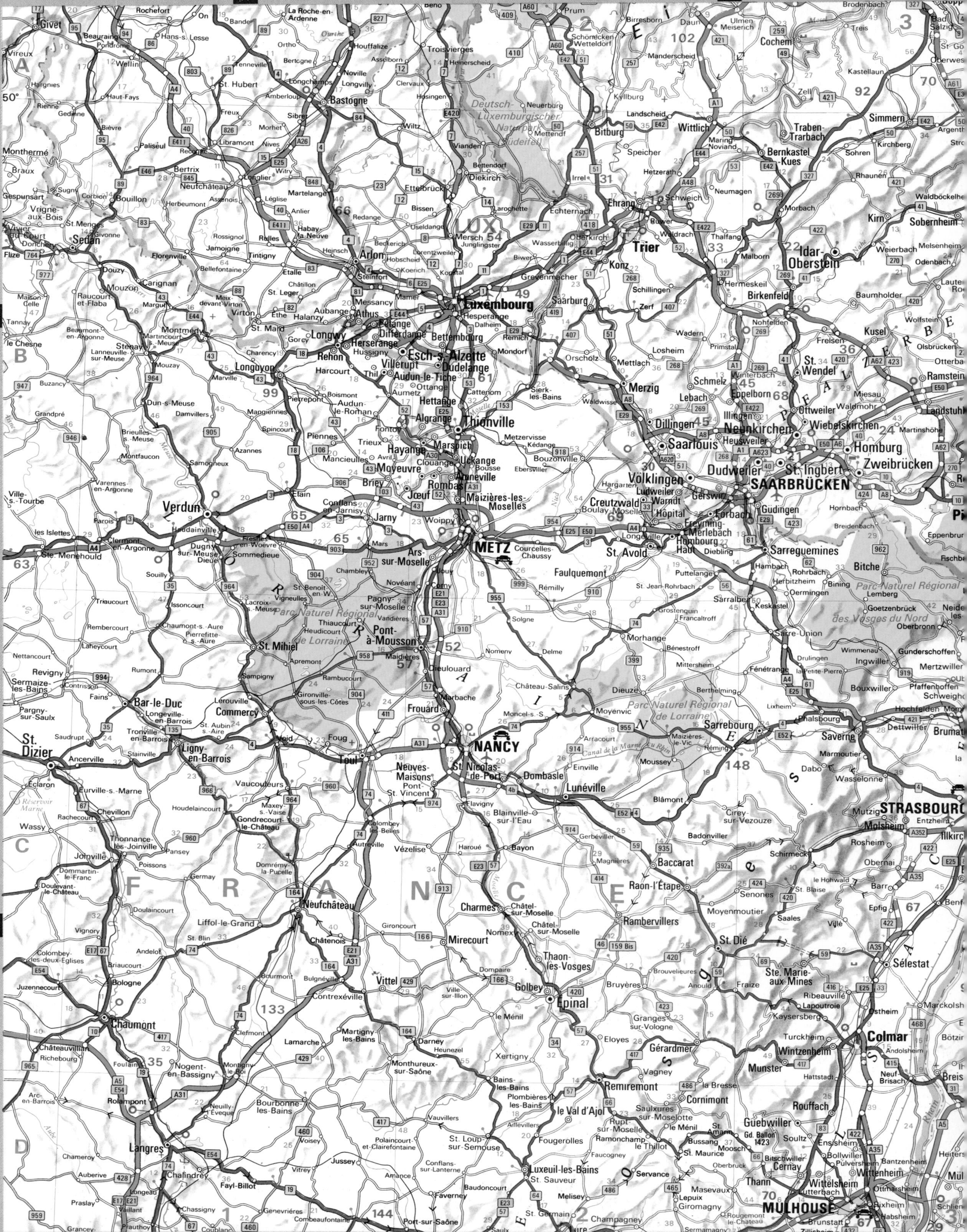

A

B

21

63

C

21

D

25   70

FRANCE

Luxembourg
LUX

Trier

SAARBRÜCKEN

METZ

NANCY

STRASBOURG

Colmar

MULHOUSE

Verdun

Bar-le-Duc

St. Dizier

Chaumont

Langres

Épinal

Bastogne

Arlon

Sedan

Bouillon

Thionville

Esch-s-Alzette

Saarlouis

Völklingen

Dudweiler

Idar-Oberstein

Homburg

Zweibrücken

Neunkirchen

Forbach

Sarreguemines

Saverne

Lunéville

St. Dié

Gérardmer

Remiremont

Parc Naturel Régional de Lorraine

Parc Naturel Régional des Vosges du Nord

Deutsch-Luxemburgischer Naturpark Südeifel

0   5   10   20   30   40 Miles

62 63

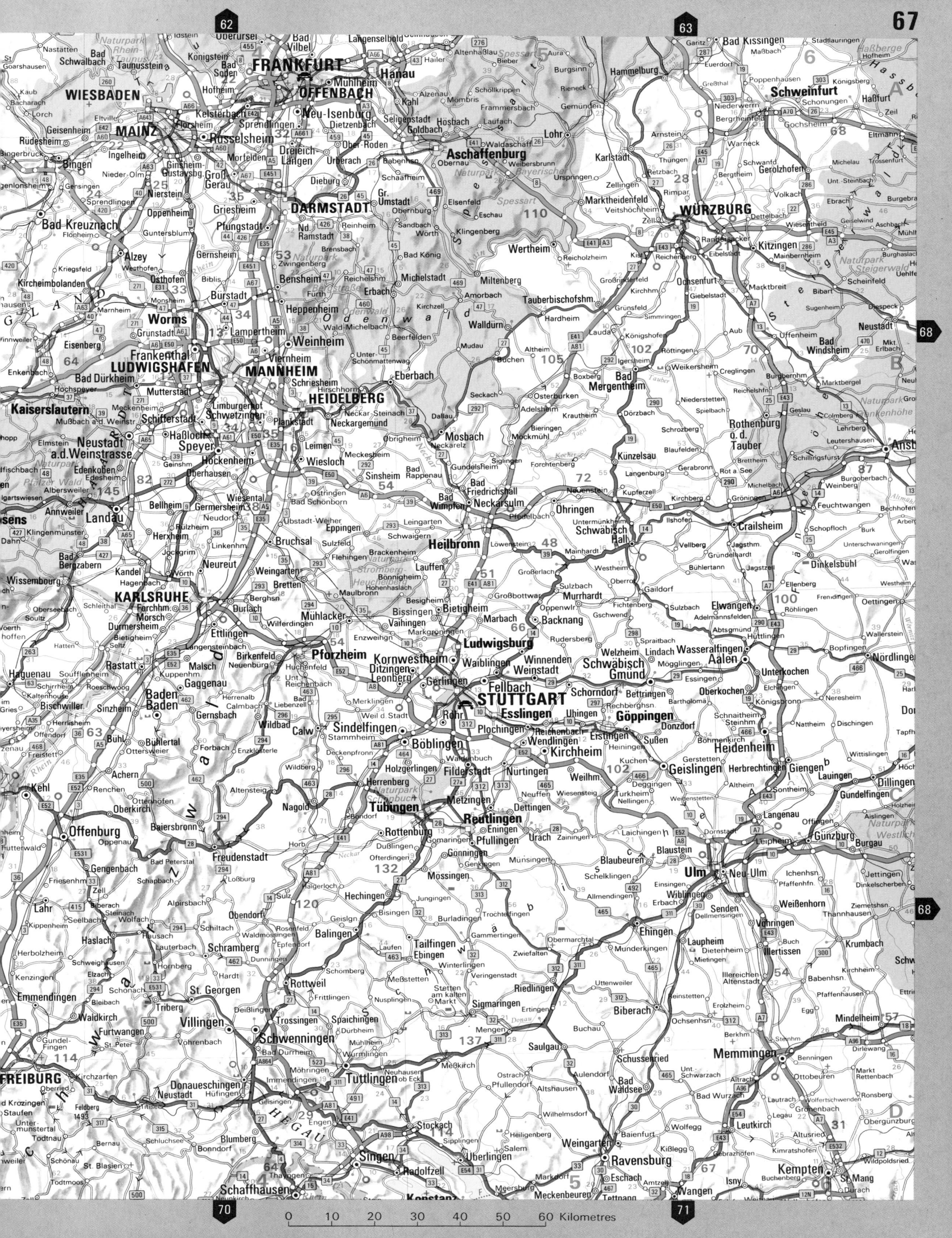
FRANKFURT
OFFENBACH
WIESBADEN
MAINZ
Hanau
Aschaffenburg
DARMSTADT
Würzburg
Schweinfurt
Kitzingen
Bad Kreuznach
Alzey
Worms
Kaiserslautern
LUDWIGSHAFEN
MANNHEIM
HEIDELBERG
Frankenthal
Bad Dürkheim
Neustadt a.d.Weinstrasse
Speyer
Landau
Weinheim
Bensheim
Heppenheim
Wertheim
Tauberbischofshm.
Bad Mergentheim
Rothenburg o.d. Tauber
Mosbach
Heilbronn
Neckarsulm
Öhringen
Schwäbisch Hall
Crailsheim
Dinkelsbühl
KARLSRUHE
Bruchsal
Pforzheim
Ludwigsburg
Bietigheim
Backnang
STUTTGART
Esslingen
Böblingen
Sindelfingen
Göppingen
Schwäbisch Gmünd
Aalen
Nördlingen
Heidenheim
Baden Baden
Rastatt
Offenburg
Kehl
Tübingen
Reutlingen
Ulm
Neu-Ulm
Günzburg
Freudenstadt
Rottweil
Villingen
Schwenningen
Tuttlingen
Sigmaringen
Biberach
Memmingen
Kempten
Ravensburg
Singen
Schaffhausen
FREIBURG
Donaueschingen
Naturpark Spessart
Odenwald
Schwarzwald
Schwäbische Alb
HEGAU

0 10 20 30 40 50 60 Kilometres

68 68 70 71

63 64

67

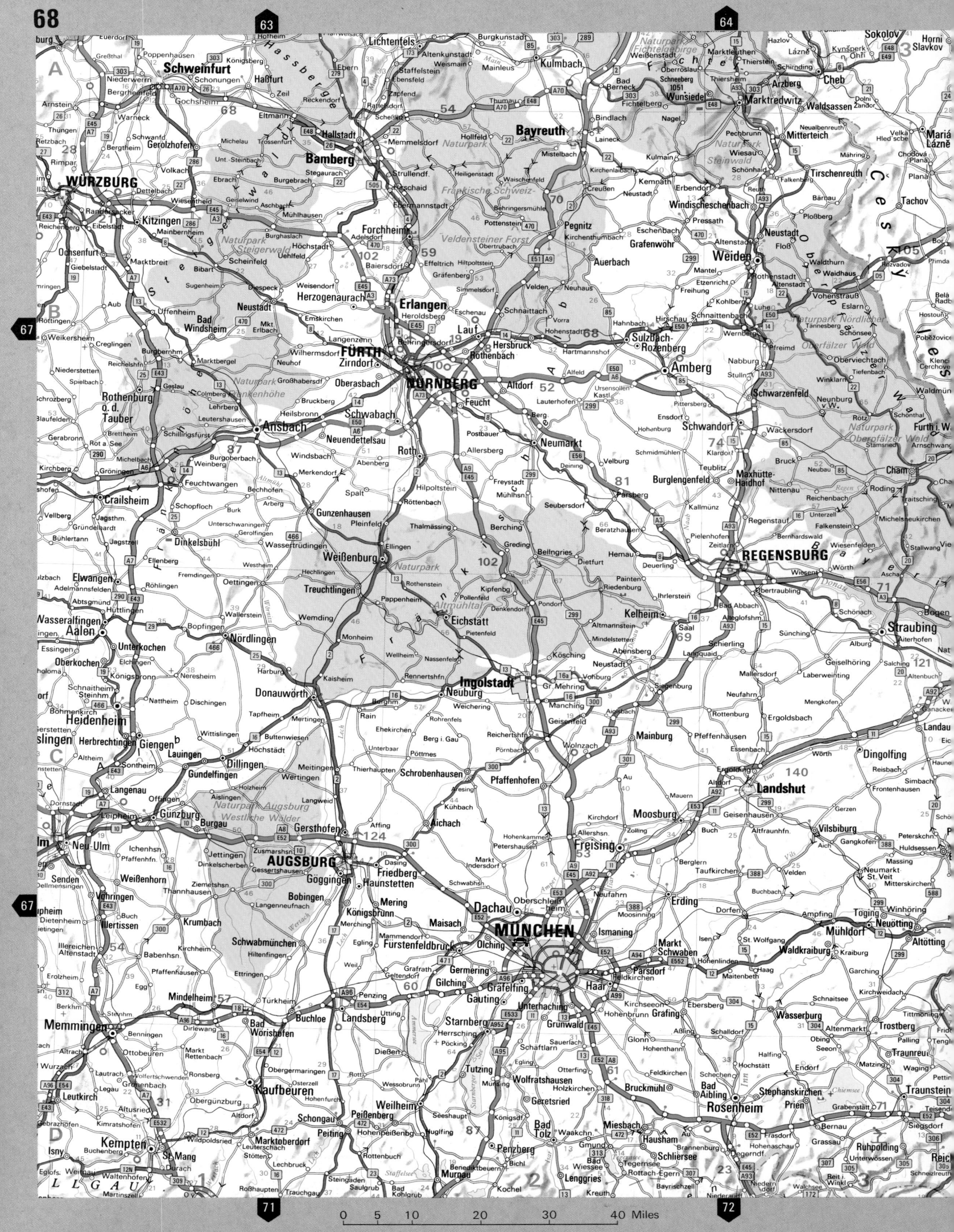
Schweinfurt
Haßfurt
Lichtenfels
Kulmbach
Bamberg
Bayreuth
Wunsiedel
Marktredwitz
Cheb
WÜRZBURG
Kitzingen
Forchheim
Erlangen
Herzogenaurach
Weiden
Neustadt
Bad Windsheim
FÜRTH
NÜRNBERG
Lauf
Hersbruck
Sulzbach-Rosenberg
Amberg
Rothenburg o. d. Tauber
Ansbach
Schwabach
Neumarkt
Schwandorf
Cham
Crailsheim
Gunzenhausen
Dinkelsbühl
Weißenburg
REGENSBURG
Straubing
Kelheim
Eichstätt
Treuchtlingen
Nördlingen
Aalen
Heidenheim
Donauwörth
Neuburg
Ingolstadt
Landshut
Dingolfing
Dillingen
Günzburg
Augsburg
Freising
Moosburg
Erding
Dachau
MÜNCHEN
Neu-Ulm
Memmingen
Kaufbeuren
Landsberg
Starnberg
Rosenheim
Traunstein
Kempten
Füssen
Bad Tölz
Miesbach
Weilheim
Mühldorf
Wasserburg
Fränkische Schweiz
Veldensteiner Forst
Naturpark Steigerwald
Naturpark Frankenhöhe
Altmühltal
Naturpark Augsburg Westliche Wälder
Český les
Oberpfälzer Wald
Bayerischer Wald
ALLGÄU

71 72

0 5 10 20 30 40 Miles

64 65

PRAHA
Kladno
Nové Strašecí
Tuchlovice
Velká Dobrá
Unhošť
Jeneč
Chýnava
Kyje
Horní Počernice
Úvaly
Český Brod
Úhříněves
Kostelec n. Černými Lesy
Sadská
Kolín
Týnec n. Labem
Přelouč
Bohdaneč
Labe
Bochov
Lubenec
Bečov n. Teplou
Jesenice
Rakovník
Žlutice
Toužim
Žihle
Čistá
Stvolny
Manětín
Kralovice
Teplá
Plasy
Kaznějov
Dolní Bělá
Úněšov
Rudná
Beroun
Radotín
Modřany
Zbraslav
Říčany
Jesenice
Mnichovice
Zásmuky
Kutná Hora
Čáslav
Nové Dvory
Heřmanův Městec
Vrdy
Slatiňany
Ronov n. Doubravou
Zdice
Řevnice
Dobřichovice
Davle
Jílové u. Prahy
Senohraby
Sázava
Uhlířské-Janovice
Mníšek p. Brdy
Štěchovice
Nový Knín
Žebrák
Hořovice
Hostomice
Zbiroh
Radnice
Mýto
Třemošná
Město Touškov
Chrást
Černošín
Stříbro
Kozolupy
Pernarec
Nýřany
PLZEŇ
Rokycany
Starý Plzenec
Strašice
Jince
Dobříš
Příbram
Poříčí n. Sázavou
Benešov
Divišov
Pyšely
Čestín
Zbraslavice
Zruč n. Sázavou
Ledeč n. Sázavou
Golčův Jeníkov
Habry
Vilémov
Trhová Kamenice
Chotěboř
Neveklov
Bystřice
Vlašim
Světlá n. Sázavou
Dolní Kralovice
Česká Bělá
Zahrádka
Havlíčkův Brod
Přibyslav
Kladruby
Chotěšov
Líně
Mirošov
Spálené Poříčí
Rožmitál p. Třemšínem
Milín
Kamýk n. Vltavou
Sedlčany
Jankov
Votice
Načeradec
Čechtice
Holýšov
Stod
Merklín
Přeštice
Seč
Blovice
Nové Mitrovice
Krásná Hora n. Vltavou
Sedlec-Prčice
Miličín
Mladá Vožice
Lukavec
Košetice
Křelovice
Humpolec
Staňkov
Horšovský Týn
Koloveč
Borovy
Březnice
Orlická přehr. n.
Stare Sedlo
Mirovice
Bělčice
Jistebnice
Ratibořské Hory
Pacov
Červená Řečice
Štoky
Polná
Dražeňov
Domažlice
Kout na Šumave
Švihov
Nepomuk
Kasejovice
Petrovice
Milevsko
Vetrny Jeníkov
Leskovice
Pelhřimov
Jihlava
Klatovy
Kdyně
Blatná
Mirotice
Zvíkovské Podhradí
Opařany
Tábor
Chýnov
Sezimovo-Ústí
Černovice
Horní Cerekev
Batelov
Luka n. Jihlavou
Všeruby
Plánice
Nalžovské Hory
Horažďovice
Velký Bor
Sedlice
Záhoří
Bernartice
Malšice
Planá n. Lužnicí
Písek
Bechyně
Sudoměřice u Bechyně
Tučapy
Kamenice n. Lipou
Počátky
Žirovnice
Třešť
Brtnice
Stonařov
Nýrsko
Janovice n. Úhlavou
Běšiny
Kolinec
Rabí
Katovice
Strakonice
Kraselov
Albrechtice n. Vltavou
Deštná
Jarošov n. Nežárkou
Okříšky
Předín
Kötzting
Lam
Sušice
Hartmanice
Drahonice
Protivín
Temelín
Týn n. Vltavou
Soběslav
Veselí n. Lužnicí
Kardašova Řečice
Studená
Strmilov
Telč
Želatava
Arnbruck
Bayerisch Eisenstein
Kašperské Hory
Volyně
Vodňany
Jindřichův Hradec
Kunžak
Budeč
Drachselsried
Gr. Arber
Bodenmais
Naturpark Bayerischer Wald
Stachy
Bavorov
Vlachovo Březí
Netolice
Hluboká n. Vltavou
Ševětín
Lomnice n. Lužnicí
Stráž n. Nežárkou
Dačice
Patersdorf
Zwiesel
Srní
Vimperk
Husinec
Prachatice
Lišov
Třeboň
Nová Bystřice
Slavonice
Jemnice
Moravské Budějovice
Dešov
Frauenau
Kvilda
České Budějovice
Chlum u Třeboně
Litschau
Kautzen
Dobersberg
Regen
Klingenbrunn
St. Oswald
Horní Vltavice
Smědeč
Ledenice
Kirchdf.
Volary
Křemže
Kamenný Újezd
Borovany
Suchdol n. Lužnicí
Brand
Heidenreichstein
Drosendorf
Raabs
Grafling
Offenberg
Metten
Lalling
Grafenau
Philippsreut
Strážný
Chvalšiny
Trhové Sviny
Waidhofen a.d. Thaya
Deggendorf
Schönberg
Velešín
Nové Hrady
Schrems
Groß-Siegharts
Geras
Plattling
Hengersbg.
Freyung
Altreichenau
Horní Planá
Český Krumlov
Větřní
Horní Stropnice
Hoheneich
Gmünd
Vitis
Schwarzenau
Göpfritz a.d. Wild
Fürstenstein
Jandelsbrunn
Kaplice
České Velenice
Weitra
Osterhofen
Winzer
Tittling
Waldkchn.
Breitenbg.
Ulrichsberg
Černá v Pošumaví
Lipenská přehr. nádrz
Benešov n. Černou
St. Martin
Allentsteig
Großglobnitz
Horn
Aicha
Prag
Aigen i. M.
Frymburk
Dolní Dvořiště
Jagenbach
Hilgartsberg
Ruderting
Hauzenberg
Vyšší Brod
Leopold schlag
Großpertholz
Zwettl
Gars-a-Kamp
Kamp
Pleinting
Vilshofen
Göttersdf
Windorf
Wegscheid
Kollerschlag
Oepping
Haslach a.d. Mühl
Karlstift
Großgerungs
Rudmanns
Aldersbach
Sandbach
Heining
Obernzell
Rohrbach
Vorderweißenbach
Rainbach i. Mühlkreis
Sandl
Gföhl
Ortenburg
Passau
Fürstenzell
Engelhartszell
Donau
Hofkirchen i.M.
Helfenbg
Bad Leonfelden
Freistadt
Liebenau
Lichtenau
Langenlois
Johanniskirchen
Schmidham
Wernstein
Munzkchn.
Lembach
Zwettl a.d. Rodl
St. Oswald b. Freist
Weitersfelden
Arbesbach
Grafenschlag
Lengenfeld
Griesbach
Neuhaus
Schärding
Altenfelden
Neufelden
Oberneukirchen
Unterweißenbach
Weißenkchn. i.d.W.
Krems a.d. Donau
Birnbch.
Ruhstorf
St. Roman
Waldkchn. a. Wesen
Reichenau i. Mühlkreis
Neumarkt i. Mühlkn.
St. Leonhard b. Freistadt
Königswiesen
Ottenschlag
Rohrend
Mautern
Taufkirchen a.d. Pram
Rotthalmünster
Pocking
Suben
Andorf
Aschach a.d. D.
Feldkirchen a.d. Donau
Gallneukirchen
Hagenberg
Pregarten
Bad Zell
Weinsberg 1039
Martinsbg
Spitz
Aggsbach Dorf
Antiesenhfn.
Raab
Peuerbach
Ottensheim
Tragwein
Pabneukirchen
St. Georgen a.W.
Laimbach a. Ostrong
Poggstall
Aggsbach Markt
Malching
Egglfing
Waizenkchn
Eferding
Wilhering
St. Georgen a.d. G.
Kreuzen
Waldhsn Str G.
Simbach
St. Martin
Riedau
Alkoven
Leonding
LINZ
Mauthausen
Perg
Grein
Pöchlarn
Melk
Loosdorf
Karlstetten
St. Pölten
Braunau
Altheim
Aurolzmünster
Kallham
Grieskirchen
Hörsching
Weng
Ried i. Innkreis
Traun
Markt St. Florian
Enns
Baumgartenbg
Persenbeug
Neukirchen
Aspach
Haag
Meggenhfn
Pichl b. Wels
Wels
St. Valentin
Strengbg
Ybbs a.d. Donau
St. Leonhard a. Forst
Ob. Grafendf
Burghausen
Hochburg-Ach
Mauerkirchen
Hohnhart
St. Johann a.W.
Eberschwang
Kematen
Steinhaus
Neuhofen
Wieselburg
Mank
Kilb
Rabenstein
Wilhelmsburg
Mattighofen
Schalchen
Ampflwang
Stadl-Paura
Lambach
Kematen a.d. Kr.
Haag
Wolfsbach
Aschbach Markt
Amstetten
Ostermiething
Munderfing
Frankenburg
Schwanenstadt
Steinerkchn a.d. Traun
Kremsmünster
Sierning
Steyr
St. Peter i.d. Au
Purgstall
Traisen
Egglesberg
Ungenach
Vöcklabruck
Sattledt
Bad Hall
Garsten
Seitenstetten Markt
Randegg
Scheibbs
Kirchberg a.d. P.
Lilienfeld
Lamprechtshsn
Vöcklamarkt
Timelkam
Lenzing
Attnang-Puchheim
Vorchdf
Wartberg
Waidhofen a.d. Ybbs
Gresten
Frankenfels
Oberndorf b. Salzburg
Strasswalchen
Frankenmarkt
Seewalchen
Schörfling
Pettenbach
Grünburg
Ternberg
Maria Neustift
Losenstein
St. Anton a.d. J.
Gaming
Puchenstuben
Türnitz
Hohenberg
Obertrum
Wallersee
Neumarkt a.W.
St. Georgen i.A.
Altmünster
Gmunden
Kirchdorf a.d. Krems
Gaflenz
Ybbsitz
Seekirchen Markt
Henndorf a.W.
Oberwang
Weyregg
Traunsee
Micheldorf
Großraming
Weyer
Opponitz
St. Georgen a.R.
Annaberg
Freilassing
Anthering
Thalgau
Mondsee
Attersee (Kammersee)
Unterach
Neukirchen
Grünau i. Almtal
Klaus a.d. Pyhrnbahn
Lunz a. See
St. Aegyd a.N.
Schwarzau i. Geb.
Anger
Lorenz
Mondsee
Ebensee
Hollenstein a.d. Ybbs
Göstling a.d. Ybbs
Göstlinger Alpen
Mariazell
SALZBURG
St. Gilgen
Sengsengebirge
Windischgarsten
Altenmarkt
Gußwerk
St. Wolfgang
Wolfgangsee
Laussa
Palfau
Mürzsteg
Grödig
Puch
Hallein
Bad Ischl
Hintersee
Totesgebirge
Hinterstoder
St. Gallen
Weißenbach a.d. E.
Gams b. Hieflau
Kapellen
Bischofswiesen
Vigaun
Bad Goisern
Potschen
Altaussee
Pyhrn Pass
Wildalpen
Enns
ČESKÁ REPUBLIKA
Brdy
Českomoravská vrchovina
Šumava
Bayerischer Wald
Otava
Vltava
Sázava
Lužnice
Dyje

96
96

0 10 20 30 40 50 60 Kilometres

66 67

25

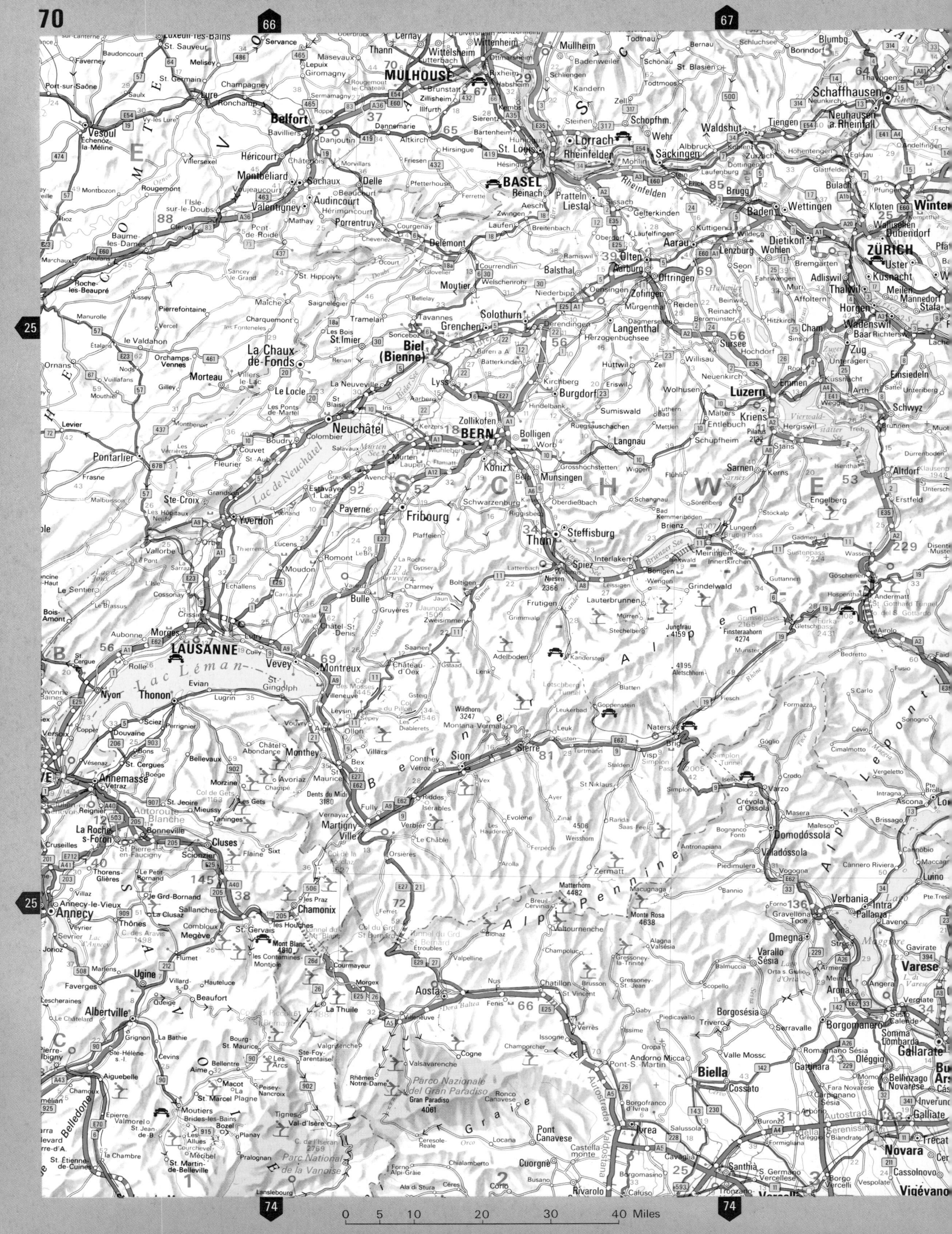
MULHOUSE
BASEL
Belfort
Montbéliard
Vesoul
Lure
Mulhouse
Lörrach
Rheinfelden
Säckingen
Waldshut
Schaffhausen
Neuhausen a. Rheinfall
Baden
Wettingen
ZÜRICH
Winterthur
Uster
Kloten
Dübendorf
Dietikon
Thalwil
Horgen
Wädenswil
Meilen
Männedorf
Stäfa
Aarau
Olten
Oftringen
Zofingen
Liestal
Pratteln
Reinach
Delémont
Porrentruy
Moutier
Solothurn
Grenchen
Biel (Bienne)
La Chaux-de-Fonds
Le Locle
Neuchâtel
BERN
Burgdorf
Langenthal
Sursee
Luzern
Kriens
Emmen
Zug
Cham
Baar
Schwyz
Einsiedeln
Altdorf
Erstfeld
Sarnen
Stans
Thun
Steffisburg
Interlaken
Spiez
Fribourg
Payerne
Yverdon
Pontarlier
Ste-Croix
Vallorbe
Morges
LAUSANNE
Vevey
Montreux
Nyon
Thonon
Evian
Annemasse
Bonneville
Cluses
Annecy
Chamonix
Mont Blanc 4810
Albertville
Ugine
Megève
Martigny
Sion
Sierre
Brig
Visp
Zermatt
Aosta
Biella
Ivrea
Domodóssola
Verbania
Varese
Gallarate
Novara
Vigévano
Borgomanero
Lac Léman
Lac de Neuchâtel
Alpi Pennine
Alpi Graie
Alpi Lepontine
Jungfrau 4159
Matterhorn 4482
Monte Rosa 4638
Gran Paradiso 4061
Parco Nazionale del Gran Paradiso
Parc National de la Vanoise
S C H W E I Z
A l p e n

0 5 10 20 30 40 Miles

25

74 74

67
68

Ravensburg
Kempten
Friedrichshafen
Konstanz
Lindau
Bregenz
Dornbirn
St. Gallen
Feldkirch
Bludenz
ALLGAU
Bodensee
Marktoberdorf
Füssen
Garmisch-Partenkirchen
Zugspitze 2963
INNSBRUCK
Solbad Hall i.T.
Imst
Landeck
Lechtaler Alpen
Stubaier Alpen
Ötztaler Alpen
Wildspitze 3774
LIECH
Chur
Davos
Silvrettahorn 3248
St. Moritz
Piz. Bernina 4055
Merano (Meran)
Bolzano (Bozen)
Brenner Pass 1374
Ortles 3899
Parco Nazionale dello Stelvio
Sóndrio
Tirano
Alpi Orobie
Trento
Rovereto
Bellinzona
Lugano
Como
Lecco
BERGAMO
BRÉSCIA
Lago di Garda
Vicenza
VERONA
MILANO
Monza
Crema
Lodi
Desenzano d. Garda
Peschiera d. Garda
Villafranca di Verona

72
72

75
75

0 10 20 30 40 50 60 Kilometres

68 69

71

SALZBURG
INNSBRUCK
Bad Reichenhall
Kufstein
Wörgl
Kitzbühel
Saalfelden
Zell am See
Bischofshofen
Hallein
Garmisch-Partenkirchen
Penzberg
Miesbach
Bad Tölz
Lenggries
Schwaz
Mayrhofen
Lienz
Spittal
Bad Ischl
Badgastein
Hohe Tauern
Zillertaler Alpen
Stubaier Alpen
Gail Taler Alpen
Alpi Carniche
Dolomiti
Merano (Meran)
Bolzano (Bozen)
Bressanone (Brixen)
Brunico (Bruneck)
Cortina d'Ampezzo
Belluno
Trento
Rovereto
Feltre
Vittorio Veneto
Conegliano
Pordenone
Udine
Gorízia
Monfalcone
TRIESTE
Treviso
Mestre
VENÉZIA
PADOVA
Vicenza
VERONA
Bassano d. Grappa
Castelfranco Veneto
Schio
Thiene
Valdagno
Asiago
Portogruaro
S. Donà di Piave
Lido di Iésolo
Grado
Cividale d. Friuli
Gemona d. Friuli
Tolmezzo
Palmanova
Latisana
Koper
Izola
Piran
Portorož

0 5 10 20 30 40 Miles

71

76 76

69
96

Ebensee
Totesgebirge
Sengsengebirge
Ennstaler Alpen
Göstlinger Alpen
Hochschwab
Liezen
Bad Mitterndorf
Admont
Eisenerz
Eisenerzer Alpen
Rottenmanner Tauern
Wölzer Tauern
Leoben
Kapfenberg
Bruck a.d. Mur
Trofaiach
Mürzzuschlag
Mürzsteg
Kindberg
Neunkirchen
Gloggnitz
Ternitz
Pottschach
Sopron
Mattersburg
Fohnsdorf
Knittelfeld
Judenburg
Zeltweg
Murau
Tamsweg
Frohnleiten
Gleinalpe
Weiz
Gratkorn
GRAZ
Köflach
Voitsberg
Barnbach
Gleisdorf
Fürstenfeld
Hartberg
Oberwart
Szombathely
Köszeg
Güssing
Szentgotthárd
Feldbach
Deutschlandsberg
Leibnitz
Wolfsberg
Friesach
St. Veit
Klagenfurt
Villach
Velden
Ferlach
Karawanken
Maribor
Murska Sobota
Gornja Radgona
Radkersburg
Ptuj
Pohorje
Slovenska Bistrica
Slovenjgradec
Ravne
Dravograd
Velenje
Celje
Jesenice
Bled
Radovljica
Kranj
Kamnik
Savinjske Alpe
Julijske Alpe
Triglav 2864
LJUBLJANA
Idrija
Trbovlje
Hrastnik
Zagorje
Litija
Bohor
SLOVENIJA
Novo Mesto
Gorjanci
Kočevje
Postojna
Cerknica
Ilirska Bistrica
Sežana
Opatija
Rijeka
Delnice
Risnjak
Karlovac
Duga Resa
ZAGREB
Samobor
Zaprešić
Medvednica
Velika Gorica
Dugo Selo
Sisak
Petrinja
Varaždin
Čakovec
Ivanšcica
Krapina
Lendava
Nedelišće
Vrbovec
Križevci
Zelina
Jastrebarsko
Metlika
Vrbovsko
Ogulin

0 10 20 30 40 50 60 Kilometres

98
98
77
77

70
70

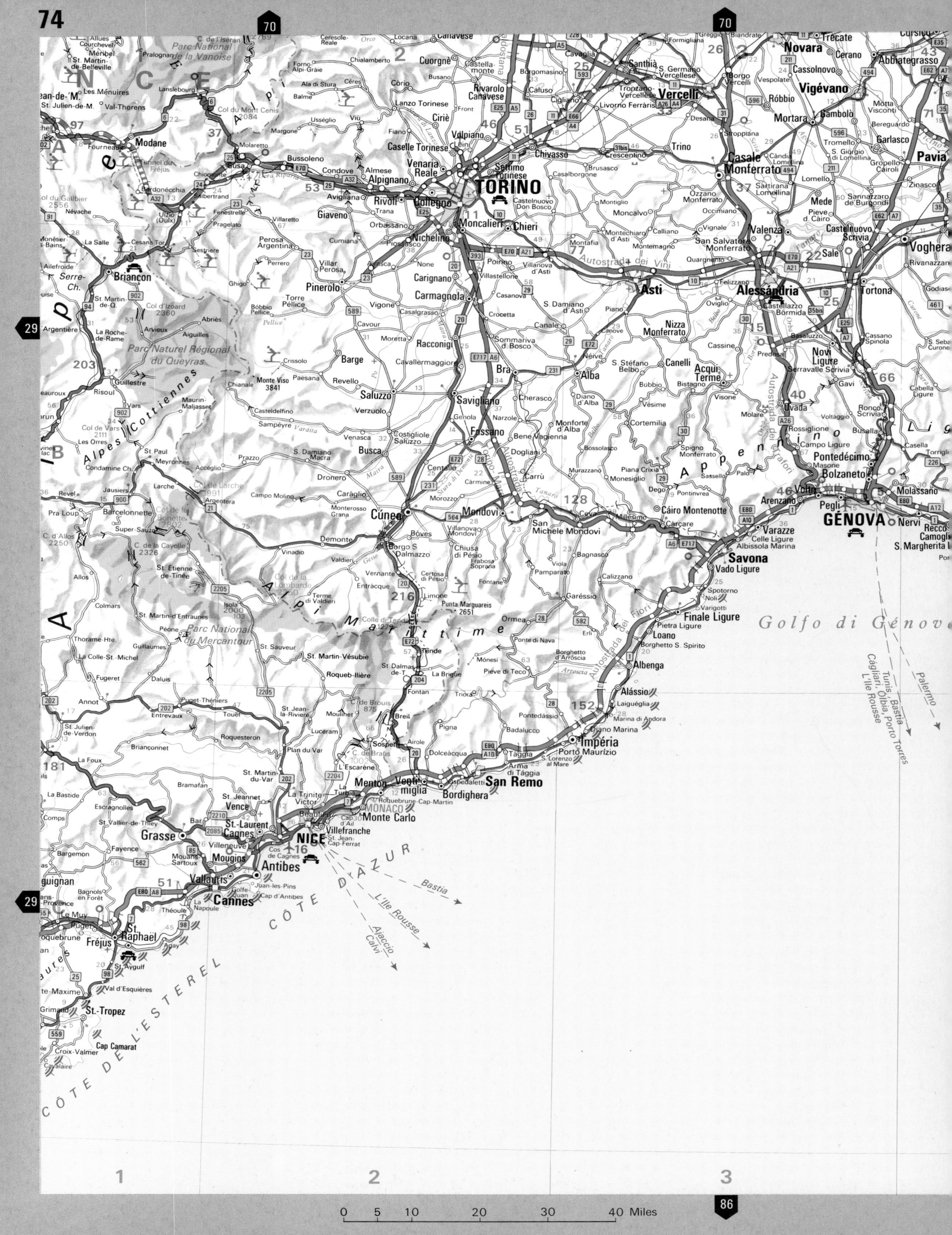

Parc National de la Vanoise
Modane
Susa
Bussoleno
Alpignano
Rivoli
Collegno
TORINO
Moncalieri
Chieri
Nichelino
Chivasso
Settimo Torinese
Venaria Reale
Caselle Torinese
Ciriè
Volpiano
Rivarolo Canavese
Cuorgnè
Ivrea
Santhià
Vercelli
Novara
Trecate
Abbiategrasso
Vigévano
Mortara
Garlasco
Pavia
Casale Monferrato
Trino
Valenza
Alessàndria
Tortona
Voghera
Asti
Alba
Bra
Carmagnola
Carignano
Pinerolo
Saluzzo
Savigliano
Fossano
Racconigi
Cuneo
Mondovì
Busca
Dronero
Barge
Giaveno
Briançon
Guillestre
Parc Naturel Régional du Queyras
Monte Viso 3841
Col d'Izoard 2360
Alpes Cottiennes
Barcelonnette
Parc National du Mercantour
Alpi Marittime
Limone
Tende
Breil
Sospel
Menton
Monaco
Monte Carlo
Ventimiglia
Bordighera
San Remo
Impéria
Porto Maurízio
Alássio
Albenga
Loano
Finale Ligure
Savona
Vado Ligure
Varazze
Arenzano
GÉNOVA
Nervi
Pegli
Bolzaneto
Pontedécimo
Novi Ligure
Ovada
Acqui Terme
Nizza Monferrato
Canelli
Cèva
Cáiro Montenotte
Ormea
Garéssio
Autostrada dei Fiori
Autostrada dei Vini
Golfo di Génova
Appennino Ligure
NICE
Villefranche
Antibes
Cannes
Grasse
Vence
Cagnes
Mougins
Vallauris
Juan-les-Pins
St. Raphaël
Fréjus
St.-Tropez
Cap Camarat
CÔTE D'AZUR
CÔTE DE L'ESTEREL
Bastia
L'Ile Rousse
Ajaccio
Calvi
Palermo
Tunis, Bastia
Cágliari, Olbia, Porto Torres
L'Ile Rousse
1
2
3

29
29
86

0 5 10 20 30 40 Miles

71

71

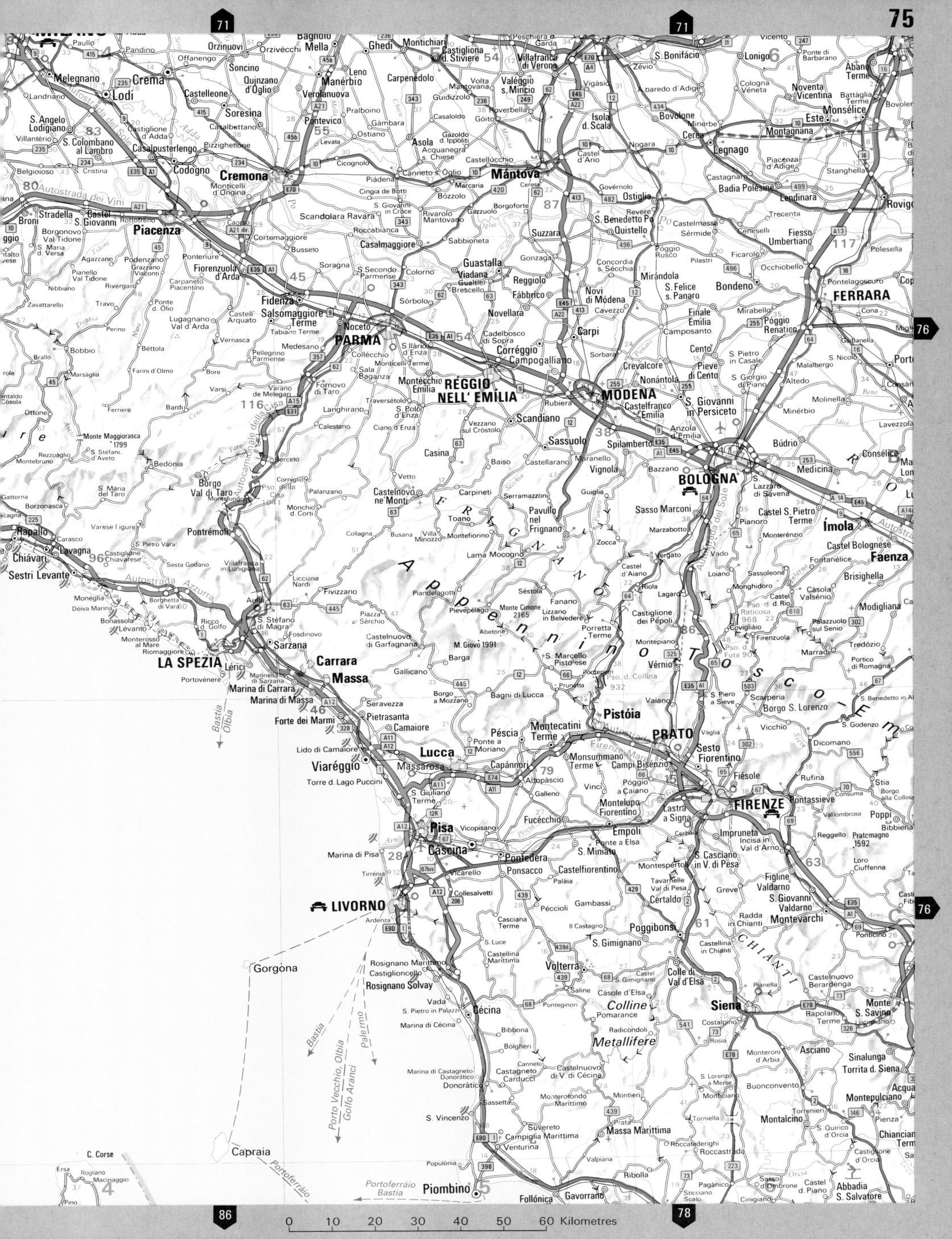

Paullo
Pandino
Orzinuovi
Orzivécchi
Bagnolo Mella
Ghedi
Montichiari
Castiglione d. Stiviere
Villafranca di Verona
Peschiera d. Garda
S. Bonifácio
Lonigo
Ponte di Barbarano
Ábano Terme
Melegnano
Offanengo
Crema
Soncino
Quinzano d'Oglio
Manérbio
Leno
Carpenédolo
Volta Mantovana
Valéggio s. Mincio
Vigásio
Zévio
Cologna Veneta
Noventa Vicentina
Battáglia Terme
Bovolenta
Landriano
Lodi
Castelleone
Soresina
Verolanuova
Guidizzolo
Roverbella
Isola d. Scala
Bovolone
Minerbe
Este
Monsélice
Montagnana
S. Angelo Lodigiano
Villantério
S. Colombano al Lambro
Castiglione d'Adda
Casalbuttano
Pontevico
Pralboino
Gámbara
Ostiano
Asola
Casaloldo
Gazoldo d. Ippoliti
Gòito
Acquanegra s. Chiese
Castellucchio
Castel d'Ario
Nogara
Cerea
Legnago
Piacenza d'Adige
Stanghella
Casalpusterlengo
Pizzighettone
Codogno
Belgioioso
S. Cristina
Cremona
Cicognolo
Canneto s. Óglio
Mantova
Piádena
Marcaria
Cerese
Gfocernolo
Ostiglia
Castagnaro
Badia Polésine
Lendinara
Rovigo
Autostrada dei Vini
Monticelli d'Ongina
Cingia de Botti
Bòzzolo
Borgoforte
Revere
S. Benedetto Po
Quistello
Castelmassa
Sérmide
Trecenta
Fiesso Umbertiano
Stradella
Broni
Castel S. Giovanni
Rottofreno
Piacenza
Caorso
S. Giovanni in Croce
Scandolara Ravara
Rivarolo Mantovano
Gazzuolo
Suzzara
Ceneselli
Polesella
Borgonovo Val Tidone
S. Maria d. Versa
Cortemaggiore
Roccabianca
Casalmaggiore
Sabbioneta
Poggio Rusco
Ficarolo
Pilastri
Occhiobello
Agazzano
Podenzano
Grazzano Visconti
Pontenure
Busseto
Soragna
Guastalla
Gonzaga
Concordia s. Sécchia
Pianello Val Tidone
Fiorenzuola d'Arda
S. Secondo Parmense
Colorno
Viadana
Reggiolo
Mirándola
S. Felice s. Panaro
Bondeno
Pontelagoscuro
Ferrara
Nibbiano
Rivergaro
Carpaneto Piacentino
Fidenza
Gualtieri
Brescello
Fábbrico
Novi di Módena
Travo
Ponte d. Ólio
Salsomaggiore Terme
Sórbolo
Novellara
Cavezzo
Finale Emília
Mirabello
Poggio Renatico
Cona
Zavattarello
Lugagnano Val d'Arda
Castell' Arquato
Tabiano Terme
Noceto
Parma
Cadelbosco di Sopra
Carpi
Camposanto
Perino
Vernasca
Medesano
S. Ilário d'Enza
Corréggio
Campogalliano
Sorbara
Cento
S. Pietro in Casale
Galbanella
Bobbio
Bettola
Pellegrino Parmense
Collécchio
Monticelli Terme
Crevalcore
Pieve di Cento
Malalbergo
S. Nicolò
Brallo
Marságlia
Farini d'Olmo
Bore
Sala Baganza
Montécchio Emília
Réggio nell' Emília
Módena
Nonántola
S. Giorgio di Piano
Altedo
Varsi
Varano de Melegari
Fornovo di Taro
Rubiera
Castelfranco Emília
S. Giovanni in Persiceto
Molinella
Ottone
Bardi
Ferriere
Autocamionale della Cisa
Langhirano
Traversétolo
S. Polo d'Enza
Scandiano
Anzola d'Emília
Minérbio
Lavezzola
Calestano
Ciano d'Enza
Vezzano sul Cróstolo
Sassuolo
Spilamberto
Búdrio
Monte Maggiorasca 1799
Rezzoágllio
S. Stéfano d'Aveto
Montebruno
Bedónia
Berceto
Casina
Baiso
Castellarano
Maranello
Vignola
Bazzano
Bologna
Medicina
Conselice
Borgo Val di Taro
Corniglio
Palanzano
Vetto
Castelnovo ne' Monti
Carpineti
Serramazzoni
Guiglia
Sasso Marconi
S. Lazzaro di Sávena
Castel S. Pietro Terme
Ímola
S. Maria del Taro
Gattorna
Borzonasca
Mónchio d. Corti
Toano
Pavullo nel Frignano
Marzabotto
Castel Bolognese
Faenza
Rapallo
Carasco
Lavagna
Chiávari
Sestri Levante
Varese Ligure
Pontrémoli
Collagna
Busana
Villa Minozzo
Montefiorino
Zocca
Pianoro
Monterénzio
Vado
Loiano
Fontanélice
Brisighella
S. Pietro Vara
Castiglione Chiavarese
Sesta Godano
Villafranca in Lunigiana
Lama Mocogno
Frignano
Appennino Tosco-Emiliano
Vergato
Castel d'Aiano
Riola
Lagaro
Sassoleone
Monghidoro
Cásola Valsénio
Modigliana
Autostrada Azzurra
Monéglia
Déiva Marina
Bonassola
Lévanto
Monterosso al Mare
Riomaggiore
Borghetta di Vara
Riccò d. Golfo
Aulla
Fivizzano
Licciana Nardi
Piandelagotti
Sestola
Fanano
Pievepélago
Monte Cimone 2165
Lizzano in Belvedere
Castiglione dei Pépoli
Raticosa 968
Palazzuolo sul Senio
Coviglíaio
Firenzuola
Marradi
Tredózio
Portico di Romagna
S. Stéfano di Magra
Fosdinovo
Sarzana
Piazza al Sérchio
Castelnuovo di Garfagnana
Abetone
M. Giovo 1991
Porretta Terme
Montepiano
Vérnio
Pso. d. Futa 903
La Spezia
Lérici
Portovénere
Carrara
Massa
Marinella di Sarzana
Marina di Carrara
Marina di Massa
Gallicano
Barga
S. Marcello Pistoiese
Pso. d. Collina 932
Bagni di Lucca
Borgo a Mozzano
Serravezza
Pietrasanta
Forte dei Marmi
Camaiore
Lido di Camaiore
Viaréggio
Massarosa
Torre d. Lago Puccini
Lucca
Péscia
Ponte a Moriano
Montecatini Terme
Pistóia
Prato
Vaiano
S. Piero a Sieve
Scarperia
Borgo S. Lorenzo
Vicchio
Dicomano
S. Benedetto in Alpe
S. Godenzo
Bastia
Olbia
Capánnori
Altopáscio
Monsummano Terme
Campi Bisénzio
Sesto Fiorentino
Fiésole
Rufina
Stia
Borgo alla Collina
Pontassieve
Consuma
Poppi
Bibbiena
S. Giuliano Terme
Galleno
Vinci
Póggio a Caiano
Montelupo Fiorentino
Lastra a Signa
Firenze
Vallombrosa
Pratomagno 1592
Pisa
Vicopisano
Fucécchio
Empoli
Impruneta
Incisa in Val d'Arno
Reggello
Loro Ciuffenna
Marina di Pisa
Cáscina
Pontedera
Ponsacco
Ponte a Elsa
S. Miniato
Castelfiorentino
Montespertoli
S. Casciano in V. di Pesa
Tavarnelle Val di Pesa
Greve
Figline Valdarno
S. Giovanni Valdarno
Montevarchi
Tirrénia
Vicarello
Collesalvetti
Paláia
Certaldo
Radda in Chianti
Livorno
Ardenza
Casciana Terme
Péccioli
Gambassi
Il Castagno
Poggibonsi
S. Gimignano
Castellina in Chianti
Chianti
Ponticino
S. Luce
Castellina Marittima
Rosignano Marittimo
Castiglioncello
Rosignano Solvay
Gorgona
Volterra
Saline
Cásole d'Elsa
Colle di Val d'Elsa
Castelnuovo Berardenga
Siena
Monte S. Savino
Vada
S. Pietro in Palazzi
Cécina
Marina di Cécina
Ponteginori
Colline Metallifere
Pomarance
Radicóndoli
Costalpino
Rosia
Rapolano Terme
Lucignano
Bibbona
Bólgheri
Asciano
Monteroni d'Arbia
Sinalunga
Torrita d. Siena
Marina di Castagneto Donorático
Castagneto Carducci
Castelnuovo di V. di Cécina
Buonconvento
Acquaviva
Montepulciano
Sassetta
Monterotondo Marittimo
Montieri
S. Lorenzo a Merse
Monticiano
Torrenieri
Pienza
S. Vincenzo
Suvereto
Campiglia Marittima
Venturina
Prata
Massa Marittima
Torniella
Montalcino
S. Quirico d'Órcia
Chianciano Terme
Capraia
C. Corse
Porto Vecchio, Olbia
Golfo Aranci
Palermo
Portoferráio
Roccastrada
Roccatederighi
Castiglione d'Órcia
Populónia
Valpiana
Ribolla
Ersa
Rogliano
Macinaggio
Pino
Portoferráio Bastia
Piombino
Follónica
Gavorrano
Paganico
Stícciano Scalo
Cinigiano
Sasso d'Ombrone
Castel d. Piano
Abbadia S. Salvatore

76

76

86

0 10 20 30 40 50 60 Kilometres

78

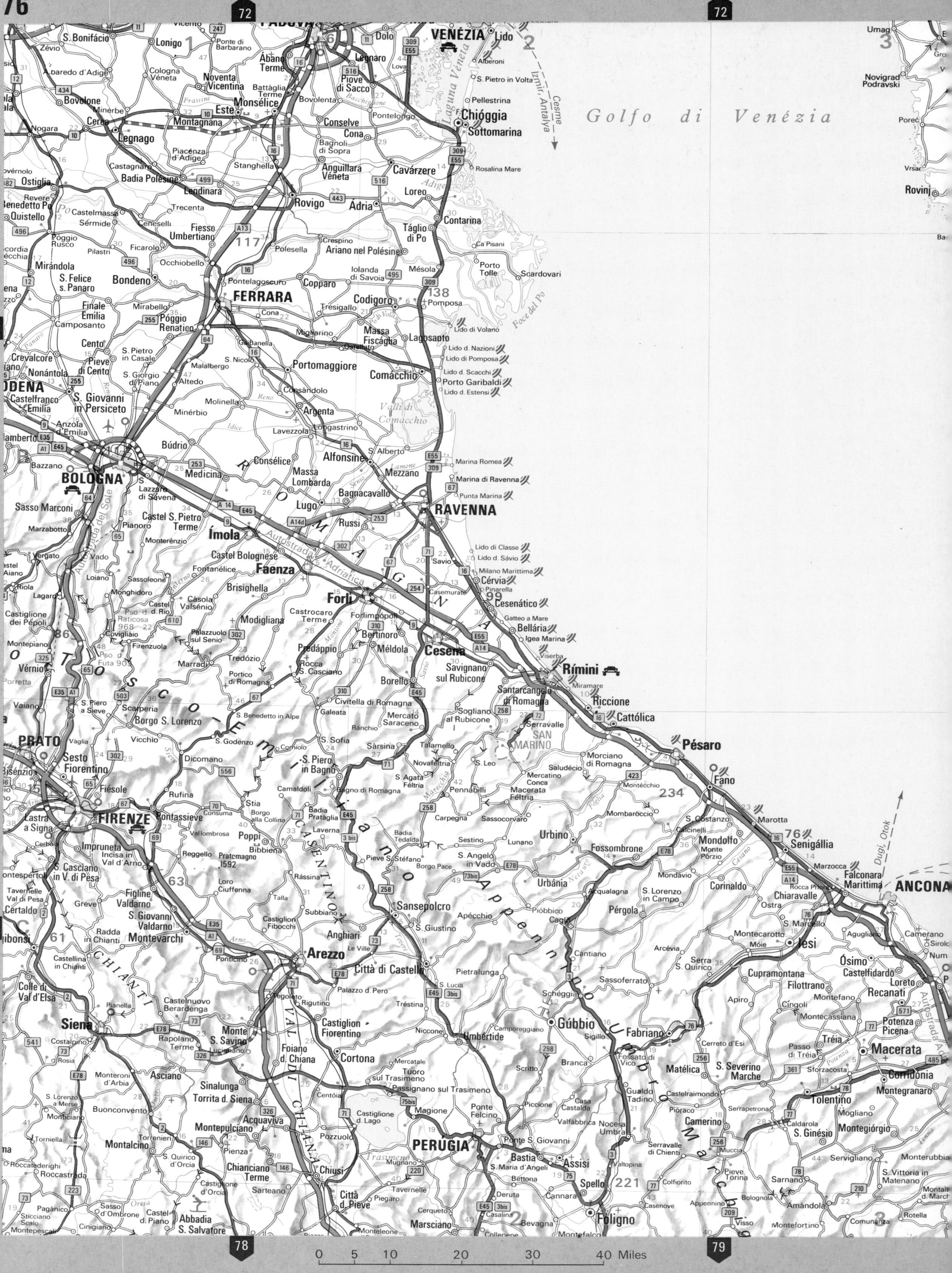
72
72
75
75
78
79
PADOVA
VENÉZIA
Lido
Golfo di Venézia
Laguna Veneta
Cesme
Izmir, Antalya
Umag
Novigrad Podravski
Poreč
Vrsar
Rovinj
S. Bonifácio
Zévio
Lonigo
Ponte di Barbarano
Dolo
Abano Terme
Legnaro
Alberoni
S. Pietro in Volta
Pellestrina
Chióggia
Sottomarina
Rosalina Mare
Cologna Véneta
Noventa Vicentina
Battáglia Terme
Piove di Sacco
Bovolone
Minerbe
Este
Monsélice
Bovolenta
Conselve
Pontelongo
Cerea
Montagnana
Legnago
Nogara
Bagnoli di Sopra
Cona
Castagnaro
Piacenza d'Adige
Stanghella
Anguillara Véneta
Cavárzere
Ostiglia
Badia Polésine
Lendinara
Loreo
Revere
Rovigo
Ádria
Quistello
Castelmassa
Trecenta
Contarina
Sérmide
Ceneselli
Fiesso Umbertiano
Táglio di Po
Poggio Rusco
Ficarolo
Pilastri
Crespino
Ariano nel Polésine
Ca'Pisani
Polesella
Mirándola
Occhiobello
Porto Tolle
Scardovari
S. Felice s. Panaro
Bondeno
Pontelagoscuro
Iolanda di Savoia
Mésola
FERRARA
Copparo
Codigoro
Pomposa
Finale Emília
Mirabello
Cona
Tresigallo
Camposanto
Póggio Renatico
Foce del Po
Lido di Volano
Cento
Migliarino
Massa Fiscáglia
Lagosanto
S. Pietro in Casale
Lido d. Nazioni
Lido di Pomposa
Crevalcore
Pieve di Cento
Portomaggiore
Nonántola
S. Giorgio di Piano
Comácchio
Lido d. Scacchi
Porto Garibaldi
Lido d. Estensi
MODENA
Altedo
Consándolo
Castelfranco Emília
S. Giovanni in Persiceto
Molinella
Argenta
Minérbio
Valli di Comacchio
Anzola d'Emília
Longastrino
Lavezzola
Búdrio
Alfonsine
S. Alberto
Marina Romea
Bazzano
Consélice
BOLOGNA
Medicina
Massa Lombarda
Mezzano
Marina di Ravenna
Lazzaro di Savena
Punta Marina
Bagnacavallo
Sasso Marconi
Lugo
RAVENNA
Castel S. Pietro Terme
Marzabotto
Pianoro
Russi
Ímola
Monterénzio
Lido di Classe
Castel Bolognese
Lido d. Sávio
Vado
Sávio
Milano Marittima
Faenza
Cérvia
Fontanélice
Loiano
Sassoleone
Pinarella
Riola
Brisighella
Lagaro
Monghidoro
Cásola Valsénio
Forlì
Cesenático
Castiglione dei Pépoli
Castrocaro Terme
Gatteo a Mare
Modigliana
Forlimpópoli
Bellária
Pso. d. Raticosa
Bertinoro
Igea Marina
Palazzuolo sul Senio
Montepiano
Firenzuola
Predáppio
Méldola
Cesena
Viserba
Vérnio
Rocca S. Casciano
Savignano sul Rubicone
Rímini
Marradi
Tredózio
Pso. d. Futa
Portico di Romagna
Porretta
Miramare
Borello
Riccione
Santarcangelo di Romagna
Civitella di Romagna
Vaiano
S. Piero a Sieve
Scarperia
Cattólica
Galeata
Sogliano al Rubicone
S. Benedetto in Alpe
Mercato Saraceno
Borgo S. Lorenzo
Serravalle
SAN MARINO
Ránchio
PRATO
Vicchio
S. Godenzo
S. Sofia
Pésaro
Váglia
Sesto Fiorentino
Corniolo
Sársina
Talamello
Novafeltria
Dicomano
S. Piero in Bagno
Morciano di Romagna
S. Leo
Saludécio
Fano
Fiésole
Mercatino Conca
S. Agata Féltria
Rufina
Camáldoli
Bagno di Romagna
Pennabilli
Montecchio
Macerata Féltria
FIRENZE
Pontassieve
Consuma
Stia
Borgo alla Collina
Lastra a Signa
Badia Pratáglia
Mombaróccio
Carpegna
Sassocorvaro
Marotta
S. Costanzo
Vallombrosa
Poppi
Laverna
Calcinelli
Badia Tedalda
Bibbiena
Sestino
Lunano
Urbino
Mondolfo
Senigállia
Impruneta
Incisa in Val d'Arno
Reggello
Pratomagno
Fossombrone
Monte Pórzio
Marzocca
S. Casciano in V. di Pesa
Pieve S. Stéfano
S. Angelo in Vado
Falconara Marittima
ANCONA
Rássina
Borgo Pace
Urbánia
Mondávio
Tavernelle Val di Pesa
Loro Ciuffenna
Corinaldo
Chiaravalle
Figline Valdarno
Acqualagna
S. Lorenzo in Campo
Certaldo
Greve
Talla
Sansepolcro
Pérgola
Ostra
S. Giovanni Valdarno
Apécchio
Piobbico
Radda in Chianti
Montevarchi
Subbiano
S. Giustino
Cagli
S. Marcello
Castiglion Fibocchi
Anghiari
Montecarotto
Camerano
Castellina in Chianti
Arcévia
Móie
Iesi
Agugliano
Le Ville
Cantiano
Serra S. Quirico
Ósimo
Ponticino
Arezzo
Città di Castello
Pietralunga
Castelfidardo
CHIANTI
Cupramontana
Loreto
Colle di Val d'Elsa
Palazzo d. Pero
Sassoferrato
Filottrano
Recanati
S. Lucia
Montefano
Pianella
Castelnuovo Berardenga
Rigutino
Tréstina
Schéggia
Apiro
Cíngoli
Potenza Picena
Montecassiana
Siena
Castiglion Fiorentino
Gúbbio
Fabriano
Niccone
Camporeggiano
Monte S. Savino
Umbértide
Tréia
Costalpino
Rapolano Terme
Foiano d. Chiana
Cortona
Sigillo
Cerreto d'Esi
Passo di Tréia
Macerata
Rosia
Asciano
Mercatale
Fossato di Vico
Matélica
S. Severino Marche
Sforzacosta
Corridonia
Tuoro sul Trasimeno
Scritto
Monteroni d'Arbia
Sinalunga
Gualdo Tadino
Castelraimondo
Tolentino
Montegranaro
Torrita d. Siena
Passignano sul Trasimeno
Ponte Felcino
Piccione
Casa Castalda
S. Lorenzo a Merse
Buonconvento
Centóia
Píoraco
Serrapetrona
Mogliano
Monticiano
Acquaviva
Castiglione d. Lago
Magione
Valfabbrica
Camerino
Caldarola
Montepulciano
Nocera Umbra
S. Ginésio
Montegiórgio
Torniella
Montalcino
Torrenieri
Pozzuolo
PERÚGIA
Ponte S. Giovanni
Serravalle di Chienti
Muccia
S. Quirico d'Orcia
Pienza
Bastia
Assisi
Roccatederighi
Chianciano Terme
Chiusi
Mugnano
S. Maria d'Angeli
Valtopina
Pieve Torina
Servigliano
Monterubbia
Roccastrada
Castiglione d'Orcia
Bettona
Sarnano
S. Vittoria in Matenano
Sarteano
Colfiorito
Città d. Pieve
Piegaro
Tavernelle
Deruta
Spello
Cannara
Bolognola
Appennino
Amándola
Casenove
Pagánico
Sasso d'Ombrone
Castel d. Piano
Abbadia S. Salvatore
Cerqueto
Casalina
Foligno
Bevagna
Visso
Montefortino
Comunanza
Rotella
Stícciano Scalo
Montepescali
Cinigiano
Monteleone
Marsciano
Collepepe
Montefalco
ROMAGNA
TOSCO EMILIANO
CASENTINO
Appennino Umbro Marchigiano
VAL DI CHIANA
Autostrada del Sole
Autostrada Adriatica
Dugi Otok
0 5 10 20 30 40 Miles

73 73

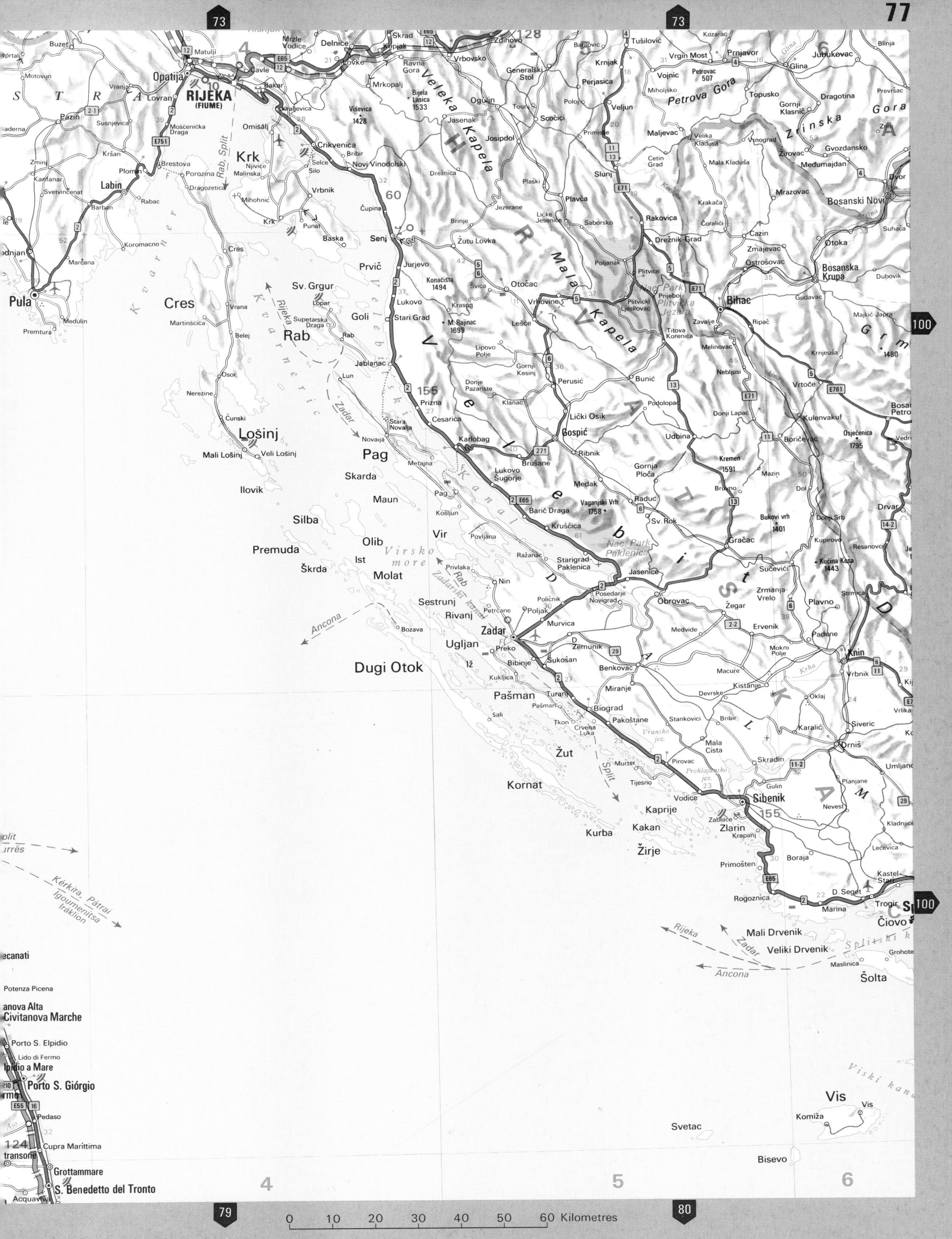
Buzet
Motovun
Opatija
Matulji
RIJEKA
(FIUME)
Delnice
Skrad
Kupjak
Vrbovsko
Zdihovo
Mrzle Vodice
Lovke
Čavle
Bakar
Ravna Gora
Mrkopalj
Lovran
Mošćenička Draga
Pazin
Sušnjevica
Kršan
Plomin
Labin
Rabac
Barban
Svetvinčenat
Kanfanar
Žminj
Brestova
Porozina
Dragozetići
Omišalj
Krk
Njivice
Malinska
Kraljevica
Crikvenica
Bribir
Selce
Silo
Novi Vinodolski
Vrbnik
Mihohnić
Punat
Baška
Senj
Čupina
Bijela Lasica 1533
Viševica 1428
Veleka Kapela
Jasenak
Ogulin
Josipdol
Drežnica
Generalski Stol
Tounj
Scočići
Plaški
Brinje
Jezerane
Lićke Jesenice
Žutu Lovka
Prvič
Jurjevo
Konačišta 1494
Švica
Otočac
Kraspa
M. Rajinac 1699
Vrhovine
Lešće
Lipovo Polje
Gornji Kesinj
Donje Pazarište
Perušić
Klanac
Lički Osik
Gospić
Ribnik
Brušane
Lukovo Šugorje
Karlobag
Cesarica
Prizna
Jablanac
Stari Grad
Lukovo
Goli
Sv. Grgur
Lopar
Supetarska Draga
Rab
Lun
Stara Novalja
Novalja
Pag
Metajna
Koromacno
Cres
Vrana
Martinšćica
Belej
Osor
Nerezine
Čunski
Lošinj
Mali Lošinj
Veli Lošinj
Ilovik
Skarda
Maun
Silba
Premuda
Olib
Ist
Škrda
Molat
Virsko more
Vir
Košljun
Povljana
Privlaka
Ražanac
Nin
Starigrad Paklenica
Jasenice
Sestrunj
Rivanj
Zadar
Petrčane
Poličnik
Posedarje
Novigrad
Poljak
Murvica
Obrovac
Bozava
Ugljan
Preko
Iž
Dugi Otok
Bibinje
Sukošan
Zemunik
Benkovac
Kukljica
Pašman
Turanj
Biograd
Pakoštane
Sali
Tkon
Crvena Luka
Žut
Murter
Tijesno
Kornat
Vodice
Šibenik
Kaprije
Kakan
Kurba
Žirje
Zlarin
Krapanj
Primošten
Rogoznica
Marina
Trogir
Čiovo
Šolta
Mali Drvenik
Veliki Drvenik
Maslinica
Grohote
Vis
Komiža
Svetac
Biševo
Pula
Medulin
Premtura
Marčana
Vodnjan
Labin
Tušilovič
Vrgin Most
Prnjavor
Kozarac
Jubukovac
Blinja
Glina
Vojnic
Petrovac 507
Krnjak
Perjasica
Veljun
Miholjsko
Petrova Gora
Topusko
Gornji Klasnič
Dragotina
Prevršac
Zrinska Gora
Maljevac
Velika Kladuša
Vrnograd
Žirovac
Gvozdansko
Cetin Grad
Mala Kladuša
Medumajdan
Slunj
Plavča
Saborsko
Rakovica
Krakača
Čoralići
Mrazovac
Bosanski Novi
Drežnik Grad
Cazin
Zmajevac
Otoka
Suhača
Poljanak
Plitvice
Ostrošovac
Bosanska Krupa
Dubovik
Plitvički Ljeskovac
Nac. Park Plitvička Jezera
Prijeboj
Bihać
Ripač
Gudavac
Majkić Japra
Mala Kapela
Titova Korenica
Zavalje
Melinovac
Grmeč 1480
Krnjeusa
Bunić
Nebljusi
Vrtoče
Podolopac
Donji Lapac
Kulenvakuf
Osječenica 1795
Udbina
Boričevac
Kremen 1591
Mazin
Gornja Ploča
Medak
Bruvno
Dol
Vaganjski Vrh 1758
Baric Draga
Kruščica
Raduc
Sv. Rok
Bukovi vrh 1401
Drvar
Donji Srb
Kupirovo
Velebit
Nac. Park Paklenica
Gračac
Resanovci
Kučina Kosa 1443
Sučević
Zrmanja-Vrelo
Žegar
Plavno
Strmica
Medvide
Ervenik
Padene
Mokro Polje
Knin
Vrbnik
Macure
Kistanje
Devrske
Miranje
Mirograd
Oklaj
Stankovici
Bribir
Karalić
Siveric
Vransko jez.
Mala Cista
Drniš
Skradin
Umljanovići
Pirovac
Proklajansko jez.
Gulin
Planjane
Nevest
Zablaće
Boraja
Kladnjice
Lećevica
Kastel Stari
D. Seget
Dalmacija
Kvarner
Kvarnerić
Velebitski Kanal
Zadarski kanal
Splitski kanal
Viški kanal
Rijeka
Zadar
Ancona
Split
Kérkira, Pátrai, Igoumenitsa, Iráklion
Recanati
Potenza Picena
Civitanova Alta
Civitanova Marche
Porto S. Elpidio
Lido di Fermo
S. Elpidio a Mare
Porto S. Giórgio
Fermo
Pedaso
Cupra Maríttima
Ripatransone
Grottammare
S. Benedetto del Tronto
Acquaviva
E65
E71
E751
E761
E55
4
5
6
0 10 20 30 40 50 60 Kilometres

100 100 79 80

Campiglia Maríttima
Venturina
Populónia
Piombino
Portoferráio
Rio Marina
Porto Azzurro
Prócchio
Cavo

Massa Maríttima
Roccatederighi
Roccastrada
Valpiana
Ribolla
Follónica
Gavorrano
Vetulónia
Batignano
Montepescali
Stícciano Scalo
Paganico
Campagnático
Grosseto
Castiglione della Pescáia
Marina di Grosseto
Principina a Mare
Rispéscia
Scansano
Magliano in Toscana
Marina di Alberese
Talamone
Fonteblanda
Albínia
Orbetello
Orbetello Scalo
Porto Santo Stefano
Port' Ercole
Gíglio
Giglio Porto

Montalcino
S. Quírico d'Orcia
Pienza
Chianciano Terme
Sarteano
Castiglione d'Orcia
Sasso d'Ombrone
Castel del Piano
Abbadia S. Salvatore
Arcidosso
Piancastagnáio
Cinigiano
Terme di Roselle
Arcille
Cana
S. Caterina
S. Fiora
Roccalbegna
Castell' Azzara
Samprugnano
Saturnia
Pitigliano
Manciano
Farnese
Ischia di Castro
Canino
Capalbio
Montalto di Castro
Tarquínia
Marina di Tarquinia
Allumiere
Tolfa
Civitavécchia
Santa Marinella
Santa Severa

MARE TIRRENO

ARCIPELAGO TOSCANO
Elba
Montecristo
Giannutri

Chiusi
Cittá d. Pieve
Tavernelle
Piegaro
Cerquéto
Casalina
Marsciano
Monteleone d'Orvieto
Ficulle
S. Casciano d. Bagni
S. Lorenzo Nuovo
Acquapendente
Orvieto
Baschi
Onano
Sorano
Grotte di Castro
Látera
Lago di Bolsena
Bolsena
Bagnorégio
Guardea
Valentano
Montefiascone
Zepponami
Marta
Viterbo
Bagnáia
Vetralla
Vignanello
Caprarola
Cívita Castellana
Roncíglione
Blera
Monte Romano
Capránica
Bassano di Sutri
Nepi
Sutri
Tuscánia
Arlena di Castro

Bástia
S. Maria d. Ángeli
Assisi
Bettona
Deruta
Bevagna
Collepepe
Montefalco
Bastardo
Todi
Massa Mártana
Spoleto
Acquásparta
San Gemini
Amélia
Terni
Attigliano
Narni
Soriano nel Cimino
Orte
Otricoli
Lugnano
Magliano Sabina
Cantalupo in Sabina
Poggio Mirteto
Fara in Sabina
Capena
Monte Libretti
Palombara Sabina
Mentana
Guidónia
Tívoli
Bagni di Tívoli

Civitavécchia
Cervéteri
Ládispoli
Palidoro
Maccarese
Fregene
Fiumicino
Acília
Lido di Óstia
Castel Fusano
Torre Nova
Cittá d. Vaticano
ROM[A]
Tomba di Nerone
la Storta
Anguillara Sabázia
Lídi di Bráccia no
Bracciano
Manziana
Trevignano Romano
Campagnano di Roma
Riano
Marino
Fráscati
Albano Laziale
Genzano di Roma
Pomézia
Tor Vaiánica
Aprília
Lavinio-Lido di Enea
Lido di Cincinnato
Ánzio
Nettu[no]

Bastia
Ólbia Golfo Aranci
Arbatax
Cágliari

0 5 10   20   30   40 Miles

A
B
C
1 2 3

76
77

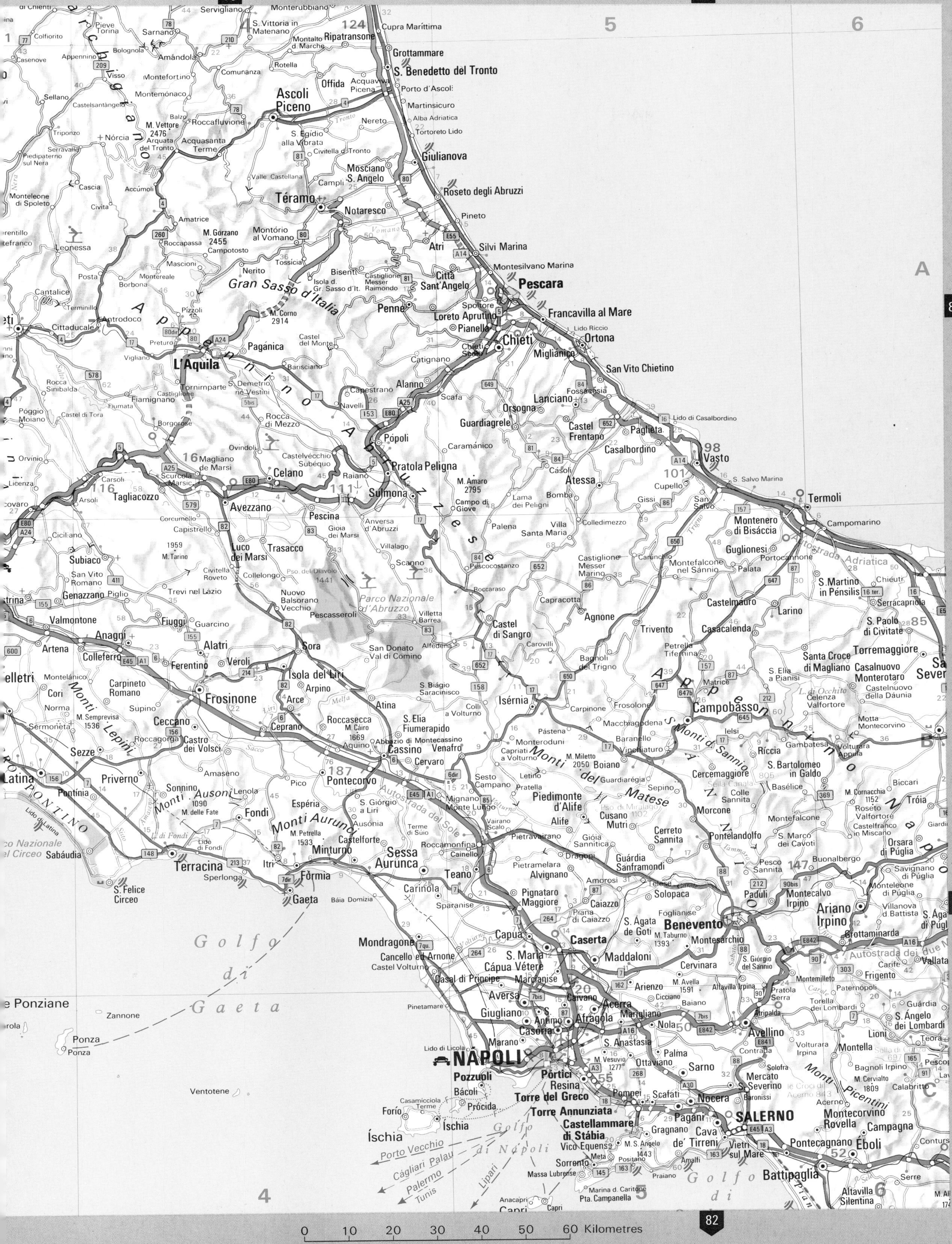
5
6
A
B
C
4
Servigliano
Monterubbiano
S. Vittoria in Matenano
Cupra Maríttima
Montalto d. Marche
Ripatransone
Grottammare
S. Benedetto del Tronto
Porto d'Ascoli
Martinsicuro
Alba Adriatica
Tortoreto Lido
Pieve Torina
Sarnano
Colfiorito
Bolognola
Amândola
Casenove
Appennino
Visso
Montefortino
Comunanza
Rotella
Offida
Acquaviva Picena
Ascoli Piceno
Sellano
Castelsantàngelo
Montemónaco
Balzo
Roccafluvione
Nereto
M. Vettore 2476
Arquata del Tronto
Acquasanta Terme
S. Egidio alla Vibrata
Civitella d. Tronto
Triponzo
Nòrcia
Serravalle
Piedipaterno sul Nera
Giulianova
Mosciano S. Angelo
Valle Castellana
Campli
Cascia
Accúmoli
Téramo
Notaresco
Roseto degli Abruzzi
Monteleone di Spoleto
Civita
Pineto
Amatrice
M. Gorzano 2455
Montório al Vomano
Atri
Leonessa
Roccapassa
Campotosto
Silvi Marina
Mascioni
Tossicia
Montesilvano Marina
Nerito
Bisenti
Castiglione Messer Raimondo
Città Sant'Angelo
Pescara
Posta
Montereale
Borbona
Isola d. Gr. Sasso d'It.
Gran Sasso d'Italia
Cantalice
Terminillo
Pizzoli
Penne
Spoltore
Antrodoco
M. Corno 2914
Loreto Aprutino
Francavilla al Mare
Cittaducale
Pianella
Lido Riccio
Ortona
Preturo
Castel del Monte
Chieti
Chieti Scalo
Paganica
Vigliano
L'Aquila
Appennino Abruzzese
Miglianico
Barisciano
Catignano
San Vito Chietino
Rocca Sinibalda
Tornimparte
S. Demetrio ne' Vestini
Castiglione
Capestrano
Alanno
Scafa
Fossacesia
Lanciano
Fiamignano
Navelli
Orsogna
Lido di Casalbordino
Poggio Moiano
Castel di Tora
Borgorose
Rocca di Mezzo
Guardiagrele
Castel Frentano
Paglieta
Pópoli
Casalbordino
Ovindoli
Caramánico
Vasto
Orvinio
Magliano de' Marsi
Castelvecchio Subéquo
Pratola Peligna
Casoli
Licenza
Scurcola Marsic.
Celano
Atessa
S. Salvo Marina
Carsoli
Tagliacozzo
Arsoli
Raiano
M. Amaro 2795
Bomba
Sulmona
Cupello
Termoli
Avezzano
Campo di Giove
Gissi
San Salvo
Lama dei Peligni
Corcumello
Pescina
Anversa d'Abruzzi
Capistrello
Gioia dei Marsi
Palena
Villa Santa Maria
Colledimezzo
Montenero di Bisáccia
Campomarino
Ciciliano
Luco dei Marsi
Trasacco
1959 M. Tarino
Villalago
Guglionesi
Portocannone
Subiaco
Castiglione Messer Marino
Montefalcone nel Sánnio
Palata
San Vito Romano
Civitella Roveto
Collelongo
Pso. del Diavolo
Scanno
Pescocostanzo
Autostrada Adriatica
Genazzano
Piglio
Trevi nel Lazio
Nuovo Balsorano Vecchio
1441
Chieuti
S. Martino in Pénsilis
Serracapriola
Roccaraso
Capracotta
Parco Nazionale d'Abruzzo
Castelmauro
Larino
Valmontone
Fiuggi
Guarcino
Pescasseroli
Agnone
Villetta Barrea
Castel di Sangro
Trivento
S. Paolo di Civitate
Casacalenda
Anagni
Alatri
Artena
Colleferro
Ferentino
Véroli
San Donato Val di Comino
Alfedena
Carovilli
Petrella Tifernina
Torremaggiore
Santa Croce di Magliano
Casalnuovo Monterotaro
Bagnoli del Trigno
Velletri
Monti Lepini
Isola del Liri
Montelánico
Carpineto Romano
Arpino
S. Biágio Saracinisco
S. Elia a Pianisi
Castelnuovo della Daunia
Cori
Frosinone
Arce
Colli a Volturno
Isérnia
Matrice
L. di Occhito
Celenza Valfortore
Norma
Supino
Atina
Carpinone
Frosolone
Campobasso
M. Semprevisa 1536
Ceccano
Roccasecca
S. Elia Fiumerapido
Macchiagodena
Motta Montecorvino
Sermoneta
Ceprano
M. Cáiro 1669
Abbazio di Montecassino
Pástena
Jelsi
Castro dei Volsci
Roccagorga
Cassino
Venafro
Monteroduni
Baranello
Vinchiaturo
Monti d. Sannio
Gambatesa
Sezze
Aquino
Capriati a Volturno
Monti del Matese
Ríccia
Volturara Appula
Latina
Privern
Cervaro
M. Miletto 2050
Boiano
Pontecorvo
Sesto Campano
S. Bartolomeo in Galdo
Cercemaggiore
Amaseno
Letino
Guardiarégia
Sepino
Biccari
Pontínia
Sonnino
Monti Ausoni
Lenola
Pico
Pratella
Piedimonte d'Alife
Colle Sannita
Basélice
Tróia
M. delle Fate 1090
Espéria
S. Giórgio a Liri
Mignano Monte Lungo
M. Cornacchia 1152
Roseto Valfortore
Morcone
Lido di Latina
Fondi
Monti Aurunci
Ausónia
Cusano Mutri
Castelfranco in Miscano
Alife
Montefalcone
Cerreto Sannita
Pso. di Miralago 1102
M. Petrella 1533
Terme di Súio
Vairano Scalo
Pietravairano
Gióia Sannitica
Pontelandolfo
S. Marco dei Cavoti
Orsara di Púglia
Parco Nazionale del Circeo
Sabáudia
Lido di Fondi
Castelforte
Minturno
Roccamonfina
Dragoni
Guárdia Sanframondi
Buonalbergo
Terracina
Itri
Sessa Aurunca
Cainello
Pietramelara
Pesco Sannita
Savignano di Púglia
Sperlonga
Fórmia
Teano
Alvignano
Amorosi
Telese
Solopaca
Paduli
Montecalvo Irpino
Monteleone di Púglia
S. Felice Circeo
Gaeta
Báia Domizia
Carinola
Pignataro Maggiore
Caiazzo
Piana di Caiazzo
Foglianise
Ariano Irpino
Villanova d. Battista
Sparanise
S. Ágata de' Goti
Benevento
Grottaminarda
M. Taburno 1393
Montesarchio
Golfo di Gaeta
Mondragone
Capua
Caserta
S. Maria Cápua Vétere
Maddaloni
S. Giórgio del Sannio
Cancello ed Arnone
Castel Volturno
Cervinara
Autostrada dei due Mari
Carife
Vallata
Frigento
Casal di Principe
Marcianise
Arienzo
M. Avella 1591
Altavilla Irpina
Montemiletto
Paternópoli
Aversa
Caivano
Acerra
Cicciano
Baiano
Pratola Serra
Torella dei Lombardi
Guárdia
Isole Ponziane
Zannone
Pinetamare
Giugliano
S. Antimo
Afragola
Marigliano
Atripalda
S. Ángelo dei Lombardi
Casoria
Nola
Avellino
Lioni
Ponza
Marano
S. Anastasia
Contrada
Volturara Irpina
Montella
Lido di Licola
NAPOLI
M. Vesuvio 1277
Ottaviano
Palma
Sarno
Bagnoli Irpino
Pozzuoli
Pórtici
Resina
Solofra
M. Cervialto 1809
Báctoli
Torre del Greco
Pompei
Scafati
Nocera
Mercato S. Severino
Baronissi
Monti Picentini
Calabritto
Ventotene
Casamicciola Terme
Prócida
Torre Annunziata
Castellammare di Stábia
Pagani
Acerno
Forio
Íschia
Gragnano
SALERNO
Montecorvino Rovella
Campagna
Golfo di Nápoli
Vico Equense
M. S. Angelo 1443
Cava de' Tirreni
Vietri sul Mare
Pontecagnano
Éboli
Porto Vecchio
Cágliari
Palau
Palermo
Tunis
Lipari
Sorrento
Meta
Positano
Amalfi
Massa Lubrense
Praiano
Golfo di
Battipaglia
Marina d. Cantone
Pta. Campanella
Anacapri
Capri
Altavilla Silentina
Serre
0 10 20 30 40 50 60 Kilometres

80
80
82

A 1 2 3

Korčulanski kanal

Svetac · Komiža

Biševo

Vela Luka · Prigradica
Korčula Blato Smokvi · Brna

Lastrovski k

B

J A D R A N S K O   M

Sušac

Ubli
Lastovo

79
avilla al Mare
Lido Riccio
Ortona
San Vito Chietino

652 Paglieta
Casalbordino Lido di Casalbordino
98
A14 **Vasto**
101 Cupello S. Salvo Marina
Gissi San 16 *Isole Trémiti*
Salvo 14
Colledimezzo 86 Termoli
650 Montenero Campomarino
di Bisáccia
157 Chiéuti Lago di Lésina Lago di
Castiglione Guglionesi Portocannone Lesina Varano
Carunchio Palata S. Martino *Rodi* Peschici
Montefalcone 87 in Pénsilis 16 ter. Poggio *Gargánico* Manacore
nel Sánnio 647 Imperiale Ischitella Vico 20
Castelmauro Serracapriola E55 del Gargano **Vieste**
Trivento Larino 16 Apricena Sannicandro 89 Carpino
Casacalenda S. Paolo 85 Gargánico Cagnano 89
Petrella di Civitate 89 Varano San Marco Pugnochiuso
Tiferinna 157 Santa Croce Torremaggiore Rignano in Lamis Báia d. Zágare
647 di Magliano Gargánico San Giovanni 36 Mattinata
Matrice Casalnuovo San Rotondo 15 Monte Sant'Angelo
Campobasso 212 Monterotaro Severo **Manfredónia**
645 Celenza Castelnuovo 160 Lido di Siponto
Macchiagodena Valfortore della Dáunia 22 *T*
Baranello Ielsi Motta Arpinova *M A R*
Vinchiaturo Montecorvino Lucera Zapponeta
Guardiarégia Sepino Ríccia 17 13 Margherita
Cercemaggiore Gambatesa Volturara 36 **FÓGGIA** A14 di Savóia
Matese S. Bartolomeo Appula Carapelle 545 159
Colle in Galdo 805 M. Cornacchia Biccari Trinitápoli
Morcone Sannita Baselice 369 1152 Tróia Carapelle 132 Barletta
Montefalcone Roseto 160 Orta Nova S. Ferdinando 16 Trani
Cerreto Valfortore Giardinetto Castelluccio di Púglia 16
Sannita Pontelandolfo S. Marco Castelfranco de' sau 161 Stornara 57 Cerignola A14 72 Biscéglie
Guárdia dei Cavoti in Miscano 90 Bovino 16 Canosa Ándria Molfetta
Sanframondi Pesco Orsara Ascoli di Púglia 98 E55 Giovinazzo
Telese Sannita 147 di Púglia Savignano Satriano 93 S. Spirito
Solopaca 212 Montecalvo di Púglia Deliceto E842 15 Minervino Corato Terlizzi
S. Agata 90bis Irpino Monteleone Accadia Murge 378 Bitonto BAR
de' Goti Fogliarise Paduli di Púglia Candela 97 170 Ruvo Palo
Benevento Ariano Villanova E842 170dir di Púglia del Colle 96 Modugno
Montesarchio Irpino d. Battista S. Agata 129 Posta Piana 170 Bitetto
Maddaloni Grottaminarda di Púglia Rocchetta Melfi Montemilone 170 Grumo Áppula Capurso
Cervinara A16 S. António Lavello Spinazzola 378 Caposl
Arienzo Carife Vallata Lacedónia Rapolla 169 Toritto Sannicandro
Cicciano Altavilla Irpina 303 Frigento Bisáccia Aquilonia 97 di Bari
Nola 50 Baiano Montemiletto Carife M. Vúlture Venosa Acquaviva
Anastasia 7bis Pratola Paternópoli 303 Andretta Rionero 168 Palazzo delle Fonti 132
Serra S. Ángelo in Vúlture S. Gervásio Cassano
Avellino dei Lombardi Calitri Ripacándida Genzano delle Murge Gióia
Ottaviano E841 Montella Teora Atella di Lucánia Altamura del Colle
Palma Contrada Lioni Forenza Santéramo
Sarno Solofra Volturara Bagnoli Irpino Acerenza Gravina in Colle
Mercato Irpina Pescopagano Bella in Púglia E843
Scafati Severino le Croci di M. Cervialto Laviano S. Fele Pietragalla Irsina Matera A14
Nocera Acerno 843 1809 Muro Aviglione Oppido
Pagani Baronissi Lucano Bella Cancellara Lucano Váglio 96 Grassano
SALERNO Montecorvino Ruoti Basilicata Tolve Tricárico Gróttole 175
Rovella Campagna S. Gregório Picerno Castellaneta
Cava Magno Ginosa
de' Tirreni Vietri Pontecagnano Éboli Contursi Buccino **Potenza** 407 109
sul Mare 52 Battipaglia Serre Auletta Tito Trivigno Garaguso Miglónico
Altavilla E847 Vietri 55 1143 Anzi
Silentina di Potenza 92
M. Alburno Caggiano Pso Croce

0 5 10 20 30 40 Miles

100
101

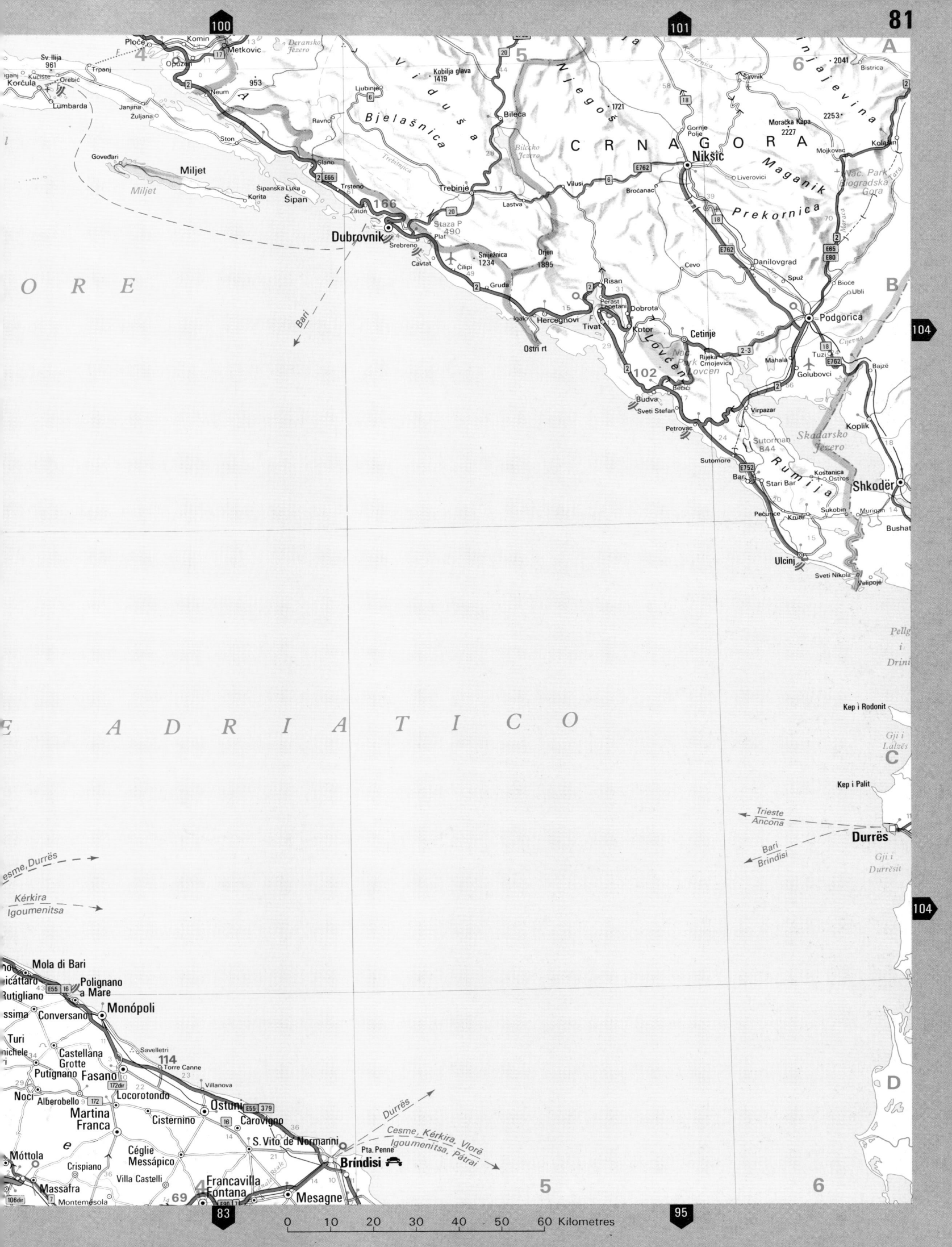
Ploče
Komin
Metkovic
Opuzen
Sv. Ilija
961
Trpanj
Kućište
Orebić
Korčula
Lumbarda
Neum
953
Janjina
Žuljana
Ston
Ravno
Ljubinje
Kobilja glava
1419
Bjelašnica
Viduša
Bileća
Bilećko Jezero
1721
Njegoš
Šavnik
Gornje Polje
Moračka Kapa
2227
2253
2041
Bistrica
Sinjajevina
Kolašin
Mojkovac
CRNA GORA
Nikšić
Maganik
Liverovici
Nac. Park Biogradska Gora
Tara
Goveđari
Miljet
Šipanska Luka
Korita
Šipan
Slano
Trsteno
Zaton
Trebinje
Lastva
Vilusi
Bročanac
Prekornica
Dubrovnik
Srebreno
Cavtat
Staza P
490
Plat
Čilipi
Snježnica
1234
Orjen
1895
Gruda
Cevo
Danilovgrad
Spuž
Bioče
Ubli
Risan
Perast
Lepetani
Dobrota
Igalo
Hercegnovi
Tivat
Kotor
Ostri rt
Cetinje
Podgorica
Lovćen
Nac. Park Lovćen
Rijeka Crnojevića
Mahala
Tuzi
Golubovci
Cijevna
Bajze
Budva
Bečići
Sveti Stefan
Petrovac
Virpazar
Skadarsko Jezero
Koplik
Sutorman
844
Sutomore
Bar
Stari Bar
Rumija
Kostanica
Ostros
Shkodër
Pečurice
Kruta
Sukobin
Murigan
Bushat
Ulcinj
Sveti Nikola
Velipoje
M O R E
Bari
Pellg i Drinit
Kep i Rodonit
Gji i Lalzës
Kep i Palit
Trieste
Ancona
Durrës
Bari
Brindisi
Gji i Durrësit
E ADRIATICO
Cesme, Durrës
Kérkira
Igoumenitsa
Mola di Bari
Polignano a Mare
Rutigliano
Monópoli
Conversano
Turi
Castellana Grotte
Savelletri
Torre Canne
Putignano
Fasano
Villanova
Noci
Alberobello
Locorotondo
Ostuni
Martina Franca
Cisternino
Carovigno
S. Vito de Normanni
Durrës
Cesme, Kérkira, Vlorë
Igoumenitsa, Pátrai
Móttola
Céglie Messápico
Pta. Penne
Bríndisi
Crispiano
Villa Castelli
Francavilla Fontana
Massafra
Montemesola
Mesagne
E65
E762
E752
E80
E55
A
B
C
D
4
5
6

104
104
83
95

0 10 20 30 40 50 60 Kilometres

Ischia

Golfo di Napoli

Castellammare di Stábia
Pagani
Gragnano
Vico Equense
Cava de' Tirreni
SALERNO
Meta
Sorrento
Positano
Amalfi
Vietri sul Mare
Massa Lubrense
Marina d. Caritone
Pta. Campanella
Praiano
60

Capri
Capri
Anacapri

Montecorvino Rovella
Campagna
Acerno
Muro Lucano
Avigliano

Pontecagnano Eboli
Battipaglia

Contursi
S. Gregório Magno
Buccino

Ruoti
Picerno

Potenza

Tricárico
Irsina

Grassano

Golfo di Salerno

Piana del Sele

Serre
Altavilla Silentina
M. Alburno 1742
Controne
Polla
Vietri di Potenza
Caggiano
Tito

Anzi
Accettura
Laurenzana
S. Mauro Forte
Stigliano

Paestum
Capáccio
Roccadáspide
Corleto Monforte
S. Rufo

Sala Consilina
Márico Nuovo
Calvello
Corleto Perticara
Cirigliano
Laurénzana

Agrópoli
Ogliastro Cilento
Teggiano
Padula
M. Volturino 1836
Viggiano
Montemurro
Missanello

CILENTO

Stio
Vallo della Lucánia
Buonabitácolo
Montesano sulla Marcellana
Spinoso
S. Arcángelo

S. Marco
Castellabate
Montecórice
Laurino M. Cervati 1899
Rofrano
Sanza
Casalbuono
Moliterno
Roccanova
S. Chírico Raparo

Pta. Licosa
Ogliastro Marina
Póllica
Ceraso
M. Sacro 1705
S. Severino Lucano
Castelsaraceno

Acciaroli
Montano Antilia
Lagonegro
M. Sirino 2005
Latrónico
Chiaromonte

Ascea
Torre Orsáia
Rivello
Episcópia
Francavilla in Sinni

Pisciotta
Fória
Sapri
Láuria
Castellúccio Inferiore

M. Bulgheria 1225
S. Giovanni a Piro
Viggianello
Terra

Capo Palinuro
Camerota
Mormanno
M. Dolcedorme 2271
Rotonda
Pollino

Marina di Camerota
Pta. d. Infreschi
Maratea
Tórtora

Golfo di Policastro

Práia a Mare
Papasidero
S. Doménica
Talao

Capo Scalea
Scalea
Morano Cálabro
Castrovillari
Cas allo

Verbicaro
Orsomarso
Czo. Pellegrino 1986
Lungro
Firmo

Cirella
Altomonte
Spe
Alb

Diamante
Buonvicino
S. Sosti
Roggiano Gravina
Társia

Belvedere Maríttimo
S. Ágata di Ésaro
Fagnano Castello
S. Marco Argentano
S. Demétri Corone

Sangineto Lido
Capo Bonifati

Cetraro
Marina di Acquappesa
Rota Greca
Bisigna

Catena Costiera
Montalto Uffugo
Luzzi
Rose

Fuscaldo

Páola
S. Fili
Cosenza
Rende

S. Lúcido
Torremezzo di Falconara
Carolei
Caroilei

Fiumefreddo Brúzio
M. Cocuzza 1541
96

Lago
278
Aiello Cálabro
Rogli

Amantea
Scigliano

Nocera Tirinese
Platania
Gizzeria

Capo Súvero
Gizzeria Lido
Santa Eufémia
Lamézia
Sambias

Golfo di S. Eufémia

Napoli

Strómboli

Pizzo
Filadélfa

Panarea
Briático
Vibo Valéntia
S. Nicolà da Crissa

Salina
Tropea
Capo Vaticano
M. Poro 710
Mileto
Soriano Cálabro

Isole Eolie o Lipari
Lípari
Lípari
Ióppolo
Golfo di Gióia
Nicótera
Dínami
Mongiana

Vulcano
Rosarno
Laureana di Borrello
Fabri

Gióia Táuro
Polístena
Cinquefrondi

Capo di Milazzo
Capo Barbi
Palmi
Seminara
Cittanova
Mámmola
Gróia

Villafranca Tirrena
Bagnara Cálabra
Óppido Mamertina
Taurianova

Milazzo
Spadafora
Torre di Faro
Scilla
S. Eufémia d'Aspromonte
Delianuova
Platì
Síder
Locri

Golfo di Patti
Spartà
Mortelle
Messina
Gerace

0 5 10 20 30 40 Miles

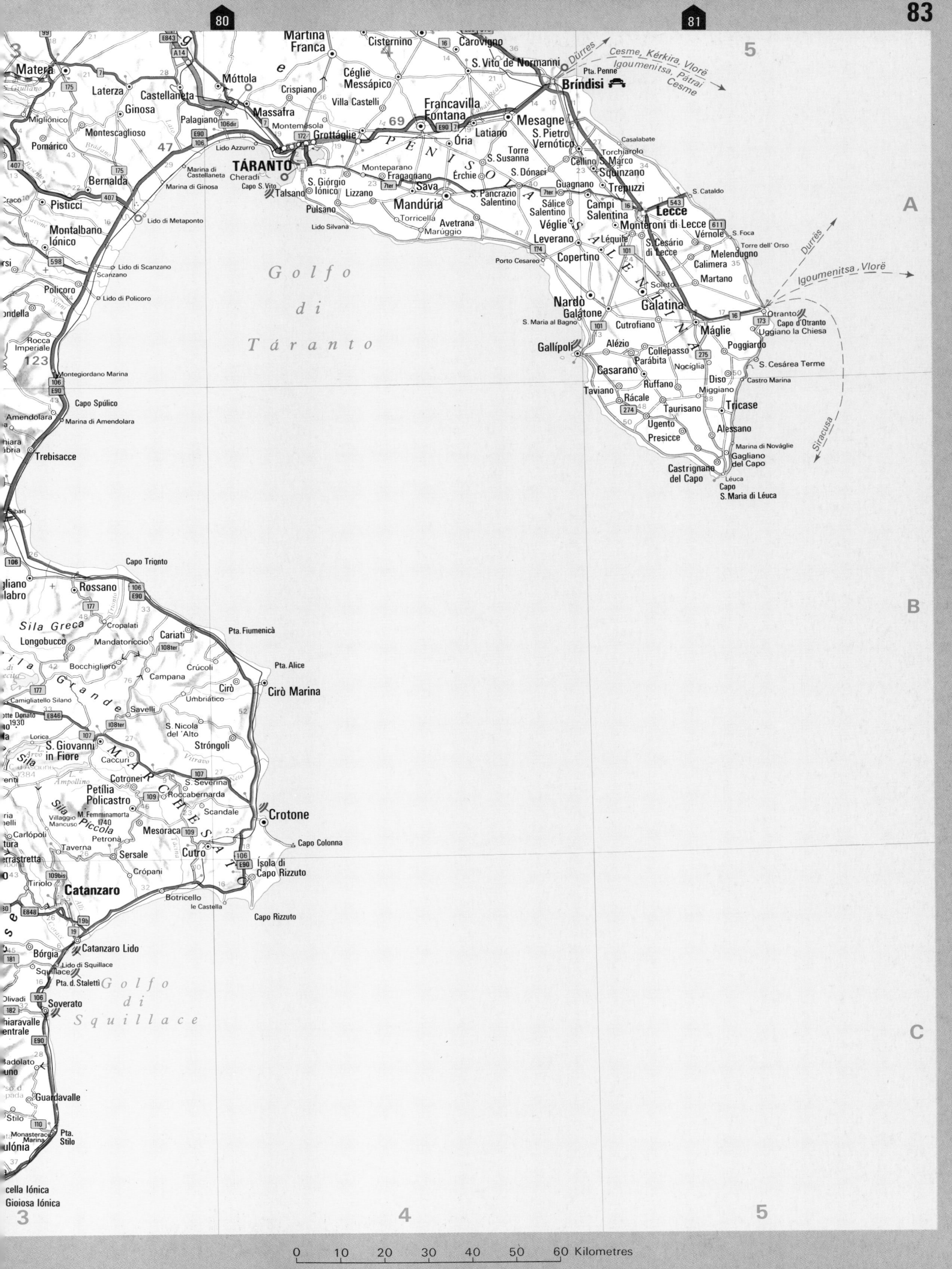

5

80   81

A

B

C

3   4   5

Matera
Laterza
Castellaneta
Ginosa
Miglionico
Montescaglioso
Pomárico
Bernalda
Pisticci
Montalbano
Iónico

Martina
Franca
Móttola
Crispiano
Massafra
Palagiano
Grottáglie
TÁRANTO
Cheradi
Marina di
Castellaneta
Marina di Ginosa
Lido Azzurro
S. Giórgio
Iónico
Talsano
Capo S. Vito
Lizzano
Pulsano
Lido di Metaponto

Cisternino
Céglie
Messápico
Villa Castelli
Montemesola
Monteparano
Sava
Fragagnano
Mandúria
Torricella
Avetrana
Marúggio
Lido Silvana

Carovigno
S. Vito de Normanni
Francavilla
Fontana
Ória
Latiano
S. Pietro
Vernótico
Torre
S. Susanna
S. Dónaci
Érchie
S. Pancrazio
Salentino
Sálice
Salentino
Véglie
Leverano
Porto Cesareo
Copertino

Brindisi
Pta. Penne
Mesagne
Casalabate
Torchiarolo
Cellino S. Marco
Squinzano
Guagnano
Trepuzzi
Campi
Salentina
Monteroni di Lecce
Léquile
S. Cesário
di Lecce
Lecce
S. Cataldo
Vérnole
S. Foca
Torre dell' Orso
Melendugno
Calimera
Martano

Durrës
Cesme, Kérkira, Vlorë
Igoumenitsa, Pátrai
Cesme

Durrës
Igoumenitsa, Vlorë

Golfo
di
Táranto

Nardò
Galátone
S. Maria al Bagno
Gallípoli
Alézio
Casarano
Taviano
Rácale
Ugento
Presicce
Castrignano
del Capo

Soleto
Cutrofiano
Galatina
Máglie
Collepasso
Parábita
Nocíglia
Ruffano
Taurisano
Alessano
Léuca
Capo
S. Maria di Léuca

Otranto
Capo d'Otranto
Uggiano la Chiesa
Poggiardo
Diso
Miggiano
Tricase
Castro Marina
S. Cesárea Terme
Marina di Nováglie
Gagliano
del Capo

Siracusa

Policoro
Lido di Policoro
Rocca
Imperiale
Montegiordano Marina
Capo Spúlico
Amendolara
Marina di Amendolara
Trebisacce
Sibari

Capo Trionto
Rossano
Sila Greca
Longobucco
Cropalati
Mandatoriccio
Bocchigliero
Campana
Umbriático
Crúcoli
Cirò
Cirò Marina
Savelli
S. Nicola
del 'Alto
Stróngoli
Caccuri

Pta. Fiumenicà
Pta. Alice

Golfo
di
Squillace

Camigliatello Silano
S. Giovanni
in Fiore
Cotronei
S. Severina
Petília
Policastro
M. Femminamorta
Villaggio
Mancuso
Mesoraca
Petronà
Sersale
Cutro
Catanzaro
Taverna
Carlópoli
Tiriolo

Roccabernarda
Scandale
Crotone
Capo Colonna
Ísola di
Capo Rizzuto
Botricello
le Castella
Capo Rizzuto

Bórgia
Catanzaro Lido
Lido di Squillace
Squillace
Pta. d. Staletti
Soverato
Chiaravalle
Guardavalle
Stilo
Monasterace
Marina
Pta.
Stilo
Gioiosa Iónica

0 10 20 30 40 50 60 Kilometres

1   2

A

Livorno
Genova
Cágliari
Tunis
Ustica Nápoli

Cágliari
Tunis

Capo S. Vito
Capo Gallo
Mondello
Isola delle
Femmine
S. Vito
lo Capo   Terrasini   Capi
Golfo   E90   27   Capaci
di   A29   **PALERMO**
Castellammare   24   Carini   7   Ficarazzi
Pizzolungo   M. Spáragio   Montelepre   63   Monreale   Bagheria
Éríce   Valdérice   1110   Scopello   Balestrate   186   Casteldáccia
Trápani   187   Castellammare   113   Partinico   Altofonte   121   113   Golfo di
Lévanzo   del Golfo   Fulgatore   113   Piana   Misilmeri   E90   Trabia   Términi
Isole Égadi   Paceco   8   Alcamo   S. Cipirello   degli Albanesi   Bolognetta   46   Términi   Cefalù
Maréttimo   113   Calatafimi   118   Marineo   Caccamo   Imerese   E90   113
Favignana   42   A29 dir.   Vita   Camporeale   Grande   Ciminna   285   Cerda   A19   Campofelice   A20   Tus
Favignana   115   Salemi   188A   A29   119   MAZARA   Mezzoiuso   Montemaggiore   Vicari   di Roccella   Collesano   Pzo.   286   Castelbuo
Stagnone   188   Salemi   E90   44   Roccamena   Rca. Busambra   Belsito   Roccapalumba   Caltavuturo   e Madonie   Carbonara   Gera
Marsala   VAL   Gibellina   624   Corleone   1613   Lercara   121   Ália   Valledolmo   62   1979   Petralia
Strasatti   Trinita   S. Ninfa   Salaparuta   Campofiorito   Plla.   Friddi   66   Resuttano   Polizzi   Sottana
42   Pa tanna   188   S. Margherita   Bisacquino   Imbriaca   189   Vallelunga   Generosa   Alimena
188   di Belice   718   Prizzi   Pratameno   Villalba   Plla. di
Mazara   E90   Castelvetrano   S. Carlo   Chiusa   Palazzo   118   S. Stéfano   Recativo   Villarc
del Vallo   A29   115   E931   Sambuca   Sclafani   Adriano   Quisquina   832   **SIC**
Campobello   Menfi   115   di Sicília   Bivona   Alessándria   Cammarata   Marianópoli   122 bis   E
di Mazara   Caltabellotta   386   della Rocca   M. Cammarata   S. Caterina   115   122
Granítola   Marinella   Ciancana   1580   Casteltérmini   64   Mussomeli   Villarrosa   **Caltanisse**
Capo Granítola   Sciacca   Ribera   Cattólica   S. Biágio   Campofranco   S. Cataldo   28   122
B   Capo S. Marco   Platani   Eraclea   Plátani   Montedoro   Serradifalco   Pietraperzia   191
Raffadali   Aragona   640   Canicatti   190   Sommatino   20
Montallegro   Racalmuto   122   Castrofilippo   17   Délia   Riesi   Ba
Siculiana   Agrigento   189   Favara   123   Naro   Ravanusa   14
Porto   115   Camastra   Campobello   33   Butera
Empédocle   Plla. di   162   Palma   di Licata   E931   115
Rocca Corvo   di Montechiaro   Salso   20
Licata   Falconara   115
Ge

MARE MEDITERRANEO   *Golfo di*

C

1   2

0   5   10   20   30   40 Miles

3 4

S. Eufémia

Isole Eolie o Lipari

Strómboli

Napoli

Panarea

Girifalco Bórgia Catanzar
Lido di Squillace
Pta. d. Staletti

Briático Pizzo Filadélfia
Tropea Vibo Valéntia Olivadi Soverato
E45 A3 110 S. Nicola Chiaravalle 106
Capo Vaticano M. Poro da Crissa Centrale
710 Soriano Simbário E90
Ióppolo Cálabro 182
Mileto 182 Serra S. Bruno Badolato
Salina Nicótera Dinami M. Pecorara
Golfo di Rosarno 18 127 1423 Guardavalle
Gióia Mongiana Pietra Spada
Lípari Laureana 1335
di Borrello Fabrízia
Gióia Táuro Polistena Cinquefrondi Stilo
Lípari 281 110 Pso. Croce Ferrata Monasterace Pta.
Capo Barbi Palmi 111 110 Caulónia Marina Stilo
Seminara Cittanova Grotteria
Vulcano Taurianova Mámmola Gioiosa Iónica
Capo Milazzo Oppido Gerace Roccella Iónica
Villafranca Spartà Mamertina 111 Marina di Gioiosa Iónica
Tirrena Mortelle Bagnara 112 Siderno
Capo Calavà Spadafora Torre Cálabra Platì Careri 106 Locri
Milazzo Villa S. Giovanni Aspromonte
Gioiosa Golfo di Patti E90 113 di Faro Scilla Delianuova 1956 S. Luca
Marea Capo Barcellona Montalto Bovalino Marina
d'Orlando Brolo Pozzo di Gotto S. Eufémia 1408 Bianco
S Ágata Naso E90 113 MESSINA d'Aspromonte Sella Entrata
di Militello Patti A20 RÉGGIO Láganadi Bova
éfano Longi Falcone S. Lucia DI CALABRIA Gambárie S. Luca
astra Caronia 105 del Mela Cardeto Bagaladi
S Mazzarrà Castroreale Pzo. Poverello Staiti
Tortorici 116 Fratello S. Andrea 1279 106 Bova
stretta Ucria Floresta S. Piero Novara A18 Pta. di Montebello Bova Marina
117 Monti Patti di Sicília Péllaro Iónico 183
Capizzi Montalbano Scaletta Mélito di Lazzaro Brancaleone Marina
Randazzo Elicona Zanclea Porto Salvo
Nebrodi M. Soro Antillo Alì Terme Capo Spartivento
Colla di Cesarò 1847 S. Doménica Roccalumera
Contrasto Vittória Francavilla S. Teresa
erlinga Cerami Troina di Sicília di Riva
120 Castiglione 97
Nicosia Maletto Bronte di Sicília Taormina
Gagliano 284 Giardini
eonforte Castelferrato Linguaglossa 114
117 Agira Adrano M. Etna Piedimonte Fiumefreddo di Sicília
Regalbuto 3340 Etneo
Centúripe Biancavilla Máscali
Assoro S. Maria Zafferana Riposto
alascibetta 94 di Licodia Nicolosi Etnea E45 Giarre
A19 192 Paternò
Valguarnera Raddusa Castel Misterbianco Trecastagni Acireale
Caropepe di Iúdica Belpasso Aci Catena
ti Ramacca Motta Aci Castello
rina Aidone S. Anastásia Otranto
117bis Palagonia CATÁNIA Valletta
S. Michele Mirabella Lido di Pláia
di Ganzaria Imbáccari Golfo
rino Mineo di
124 Scórdia Lentini Catánia
Caltagirone Militello Carlentini Capo S. Croce
417 in Val di Francofonte
Grammichele Catánia Melilli Augusta
Niscemi Vizzini Sortino Priolo Golfo di
S Pietro Licodia Bucchéri Gargallo Augusta Otranto
Monterosso Almo Eubea Ferla
Chiaramonte M. Láuro Giarratana Solarino Siracusa
Acate Gulfi 986 124 Floridia
E45 Palazzolo A18
Vittória Acréide Canicattini Capo Murro
221 Bagni di Porco
Cómiso Ragusa Cassibile Valletta
Scoglitti 115 Módica Noto 115 Ávola
S. Croce Golfo
Camerina Scicli Íspica di
Marina di Ragusa Rosolini Noto
Donnalucata Marzamemi
Sampieri Pozzallo Pachino
Capo Pássero
Portopalo

LIA A L DI M O T O

0 10 20 30 40 50 60 Kilometres

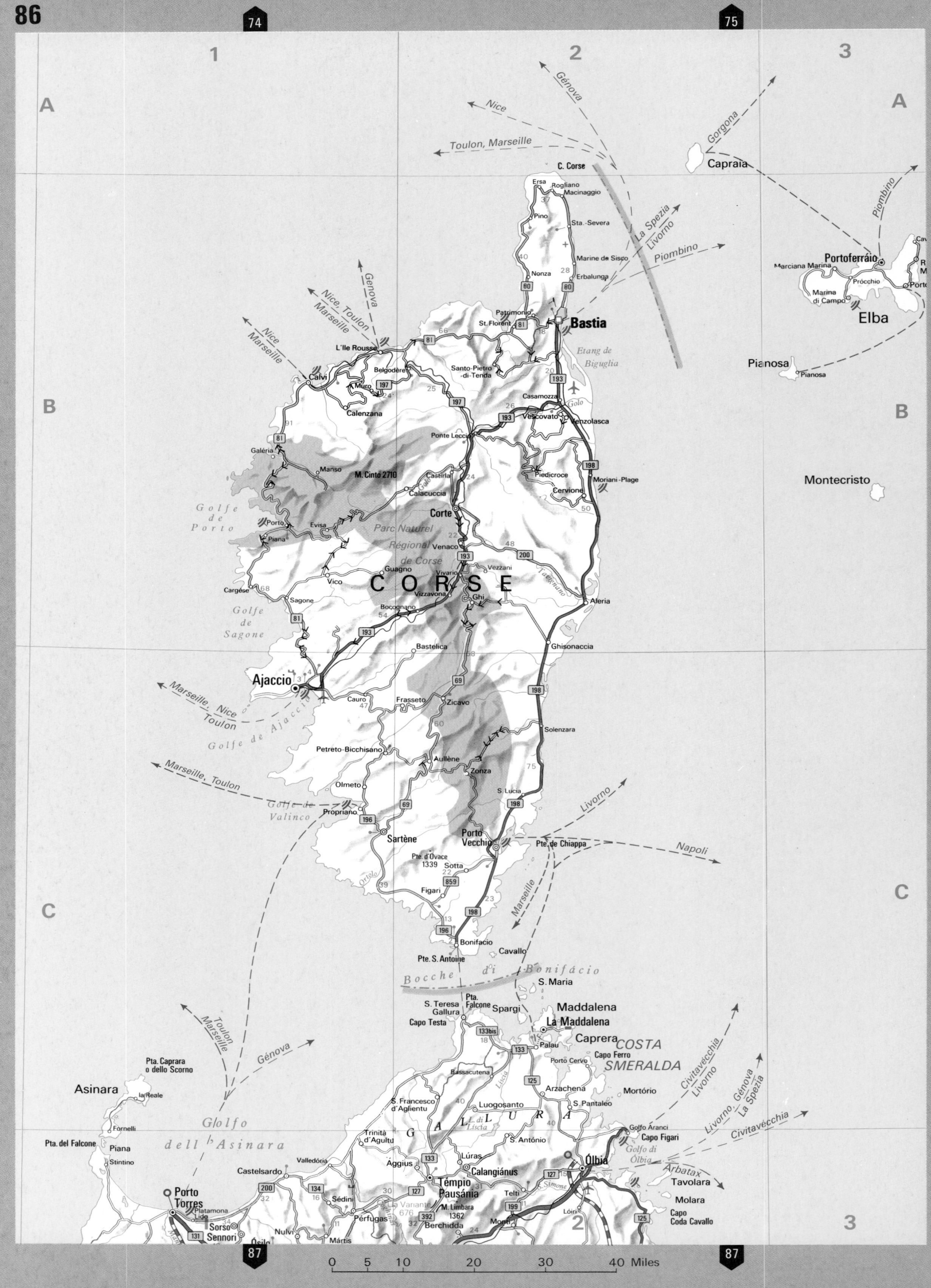

74   75

1   2   3

A   A

C. Corse

Ersa
Rogliano
Macinaggio

Nice

Toulon, Marseille

Pino

Sta.-Severa

Gorgona

Capraia

La Spezia
Livorno

Piombino

Marciana Marina
Marine de Sisco

Próccio

Marina
di Campo

Portoferráio

Elba

Nonza   28   Erbalunga

Pianosa

Pianosa

Génova

Nice, Toulon
Marseille

Nice
Marseille

Patrimonio

St. Florent   Bastia

L'Ile Rousse

Calvi

Belgodère
Muro   197

Calenzana

Santo-Pietro
-di-Tenda

Etang de
Biguglia

B   B

Galéria

Manso

M. Cinto 2710

Calenzana

Ponte Leccia

Piedicroce

Casamozza

Vescovato
Venzolasca

Golo

198

Moriani-Plage

Montecristo

Calacuccia

Castirla

Corte

Cervione

50

Parc Naturel

Golfe
de
Porto

Porto

Evisa

Piana

Régional
de Corse

Venaco   193   200

Vezzani

Cargése   68

Sagone

Guagno
Vico

Vivario

Vizzavona

Aferia

Bocognano   54

Ghi

Golfe
de
Sagone

81

193

Bastelica

Ghisonaccia

Ajaccio

Cauro   47

Frasseto

Zicavo

69

198

Marseille, Nice
Toulon

Golfe de Ajaccio

Petreto-Bicchisano

Aullène

Zonza

Solenzara

Marseille, Toulon

Olmeto

Golfe de
Valinco

Propriano

196

Sartène

69

S. Lucia   198

Livorno

Porto
Vecchio

Pte. de Chiappa   Napoli

Pte. d'Ovace
1339   Sotta

859

22

Marseille

C   C

Figari

Oriele   39

196   198   23

Bonifacio

Cavallo

Pte. S. Antoine

Bocche   d'i   Bonifácio

S. Maria

S. Teresa
Gallura   Pta.
Falcone   Spargi   Maddalena

Toulon
Marseille

Génova

Capo Testa   133bis   La Maddalena

Palau   Caprera

COSTA
SMERALDA

Civitavécchia
Livorno

133

Portó Cervo   Capo Ferro

Asinara

Pta. Caprara
o dello Scorno

la Reale

Bassacutena

125

Arzachena

Mortório

S. Pantaleo

Livorno-Génova
La Spezia

Golfo
dell' Asinara

Fornelli

Piana

Pta. del Falcone

S. Francesco
d'Aglientu

G   Luogosanto   40   S. António

A   L   L   U   R   A

Golfo Áranci

Capo Figari

Civitavécchia

Stintino

Trinità
d'Agultu

Lisca   S. António

Golfo di
Ólbia

Arbatax

Castelsardo

Valledória

Aggius   133

Lúras

Calangiánus

Ólbia

Tavolara

Porto
Torres

200   134

Sédini
16

30

127

Témpio
Pausánia

Telti

127

199

Simone

Molara

Platamona
Lido   32

Pérfugas

Variante
676   392

Berchidda

M. Limbara
1362

Lóiri

24

Capo
Coda Cavallo

Sorso
Sennori   131

Nulvi
Ósila   Mártis

125

3

87   87

0   5   10   20   30   40 Miles

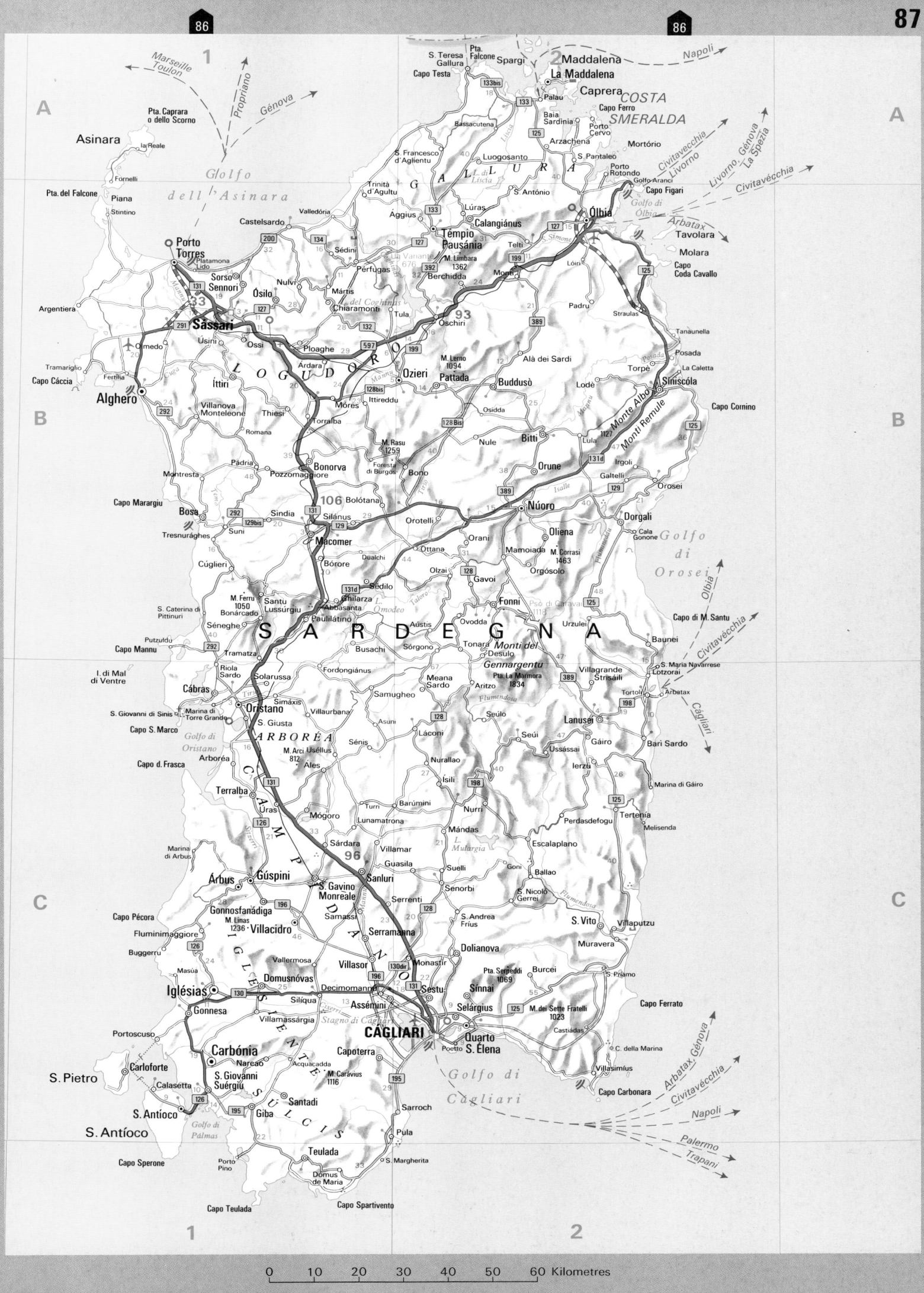
Marseille
Toulon
Propriano
Génova
Napoli
Asinara
Pta. Caprara o dello Scorno
la Reale
Fornelli
Golfo dell'Asinara
Pta. del Falcone
Piana
Stintino
Castelsardo
Valledória
Porto Torres
Platamona Lido
Sorso
Sennori
Sássari
Ósilo
Argentiera
Olmedo
Úsini
Ossi
Tramariglio
Capo Cáccia
Fertilia
Alghero
Íttiri
Villanova Monteleone
Thiesi
Romana
Pádria
Montresta
Pozzomaggiore
Bonorva
Capo Marargiu
Bosa
Sindia
Tresnuraghes
Suni
Macomer
Cúglieri
M. Ferru 1050
Bonárcado
Santu Lussúrgiu
S. Caterina di Pittinuri
Séneghe
Putzuldu
Capo Mannu
Tramatza
I. di Mal di Ventre
Riola Sardo
Cábras
S. Giovanni di Sinis
Marina di Torre Grande
Oristano
Capo S. Marco
Golfo di Oristano
Capo d. Frasca
Arboréa
Terralba
Uras
Marina di Arbus
Árbus
Gúspini
Capo Pécora
Gonnosfanádiga
M. Linas 1236
Villacidro
Fluminimaggiore
Buggerru
Masúa
Iglésias
Gonnesa
Portoscuso
Carbónia
Carloforte
S. Pietro
Calasetta
S. Giovanni Suérgiu
S. Antíoco
Golfo di Pálmas
Capo Sperone
Porto Pino
Capo Teulada
Giba
Santadi
Teulada
Domus de Maria
Capo Spartivento
S. Margherita
Pula
Sarroch
Capoterra
Acquacadda
M. Caravius 1116
Nareao
Villamassárgia
Siliqua
Decimomannu
Assémini
Domusnóvas
Vallermosa
Villasor
CAGLIARI
Stagno di Cagliari
Poetto
Quartu S. Élena
Golfo di Cagliari
Arbatax, Génova
Civitavécchia
Palermo
Trapani
Capo Carbonara
Villasimíus
C. della Marina
Castiádas
M. dei Sette Fratelli 1023
Capo Ferrato
Burcei
Sínnai
Pta. Serpeddi 1069
Selárgius
Sestu
Monastir
S. Priamo
Muravera
Villaputzu
S. Vito
Dolianova
Serramanna
Samassi
S. Andrea Frius
Senorbì
Serrenti
Sanluri
S. Gavino Monreale
Guasila
Suelli
Sárdara
Villamar
Mógoro
Lunamatrona
Turri
Barúmini
Mándas
Nurri
Ísili
Nurallao
Láconi
L. Mulargia
Escalaplano
Ballao
Goni
S. Nicolò Gerrei
Flumendosa
Perdasdefogu
Tertenía
Melisenda
Marina di Gáiro
Gáiro
Ierzu
Ussássai
Seúi
Seúlo
Bari Sardo
Lanusei
Tortolì
Arbatax
Cágliari
Villagrande Strisáili
Lotzorai
S. Maria Navarrese
Baunei
Capo di M. Santu
Urzulei
Olbia
Civitavécchia
Gennargentu
Monti del Gennargentu
Pta. La Marmora 1834
Aritzo
Desulo
Tonara
Meana Sardo
Samugheo
Sórgono
Atzara
Ovodda
Áustis
Busachi
Fordongiánus
Villaurbana
Simáxis
Solarussa
S. Giusta
ARBORÉA
M. Arci 812
Usellus
Ales
Sénis
Asuni
SARDEGNA
CAMPIDANO
IGLESIENTE
SULCIS
Paulilátino
Abbasanta
Ghilarza
L. Omodeo
Sédilo
Bórore
Dualchi
Ottana
Olzai
Gavoi
Fonni
Orgósolo
Mamoiada
M. Corrasi 1463
Oliena
Orani
Orotelli
Núoro
Dorgali
Cala Gonone
Golfo di Orosei
Orosei
Galtelli
Irgoli
Lula
Orune
Bitti
Nule
Osidda
Monte Albo
Monti Remule
Lodè
Siniscóla
Capo Comino
La Caletta
Posada
Torpè
Tanaunella
Alà dei Sardi
Buddusò
Pattada
M. Lerno 1094
Ozieri
Ittireddu
Móres
Torralba
M. Rasu 1259
Foresta di Burgos
Bono
Bolótana
Silánus
LOGUDORO
Árdara
Ploaghe
Chiaramonti
Mártis
Nulvi
Pérfugas
Sédini
Tula
Óschiri
Berchidda
M. Limbara 1362
Monti
Tempio Pausánia
Calangiánus
Lúras
Ággius
Trinità d'Agultu
S. Francesco d'Aglientu
Luogosanto
GALLURA
L. di Líscia
S. António
Telti
Ólbia
Golfo di Ólbia
Lóiri
Padru
Straulas
Capo Coda Cavallo
Molara
Tavolara
Capo Figari
Golfo Aranci
Porto Rotondo
S. Pantaleo
Arzachena
Mortório
Porto Cervo
Baia Sardinia
Capo Ferro
COSTA SMERALDA
Palau
Caprera
La Maddalena
Maddalena
Spargi
Pta. Falcone
S. Teresa Gallura
Capo Testa
Bassacutena
Livorno
La Spezia
A
B
C
1
2
0 10 20 30 40 50 60 Kilometres

57
92
61

1
2
3
A
B
C
Łeba
J. Łebsko
J. Sarbsko
Sasino
Żarnowiec
Choczewo
Żelazno
Wicko
Kostkowo
Rowy
J. Gardno
Główczyce
Cecenowo
Żelkowo
Gościcino
Ustka
Duninowo
J. Wicko
Jarosławiec
J. Kopań
Postomino
Lubuczewo
Lębork
Bożepole Wielkie
Pogorzelice
Mianowice
Potęgowo
Słupsk
Sycewice
Wieprza
Darłowo
Stary Jarosław
Łupawa
Linia
Strzepcz
Kwakowo
Sławno
Bukowo Morskie
Czarna-Dąbrówka
Budowo
Sierakowice
Unieście
Mielno
Sarbinowo
Ustronie Morskie
Mielechowo
Ostrowiec
Korzybie
Barcino
Suchorze
Unichowo
Kołczygłowy
Brodnica Graniczna
Jamno
J. Jamno
Kołobrzeg
Koszalin
Sianów
Kępice
Krąg
Trzebielino
Borzytuchom
Stężyca
Mrzeżyno
Dygowo
Dobrzyca
Nacław
Bytów
Nakło
Kalisko
Niechorze
Trzebiatów
Wrzosowo
Manowo
Polanów
Dretyń
Niezabyszewo
Tuchomie
Półczno
Korne
Kościerzyna
Gołańcz Pomorska
Gościno
Karlino
Niedalino
Mostowo
Kawcze
Studzienice
Lipusz
Cerkwica
Białogard
Radew
Miastko
Piaszczyna
Borzyszkowy
Sominy
Świerzno
Gorawino
Świetlino
Drzewiany
Dziemiany
Kiszewa Stara
Gryfice
Rymań
Bobolice
Lipnica
J. Wdzydze
Sławoborze
Tychowo
Biały Bór
Koczała
Brusy
Karsin
Rabino
Tychówko
Grzmiąca
Wierzchowo
Brzezie
Konarzyny
Płoty
Resko
Świdwin
Sława
Połczyn-Zdrój
Parsęta
Przechlewo
Mecikał
Czersk
Starogard
Barwice
Rzeczenica
J. Charzykowskie
Rytel
Bierzwina
Ostropole
J. Wielimie
Gwda Wielka
Szczecinek
Charzykowy
Chojnice
Legbąd
Śliwice
Nowogard
Wierzbięcin
Łobez
Gawroniec
Kluczewo
Połne
Jeleniino
Czarne
Człuchów
Silno
Dobra
J. Siecino
J. Drawsko
J. Pile
Lotyń
Barkowo
Zamarte
Tuchola
Węgorzyno
Drawsko Pomorskie
Złocieniec
Czaplinek
Łubowo
Okonek
Cierznie
Debrzno
Kamień Kraj.
Pamiętowo
Bysław
Kania
Broczyno
Lędyczek
Gostycyn
Chociwel
Wierzchowo
Podgaje
Lipka
Kamionka
Ińsko
Lubieszewo
Iłowiec
Sypniewo
Sępólno-Krajeńskie
J. Koronowskie
Ciemnik
Jastrowie
Glomia
Złotów
Makowarsko
Stargard Szczeciński
Dobrzany
Pożrzadło Wlp.
Mirosławiec
Piecnik
Szwecja
Płytnica
Sypniewo
Więcbork
Koronowo
Suliborz
Kalisz Pomorski
J. Bytyńskie
Wałcz
Piława
Krępsko
Suchań
Wapnica
Recz
Marcinkowice
Kotomierz
Dolice
Drawno
Tryszczyn
Łobżenica
Mrocza
Lubiatowo
Tuczno
Gostomia
Dobrzyca
Wysoka
Choszczno
Suliszewo
Rusinowo
Szydłowo
Piła
Śmiłowo
Wyrzysk
Sadki
Nakło n. N.
Kanał Bydgoski
BYDGOSZCZ
Fordon
Osielsko
Zieleniewo
Człopa
Stobno
Osiek
Białe Błota
Krzęcin
Szczuczarz
Ujście
Miasteczko Krajeńskie
Białośliwie
Pełczyce
Bierzwnik
Trzcianka
Samocin
Smogulec
Rynarzewo
Mostkowo
Kuźnica Żelichowska
Siedlisko
Chodzież
Margonin
Szubin
Bobrówko
Dobiegniew
Kuźnica Czarnkowska
Kcynia
Łabiszyn
Gołańcz
Muranowo
Nowa Wieś Wielka
Strzelce Krajeńskie
Krzyż
Wieleń
Czarnków
Czeszewo
Wapno
Złotniki Kujawskie
Przyłęg
Huta
Budzyń
Kłodawa
Drezdenko
Lubasz
Barcin
Żnin
Puszcza Notecka
Ryczywół
Wągrowiec
Domasławek
Piechcin
Gorzów Wielkopolski
Noteć
Santok
Klempicz
Wenecja
Goszczanowo
Ludomy
Rogoźno
Mieścisko
Dąbrowa
Bogdaniec
Chojno
Wronki
Obrzycko
Janowiec Wielkopolski
Rogowo
Janikowo
Biezdrowo
Popowo Kościelne
Murzynowo
Sieraków
Warta
Oborniki
Skoki
Mogilno
Skwierzyna
Międzychód
Szamotuły
Kłecko
Modliszewko
Przytoczna
Wierzbno
Nojewo
Murowana Goślina
Kiszkowo
Lubniewice
Kwilcz
Kaźmierz
Chludowo
Trzemeszno
Jankowo Dolne
Pniewy
Rokietnica
Owińska
Gniezno
Orchowo
Pszczew
Międzyrzecz
Bytyń
Pobiedziska
Łubowo
Żydowo
Witkowo
Trzemeszno Lubuskie
Lwówek
Lusówko
Swarzędz
Anastazewo
Bolewice
Kostrzyn
Powidz
J. Powidzkie
Boryszyn
Trzciel
Buk
POZNAŃ
Nekla
Torzym
Łagów
Jordanowo
Nowy Tomyśl
Komorniki
Luboń
Jabłonka
Września
P O M O R S K I E
P O J E Z I E R Z E
Tu

61
65
90

0 5 10 20 30 40 Miles

92
93

Zatoka Gdańska
Mierzeja Helska
Kurskaya Kosa
Mierzeja Wiślana
Zalew Wiślany
Kaliningradskiy Zaliv
Oxelösund
Karlskrona
KALININGRAD
Guryevsk
Konstantinovka
Svetlyy
Baltiysk
Primorsk
Komsomolsk
Ozierki
Gvardieysk
Znamiensk
Talpaki
Darnieye
Vysokye
Niviehskoye
Ludushkin
Pyatidorozhnoye
Marmanovo
Kornievo
Gvardeyskoye
Druzba
Pravdinsk
Mozy
Lipniaki
Bagrationovsk
Szyrokoye
Zheleznodorozhny
Jastrzębia Góra
Rozewie
Władysławowo
Chałupy
Puck
Jastarnia
Jurata
Hel
Wejherowo
Reda
Rewa
Rumia
GDYNIA
Sopot
GDAŃSK
Kokoszki
Borkowo
Koszwały
Kiezmark
Rybina
Sztutowo
Krynica Morska
Przebrno
Frambork
Braniewo
Tolkmicko
Pogrodzie
Łęcze
Milejewo
Pruszcz Gd.
Łęgowo
Przywidz
Sobowidz
Pszczółki
Nowy Dwór Gd.
Nw. Staw
Elbląg
Gronowo
Jegłownik
Bogaczewo
Pasłęk
Godziszewo
Skarszewy
Tczew
Czarlin
Malbork
Stare Pole
Zwierzno
Starogard Gd.
Pelplin
Rudno
Sztum
Tropy
Dzierzgoń
Rychliki
Kwietniewo
Zielonka Pasłęcka
Młynary
Wilczęta
Lipowina
Lelkowo
Kandyty
Górowo Iławeckie
Wojciechy
Bartoszyce
Sępopol
Barciany
Srokowo
Łabędnik
Pieszkowo
Pieniężno
Płoty
Henrykowo
Runowo
Rogóż
Orneta
Lidzbark Warm.
Kiwity
Bisztynek
Samulewo
Kraskowo
Kętrzyn
Reszel
Godkowo
Lubomino
Miłogórze
Frankowo
Lutry
Kolno
Wilkowo
Miłakowo
Radostowo
Dobre Miasto
Jeziorany
Lężany
Morąg
Boguchwały
Świątki
Czerwonka
Szestno
Mrągowo
Sorkwity
Biskupiec
Sprecowo
Dywity
Barczewo
Mostkowo
Łukta
Morzeszczyn
Gniew
Mikołajki Pomorskie
Stary Dzierzgoń
Zalewo
Nowa Wieś
Ryjewo
Lubichowo
Skórcz
Osiek
Smętowo
Prabuty
Kwidzyn
Jerzwałd
Siemiany
Susz
Miłomłyn
Piławki
Ostróda
Podlejki
Kudypy
Olsztyn
Kortowo
Klewki
Stare Jabłonki
Dorotowo
Dźwierzuty
Nowe Kiejkuty
Babięta
Piecki
Nawiady
Pasym
Grom
Świętajno
Spychowo
Szczytno
Rozogi
Samborowo
Zabrowo
Jedrychowo
Kisielice
Iława
Gardeja
Bądki
Warlubie
Osie
Rychnowo
Olsztynek
Butryny
Rożental
Lubawa
Marwałd
Kurki
Jedwabno
Grunwald
Wapłewo
Dąbrówno
Zimna Woda
Napiwoda
Księży Lasek
Myszyniec
Wielbark
Muszaki
Nidzica
Puchałowo
Dusocin
Łasin
Jeżowo
Grupa
Graniczna
Grudziądz
Biskupiec
Samplawa
Nowe Miasto Lubawskie
Kiełpiny
Brzozie Lubawskie
Mroczno
Uzdowo
Janowo
Surowe
Zaręby
Zawady
Świecie
Przechowo
Chełmno
Okonin
Radzyń Chełm.
Jabłonowo
Paparzyn
Stolno
Zbrachlin
Płużnica
Wąbrzeżno
Dębowa Łąka
Małki
Brodnica
Grążawy
Lidzbark
Działdowo
Gródki
Chorzele
Świętosław
Unisław
Chełmża
Lipnica
Wrocki
Górzno
Osiek
Świedziebnia
Zieluń
Iłowo
Kuklin
Krzynowłoga Mała
Parciaki
Jednorożec
Grzywna
Kowalewo Pom.
Wielka Łąka
Golub-Dobrzyń
Strzygi
Radomin
Lubowidz
Mława
Szydłowo
Dzierzgowo
Drążdżewo
Nowa Wieś
Mchowo
Czarnowo
Pędzewo
Łysomice
Grębocin
TORUŃ
Rypin
Okalewo
Kuczbork
Żuromin
Wiśniewo
Grudusk
Krasnosielc
Przasnysz
Sypniewo
Dobrzejewice
Czerniewice
Cierpice
Puszcza Bydgoska
Szreńsk
Konopki
Mdzewo
Urszulewo
Bieżuń
Rodzanów
Strzegowo
Szczuki
Sieluń
Krasne
Maków Mazowiecki
Ciechanów
Gniewkowo
Czernikowo
Otłoczyn
Kikół
Gójsk
Skępe
Rościszewo
Gradzanowo Kościelne
Aleksandrów Kujawski
Ciechocinek
Nieszawa
Lipno
Sierpc
Glinojeck
Ościsłowo
Gołymin Stary
Szelków
Lubiel Nowy
Inowrocław
Radomice
Mochowo
Jeżewo
Raciąż
Ojrzeń
Przewodowo Parcele
Kleszewo
Tupadły
Pieranie
Tłuchowo
Drobin
Strzegocin
Pułtusk
Rząśnik
Kruszwica
Dobre
Szpetal Graniczny
Nowe Miasto
Pniewo
Zelno
Radziejów
Włocławek
Dobrzyń nad Wisłą
Sikórz
Bielsk
Góra
Dzierzążnia
Płońsk
Strzyże
Nasielsk
Sierakowo
Brześć Kuj.
Kruszyn
Goślice
Kucice
Wróblewo
Cieksyn
Wierzbica
Serock
Popowo Kościelne
Piotrków Kujawski
Lubraniec
Płock
Bulkowo
Przyborowice
Pomiechówek
Dębe
Zegrzynek
Zegrze
Kowal
Czarne
Bodzanów
Kobylniki
Zakroczym
Modlin
Nowy-Dwór Mazowiecki
Nieporęt
Radzymin
Miłżyn
Orle
Łąck
Tomisławice
Gostynin
Kępa Polska
Legionowo
Jabłonna
Izbica Kujawska
Lubień Kujawski
Gabin
Wyszogród
Kampinos
Palmiry
Łomianki
Marki
Wołomin
Kobyłka
Zielonka
Sompolno
Chodecz
Sanniki
Ślesin
Brdów
Strzelce
Puszcza
Zatoka
Wisła
Pregola
Drwęca
Osa
Wkra
Nida
Omulew
Narew
Sona
Łydynia
Skrwa
Płonka
Raciążnica
Działdówka
Pasłęka
Wałsza
Nogat
J. Drużno
Kanał Elbląski
J. Narie
J. Ruda Woda
J. Jeziorak
J. Dzierzgoń
J. Plusne
J. Łańskie
J. Dadaj
J. Ryńskie
J. Zegrzyńskie
J. Gopło
J. Głuszyńskie
Bory Tucholskie
POJEZIERZE MAZURSKIE
4
5
6
7
A
B
C
E28
E77
E75
E261
1
7
10
16
22
25
50
51
52
53
60
61
62
191
192
193
194
196
216
229
245
298
508
38
47
53
62
69
75
84
89
93
103
27
32
52

0 10 20 30 40 50 60 Kilometres

93
93

88
89
65

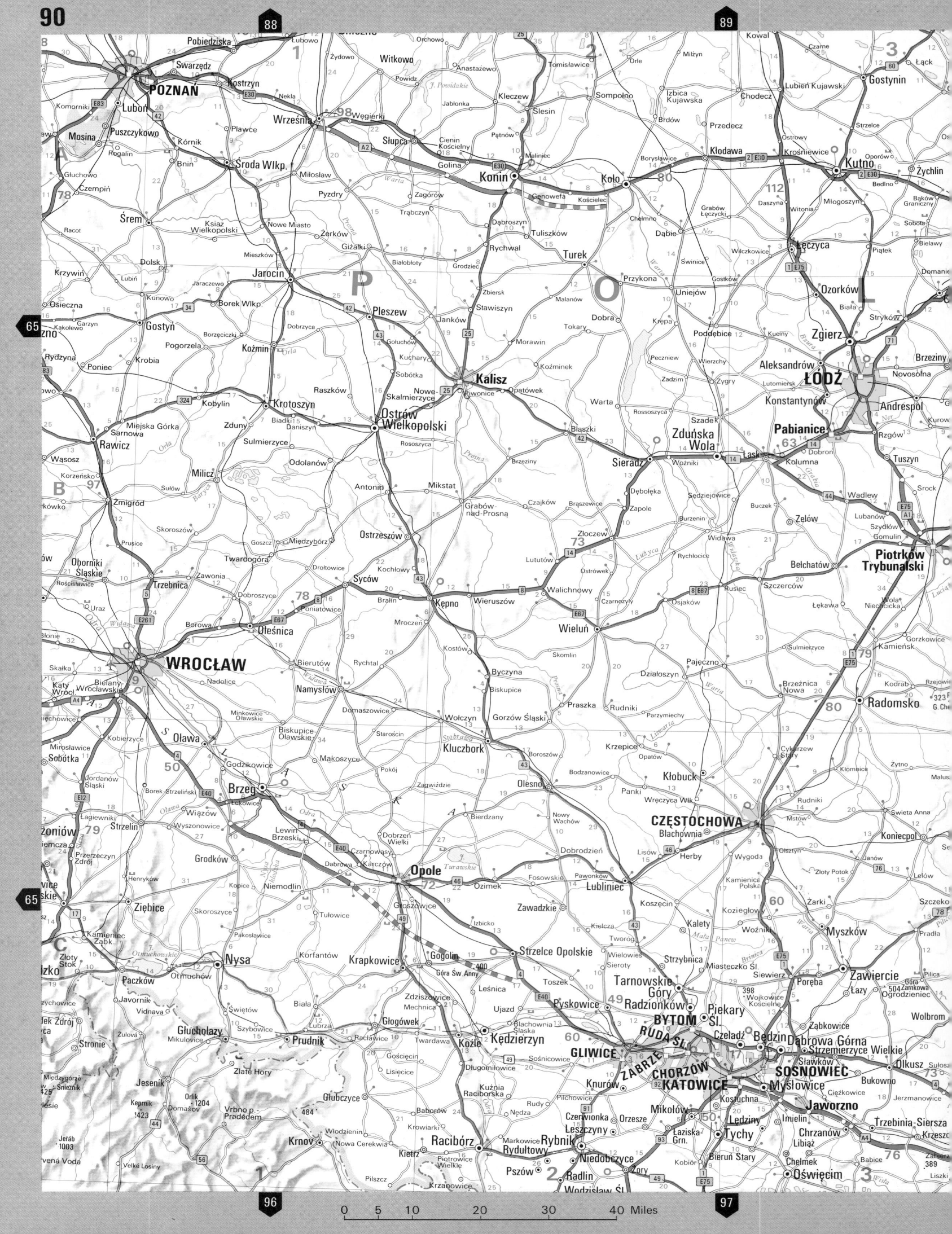
POZNAŃ
Swarzędz
Kostrzyn
Luboń
Mosina
Puszczykowo
Kórnik
Środa Wlkp.
Września
Września
Słupca
Witkowo
Konin
Koło
Kłodawa
Kutno
Gostynin
Łęczyca
Ozorków
Zgierz
ŁÓDŹ
Aleksandrów
Konstantynów
Pabianice
Andrespol
Tuszyn
Zduńska Wola
Sieradz
Turek
Uniejów
Poddębice
Kalisz
Ostrów Wielkopolski
Pleszew
Jarocin
Krotoszyn
Koźmin
Gostyń
Śrem
Rawicz
Milicz
Żmigród
Trzebnica
Oleśnica
WROCŁAW
Oława
Brzeg
Namysłów
Kępno
Syców
Ostrzeszów
Wieruszów
Wieluń
Kluczbork
Olesno
Opole
Nysa
Krapkowice
Kędzierzyn
Koźle
Racibórz
Rybnik
Gliwice
Zabrze
Bytom
Ruda Śl.
Chorzów
Katowice
Sosnowiec
Będzin
Dąbrowa Górna
Tychy
Jaworzno
Mysłowice
Oświęcim
Chrzanów
Olkusz
Zawiercie
Myszków
Tarnowskie Góry
Lubliniec
Częstochowa
Kłobuck
Radomsko
Bełchatów
Piotrków Trybunalski
Prudnik
Głuchołazy
Strzelce Opolskie
Ziębice
Strzelin
Grodków
Niemodlin
Jeseník
Krnov
P
O
L
S
L
A
S
K
A

0 5 10 20 30 40 Miles

65
96
97

89
93

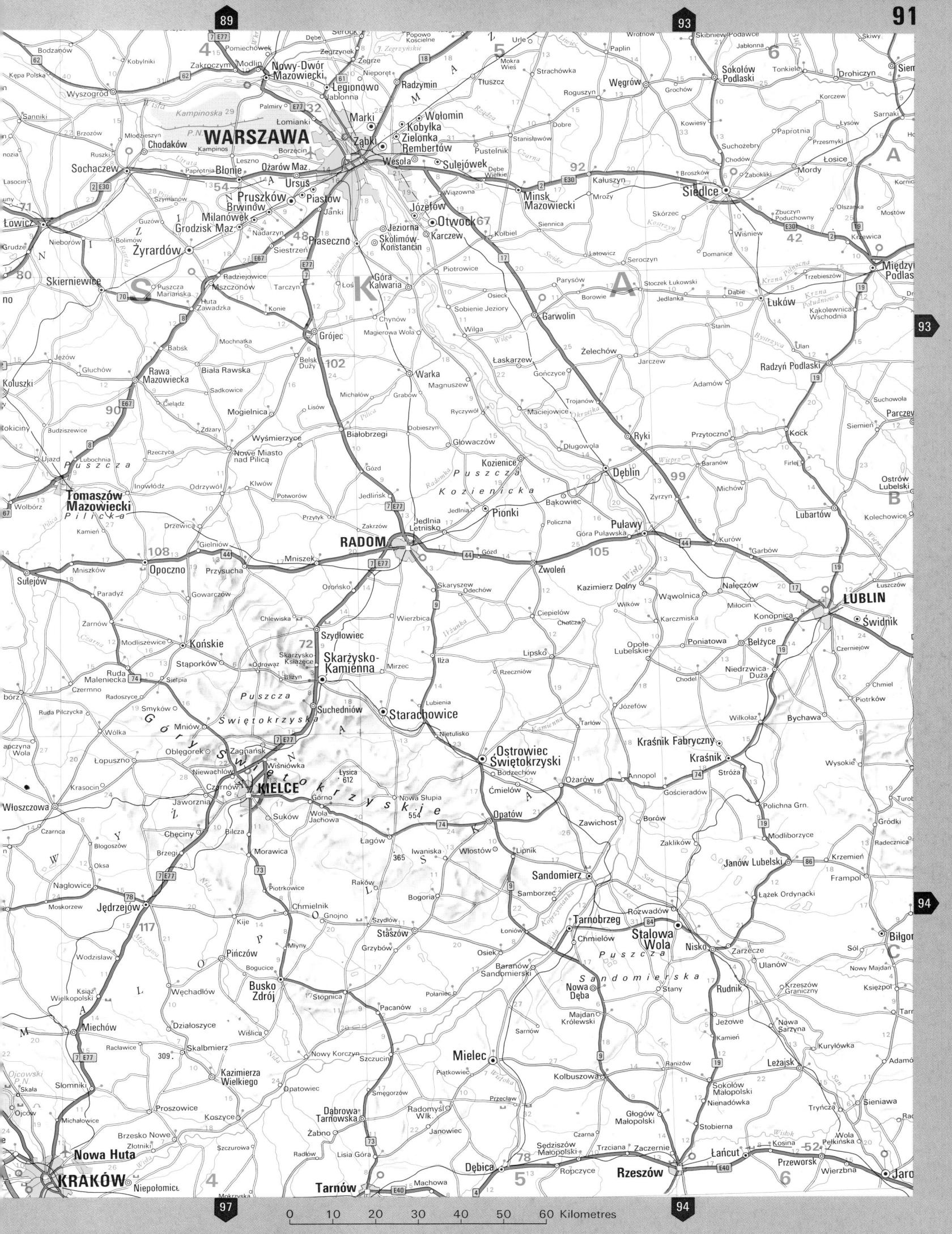

WARSZAWA
Nowy-Dwór Mazowiecki
Legionowo
Jabłonna
Radzymin
Modlin
Zakroczym
Pomiechówek
Wyszogród
Kampinoska
Marki
Ząbki
Wołomin
Kobyłka
Zielonka
Rembertów
Wesoła
Sulejówek
Łomianki
Borzęcin
Chodaków
Sochaczew
Błonie
Ożarów Maz.
Ursus
Pruszków
Piastów
Brwinów
Milanówek
Grodzisk Maz.
Żyrardów
Łowicz
Skierniewice
Piaseczno
Józefów
Otwock
Karczew
Jeziorna
Skolimów-Konstancin
Góra Kalwaria
Mińsk Mazowiecki
Kałuszyn
Siedlce
Węgrów
Sokołów Podlaski
Drohiczyn
Łosice
Międzyrzec Podlaski
Łuków
Garwolin
Żelechów
Radzyń Podlaski
Grójec
Warka
Rawa Mazowiecka
Mogielnica
Białobrzegi
Tomaszów Mazowiecki
Kozienice
Dęblin
Ryki
Puławy
Pionki
Jedlnia Letnisko
RADOM
Opoczno
Przysucha
Sulejów
Zwoleń
Kazimierz Dolny
Nałęczów
LUBLIN
Świdnik
Lubartów
Kock
Parczew
Ostrów Lubelski
Końskie
Szydłowiec
Skarżysko-Kamienna
Iłża
Starachowice
Suchedniów
Ostrowiec Świętokrzyski
Opole Lubelskie
Bełżyce
Kraśnik
Kraśnik Fabryczny
Bychawa
KIELCE
Chęciny
Włoszczowa
Nowa Słupia
Opatów
Ożarów
Zawichost
Sandomierz
Janów Lubelski
Tarnobrzeg
Stalowa Wola
Nisko
Rudnik
Biłgoraj
Jędrzejów
Pińczów
Busko Zdrój
Staszów
Chmielnik
Miechów
Kazimierza Wielkiego
Mielec
Kolbuszowa
Nowa Dęba
Leżajsk
Łańcut
Przeworsk
Rzeszów
Dębica
Tarnów
Dąbrowa Tarnowska
Nowa Huta
KRAKÓW
Niepołomice
Puszcza Kozienicka
Puszcza Świętokrzyska
Puszcza Sandomierska
Góry Świętokrzyskie
Wisła
Łysica 612
E7
E30
E40
E67
E77

0 10 20 30 40 50 60 Kilometres

97
94

46 47

OSLO
Drammen
Moss
Sarpsborg
Fredrikstad
Tönsberg
Larvik
Skien
Kristiansand
Arendal
Mandal
Lindesnes
Egersund
Sandnes
Karlstad
Kristinehamn
Örebro
Arboga
Köping
Västerås
Enköping
Uppsala
STOCKHOLM
Södertälje
Nynäshamn
Norrköping
Linköping
Motala
Vänern
Vättern
Mälaren
Skagerrak
Kattegat
Göteborg
Uddevalla
Vänersborg
Trollhättan
Borås
Jönköping
Huskvarna
Växjö
Kalmar
Karlskrona
Karlshamn
Kristianstad
Halmstad
Helsingborg
Helsingør
Landskrona
Malmö
Lund
Trelleborg
Ystad
Öland
Gotland
Visby
Bornholm (Dan.)
Rønne
Ostsee
Østersøen
KØBENHAVN
Roskilde
Køge
Sjælland
Odense
Fredericia
Kolding
Esbjerg
Vejle
Horsens
Århus
Silkeborg
Viborg
Randers
Ålborg
Frederikshavn
Skagen
Hjørring
Limfjorden
Flensburg
Schleswig
Kiel
Rendsburg
Fehmarn
Lübeck
Wismar
Rostock
Stralsund
Rügen
Sassnitz
HAMBURG
Bremen
Bremerhaven
Wilhelmshaven
Cuxhaven
Oldenburg
Osnabrück
Bielefeld
Hannover
Braunschweig
Magdeburg
BERLIN
Potsdam
Frankfurt
Halle
LEIPZIG
DRESDEN
Chemnitz
Zwickau
Erfurt
Kassel
Göttingen
FRANKFURT
Szczecin (Stettin)
Koszalin
Słupsk
Gdańsk (Danzig)
Gdynia
Sopot
Elbląg
Bydgoszcz
Toruń
Poznań
Gniezno
Wrocław
Łódź
Kalisz
Opole
Częstochowa
Ostsee
Gotska Sandön
Åland (Ahvenanmaa)

0 20 40 60 80 100 120 140 160 Miles

63 90 59

47

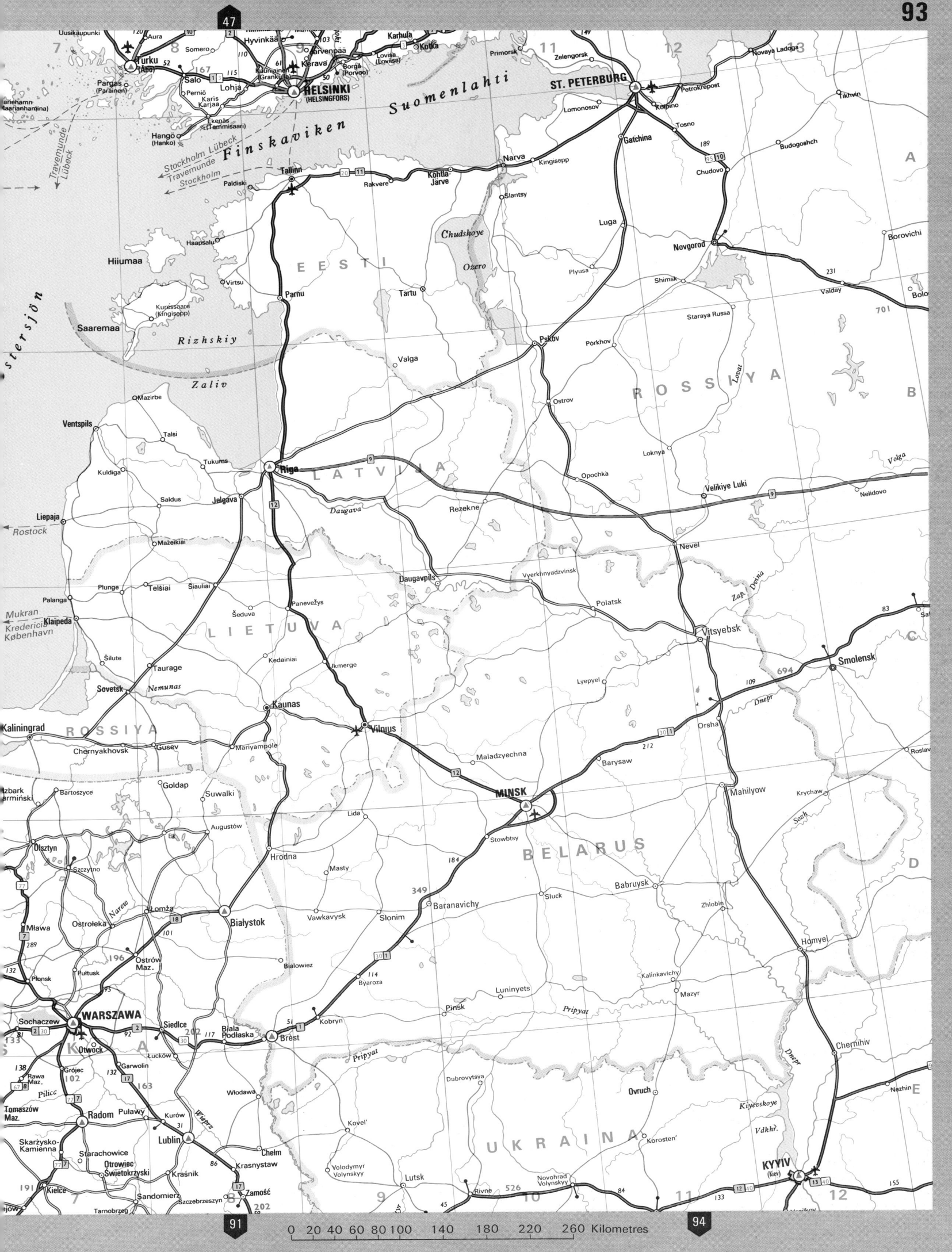

Suomenlahti
Finskaviken
Rizhskiy
Zaliv
Chudskoye
Ozero
EESTI
LATVIJA
LIETUVA
ROSSIYA
BELARUS
UKRAINA
HELSINKI
(HELSINGFORS)
ST. PETERBURG
Tallinn
Riga
Vilnius
MINSK
WARSZAWA
KYYIV
(Kiev)
Turku
(Åbo)
Salo
Lohja
Porvoo
Kotka
Karhula
Hyvinkää
Järvenpää
Kerava
Hangö
(Hanko)
Ekenäs
(Tammisaari)
Pargas
(Parainen)
Primorsk
Zelengorsk
Novaya Ladoga
Petrokrepost
Tikhvin
Lomonosov
Kolpino
Tosno
Gatchina
Budogoshch
Chudovo
Narva
Kingisepp
Kohtla-Järve
Rakvere
Paldiski
Slantsy
Luga
Novgorod
Borovichi
Haapsalu
Hiiumaa
Saaremaa
Kuressaare
(Kingisepp)
Virtsu
Parnu
Tartu
Plyusa
Shimsk
Valday
Staraya Russa
Pskov
Porkhov
Valga
Ostrov
Lovat
Mazirbe
Ventspils
Talsi
Tukums
Kuldiga
Loknya
Opochka
Velikiye Luki
Nelidovo
Volga
Saldus
Jelgava
Liepaja
Rostock
Daugava
Rezekne
Nevel
Mažeikiai
Daugavpils
Vyerkhnyadzvinsk
Zap. Dvina
Polatsk
Plunge
Telšiai
Šiauliai
Palanga
Klaipeda
Mukran
København
Šeduva
Panevežys
Vitsyebsk
Smolensk
Šilute
Taurage
Kedainiai
Ukmerge
Lyepyel
Sovetsk
Nemunas
Kaunas
Dnepr
Orsha
Kaliningrad
Chernyakhovsk
Gusev
Mariyampole
Maladzyechna
Barysaw
Roslavl
Goldap
Suwałki
Bartoszyce
Lida
Mahilyow
Krychaw
Sozh
Olsztyn
Augustów
Ełk
Stowbtsy
Szczytno
Hrodna
Masty
Babruysk
Narew
Łomża
Białystok
Vawkavysk
Slonim
Baranavichy
Sluck
Zhlobin
Mława
Ostrołęka
Ostrów Maz.
Homyel
Pułtusk
Płońsk
Bialowiez
Byaroza
Kalinkavichy
Mazyr
Luninyets
Pinsk
Pripyat
Kobryn
Brest
Biała Podlaska
Siedlce
Sochaczew
Otwock
Garwolin
Łuków
Chernihiv
Grójec
Rawa Maz.
Pilica
Włodawa
Dubrovytsya
Ovruch
Nezhin
Tomaszów Maz.
Radom
Puławy
Kurów
Wieprz
Kovel'
Kiyevskoye
Vdkhr.
Lublin
Chełm
Korosten'
Skarżysko-Kamienna
Starachowice
Ostrowiec Świetokrzyski
Kraśnik
Krasnystaw
Volodymyr Volynskyy
Lutsk
Rivne
Novohrad Volynskyy
Kielce
Sandomierz
Zamość
Szczebrzeszyn
Tarnobrzeg

91

0 20 40 60 80 100 140 180 220 260 Kilometres

94

93

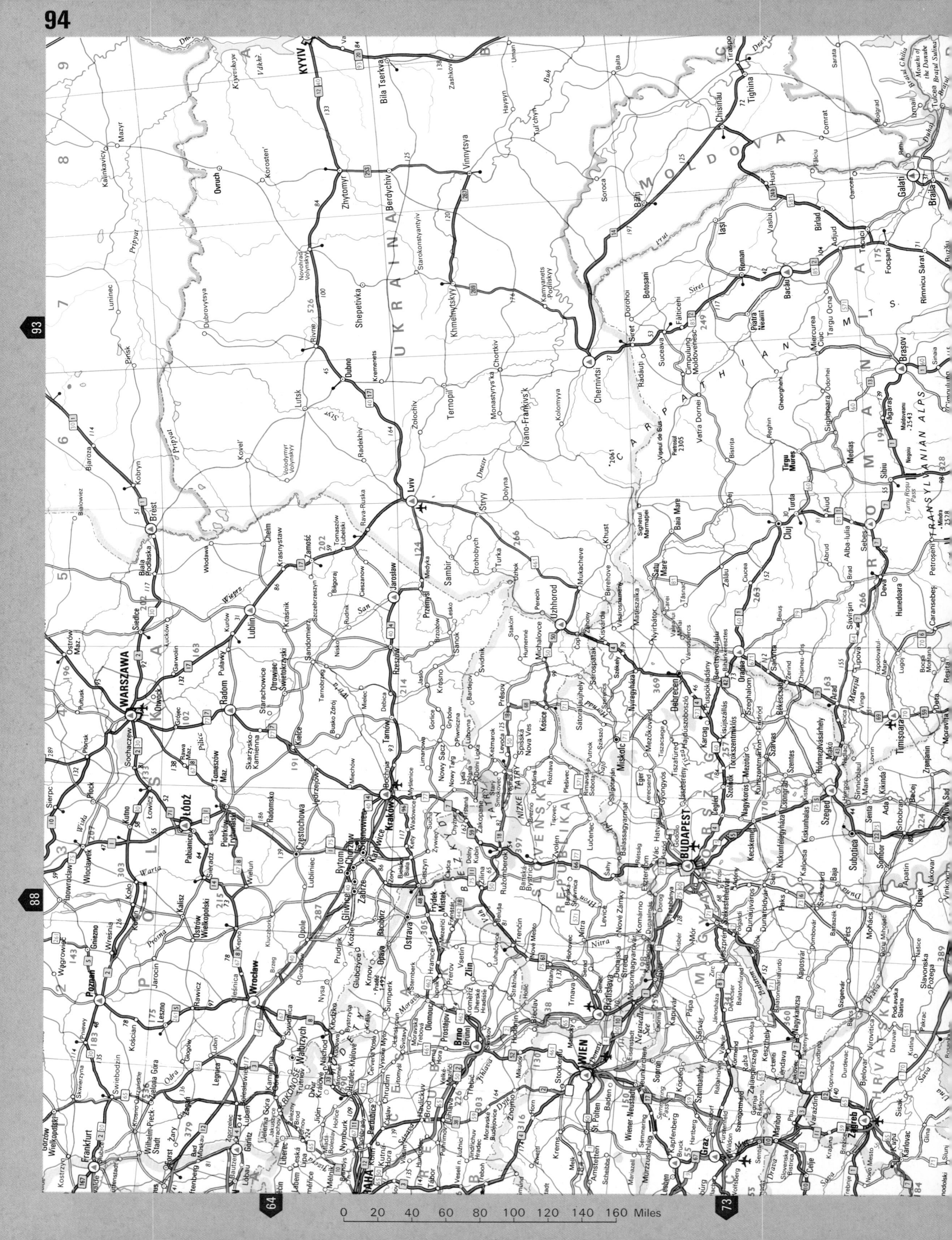
KYYIV
Bila Tserkva
Zhytomyr
Berdychiv
Vinnytsya
Ovruch
Mazyr
Pinsk
Rivne
Dubno
Lutsk
Kovel'
Lviv
Ternopil'
Khmel'nytskyy
Kamyanets-Podil'skyy
Chernivtsi
Ivano-Frankivs'k
Stryy
Uzhhorod
Mukacheve
Chişinău
Tighina
Bălţi
Iaşi
Galaţi
Brăila
Bacău
Roman
Suceava
Cluj
Braşov
Sibiu
Tirgu Mureş
Oradea
Arad
Timişoara
Satu Mare
Baia Mare
Debrecen
Miskolc
Košice
Prešov
BUDAPEST
Szeged
Kecskemét
Pécs
Győr
Bratislava
WIEN
Graz
Maribor
Zagreb
Brno
Olomouc
Ostrava
Katowice
Kraków
Częstochowa
Łódź
WARSZAWA
Radom
Lublin
Kielce
Rzeszów
Przemyśl
Tarnów
Wrocław
Poznań
Opole
Legnica
Frankfurt
Brest
Siedlce
Zamość
Zilina
Trenčín
Nitra
U K R A I N A
M O L D O V A
P O L S K A
C A R P A T H I A N S
T R A N S Y L V A N I A N   A L P S
SLOVENSKÁ REPUBLIKA
M A G Y A R O R S Z Á G
HRVATSKA
Dnestr
Wisła
Warta
Prut
Siret
Dunaj
Drava
Sava

88

64

0 20 40 60 80 100 120 140 160 Miles

73

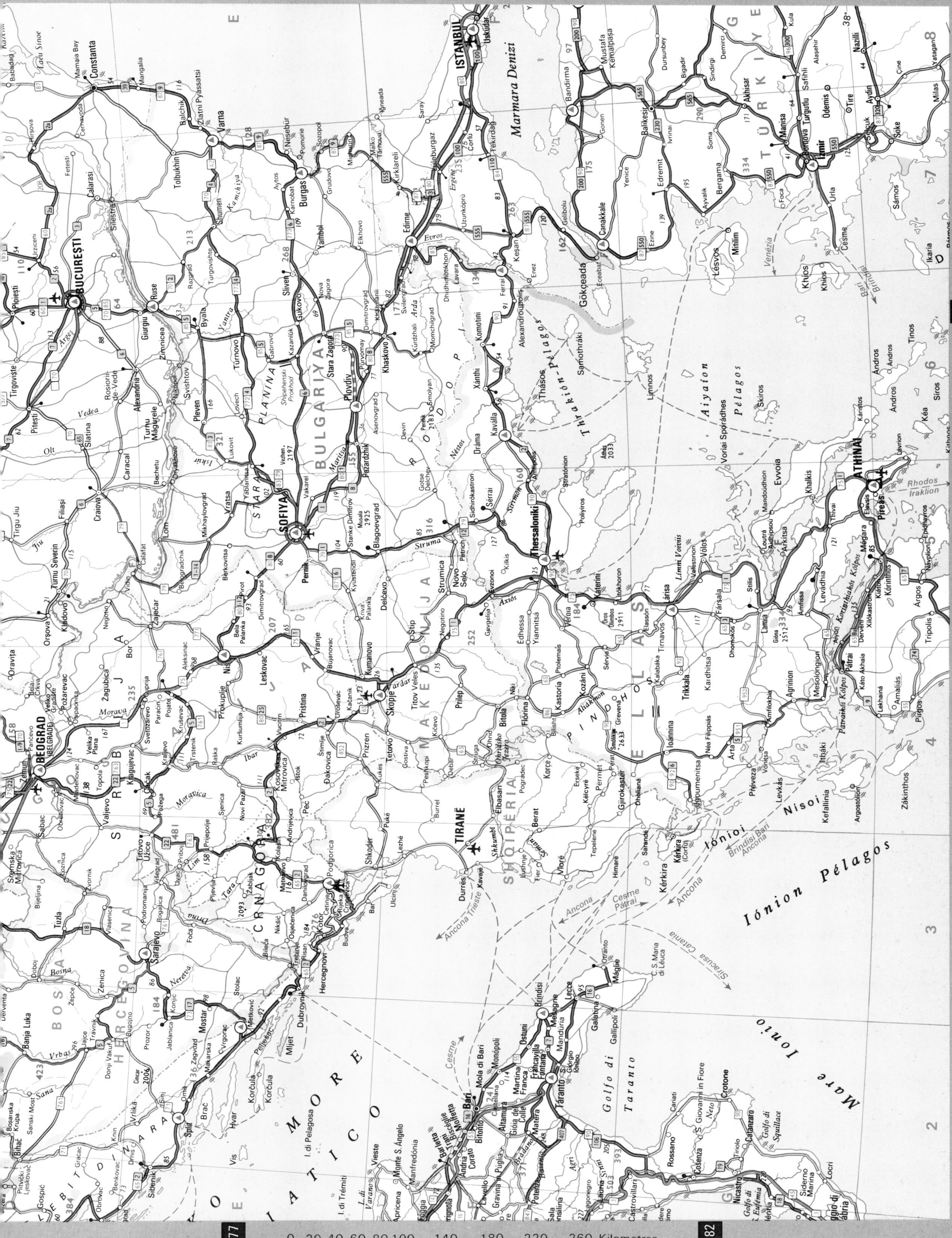

0 20 40 60 80 100 140 180 220 260 Kilometres

65
90
69

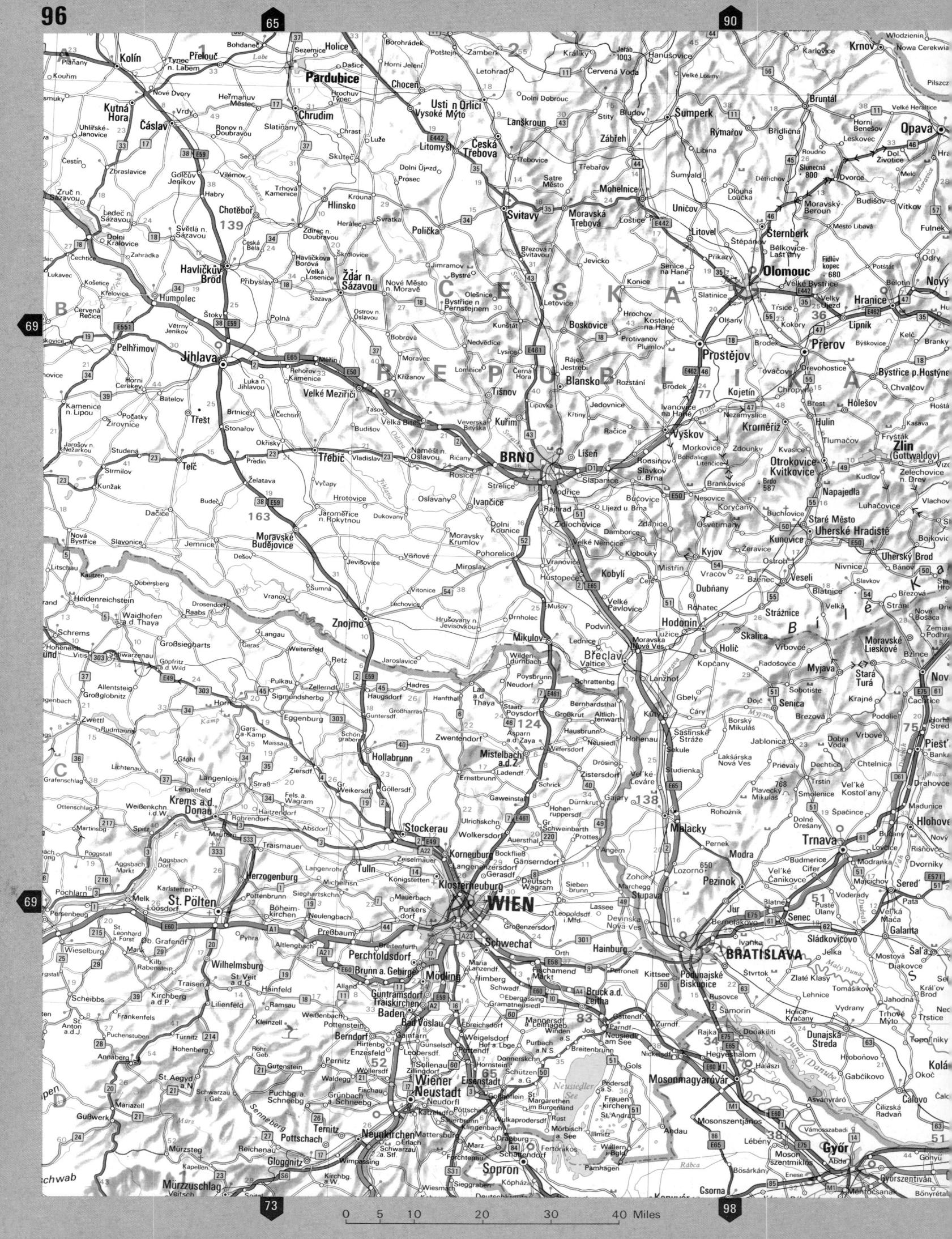

ČESKÁ REPUBLIKA
Kolín
Pardubice
Kutná Hora
Čáslav
Chrudim
Ústí n. Orlicí
Česká Třebová
Litomyšl
Šumperk
Bruntál
Krnov
Opava
Havlíčkův Brod
Žďár n. Sázavou
Svitavy
Polička
Mohelnice
Olomouc
Prostějov
Přerov
Hranice
Jihlava
Pelhřimov
Třebíč
Velké Meziříčí
Telč
BRNO
Blansko
Boskovice
Vyškov
Kroměříž
Zlín (Gottwaldov)
Uherské Hradiště
Znojmo
Mikulov
Břeclav
Hodonín
Moravské Budějovice
Hollabrunn
Stockerau
Mistelbach a.d.Z.
Krems a.d. Donau
St. Pölten
Tulln
Klosterneuburg
WIEN
Schwechat
Mödling
Baden
Wiener Neustadt
Neunkirchen
Eisenstadt
Sopron
BRATISLAVA
Trnava
Pezinok
Malacky
Senica
Mosonmagyaróvár
Győr
Neusiedler See
Dunaj (Danube)
Bílé Karpaty

0 5 10 20 30 40 Miles

73
98

90 91

Racibórz
Rybnik
Wodzisław Śl.
Pszczyna
Oświęcim
Kraków
Nowa Huta
Wieliczka
Niepołomice
Bochnia
Brzesko
Tarnów
Ostrava
Havířov
Karviná
Bielsko-Biała
Czechowice-Dziedzice
Cieszyn
Český Těšín
Frýdeck-Místek
Třinec
Wadowice
Andrychów
Żywiec
Myślenice
Limanowa
Nowy Sącz
Stary Sącz
Rabka
Nowy Targ
Zakopane
Beskid Śląski
Beskidy
Beskid Sądecki
Beskid Wyspowy
Gorczański P. N.
Tatrzański P. N.
Tatry
Vysoké
Západné
Nízke Tatry
Javorníky
Malá Fatra
Moravskoslezské Beskydy
Čadca
Žilina
Martin
Ružomberok
Liptovský Mikuláš
Poprad
Kežmarok
Levoča
Spišská Nová Ves
Považská Bystrica
Púchov
Trenčín
Prievidza
Handlová
Kremnica
Banská Bystrica
Brezno
Zvolen
Slovenské rudohorie
Rožňava
Rimavská Sobota
Lučenec
Banská Štiavnica
Levice
Nitra
Nové Zámky
Komárno
Slovenská Republika
Salgótarján
Balassagyarmat
Ózd
Kazincbarcika
Miskolc
Bükk
Eger
Mátra
Cserhát
Gyöngyös
Hatvan
Vác
Esztergom
Szentendre
Mezőkövesd
Füzesabony
Tata

94 94

98 99

0 10 20 30 40 50 60 Kilometres

Schneebg. a. Schneeberg Neudorfl Margarethen im Burgenland Frauen-kirchen St. Andra Asvanyraro Caltovo Čilizská Radvaň Zlatná n. O. Kamenicná Komárno Marcelova Peter

Ternitz Neunkirchen Katzelsdorf Pottsching Wulkaprodersdorf Rust Illmitz Andau Mosonszentjanos E60 Vámosszabadi M1 14 Győr Abda Szőny Dunaalmás Almásfüzitő Komárom Komárno

Reichenau Pottschach Erlach Schwarzau a. Stf. Marz Schattendorf Möbisch a. See Wällern i. Bgld. Lébény Moson-szentmiklós Nagybaráti Pér Bőnyrétalap Bábolna Nagyigmánd Kocs Tata

Gloggnitz Wimpassing Sopron Kópháza Nagycenk Fertőszentmiklós Csorna Kapuvár Rábapatona Kóny Enese Győrszentiván E75 E60 Ács Mocsa Környe Orosz

Szombathely Kőszeg Csepreg Bük Répcelak Beled Szany Vág Gyarmat Gic Pápa Pannonhalma Császár Kisbér Bokod Oroszlány

Körmend Vasvár Rum Sárvár Celldömölk Ostffyasszonyfa Nemeskér Pápateszér Bakonyszentkirály Mór Csákberény Bodajk

Zalaegerszeg Zalalövő Nádasd Győrvár Zalaszentgrót Sümeg Devecser Ajka Veszprém Várpalota Székesfehérvár Szabadbattyán

MAGYAR... A

Keszthely Hévíz Balatonederics Tapolca Badacsonytomaj Balatonfüred Tihany Siófok Balatonszabadi Enying

Balaton

Nagykanizsa Letenye Csurgó Nagyatád Kaposvár Dombóvár Komló PÉCS Szigetvár Szentlőrinc

Maribor Murska Sobota Ptuj Ormož Čakovec Varaždin Nedelišče Prelog Legrad Koprivnica Đurđevac Virovitica Podravska Slatina Donji Miholjac Valpovo

ZAGREB Velika Gorica Dugo Selo Ivanić Grad Čazma Bjelovar Daruvar Pakrac Lipik

HRVATSKA

Sisak Petrinja Kutina Novska Slavonska

Medvednica Sljeme 1035 Moslavačka gora G. Humka 489

0 5 10 20 30 40 Miles

97
97

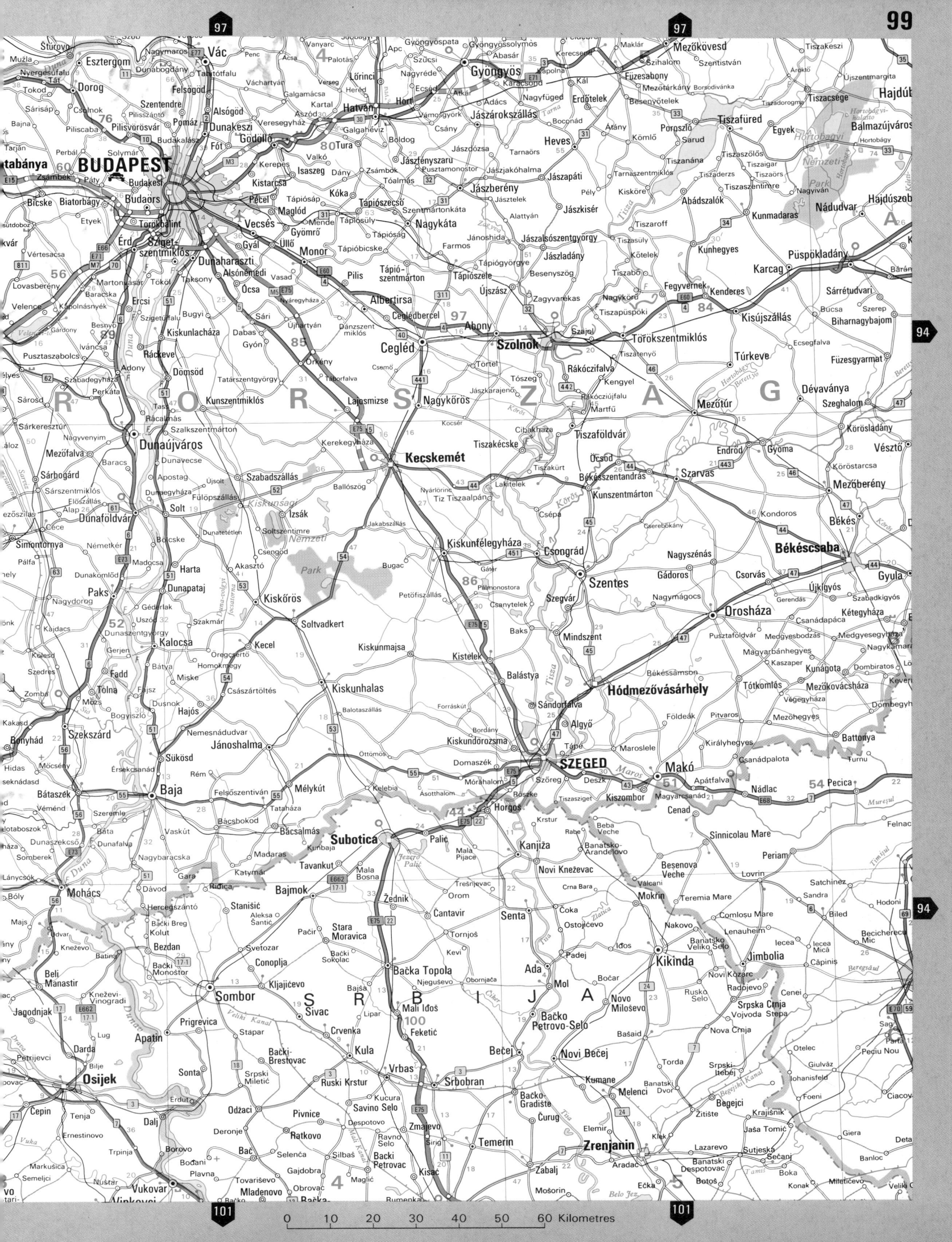

BUDAPEST
Vác
Esztergom
Szentendre
Gödöllő
Dunakeszi
Budaörs
Érd
Vecsés
Monor
Cegléd
Abony
Szolnok
Hatvan
Gyöngyös
Jászberény
Mezőkövesd
Füzesabony
Tiszafüred
Heves
Nagykáta
Albertirsa
Törökszentmiklós
Kisújszállás
Karcag
Püspökladány
Nádudvar
Mezőtúr
Túrkeve
Dévaványa
Szeghalom
Gyoma
Endrőd
Szarvas
Mezőberény
Békés
Békéscsaba
Gyula
Orosháza
Szentes
Csongrád
Kecskemét
Nagykőrös
Lajosmizse
Kiskunfélegyháza
Kiskunhalas
Kiskőrös
Kalocsa
Dunaújváros
Dunaföldvár
Paks
Szekszárd
Tolna
Baja
Mohács
Hódmezővásárhely
SZEGED
Makó
Mindszent
Kistelek
Soltvadkert
Jánoshalma
Mélykút
Tiszakécske
Kunszentmárton
Kunszentmiklós
Ráckeve
Solt
Harta
Tiszaföldvár
Martfű
Nagymágocs
Battonya
Mezőhegyes
Tótkomlós
Dunaharaszti
Gyál
Üllő
Pilis
Isaszeg
Kerepes
Kistarcsa
Pécel
Maglód
Tápiószecső
Tápiószele
Újszász
Jászapáti
Jászkisér
Kunhegyes
Kunmadaras
Balmazújváros
Hajdúszob
Kenderes
Fegyvernek
Sárrétudvari
Biharnagybajom
Füzesgyarmat
Vésztő
Körösladány
Sarkad
Csorvás
Újkígyós
Mezőkovácsháza
Kunágota
Pitvaros
Földeák
Kiszombor
Pecica
Nădlac
Sânnicolau Mare
Jimbolia
Kikinda
Novi Kneževac
Kanjiža
Senta
Ada
Mol
Bečej
Novi Bečej
Zrenjanin
Subotica
Palić
Bačka Topola
Mali Iđoš
Feketić
Kula
Vrbas
Srbobran
Temerin
Sombor
Apatin
Osijek
Vukovar
Bajmok
Horgoš
Röszke
Mórahalom
S R B I J A
O R S Z Á G
Kiskunsági Nemzeti Park
Hortobágyi Nemzeti Park
Duna
Tisza
Maros
Körös
Zagyva
Tarna
Lake Tisza
E75
E60
E71
E73
E662
E68
E79
M3
M5
M7

0 10 20 30 40 50 60 Kilometres

94
94
101
101

98 98 77 77

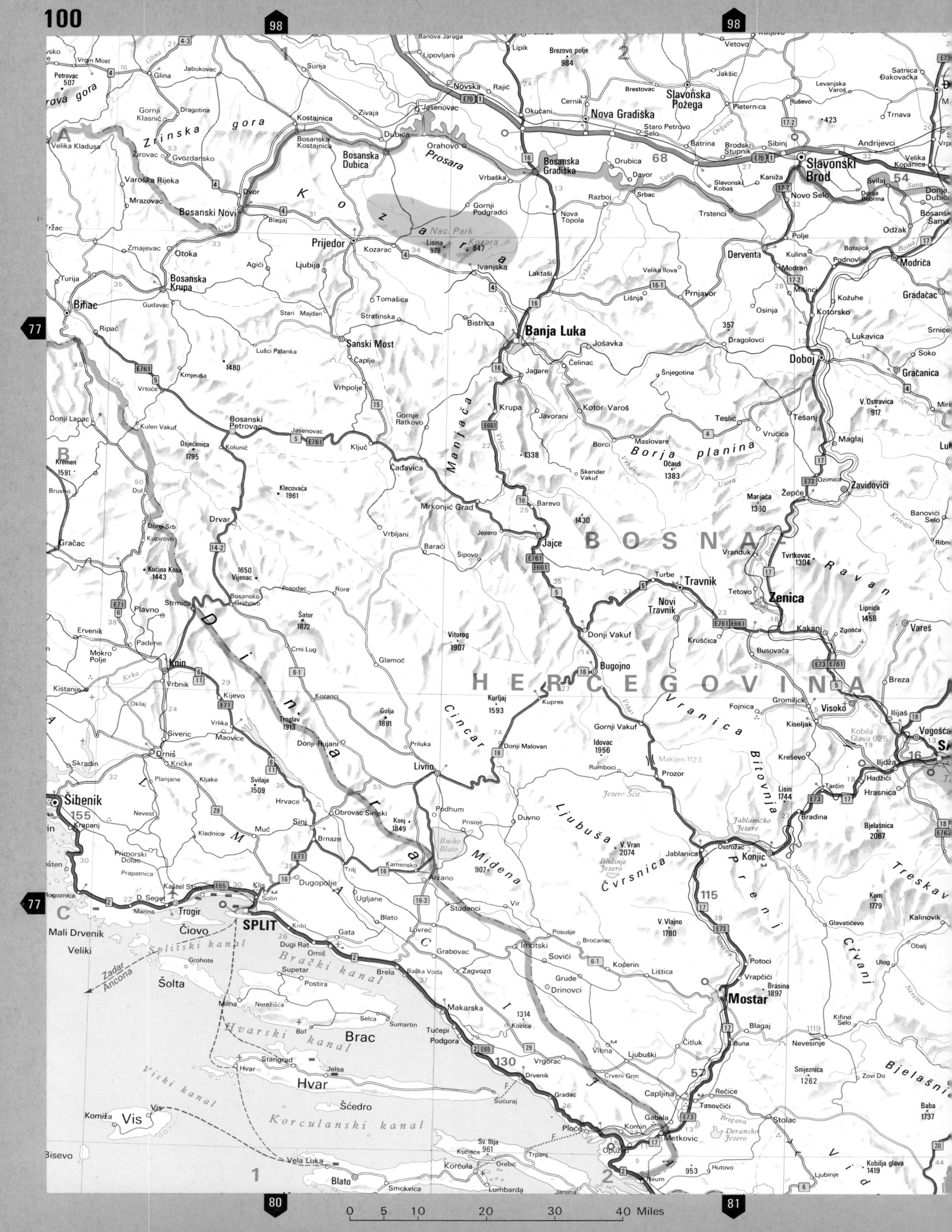
Banja Luka
Bosanska Gradiška
Slavonski Brod
Nova Gradiška
Slavonska Požega
Bosanski Novi
Bosanska Dubica
Bosanska Krupa
Prijedor
Bihać
Sanski Most
Bosanski Petrovac
Drvar
Ključ
Mrkonjić Grad
Jajce
Kotor Varoš
Derventa
Doboj
Modriča
Gradačac
Gračanica
Tešanj
Maglaj
Zavidovići
Zenica
Travnik
Novi Travnik
Donji Vakuf
Bugojno
Kakanj
Visoko
Vareš
Kiseljak
Kreševo
Fojnica
Kupres
Livno
Glamoč
Knin
Drniš
Šibenik
Sinj
Trogir
SPLIT
Omiš
Makarska
Imotski
Duvno
Prozor
Jablanica
Konjic
Mostar
Čitluk
Ljubuški
Čapljina
Metković
Ploče
Stolac
Posušje
Široki Brijeg
Brac
Hvar
Vis
Šolta
Korčula
Vela Luka
Blato
Zrinska gora
Kozara
Prosara
Nac. Park Kozara
Manjača
Borja planina
Dinara
Cincar
Vranica
Bitovnja
Prenj
Čvrsnica
Ljubuša
Midena
Biokovo
Treskavica
Crvanj
BOSNA
HERCEGOVINA
Bosna
Sava
Una
Vrbas
Neretva
Krka
Spiltski kanal
Brački kanal
Hvarski kanal
Viški kanal
Korčulanski kanal
Busko Blato
Jablaničko Jezero
Deransko Jezero
Zadar Ancona
E70
E71
E73
E761
E661
E65
0 5 10 20 30 40 Miles

80 81

99
99

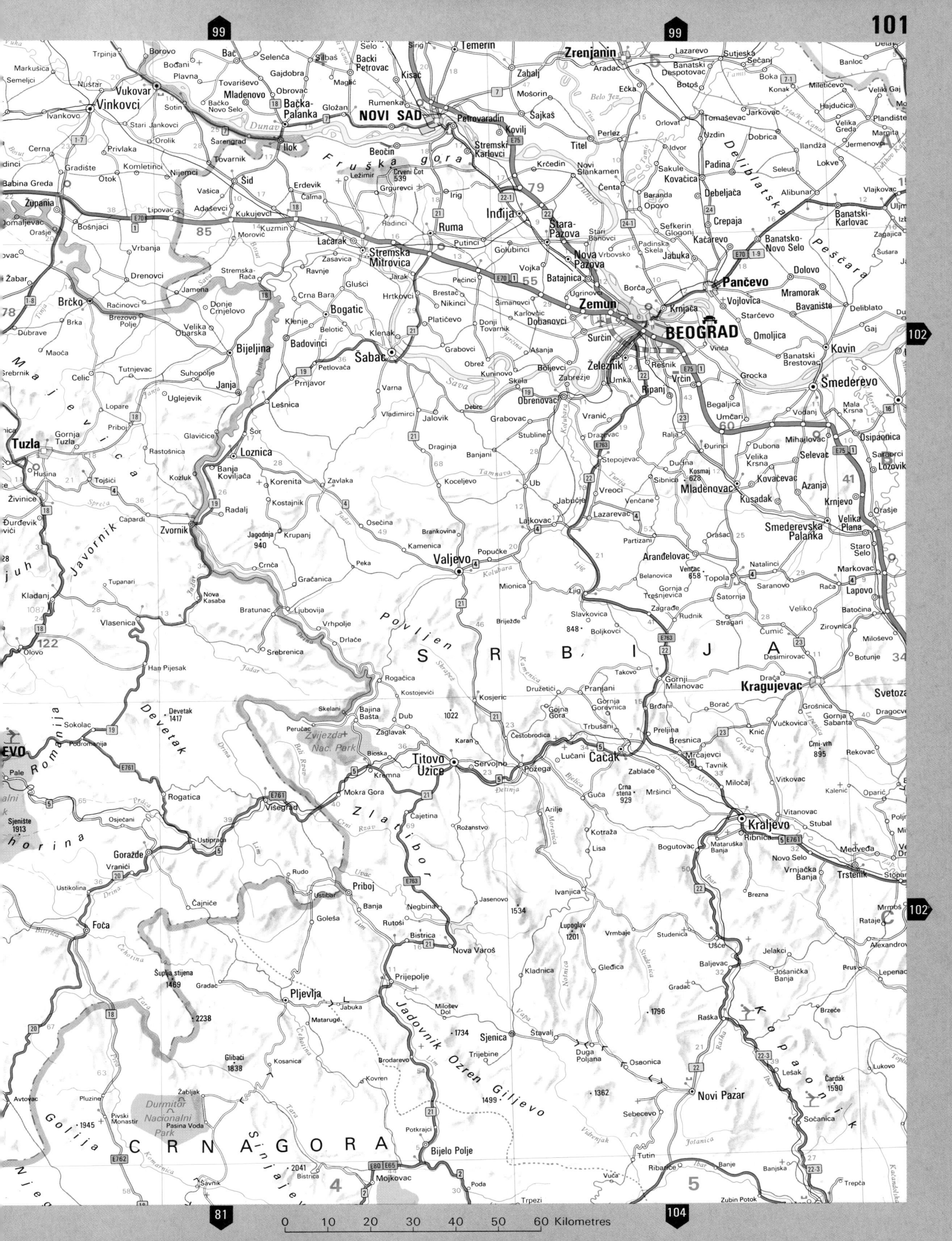
Zrenjanin
Temerin
Vukovar
Vinkovci
NOVI SAD
Bačka Palanka
Petrovaradin
Sremski Karlovci
Fruška gora
Ilok
Šid
Inđija
Ruma
Stara Pazova
Nova Pazova
Sremska Mitrovica
Pančevo
Zemun
BEOGRAD
Kovin
Smederevo
Brčko
Bijeljina
Šabac
Bogatić
Loznica
Zvornik
Tuzla
Obrenovac
Mladenovac
Smederevska Palanka
Aranđelovac
Valjevo
Ljig
Lajkovac
Ub
Kragujevac
Gornji Milanovac
Čačak
Titovo Užice
Požega
Kraljevo
Trstenik
Vrnjačka Banja
Ivanjica
Novi Pazar
Raška
Sjenica
Nova Varoš
Prijepolje
Priboj
Pljevlja
Bijelo Polje
Mojkovac
Foča
Goražde
Višegrad
Rogatica
Srebrenica
Ljubovija
Bajina Bašta
Zvijezda Nac. Park
Durmitor Nacionalni Park
Zlatibor
Povljen
Majevica
Javornik
Devetak
Romanija
Jadovnik
Ozren
Giljevo
Kopaonik
Deliblatska Peščara
Dunav
Sava
Drina
Tisa
Morava
Ibar
Lim
S R B I J A
C R N A G O R A
0 10 20 30 40 50 60 Kilometres

102
102
81
104

94

94

101

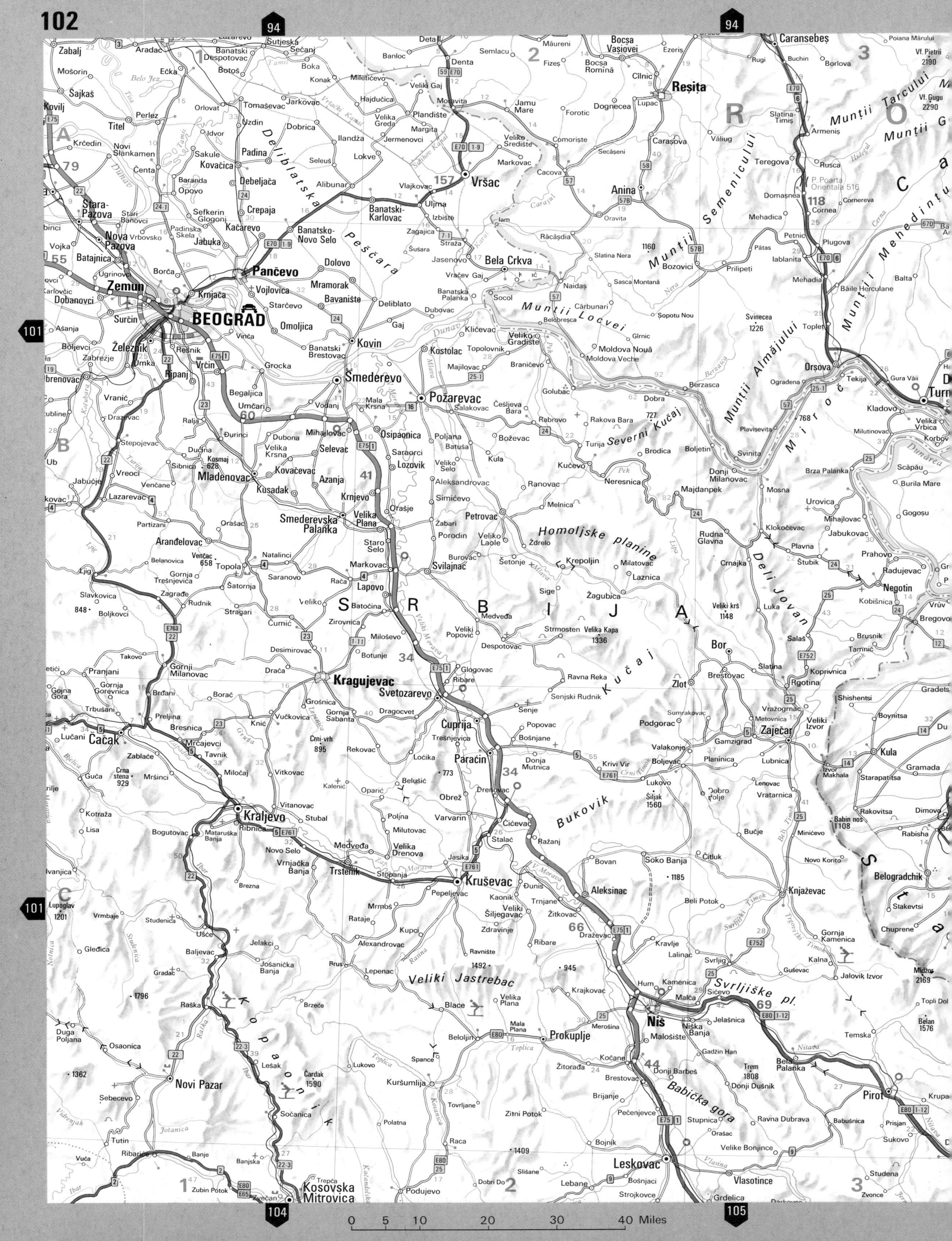
Zabalj
Aradac
Banatski Despotovac
Sutjeska
Sečanj
Mošorin
Ečka
Botoš
Boka
Belo Jez.
Konak
Šajkaš
Kovilj
Perlez
Orlovat
Tomaševac
Jarkovac
Titel
Uzdin
Idvor
Krčedin
Novi Slankamen
Sakule
Padina
Kovačica
Čenta
Baranda
Opovo
Debeljača
Stara Pazova
Stari Banovci
Sefkerin
Glogonj
Crepaja
Padinska Skela
Kačarevo
Nova Pazova
Vrbovsko
Jabuka
Vojka
Batajnica
Ugrinovci
Borča
Pančevo
Zemun
Krnjača
Vojlovica
Dobanovci
Surčin
BEOGRAD
Starčevo
Omoljica
Ašanja
Boljevci
Železnik
Zabrezje
Umka
Resnik
Vrčin
Ripanj
Vinča
Grocka
Banatski Brestovac
Kovin
Smederevo
Begaljica
Umčari
Vranić
Ralja
Vodanj
Mala Krsna
Požarevac
Dražavac
Stepojevac
Đurinci
Dubona
Mihajlovac
Velika Krsna
Selevac
Osipaonica
Sibnica
Dučina
Kosmaj 628
Mladenovac
Kovačevac
Azanja
Lozovik
Sararci
Ub
Vreoci
Jabučje
Venčane
Kusadak
Krnjevo
Lazarevac
Velika Plana
Smederevska Palanka
Oršaje
Partizani
Orašac
Aranđelovac
Staro Selo
Natalinci
Venčac 658
Topola
Belanovica
Gornja Trešnjevica
Šatornja
Ljig
Saranovo
Markovac
Rača
Lapovo
Svilajnac
Slavkovica
Zagrađe
Rudnik
Stragari
Batočina
Boljkovci
Čumić
Zirovnica
Miloševo
Botunje
Desimirovac
Takovo
Gornji Milanovac
Pranjani
Gornja Gorevnica
Brđani
Kragujevac
Svetozarevo
Dragocvet
Grošnica
Gornja Sabanta
Borač
Trbušani
Preljina
Vučkovica
Knić
Bresnica
Lučani
Čačak
Mrčajevci
Zablaće
Tavnik
Crni-vrh 895
Rekovac
Ćuprija
Trešnjevica
Paraćin
Guča
Crna stena 929
Mršinci
Miločaj
Vitkovac
Kalenić
Oparić
Belušić
Obrež
Kotraža
Lisa
Kraljevo
Ribnica
Vitanovac
Stubal
Poljna
Milutovac
Varvarin
Bogutovac
Mataruška Banja
Novo Selo
Medveđa
Velika Drenova
Vrnjačka Banja
Trstenik
Stopanja
Jasika
Kruševac
Pepeljevac
Ivanjica
Lupoglav 1201
Vrmbaje
Studenica
Brezna
Mrmoš
Rataje
Kupci
Ušće
Jelakci
Aleksandrovac
Gleđica
Baljevac
Gradac
Jošanička Banja
Brus
Lepenac
Veliki Jastrebac
1796
Raška
Brzeće
Blace
Kopaonik
Duga Poljana
Osaonica
Lešak
Čardak 1590
Lukovo
Spance
1362
Novi Pazar
Kuršumlija
Sebecevo
Sočanica
Tovrljane
Josanica
Polatna
Tutin
Ribariće
Banje
Banjska
Raca
Vuča
Zubin Potok
Kosovska Mitrovica
Trepča
Zvečan
Podujevo
Dobri Do
Deta
Banloc
Semlacu
Denta
Veliki Gaj
Meticevo
Hajdučica
Moravita
Jamu Mare
Velika Greda
Plandište
Margita
Jermenovci
Dobrica
Ilandža
Seleuš
Lokve
Alibunar
Deliblatska Peščara
Vlajkovac
Vršac
Banatski Karlovac
Uljma
Izbište
Banatsko Novo Selo
Zagajica
Šušara
Straža
Jasenovo
Dolovo
Mramorak
Bavanište
Deliblato
Bela Crkva
Vračev Gaj
Banatska Palanka
Dubovac
Socol
Gaj
Dunav
Kličevac
Kostolac
Veliko Gradište
Topolovnik
Majilovac
Braničevo
Golubac
Češljeva Bara
Salakovac
Rabrovo
Rakova Bara
Poljana
Batuša
Božovac
Kula
Veliko Selo
Aleksandrovac
Simićevo
Ranovac
Žabari
Porodin
Petrovac
Veliko Laole
Ždrelo
Melnica
Homoljske planine
Burovac
Šetonje
Krepoljin
Milatovac
Laznica
Sige
Žagubica
Veliko Popović
Medveđa
Despotovac
Strmosten
Velika Kapa 1336
Glogovac
Ribare
Ravna Reka
Senjski Rudnik
Kučaj
Senje
Popovac
Bošnjane
Donja Mutnica
773
Drenovac
Ćićevac
Stalać
Ražanj
Bukovik
Đunis
Kaonik
Veliki Šiljegovac
Trnjane
Žitkovac
Zdravinje
Ribare
Ravnište
1492
945
Dražavac
Aleksinac
Bovan
Soko Banja
1185
Krajkovac
Velika Plana
Mala Plana
Beloljin
Prokuplje
Toplica
Merošina
Žitorađa
Kočane
Brestovac
Brijanje
Pečenjevce
Zitni Potok
1409
Slišane
Lebane
Bojnik
Leskovac
Bošnjaci
Strojkovce
Māureni
Bocşa Vasiovei
Bocşa Romînă
Fizeş
Ezeriş
Cîlnic
Reşiţa
Dognecea
Lupac
Forotic
Comorişte
Carașova
Secăşeni
Cacova
Anina
Oraviţa
Răcăşdia
Slatina Nera
1160
Munţii Bozovici
Naidaş
Sasca Montană
Cărbunari
Munții Locvei
Belobresca
Gîrnic
Moldova Nouă
Moldova Veche
Şopotu Nou
Dobra
Berzasca
727
Severni Kučaj
Turija
Brodica
Boljetin
Kučevo
Neresnica
Majdanpek
Rudna Glavna
Crnajka
Deli Jovan
Veliki krš 1148
Luka
Bor
Zlot
Brestovac
Slatina
Sumrakovac
Podgorac
Valakonje
Gamzigrad
Krivi Vir
Boljevac
Lukovo
Šiljak 1560
Dobro Polje
Planinica
Zaječar
Lubnica
Lenovac
Vratarnica
Bučje
Minićevo
Knjaževac
Beli Potok
Čitluk
Kravlje
Lalinac
Svrljig
Gusevac
Gornja Kamenica
Kalna
Hum
Kamenica
Mala
Svrljiške pl.
Sićevo
Niš
Jelašnica
Niška Banja
Malošište
Gadžin Han
Trem 1808
Donji Barbeš
Donji Dušnik
Babička gora
Stupnica
Orašac
Ravna Dubrava
Velike Bonjince
Vlasotince
Grdelica
Caransebeş
Rugi
Buchin
Borlova
Poiana Mărului
Vf. Pietrii 2190
Munții Țarcului
Vf. Gugu 2290
Munții Godeanu
Slatina-Timiş
Armeniş
Văliug
Teregova
Semenicului
Rusca
P. Poarta Orientala 516
Domaşnea
Cornea
Cornereva
Mehadica
Petnic
Pătas
Plugova
Iablaniţa
Prilipeţi
Mehadia
Băile Herculane
Balta
Munții Mehedinți
Svinecea 1226
Topleţ
Munţii Almăjului
Orşova
Ogradena
Tekija
Gura Văii
Turnu Severin
Plavişevita
Mirocč
768
Kladovo
Velika Vrbica
Milutinovac
Korbovo
Svinita
Donji Milanovac
Brza Palanka
Scăpău
Burila Mare
Dunărea
Mosna
Urovica
Gogoşu
Mihajlovac
Klokočevac
Jabukovac
Plavna
Prahovo
Štubik
Radujevac
Negotin
Kobišnica
Vrav
Bregovo
Brusnik
Tamnič
Salaš
Timok
Koprivnica
Rgotina
Gradets
Shishentsi
Vražogrnac
Metovnica
Veliki Izvor
Boynitsa
Kula
Izvor Makhala
Starapatitsa
Gramada
Rakovitsa
Dimovo
Babin nos 1108
Rabrisha
Novo Korito
Belogradchik
Stakevtsi
Chuprene
Midžor 2169
Jalovik Izvor
Topli Dol
Belan 1576
Temska
Bela Palanka
Pirot
Krupac
Prisjan
Babušnica
Sukovo
Studena
Zvonce
Izvor
SRBIJA
ROMÂNIA
Dunav
Morava
Velika Morava
Ibar
Toplica
Nišava
Crni Timok
Beli Timok
Mlava
Pek
Kolubara
Tisa
Tamiš
Rasina
Studenica
Kosanica

0 5 10 20 30 40 Miles

101

104

105

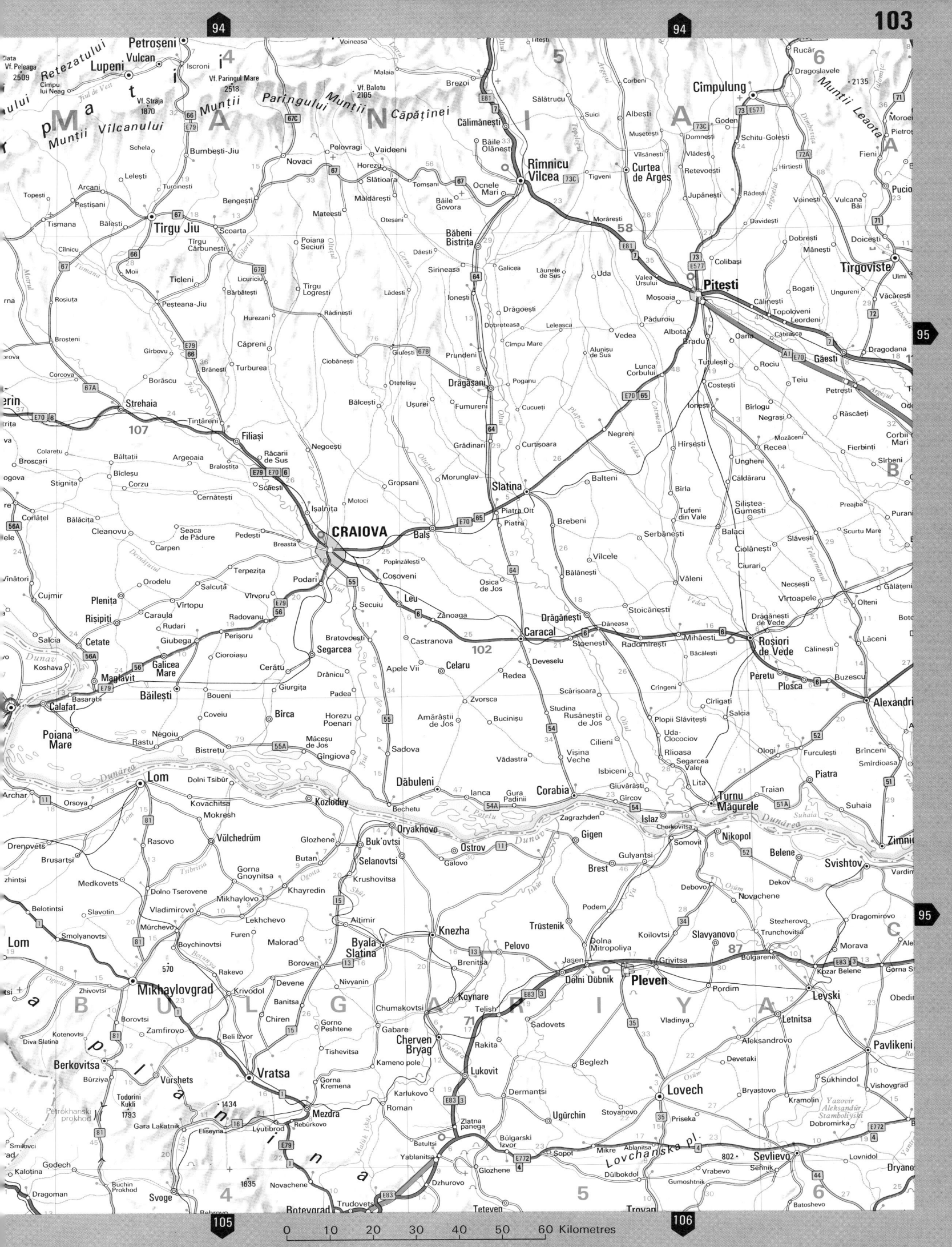

Vf. Peleaga
2509
Retezatului
Muntii
Petroseni
Lupeni
Vulcan
Iscroni
Vf. Paringul Mare
2518
Vf. Balotu
2105
Voinesa
Malaia
Brezoi
Pitesti
Rucăr
Dragoslavele
2135

Cimpu
lui Neag
Muntii Vilcanului
Vf. Straja
1870
Muntii Paringului
Muntii
Căpățînei
Cimpulung
Goden
Schitu-Golesti
Moroe
Pietroș

Schela
Bumbesti-Jiu
Polovragi
Vaideeni
Băile
Olănesti
Rimnicu
Vilcea
Curtea
de Arges
Domnesti
Vlădesti
Rădesti
Vilsănesti
Hirtiesti
Fieni
Arcani
Lelesti
Novaci
Horezu
Slătioara
Tomsani
Ocnele
Mari
Tigveni
Musetesti
Sălătrucu
Albesti
Suici
Retevoesti
Jupânesti
Voinesti
Vulcana
Băi

Tigrovista

Tirgu Jiu
Tirgu
Cărbunesti
Moii
Mateesti
Otesani
Băile
Govora
Morăresti
58
Bogati
Ungureni
Văcăresti

Ticleni
Licuriciu
Tirgu
Logresti
Lădesti
Băbeni
Bistrita
Galicea
Pitesti
Colibasi
Ulmi

0   10   20   30   40   50   60 Kilometres

101 1 2 102

A 1 2

Pasina Voda
Komarnica
Sinjajevina
·2041
Bistrica
44 Mojkovac 6 Poda
Biogradsko Nac. Park
Potkrajci 21
Bijelo Polje
30
Trpezi
Sebecevo
Jošanica
Tutin
Ribariće
Vuča
Banje
Banjska
22-3
Tovrljane
Polatna
Raca
27
Sočanica
25
29

Savnik
2253
Bjelasica
Crna glava 2137
Ivangrad
Kaliče Rožaj
E65 2 E80
Zubin Potok
Zvečan
Trepča
Kosovska Mitrovica
Makovac
Kačikol
E80

Gornje Polje
Moračka Kapa 2227
Liverovici
Kolašin
Vinicka 18
Matesevo
Tresnjevik 1598
Istok
Mokra gora
Rudnik
Gornja Klina
Glavnik
Donje Ljupče
Orlane
Batlava
Podujevo
25

Nikšic
Maganik
Prekornica
E762
39
70
Andrijevica
Murino Velika Brezojevice
Plav
Marijaš 2530
Peć
Bistrica
Novo Selo
Đurakovac
Srbica
Trstenik
Vučitrn
36
Obilić
Pristina
Novo Brdo

B
Cevo
55
Danilovgrad
Spuž
E65 E80 2
Bioče Ubli
Podgorica
Selce
Bogě
Gusinje
Jezerce 2694 Theth
Prokletije
Kučiste
Pečka
Vitomirica
Ljesane 9
Klina Klina
Iglarevo
Komoran
Orlate
Magura
Lipljan E65
Gračanica
Janjevo
25-2
Paralovo
Brasalice

81
Cetinje
45
Rijeka Crnojevica Mahala
Tuzi
Golubovci
2-3
Virpazar
Sutorman 844
Bajze
Skadarsko Jezero
Koplik
Junik
21
Skivjani
Dečani
Đakovica
Zrze
Ratkovac
Studenčane
Orahovac
Suva Reka
Velika Kruša
Banja
Crnoljevo
Blace
Štimlje
Uroševac
15
Donji Livoč
Požaranje
Vitina
32

Bar
Stari Bar
Rumija
Sutomore
Pečurice Krute Sukobin
Murigan
Ulcinj
Sveti Nikola
Veljpoje
24
Drin
Mes
Shkodër
Bushat
Ure Shtrenjtë
Kiri
Kukěs
Kušnin
Zjum
Pirane
E851
25
Prizren
Beli Drim
Zur
Vrbica
Sredska
Dragaš
2499 Ljuboten
Štrpce
Vratnica
Globočnica
Skopska
42

Kep i Rodonit
Dajč
Kashnjet
Lezhě
16
Rubik
Reshen
Blinisht
Fushe-Lure
Suhodoll
Žirovnica
Debar
Galičica
Sar planina
58
Dobroste
Tearce
Kuckovo
Tetovo
Vardar
Dorče Petrov
Gorno Nerezi
E65

C
Gji i Lalzěs
Kep i Palit
Ishm
Milot
Laç
Mamurras
Burrel
Kurbnesh
Lunar
Maqellarě
Galičnik
Rostuša
Zajas
Mavrovi Hanovi
Simnica
46
Mavrovo Nac. Park
Bistra Pl.
Kičevo
Brod
Debriste
Ropotovo
Zelino
Kamenjane
Grupčin
Matka
14
25
Vrapčište Cegrane Forino
Zdunje
Gostivar
Kodra Taurli 1853
Suva Gora
Nova Breznica
Kruševo
Krivogaštani
Malo i...
Obršani
Jakupi
Solunska Glava 2540
26

Trieste Ancona
Bari Brindisi Otranto
Durrěs
Shijak
11
Vore
12 15
TIRANË
Vaqarr
Petrelě
Vrrě
Peshk
Ostren i math
Klenjě
Lukovo
63
Labuništa
Vevčani Veleshta
Mešeišta
Trebiniste
Struga
Kosel
Radožda
E852
Kališta
15
Jablanica
Crni Drim
Ilinska Pl.
Belčiste
Botun
Lešani
Sopotnica
20
Plačenska Pl.
Crna
Bučin
Murgaševo
Topolčani
22
Lopatica
E65

81
Ndroq
Kavajě
Zgozdh
Mesqetě
Gracen
28
Labinot-Mal
25
Librazhd
6
Elbasan
38
Prrenjas
Ohridsko Jezero
Ohrid
Galičica Nac. Park
Peštani
Radožda
Carev Dvor
Resen
Kukurecani
36
Capari
2600 Bitola
Bukovo
Pelister Nac. Park
26 E65
16
12

D
Kryevidh
Rrogozhinë
Peqin
Cerme Proske
8
Čerrik
Shkumbi
Gostimě
Belsh
Drizě
Gramsh
32
Radokal i Poshtěm
Pogradec
Pogori
Ljubaništa
Stenje
Prespansko Jezero
Ljubojno
Medzitlija
L. Megáli Préspa
Flórina
Ándartikón
Alónas
Skopiá
E86

Lushnje
Fier
Patos
Seman
Roskovec
Libofshë
Levan
Novosele
Ure Vajgurore
Kuçove
Fier-Shegan
Devoll
Berat
Uznove
Mali i Tomorr
Sojnik
Moglicě
Maliq
Pustec
Voskopojě
2128
Vissinia
Vronterón
Vatokhórion
Polipótamon
Melás
Makrokhórion
Vérnc

1 2

108 108

0 5 10 20 30 40 Miles

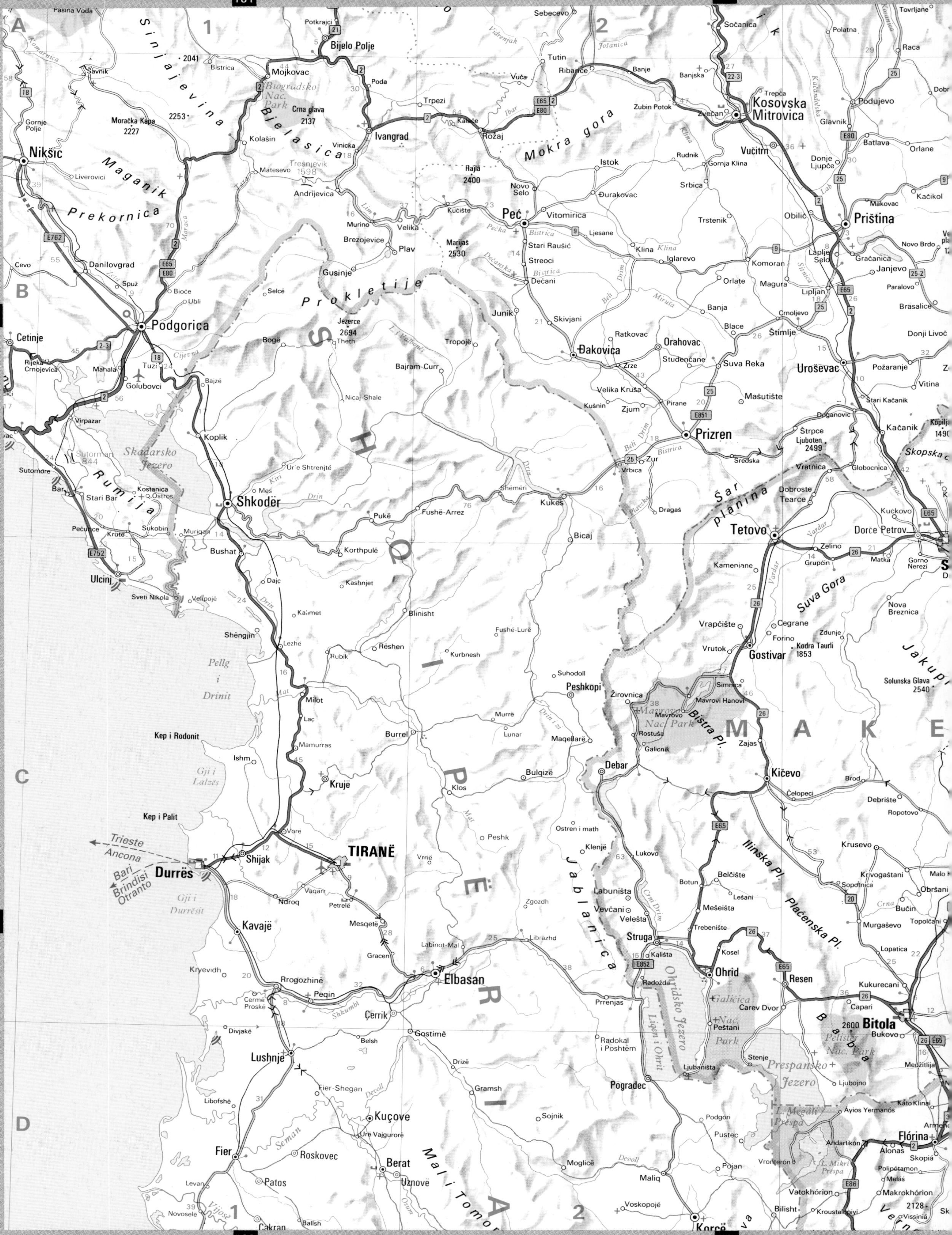

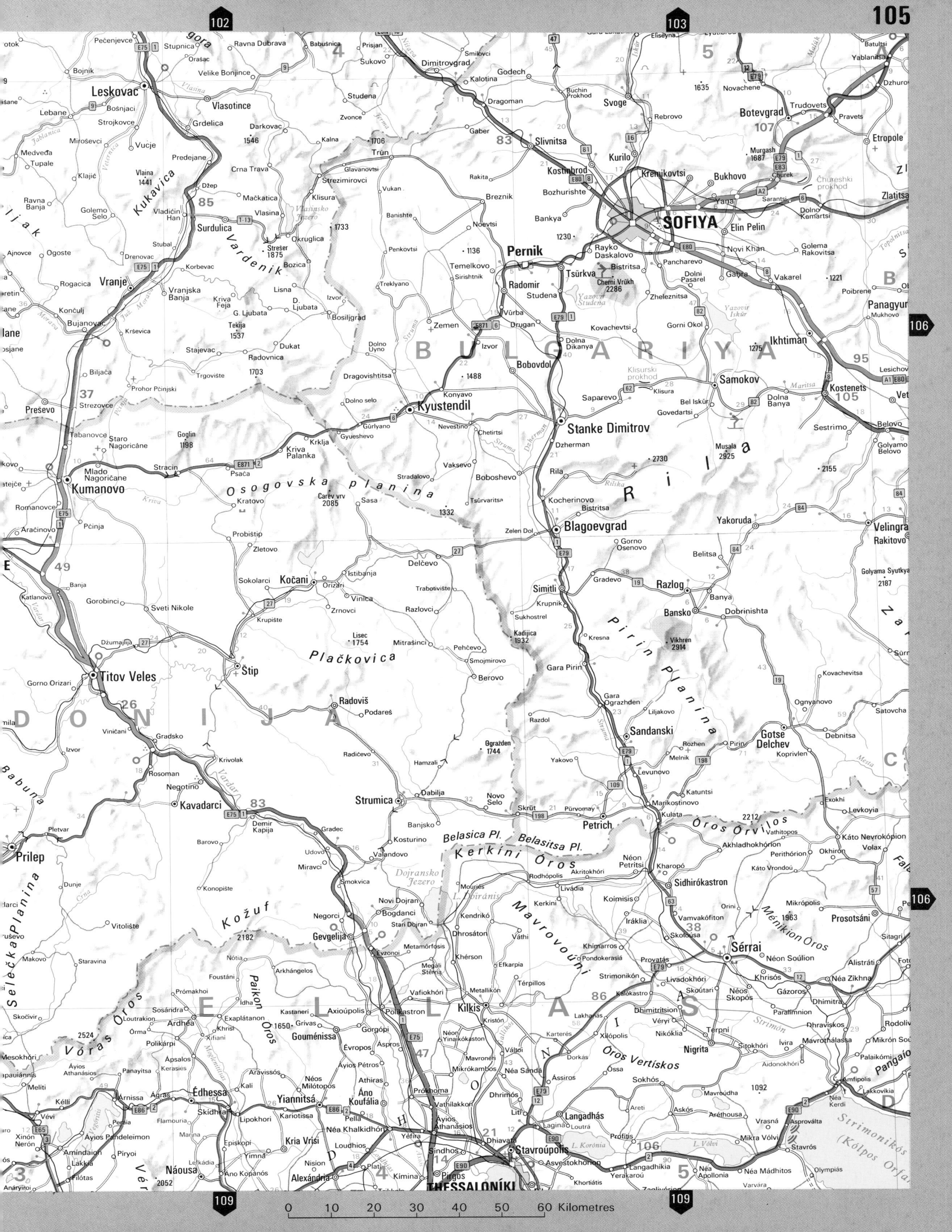
102
103
106
109
BULGARIYA
SOFIYA
Pernik
Kyustendil
Stanke Dimitrov
Blagoevgrad
Samokov
Ikhtiman
Kostenets
Botevgrad
Etropole
Pravets
Trudovets
Novachene
Svoge
Kostinbrod
Slivnitsa
Dragoman
Dimitrovgrad
Godech
Kalotina
Kremikovtsi
Bukhovo
Elin Pelin
Novi Khan
Vakarel
Zlatitsa
Panagyurishte
Belovo
Velingrad
Rakitovo
Yakoruda
Razlog
Bansko
Dobrinishta
Simitli
Kresna
Sandanski
Gotse Delchev
Petrich
Kulata
Melnik
Radomir
Bobovdol
Dupnitsa
Rila
Kocherinovo
Boboshevo
Nevestino
Rila
Musala 2925
Vikhren 2914
Pirin Planina
Osogovska planina
Plačkovica
Leskovac
Vlasotince
Surdulica
Vranje
Bujanovac
Preševo
Kumanovo
Kriva Palanka
Kratovo
Kočani
Sveti Nikole
Štip
Titov Veles
Radoviš
Strumica
Kavadarci
Negotino
Gevgelija
Prilep
Kožuf
Babuna
Belasica Pl.
Belasitsa Pl.
Kerkíni Óros
Óros Órvilos
DONIJA
ELLAS
Sidhirókastron
Sérrai
Néa Zíkhna
Nigrita
Kilkís
Políkastron
Goumenissa
Yiannitsá
Édhessa
Náousa
Alexándria
Langadhás
Stavroúpolis
THESSALONÍKI
Amfipolis
Strimonikós (Kólpos Orfanoú)
Mavrovoúni
Óros Vertískos
Vóras Óros
Paikon Óros
0 10 20 30 40 50 60 Kilometres

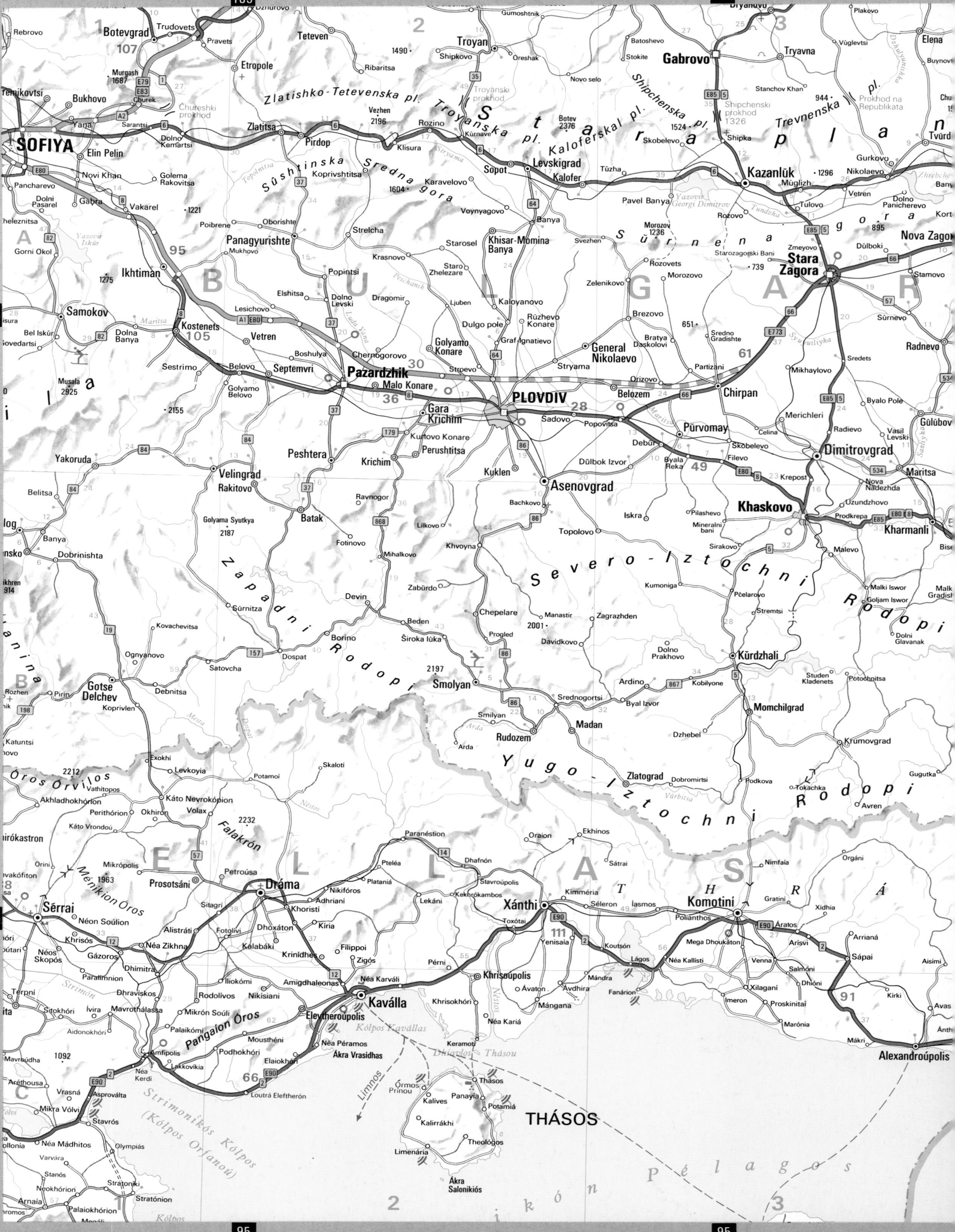
103
103
105
105
95
95
SOFIYA
Botevgrad
Trudovets
Pravets
Teteven
Etropole
Troyan
Shipkovo
Oreshak
Gumoshtnik
Ribaritsa
Gabrovo
Batoshevo
Stokite
Tryavna
Vŭglevtsi
Plakovo
Elena
Buynovt
Novo selo
Stanchov Khan
Prokhod na Republikata
Shipchenski prokhod 1326
Troyanski prokhod
Chureshki prokhod
Zlatishko-Tetevenska pl.
Troyanska pl.
Kaloferska pl.
Shipchenska pl.
Trevnenska pl.
Stara planina
Bukhovo
Yana
Sarantsi
Zlatitsa
Pirdop
Vezhen 2196
Rozino
Klisura
Kŭrnare
Botev 2376
Skobelevo
Shipka
Tvŭrdi
Elin Pelin
Dolno Kamartsi
Novi Khan
Golema Rakovitsa
Sredna gora
Sŭshtinska
Koprivshtitsa
Karavelovo
Sopot
Levskigrad
Kalofer
Tŭzha
Kazanlŭk
Mŭglizh
Gurkovo
Nikolaevo
Pavel Banya
Yazovir Georgi Dimitrov
Tulovo
Dolno Panicherevo
Rozovo
Vetren
Pancharevo
Dolni Pasarel
Gabra
Vakarel
Poibrene
Oboriste
Voynyagovo
Banya
Morozov 1236
Sŭrnena gora
Kort
Nova Zagora
Zmeyovo
Dŭlboki
Stara Zagora
Starozagorski Bani
Iskŭr
Gorni Okol
Panagyurishte
Mukhovo
Strelcha
Khisar-Momina Banya
Starosel
Svezhen
Rozovets
Morozovo
Ikhtiman
Krasnovo
Staro Zhelezare
Zelenikovo
Stamovo
Popintsi
Elshitsa
Dolno Levski
Dragomir
Ljuben
Kaloyanovo
Brezovo
Samokov
Lesichovo
Dulgo pole
Rŭzhevo Konare
Bratya Daskolovi
Sredno Gradishte
Sŭrnevo
Bel Iskŭr
Kostenets
Dolna Banya
Vetren
Golyamo Konare
Graf-Ignatievo
General Nikolaevo
Radnevo
Maritsa
Boshulya
Chernogorovo
Sestrimo
Belovo
Septemvri
Pazardzhik
Malo Konare
Stroevo
Stryama
Partizani
Mikhaylovo
Sredets
Musala 2925
Golyamo Belovo
PLOVDIV
Orizovo
Belozem
Chirpan
Byalo Pole
Gara Krichim
Sadovo
Popovitsa
Pŭrvomay
Merichleri
Celina
Radievo
Vasil Levski
Gŭlŭbovo
Kurtovo Konare
Perushtitsa
Debŭr
Skobelevo
Dimitrovgrad
Yakoruda
Peshtera
Krichim
Kuklen
Dŭlbok Izvor
Byala Reka
Filevo
Velingrad
Rakitovo
Asenovgrad
Krepost
Maritsa
Nova Nadezhda
Belitsa
Ravnogor
Bachkovo
Khaskovo
Uzundzhovo
Golyama Syutkya 2187
Batak
Lilkovo
Iskra
Pilashevo
Mineralni bani
Prodkrepa
Kharmanli
Banya
Topolovo
Sirakovo
Malevo
Dobrinishta
Fotinovo
Khvoyna
Mihalkovo
Severo-Iztochni Rodopi
Kumoniga
Malki Iswor
Goljam Iswor
Zapadni Rodopi
Zabŭrdo
Pčelarovo
Devin
Sŭrnitsa
Chepelare
Manastir
Zagrazhden
Stremtsi
Kovachevitsa
Beden
Borino
Široka lŭka
Progled
2001
Davidkovo
Dolni Glavanak
Ognyanovo
Dospat
Satovcha
Dolno Prakhovo
Kŭrdzhali
Smolyan
2197
Ardino
Kobilyone
Studen Kladenets
Potochnitsa
Gotse Delchev
Debnitsa
Koprivlen
Srednogortsi
Byal Izvor
Momchilgrad
Smilyan
Rudozem
Madan
Arda
Dzhebel
Krumovgrad
Katuntsi
Skaloti
Exokhí
Levkoyia
Potamoi
Zlatograd
Dobromirtsi
Yugo-Iztochni Rodopi
Podkova
Tokachka
Gugutka
Avren
Óros Órvilos 2212
Vathitopos
Akhladhokhórion
Káto Nevrokópion
Perithórion
Okhiron
Volax
2232
Falakrón
Káto Vrondoú
Nestos
Paranéstion
Oraion
Ekhinos
Mikrópolis
1963
Orini
Ménikion Óros
Prosotsáni
Petroúsa
Dráma
Pteléa
Dhafnón
Sátrai
Nimfaía
Orgáni
Nikifóros
Plataniá
Stavroúpolis
Kekhrókambos
Kimmería
Adhrianí
Lekáni
Xánthi
Séleron
Íasmos
Komotini
Gratini
Xidhia
Sérrai
Néon Soúlion
Sitagri
Khoristí
Toxótai
Polianthos
Alistráti
Fotolivi
Dhoxáton
Kiria
Yenisaía
Koutsón
Áratos
Arrianá
Khrisós
Néa Zíkhna
Kalabáki
Filippoi
Mega Dhoukáton
Arísvi
Sápai
Néos Skopós
Gázoros
Krinídhes
Zigós
Pérni
Lágos
Néa Kallísti
Venna
Aisimi
Dhimítra
Paralimnion
Iliokómi
Amigdhaleonas
Néa Karváli
Khrisoúpolis
Ávaton
Ávdhira
Mándra
Salmóni
Dhióni
Strimon
Terpní
Dhraviskos
Rodolivos
Nikisiani
Kaválla
Khrisokhóri
Fanárion
Xilaganí
Kirki
Sitokhóri
Ívira
Mavrothálassa
Mikrón Soúli
Eleýtheroúpolis
Mángana
Imeron
Proskinitaí
Aidonokhóri
Palaikómi
Pangaíon Óros
Néa Kariá
Maróneia
Mousthéni
Kólpos Kavállas
Keramoti
Dhiavlos Thásou
Mákri
Amfípolis
Néa Péramos
Ákra Vrasídhas
Alexandroúpolis
Mavrobúdha
1092
Podhokhóri
Lakkovíkia
Néa Kerdi
Elaiokhóri
Thásos
Aréthousa
Vrasná
Asprovalta
Loutrá Eleftherón
Órmos Prínou
Panayía
Kalíves
Límnos
Mikra Vólvi
Stavrós
Potamiá
THÁSOS
Kalirrákhi
Strimonikós Kólpos (Kólpos Orfanoú)
Néa Mádhitos
Olympiás
Theológos
Limenária
Varvára
Stanós
Ákra Salonikiós
Neokhórion
Stratóniki
Arnaía
Stratónion
Palaiokhórion
Thrakikón Pélagos
BULGARIA
ELLAS
0 5 10 20 30 40 Miles

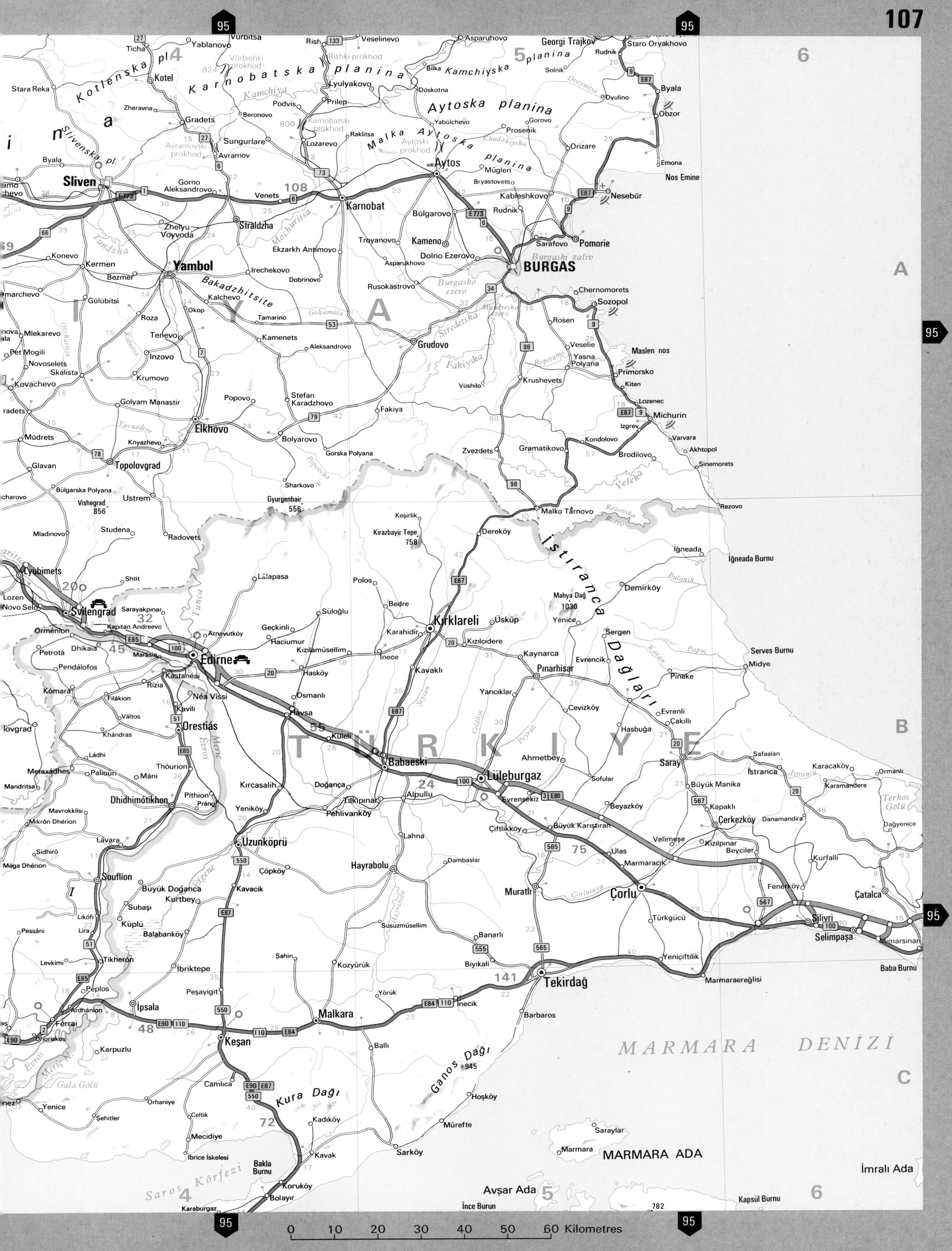
95
95
95
95
95
95
Sliven
Kotel
Karnobatska planina
Kotlenska pl.
Slivenska pl.
Aytoska planina
Kamchiyska planina
Malka Aytoska planina
Aytos
Karnobat
Yambol
BURGAS
Burgaski zaliv
Nesebŭr
Pomorie
Sarafovo
Obzor
Byala
Emona
Nos Emine
Chernomorets
Sozopol
Primorsko
Kiten
Lozenec
Michurin
Varvara
Akhtopol
Sinemorets
Rezovo
Maslen nos
Grudovo
Elkhovo
Topolovgrad
Straldzha
Bolyarovo
Malko Tărnovo
Svilengrad
Lyubimets
Edirne
Kırklareli
Babaeski
Lüleburgaz
Uzunköprü
Hayrabolu
Çorlu
Tekirdağ
Malkara
Keşan
İpsala
Silivri
Selimpaşa
Çatalca
Saray
Çerkezköy
Pınarhisar
Vize
Demirköy
İğneada
İğneada Burnu
Serves Burnu
Midye
Istranca Dağları
Mahya Dağ 1030
Ganos Dağı 945
Kura Dağı
Şarköy
Mürefte
Barbaros
Marmaraereğlisi
Saros Körfezi
Bakla Burnu
MARMARA DENİZİ
MARMARA ADA
Marmara
Avşar Ada
İmralı Ada
Kapsül Burnu
Baba Burnu
Orestiás
Dhidhimótikhon
Souflion
Férrai
Kastanéai
Orménion
Évros
Meriç
Tundzha
Terkos Gölü
TÜRKIYE
A
B
C
4
5
6
0 10 20 30 40 50 60 Kilometres

104 104

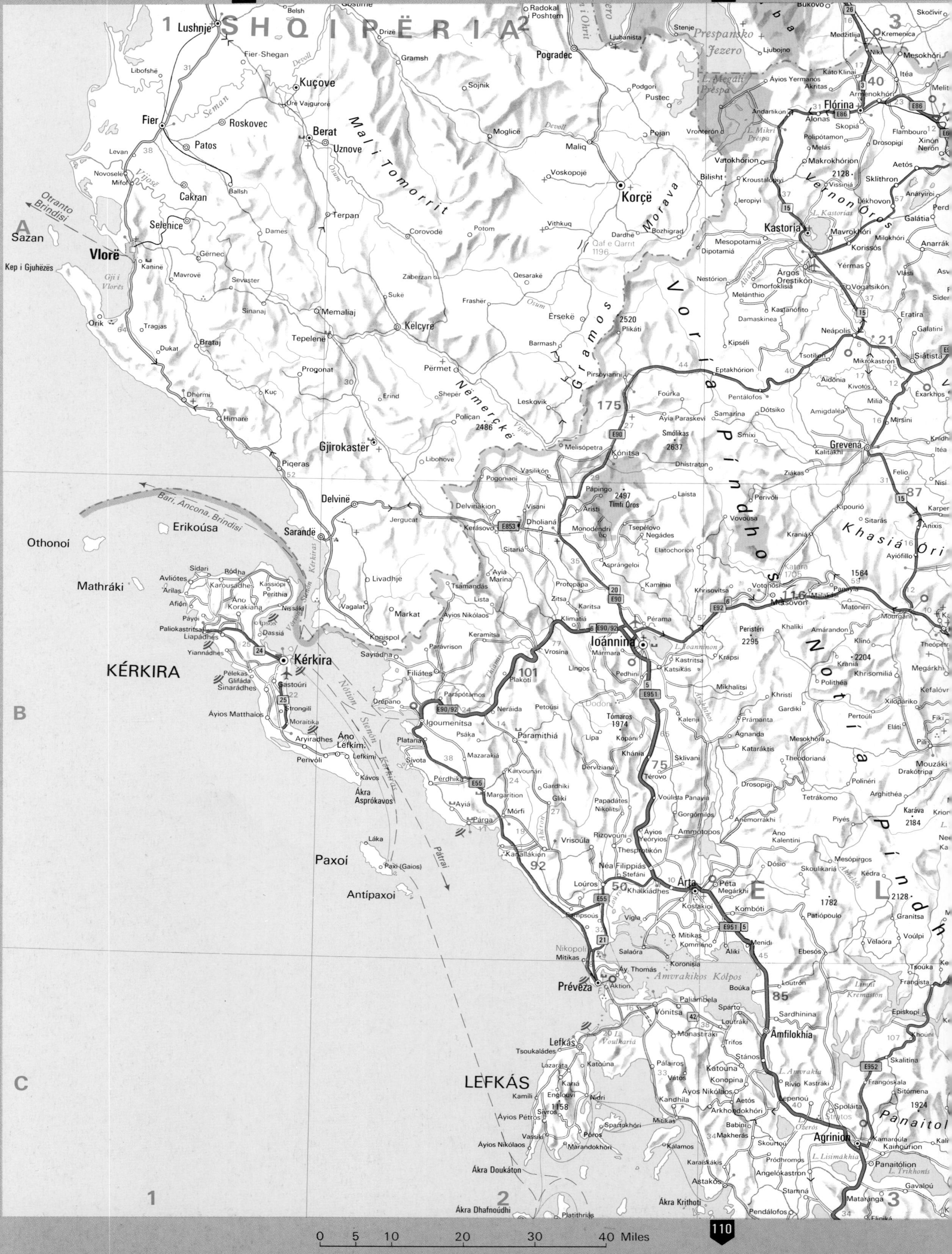
SHQIPËRIA
Lushnje
Fier
Kuçove
Berat
Roskovec
Patos
Uznove
Mali Tomorrit
Pogradec
Korçë
Vlorë
Sazan
Kep i Gjuhëzës
Selenice
Cakran
Otranto
Brindisi
Tepelenë
Këlcyrë
Përmet
Gjirokastër
Nëmerçkë
Gramos
Himare
Piqeras
Delvinë
Sarandë
Konispol
Ersekë
Bilisht
Flórina
Kastoria
Vórion Óros
Voría Píndhos
Nótia Píndhos
Khasiá Óri
Grevená
Kónitsa
Smólikas 2637
Ioánnina
Métsovon
Igoumenitsa
Paramithiá
Párga
Préveza
Árta
Amfilokhía
Agrinion
Lefkás
LEFKÁS
Kérkira
KÉRKIRA
Othonoí
Erikoúsa
Mathráki
Paxoí
Antípaxoi
Ákra Asprókavos
Ákra Doukáton
Ákra Dhafnoúdhi
Amvrakikós Kólpos
Bari, Ancona, Brindisi
Pátrai
Panaitolikón
E
L
A
B
C
1
2
3
0 5 10 20 30 40 Miles

110

105
105
95
95

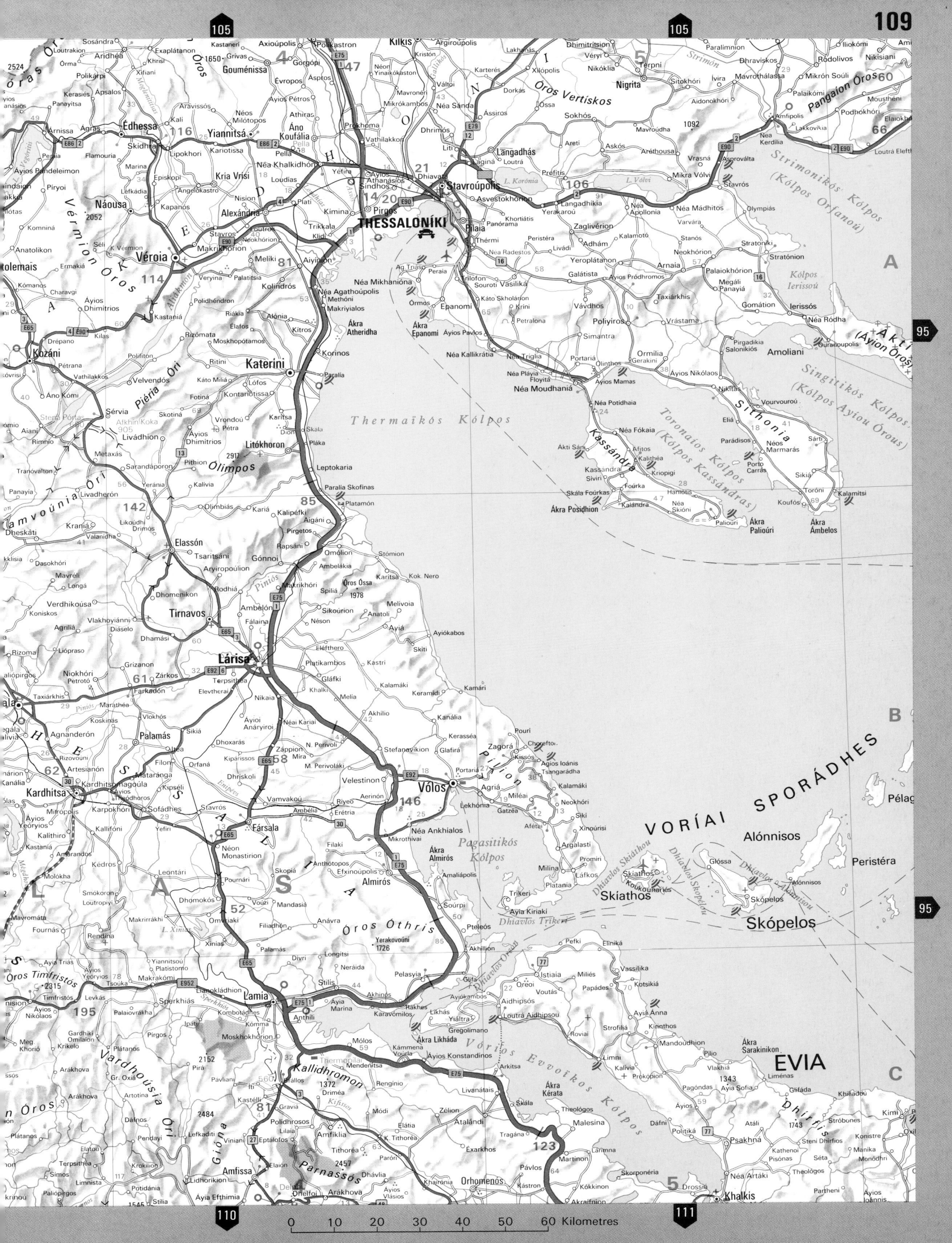
THESSALONÍKI
Kilkis
Nigrita
Óros Vertískos
Pangaíon Óros
Édhessa
Yiannitsá
Gouménissa
Náousa
Véroia
Alexándria
Kozáni
Kateríni
Stavroúpolis
Langadhás
Strimonikós Kólpos (Kólpos Orfanoú)
Kólpos Ierissoú
Thermaïkós Kólpos
Néa Moudhania
Kassándra
Toronaíos Kólpos (Kólpos Kassándras)
Sithonía
Singitikós Kólpos (Kólpos Ayíou Órous)
Akti (Ayion Óros)
Amoliani
Ierissós
Políyiros
Arnaía
Vérmion Óros
Piéria Óri
Ólimpos
Litókhoron
Elassón
Tirnavos
Lárisa
Kardhitsa
Palamás
Farsala
Vólos
Pílion
Zagorá
Pagasitikós Kólpos
VORÍAI SPORÁDHES
Skíathos
Skópelos
Alónnisos
Peristéra
Óros Óthris
Almirós
Lamia
Stilís
Vórios Evvoïkós Kólpos
EVIA
Limni
Istiaia
Amfissa
Parnassós
Gióna
Vardhoúsia Óri
Atalándi
Khalkis
0 10 20 30 40 50 60 Kilometres

110
111

108
109

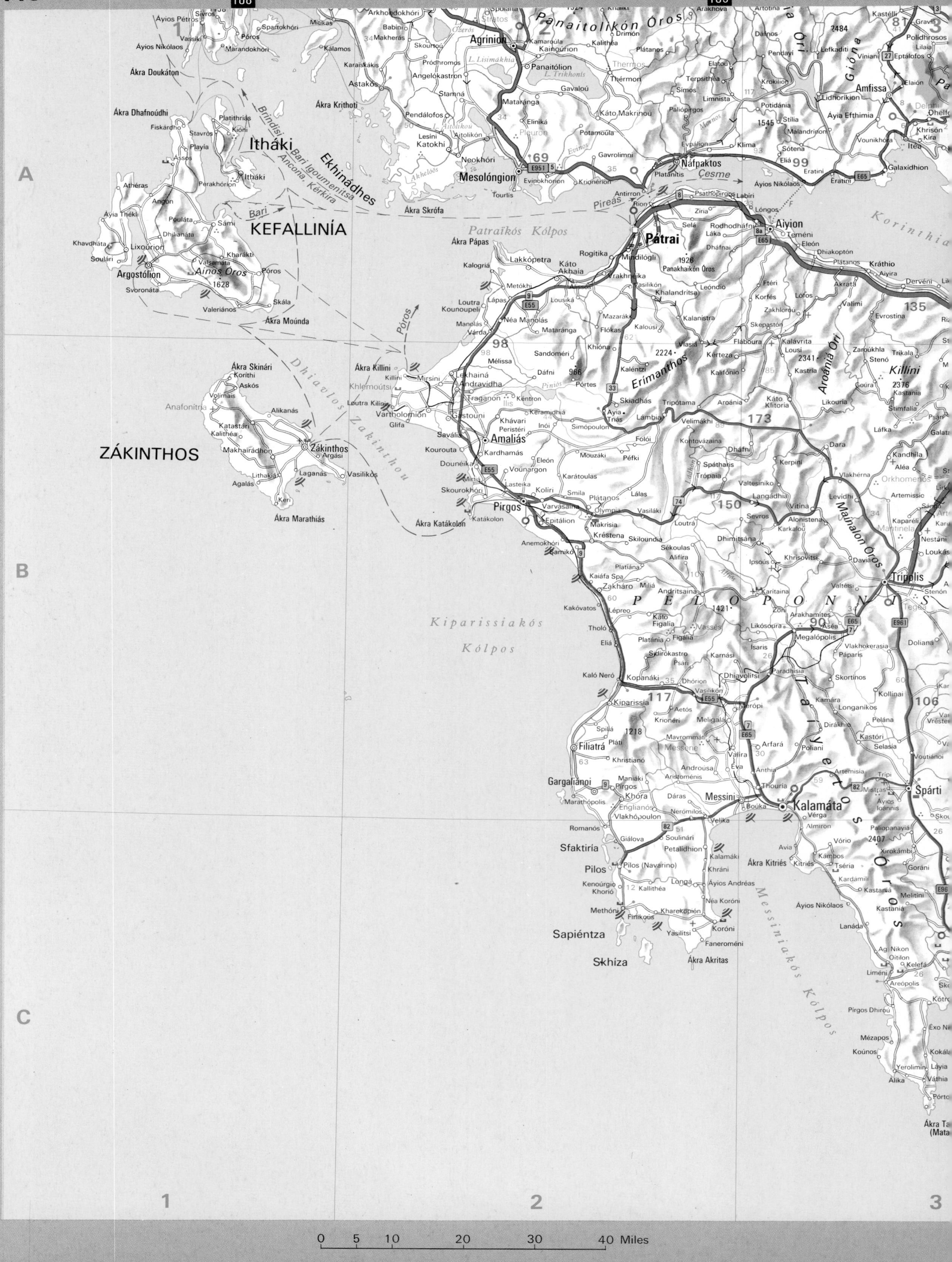
1
2
3
A
B
C
Ith//aki
KEFALLINÍA
ZÁKINTHOS
Ekhinádhes
Brindisi
Bari Igoumenitsa
Ancona Kérkira
Bari
Pireas
Çesme
Póros
Dhiavlos Zakinthou
Patraïkós Kólpos
Kiparissiakós Kólpos
Messiniakós Kólpos
Korinthiakós
PELOPONNISOS
Panaitolikón Óros
Erímanthos
Mainalon Óros
Taïyetos Óros
Aroánia Óri
Killíni
Gióna
Ainos Óros
Áyios Pétros
Sívros
Vassikí
Áyios Nikólaos
Póros
Marandokhóri
Spartokhóri
Mitikas
Kálamos
Kastós
Akra Doukáton
Akra Dhafnoúdhi
Fiskárdho
Stavrós
Platithriás
Kióni
Playia
Assos
Itháki
Perakhórion
Athéras
Angon
Áyia Thékli
Poulata
Sámi
Dhilianata
Khavdháta
Lixoúrion
Souláki
Valsamata
Kharákti
Argostólion
Póros
Svoronáta
Valeriános
Skála
Akra Moúnda
1628
Akra Skinári
Koríthi
Askós
Volímais
Anafonítria
Alikanás
Katastári
Kalithéa
Makhairádhon
Zákinthos
Argási
Lithakiá
Laganás
Vasilikós
Agalás
Keri
Akra Marathiás
Arkhontokhóri
Babini
Makheras
Skourtoú
Karaïskákis
Astakós
Akra Krithotí
Pendálofos
Lesini
Katokhí
Aitolikón
Neokhóri
Mesolóngion
Evinokhórion
Tourlis
Akra Skrófa
Angelókastron
Stamná
Prodhromos
Agrínion
Stratos
Kainoúrion
Kamaroúla
Panaitólion
L. Lisimákhia
L. Trikhonis
L. Aitolikou
Matarángá
Eliniká
Pleuron
Gavaloú
Thérmon
Thermos
Kalithéa
Plátanos
Drimón
Elatoú
Terpsithéa
Símos
Limnista
Páliopirgos
Káto Makrinoú
Potamoúla
Gavrolimni
Krionérion
Evinos
Mornos
Klima
Náfpaktos
Platanítis
Antírrion
Ríon
Psathópirgos
Labiri
Longos
Aíyion
Teméni
Eleón
Dhiakoptón
Plátanos
Kráthio
Aiyira
Dervéni
Zíria
Selá
Rodhodháfni
Láka
Dháfnai
Pátrai
Mindilógli
Panakhaikón Óros
1926
Rogitika
Akra Pápas
Kalogriá
Lakkópetra
Káto Akhaia
Vrakhnéika
Alissós
Metókhi
Lápas
Loutra Kounoupeli
Manolás
Várda
Néa Manolás
Lousiká
Mazaráki
Matarángá
Flókas
Kalousi
Vasilikón
Khalandritsa
Leóndio
Kalanistra
Skepastón
Ftéri
Korfés
Lofos
Zakhloroú
Akrata
Válimi
Evrostina
Kalávrita
Lousi
Flamboura
Vlasia
Kerteza
Kalifónio
Kastria
2224
2341
Khióna
Sandoméri
Mélissa
Dáfni
966
Pórtes
Kaléntzi
Akra Killíni
Killíni
Khlemoútsi
Loutra Kilinis
Mirsini
Lekhainá
Andravidha
Traganon
Kéntron
Ilis
Vartholomión
Glífa
Gastoúni
Savália
Keramidhiá
Khávari
Peristéri
Inói
Simópoulon
Skiadhás
Ayia Triás
Lámbia
Tripótama
Aroánia
Káto Klitoria
Likouria
Kourouta
Amaliás
Kardhamás
Douneika
Eleón
Vounargon
Mouzáki
Péfki
Karátoulas
Folói
Kontovázaina
Dháfni
Kerpiní
Dara
Spátharis
Tropaia
Valtesiniko
Langádhia
Vlakhérna
Kandhila
Aléa
Orkhomenós
Artemissio
Levídhi
Kaparéli
Mantinela
Lasteika
Skourokhóri
Kolíri
Smila
Plátanos
Lálas
Pírgos
Varvásaina
Olympia
Vasiláki
Loutrá
Vitina
Alonistena
Karkalou
Akra Katákolon
Katákolon
Epitálion
Makrisia
Kréstena
Skilloundia
Dhimitsána
Anemokhóri
Samikó
Sékoulas
Alifíra
Khrisovitsi
Ipsoús
Davia
Trípolis
Platiána
Kaiáfa Spa
Zakháro
Miliá
Andritsaina
Kakóvatos
Lépreo
Káto Figalia
1421
Zoni
Arakhamites
Aséa
Valtétsi
Stenón
Tegea
Tholó
Vassés
Figália
Likósoura
Megalópolis
Eliá
Plátania
Skirokastro
Psári
Karnási
Isaris
Vlakhokerasia
Páparis
Doliana
Kaló Neró
Kopanáki
Dhórion
Dhiavolitsi
Paradhisia
Skortinos
Kiparissía
Vasilikón
Merópi
Kollinai
Aetós
Kamára
Longanikos
Krionéri
Meligalá
Spiliá
1218
Dirákhio
Pelána
Mavrommati
Messene
Filiatrá
Khristianó
Arfará
Valira
Eva
Poliani
Kastóri
Selasia
Voutiáno
Androusa
Aristoménis
Anthia
Artemisía
Tripi
Gargaliánoi
Maniáki
Pírgos
Khóra
Dáras
Messíni
Thouria
Kalamáta
Mistras
Áyios Ioánnis
Spárti
Marathópolis
Englianós
Vlakhópoulon
Nerómilos
Boúka
Vérga
Almiron
Romanós
Giálova
Velíka
Soulinári
Petalidhion
Paliopanayia
Vório
2407
Xirokámbi
Sfaktiría
Pílos
Pilos (Navarino)
Kalamáki
Khráni
Avia
Akra Kitriés
Kitriés
Kámbos
Tséria
Kardamili
Gorani
Kenoúrgio Khorió
Kalithéa
Longá
Áyios Andréas
Kastania
Melitini
Néa Koróni
Methóni
Finikous
Kharakopión
Áyios Nikólaos
Kastania
Sapiéntza
Yasilitsi
Koróni
Lanáda
Faneroméni
Skhíza
Akra Akritas
Ag. Nikon
Oitilon
Kelefá
Liméni
Areópolis
Pirgos Dhiroú
Mézapos
Koúnos
Yerolimín
Láyia
Vathia
Álika
Pórto
Akra Tainaron (Matapan)
Kastélli
Gravia
Polidhrosos
Lilaia
Viniani
Eptálofos
Dáfnos
Penáyi
Lefkadíti
2484
Krokílion
Lidhoríkion
Amfissa
Elaión
Delphi
Dhelfoí
Potidánia
Stília
1545
Malandrinon
Áyia Efthimia
Khrisón
Kira
Itéa
Vounikhóra
Sótena
Eliá
Galaxídhion
Eratiní
Áyios Nikólaos
E55
E65
E951
E961
E96
69
98
99
117
135
150
173
90
106
0
5
10
20
30
40 Miles

5

Pagondas · Ayia Sofía
Glifáda · Khiliadóú
Ákra Kimis
Kimi
Peralia Kimis

Livanátais
Módi · Zélion · Skála
Kérata · Theológos
Dháfni · Politiká
Atáli · Stróbones
Konistra
Oxilithos

Elátia · K. Tithoréa · Atalándi · Malesina
Áyios · 59
Psakhná · Steni Dhirfíos · Manika · Monódhri

Tragána
123 · Exarkhos · Pávlos · Martinón · Skorponéria
Néa Artáki · Theológos · Séta · Oktoniá · Akhladeri

Orhomenós · Kókkinon · Drosiá
Khalkís · Afráti · Yimnón · Ayii Ioánnis · Ayii Apóstoli

Aliartos · Akraifnion · Mouriki · 44 · Alivérion · Véles · Kóskina

Levádhia · 103 · Thivai · 1 E75 · Vathi · Lefkanti · Amárinthos · L. Dhístos

A

Nótios Evvoikos Kólpos
Ákra Kafiréas

ÁNDROS

Salamis · PIREÁS · ATHÍNAI

Makronísi

Kéa · Yiaros

B

Kíthnos · Ermoúpolis

Sérifos

Mírtóön
Pélagos
Sífnos

Parapóla

Kímolos · Kímolos · Poliáigos
Andímilos · Mílos

C

KÍTHIRA

0 10 20 30 40 50 60 Kilometres

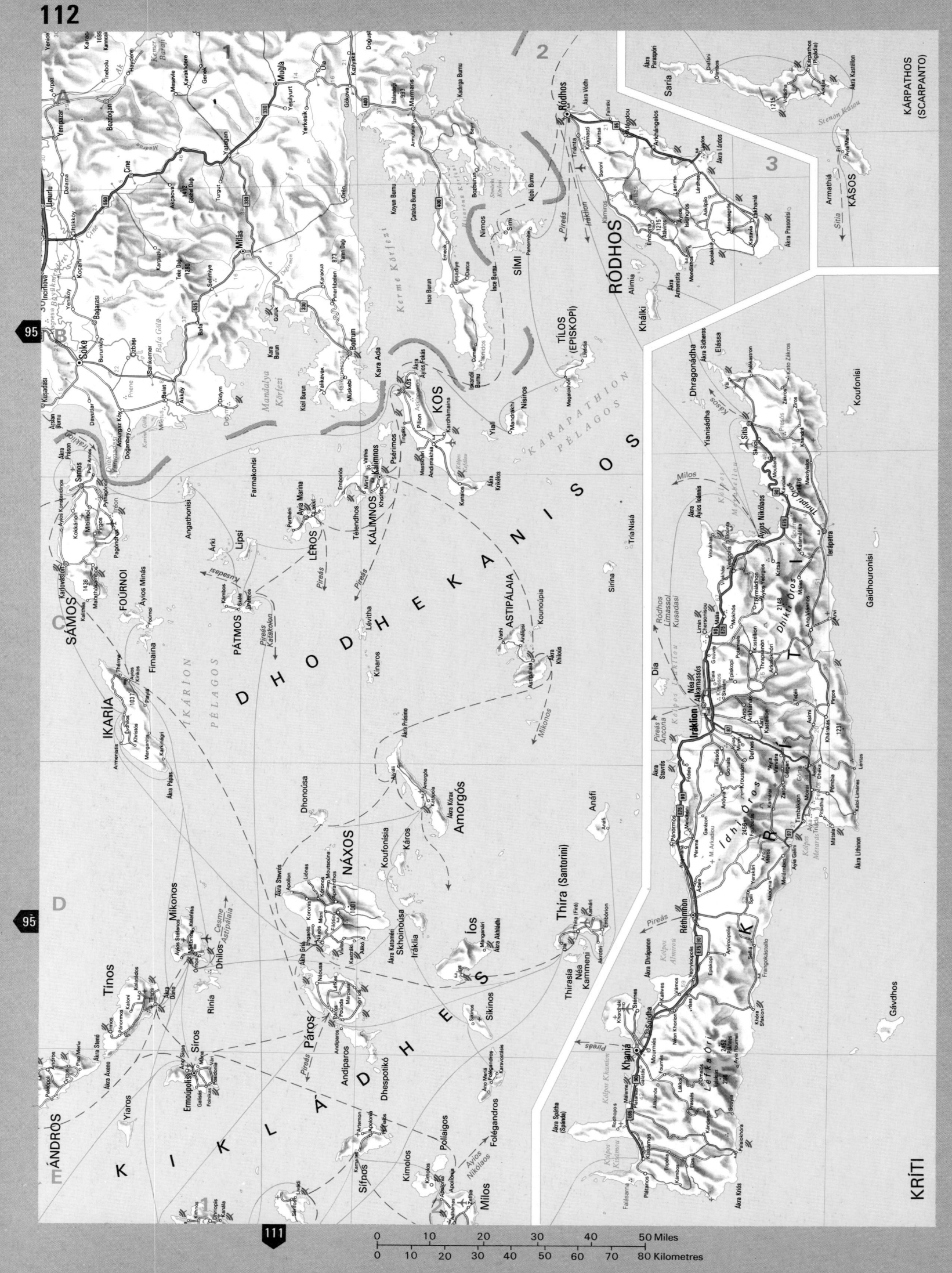

0	10	20	30	40	50 Miles

0	10	20	30	40	50	60	70	80 Kilometres

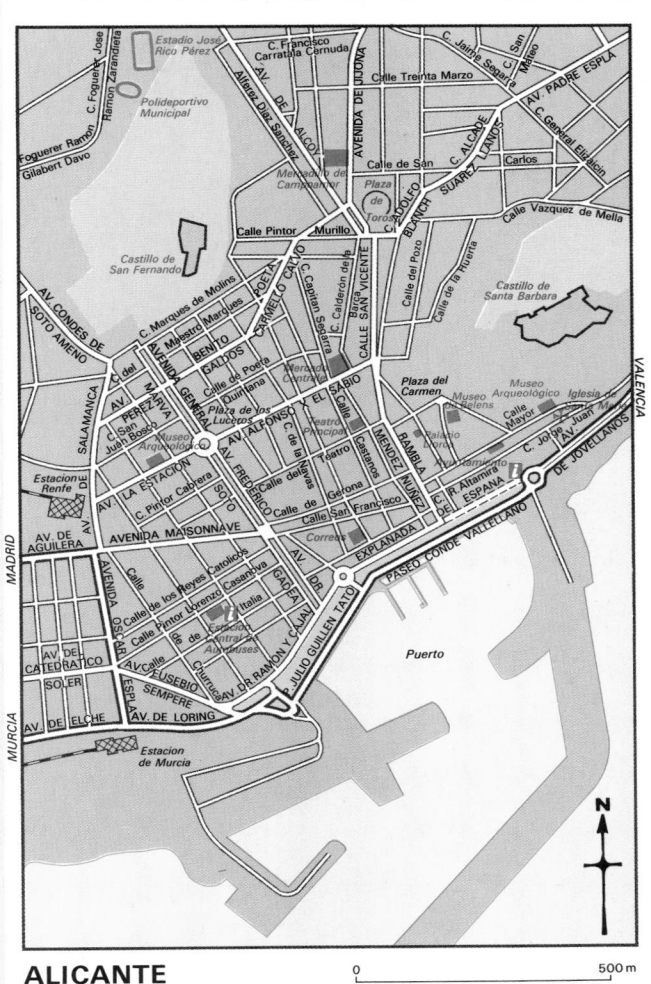

ALICANTE

0   500 m

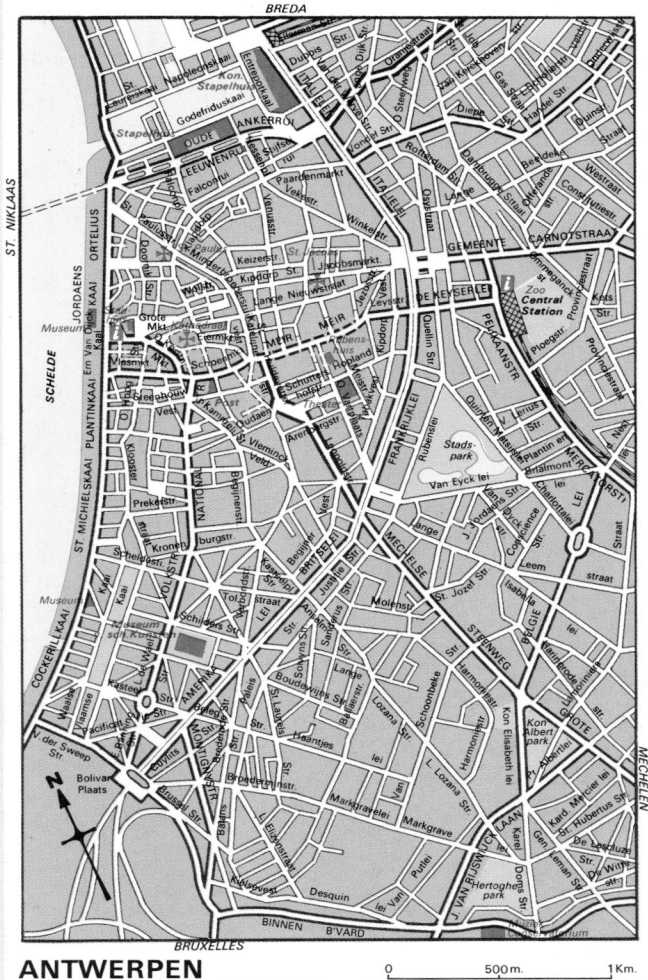

ANTWERPEN

0   500 m.   1 Km.

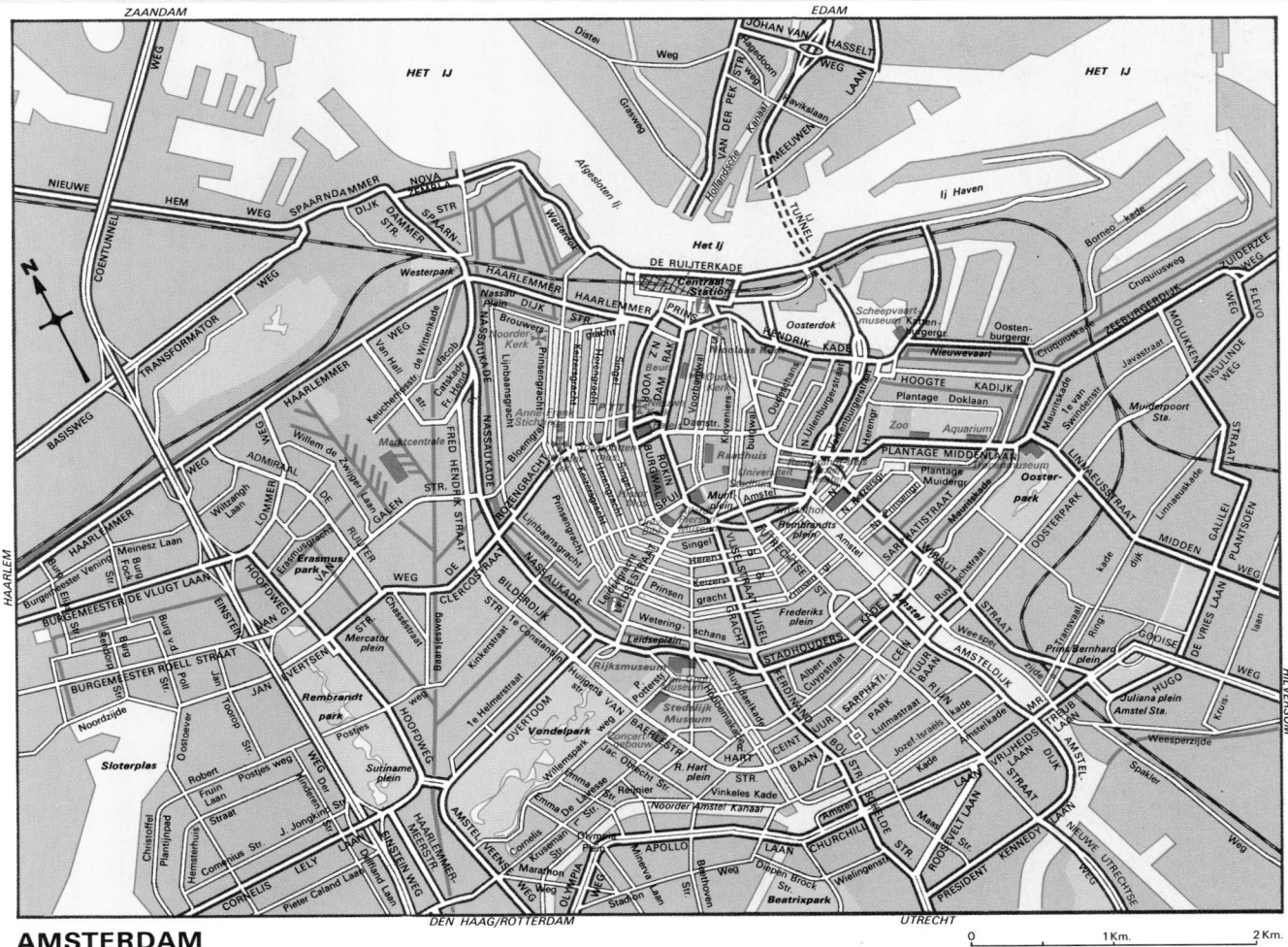

AMSTERDAM

0   1 Km.   2 Km.

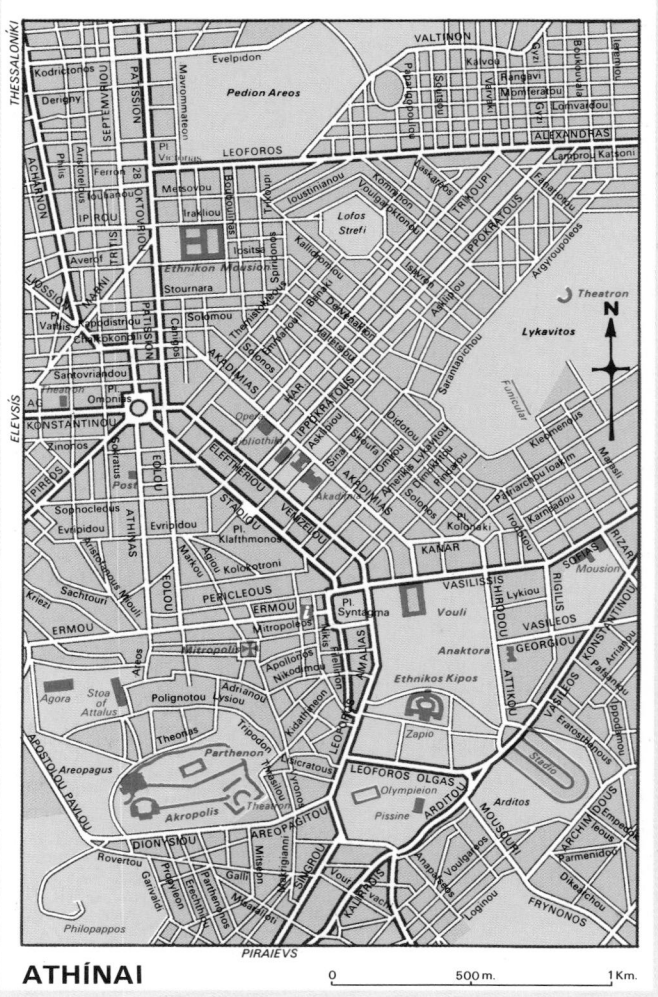

ATHÍNAI

0   500 m.   1 Km.

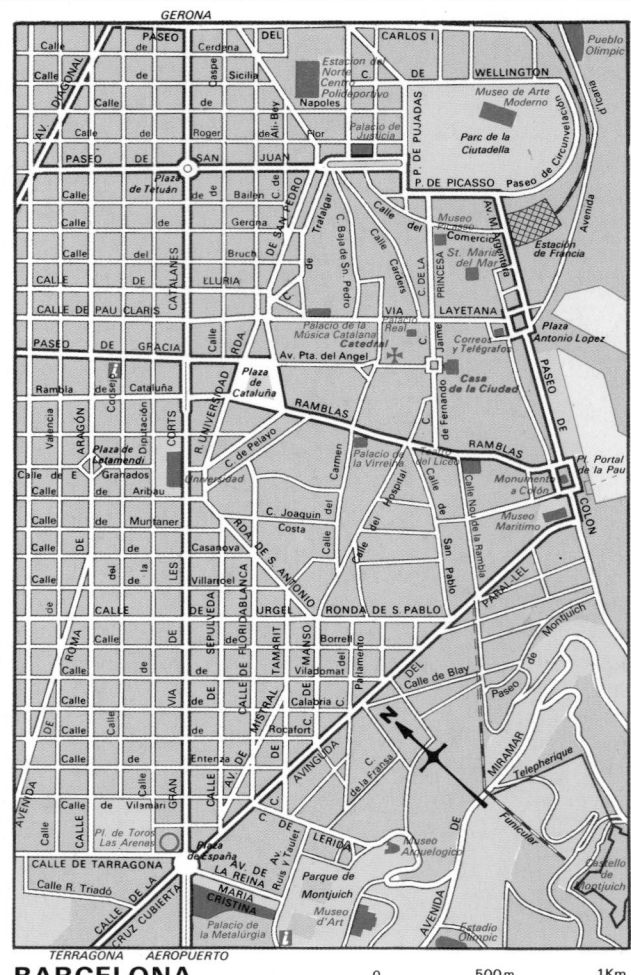

BARCELONA

0   500 m.   1 Km.

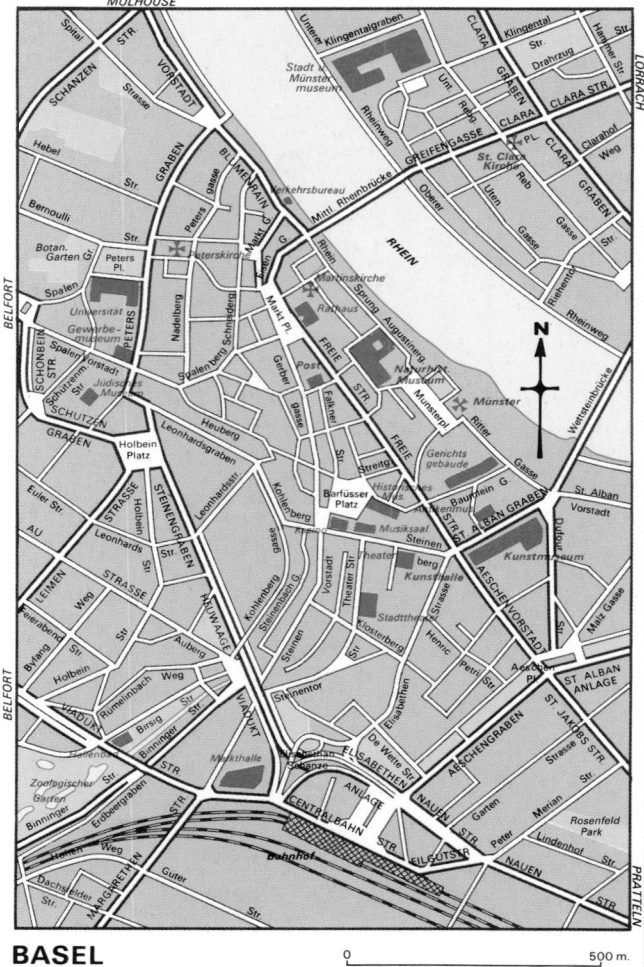

BASEL

0   500 m.

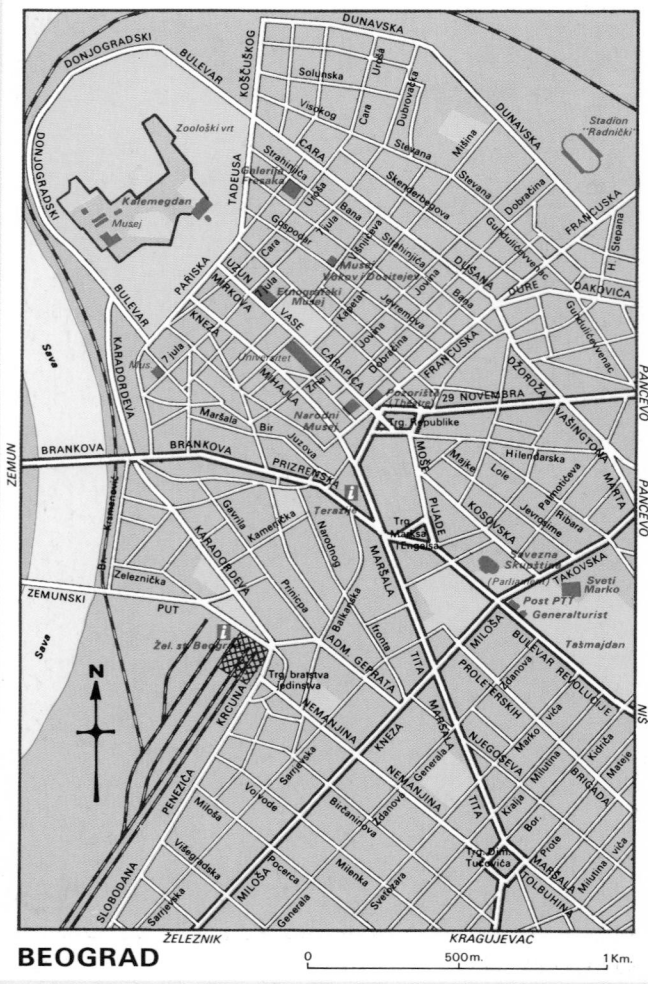

BEOGRAD

0   500 m.   1 Km.

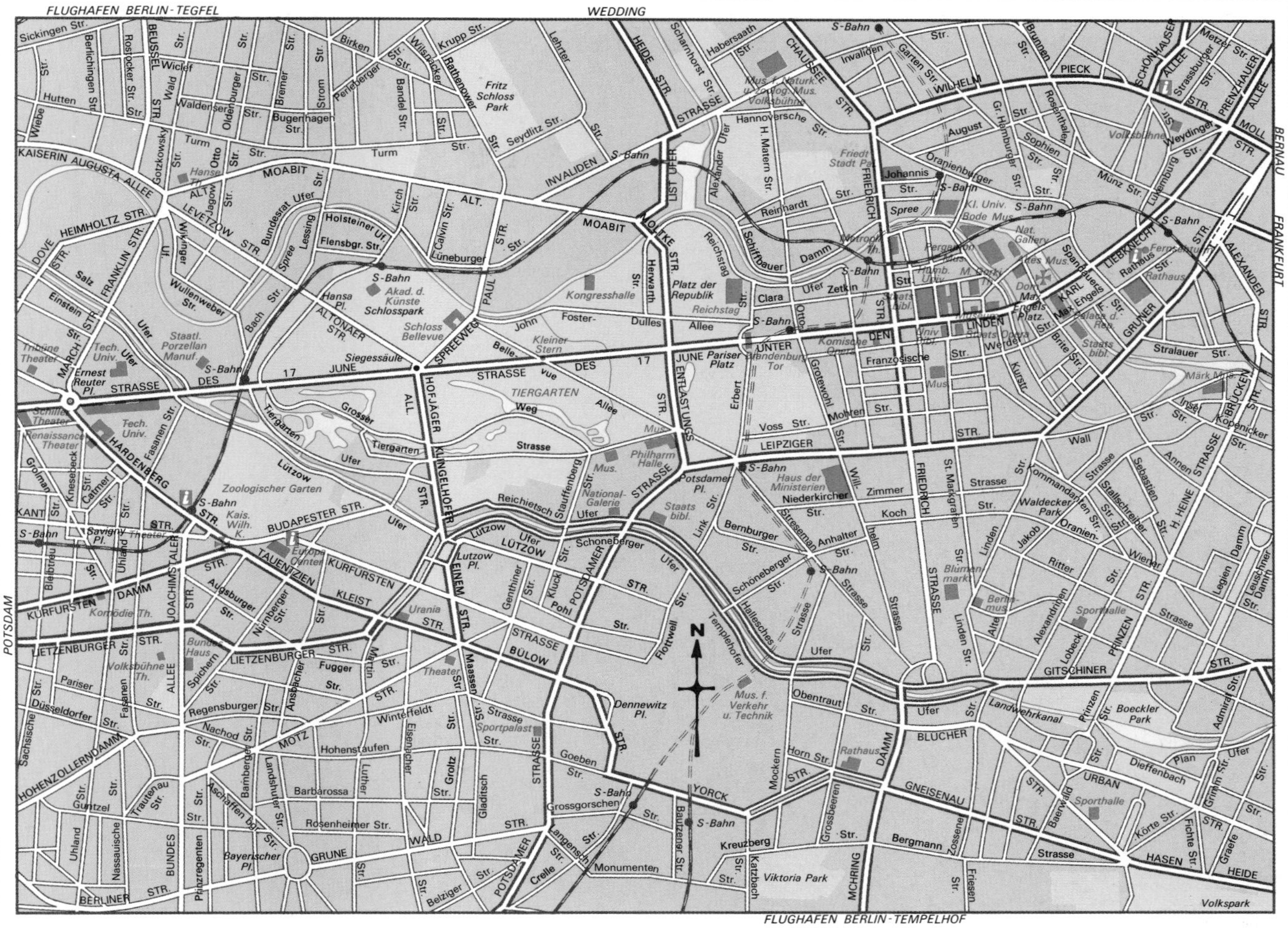

BERLIN

0 1 Km.

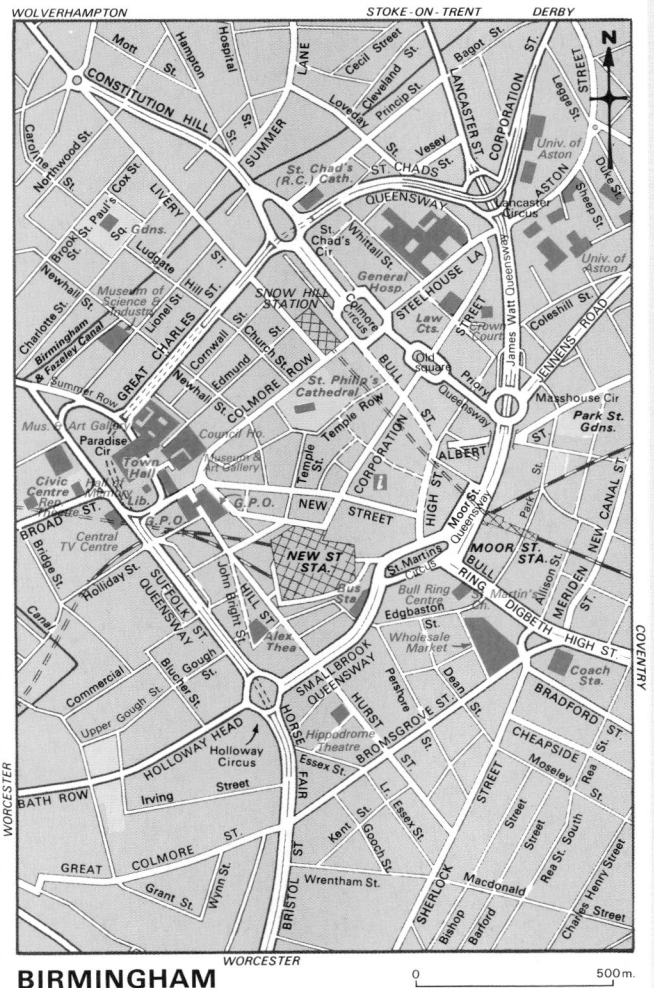

BIRMINGHAM

0 500 m.

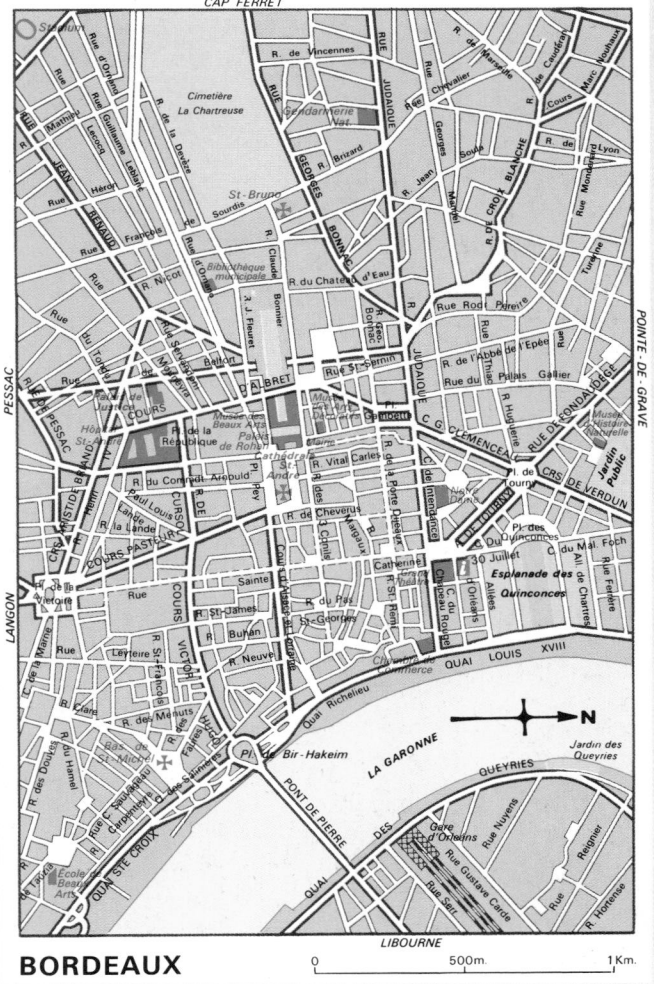

BORDEAUX

0 500 m. 1 Km.

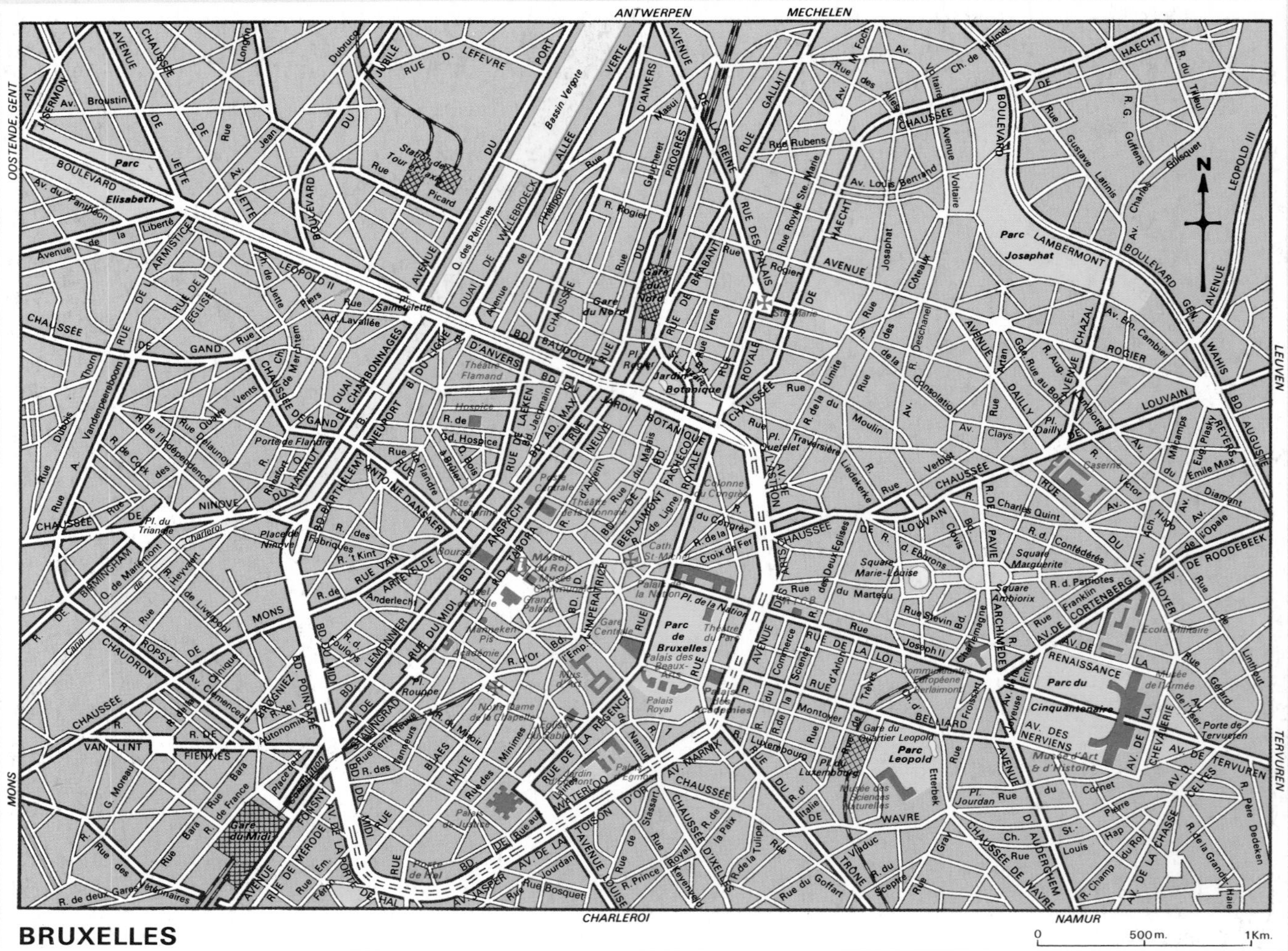

BRUXELLES

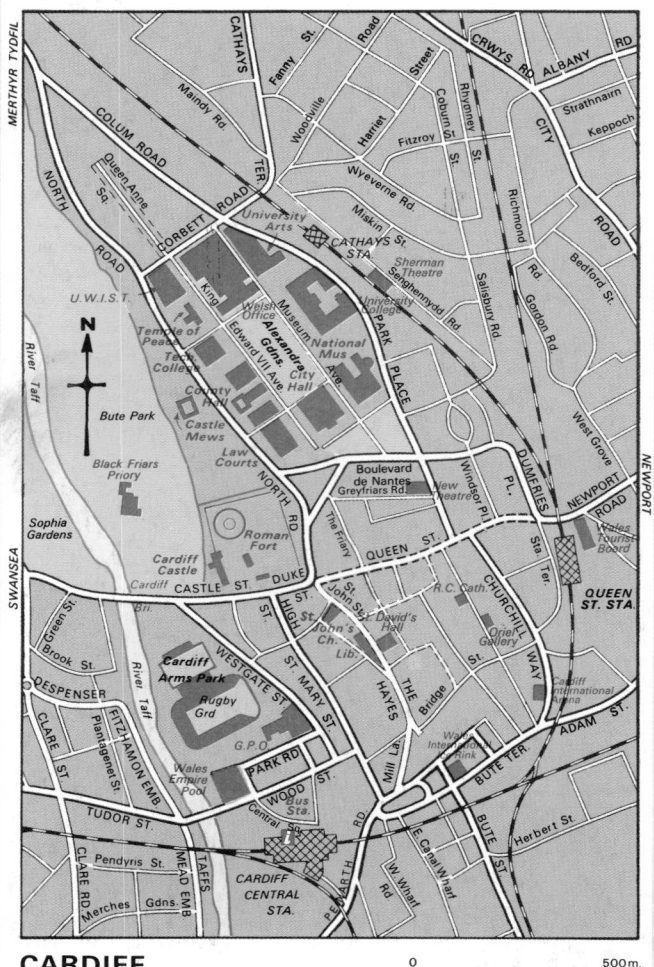

CARDIFF

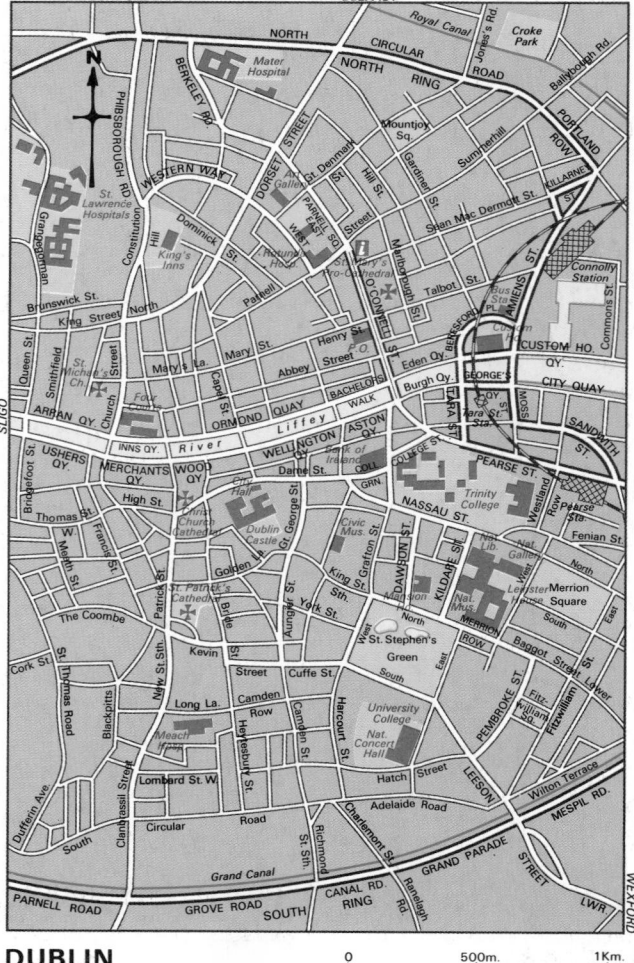

DUBLIN

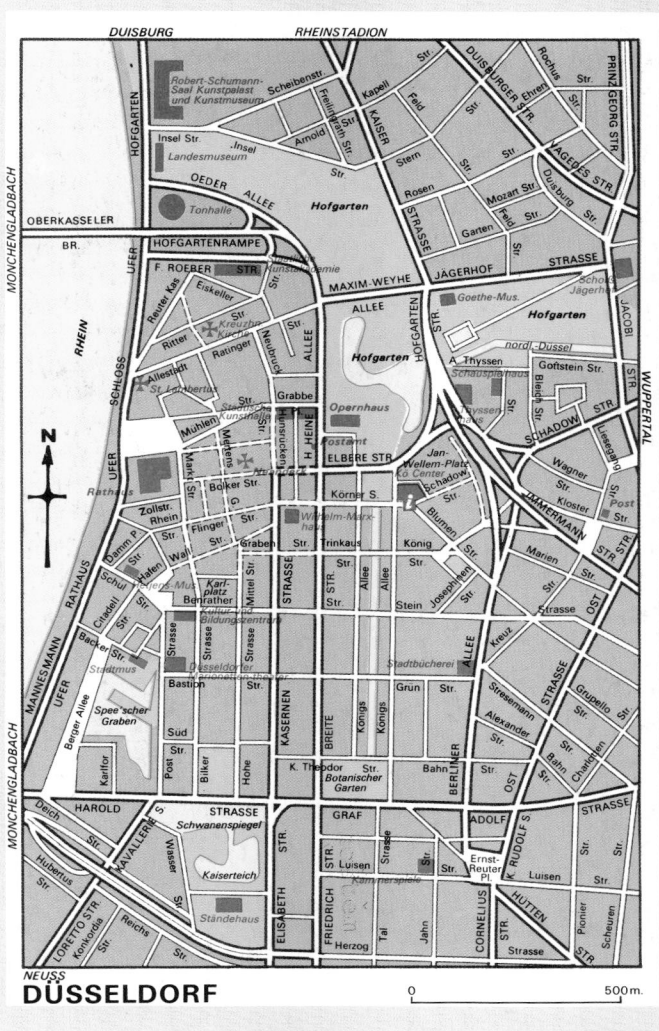

DÜSSELDORF

0   500 m.

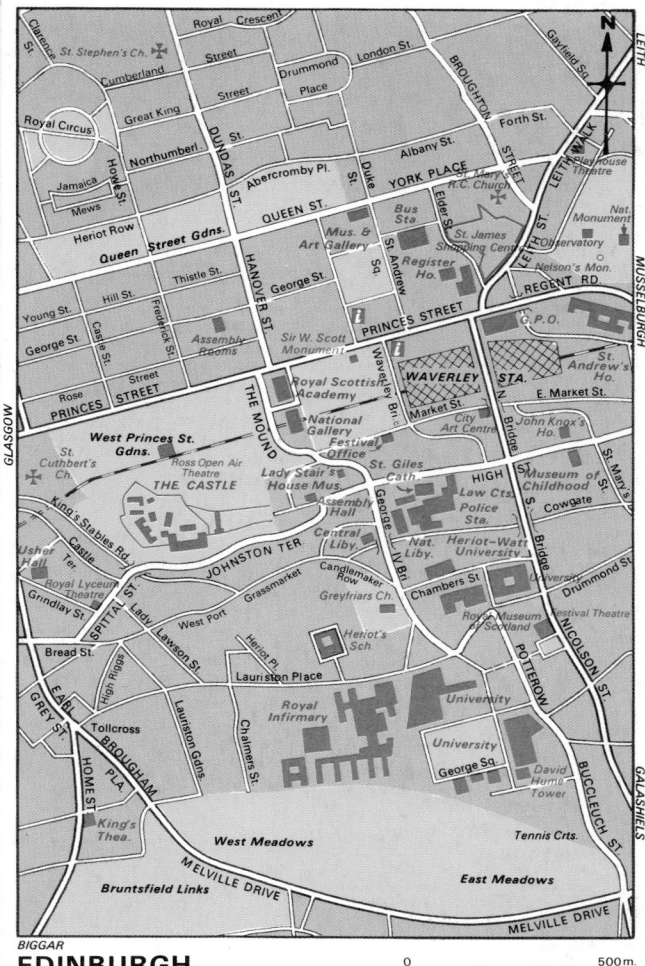

EDINBURGH

0   500 m.

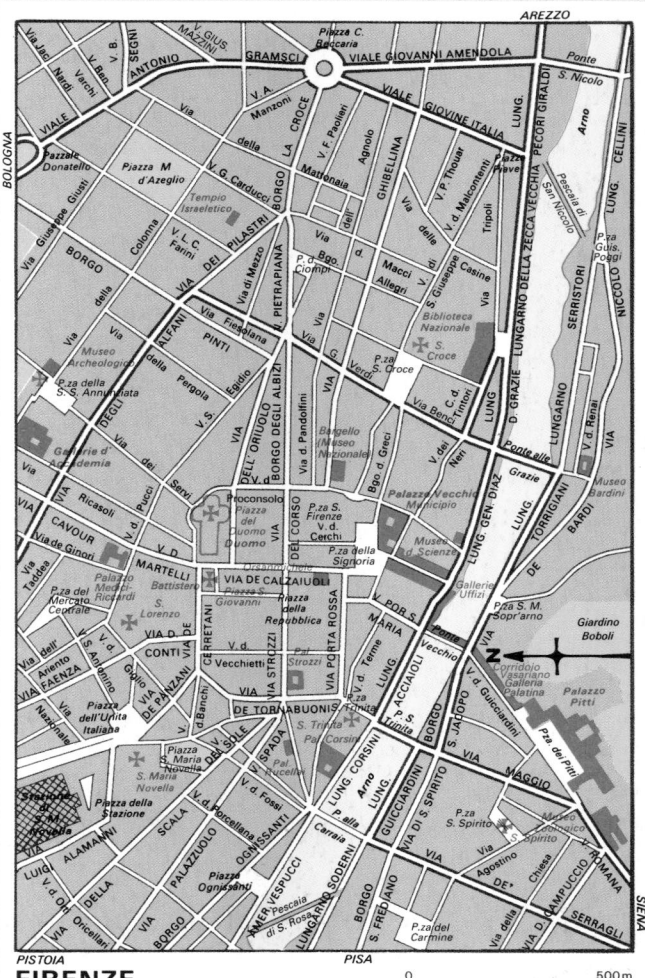

FIRENZE

0   500 m.

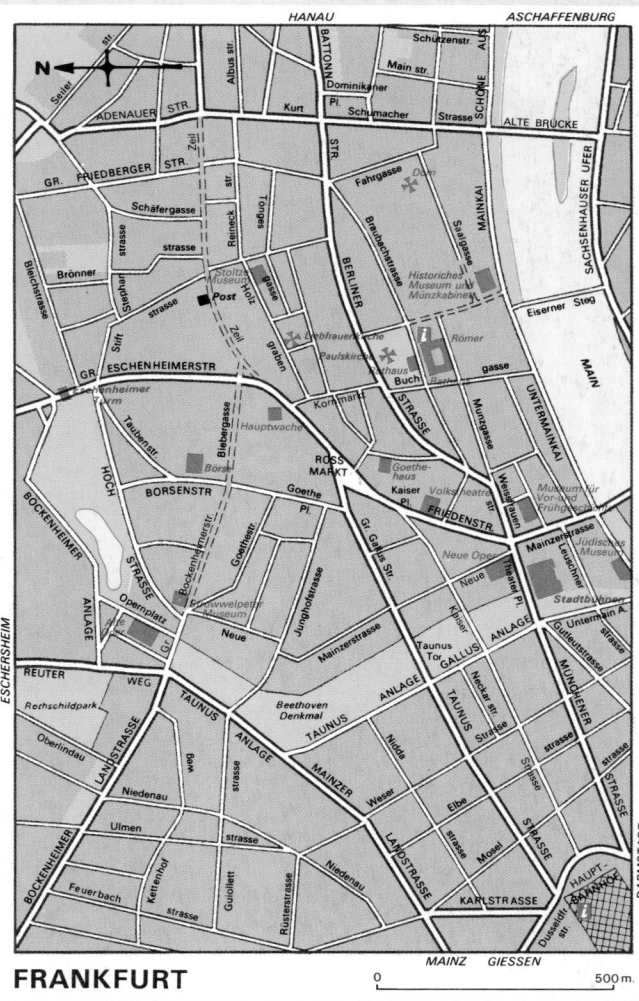

FRANKFURT

0   500 m.

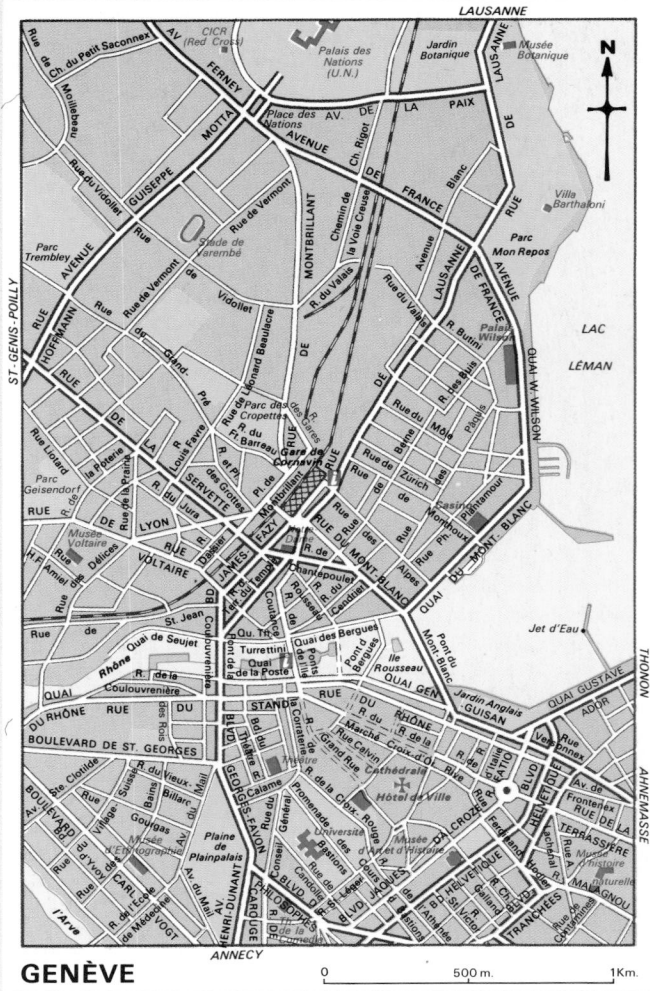

GENÈVE

0   500 m.   1 Km.

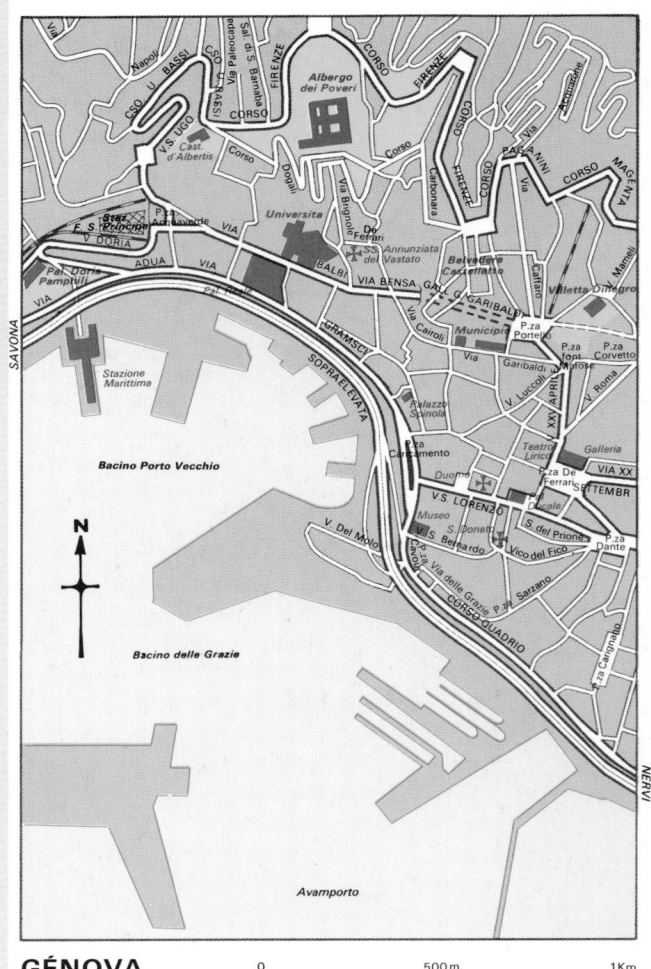

GÉNOVA

0   500 m.   1 Km.

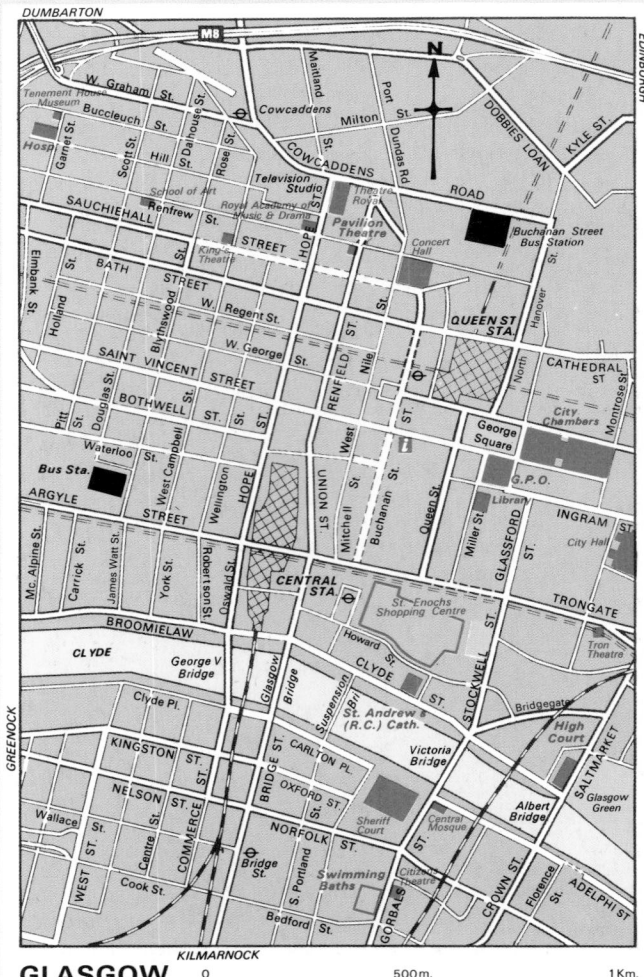

GLASGOW

0   500 m.   1 Km.

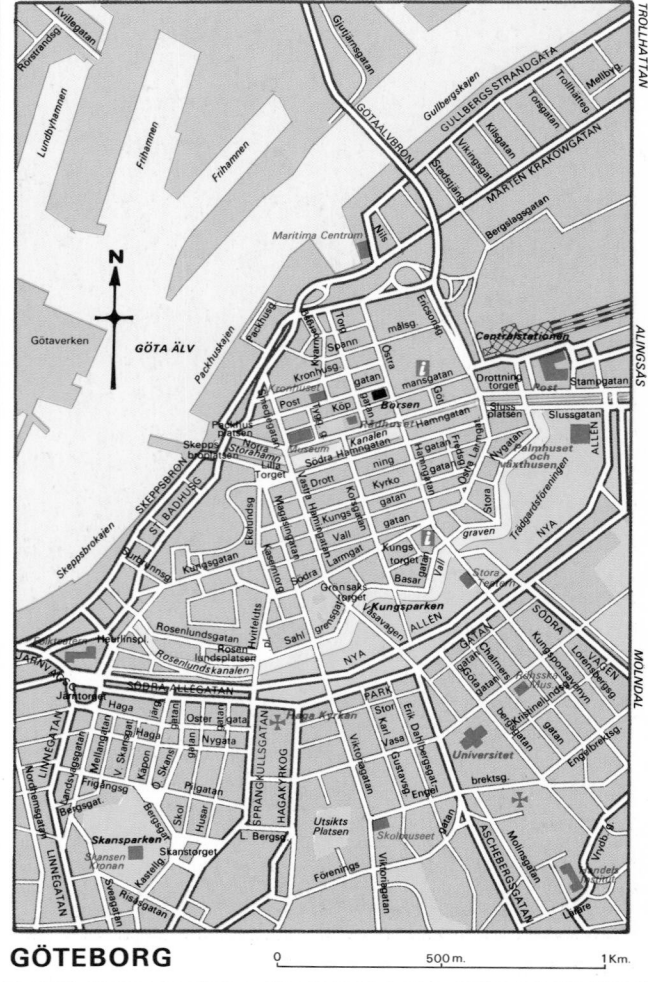

GÖTEBORG

0   500 m.   1 Km.

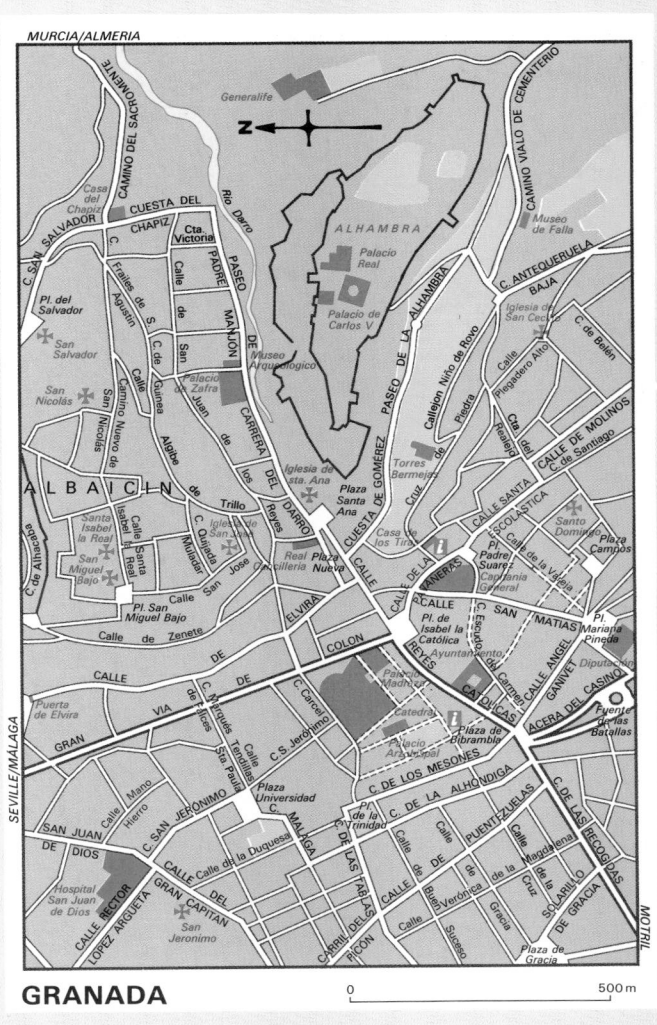

GRANADA

0   500 m

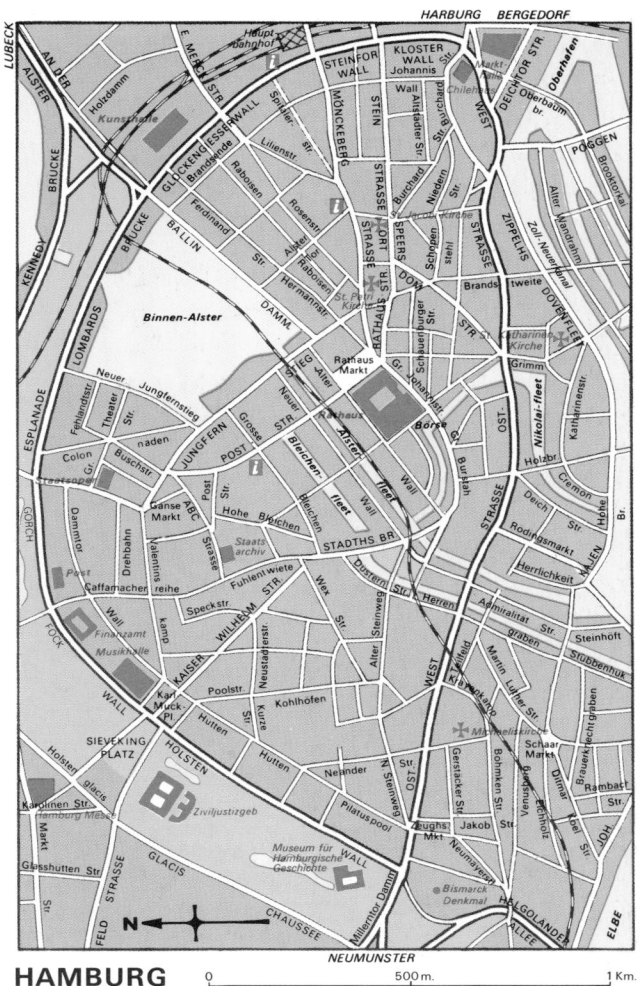

HAMBURG

0   500 m.   1 Km.

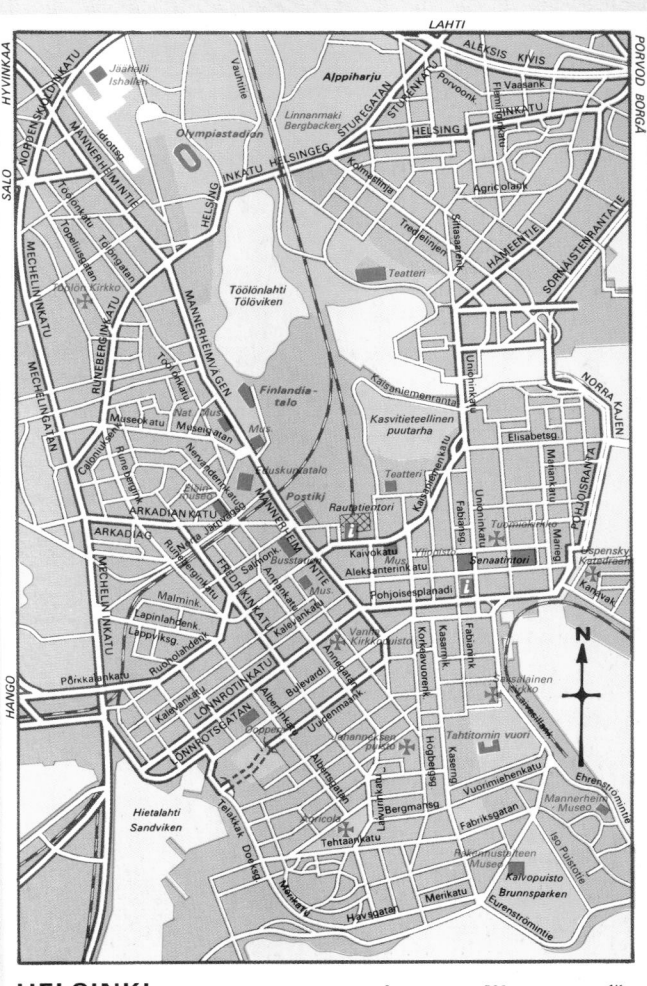

HELSINKI

0   500 m.   1 Km.

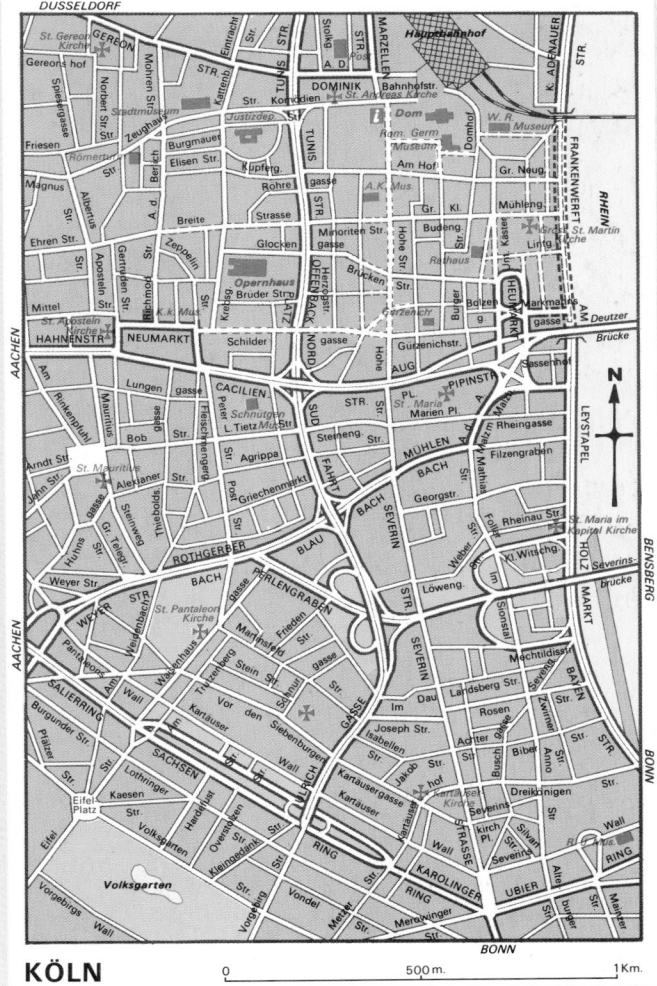

KÖLN

0   500 m.   1 Km.

KØBENHAVN

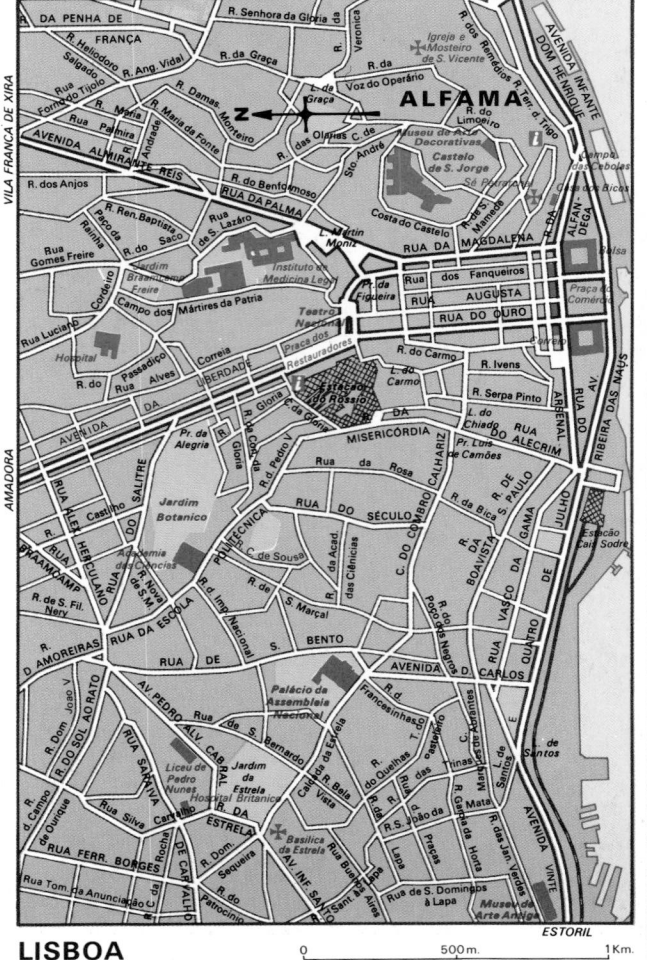

LISBOA

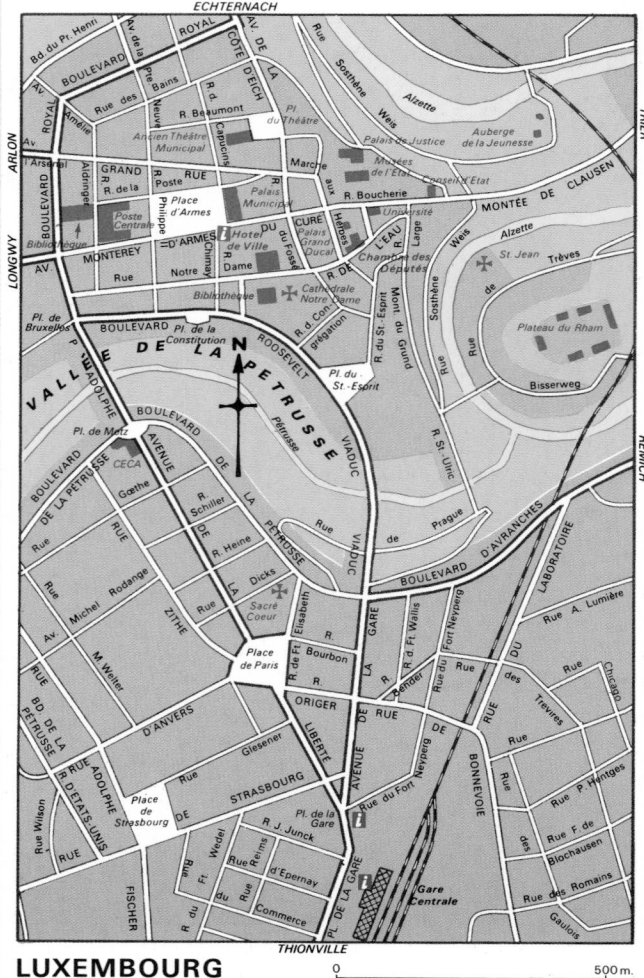

LUXEMBOURG

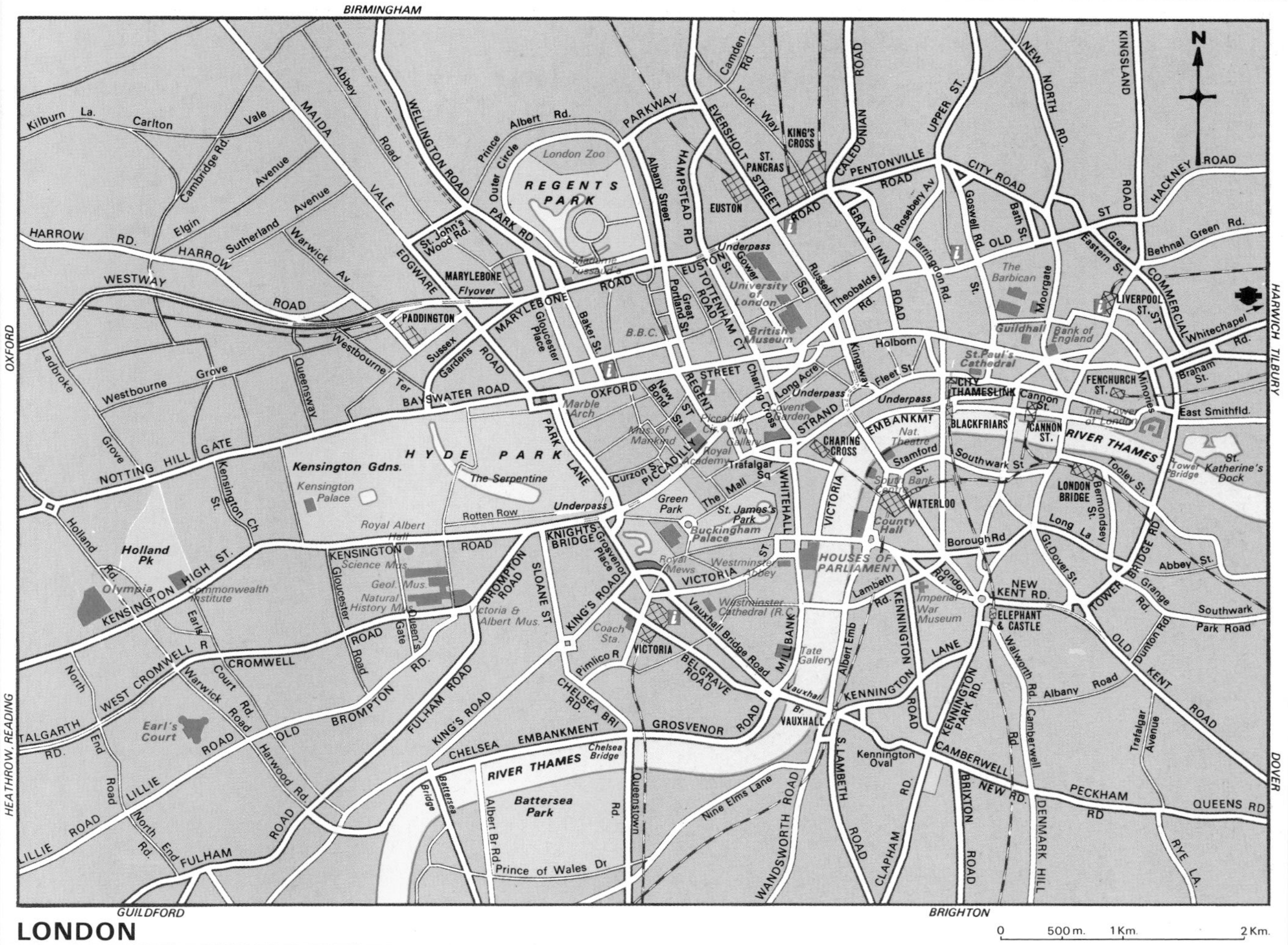
BIRMINGHAM
OXFORD
HARWICH TILBURY
HEATHROW, READING
DOVER
GUILDFORD
BRIGHTON
REGENTS PARK
London Zoo
HYDE PARK
Kensington Gdns.
The Serpentine
Kensington Palace
Rotten Row
Holland Pk
Olympia
Commonwealth Institute
Earl's Court
Science Mus.
Geol. Mus.
Natural History Mus.
Victoria & Albert Mus.
Royal Albert Hall
Marble Arch
Green Park
St. James's Park
Buckingham Palace
Trafalgar Sq
HOUSES OF PARLIAMENT
Westminster Abbey
Westminster Cathedral (R.C.)
Tate Gallery
County Hall
Nat. Theatre
Imperial War Museum
St. Paul's Cathedral
Guildhall
Bank of England
The Barbican
The Tower of London
Tower Bridge
St. Katherine's Dock
British Museum
University of London
B.B.C.
RIVER THAMES
Battersea Park
Chelsea Bridge
Battersea Bridge
PADDINGTON
MARYLEBONE
EUSTON
ST. PANCRAS
KING'S CROSS
LIVERPOOL ST.
FENCHURCH ST.
CANNON ST.
BLACKFRIARS
CHARING CROSS
WATERLOO
LONDON BRIDGE
VICTORIA
ELEPHANT & CASTLE
Kennington Oval
VAUXHALL
CITY THAMESLINK
Coach Sta.
Royal Mews
Royal Academy
Mus. of Mankind
National Gallery
Covent Garden
South Bank Centre
BAYSWATER ROAD
NOTTING HILL GATE
KENSINGTON HIGH ST.
CROMWELL
WEST CROMWELL R
BROMPTON
FULHAM ROAD
KING'S ROAD
CHELSEA EMBANKMENT
GROSVENOR ROAD
PARK LANE
PICCADILLY
OXFORD STREET
REGENT ST
STRAND
WHITEHALL
EMBANKMENT
MARYLEBONE ROAD
EUSTON ROAD
PENTONVILLE ROAD
CITY ROAD
WESTWAY
HARROW RD.
EDGWARE ROAD
PARK RD
WELLINGTON ROAD
PARKWAY
HAMPSTEAD RD
EVERSHOLT STREET
CALEDONIAN ROAD
UPPER ST.
NEW NORTH RD.
KINGSLAND ROAD
HACKNEY ROAD
COMMERCIAL ST.
Whitechapel
Bethnal Green Rd.
East Smithfld.
Tooley St.
Southwark St
Borough Rd
NEW KENT RD.
OLD KENT ROAD
KENNINGTON LANE
KENNINGTON PARK RD
CAMBERWELL NEW RD.
PECKHAM RD
QUEENS RD
RYE LA.
DENMARK HILL
BRIXTON ROAD
CLAPHAM RD.
WANDSWORTH ROAD
S. LAMBETH ROAD
Nine Elms Lane
Queenstown Rd.
Prince of Wales Dr
SLOANE ST
KNIGHTSBRIDGE
BELGRAVE ROAD
VAUXHALL BRIDGE ROAD
MILLBANK
LILLIE ROAD
FULHAM
TALGARTH RD.
Kilburn La.
Carlton Vale
MAIDA VALE
Abbey Road
Prince Albert Rd.
Outer Circle
Albany Street
TOTTENHAM CT. RD
Baker St.
Gloucester Place
Sussex Gardens
Westbourne Grove
Queensway
Ladbroke Grove
Holland Rd
Kensington Ch. St.
Gloucester Rd
Queen's Gate
Warwick Rd
North End Rd
Earls Court Rd.
Harwood Rd
Underpass
Theobalds Rd.
Holborn
Fleet St.
Kingsway
GRAY'S INN RD
Farringdon Rd.
Goswell Rd
Rosebery Av
Moorgate
Great Eastern St
Minories
Braham St
Long La
Bermondsey St.
TOWER BRIDGE RD
Grange Rd
Abbey St.
Southwark Park Road
Dunton Rd
Albany Road
Trafalgar Avenue
Walworth Rd.
Camberwell Rd
Lambeth Rd
Albert Emb
Stamford St
The Mall
Curzon St
Grosvenor Place
Pimlico R
CHELSEA BRI RD.
Flyover
St. John's Wood Rd

LONDON

0 500 m. 1 Km. 2 Km.

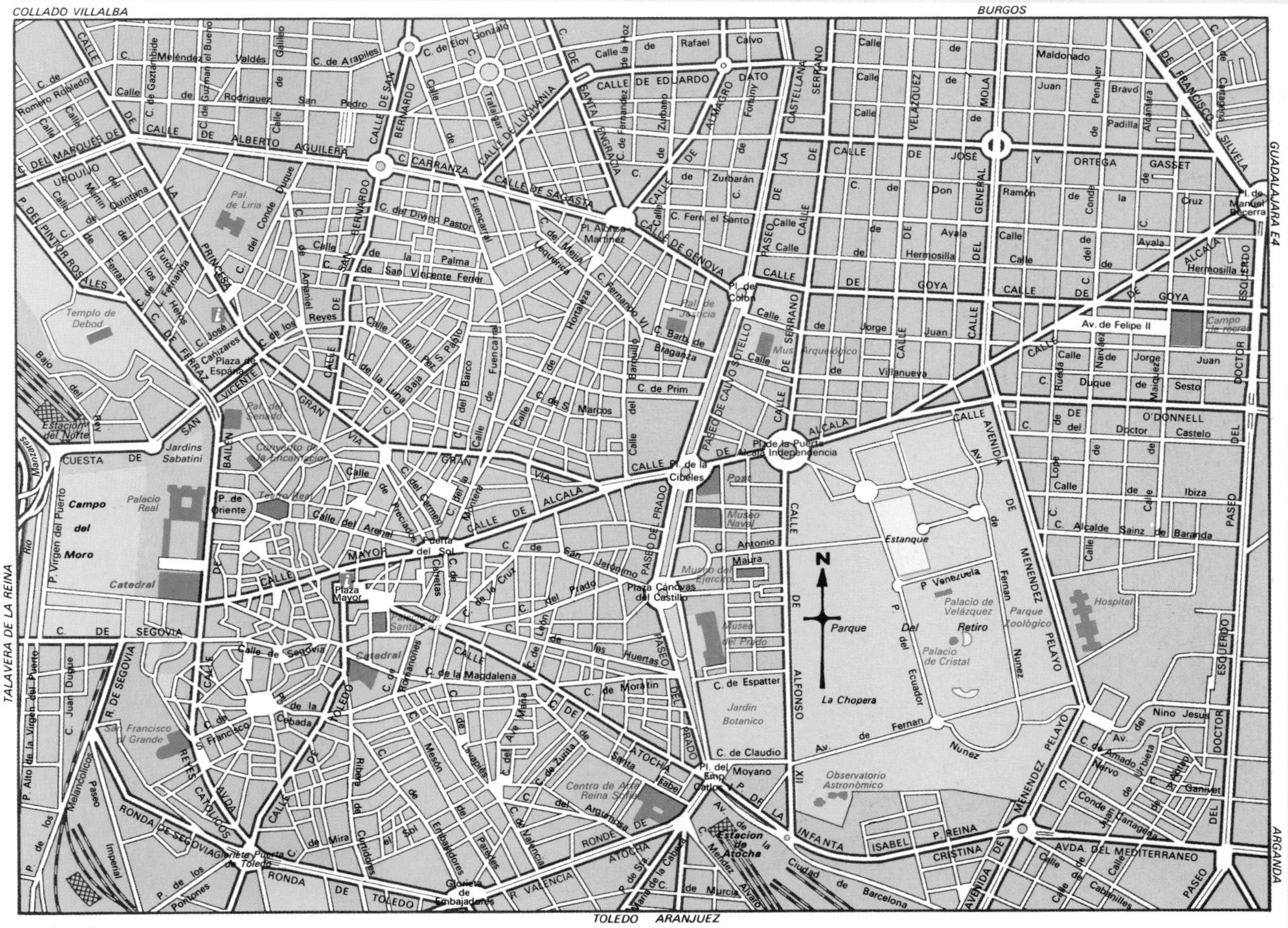
COLLADO VILLALBA
BURGOS
GUADALAJARA E4
ARGANDA
TALAVERA DE LA REINA
TOLEDO
ARANJUEZ
Templo de Debod
Pal. de Liria
Plaza de España
Estación del Norte
Jardins Sabatini
Campo del Moro
Palacio Real
Catedral
P. de Oriente
Teatro Real
Plaza Mayor
Puerta del Sol
San Francisco el Grande
Glorieta Puerta de Toledo
Glorieta de Embajadores
Centro de Arte Reina Sofía
Estación de Atocha
Pl. del Emp. Carlos V
Jardín Botánico
Museo del Prado
Plaza Cánovas del Castillo
Museo del Ejército
Museo Naval
Pl. de la Cibeles
Pl. de la Puerta de la Independencia
Estanque
Parque del Retiro
Palacio de Velázquez
Palacio de Cristal
Parque Zoológico
La Chopera
Observatorio Astronómico
Hospital
Campo de Toros
Pl. de Colón
Mus. Arqueológico
Pal. de Justicia
Pl. Alonso Martínez
Pl. de Manuel Becerra
Av. de Felipe II
GRAN VIA
CALLE DE ALCALA
ALCALA
MAYOR
C. DE SEGOVIA
CALLE DE GENOVA
CALLE DE SAGASTA
CARRANZA
ALBERTO AGUILERA
CALLE DE SAN BERNARDO
PASEO DE LA CASTELLANA
SERRANO
VELAZQUEZ
GENERAL MOLA
CALLE DE JOSE ORTEGA Y GASSET
CALLE DE GOYA
CALLE DE HERMOSILLA
CALLE DE AYALA
CALLE DE JORGE JUAN
C. DE VILLANUEVA
DOCTOR ESQUERDO
O'DONNELL
C. Alcalde Sainz de Baranda
Ibiza
Menéndez Pelayo
PASEO DEL PRADO
PASEO DE RECOLETOS
CALLE ALFONSO XII
C. de Espalter
C. de Claudio Moyano
Av. de Fernan Nunez
P. Venezuela
P. REINA CRISTINA
INFANTA ISABEL
AVDA DEL MEDITERRANEO
AVENIDA CIUDAD DE BARCELONA
RONDA DE ATOCHA
RONDA DE VALENCIA
RONDA DE TOLEDO
RONDA DE SEGOVIA
CALLE DE TOLEDO
C. de Embajadores
C. de la Magdalena
C. de Moratín
Huertas
C. de San Jerónimo
Atocha
P. Virgen del Puerto
CUESTA
BAILEN
SAN VICENTE
C. DE LA PRINCESA
P. DEL PINTOR ROSALES
C. DEL MARQUES DE URQUIJO
C. de Fuencarral
C. de Hortaleza
Conde Duque
C. de Eloy Gonzalo
C. de Arapiles
C. de Bravo Murillo
C. de Francisco Silvela
C. de Cartagena
C. de Maldonado
C. de Fernán el Santo
C. de Prim
C. de S. Marcos
C. de Antonio Maura
C. de Segovia
Glorieta de Embajadores
Paseo Imperial
P. de los Melancólicos
P. de los Pontones

MADRID

0 500 m. 1 Km.

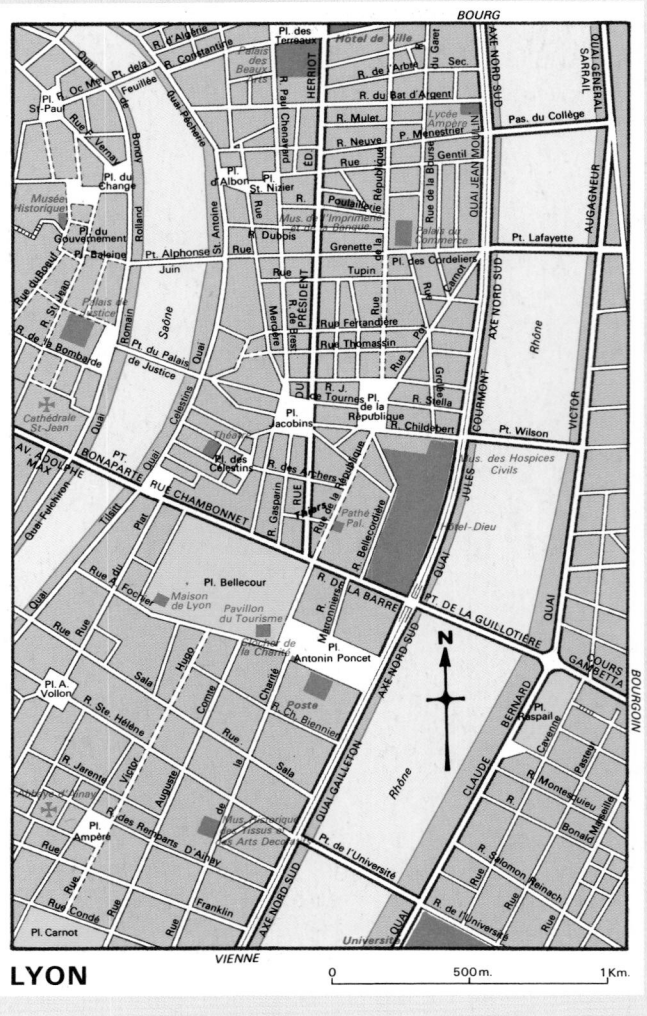

LYON

0   500 m.   1 Km.

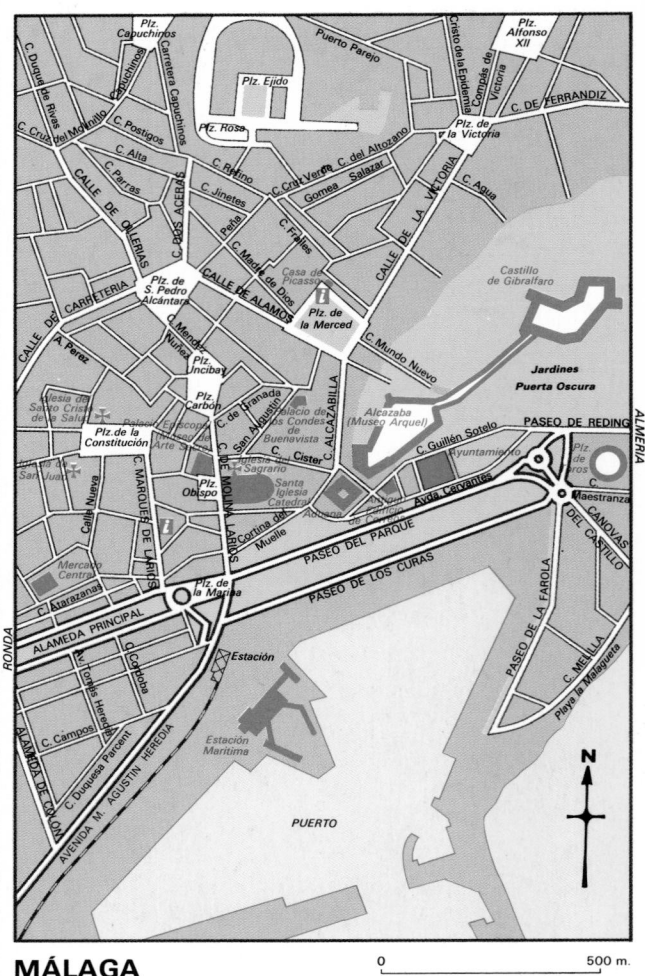

MÁLAGA

0   500 m.

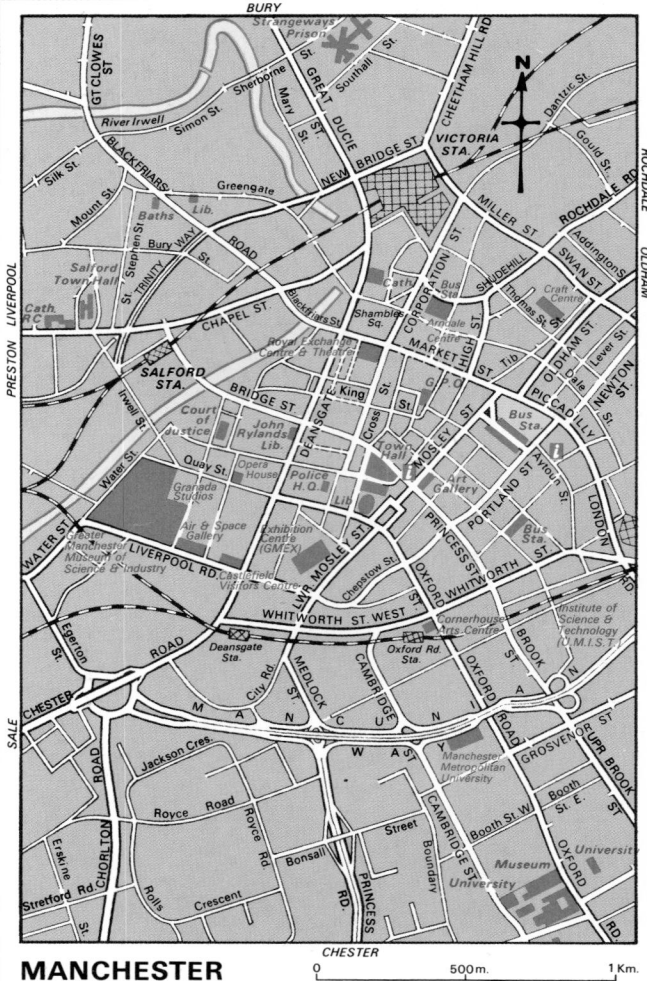

MANCHESTER

0   500 m.   1 Km.

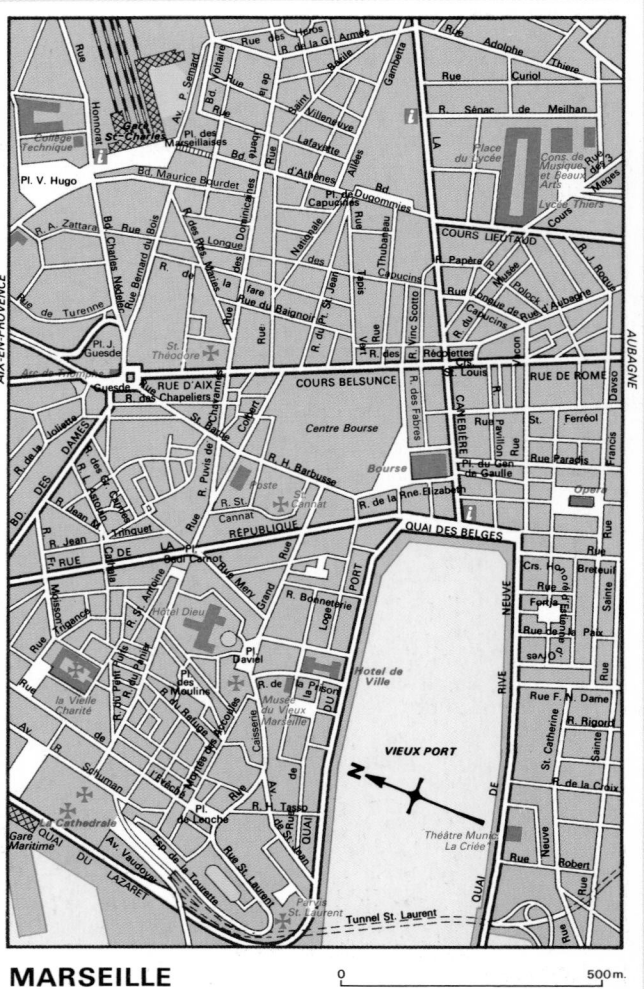

MARSEILLE

0   500 m.

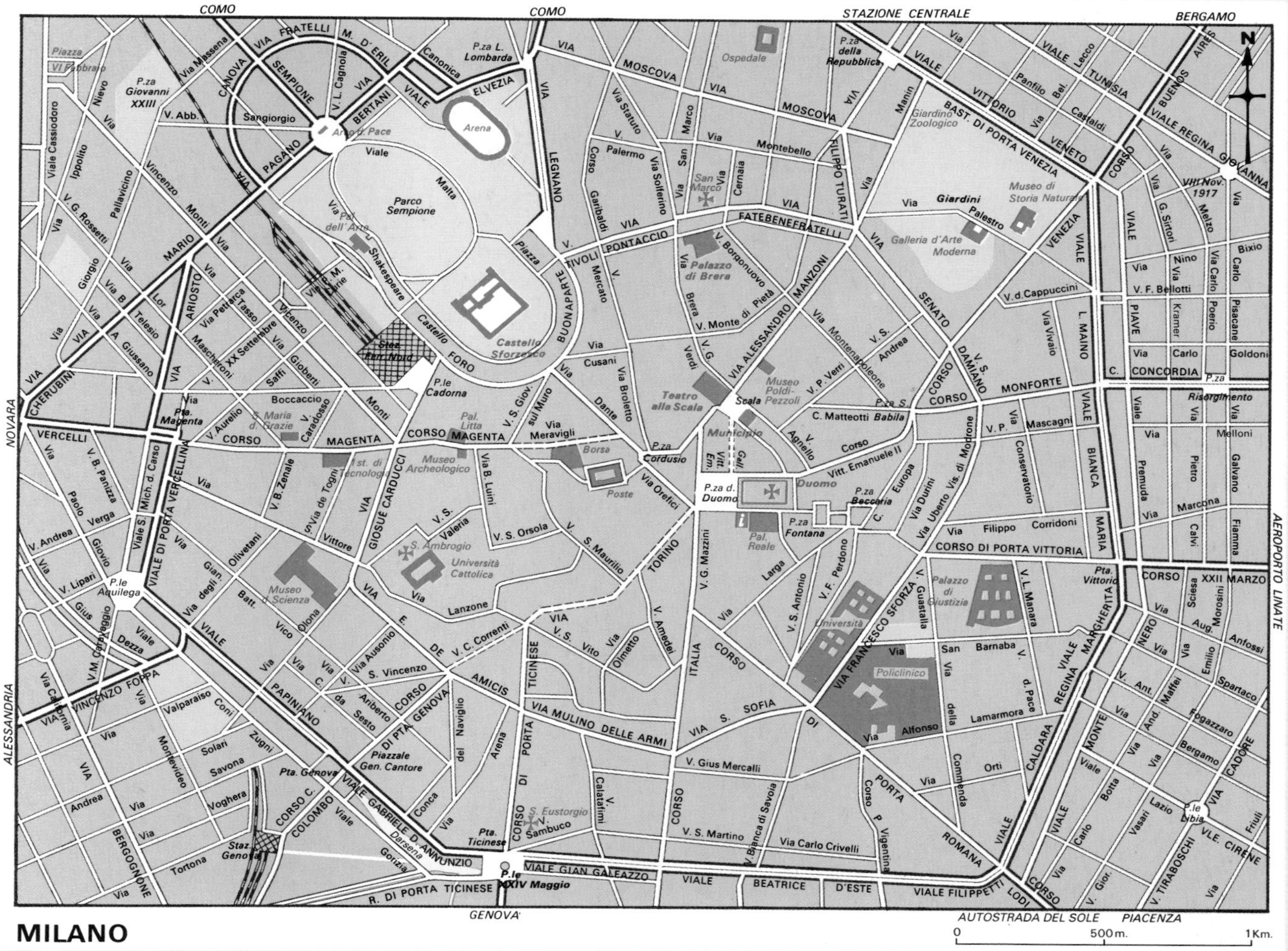
COMO
COMO
STAZIONE CENTRALE
BERGAMO
N
NOVARA
ALESSANDRIA
AEROPORTO LINATE
GENOVA
AUTOSTRADA DEL SOLE
PIACENZA
0
500 m.
1 Km.
Parco Sempione
Arena
Arco d. Pace
Castello Sforzesco
Staz. Ferr. Nord
P.le Cadorna
Ospedale
P.za della Repubblica
Giardino Zoologico
Giardini
Museo di Storia Naturale
Galleria d'Arte Moderna
Palazzo di Brera
Teatro alla Scala
Museo Poldi-Pezzoli
Municipio
P.za d. Duomo
Duomo
Pal. Reale
Borsa
Poste
P.za Cordusio
P.za Fontana
P.za Beccaria
Museo Archeologico
Ist. di Tecnologia
S. Ambrogio
Università Cattolica
Museo d. Scienza
S. Maria d. Grazie
Pal. Litta
P.le Aquileja
Palazzo di Giustizia
Università
Policlinico
S. Eustorgio
Darsena
P.le XXIV Maggio
Pta. Ticinese
Pta. Genova
Staz. Genova
Piazzale Gen. Cantore
Pta. Vittoria
P.le Libia
P.za L. Lombarda
P.za Giovanni XXIII
Piazza VI Febbraio
CORSO MAGENTA
CORSO VERCELLI
VIALE DI PORTA VERCELLINA
VIALE PAPINIANO
VIALE GABRIELE D'ANNUNZIO
VIALE GIAN GALEAZZO
VIALE BEATRICE D'ESTE
VIALE FILIPPETTI
CORSO DI PORTA ROMANA
CORSO DI PORTA VITTORIA
CORSO XXII MARZO
VIA FRANCESCO SFORZA
VIA ALESSANDRO MANZONI
VIA FATEBENEFRATELLI
VIA MOSCOVA
VIALE MONTE NERO
VIALE REGINA MARGHERITA
BAST. DI PORTA VENEZIA
VIALE VITTORIO VENETO
VIALE TUNISIA
VIALE REGINA GIOVANNA
CORSO BUENOS AIRES
VIA FILIPPO TURATI
CORSO MONFORTE
VIA MULINO DELLE ARMI
CORSO DI PORTA TICINESE
CORSO ITALIA
VIA TORINO
VIA DANTE
FORO BUONAPARTE
CORSO SEMPIONE
VIA LEGNANO
VIALE ELVEZIA
VIA CANONICA
VIALE CERUBINI
CORSO COLOMBO
VIA VINCENZO FOPPA
VIALE TIBALDI

MILANO

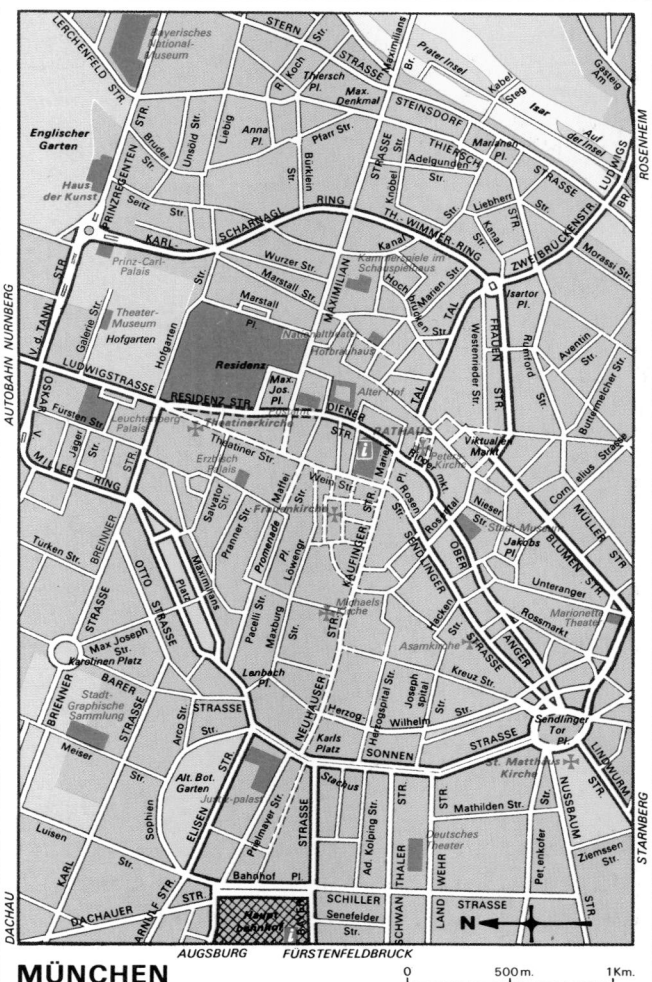
ROSENHEIM
AUTOBAHN NURNBERG
DACHAU
AUGSBURG
FÜRSTENFELDBRUCK
STARNBERG
Englischer Garten
Bayerisches National-Museum
Haus der Kunst
Prinz-Carl-Palais
Theater-Museum
Hofgarten
Residenz
Max. Jos. Pl.
Alter Hof
Rathaus
Theatinerkirche
Frauenkirche
Michaelskirche
Asamkirche
Viktualien Markt
Stadt. Museum
Marionetten Theater
Karolinen Platz
Stadt. Graphische Sammlung
Lenbach Pl.
Karls Platz
Stachus
Alt. Bot. Garten
Justiz-palast
St. Matthäus Kirche
Sendlinger Tor Pl.
Deutsches Theater
Hauptbahnhof
Prater Insel
Isar
Auf der Insel
Isartor Pl.
Mariahilf Pl.
Wiener Pl.
Pl.
Odeons Pl.
PRINZREGENTEN STR.
MAXIMILIAN STR.
BRIENNER STR.
LUDWIGSTRASSE
RESIDENZ STR.
DIENER STR.
KAUFINGER STR.
NEUHAUSER STR.
SENDLINGER STR.
SONNENSTRASSE
BAYER STR.
SCHILLER STR.
LANDWEHR STR.
LINDWURM STR.
MÜLLER STR.
OTTO STRASSE
ARNULF STR.
DACHAUER STR.
ZWEIBRÜCKENSTR.
THIERSCH STR.
STEINSDORF STR.
OSKAR V. MILLER RING
ALTHEIMER ECK
TAL
N
0
500 m.
1 Km.

MÜNCHEN

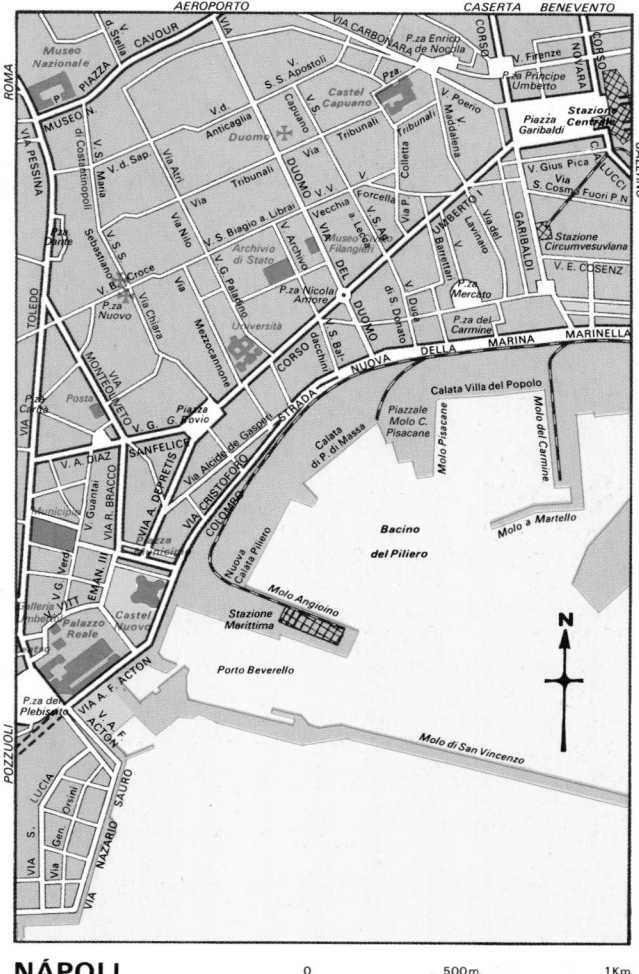
AEROPORTO
CASERTA
BENEVENTO
ROMA
SALERNO
POZZUOLI
N
Museo Nazionale
Castel Capuano
Duomo
Piazza Garibaldi
Stazione Centrale
P.za Principe Umberto
P.za Enrico de Nicola
Stazione Circumvesuviana
Archivio di Stato
Museo Filangieri
Università
P.za Dante
P.za Nuovo
P.za G. Bovio
P.za Nicola Amore
P.za Mercato
P.za del Carmine
P.za Carità
Posta
Galleria Umberto
Palazzo Reale
Castel Nuovo
P.za del Plebiscito
Stazione Marittima
Molo Angioino
Porto Beverello
Molo di San Vincenzo
Bacino del Piliero
Calata Villa del Popolo
Piazzale Molo C. Pisacane
Molo Pisacane
Molo del Carmine
Molo a Martello
Calata di P. di Massa
Calata Piliero
VIA PESSINA
VIA TOLEDO
VIA DUOMO
CORSO UMBERTO I
CORSO GARIBALDI
VIA NUOVA DELLA MARINA
VIA A. DEPRETIS
VIA CRISTOFORO COLOMBO
VIA MONTEOLIVETO
VIA SANFELICE
VIA CARBONARA
VIA CAVOUR
VIA FORIA
VIA S. LUCIA
VIA NAZARIO SAURO
VIA ACTON
0
500 m.
1 Km.

NÁPOLI

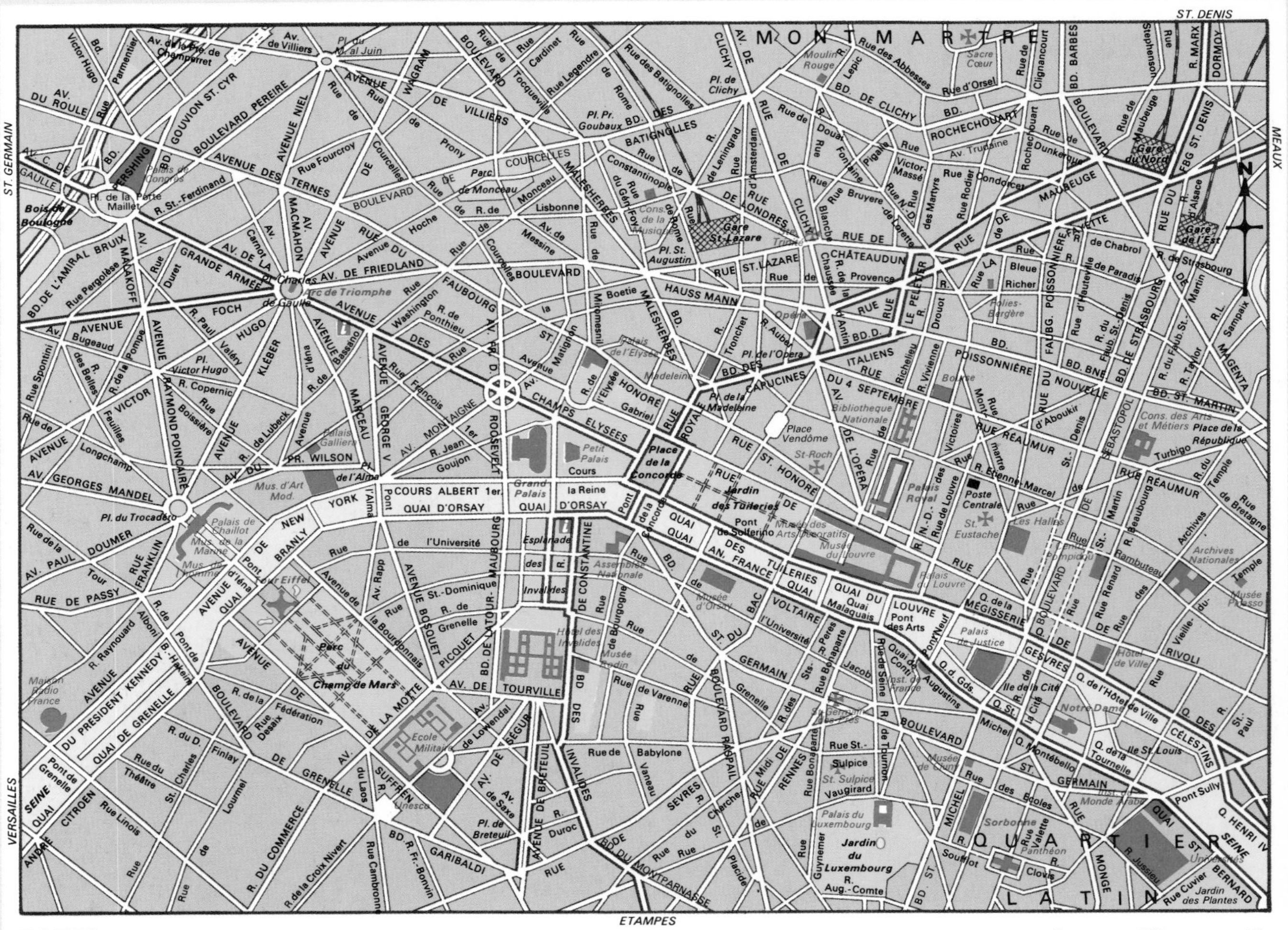
ST. DENIS
MEAUX
ST. GERMAIN
VERSAILLES
ETAMPES
MONTMARTRE
QUARTIER
LATIN
Sacre Cœur
Moulin Rouge
Gare du Nord
Gare de l'Est
Gare St. Lazare
Pl. de Clichy
BD. DE CLICHY
BD. ROCHECHOUART
BD. BARBES
BD. DES BATIGNOLLES
BOULEVARD PEREIRE
BOULEVARD MALESHERBES
BOULEVARD HAUSSMANN
BD. DE COURCELLES
Parc de Monceau
AVENUE DE WAGRAM
AVENUE DES TERNES
AVENUE NIEL
AVENUE MAC MAHON
AV. DE LA GRANDE ARMEE
AV. DE FRIEDLAND
Pl. Charles de Gaulle
Arc de Triomphe
AVENUE FOCH
AVENUE KLEBER
AVENUE VICTOR HUGO
AVENUE RAYMOND POINCARE
AVENUE D'IENA
AVENUE MARCEAU
AVENUE GEORGE V
AVENUE MONTAIGNE
AV. DES CHAMPS ELYSEES
Pl. du Trocadéro
Palais de Chaillot
AV. GEORGES MANDEL
AV. PAUL DOUMER
RUE DE PASSY
AV. DE NEW YORK
COURS ALBERT 1er.
QUAI D'ORSAY
QUAI BRANLY
Tour Eiffel
Parc du Champ de Mars
Ecole Militaire
Unesco
AV. DE LA MOTTE PICQUET
AVENUE BOSQUET
AVENUE RAPP
AV. DE SUFFREN
AV. DE SEGUR
AVENUE DE BRETEUIL
BD. DES INVALIDES
BD. DE LA TOUR MAUBOURG
Esplanade des Invalides
Hôtel des Invalides
Musée Rodin
RUE DE VARENNE
RUE DE GRENELLE
RUE DE VAUGIRARD
RUE DE SEVRES
BD. DE GRENELLE
BOULEVARD GARIBALDI
RUE DU COMMERCE
QUAI DE GRENELLE
QUAI ANDRE CITROEN
AV. DU PRESIDENT KENNEDY
Maison de Radio France
Place de la Concorde
Jardin des Tuileries
Place Vendôme
AV. DE L'OPERA
Opera
RUE ST. HONORE
RUE DE RIVOLI
Musée du Louvre
Palais Royal
Les Halles
St. Eustache
Bourse
Bibliotheque Nationale
BD. POISSONNIERE
BD. BONNE NOUVELLE
BD. ST. MARTIN
BD. DE SEBASTOPOL
BD. DE STRASBOURG
BD. DE MAGENTA
RUE REAUMUR
RUE ETIENNE MARCEL
RUE DE RIVOLI
Hôtel de Ville
Centre Pompidou
Place de la République
Archives Nationales
Musée Picasso
Ile de la Cité
Notre Dame
Ile St. Louis
Palais de Justice
BOULEVARD ST. GERMAIN
BOULEVARD RASPAIL
BD. ST. MICHEL
Jardin du Luxembourg
Palais du Luxembourg
St. Sulpice
Sorbonne
Panthéon
Musée de Cluny
Inst. du Monde Arabe
Jardin des Plantes
QUAI ST. BERNARD
Pont Sully
QUAI HENRI IV
BD. DU MONTPARNASSE
SEINE
0 500m. 1Km.

PARIS

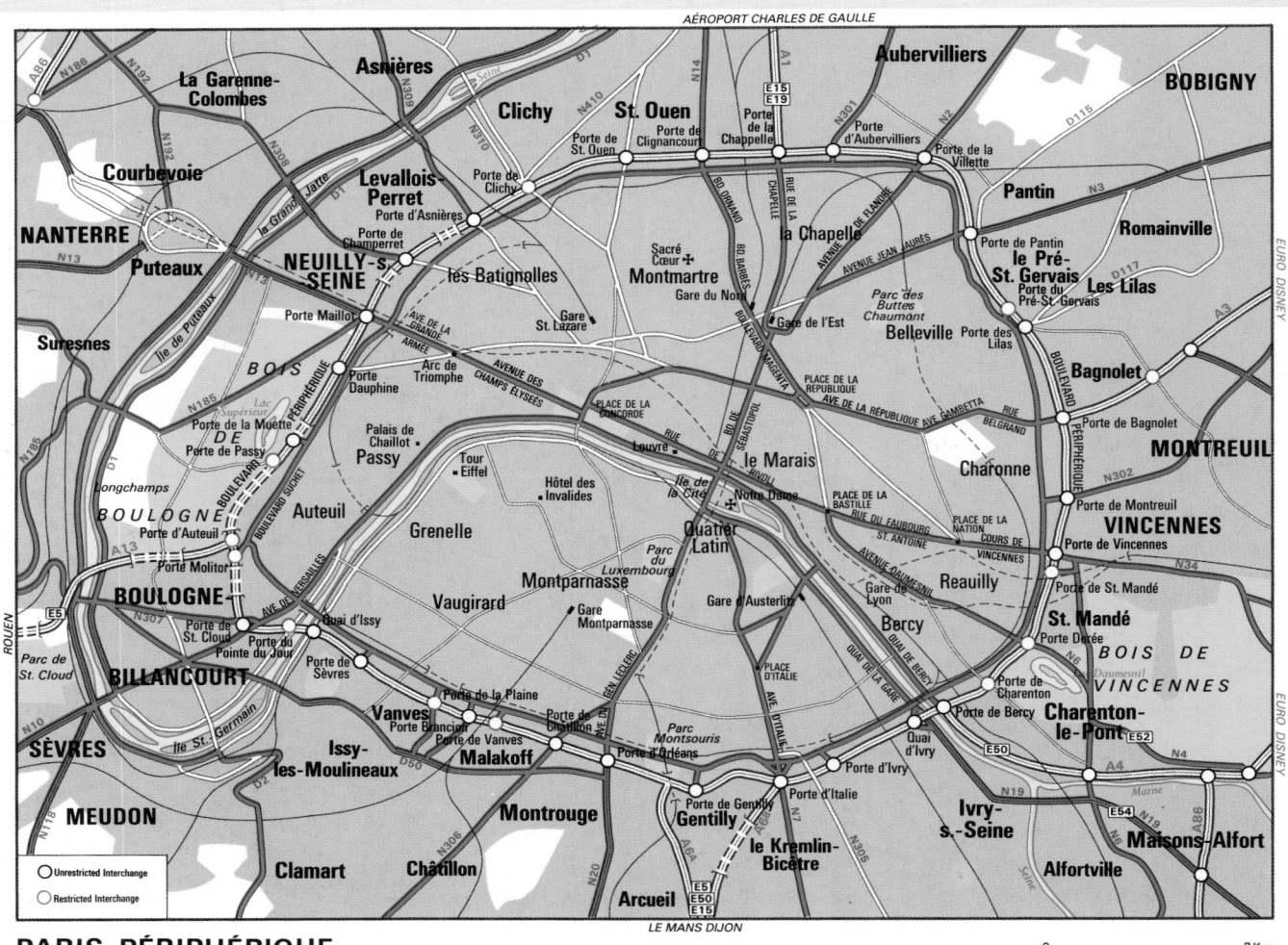
AÉROPORT CHARLES DE GAULLE
EURO DISNEY
ROUEN
LE MANS DIJON
Asnières
Aubervilliers
BOBIGNY
La Garenne-Colombes
Clichy
St. Ouen
Courbevoie
Levallois-Perret
Pantin
Romainville
NANTERRE
Puteaux
NEUILLY-s.-SEINE
les Batignolles
Montmartre
la Chapelle
le Pré-St. Gervais
Les Lilas
Suresnes
BOIS DE BOULOGNE
Belleville
Bagnolet
MONTREUIL
Passy
le Marais
Charonne
VINCENNES
Auteuil
Grenelle
Quatier Latin
BOULOGNE-BILLANCOURT
Vaugirard
Montparnasse
Reauilly
St. Mandé
BOIS DE VINCENNES
Bercy
Charenton-le-Pont
SÈVRES
Vanves
Issy-les-Moulineaux
Malakoff
MEUDON
Montrouge
Gentilly
le Kremlin-Bicêtre
Ivry-s.-Seine
Maisons-Alfort
Alfortville
Clamart
Châtillon
Arcueil
Parc de St. Cloud
Porte de St. Ouen
Porte de Clignancourt
Porte de la Chapelle
Porte d'Aubervilliers
Porte de la Villette
Porte de Clichy
Porte d'Asnières
Porte de Champerret
Porte Maillot
Porte Dauphine
Porte de la Muette
Porte de Passy
Porte d'Auteuil
Porte Molitor
Porte de St. Cloud
Porte du Pointe du Jour
Quai d'Issy
Porte de Sèvres
Porte de la Plaine
Porte Brancion
Porte de Vanves
Porte de Châtillon
Porte d'Orléans
Porte de Gentilly
Porte d'Italie
Porte d'Ivry
Quai d'Ivry
Porte de Bercy
Porte de Charenton
Porte Dorée
Porte de St. Mandé
Porte de Vincennes
Porte de Montreuil
Porte de Bagnolet
Porte des Lilas
Porte du Pré-St. Gervais
Porte de Pantin
Sacré Cœur
Gare du Nord
Gare de l'Est
Gare St. Lazare
Arc de Triomphe
Palais de Chaillot
Tour Eiffel
Hôtel des Invalides
Louvre
Notre Dame
Parc du Luxembourg
Gare Montparnasse
Gare d'Austerlitz
Gare de Lyon
Parc des Buttes Chaumont
Parc Montsouris
Lac Supérieur
Longchamps
BOULEVARD PÉRIPHÉRIQUE
AVENUE DES CHAMPS ELYSÉES
AVE DE LA RÉPUBLIQUE
AVE GAMBETTA
PLACE DE LA RÉPUBLIQUE
PLACE DE LA CONCORDE
PLACE DE LA BASTILLE
RUE DU FAUBOURG ST. ANTOINE
PLACE DE LA NATION
COURS DE VINCENNES
AVENUE DAUMESNIL
PLACE D'ITALIE
AVE. D'ITALIE
BD DE SÉBASTOPOL
BD. DE MAGENTA
AVENUE JEAN JAURÈS
AVENUE DE FLANDRE
AVE DE VERSAILLES
QUAI DE BERCY
QUAI DE LA GARE
Seine
Marne
A1
A3
A4
A6
A13
A86
E5
E15
E19
E50
E52
E54
N1
N2
N3
N4
N6
N7
N10
N13
N14
N19
N20
N34
N118
N185
N186
N192
N301
N302
N305
N306
N307
N308
N309
N310
N410
D1
D115
D117
Unrestricted Interchange
Restricted Interchange
0 3Km.

PARIS PÉRIPHÉRIQUE

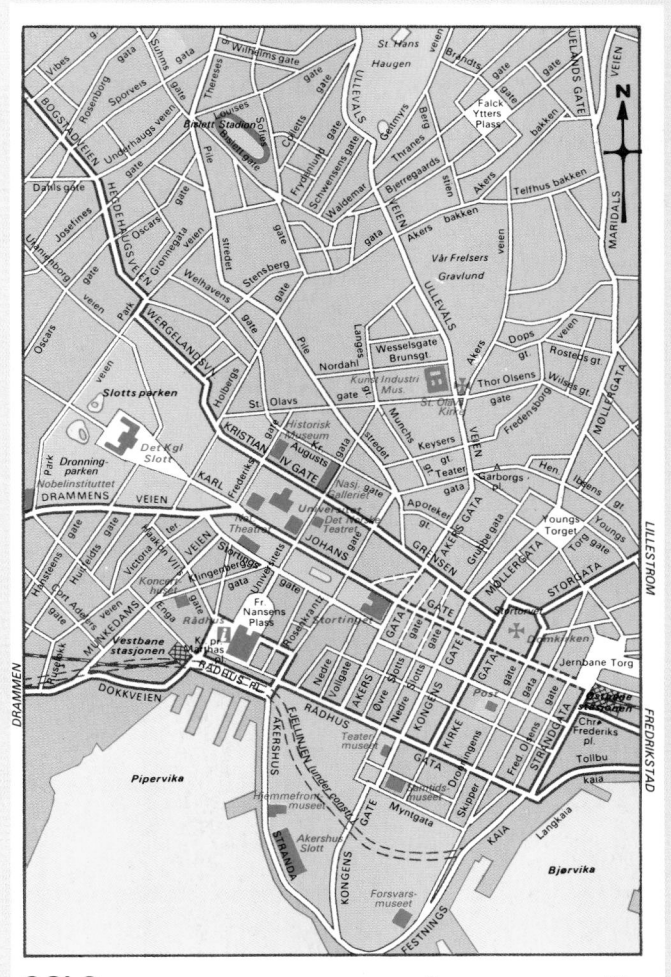
DRAMMEN
LILLESTROM
FREDRIKSTAD
Slotts parken
Pipervika
Bjørvika
0
500 m.

OSLO

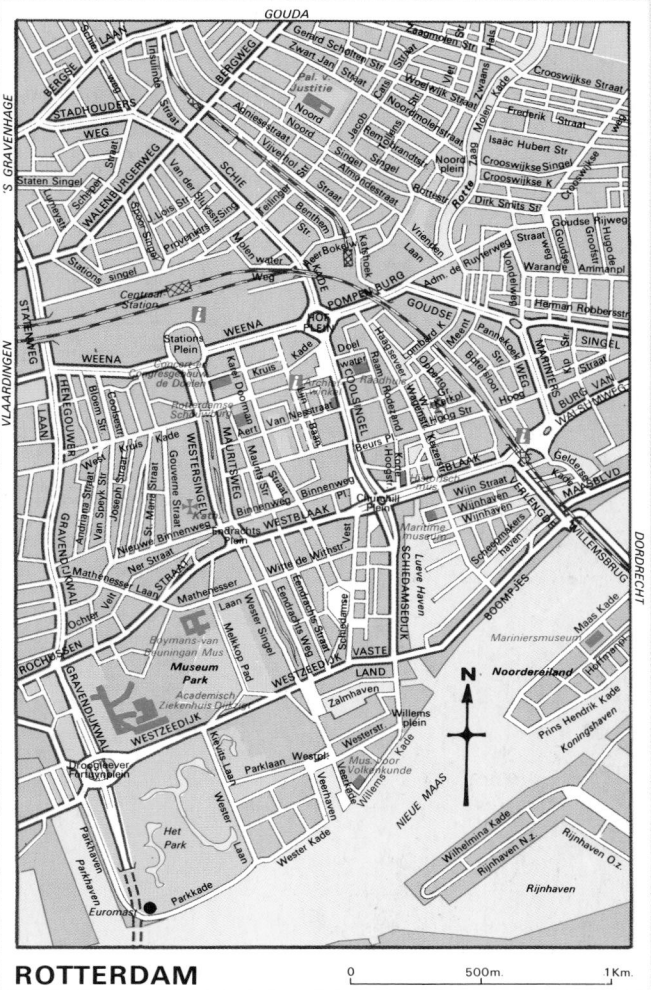
GOUDA
'S GRAVENHAGE
VLAARDINGEN
DORDRECHT
NIEUWE MAAS
Het Park
Rijnhaven
0
500m.
1Km.

ROTTERDAM

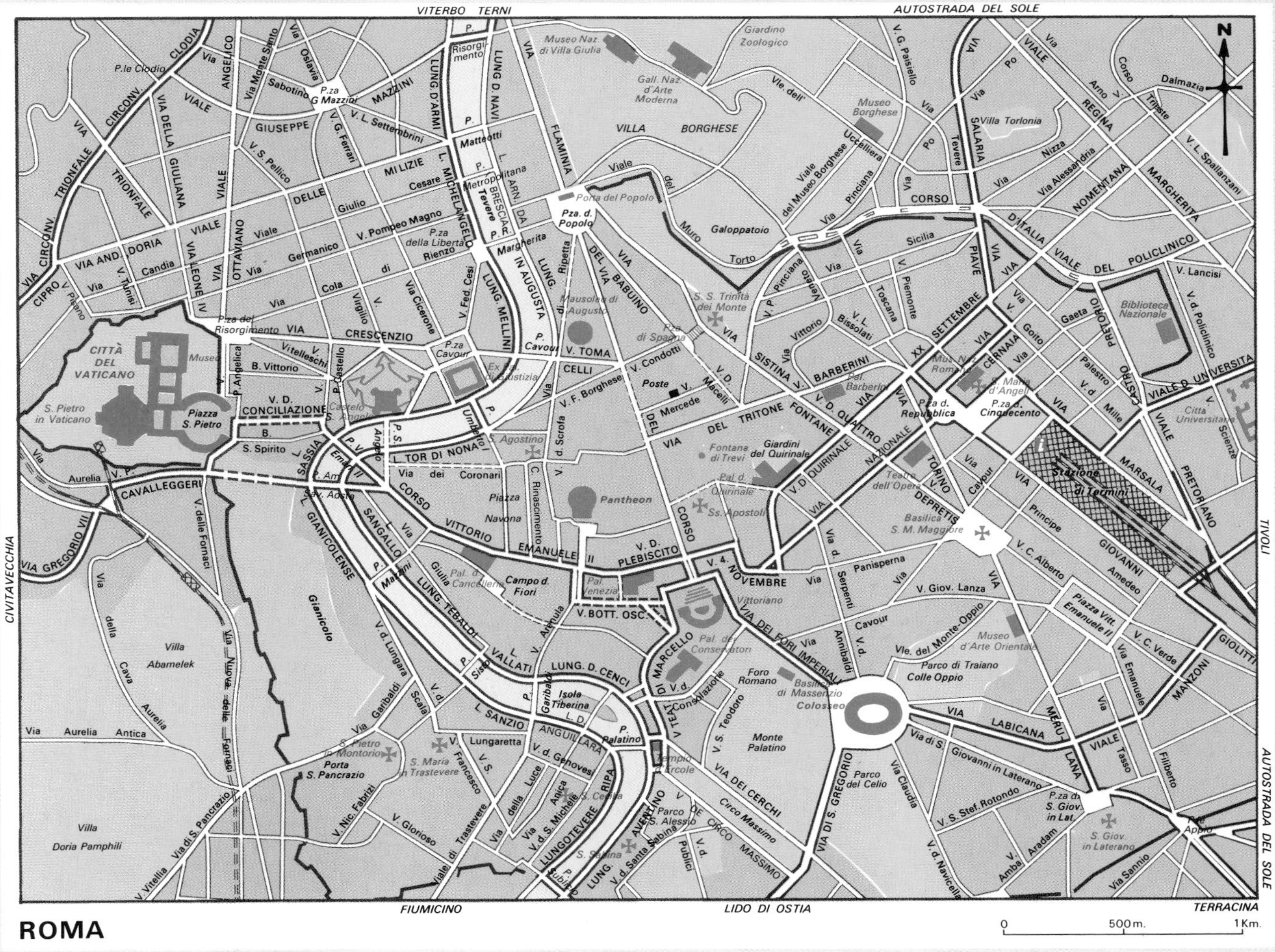
VITERBO TERNI
AUTOSTRADA DEL SOLE
CIVITAVECCHIA
TIVOLI
FIUMICINO
LIDO DI OSTIA
TERRACINA
VILLA BORGHESE
CITTÀ DEL VATICANO
Gianicolo
0
500m.
1Km.

ROMA

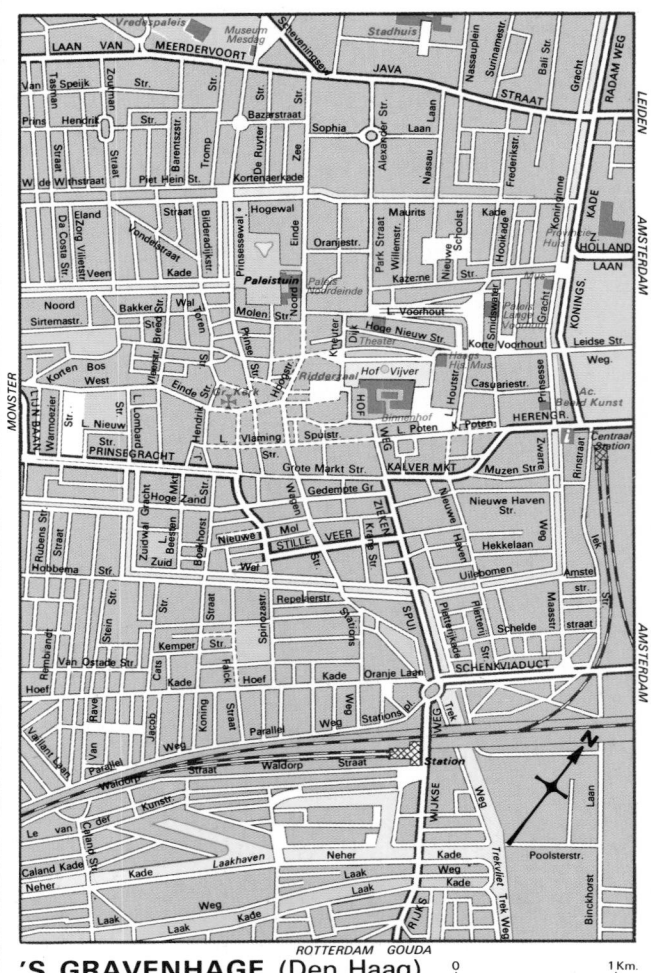

'S GRAVENHAGE (Den Haag)

0   1 Km.

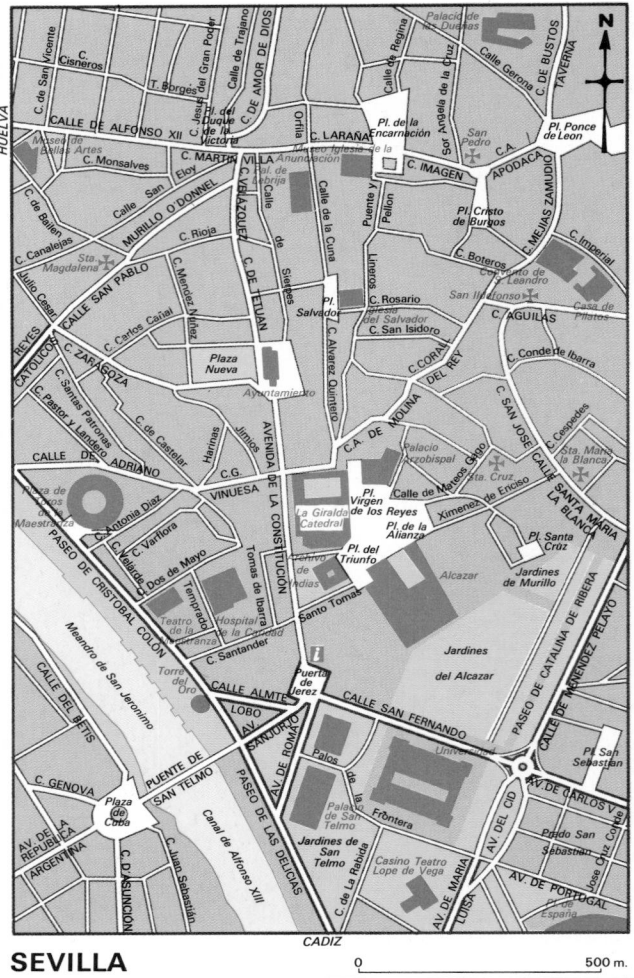

SEVILLA

0   500 m.

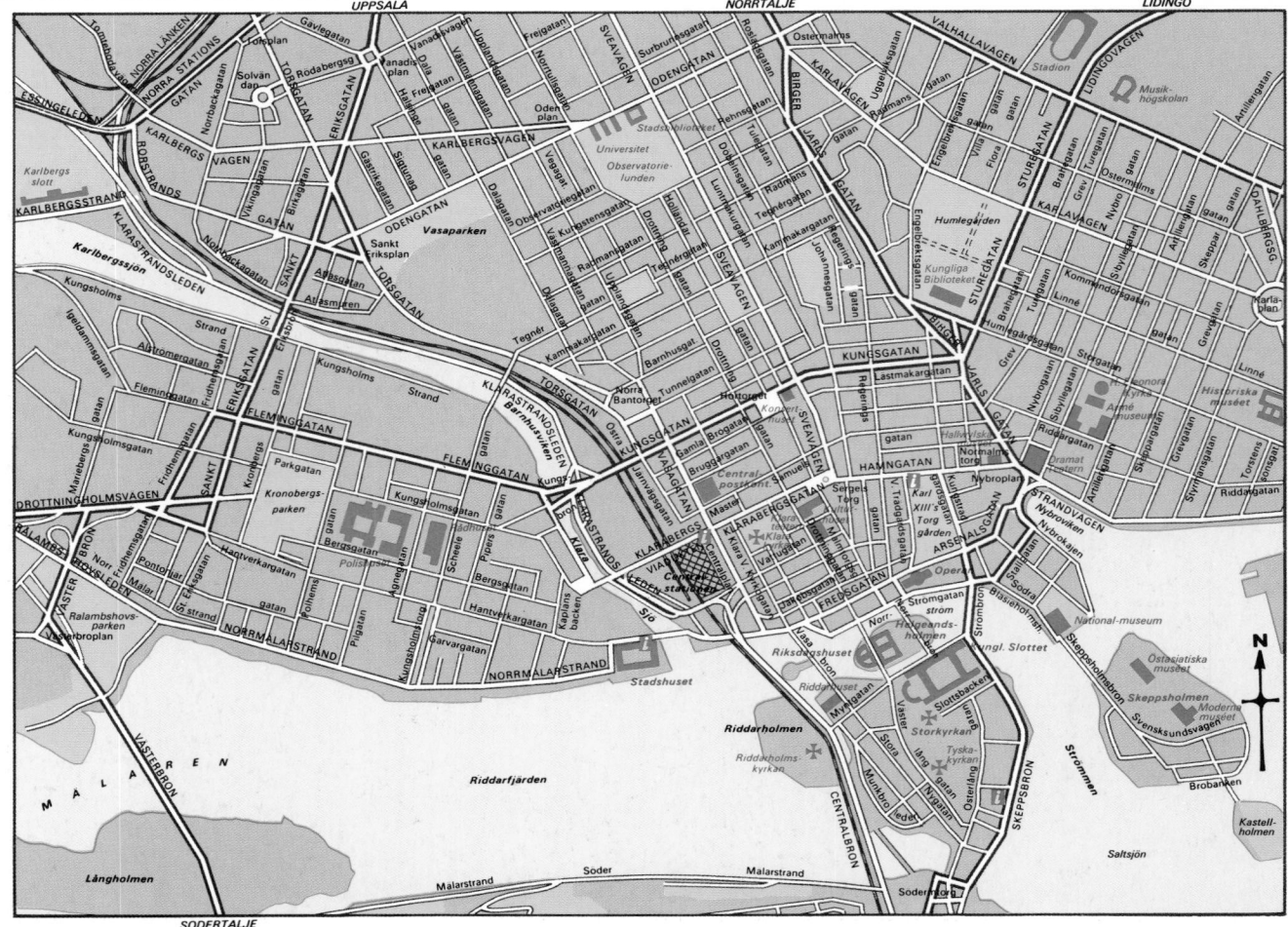

STOCKHOLM

0   500 m.   1 Km.

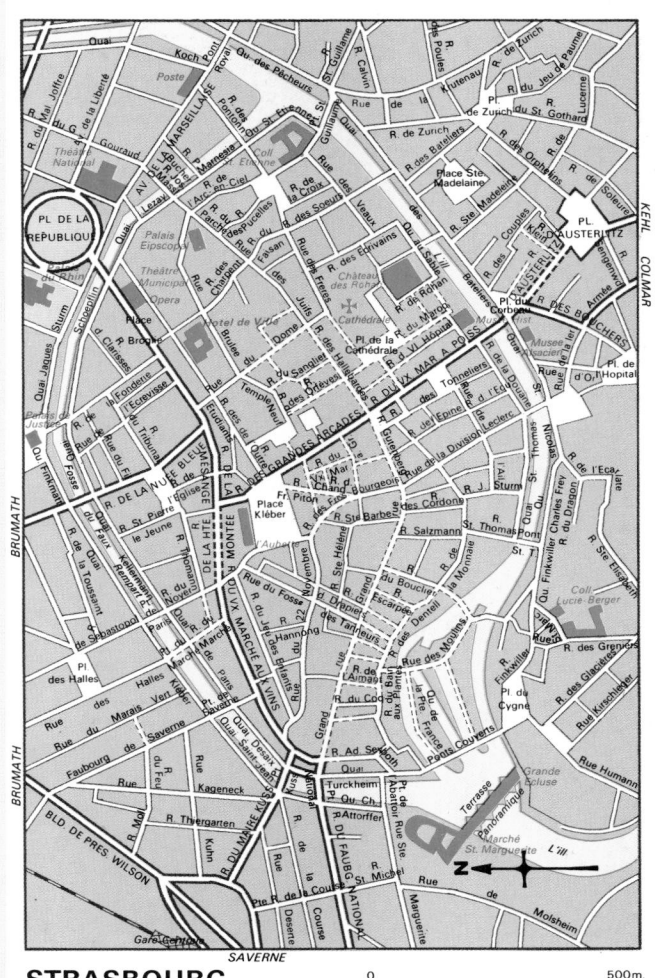

STRASBOURG

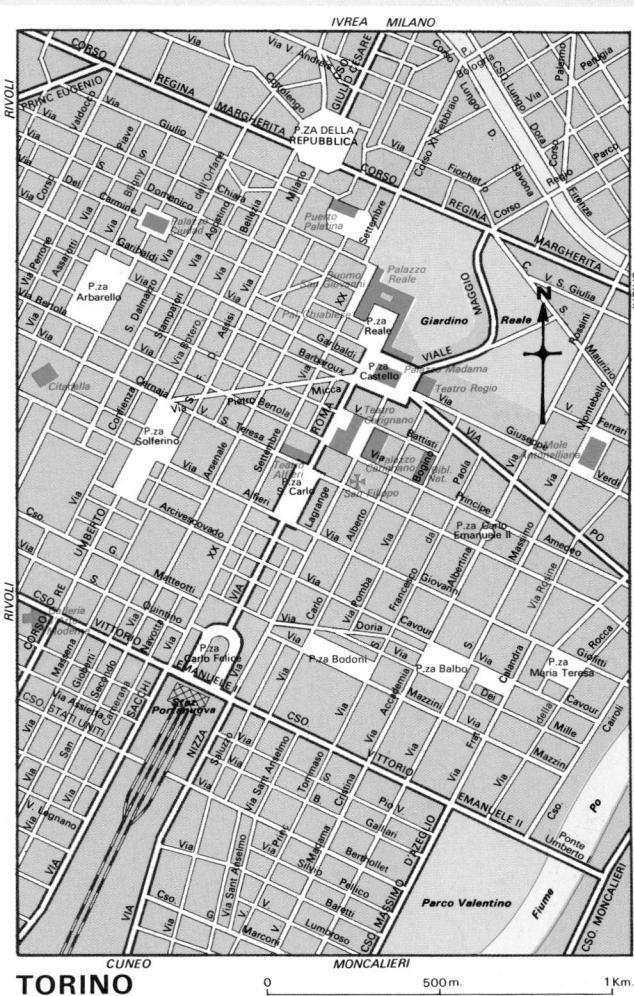

TORINO

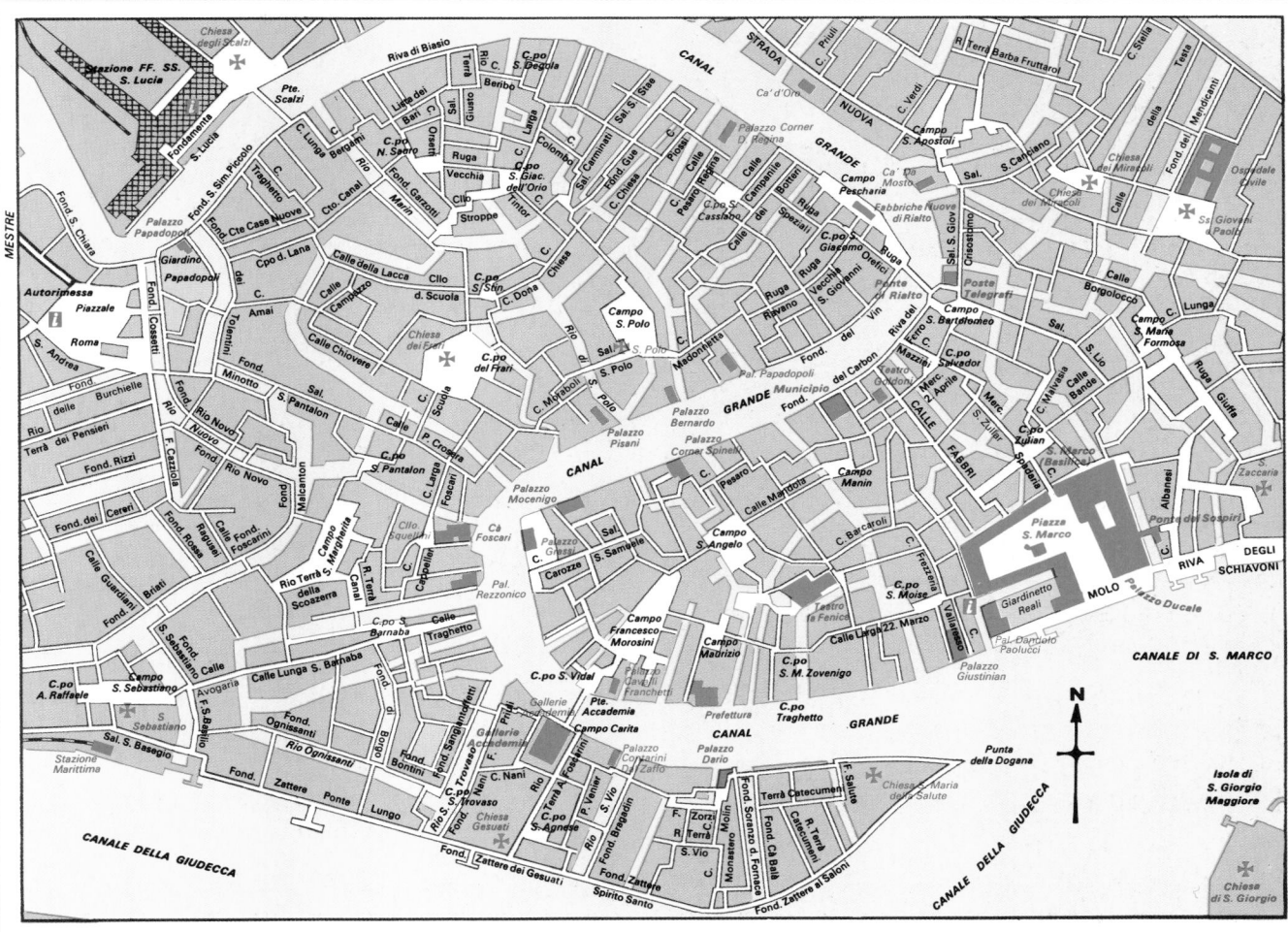

VENÉZIA

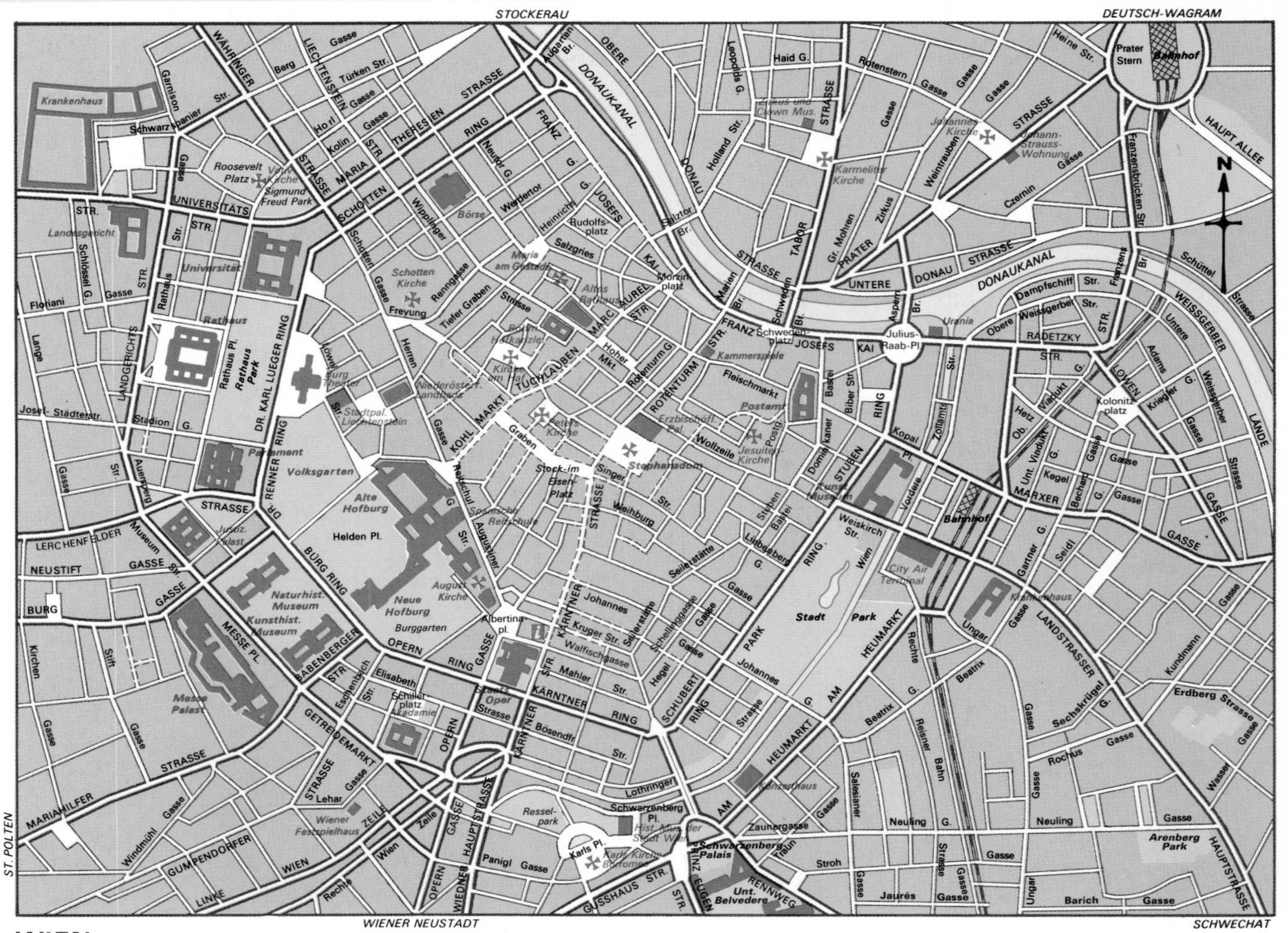
STOCKERAU
DEUTSCH-WAGRAM
ST. POLTEN
WIENER NEUSTADT
SCHWECHAT
Krankenhaus
Garnison
WÄHRINGER
LIECHTENSTEIN
Türken Str.
Berg
Gasse
Schwarzspanier Str.
Roosevelt Platz
Votiv Kirche
Sigmund Freud Park
UNIVERSITÄTS STR.
Universität
Landesgericht
Schlössel G.
Florianí
Lange
Rathaus
Rathaus Pl.
Rathaus Park
DR. KARL LUEGER RING
LANDGERICHTS STR.
Josef- Städterstr.
Stadion G.
Parlament
Volksgarten
DR RENNER RING
Auerspera
STRASSE
LERCHENFELDER
NEUSTIFT
GASSE
BURG
Museum
Justiz Palast
BURG RING
Helden Pl.
Alte Hofburg
Naturhist. Museum
Kunsthist. Museum
MESSE PL.
Messe Palast
BABENBERGER
Neue Hofburg
Burggarten
Augustiner Kirche
Albertina pl.
OPERN
RING
GASSE
Elisabeth
Schiller platz
Akademie
Staats Oper
Eschenbach
GETREIDEMARKT
Lehar
Wiener Festspielhaus
ZEILE
Wien
MARIAHILFER
Windmühl Gasse
GUMPENDORFER
WIEN
Rechte
LINKE
Stiftg.
Kirchen
Gasse
OPERN
WIEDNER HAUPTSTRASSE
KÄRNTNER
Bösendrf.
Panigl Gasse
Ressel- park
Karls Pl.
Karls Kirche
GUSSHAUS STR.
Schwarzenberg Pl.
Hist. Museum der Stadt Wien
Schwarzenberg Palais
PRINZ EUGEN STR.
Unt. Belvedere
RENNWEG
Lothringer
Zaunergasse
Stroh
Jaurés
Gasse
Salesianer
Neuling G.
Barich
Gasse
Arenberg Park
HAUPTSTRASSE
Rochus
Ungar
HEUMARKT
Konzerthaus
Beatrix
Reisner
Bahn
Stadt Park
PARK RING
SCHUBERT RING
Johannes
Hegel
Mahler
Walfischgasse
Kruger Str.
Seilerstätte
Weihburg
Singer
Stock-im Eisen- Platz
Stephansdom
Graben
KOHL MARKT
Reitschul G.
Spanische Reitschule
Augustiner Str.
Petruskirche
Wollzeile
Jesuiten Kirche
Postamt
Erzbischöfl. Pal.
ROTENTURM
Fleischmarkt
Kammerspiele
Hoher Mkt.
Rotenturm G.
TUCHLAUBEN
MARC AUREL STR.
Kirche am Hof
Bürgerl. Zeughaus
Burg Theater
Löwel
Herren
Niederösterr. Landhaus
Stadtpal. Liechtenstein
Freyung
Schotten Kirche
Tiefer Graben
Renngasse
Maria am Gestade
Altes Rathaus
Salzgries
Rudolfs- platz
Heinrichs G.
JOSEFS KAI
Wipplinger
Börse
Werdertor
Neutor G.
SCHOTTEN RING
MARIA THERESIEN STR.
Kolin
Hörl
RING
FRANZ JOSEFS KAI
Augarten Br.
OBERE
DONAUKANAL
Morzin platz
Salztor Br.
Marien Br.
Schwedenbr.
Schweden Pl.
TABOR STRASSE
Leopolds G.
Haid G.
Holland Str.
Zirkus und Clown Mus.
Karmeliter Kirche
Rotenstern Gasse
Johannes Kirche
Johann- Strauss- Wohnung
Weintrauben G.
Czernin
PRATER STRASSE
Gr. Mohren
Zirkus
Prater Stern
Bahnhof
Franzensbrücken Str.
HAUPT ALLEE
Heine Str.
UNTERE DONAU STRASSE
Aspern Br.
Julius- Raab-Pl.
Urania
Radetzky
Obere Weissgerber Str.
Dampfschiff Str.
Franzens Br.
Schüttel Strasse
WEISSGERBER
Untere
LÄNDE
Löwen
Krieglar
Kolonitz platz
Adams
Hetz
Ob. Viadukt
Unt. Viadukt
Kegel
Bachen
Marxer
Stuben Bastei
Dominikaner Bastei
STUBEN RING
Kunst Museum
Weiskirch Str.
Vordere
Bahnhof
City Air Terminal
Krankenhaus
Ungar
LANDSTRASSER
Erdberg Strasse
Kundmann
Sechskrügel
Wasser Gasse
Rechte
Zollamts
Biber Str.
Postg.
Liebenberg G.

WIEN

0 500 m. 1 Km.

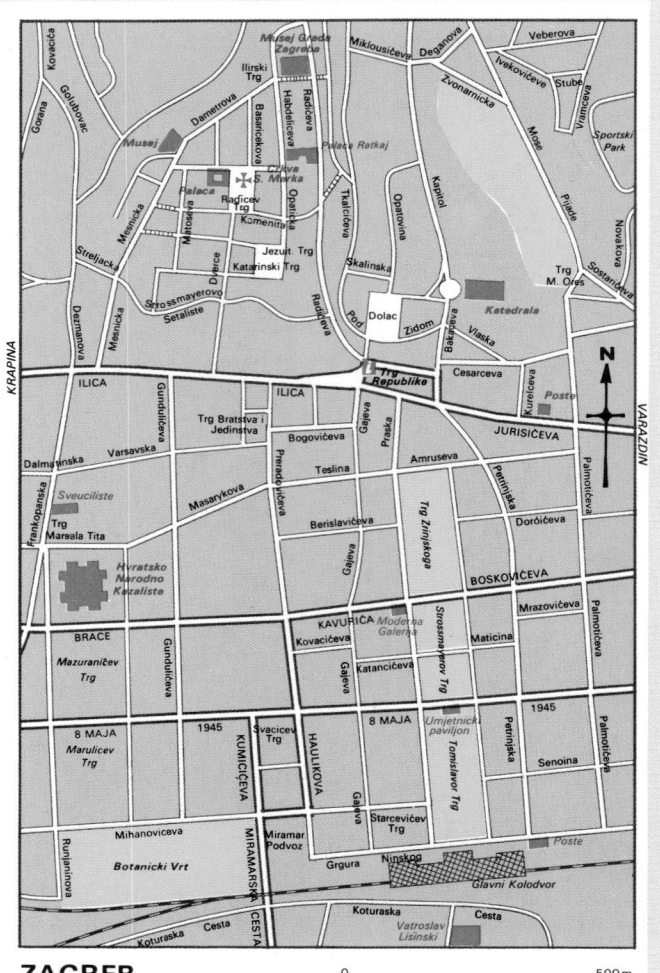
KRAPINA
VARAŽDIN
Kovačića
Gorana
Golubovac
Musej Grada Zagreba
Miklouščeva
Deganova
Veberova
Ilirski Trg
Radićeva
Habdelićeva
Basaričekova
Dametrova
Palača Ratkaj
Muzej
Palača
Crkva S. Marka
Radićev Trg
Kamenita
Opatička
Tkalčićeva
Mesnička
Matoševa
Strejacka
Jezuit. Trg
Katarinski Trg
Dverce
Strossmayerovo
Setalište
Dermanova
Mesnička
Zvonarnička
Ivekovićeve
Stube
Vramceva
Mose
Sportski Park
Kaptol
Opatovina
Skalinska
Pijacia
Novakova
Trg M. Ores
Sosaričeva
Radićeva
Pod Zidom
Dolac
Bakačeva
Vlaska
Katedrala
Trg Republike
Cesarčeva
Kurelčeva
Poste
ILICA
Gundulićeva
Trg Bratstva i Jedinstva
Bogovićeva
Gajeva
Praska
JURIŠIĆEVA
Dalmatinska
Varsavska
Teslina
Amruseva
Preradovićeva
Petrinjska
Palmotićeva
Frankopanska
Sveučilište
Trg Maršala Tita
Masarykova
Berislavićeva
Doročićeva
Trg Zrinjskoga
Hrvatsko Narodno Kazalište
BOSKOVIĆEVA
BRACE KAVURIĆA
Kovačićeva
Moderna Galerija
Mrazovićeva
Mazuraničev Trg
Katančićeva
Strossmayerov Trg
Maticina
Palmotićeva
8 MAJA
1945
Svačićev Trg
KUMIČIĆEVA
HAULIKOVA
Umjetnički paviljon
Tomislavov Trg
Petrinjska
Senoina
Marulićev Trg
Starčevićev Trg
Mihanovićeva
Runjaninova
Botanički Vrt
Miramar Podvoz
MIRAMARSKA
Poste
Grgura Ninskog
Glavni Kolodvor
Koturaska Cesta
Vatroslav Lisinski
Cesta

ZAGREB

0 500 m.

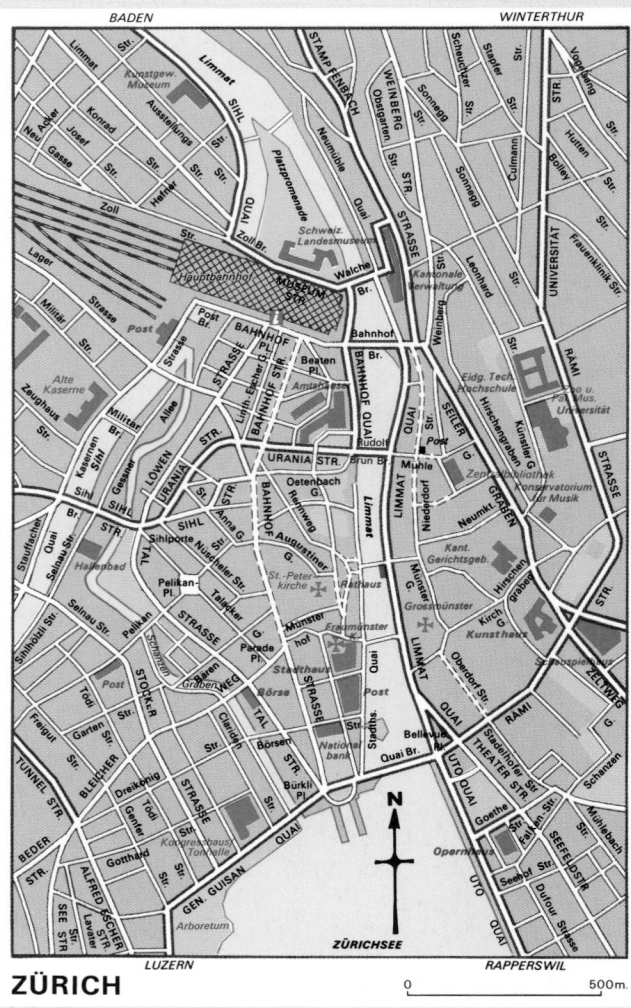
BADEN
WINTERTHUR
LUZERN
RAPPERSWIL
Limmat Str.
Limmat
SIHL QUAI
Kunstgew. Museum
Ausstellungs Str.
Konrad
Josef
Neue Adler Gasse
Hafner
Zoll
STAMPFENBACH
Neumühle Quai
WEINBERG
Obstgarten Str.
Sonnegg
Scheuchzer Str.
Stapfer Str.
Platzpromenade
Schweiz. Landesmuseum
Walche
Zoll Br.
Hauptbahnhof
MUSEUM STR.
Kantonale Verwaltung
Leonhard
Culmann
UNIVERSITÄT
Frauenklinik Str.
Lager
Militär
Strasse
Post
Post Br.
BAHNHOF PL.
Bahnhof Br.
Beaten Pl.
Amtshaus
Bahnhof
Weinberg
RÄMI
Eidg. Tech. Hochschule
Kunst u. Kunstg. Mus.
Universität
Hirschengraben
Künstler G.
Alte Kaserne
Zeughaus
Kasernen Str.
Militär Br.
Allee
Löwen
URANIA
Lindenhof
Bahnhof Str.
BAHNHOF QUAI
URANIA STR.
Rudolf Brun Br.
SELLER GRABEN
Mühle
Post
Oetenbach
Rennweg
Augustiner G.
Limmat
LIMMAT QUAI
Niederdorf Str.
Zentralbibliothek
Konservatorium für Musik
Neumkt.
Kant. Gerichtsgeb.
STRASSE
Hallenbad
Stauffacher Quai
Selnau Str.
Sihlporte
Nuschel Str.
Pelikan Pl.
Talacker
St. Peter kirche
Rathaus
Münster hof
Fraumünster
Grossmünster
Kirch Gasse
Hirschen graben
Kunsthaus
Heimplatz
ZELTWEG
Pelikan
STRASSE
Parade Pl.
Stadthaus
Börse
Post
Schanzen graben
Bären Gasse
Sihlhölzli Str.
Freigut
Todi
Garten Str.
STOCKER
TAL STR.
Clariden
Börsen Str.
National bank
Stadth. Quai
Bellevue Pl.
Quai Br.
UTO QUAI
Stadelhofer Str.
Oberdorf Str.
RÄMI
THEATER STR.
Schanzen
TUNNEL STR.
BLEICHER
Dreikönig
Genfer Str.
STRASSE
Bürkli Pl.
Kongresshaus/ Tonhalle
Goethe Str.
Falken Str.
Mühlebach
SEEFELD STR.
Opernhaus
Seefeld
Dufour Strasse
BEDER STR.
Gotthard
ALFRED ESCHER STR.
SEE STR.
Lavater
GEN. GUISAN QUAI
Arboretum
ZÜRICHSEE

ZÜRICH

0 500 m.

GB	F		D	I
Austria	Autriche	**A**	Österreich	Austria
Albania	Albanie	**AL**	Albanien	Albania
Andorra	Andorre	**AND**	Andorra	Andorra
Belgium	Belgique	**B**	Belgien	Belgio
Bulgaria	Bulgarie	**BG**	Bulgarien	Bulgaria
Belorussia	Belarus	**BL**	Weißrussland	Bielorussia
Bosnia-Hercegovina	Bosnia-Herzegovine	**BO**	Bosnien-Herzegowina	Bosnia-Herzegovina
Switzerland	Suisse	**CH**	Schweiz	Svizzera
Croatia	Croatie	**CRO**	Kroatien	Croazia
Czech Republic	République Tchèque	**CZ**	Tschechische Republik	Repubblica Ceca
Germany	Allemagne	**D**	Deutschland	Germania
Denmark	Danemark	**DK**	Dänemark	Danimarca
Spain	Espagne	**E**	Spanien	Spagna
Estonia	Estonie	**EW**	Estland	Estonia
France	France	**F**	Frankreich	Francia
Liechtenstein	Liechtenstein	**FL**	Liechtenstein	Liechtenstein
United Kingdom	Royaume Uni	**GB**	Großbritannien und Nordirland	Regno Unito
Gibraltar	Gibraltar	**GBZ**	Gibraltar	Gibilterra
Greece	Grèce	**GR**	Greichenland	Grecia
Hungary	Hongrie	**H**	Ungarn	Ungheria
Italy	Italie	**I**	Italien	Italia
Ireland	Irlande	**IRL**	Irland	Irlanda
Luxembourg	Luxembourg	**L**	Luxemburg	Lussemburgo
Lithuania	Lituanie	**LT**	Litauen	Lituania
Latvia	Lettonie	**LV**	Lettland	Lettonia
Macedonia	Macédoine	**MAK**	Makedonien	Macedonia
Monaco	Monaco	**MC**	Monaco	Monaco
Moldavia	Moldavie	**MD**	Moldawien	Moldavia
Norway	Norvège	**N**	Norwegen	Norvegia
Netherlands	Pays-Bas	**NL**	Niederlande	Paesi Bassi
Portugal	Portugal	**P**	Portugal	Portogallo
Poland	Pologne	**PL**	Polen	Polonia
Russia	Russie	**R**	Russland	Russia
Rumania	Roumanie	**RO**	Rumanien	Romania
San Marino	Saint-Marin	**RSM**	San Marino	San Marino
Sweden	Suède	**S**	Schweden	Svezia
Finland	Finlande	**SF**	Finnland	Finlandia
Slovenia	Slovénie	**SL**	Slowenien	Slovenia
Slovak Republic	République Slovaque	**SQ**	Slowak Republik	Repubblica Slovacca
Turkey	Turquie	**TR**	Türkei	Turchia
Ukraine	Ukraine	**U**	Ukraine	Ucraina
Yugoslavia	Yougoslavie	**YU**	Jugoslawien	Jugoslavia

A

30 A Coruña E A2
30 A Pontenova E A3
31 A-Ver-o-Mar P C2
71 Aach D A4
17 Aachen D C6
67 Aalen D C6
17 Aalsmeer NL A4
17 Aalst B C4
17 Aalst NL B5
62 Aalten NL B1
47 Äänekoski SF E12
70 Aarau CH A3
70 Aarberg CH A2
70 Aarburg CH A2
16 Aardenburg NL B3
17 Aarschot B C4
47 Aavasaksa SF C11
99 Aba H A3
39 Abádanes E B4
38 Abades E B2
99 Abádszalók H A5
98 Abaliget H B3
72 Ábano Terme I C1
45 Abarán E A5
97 Abasár H D6
78 Abbadia S. Salvatore I A2
59 Abbehausen D B5
57 Abbekäs S D2
16 Abbeville F C1
4 Abbey IRL A3
9 Abbey Town GB D4
4 Abbeyfeale IRL B2
5 Abbeyleix IRL B4
5 Abbeyside IRL B4
71 Abbiategrasso I C3
11 Abbot's Bromley GB C4
13 Abbotsbury GB C5
98 Abda H A2
33 Abejar E C4
42 Abela P B1
68 Abenberg D B1
38 Abenojar E D2
55 Åbenrå DK C2
68 Abensberg D C2
[illegible] Aberaeron GB A3
13 Abercarn GB B4
7 Aberchirder GB C6
13 Aberdare GB B4
10 Aberdaron GB C1
9 Aberdeen GB A5
9 Aberdour GB B4
10 Aberdovey GB C1
9 Aberfeldy GB B4
10 Aberffraw GB B1
8 Aberfoyle GB B3
13 Abergavenny GB B4
10 Abergele GB B2
13 Aberkenfig GB B4
9 Abernethy GB B4
12 Aberporth GB A3
10 Abersoch GB C1
13 Abertillery GB B4
37 Abertura E B5
10 Aberystwyth GB C1
75 Abetone I B5
72 Abfaltersbach A B2
34 Abiego E A2
55 Abild DK D1
15 Abingdon GB C1
9 Abington GB C4
36 Abiul P B2
45 Abla E B4
103 Ablanitsa BG C5
20 Ablis F C2
47 Åbo SF F11
70 Abondance F B1
99 Abony H A5
9 Aboyne GB A5
36 Abrantes P B2
24 Abrest F B3
29 Abriès F B5
94 Abrud RO C5
96 Absdorf A C1
72 Abtenau A A3
67 Abtsgmünd D C6
31 Abusejo E D4
56 Åby,*Kronoberg* S C3
53 Åby,*Östergötland* S D2
54 Åbybro DK A2
56 Åbyfors S B3
52 Åbyggeby S B3
53 Åbytorp S C1
85 Acate I B3
80 Accadia I C2
74 Accéglio I B1
82 Accettura I A3
82 Acciaroli I A2
26 Accous F C3
10 Accrington GB B3
79 Accúmoli I A4
37 Acedera E B5
37 Acehuche E B4
39 Acered E A5
80 Acerenza I D2
80 Acerno I D2
79 Acerra I C5
37 Aceuchal E C4
7 Achavanich GB B5
17 Achel B B5
17 Achene B C5
72 Achensee A A1
72 Achenthal A A1
67 Achern D C4
20 Acheux en Amienois F A3
6 Achfary GB B4
2 Achill IRL C2
59 Achim D B6
6 Achnasheen GB C3
6 Achnashellach Lodge GB C3
8 Achosnich GB B1
85 Aci Castello I B4
85 Aci Catena I B4
78 Acilia I B3
85 Acireale I B4
14 Acle GB B4
87 Acquacadda I C1
76 Acqualagna I C2
75 Acquanegra sul Chiese I A5
78 Acquapendente I A2
79 Acquasanta Terme I A4
78 Acquasparta I A3
76 Acquaviva I C1
80 Acquaviva delle Fonti I D3
79 Acquaviva Picena I A4
74 Acqui Terme I B3
20 Acquigny F B2
82 Acri I B3
98 Ács H A3
97 Acsa H D5
21 Acy-en-Multien F B3
99 Ada CRO C5
99 Adács H A5
50 Adalsbruk N B2
91 Adamów PL B6
44 Adamuz E A2
98 Ádánd H B3
38 Adanero E B2
4 Adare IRL B3
101 Adaševci YU A4
11 Addingham GB B4
33 Adeanueva de Ebro E B5
16 Adegem B B3
70 Adelboden CH B2
112 Adele,*Kriti* GR
63 Adelebsen D B4
80 Adélfia I C3
67 Adelmannsfelden D C6
68 Adelsdorf D B1
67 Adelsheim D B5
53 Adelsö S C3
40 Ademuz E A1
62 Adenau D C1
60 Adendorf D B1
109 Adhám GR A5
111 Adhámas GR C5
111 Adhámi GR B4
106 Adhriani GR B2
16 Adinkerke B B2
94 Adjud RO C7
73 Adlešiči SL C5
70 Adliswil CH A3
73 Admont A A4
48 Adneran N B3
53 Adolfsberg S C1
99 Adony H A3
62 Adorf,*Hessen* D B3
64 Adorf,*Sachsen* D C2
44 Adra E C3
33 Adradas E C4
36 Adraga P C1
4 Adrahan IRL A3
85 Adrano I B3
76 Ádria I A2
11 Adwick le Street GB B4
40 Adzaneta E A2
109 Aerinón GR B4
55 Ærøskøbing DK D3
70 Aesch CH A2
108 Aetós,*Aitolía kai Acarnanía* GR C3
108 Aetós,*Florina* GR A3
110 Aetós,*Messinía* GR B2
112 Afándou GR A2
109 Afétai GR B5
63 Afferde D A4
68 Affing D C1
70 Affoltern CH A3
108 Afión GR B1
109 Áfitos GR A5
46 Åfjord N E5
79 Afragola I C5
111 Afráti GR A4
73 Afritz A B3
110 Agalás GR B1
109 Aganderón GR B3
74 Agay F C1
75 Agazzano I B4
28 Agde F C2
27 Agen F B4
34 Ager E A3
55 Agerbæk DK C1
55 Agerskov DK C2
54 Agger DK B1
54 Aggersund DK A2
87 Ággius I B2
96 Aggsbach Dorf A C1
69 Aggsbach Markt A C6
3 Aghalee GB B5
100 Agiči BO B1
109 Agios Ioánis GR B5
85 Agira I B3
105 Agiroúpolis GR D4
108 Ágnanda GR B3
54 Agnesberg S A5
29 Agnières F B4
70 Agno CH C3
79 Agnone I B5
72 Agordo I B2
40 Agost E C2
45 Agramón E A5
35 Agramunt E B4
109 Ágras GR A3
33 Agreda E C5
109 Agriá GR B5
84 Agrigento I B2
109 Agriliá GR B3
108 Agrínion GR C3
44 Agrón E B3
82 Agrópoli I A1
31 Agua Longa P C2
45 Aguadulce,*Almería* E C4
43 Aguadulce,*Sevilla* E B5
30 Agualada E A2
34 Aguarón E B1
34 Aguas E A2
36 Aguas Belas P B2
40 Aguas de Busot E C2
36 Aguas de Moura P C2
31 Aguas Santas P C2
34 Aguaviva E C2
33 Aguaviva de la Vega E C4
38 Agudo E D2
31 Agueda P D2
28 Aguessac F B2
76 Agugliano I C3
36 Aguiar P C3
31 Aguiàr da Beira P D3
38 Aguilafuente E A2
32 Aguilar de Campóo E B2
44 Aguilar de la Frontera E B2
45 Aguilas E B5
34 Aguinaliu E A3
62 Ahaus D A2
37 Ahigal E A4
31 Ahigal de Villarino E C4
43 Ahillones E A4
61 Ahlbeck D B5
62 Ahlen D B2
63 Ahlten D A4
107 Ahmetbey TR B5
3 Ahogill GB B5
60 Ahrensbök D A1
59 Ahrensburg D B7
62 Ahrweiler D C2
24 Ahun F B2
57 Åhus S D3
109 Aiani GR A3
33 Aibar E B5
68 Aich D C3
69 Aicha D C4
68 Aichach D C2
109 Aidhipsós GR C5
85 Aidone I B3
108 Aidónia GR A3
109 Aidonokhóri GR A5
82 Aiello Cálabro I B3
109 Aigáni GR B4
69 Aigen i. M. A C4
70 Aigle CH B1
68 Aiglsbach D C2
26 Aignan F C4
25 Aignay-le-Duc F A4
23 Aigre F C5
22 Aigrefeuille-d'Aunis F B4
22 Aigrefeuille-sur-Maine F A3
35 Aiguablava E B6
25 Aiguebelle F C6
24 Aigueperse F B3
28 Aigues-Mortes F C3
28 Aigues-Vives F C1
29 Aiguilles F B5
27 Aiguillon F B4
24 Aigurande F B1
29 Ailefroide F B5
21 Aillant-sur-Tholon F D4
66 Aillevillers F D2
20 Ailly-sur-Somme F B3
28 Aimargues F C3
70 Aime F C1
72 Ainet A B2
34 Ainsa E A3
74 Airasca I B2
8 Aird GB B2
6 Aird Uig GB B1
9 Airdrie GB C4
26 Aire-sur-l'Adour F C3
16 Aire-sur-la-Lys F C2
74 Airole I C2
70 Airolo CH B3
23 Airvault F B4
25 Aisey-sur-Seine F A4
10 Aisgill GB A3
106 Aisimi GR B3
68 Aislingen D C1
25 Aissey F A6
25 Aisy-sur-Armançon F A4
68 Aiterhofen D C3
7 Aith,*Orkney Is.* GB A6
6 Aith,*Shetland Is.* GB
110 Aitolikón GR A2
94 Aiud RO C5
21 Aix-en-Othe F C4
29 Aix-en-Provence F C4
25 Aix-les-Bains F C5
23 Aixe-sur-Vienne F C6
112 Aiyiáli GR D2
111 Aiyina GR B4
109 Aiyinion GR A4
110 Aíyion GR A3
110 Aiyira GR A3
22 Aizenay F B3
86 Ajaccio F C1
24 Ajain F B2
73 Ajdovščina SL C3
98 Ajka H A2
105 Ajnovce YU B3
38 Ajofrin E C3
107 Ajtos BG A5
37 Ajuda P C3
57 Åkarp S D2
99 Akasztó H B4
112 Akçaova TR A1
64 Aken D B2
52 Åkerby S B3
48 Åkernes N C4
53 Åkers styckebruk S C3
53 Åkersberga S C4
111 Akharnai GR A4
109 Akhilio GR B4
109 Akhillion GR B4
109 Akhinós GR C4
95 Akhisar TR G7
111 Akhladeri GR A5
111 Akhladhókambos GR B3
107 Akhtobol BG A5
57 Åkirkeby DK D3
112 Akköy TR B1
58 Akkrum NL B2
105 Akladhokhórion GR C5
112 Akoúmia,*Kriti* GR
48 Åkra N B3
111 Akraifnion GR A4
110 Akráta GR A3
48 Åkrehamn N B2
108 Akritas GR A3
105 Akritokhóri GR C5
112 Akrotiri GR D2
111 Akti Idras GR B4
109 Akti Sáni GR A5
108 Aktion GR C2
46 Ål N F4
71 Ala I C6
87 Alà dei Sardi I B2
74 Ala di Stura I A2
32 Alaejos E C1
54 Alafors S A5
70 Alagna Valsésia I C2
34 Alagón E B1
40 Alaguas E B2
43 Alájar E B3
47 Alajärvi SF E11
44 Alameda E B2
38 Alameda de la Sagra E B3
44 Alamedilla E B3
44 Alamillo E A2
39 Alaminos E B4
36 Alandroal P C3
37 Alange E C4
43 Alanis E A4
79 Alanno I A4
99 Alap H B3
32 Alar del Rey E B2
38 Alaraz E B1
39 Alarcón E C4
41 Alaró,*Mallorca* E
95 Alaşehir TR G8
74 Alássio I B3
40 Alatoz E B1
79 Alatri I B4
99 Alattyán H A5
47 Alavus SF E11
41 Alayor,*Menorca* E
40 Alba E A1
74 Alba I B3
79 Alba Adriatica I A4
38 Alba de Tormes E B1
94 Alba-Iulia RO C5
39 Albacete E D5
62 Albachten D B2
54 Albæk DK A3
34 Albafarrech E B3
34 Albages E B3
40 Albaida E C2
27 Albais F B5
37 Albala del Caudillo E B4
45 Albaladejo E A4
40 Albalat E B2
34 Albalate de Cinca E B3
39 Albalete de Zorita E B4
34 Albalete del Arzobispo E B2
28 Alban F C1
35 Albaná E A5
45 Albánchez E B4
44 Albanchez de Ubeda E B3
45 Albanilla E A5
78 Albano Laziale I B3
75 Albaredo d'Adige I A6
40 Albarracin E A1
40 Albatana E C1
45 Albatera E A6
70 Albbruck D A3
44 Albedin E B2
33 Albelda E B4
74 Albenga I B3
25 Albens F C5
53 Alberga S D2
31 Albergaria-a-Nova P D2
31 Albergaria-a-Velha P D2
36 Albergaria dos Doze P B2
36 Alberge P C2
31 Albergueria E B3
37 Albergueria de Argañán E A4
40 Alberique E B2
42 Albernoa P B2
81 Alberobello I D4
72 Alberoni I C2
59 Albersdorf D A6
62 Albersloh D B2
67 Albersweiler D B4
20 Albert F A3
99 Albertirsa H A4
25 Albertville F C6
103 Albesti RO A5
27 Albi F C6
83 Albidona I B3
78 Albinia I A2
71 Albino I C4
32 Albires E B1
74 Albisola Marina I B3
17 Alblasserdam NL B4
40 Albocácer E A3
44 Albolote E B3
44 Albondón E C3
40 Alboraya E B2
40 Alborea E B1
54 Ålborg DK A2
103 Albota RO B5
45 Albox E B4
69 Albrechtice n. Vitavou CZ B5
42 Albufeira P B1
44 Albuñol E C3
44 Albuñuelas E C3
68 Alburg D C3
37 Alburquerque E B4
46 Alby S E7
36 Alcácer do Sal P C2
36 Alcáçovas P C2
45 Alcadozo E A5
37 Alcafoces P B3
36 Alcainça P C1
36 Alcains P B3
40 Alcalá de Chisvert E A3
43 Alcalá de Guadaira E B4
34 Alcalá de Gurrea E A2
39 Alcalá de Henares E B3
40 Alcalá de la Selva E A2
43 Alcalá de los Gazules E C4
40 Alcalá del Júcar E B1
43 Alcala del Rio E B4
43 Alcalá del Valle E C4
44 Alcalá la Real E B3
84 Alcamo I B1
34 Alcampel E B3
33 Alcanadre E B4
41 Alcanar E A3
36 Alcanede P B2
31 Alcañices E C4
34 Alcañiz E B2
37 Alcántara E B4
42 Alcantarilha P B1
45 Alcantarilla E B5
44 Alcaracejos E A2
45 Alcaraz E A4
42 Alcaria Ruiva P B2
34 Alcarraz E B3
44 Alcaudete E B2
38 Alcaudete de la Jara E C2
39 Alcázar de San Juan E C3
32 Alcazarén E C2
13 Alcester GB A6
38 Alcoba E C2
36 Alcobaça P B1
39 Alcobendas E B3
40 Alcoceber E A3
39 Alcocer E B4
36 Alcochete P C2
36 Alcoentre P B2
39 Alcohujate E B4
44 Alcolea,*Almería* E C4
44 Alcolea,*Córdoba* E B2
38 Alcolea de Calatrava E D2
34 Alcolea de Cinca E B3
38 Alcolea de Tajo E C1
39 Alcolea del Pinar E A4
43 Alcolea del Rio E B4
37 Alcollarin E B5
14 Alconbury Hill GB B2
37 Alconchel E C3
37 Alconera E C4
45 Alcontar E B4
40 Alcora E A2
38 Alcorcón E B3
34 Alcorisa E C2
42 Alcoutim P B2
35 Alcover E B4
40 Alcoy E C2
99 Alcsútdoboz H A3
34 Alcubierre E B2
33 Alcubilla de Avellaneda E C3
32 Alcubilla de Nogales E B1
44 Alcubillas E A3
40 Alcublas E B2
41 Alcudía,*Mallorca* E
44 Alcudia de Guadix E B3
37 Alcuéscar E B4
40 Aldaya E B2
13 Aldbourne GB B6
11 Aldbrough GB B5
34 Aldea E C3
37 Aldea de Trujillo E B5
37 Aldea del Cano E B4
38 Aldea del Fresno E B2
31 Aldea del Obispo E D4
31 Aldea del Obispo P D4
44 Aldea del Rey E A3
38 Aldea Real E A2
37 Aldeacentenera E B5
31 Aldeadávila de la Ribera E C4
32 Aldealcorvo E C3
33 Aldealuenga de Sta. Maria E C3
32 Aldeamayor de San Martin E C2
38 Aldeanueva de Barbarroya E C1
38 Aldeanueva de S. Bartolomé E C1
37 Aldeanueva del Camino E A5
38 Aldeanueva del Codonal E A2
33 Aldeapozo E C4
44 Aldeaquemada E A3
38 Aldearrubia E A1
38 Aldeaseca de la Frontera E B1
32 Aldeasoña E C2
38 Aldeatejada E B1
14 Aldeburgh GB B4
40 Aldehuela E A1
33 Aldehuela de Calatañazor E C4
31 Aldehuela de Yeltes E D4
36 Aldeia da Serra P C3
37 Aldeia do Bispo P A4
36 Aldeia do Mato P B2
36 Aldeia Gavinha P B1
42 Aldeia Nova P B2
44 Aldeire E B3
17 Aldekerk D B6
17 Aldenhoven D C6
13 Alderbury GB B6
15 Aldermaston GB C1
69 Aldersbach D C4
15 Aldershot GB C2
104 Aldince MAK C3
11 Aldridge GB C4
110 Aléa GR B3
56 Åled S C1
45 Aledo E B5
33 Alegia Dulantzi E B4
99 Aleksa Šantić CRO C4
102 Aleksandrovac YU B2
103 Aleksandrovo BG C5
107 Aleksandrovo BG A4
90 Aleksandrów PL B3
89 Aleksandrów Kujawski PL C4
102 Aleksinac YU C2
56 Ålem S C5
19 Alençon F B6
36 Alenquer P B1
35 Alenya F A6
86 Aleria F B2
28 Alès F B3
87 Áles I C1
74 Alessándria I B3
84 Alessándria della Rocca I B2
83 Alessano I B5
54 Ålestrup DK B2
46 Ålesund N E3
35 Alet-les-Bains F A5
8 Alexandria GB C3
109 Alexándria GR A4
95 Alexandria RO E6
106 Alexandroúpolis GR C3
102 Alexandrovac YU C2
29 Aleyrac F B3
83 Alézio I A5
44 Alfacar E B3
37 Alfaiates P A4
34 Alfajarin E B2
40 Alfambra E A1
42 Alfambra P B1
31 Alfândega da Fé P C4
31 Alfarela de Jafes P C3
36 Alfarelos P A2
36 Alfarim P C1
44 Alfarnate E C2
33 Alfaro E B5
34 Alfarrás E B3
79 Alfedena I B5
36 Alfeizarão P B1
68 Alfeld,*Bayern* D B2
63 Alfeld, *Niedersachsen* D B4
31 Alfena P C2
42 Alferce P B1
59 Alfhausen D C4
76 Alfonsine I B2
7 Alford,*Grampian* GB C6
11 Alford,*Lincolnshire* GB B6
35 Alforja E B3
11 Alfreton GB B4
52 Alfta S A2
42 Alfundão P A1
41 Algaida,*Mallorca* E
43 Algar,*Cádiz* E C4
45 Algar,*Murcia* E B6
51 Älgaräs S D5
48 Ålgård N C2
44 Algarinejo E B2
44 Algarrobo E C2
43 Algatocin E C4
43 Algeciras E C4
40 Algemesí E B2
36 Algés P C1
39 Algete E B3
87 Alghero I B1
56 Älghult S B4
40 Alginet E B2
43 Algodonales E C4
38 Algodor E C3
42 Algodor P B2
39 Algora E B4
33 Algorta E A4
42 Algoz P B1
66 Algrange F B2
34 Alguaire E B3
45 Alguazas E A5
99 Algyö H B5
45 Alhama de Almeria E C4
33 Alhama de Aragón E C5
44 Alhama de Granada E C3
45 Alhama de Murcia E B5
39 Alhambra E D3
36 Alhandra P C1
44 Alhaurin de la Torre E C2
44 Alhaurin el Grande E C2
44 Alhendin E B3
39 Alhóndiga E B4
36 Alhos Vedros P C1
85 Ali Terme I B4
38 Alia E C1
84 Ália I B2
34 Aliaga E C2
111 Aliartos GR A4
101 Alibunar YU A5
40 Alicante E C2
44 Alicún de Ortega E B3
79 Alife I B5
110 Alifira GR B2
32 Alija del Infantado E B1
31 Alijo P C3
110 Alika GR C3
110 Alikanás GR B1
108 Aliki,*Árta* GR B3
111 Aliki,*Voiotia* GR A4
112 Alikianós,*Kriti* GR
112 Alikó GR D2
84 Alimena I B3
35 Aliña E A4
56 Alingsås S B1
25 Alise-Ste. Reine F A4
37 Aliseda E B4
110 Alissós GR A2
106 Alistráti GR B1
111 Alivérion GR A5
29 Alixan F B4
42 Aljaraque E B2
30 Aljariz E B3
42 Aljezur P B1
45 Aljorra E B5
36 Aljubarrota P B2
37 Aljucen E B4
42 Aljustrel P B1
17 Alken B C5
58 Alkmaar NL C1
69 Alkoven A C5
62 Allagen D B3
20 Allaines F C2
22 Allaire F A2
28 Allanche F A1
96 Alland A C2
30 Allande E A4
27 Allasac F A5
29 Allauch F C4
28 Allegre F A2
29 Allemagne-en-Provence F C5
29 Allemont F A5
9 Allendale Town GB D5
62 Allendorf D C3
69 Allentsteig A C6
5 Allenwood IRL A5
40 Allepuz E A2
68 Allersberg D B2
68 Allershausen D C2
29 Allevard F A5
29 Allex F B3
54 Allingåbro DK B3
57 Allinge DK D3
67 Allmendingen D C5
33 Allo E B4
9 Alloa GB B4
24 Allogny F A2
10 Allonby GB A2
20 Allones F C2
26 Allons F B3
29 Allos F B5
63 Allstedt D B6
78 Allumiere I A2
36 Almaceda P B3
34 Almacellas E B3
44 Almachar E C2
36 Almada P C1
44 Almadén E A2
43 Almadén de la Plata E B3
44 Almadenejos E A2
39 Almadrones E B4
38 Almagro E D3
33 Almajano E C4
40 Almansa E C1
42 Almansil P B1
32 Almanza E B1
37 Almaraz E B5
42 Almareleja P A2
43 Almargen E C4
33 Almarza E C4
98 Almásfüzitö H A3
33 Almazán E C4
40 Almazora E B2
33 Almazul E C4
62 Alme D B3
44 Almedinilla E B2
31 Almeida E C4
31 Almeida P D4
36 Almeirim P B2
62 Almelo NL A1
34 Almenar E B3
33 Almenar de Soria E C4
40 Almenara E B2
31 Almendra P D3
37 Almendral E C4
38 Almendral de la Cañada E B2
37 Almendralejo E C4
71 Almenno S. Bart I C4
17 Almere NL A5
45 Almería E C4
45 Almerimar E C4
74 Almese I A2
42 Almexial P B2
56 Älmhult S C3
111 Almiri GR B4
110 Almiron GR C3
111 Almiropótamos GR A5
109 Almirós GR B4
42 Almodôvar P B1
44 Almodóvar del Campo E A2
39 Almodóvar del Pinar E C5
43 Almodóvar del Rio E B4
31 Almofala P D3
44 Almogia E C2
37 Almoharin E B4
34 Almonacid de la Sierra E B1
38 Almonacid de Toledo E C3
43 Almonaster la Real E B3
13 Almondsbury GB B5
43 Almonte E B3
45 Almoradi E A6
43 Almoraima E C4
38 Almorox E B2
36 Almoster P B2
52 Älmsta S C4
45 Almudena E A5
34 Almudévar E A2
44 Almuñecar E C3
52 Almunge S C4
44 Almuradiel E A3
7 Alness GB C4
9 Alnmouth GB C6
9 Alnwick GB C6
108 Álonas GR A3
109 Alónia GR A4
110 Alonistena GR B3
109 Alónnisos GR B5
44 Alora E C2
35 Alos de Isil E A4
42 Alosno E B2
25 Aloxe-Corton F A4
44 Alozaina E C2
72 Alpbach A A1
39 Alpedrete E B3
17 Alpen D B6
40 Alpera E C1
17 Alphen NL B4
17 Alphen a/d Rijn NL A4
13 Alphington GB C4
36 Alpiarca P B2
74 Alpignano I A2
67 Alpirsbach D C4
40 Alpuente E B1
107 Alpullu TR B5
42 Alqueva P A2
34 Alquézar E A3
10 Alsager GB B3
33 Alsasua E B4
17 Alsdorf D C6
55 Alselv DK C1
63 Alsfeld D C4
52 Alsike S C3
63 Alsleben D B6
99 Alsógod H A4
99 Alsónémedi H A4
62 Alstätte D A1
56 Alsterbro S C4
9 Alston GB D5
46 Alta N B11
80 Altamura I D3
39 Altarejos E C4
73 Altaussee A A3
79 Altavilla Irpina I B5
82 Altavilla Silentina I A2
64 Altdöbern D B4
70 Altdorf CH B3
68 Altdorf,*Bayern* D B2
68 Altdorf,*Bayern* D C3
68 Altdorf,*Bayern* D D1
42 Alte P B1
40 Altea E C2
76 Altedo I B1
68 Alteglofsheim D C3
46 Alteidet N A11
62 Altena D B2
63 Altenau D B5
64 Altenberg D C3
62 Altenberge D A2
62 Altenbögge-Bönen D B2
59 Altenbruch D B5
68 Altenbuch D C3
64 Altenburg D C2
59 Altenesch D B5
69 Altenfelden A C4
63 Altengronau D C4
62 Altenhaßlau D C4
67 Altenheim D C3
62 Altenhundem D B3
61 Altenkirchen, *Mecklenburg-Vorpommern* D A4
62 Altenkirchen, *Radom* D C2
60 Altenkrempe D A1
68 Altenkunstadt D A2
62 Altenlünne D A2
68 Altenmarkt D C3
72 Altenmarkt, *Salzburg* A A3
73 Altenmarkt, *Steiermark* A A4
59 Altenoythe D B4
67 Altensteig D C4
61 Altentreptow D B4
59 Altenwalde D B5
63 Altenweddingen D A6
36 Alter do Chão P B3
68 Altfraunhofen D C3
69 Altheim A C4
67 Altheim,*Baden-Württemberg* D B5
67 Altheim,*Baden-Württemberg* D C6
73 Althofen A B4
103 Altimir BG C4

102 Bozovici RO B2
75 Bózzolo I A5
74 Bra I B2
56 Braås S B4
55 Brabrand DK B3
6 Bracadale GB C2
78 Bracciano I A3
11 Bracebridge Heath GB B5
64 Brachstedt D B2
24 Bracieux F A1
46 Bräcke S E7
67 Brackenheim D B5
15 Brackley GB B1
57 Bräckne-Hoby S C4
15 Bracknell GB C2
62 Brackwede D B3
9 Braco GB B4
94 Brad RO C5
11 Bradford GB B4
13 Bradford on Avon GB B5
100 Bradina BO C3
15 Bradwell on Sea GB C3
6 Brae, *Shetland Is.* GB
55 Brædstrup DK C2
9 Braemar GB B4
6 Braemore GB C3
7 Braeswick GB A6
31 Braga P C2
31 Bragança P C4
94 Braila RO D7
11 Brailsford GB C4
23 Brain-s-Allonnes F A5
21 Braine F B4
17 Braine-l'Alleud B C4
17 Braine-le-Comte B C4
15 Braintree GB C3
17 Braives B C5
59 Brake, *Niedersachsen* D B5
62 Brake, *Nordrhein-Westfalen* D A3
62 Brakel D B4
51 Brålanda S D3
90 Bralin PL B1
75 Brallo I B4
109 Brállos GR C4
103 Braloştiţa RO B4
27 Bram F C6
74 Bramafan F C1
72 Bramberg am Wildkogel A A2
55 Bramdrup DK C2
15 Bramford GB B4
55 Bramminge DK C1
14 Brampton, *Cambridgeshire* GB B2
9 Brampton, *Cumbria* GB D5
14 Brampton, *Suffolk* GB B4
62 Bramsche D A2
59 Bramstedt D C5
76 Branca I C2
85 Brancaleone Marina I B5
14 Brancaster GB B3
69 Brand, *Nieder Östereich* A C6
71 Brand, *Vorarlberg* A A4
64 Brand-Erbisdorf D C3
50 Brandbu N B1
55 Brande DK C2
59 Brande-Hornerkirchen D B6
72 Brandenberg A A1
64 Brandenburg D A2
64 Brandis D B2
62 Brandlecht D A2
30 Brandomil E A2
11 Brandon, *Durham* GB A4
14 Brandon, *Norfolk* GB B3
61 Brandshagen D A4
50 Brandval N B3
65 Brandýs n. Labem-Stará Boleslav CZ C4
103 Brănesti RO B4
102 Braničevo YU B2
89 Braniewo PL A5
96 Brankovice CZ B3
101 Brankovina YU B4
96 Branky CZ B3
51 Bränna S D3
26 Branne F B3
68 Brannenburg D D3
27 Brantôme F A4
51 Bras S D2
29 Bras d'Asse F C5
104 Brasalice YU B3
50 Braskereidfoss N B2
94 Braşov RO D6
18 Brasparts F B2
28 Brassac F C1
24 Brassac-les-Mines F C3
17 Brasschaat B B4
51 Brastad S D2
69 Břasy CZ B4
90 Brąszewice PL B2
108 Brataj AL A1
51 Bräte N C2
73 Bratina CRO C5
96 Bratislava SQ C3
103 Bratovoeşti RO B4
51 Brattfors S C5
13 Bratton GB B5
101 Bratunac BO B4
106 Bratya Daskolvi BG A3
62 Braubach D C2
69 Braunau A C4
62 Braunfels D C3
63 Braunlage D B5
63 Braunschweig D A5
12 Braunton GB B3
21 Braux F B5
71 Bravuogn CH B4
5 Bray IRL A5
16 Bray Dunes F B2
21 Bray-sur-Seine F C4
21 Bray-sur-Somme F B3
42 Braz P B2
44 Brazatortas E A2
25 Brazey F A5
101 Brčko BO B3
98 Brckovljani CRO C1
101 Brdani YU C5
90 Brdów PL A2
39 Brea de Tajo E B3
103 Breasta RO B4
103 Brebeni RO B5
19 Brécey F B4
9 Brechin GB B5
17 Brecht B B4
62 Brecketfeld D B2
96 Břeclav CZ C2
13 Brecon GB B4
24 Brécy F A2
35 Breda E B5
17 Breda NL B4
56 Bredaryd S B2
15 Brede GB D3
55 Bredebro DK C1
62 Bredelar D B3
16 Bredene B B2
61 Bredenfelde D B4
62 Bredevoort NL B1
50 Bredsjö S C5
59 Bredstedt D A5
55 Bredsten DK C2
17 Bree B B5
58 Breezand NL C1
72 Breganze I C1
71 Bregenz A A4
102 Bregovo BG B3
19 Bréhal F B4
64 Brehna D B2
97 Brehy SQ C4
66 Breidenbach F B3
74 Breil F C2
46 Breim N F3
66 Breisach D C3
70 Breitenbach CH A2
63 Breitenbach D C4
69 Breitenberg D C4
96 Breitenbrunn A D2
60 Breitenfelde D B1
96 Breitenfurth A C2
63 Breitenworbis D B5
55 Brejning DK C2
49 Brekkesto N C5
100 Brela CRO C1
59 Bremen D B5
59 Bremerhaven D B5
59 Bremervörde D B6
70 Bremgarten CH A3
48 Bremnes N B2
55 Brenderup DK C2
63 Brendlorenzen D C5
43 Brenes E B4
103 Brenitsa BG C5
97 Brenna PL B4
72 Brenner I A1
71 Breno I C5
25 Brénod F B5
67 Brensbach D B4
15 Brent GB C2
15 Brentwood GB C3
75 Brescello I B5
71 Bréscia I C5
16 Breskens NL B3
20 Bresles F B3
101 Bresnica YU C5
74 Bressana I A4
72 Bressanone (Brixen) I B1
24 Bressole F B3
23 Bressuire F B4
103 Brest BG C5
93 Brèst BL D8
96 Brest CZ B3
18 Brest F B1
101 Brestac YU B4
73 Brestanica SL B5
77 Brestova CRO A4
100 Brestovac CRO A2
102 Brestovac YU B3
102 Brestovad YU C2
27 Bretenoux F B5
20 Breteuil, *Eure* F C1
20 Breteuil, *Oise* F B3
20 Brétigny-sur-Orge F C3
64 Bretnig D B4
67 Bretten D B4
19 Bretteville-sur-Laize F A5
67 Brettheim D B6
70 Breuil-Cervinia I C2
17 Breukelen NL A5
53 Breven S C1
49 Brevik N B6
100 Breza BO B3
73 Brežice SL C5
29 Bréziers F B5
101 Brezna YU C5
98 Breznica CRO B1
98 Breznica Našička CRO C3
69 Březnice CZ B4
105 Breznik BG B4
97 Brezno SQ C5
103 Brezoi RO A5
104 Brezojevice YU B1
20 Brezolles F C2
96 Brezová CZ C3
96 Březová n Svitavou CZ B2
106 Brezovo BG A3
101 Brezovo Polje BO B3
29 Briançon F B5
29 Brianconnet F C5
24 Briare F A2
27 Briatexte F C5
82 Briático I C3
21 Briaucourt F C6
77 Bribir CRO A4
77 Bribir CRO C5
19 Bricquebec F A4
70 Brides-les-Bains F C1
12 Bridestowe GB C3
4 Brideswell IRL A3
15 Bridge GB C4
7 Bridge of Alford GB C6
9 Bridge of Allan GB B4
9 Bridge of Cally GB B4
7 Bridge of Don GB C6
9 Bridge of Earn GB B4
7 Bridge of Forss GB B5
8 Bridge of Orchy GB B3
6 Bridge of Walls, *Shetland Is.* GB
8 Bridge of Weir GB C3
8 Bridgend, *Islay* GB C1
13 Bridgend, *Mid Glamorgan* GB B4
10 Bridgenorth GB C3
11 Bridghouse GB B4
13 Bridgwater GB B5
96 Bridlična CZ B3
11 Bridlington GB A5
18 Bridnogan F B1
13 Bridport GB C5
13 Bridstow GB B5
20 Brie-Comte-Robert F C3
18 Briec F B2
17 Brielle NL B4
60 Brielow D C3
21 Brienne-le-Château F C5
70 Brienz CH B3
82 Brienza I A2
64 Brieskow Finkenheerd D A4
60 Brietlingen D B1
21 Brieulles-sur-Meuse F B6
33 Brieva E B4
66 Briey F B1
70 Brig CH B3
11 Brigg GB B5
15 Brighstone GB D1
15 Brightlingsea GB C3
15 Brighton GB D2
29 Brignoles F C5
14 Brigstock GB B2
39 Brihuega E B4
102 Brijanje YU C2
101 Briježde YU B5
77 Brijuni CRO B3
62 Brilon D B3
42 Brinches P A2
81 Bríndisi I D4
77 Brinje CRO A5
24 Brinon-sur-Beuvron F A3
24 Brinon-sur-Sauldre F A2
7 Brinyan GB A5
30 Brión E B2
33 Briones E B4
20 Brionne F B1
21 Brionon-sur-Armançon F D4
28 Brioude F A2
23 Brioux-sur-Boutonne F B4
19 Briouze F B5
26 Briscous F C2
76 Brisighella I B1
25 Brison F C5
23 Brissac-Quincé F A4
70 Brissago CH B3
13 Bristol GB B5
5 Brittas IRL A5
27 Brive-la-Gaillarde F A5
33 Briviesca E B3
13 Brixham GB C4
72 Brixlegg A A1
14 Brixworth GB B2
101 Brka BO B3
80 Brna CRO B3
100 Brnaze CRO C1
96 Brno CZ B2
51 Bro, *Göteborg och Bohus* S D2
13 Broad Clyst GB C4
6 Broadford GB C3
15 Broadstairs GB C4
13 Broadway GB A6
13 Broadwey GB C5
13 Broadwindsor GB C5
55 Broager DK D2
56 Broaryd S B2
57 Broby S C3
100 Broćanac BO C2
81 Broćanac YU B5
26 Brocas F B3
62 Brock D A2
59 Brockel D B6
13 Brockenhurst GB C6
13 Brockworth GB B5
88 Broczyno PL B2
104 Brod MAK C3
73 Brod na Kupi CRO C4
101 Brodarevo YU C4
52 Broddbo S C2
96 Brodek CZ B3
62 Brodenbach D C2
102 Brodica YU B2
8 Brodick GB C2
107 Brodilovo BG A5
89 Brodnica PL B5
88 Brodnica Graniczna PL A4
100 Brodski Stupnik CRO A2
65 Brody PL B4
58 Broek op Langendijk NL C1
20 Broglie F B1
65 Brójce PL A5
53 Brokind S D1
85 Brolo I A3
60 Brome D C1
15 Bromley GB C2
57 Bromölla S C3
24 Bromont-Lamothe F C2
57 Brömsebro S C4
13 Bromsgrove GB A5
13 Bromyard GB A5
40 Bronchales E A1
37 Bronco E A4
54 Brønderslev DK A2
75 Broni I A4
13 Bronllys GB A4
46 Brønnøysund N D6
55 Brøns DK C1
85 Bronte I B3
72 Bronzolo (Branzoll) I B1
3 Brookeborough GB B4
9 Broomhill GB C6
18 Broons F B3
28 Broquies F B1
7 Brora GB B5
55 Brørup DK C2
57 Brösarp S D3
103 Broscari RO B3
103 Brosteni RO B3
49 Brøstrud N A5
91 Broszków PL A6
36 Brotas P C2
50 Brötjärna S B6
34 Broto E A2
50 Brøttum N A1
20 Brou F C2
10 Brough, *Cumbria* GB A3
6 Brough, *Shetland Is.* GB
6 Brough Lodge, *Shetland Is.* GB
3 Broughshane GB B5
9 Broughton, *Borders* GB C4
11 Broughton, *Lincolnshire* GB B5
14 Broughton, *Northamptonshire* GB B2
10 Broughton in Furness GB A2
65 Broumov CZ C6
21 Broussy le Grand F C4
24 Brout-Vernet F B3
66 Brouvelieures F C2
16 Brouwershaven NL B3
54 Brovst DK A2
11 Brownhills GB C4
25 Broye F B4
37 Brozas E B4
71 Brozzo I C5
96 Brtnice CZ B1
16 Bruay-en-Artois F C2
35 Bruch E B4
59 Bruchhausen-Vilsen D C5
67 Bruchsal D B4
72 Bruck A A2
68 Bruck D B3
64 Brück, *Brandenburg* D A2
96 Bruck a.d. Leitha A C2
73 Bruck a.d. Mur A A5
68 Bruckberg D B1
73 Brückl A B4
68 Bruckmühl D D2
29 Brue-Auriac F C4
60 Brüel D B2
24 Bruère-Allichamps F B2
4 Bruff IRL B3
70 Brugg CH A3
16 Brugge B B3
17 Brüggen D B6
24 Brugneas F B3
62 Brühl D C1
17 Bruinisse NL B4
19 Brûlon F C5
71 Brumano I C4
66 Brumath F C3
17 Brummen NL A6
50 Brumunddal N B1
60 Brunau D C2
55 Brundby DK C3
21 Brunehamel F B5
62 Brünen D B1
46 Brunflo S E7
72 Brunico (Bruneck) I B1
49 Brunkeberg N B5
96 Brunn a. Gebirge A C2
52 Brunna S C3
70 Brunnen CH B3
50 Brunnsberg S A4
50 Brunnsvik S B6
59 Brunsbüttel D B6
17 Brunssum NL C5
70 Brunstatt F A2
96 Bruntál CZ B3
102 Brus YU C2
77 Brušane CRO B5
103 Brusartsi BG C4
74 Brusasco I A3
71 Brusio CH B5
102 Brusnik YU B3
28 Brusque F C1
70 Brusson I C2
61 Brüssow D B5
88 Brusy PL B3
13 Bruton GB B5
77 Bruvno CRO B5
50 Bruvoll N B2
17 Bruxelles B C4
66 Bruyères F C2
19 Bruz F B4
56 Bruzaholm S B4
91 Brwinow PL A4
107 Bryastovets BG A5
103 Bryastovo BG C5
10 Bryn-Eden GB C2
12 Brynamman GB B4
48 Bryne N C2
13 Brynmawr GB B4
102 Brza Palanka YU B3
102 Brzeče YU C1
90 Brzeg PL C1
65 Brzeg Dolny PL B6
91 Brzegi PL C4
89 Brzesć Kuj PL C4
91 Brzesko Nowe PL C4
97 Brzeszcze PL B5
88 Brzezie PL B2
90 Brzeziny, *Kalisz* PL B3
90 Brzeziny, *Skierniewice* PL B2
90 Brzeżnica Nowa PL B3
97 Brzotin SQ C6
89 Brzozie Lubawskie PL B5
91 Brzozów PL A4
94 Brzozów PL B5
54 Bua S A5
36 Buarcos P A2
48 Buaveg N B2
74 Bubbio I B3
18 Bubry F C2
96 Bučany SQ C3
85 Buccheri I B3
80 Buccino I D2
36 Bucelas P C1
67 Buch, *Bayern* D C6
68 Buch, *Bayern* D C3
67 Buchau D C5
68 Buchbach D C3
71 Buchboden A A4
67 Buchen, *Baden-Württemberg* D B5
60 Büchen, *Schleswig-Holstein* D B1
71 Buchenberg D A5
21 Buchères F C5
59 Buchholz, *Niedersachsen* D B6
63 Buchholz, *Thüringen* D B5
103 Buchin Prokhod BG D4
68 Buchloe D C1
96 Buchlovice CZ B3
8 Buchlyvie GB B3
60 Bucholz D B3
71 Buchs CH A4
20 Buchy F B2
104 Bučin MAK C3
103 Bucinişu RO C5
102 Bučje YU C3
14 Buckden GB B2
62 Bückeburg D A4
12 Buckfastleigh GB C4
9 Buckhaven GB B4
7 Buckie GB C6
15 Buckingham GB C1
10 Buckley GB B2
61 Buckow D C5
9 Bucksburn GB A5
60 Bückwitz D C3
96 Bučovice CZ B2
95 Bucureşti RO D7
21 Bucy F B4
21 Bucy-lés-Pierreport F B4
90 Buczek PL B3
99 Budakalasz H A4
99 Budakesi H A3
99 Budaörs H A3
99 Budapest H A3
87 Buddusó I B2
12 Bude GB C3
96 Budec CZ B1
17 Budel NL B5
59 Büdelsdorf D A6
42 Budens P B1
62 Büderich D B1
39 Budia E B4
62 Büdingen D C4
98 Budinšćina CRO B1
96 Budišov, *Jihomoravský* CZ B2
96 Budišov, *Severomoravsky* CZ B3
13 Budleigh Salterton GB C4
96 Budmerice SQ C3
93 Budogoshch R A13
88 Budowo PL A3
76 Búdrio I B1
81 Budva YU B5
64 Budyně n. Ohří CZ C4
91 Budziszewice PL B3
97 Budzów PL B5
88 Budzyń PL C3
48 Bue N C2
34 Bueña E C1
39 Buenache de Alarcón E C4
39 Buenache de la Sierra E B5
38 Buenaventura E B2
32 Buenavista de Valdavia E B2
39 Buendia E B4
62 Buer D A3
30 Bueu E B2
33 Buezo E B3
99 Bugac H B4
24 Bugeat F C1
87 Buggerru I C1
12 Bugle GB C3
100 Bugojno BO B2
99 Bugyi H A4
67 Bühl, *Baden-Württemberg* D C4
71 Bühl, *Bayern* D A5
67 Bühlertal D C4
67 Bühlertann D B5
72 Buia I B3
13 Builth Wells GB A4
29 Buis-les-Baronnies F B4
58 Buitenpost NL B3
39 Buitrago E B3
97 Buják H D5
44 Bujalance E B2
105 Bujanovac YU B3
34 Bujaraloz E B2
72 Buje CRO C3
33 Bujedo E B3
98 Bük H A1
65 Buk PL A6
103 Buk'ovtsi BG C4
105 Bukhovo BG B5
98 Bükkösd H B2
73 Bukovici SL B5
104 Bukovo MAK C3
65 Bukowiec PL A6
97 Bukowina PL B6
90 Bukowno PL C3
88 Bukowo Morskie PL A2
70 Bülach CH A3
62 Buldern D B2
7 Buldoo GB B5
103 Bulgarene BG C6
107 Bulgarovo BG A5
107 Búlgarska Polyana BG A4
103 Búlgarski Izvor BG C5
66 Bulgnéville F C1
59 Bülkau D B5
46 Bulken N F3
89 Bulkowo PL C6
17 Bullange B C6
45 Bullas E A5
70 Bulle CH B2
15 Bullington Cross Inn GB C1
16 Bully F C2
97 Bulowice PL B5
104 Bulqizë AL C2
103 Bumbeşti-jiu RO A4
2 Bunbeg IRL A3
5 Bunclody IRL B5
3 Buncrana IRL A4
58 Bunde, *Niedersachsen* D B4
62 Bunde, *Nordrhein-Westfalen* D A3
63 Bundheim D B5
2 Bundoran IRL B3
8 Bunessan GB B1
14 Bungay GB B4
77 Bunič CRO B5
5 Bunmahon IRL B4
30 Buño E A2
40 Buñol E B2
41 Buñola, *Mallorca* E
17 Bunsbeek B C4
15 Buntingford GB C2
33 Buñuel E C5
82 Buonabitácolo I A2
80 Buonalbergo I C1
75 Buonconvento I C6
82 Buonvicino I B2
72 Burano I C2
62 Burbach D C3
13 Burbage GB B6
39 Burbáguena E A5
87 Burcei I C2
47 Bureå S D10
30 Burella de Cabo E A3
62 Büren D B3
70 Büren an der Aare CH A2
13 Burford GB B6
64 Burg, *Cottbus* D B4
63 Burg, *Magdeburg* D A6
59 Burg, *Schleswig-Holstein* D B6
60 Burg, *Schleswig-Holstein* D A2
61 Burg Stargard D B4
107 Burgas BG A5
73 Burgau A A6
68 Burgau D C1
42 Burgau P B1
67 Burgbernheim D B6
70 Burgdorf CH A2
59 Burgdorf D C7
68 Burgebrach D B1
63 Bürgel D C6
15 Burgess Hill GB D2
11 Burgh le Marsh GB B6
68 Burghaslach D B1
63 Burghaun D C4
69 Burghausen D C3
7 Burghead GB C5
68 Burgheim D C2
84 Búrgio I B2
63 Burgkunstadt D C6
68 Burglengenfeld D B3
43 Burgo E C5
31 Burgo P D2
68 Burgoberbach D B1
38 Burgohondo E B2
33 Burgos E B3
67 Burgsinn D A5
64 Burgstädt D C2
63 Burgstall D A6
92 Burgsvik S B6
34 Burguete E A1
34 Burgui E A2
43 Burguillos E B4
38 Burguillos de Toledo E C3
37 Burguillos del Cerro E C4
59 Burhave D B5
23 Burie F C4
102 Burila Mare RO B3
40 Burjaso E B2
68 Burk D B1
64 Burkau D B4
64 Burkhardtsdorf D C2
67 Burladingen D C5
59 Burlage D B4
11 Burley in Wharfedale GB B4
7 Burness GB A6
3 Burnfoot IRL A4
14 Burnham Market GB B3
15 Burnham-on-Crouch GB C3
13 Burnham-on-Sea GB B5
11 Burnley GB B3
9 Burnmouth GB C5
9 Burntisland GB B4
32 Burón E A1
70 Buronzo I C3
102 Burovac YU B2
61 Burow D B4
6 Burrafirth, *Shetland Is.* GB
6 Burravoe, *Shetland Is.* GB
104 Burrel AL C2
9 Burrelton GB B4
4 Burren IRL A2
35 Burret F A4
40 Burriana E B2
12 Burry Port GB B3
71 Burs A A4
56 Burseryd S B2
67 Bürstadt D B4
10 Burton GB A3
11 Burton Agnes GB A5
13 Burton Bradstock GB C5
14 Burton Latimer GB B2
11 Burton upon Trent GB C4
2 Burtonport IRL B3
38 Burujón E C2
112 Burunköy TR B1
98 Bürüs H C2
15 Burwash GB D3
7 Burwick GB B6
10 Bury GB B3
14 Bury St. Edmunds GB B3
90 Burzenin PL B2
103 Búrziya BG C4
87 Busachi I B1
74 Busalla I B3
75 Busana I B5
74 Busano I A2
74 Busca I B2
60 Busch D C2
98 Buševec CRO C1
104 Bushat AL C1
15 Bushey GB C2
3 Bushmills GB A5
97 Bušince SQ C5
53 Buskhyttan S D2
91 Busko Zdrój PL C4
40 Busot E C2
100 Busovača BO B2
44 Busquistar E C3
66 Bussang F D2
75 Busseto I B5
23 Bussière-Poitevine F B5
25 Bussières F C4
71 Bussolengo I C5
74 Bussoleno I A2
17 Bussum NL A5
71 Busto Arsizio I C3
59 Büsum D A5
103 Butan BG C4
84 Butera I B3
17 Butgenbach B C6
89 Butryny PL B6
71 Bütschwil CH A4
68 Buttenwiesen D C1
10 Buttermere GB A2
4 Buttevant IRL B3
63 Buttstädt D B6
62 Butzbach D C3
59 Bützfleth D B6
60 Bützow D B2
24 Buxières F B2
59 Buxtehude D B6
11 Buxton GB B4
25 Buxy F B4
106 Buynovtsi BG A3
107 Büyük Doğanca TR B4
107 Büyük Karistiran TR B5
107 Büyük Manika TR B5
23 Buzancais F B6
21 Buzancy F B5
94 Buzău RO D7
73 Buzet CRO C3
98 Buzsák H B2
26 Buzy F C3
13 Bwlch GB B4
52 By S B2
106 Byal Izvor BG B3
95 Byala BG E6
107 Byala, *Sliven* BG A4
106 Byala Reka BG A3
103 Byala Slatina BG C4
106 Byalo Pole BG A3
93 Byaroza BL D9
91 Bychawa PL B6
90 Byczyna PL B2
88 Bydgoszcz PL B3
14 Byfield GB B1
46 Bygdin N F4
49 Bygland N C4
49 Byglandsfjord N C4
48 Bykle N B4
10 Bylchau GB B2
55 Bylderup DK D2
97 Bylnice CZ B4
54 Byrum DK A3
65 Byšice Liblice CZ C4
47 Byske S D10
96 Býškovice CZ B3
88 Byslaw PL B3
96 Bystré CZ B2
97 Bystrice, *Stredočeský* CZ B4
69 Bystřice, *Stredočeský* CZ B5
96 Bystřice n Pernstejnem CZ B2
96 Bystřice p. Hostýnem CZ B3
65 Bystrzyca Klodzka PL C6
97 Bytča SQ B4
90 Bytom PL C2
65 Bytom Odrz PL B5
88 Byton PL C2
88 Bytów PL A3
92 Byxelkrok, *Öland* S B5
96 Bzenec CZ C3
96 Bzince SQ C3

C

41 C'an Pastilla, *Mallorca* E
41 C'an Picafort, *Mallorca* E
76 Ca'Pisani I B2
36 Cabacos P B2
26 Cabanac-et-Villagrains F B3
32 Cabañaquinta E A1
30 Cabañas E A2
42 Cabanas P B2
39 Cabañas de Yepes E C3
37 Cabañas del Castillo E B5
35 Cabanellas E A5
40 Cabanes E A3
33 Cabanillas E B5
73 Cabar CRO C4
29 Cabasse F C5
31 Cabeceiras de Basto P C2
36 Cabeço de Vide P B3
74 Cabella Ligure I B4
37 Cabeza del Buey E C5
43 Cabeza la Vaca E A3
39 Cabezamesada E C3
38 Cabezarados E D2
44 Cabezarrubias del Puerto E A2
38 Cabezas del Villar E B1
42 Cabezas Rubias E B2
32 Cabezón E C2
32 Cabezón de la Sal E A2
32 Cabezón de Liébana E A2
32 Cabezuela E C3
37 Cabezuela del Valle E A5
39 Cabolafuenta E A4
19 Cabourg F A5
44 Cabra E B2
31 Cabra P D3
44 Cabra del Sto. Cristo E B3
7 Cabrach GB C5
32 Cabrales (Carreña) E A2
87 Cábras I C1
31 Cabreiro P C2
30 Cabreiros E A3
39 Cabrejas E B4
36 Cabrela P C2
28 Cabrières F C2
30 Cacabelos E B4
101 Čačak YU C5
84 Cáccamo I B2
83 Caccuri I B3
42 Cacela P B2
37 Cáceres E B4
30 Cachafeiro E B2
42 Cachopo P B2
96 Cachtice SQ C3
44 Cacin E B3
98 Čačinci CRO C2
102 Cacova RO A2
36 Cadafais P C1
27 Cadalen F C6
37 Cadalso E A4
5 Cadamstown IRL A4
35 Cadaqués E A6
36 Cadaval P B1
30 Cadavedo E A4
100 Čadavica BO B1
98 Cadavica CRO C2
97 Čadca SQ B4
34 Cadéac F A3
75 Cadelbosco di Sopra I B5
71 Cadenazzo CH B3
59 Cadenberge D B6
29 Cadenet F C4
22 Cadeuil F C4
26 Cadillac F B3
43 Cádiz E C3
13 Cadnam GB C6
27 Cadouin F B4
34 Cadrete E B2
19 Caen F A5
11 Caenby Corner GB B5
10 Caergwrle GB B2
10 Caernarfon GB B1
13 Caerphilly GB B4
10 Caersws GB C2
36 Cafede P B3
82 Caggiano I A2
76 Cagli I C2
87 Cágliari I C2
80 Cagnano Varano I C2
5 Caher IRL B4
4 Cahercornish IRL B3
4 Cahermore IRL C1
4 Cahersiveen IRL C1
27 Cahors F B5
79 Caianello I B5
79 Caiazzo I B5
8 Cairnoch GB B3
8 Cairnryan GB D2
74 Cáiro Montenotte I B3
14 Caister-on-Sea GB B4
11 Caistor GB B5
79 Caivano I C5
35 Caixans E A4
27 Cajarc F B5
101 Cajetina YU C4
97 Čajkov SQ C4
101 Čajniče BO C4
97 Čaka SQ C4
97 Čakajovce SQ C4
107 Çakilli TR B5
98 Čakovec CRO B1
64 Čakovice CZ C4
108 Cakran AL A1
43 Cala E B3
41 Cala d'Or, *Mallorca* E
41 Cala Foreat, *Menorca* E
87 Cala Gonone I B2
41 Cala Llonga, *Ibiza* E
41 Cala Millor, *Mallorca* E
41 Cala Ratjada, *Mallorca* E
80 Calabritto I D2
34 Calaceite E B3
86 Calacuccia F B2
35 Calaf E B4
103 Calafat RO C3
35 Calafell E B4
44 Calahonda E C3
33 Calahorra E B5
16 Calais F C1
72 Calalzo I B2
34 Calamocha E C1
37 Calamonte E C4
43 Calañas E B3
34 Calanda E C2
87 Calangiánus I B2
95 Calarasi RO D7
41 Calas de Mallorca, *Mallorca* E
85 Calascibetta I B3
87 Calasetta I C1
45 Calasparra E A5
84 Calatafimi I B1
33 Calatayud E C5
33 Calatorao E C5
64 Calau D B3
63 Calbe D B6
33 Calcena E C5
76 Calcinelli I C2
71 Calco I C4
103 Căldăraru RO B5
71 Caldaro (Kaltern) I B6
76 Caldarola I C3
36 Caldas da Rainha P B1
34 Caldas de Bohi E A3
35 Caldas de Malavella E B5
35 Caldas de Montbúy E B5
30 Caldas de Reyes E B2
31 Caldas de San Jorge P D2
31 Caldas de Vizela P C2
38 Caldaso de los Vidrios E B2
9 Calder GB C4
10 Calder Bridge GB A2
35 Calders E B4
75 Caldirola I B4
3 Caledon GB B5
35 Calella, *Barcelona* E B5
35 Calella, *Gerona* E B6
86 Calenzana F B1
43 Calera de León E A3
38 Calera y Chozas E C2
33 Caleruega E C3
38 Caleruela E C1
75 Calestano I B5
8 Calgary GB B1
103 Călimăneşti RO A5
83 Calimera I A5
103 Călineşti RO B6
80 Calitri I D2
74 Calizzano I B3
18 Callac F B2
5 Callan IRL B4
8 Callander GB B3
29 Callas F C5
74 Calliano, *Piemonte* I A3
71 Calliano, *Trentino Alto Adige* I C6
12 Callington GB C3
40 Callosa de Ensarriá E C2
45 Callosa de Segura E A6
2 Callow IRL C2
35 Callús E B4
101 Čalma YU A4
67 Calmbach D C4
13 Calne GB B6
71 Calolziocorte I C4
35 Calonge E B6
96 Čalovec SQ D3
96 Čalovo SQ D3
40 Calpe E C3
13 Calshot GB C6
84 Caltabellotta I B2
85 Caltagirone I B3
84 Caltanissetta I B3
84 Caltavuturo I B2
33 Caltojar E C4
74 Caluso I A2
31 Calvario E C2
82 Calvello I A2
86 Calvi F B1
41 Calviá, *Mallorca* E
28 Calvisson F C3
63 Calvörde D A6
67 Calw D C4
44 Calzada de Calatrava E A3
38 Calzada de Valdunciel E A1
37 Calzadilla de los Barros E C4
75 Camaiore I C5
76 Camaldoli I C1
34 Camarasa E B3
38 Camarena E B2
28 Camarès F C1
18 Camaret F B1
29 Camaret-sur-Aigues F B3
32 Camargo E A3
40 Camarillas E A2
30 Camariñas E A1
39 Camarma E B3
31 Camarzana de Tera E B4
43 Camas E B3
84 Camastra I B2
6 Camb, *Shetland Is.* GB
30 Cambados E B2
31 Cambarinho P D2
15 Camberley GB C2
44 Cambil E B3
9 Cambo GB C6
26 Cambo-les-Bains F C2
12 Camborne GB C2
16 Cambrai F C3
30 Cambre E A2
14 Cambridge GB B3
35 Cambrils E B4
60 Cambs D B2
63 Camburg D B6
3 Camdonagh IRL A4
32 Cameleño E A2
12 Camelford GB C3
30 Camelle E A1
76 Camerano I C3
76 Camerino I C3
82 Camerota I A2
83 Cami Salentina I A5
83 Camigliatello Silano I B3
31 Caminha P C2
37 Caminomorisco E A4
39 Caminreal E B5
72 Camisano Vicentino I C1
107 Camlica TR C4
9 Cammachmore GB A5
84 Cammarata I B2
74 Camogli I B4
5 Camolin IRL B5
18 Camors F C3
80 Campagna I D2
78 Campagnano di Roma I A3
78 Campagnático I A2
27 Campan F C4
83 Campana I B3
37 Campanario E C5
44 Campanillas E C2
43 Campano E C3
32 Campaspero E C2
7 Campbelltown GB C4
8 Campbeltown GB C2
40 Campello E C2
36 Campelos P B1
75 Campi Bisénzio I C6
45 Campico López E B5
75 Campíglia Marittima I C5
38 Campillo E B1
39 Campillo de Altobuey E C5
39 Campillo de Aragón E A5
44 Campillo de Arenas E B3
37 Campillo de Llerena E C5
44 Campillos E B2
79 Campli I A4
34 Campo E A3
31 Campo P C2
31 Campo de Bacerros E B3
32 Campo de Caso E A1
39 Campo de Criptana E C3
79 Campo di Giove I A5
74 Campo Ligure I B3
37 Campo Maior P B3
74 Campo Molino I B2
39 Campo Real E B3
72 Campo Tures (Taufers) I B1
79 Campobasso I B5
84 Campobello di Licata I B2
84 Campobello di Mazara I B1
72 Campodársego I C1
71 Campodolcino I B4
84 Campofelice di Roccella I B2
84 Campofiorito I B2
72 Campofórmide I B3
84 Campofranco I B2
43 Campofrio E B3
75 Campogalliano I B5
72 Campolongo I B2
32 Campomanes E A1
80 Campomarino I C2
84 Camporeale I B2
76 Camporeggiano I C2
34 Camporrells E B3
40 Camporrobles E B1
31 Campos P C3
41 Campos del Puerto, *Mallorca* E
31 Camposa P C2
72 Camposampiero I C1
75 Camposanto I B6
34 Camposines E B3

11 Easington GB B6
9 Easington Colliery GB D6
11 Easingwold GB A4
2 Easky IRL B3
15 East Adderbury GB B1
13 East Brent GB B5
14 East Dereham GB B3
15 East Grinstead GB C2
14 East Harling GB B3
15 East Hoathly GB D3
15 East Ilsley GB C1
8 East Kilbride GB C3
9 East Linton GB C5
11 East Markham GB B5
11 East Retford GB B5
14 East Rudham GB B3
9 East Wemyss GB B4
15 Eastbourne GB D3
7 Easter Fearn GB C4
6 Easter Quarff, *Shetland Is.* GB
15 Eastleigh GB D1
13 Easton GB C5
15 Eastry GB C4
11 Eastwood GB B4
14 Eaton Socon GB B2
34 Eaux-Bonnes F A2
26 Eauze F C4
55 Ebberup DK C2
72 Ebbs A A2
13 Ebbw Vale GB B4
63 Ebeleben D B5
55 Ebeltoft DK B3
72 Eben im Pongau A A3
69 Ebensee A D4
68 Ebensfeld D A1
67 Eberbach D B4
96 Ebergassing A C2
63 Ebergötzen D B5
68 Ebermannstadt D B2
68 Ebern D A1
73 Eberndorf A B4
64 Ebersbach D B4
68 Ebersberg D C2
69 Eberschwang A C4
63 Ebersdorf, *Bayern* D C6
59 Ebersdorf, *Niedersachsen* D B6
73 Eberstein A B4
66 Ebersviller F B2
61 Eberswalde D C4
108 Ebesós GR B3
67 Ebingen D C5
71 Ebnat-Kappel CH A4
80 Éboli I D2
68 Ebrach D B1
96 Ebreichsdorf A D2
24 Ebreuil F B3
60 Ebstorf D B1
17 Ecaussinnes-d'Enghien B C4
9 Ecclefechan GB C4
10 Eccleshall GB C3
95 Eceabat TR F7
70 Echallens CH B1
33 Echarri-Aranaz E B4
33 Echauri E B5
25 Échenoz-la-Méline F A6
23 Echiré F B4
29 Echirolles F A4
27 Echourgnac F A4
9 Echt GB A5
17 Echt NL B5
63 Echte D B5
66 Echternach L B2
43 Ecija E B4
101 Ećka YU A5
63 Eckartsberga D B6
63 Eckelshausen D C3
62 Eckenhagen D C2
59 Eckernförde D A6
11 Eckington GB B4
21 Éclaron F C5
20 Ecommoy F D1
19 Ecouché F B5
20 Ecouen F B3
20 Ecouis F B2
98 Ecs H A2
99 Ecséd H A4
23 Ecuellé F A6
51 Ed S D2
50 Eda S C3
50 Eda glasbruk S C3
58 Edam NL C2
52 Edane S C3
64 Edderitz D B1
9 Eddleston GB C4
17 Ede NL A5
50 Edebäck S B4
52 Edebo S B4
47 Edefors Harads S C10
63 Edemissen D A5
3 Eden GB B6
15 Edenbridge GB C3
5 Edenderry IRL A4
67 Edenkoben D B4
3 Ederny GB B4
67 Edesheim D B4
59 Edewecht D B4
17 Edegem B B4
109 Édhessa GR A4
9 Edinburgh GB C4
107 Edirne TR B4
48 Edland N B4
73 Edlitz A A6
9 Edmondbyers GB D6
71 Édolo I B5
95 Edremit TR G7
52 Edsbro S C4
56 Edsbruk S A5
52 Edsbyn S A1
51 Edsgatan S C4
51 Edsleskog S C3
51 Edsvalla S C4
9 Edzell GB B5
17 Eefde NL A6
16 Eeklo B B3
17 Eerbeek NL A6
16 Eernegem B B3
17 Eersel NL B5
58 Eexta NL B3
69 Eferding A C5
68 Effeltrich D B2
24 Effiat F B3
105 Efkarpia GR C4
109 Efxinoúpolis GR B4
63 Egeln D B6
97 Eger H D6
97 Egerbakta H D6
55 Egernsund DK D2
48 Egersund N C3
97 Egerszólát H D6
71 Egg A A4
68 Egg D C1
49 Eggedal N A6
96 Eggenburg A C1
68 Eggenfelden D C3
61 Eggesin D B5
69 Egglesberg A C4
69 Egglfing D C4
15 Egham GB C2
17 Eghezée B C4
89 Egiertowo PL A4
24 Egletons F C2
68 Egling, *Bayern* D C1
68 Egling, *Bayern* D D2
3 Eglinton GB A4
70 Eglisau CH A3
28 Égliseneuve-d'Entraigues F A1
71 Eglofs D A4
12 Eglwyswrw GB A3
58 Egmond aan Zee NL C1
71 Egna (Neumarkt) I B6
111 Egósthena GR A4
10 Egremont GB A2
55 Egtved DK C2
29 Eguilles F C4
21 Eguilly-sous-Bois F C5
24 Eguzon F B1
98 Egyházasrádóc H A1
68 Ehekirchen D C2
67 Ehingen D C5
63 Ehmen D A5
60 Ehra-Lessien D C1
66 Ehrang D B2
64 Ehrenfriedersdorf D C2
64 Ehrenhain D C2
62 Ehringshausen D C3
71 Ehrwald A A5
33 Eibar E A4
65 Eibau D C4
67 Eibelstadt D B6
64 Eibenstock D C2
62 Eibergen NL A1
73 Eibiswald A B5
63 Eichenbarleben D A6
69 Eichendorf D C3
68 Eichstätt D C2
62 Eickelborn D B3
46 Eidfjord N F3
51 Eidsberg N C2
49 Eidsfoss N B7
50 Eidskog N B3
48 Eidsvåg N A2
50 Eidsvoll N B2
46 Eikefjord N F2
48 Eikelandsosen N A2
48 Eiken N C4
64 Eilenburg D B2
17 Eilendorf D C6
63 Eilsleben D A6
50 Eina N B1
63 Einbeck D B4
17 Eindhoven NL B5
16 Eine B C3
59 Einfeld D A6
70 Einsiedeln CH A3
67 Einsingen D C5
66 Einville F C2
63 Eisenach D C5
67 Eisenberg, *Rheinland-Pfalz* D B4
64 Eisenberg, *Thüringen* D C1
73 Eisenerz A A4
64 Eisenhüttenstadt D A4
73 Eisenkappel A B4
96 Eisenstadt A D2
72 Eisentratten A B3
62 Eiserfeld D C2
63 Eisfeld D C5
63 Eisleben D B6
67 Eistingen D C5
63 Eiterfeld D C4
62 Eitorf D C2
41 Eivissa, *Ibiza* E
31 Eixo P D2
55 Ejby DK C2
34 Ejea de' los Caballeros E A1
55 Ejstrup DK C2
34 Ejulve E C2
111 Ekáli GR A4
16 Eke B C3
51 Ekeby, *Östergötland* S D6
52 Ekeby, *Uppsala* S B4
47 Ekenäs SF G11
56 Ekenässjön S B4
17 Ekeren B B4
57 Eket S C2
106 Ekhinos GR B2
17 Eksel B B5
50 Ekshärad S B4
56 Eksjö S B3
107 Ekzarkh Antimovo BG A4
43 El Aguila E B4
38 El Alamo, *Madrid* E B3
43 El Alamo, *Sevilla* E B3
42 El Almendro E B2
33 El Almiñe E B3
45 El Alquián E C4
43 El Arahal E B4
38 El Arenal, *Avila* E B1
41 El Arenal, *Mallorca* E
45 El Arguellite E A4
32 El Astillero E A3
45 El Ballestero E A4
37 El Barco de Avila E A5
39 El Berrueco E B3
37 El Bodón E A4
30 El Bollo E B3
39 El Bonillo E D4
43 El Bosque E C4
38 El Bullaque E C2
34 El Burgo de Ebro E B2
33 El Burgo de Osma E C3
32 El Burgo Ranero E B1
33 El Buste E C5
31 El Cabaco E D4
45 El Cabo de Gata E C4
33 El Callejo E A3
43 El Campillo E B3
38 El Campillo de la Jara E C1
37 El Campo E B5
39 El Cañavete E C4
45 El Cantal E B5
44 El Carpio E B2
38 El Carpio de Tajo E C2
38 El Casar de Escalona E B2
33 El Castaño E A3
43 El Castillo de las Guardas E B3
44 El Centenillo E A3
37 El Cerro E A5
43 El Cerro de Andévalo E B3
43 El Comenar E C4
43 El Coronil E B4
32 El Cubo de Tierra del Vino E C1
43 El Cuervo E C3
45 El Ejido E C4
45 El Eljido E C4
45 El Entredicho E A4
38 El Escorial E B2
38 El Espinar E B2
30 El Ferrol E A2
34 El Frago E A2
30 El Franco E A4
33 El Frasno E C5
43 El Garrobo E B3
43 El Gastor E C4
38 El Gordo E C1
34 El Grado E A3
42 El Granado E B2
40 El Grao E B3
44 El Higuera E B2
38 El Hoya de Pinares E B2
44 El Hoyo E A3
43 El Madroño E B3
31 El Maillo E D4
38 El Mirón E B1
39 El Molar E B3
38 El Molinillo E C2
33 El Muyo E C3
33 El Olmo E C3
38 El Pardo E B3
37 El Payo E A4
39 El Pedernoso E C4
43 El Pedroso E B4
39 El Peral E C5
40 El Perelló E B2
39 El Picazo E C4
32 El Piñero E C1
40 El Pobo E A2
39 El Pobo de Dueñas E B5
39 El Pozo de Guadalajara E B3
39 El Provencio E C4
38 El Puente del Arzobispo E C1
43 El Puerto de Santa Maria E C3
33 El Quintanar E C4
43 El Real de la Jara E B3
38 El Real de S. Vincente E B2
43 El Rinconcillo E C4
38 El Robledo E C2
43 El Rocio E B3
42 El Rompido E B2
43 El Ronquillo E B3
33 El Royo E C4
43 El Rubio E B5
40 El Saler E B2
43 El Saucejo E B4
35 El Serratt AND A4
34 El Temple E B2
38 El Tiemblo E B2
39 El Toboso E C4
44 El Tocón E B3
34 El Tormillo E B2
37 El Torno E A5
32 El Valle de las Casas E B1
39 El Vellón E B3
35 El Vendrell E B4
44 El Viso E A2
43 El Viso del Alcor E B4
44 El Viso del Marqués E A3
109 Elafos GR A4
112 Elaia, *Kriti* GR
111 Elaia, *Lakonía* GR C3
106 Elaiokhóri GR C2
110 Elaión GR A3
109 Elassón GR B4
108 Eláti GR B3
109 Elátia GR C4
108 Elatochorion GR B2
110 Elatou GR A2
104 Elbasan AL C2
20 Elbeuf F B1
63 Elbingerode D B5
89 Elblag PL A5
17 Elburg NL A5
40 Elche E C2
45 Elche de la Sierra E A4
67 Elchingen D C6
40 Elda E C2
63 Eldagsen D A4
60 Eldena D B2
56 Eldsberga S C1
111 Elefsis GR A4
109 Elefthero GR B4
99 Elemir CRO C5
106 Elena BG A3
110 Eleón, *Akhaia* GR A3
110 Eleón, *Ilía* GR B2
111 Eleón, *Voiotía* GR A4
111 Elevtherai GR B4
106 Elevtheroupolis GR C2
63 Elgershausen D B4
7 Elgin GB C5
33 Elgóibar E A4
8 Elgol GB A1
110 Eliá, *Fokís* GR A3
109 Eliá, *Khalkidhikí* GR A5
110 Eliá, *Messinía* GR B2
9 Elie GB B5
111 Elika GR C3
105 Elin Pelin BG B5
110 Eliniká, *Aitolía kai Acarnanía* GR A2
109 Eliniká, *Évia* GR B5
111 Elinikó GR C3
103 Eliseyna BG C4
9 Elishaw GB C5
33 Elizondo E A5
107 Elkhovo BG A4
67 Ellenberg D B6
11 Eller Beck Bridge GB A5
10 Ellesmere GB B3
10 Ellesmere Port GB B3
16 Ellezelles B C3
68 Ellingen D B1
9 Ellington GB C6
111 Ellinikó GR B4
72 Ellmau A A2
7 Ellon GB C6
51 Ellös S D2
11 Elloughton GB B5
63 Ellrich D B5
71 Elm CH B4
59 Elm D B6
59 Elmshorn D B6
67 Elmstein D B3
35 Elne F A5
33 Elorrio E A4
112 Elos, *Kriti* GR
99 Előszállás H B3
112 Elounta, *Kriti* GR
66 Eloyes F C2
6 Elphin GB B3
67 Elsdorf D C6
67 Elsenfeld D B5
59 Elsfleth D B5
106 Elshitsa BG A2
62 Elspe D B3
17 Elspeet NL A5
17 Elst NL B5
64 Elster D B2
64 Elsterberg D C2
64 Elsterwerda D B3
64 Elstra D B4
68 Eltmann D B1
67 Eltville D A4
37 Elvas P C3
14 Elveden GB B3
16 Elven F C3
16 Elverdinge B C2
50 Elverum N B2
67 Elwangen D C6
40 Elx E C2
63 Elxleben D B5
14 Ely GB B3
62 Elz D C3
67 Elzach D C4
63 Elze D A4
50 Emådelen S A5
9 Embleton GB C6
112 Émbona GR B2
112 Embórion GR D2
112 Emboriós GR C1
29 Embrun F B5
34 Embún E A2
58 Emden D B4
112 Emecik TR B2
58 Emlichheim D C3
4 Emly IRL B3
56 Emmaboda S C4
57 Emmaljunga S C2
58 Emmeloord NL C2
70 Emmen CH A3
58 Emmen NL C3
67 Emmendinger D C3
58 Emmer-Compascuum NL C4
58 Emmer-Erfscheidenveen NL C4
17 Emmerich D B6
63 Emmern D A4
107 Emona BG A5
75 Empoli I C5
62 Emsbüren D A2
62 Emsdetten D A2
56 Emsfors S B5
68 Emskirchen D B1
59 Emstek D C5
15 Emsworth GB D2
3 Emyvale IRL B5
46 Enafors S E6
35 Encamp AND A4
36 Encarnação P C1
38 Encinas de Abajo E B1
32 Encinas de Esgueva E C2
44 Encinas Reales E B2
43 Encinasola E A3
33 Encio E B3
33 Enciso E B4
66 Endingen D C3
68 Endorf D D3
38 Endrinal E B1
94 Endrőd H C4
99 Endrőd H B5
50 Enebakk N C2
56 Eneryda S C3
98 Enese H A2
107 Enez TR C4
15 Enfield GB C2
72 Eng A A1
112 Engarés GR D1
70 Engelberg CH B3
69 Engelhartszell A C4
62 Engelskirchen D C2
67 Engen D D4
62 Enger D A3
46 Engerdal N F5
55 Engesvang DK B2
17 Enghien B C4
69 Englmar D B3
108 Englouvi GR C2
62 Engter D A3
40 Enguera E C2
39 Enguidanos E C5
67 Eningen D C5
67 Enkenbach D B3
58 Enkhuizen NL C2
53 Enköping S C3
49 Enkstrand N B6
85 Enna I B3
62 Ennepetal D B2
24 Ennezat F C3
62 Ennigerloh D B3
62 Ennigloh D A3
51 Enningdal N D2
4 Ennis IRL B3
5 Enniscorthy IRL B5
4 Enniskean IRL C3
5 Enniskerry IRL A5
3 Enniskillen GB B4
4 Ennistimon IRL B2
69 Enns A C5
58 Ens NL C2
62 Enschede NL A1
68 Ensdorf D B2
66 Ensisheim F D3
17 Ensival B C5
53 Enstaberga S D2
15 Enstone GB C1
70 Entlebuch CH B3
74 Entrácque I B2
42 Entradas P B1
24 Entrains-sur-Nohain F A3
33 Entrambasaguas E A3
33 Entrambasmestas E A3
28 Entraygues-sur-Truyère F B1
31 Entre-os-Rios P C2
25 Entremont-le-Vieux F C5
29 Entrevaux F C5
37 Entrin Bajo E C4
36 Entroncamento P B2
66 Entzheim F C3
20 Envermeu F B2
55 Enviken S B1
98 Enying H B3
96 Enzesfeld A D2
72 Enzingerboden A C2
67 Enzklösterle D C4
67 Enzweihagen D C5
21 Épagny F B4
23 Epannes F B4
109 Epanomi GR A4
62 Epe D A2
17 Epe NL A5
21 Epehy F A4
21 Épernay F B4
20 Epernon F C2
67 Epfendorf D C4
66 Epfig F C3
25 Epierre F C6
34 Épila E B1
25 Epinac-les-Mines F B4
66 Épinal F C2
82 Episcopia I A3
108 Episkopi, *Evritania* GR C3
112 Episkopi, *Iráklion, Kriti* GR
109 Episkopi, *Pélla* GR A4
112 Episkopi, *Réthimnon, Kriti* GR
110 Epitálion GR B2
25 Epoisses F A4
17 Eppegem B C4
66 Eppelborn D B3
66 Eppenbrunn D B3
64 Eppendorf D C3
15 Epping GB C3
67 Eppingen D B4
15 Epsom GB C2
108 Eptakhórion GR A3
109 Eptálofos GR C4
11 Epworth GB B5
72 Eraclea I C2
72 Eraclea Mare I C2
110 Eratini GR A3
108 Eratira GR A3
71 Erba I C4
67 Erbach, *Baden-Württemberg* D C5
67 Erbach, *Hessen* D B4
86 Erbalunga F B2
68 Erbendorf D B3
83 Érchie I A4
99 Ercsi H A3
99 Érd H A3
101 Erdevik YU A4
68 Erding D C2
99 Erdőtelek H A5
99 Erdut CRO C4
111 Erétria, *Évia* GR A4
109 Erétria, *Magnisía* GR B4
59 Erfde D A6
48 Erfjord N B3
62 Erftstadt D C1
63 Erfurt D C5
68 Ergolding D C3
68 Ergoldsbach D C3
58 Erica NL C3
84 Érice I A1
36 Ericeira P C1
56 Eriksmåla S C4
51 Erikstad S D3
108 Erind AL A2
57 Eringsboda S C4
70 Eriswil CH A2
111 Erithrai GR A4
17 Erkelenz D B6
61 Erkner D C4
62 Erkrath D B1
34 Erla E A2
96 Erlach A D2
68 Erlangen D B2
74 Erli I B3
72 Erlsbach A B2
109 Ermakiá GR A3
17 Ermelo NL A5
20 Ermenonville F B3
31 Ermezinde P C2
42 Ermidas P B1
111 Ermióni GR B4
112 Ermoúpolis GR E1
63 Ermsleben D B6
62 Erndtebrück D C3
19 Ernée F B5
99 Ernestinovo CRO C3
96 Ernstbrunn A C2
67 Erolzheim D C6
47 Erontekiö SF B11
17 Erquelinnes B C4
18 Erquy F B3
36 Erra P C2
33 Errazu E A5
55 Errindlev DK D4
33 Erro E B5
7 Errogie GB C4
9 Errol GB B4
86 Ersa F B2
99 Érsekcsanád H B3
108 Ersekë AL A2
97 Érsekvadkert H D5
66 Erstein F C3
70 Erstfeld CH B3
54 Ertebølle DK B2
67 Ertingen D C5
36 Ervedal, *Coimbra* P A2
36 Ervedal, *Portalegre* P B3
77 Ervenik CRO B5
42 Ervidel P B1
21 Ervy F C4
62 Erwitte D B3
63 Erxleben D A6
41 Es Caná, *Ibiza* E
41 Es Pujols, *Formentera* E
55 Esbjerg DK C1
21 Esbly F C3
43 Escacena del Campo E B3
30 Escairon E B3
32 Escalada E B3
33 Escalante E A3
87 Escalaplano I C2
38 Escalona E B2
38 Escalona del Prado E A2
38 Escalonilla E C2
36 Escalos de Baixo P B3
36 Escalos de Cima P B3
39 Escamilla E B4
44 Escañuela E B2
34 Escároz E A1
34 Escatrón E B2
66 Esch-sur-Alzette L B1
71 Eschach D A4
67 Eschau D B5
60 Eschede D C1
68 Eschenau D B2
68 Eschenbach D B2
71 Eschenz CH A3
63 Escherhausen D B4
63 Eschwege D B5
17 Eschweiler D C6
33 Escobasa de Almazán E C4
16 Escoeuilles F C1
45 Escombreras E B6
26 Escos F C4
26 Escource F B2
29 Escragnolles F C5
37 Escurial E B5
31 Escurial de la Sierra E D5
59 Esens D B4
30 Esgos E B3
15 Esher GB C2
9 Eskaalemuir GB C4
51 Eskilsäter S D4
55 Eskilstrup DK D4
53 Eskilstuna S C2
48 Eslarn D B3
33 Eslava E B5
45 Eslida E B2
62 Eslohe D B3
57 Eslöv S D2
21 Esnes F A4
50 Espa N B2
28 Espalion F B1
28 Espaly-St.-Marcel F A2
37 Esparragalejo E C4
38 Esparragosa del Caudillo E D1
37 Esparragossa de la Serena E C5
35 Esparraguera E C4
29 Esparron F C4
48 Espedal N C3
33 Espejo, *Alava* E B3
44 Espejo, *Córdoba* E B2
48 Espeland N A2
26 Espelette F C2
62 Espelkamp D A3
29 Espeluche F B3
44 Espeluy E A3
43 Espera E C4
37 Esperança P B3
35 Espéraza F A5
79 Espéria I B4
43 Espiel E A4
32 Espinama E A2
30 Espiñaredo E A3
35 Espinelvas E B5
36 Espinhal P A2
31 Espinho P C2
32 Espinilla E A2
32 Espinosa de Cerrato E C3
33 Espinosa de los Monteros E A3
42 Espirito Santo P B2
35 Espluga de Francolí E B4
34 Esplús E B3
35 Espolla E A5
41 Esporlas, *Mallorca* E
31 Esposende P C2
35 Espot E A4
35 Espunyola E A4
34 Esquedas E A2
38 Esquivias E B3
17 Essen B B4
59 Essen, *Niedersachsen* D C4
62 Essen, *Nordrhein-Westfalen* D B2
68 Essenbach D C3
20 Essertaux F B3
67 Essingen D C6
67 Esslingen D C5
21 Essoyes F C5
41 Establiments, *Mallorca* E
30 Estacas E B2
34 Estadilla E A3
35 Estagel F A5
16 Estaires F C2
26 Estang F C3
35 Estany E B5
31 Estarreja P D2
35 Estartit E A6
70 Estavayer-le-Lac CH B1
76 Este I A1
30 Esteiro E A2
31 Estela P C2
33 Estella E B4
41 Estellenchs, *Mallorca* E
44 Estepa E B2
32 Estépar E B3
43 Estepona E C4
21 Esternay F C4
35 Esterri de Aneu E A4
59 Esterwegen D C4
21 Estissac F C4
31 Estivadas E B3
24 Estivareilles F B2
40 Estivella E B2
42 Estói P B2
34 Estopiñán E B3
36 Estoril P C1
29 Estoublon F C5
16 Estrée-Blanche F C2
20 Estrées-St. Denis F B3
42 Estrela P A2
39 Estremera E B3
36 Estremoz P C3
52 Estuna S C4
23 Esyres F A5
97 Esztergom H D4
18 Etables-sur-Mer F B3
66 Étain F B1
25 Étalans F A6
66 Etalle B B1
20 Étampes F C3
25 Etang-sur-Arroux F B4
16 Étaples F C1
26 Étauliers F A3
66 Ethe B B1
48 Etne N B2
21 Etoges F C4
21 Etréaupont F B4
20 Étréchy F C3
20 Étrépagny F B2
20 Étretat F B1
21 Étrœungt F A4
106 Etropole BG A2
70 Étroubles I C2
71 Ettal D A6
66 Ettelbrück L B2
17 Etten NL B4
67 Ettenheim D C3
14 Ettington GB B1
67 Ettlingen D C4
68 Ettringen, *Bayern* D C1
62 Ettringen, *Rheinland-Pfalz* D C2
99 Etyek H A3
68 Etzenricht D B3
20 Eu F A2
63 Euerdorf D C5
33 Eulate E B4
17 Eupen B C6
17 Europoort NL B4
21 Eurville-sur-Marne F C6
62 Euskirchen D C1
60 Eutin D A1
21 Euvy F C5
10 Euxton GB B3
110 Eva GR B2
24 Evaux-les-Bains F B2
112 Évdhilos GR C1
50 Evenstad N A2
13 Evercreech GB B5
16 Evergem B B3
57 Everöd S D3
62 Eversberg D B3
62 Everswinkel D B2
50 Evertsberg S A4
13 Evesham GB A6
70 Évian F B1
110 Evinokhorion GR A2
86 Evisa F B1
49 Evje N C4
70 Evolène CH B2
36 Évora P C3
36 Evoramonte P C3
110 Evpálion GR A2
19 Evran F B4
19 Evrecy F A5
107 Evrencik TR B5
107 Evrenli TR B5
107 Evrensekiz TR B5
20 Évreux F B2
19 Évron F B5
105 Évropos GR D4
110 Evrostina GR A3
20 Évry F C3
105 Évzonoi GR C4
15 Ewell GB C2
62 Ewersbach D C3
15 Ewhurst GB C2
111 Examillia GR B3
105 Exaplátanon GR D4
108 Exarkhos, *Fthiótis* GR C4
108 Exarkhos, *Grevená* GR A3
27 Excideuil F A5
13 Exeter GB C4
20 Exmes F C1
13 Exminster GB C4
13 Exmouth GB C4
110 Exo Nimfio GR C3
106 Exokhi GR B1
62 Exter D A3
31 Extremo P C2
49 Eydehamn N C5
14 Eye, *Cambridgeshire* GB B2
14 Eye, *Suffolk* GB B4
9 Eyemouth GB C5
29 Eyguians F B4
29 Eyguières F C3
24 Eygurande F C2
34 Eylie F A3
27 Eymet F B4
24 Eymoutiers F C1
15 Eynsham GB C1
59 Eystrup D C6
30 Ezaro E B1
95 Ezine TR G7
31 Ezmoriz P D2

F

34 Fabara E B3
75 Fábbrico I B5
50 Fåberg, *Oppland* N A1
30 Fabero E B4
55 Fåborg DK C3
28 Fabrègues F C2
76 Fabriano I C2
82 Fabrizia I C3
31 Facha P C2
43 Facinas E C4
97 Fačkov SQ B4
26 Facture F B3
36 Fadagosa P B3
99 Fadd H B3
72 Faédis I B3
76 Faenza I B1
31 Fafe P C2
72 Fagagna I B3
94 Făgăraş RO D6
56 Fågelfors S B4
57 Fågelmara S C4
51 Fågelsta S D6
49 Fagerheim N A4
56 Fagerhult S B4
46 Fagernes, *Oppland* N F4
51 Fagersanna S D5
52 Fagersta S B1
56 Fåglavik S A2
82 Fagnano Castello I B3
70 Fahrwangen CH A3
70 Faido CH B3
21 Fains F C6
10 Fairbourne GB C1
13 Fairford GB B6
8 Fairlie GB C3
99 Fajsz H B3
14 Fakenham GB B3
107 Fakiya BG A5
55 Fakse DK C5
55 Fakse Ladeplads DK C5
109 Fálaina GR B4
19 Falaise F B5
72 Falcade I B1
2 Falcarragh IRL A3
33 Falces E B5
94 Fălciu RO C8
84 Falconara I B3
76 Falconara Marittima I C3
85 Falcone I A4
11 Faldingworth GB B5
53 Falerum S D2
42 Falésia P B1
112 Faliráki GR A2
56 Falkenberg S C1
68 Falkenberg, *Bayern* D B3
61 Falkenberg, *Brandenburg* D C4
64 Falkenberg, *Brandenburg* D B3
61 Falkensee D C4
68 Falkenstein, *Bayern* D B3
64 Falkenstein, *Sachsen* D C2
61 Falkenthal D C4
9 Falkirk GB C4
9 Falkland GB B4
51 Falköping S D4
72 Fall D A1
53 Falla S D1
63 Fallersleben D A5
59 Fallingbostel D C6
12 Falmouth GB C2
34 Falset E B3
57 Falsterbo S D1
94 Fălticeni RO C7
52 Falun S B1
48 Fana N A2
75 Fanano I B5
109 Fanárion, *Kardhítsa* GR B3
106 Fanárion, *Rodhópi* GR C3
110 Faneroméni GR C2
55 Fangel DK C3
27 Fanjeaux F C6
76 Fano I C3
53 Fanthyttan S C1
78 Fara in Sabina I A3
70 Fara Novarese I C3
32 Faramontanos de Tábara E C1
34 Farasdues E A1
56 Fårbo S B5
15 Fareham GB D1
35 Farga Moles E A4
57 Färgelanda S D2
21 Fargniers F B4
46 Färila S F7
13 Faringdon GB B6
52 Faringe S C4
75 Farini d'Olmo I B4
31 Fariza E C4
56 Färjestaden, *Öland* S C5
109 Farkadón GR B4
34 Farlete E B2
57 Färlöv S C3
99 Farmos H A4
52 Färna S C1
97 Farnă SQ C4
50 Färnäs S A5
15 Farnborough GB C2
78 Farnese I A2
15 Farnham GB C2
63 Farnroda D C5
63 Farnstädt D B6
42 Faro P B2
92 Fårösund S B6
7 Farr GB C4
72 Farra d'Alpago I B2
4 Farranfore IRL B2
109 Fársala GR B4
54 Farsø DK B2
56 Farstorp S B4
48 Farsund N C3
55 Farum DK C5
54 Fårup DK B2
81 Fasano I D4
60 Faßberg D C1
52 Fasterna S C4
34 Fatarella E B3
36 Fátima P B2
66 Faucogney F D2
29 Faucon-du-Caire F B5
27 Faugerolles F B4
9 Fauldhouse GB C4
61 Faulenrost D B3
66 Faulquemont F B2
16 Fauquembergues F C2
46 Fauske N C7
25 Fauverney F A5
20 Fauville-en-Caux F B1
84 Favaro I B2
25 Faverges F C6
66 Faverney F D2
15 Faversham GB C3
84 Favignana I B1
13 Fawley GB C6
20 Fay-aux-Loges F D3
29 Fayence F C5
66 Fayl-Billot F D1
34 Fayón E B3
7 Fearn GB C5
8 Fearnan GB B3
20 Fécamp F B1
3 Feeny GB B4
56 Fegen S B2
99 Fegyvernek H A5
61 Fehrbellin D C3
73 Fehring A B6
50 Feiring N B2
73 Feistritz i. Rosental A B4
99 Feketić CRO C4
41 Felanitx, *Mallorca* E
61 Felchow D B5
73 Feld a. See A B3
73 Feldbach A B5
61 Feldberg D B4
59 Felde D A6
97 Feldebrö H D6
71 Feldkirch A A4
68 Feldkirchen, *Bayern* D C2
68 Feldkirchen, *Bayern* D D2
69 Feldkirchen a.d. Donau A C5
73 Feldkirchen i. Kärnten A B4
31 Felgueiras P C2
108 Felio GR A3
82 Felitto I A2
45 Félix E C4
15 Felixstowe GB C4
74 Felizzano I B3
67 Fellbach D C5
24 Felletin F C2
53 Fellingsbro S C1
97 Felnémet H D6
98 Felpéc H A2
96 Fels a. Wagram A C1
98 Felsöbagod H B1
99 Felsögöd H A4
98 Felsönyék H B3
99 Felsöszentiván H B4
98 Felsöszentmárton H C2
9 Felton GB C6
72 Feltre I B1
14 Feltwell GB B3
3 Fenagh IRL B4
107 Fenerköy TR B6
74 Fenestrelle I A2
66 Fénétrange F C3
23 Feneu F A4
51 Fengersfors S D3
70 Fenis I C2
55 Fensmark DK C4
8 Fenwick GB C3
8 Feolin Ferry GB C1
5 Ferbane IRL A4
60 Ferchland D C3
98 Ferdinandovac CRO B2
61 Ferdinandshof D B4
21 Fère-Champenoise F C5
21 Fère-en-Tardenois F B4
79 Ferentillo I A3
79 Ferentino I B4
37 Feria E C4
98 Feričanci CRO C2
85 Ferla I B3
73 Ferlach A B4
72 Ferleiten A A2
31 Fermil P C2
76 Fermo I C3
31 Fermoselle E C4
4 Fermoy IRL B3
44 Fernán-Núnez E B2
45 Fernán Peréz E C4
38 Fernancabellero E C3
36 Fernão Ferro P C1
25 Fernay-Voltaire F B6
13 Ferndown GB C6
7 Ferness GB C5
6 Fernilea GB C2
5 Ferns IRL B5
70 Ferpécle CH B2
107 Ferrai GR C4
28 Ferrals F C1
83 Ferrandina I A3
76 Ferrara I B1
71 Ferrara di M. Baldo I C5
30 Ferreira E A3
42 Ferreira do Alentejo P A1
36 Ferreira do Zêzere P B2
31 Ferreras de Abajo E C4
31 Ferreras de Arriba E C4
41 Ferrerias, *Menorca* E
34 Ferreruela, *Teruel* E B1
31 Ferreruela, *Zamora* E C4
71 Ferret CH C2
70 Ferrette F A2
75 Ferriere I B4
17 Ferrière-la-Grande F C3
24 Ferrières, *Allier* F B3
21 Ferrières, *Loiret* F C3
20 Ferrières, *Oise* F B3
28 Ferrières-St.-Mary F A2
11 Ferryhill GB A4
98 Fertörakos H A1
98 Fertöszentmiklós H A1
58 Ferwerd NL B2
21 Festieux F B4
95 Feteşti RO D7
5 Fethard IRL B4
50 Fetsund N C2
9 Fettercairn GB B5
68 Feucht D B2
71 Feuchten A A5
68 Feuchtwangen D B1
62 Feudingen D C3
20 Feuquières F B2
25 Feurs F C4
49 Fevik N C5
10 Ffestiniog GB C2
79 Fiamignano I A4
74 Fiano I A2
84 Ficarazzi I A2
75 Ficarolo I B6
68 Fichtelberg D A2
67 Fichtenberg D C5
78 Ficulle I A3
75 Fidenza I B5
48 Fidjeland N C3
72 Fieberbrunn A A2
108 Fier AL A1
104 Fier-Shegan AL D1
72 Fiera di Primiero I B1
70 Fiesch CH B3
75 Fiésole I C6
76 Fiesso Umbertiano I B1
110 Figalia GR B2
86 Figari F C2
27 Figeac F B5
56 Figeholm S B5
48 Figgjo N C2
75 Figline Valdarno I C6
34 Figols E A3
36 Figueira da Foz P A2
31 Figueira de Gastelo Rodrigo P D4
42 Figueira dos Caveleiros P A1
36 Figueiredo P B3
31 Figueiredo de Alva P D3
36 Figueiró dos Vinhos P B2
35 Figueras E A5
40 Figueroles E A2
31 Figueruela de Arriba E C4

44 Gilena E B2
3 Gilford GB B5
51 Gillberga S C3
57 Gilleleje DK C1
70 Gilley, *Doubs* F A1
24 Gilley, *Saône-et-Loire* F B3
13 Gillingham, *Dorset* GB B5
15 Gillingham, *Kent* GB C3
9 Gillroanie GB D3
21 Gilocourt F B3
62 Gilserberg D C4
13 Gilwern GB B4
17 Gilze NL B4
62 Gimborn D B2
111 Gimnó GR B3
52 Gimo S B4
27 Gimont F C4
29 Ginasservis F C4
17 Gingelom B C5
103 Giṅgiova RO C4
61 Gingst D A4
83 Ginosa I A3
67 Ginsheim-Gustavsberg D B4
72 Ginzling A A1
42 Giöes P B2
79 Gioia dei Marsi I B4
80 Gióia del Colle I D3
79 Gióia Sannitica I B5
82 Gióia Táuro I C2
85 Gioiosa Iónica I A5
85 Gioiosa Marea I A3
80 Giovinazzo I C3
103 Girbovu RO B4
103 Gircov RO C5
83 Girifalco I C3
102 Girnic RO B2
66 Giromagny F D2
35 Girona see Gerona E B5
66 Gironcourt F C1
35 Gironella E A4
66 Gironville-sous-les-Côtes F C1
8 Girvan GB C3
10 Gisburn GB B3
6 Gisla GB B2
56 Gislaved S B2
55 Gislev DK C3
57 Gislövsläge S D2
20 Gisors F B2
79 Gissi I A5
53 Gisslarbo S C1
53 Gistad S D1
16 Gistel B B2
54 Gistrup DK B3
103 Giubega RO B4
71 Giubiasco CH B4
79 Giugliano I C5
103 Giuleşti RO B4
79 Giulianova I A4
95 Giurgiu RO E6
103 Giuvărăşti RO C5
55 Give DK C2
21 Givet F A5
21 Givonne F B6
25 Givors F C4
17 Givry B C4
25 Givry F B4
55 Givskud DK C2
90 Giźalki PL A1
23 Gizeux F A5
82 Gizzeria I C3
82 Gizzeria Lido I C3
55 Gjedved DK C2
54 Gjerlev DK B3
48 Gjermundshamn N A2
54 Gjerrild DK B3
49 Gjerstad N C6
50 Gjesås N B3
108 Gjirokastër AL A2
54 Gjøl DK A2
49 Gjøvdal N C5
50 Gjøvik N B1
62 Gladbach D C1
62 Gladbeck D B1
62 Gladenbach D C3
109 Glafirá GR B4
109 Gláfki GR B4
9 Glamis GB B5
100 Glamoč BO B1
55 Glamsbjerg DK C3
29 Glandage F B4
62 Glandorf D A2
73 Glanegg A B4
62 Glanerbrug NL A1
53 Glanshammar S C1
71 Glarus CH A4
3 Glasdrummond GB B6
8 Glasgow GB C3
72 Glashütte, *Bayern* D A1
59 Glashütte, *Hamburg* D B7
64 Glashütte, *Sachsen* D C3
13 Glastonbury GB B5
70 Glattfelden CH A3
64 Glauchau D C2
51 Glava S C3
51 Glavaglasbruk S C3
107 Glavan BG A4
105 Glavanovisi BG B4
100 Glavatičevo BO C3
101 Glavičice BO B4
104 Glavnik YU B3
97 Glebowice PL B5
101 Gledica YU C5
17 Glehn D B6
73 Gleisdorf A A5
14 Glemsford GB B3
2 Glenade IRL B3
2 Glenamoy IRL B2
3 Glenarm GB B6
3 Glenavy GB B5
8 Glenbarr GB C2
4 Glenbeigh IRL B2
8 Glencoe GB B2
2 Glencolumbkille IRL B3
5 Glenealy IRL B5
3 Gleneely IRL A4
6 Glenelg GB C3
3 Glenfarne IRL B4
8 Glenfinnan GB B2
4 Glengarriff IRL C2
9 Glenkerry GB C4
8 Glenluce GB D3
23 Glénouze F B4
9 Glenrothes GB B4
2 Glenties IRL B3
60 Gleschendorf D A1
64 Glesien D B2
70 Gletsch CH B3
109 Glifa, *Fthiótis* GR C4
110 Glifa, *Ilía* GR B2
109 Glifáda, *Évia* GR C5
108 Glifáda, *Kérkira* GR B1
111 Glifádha GR B4
108 Gliki GR B2
57 Glimåkra S C3
4 Glin IRL B2
100 Glina CRO A1
59 Glinde D B7
89 Glinojeck PL C6
4 Glinsk IRL A2
90 Gliwice PL C2
104 Globocnica YU B3
73 Glödnitz A B4
73 Gloggnitz A A5
97 Glogoczów PL B5
101 Glogonj YU B5
102 Glogovac YU B2
65 Głogów PL B6
91 Glogów Małoposki PL C5
90 Glogówek PL C1
18 Glomel F B2
56 Glommen S C1
47 Glommersträsk S D9
68 Glonn D D2
71 Glorenza (Glurns) I B5
36 Gloria P B2
109 Glośsa GR B5
54 Glöstorp S A4
13 Gloucester GB B5
70 Glovelier CH A2
91 Glowaczów PL B5
88 Glówczyce PL A3
60 Glöwen D C3
90 Glówno PL B3
101 Gložan YU A4
103 Glozhene BG C4
103 Glozhene BG C5
90 Głubczyce PL C1
90 Glucholazy PL C1
91 Gluchów PL B4
65 Głuchowo PL A6
55 Glücksburg D D2
59 Glückstadt D B6
55 Glumsø DK C4
101 Glušci YU B4
65 Gluszyca PL C6
13 Glyn Neath GB B4
54 Glyngøre DK B1
68 Gmund D D2
72 Gmünd, *Karnten* A B3
69 Gmünd, *Nieder Östereich* A C5
69 Gmunden A D4
73 Gnesau A B3
53 Gnesta S C3
65 Gnięchowice PL C6
89 Gniew PL B4
89 Gniewkowo PL C4
88 Gniezno PL C3
104 Gnjilane YU B3
61 Gnoien D B3
91 Gnojno PL C4
11 Gnosall GB C3
56 Gnosjö S B2
10 Gobowen GB C2
17 Goch D B6
68 Gochsheim D A1
15 Godalming GB C2
62 Goddelsheim D B3
103 Godech BG C4
72 Gódega di S. Urbano I C2
53 Godegård S D1
63 Godelheim D B4
103 Goden RO A5
20 Goderville F B1
74 Godiasco I B4
89 Godkowo PL A5
14 Godmanchester GB B2
99 Gödöllo H A4
98 Gödreszentmárton H B2
15 Godshill GB D1
15 Godstone GB C2
90 Godzikowice PL C1
89 Godziszewo PL A4
16 Goes NL B3
66 Goetzenbrück F C3
68 Göggingen D C1
10 Goginan GB C2
70 Góglio I B3
90 Gogolin PL C2
102 Gogoşu RO B3
62 Gohfeld D A3
61 Göhren D A4
17 Goirle NL B5
36 Góis P A2
75 Góito I A5
33 Goizueta E A5
101 Gojna Gora YU C5
89 Gójsk PL C5
112 Gökova TR A1
46 Gol N F4
30 Golada E B2
88 Golańcz PL C3
61 Golańcz-Pomorska PL A6
66 Golbey F C2
96 Golčuv Jenikov CZ B1
61 Golczewo PL B5
71 Goldach CH A4
93 Goldap PL C8
67 Goldbach D A5
60 Goldbeck D C2
60 Goldberg D B3
59 Goldenstedt D C5
11 Goldthorpe GB B4
4 Goleen IRL C2
36 Golega P B2
105 Golema Rakovitsa BG B5
105 Golemo Selo YU B3
61 Goleniów PL B5
101 Goleša YU C4
87 Golfo Aranci I B2
90 Golina PL A2
106 Goljam Iswor BG B3
98 Gölle H B3
96 Göllersdorf A C2
61 Gollin D B4
72 Golling A A3
39 Gollocanta E B5
96 Gols A D2
7 Golspie GB C5
64 Golßen D B3
89 Golub-Dobrzyń PL B5
102 Golubac YU B2
101 Golubinci YU B5
104 Golubovci YU B1
90 Goluchów PL B1
107 Golyam Manastir BG A4
106 Golyamo Belovo BG A2
106 Golyamo Konare BG A2
107 Golyamo Shivachevo BG A4
89 Golynim Stary PL C6
64 Golzow D A2
71 Gomagoi I B5
33 Gómara E C4
67 Gomaringen D C5
109 Gomátion GR A5
42 Gomes Aires P B1
32 Gómezserracin E C2
63 Gommern D A6
90 Gomulin PL B3
50 Gonäs S B6
29 Goncelin F A5
91 Gończyce PL B5
30 Gondomar E B2
31 Gondomar P C2
66 Gondrecourt-le-Château F C1
27 Gondrin F C4
95 Gönen TR F7
29 Gonfaron F C5
33 Goñi E B5
87 Goni I C2
112 Goniais, *Kriti* GR
87 Gonnesa I C1
67 Gönningen D C5
109 Gónnoi GR B4
87 Gonnosfanádiga I C1
98 Gönyü H A2
75 Gonzaga I B5
12 Goodwick GB A3
17 Gooik B C4
11 Goole GB B5
17 Goor NL A6
96 Göpfritz a. d. Wild A C1
70 Goppenstein CH B2
67 Göppingen D C5
44 Gor E B4
65 Góra PL B6
89 Góra PL C6
91 Góra Kalwaria PL B5
91 Góra Pulawska PL B5
44 Gorafe E B3
110 Goráni GR C3
61 Gorawino PL B6
101 Goražde BO C3
65 Gorce PL C6
66 Gorcy F B1
32 Gordaliza del Pino E B1
33 Gordejuela E A3
55 Gørding DK C1
71 Górdola CH B3
9 Gordon GB C5
32 Gordoncillo E B1
5 Gorey IRL B5
108 Gorgómilos GR B2
71 Gorgonzola I C4
105 Gorgópi GR D4
98 Gorican CRO B1
17 Gorinchem NL B4
15 Goring GB C1
64 Göritz, *Brandenburg* D A2
61 Göritz, *Mecklenburg-Vorpommern* D B4
111 Goritzá GR B3
72 Gorízia I C3
60 Gorleben D B2
55 Gørlev DK C4
94 Gorlice PL B4
65 Görlitz D B4
33 Górliz E A4
61 Görmin D B4
103 Gorna Gnoynitsa BG C4
103 Gorna Kremena BG C4
105 Gorni Okol BG B5
101 Gornja Gorevnica YU C5
102 Gornja Kamenica YU C3
104 Gornja Klina YU B2
105 Gornja Ljubata YU B4
77 Gornja Ploča CRO B5
73 Gornja Radgona SL B5
102 Gornja Sabanta YU C2
101 Gornja Trešnjevica YU B5
101 Gornja Tuzla BO B3
81 Gornje Polje YU B5
100 Gornje Ratkovo BO B1
73 Gornji Grad SL B4
100 Gornji Klasnic CRO A1
77 Gornji Kosinj CRO B5
101 Gornji Milanovac YU B5
100 Gornji Podgradci BO A2
100 Gornji Vakuf BO C2
101 Gornji Žabar BO B3
91 Górno PL C4
107 Gorno Aleksandrovo BG A4
104 Gorno Nerezi MAK C3
105 Gorno Orizari MAK C3
105 Gorno Osenovo BG C5
103 Gorno Peshtene BG C4
105 Gorobinci MAK C3
107 Gorovo BG A5
89 Górowo Iławeckie PL A6
58 Gorredijk NL B3
19 Gorron F B5
12 Gorseinon GB B3
107 Gorska Polyana BG A4
17 Gorssel NL A6
7 Gorstan GB C4
4 Gort IRL A3
3 Gortin GB B4
64 Görzke D A2
90 Gorzkowice PL B3
89 Górzno PL B5
90 Gorzów Sląski PL B2
61 Gorzów Wielkopolski PL C6
61 Górzyca PL C5
97 Gorzyce PL B4
65 Górzyn PL B4
72 Gosaldo I B1
72 Gosau A A3
14 Gosberton GB B2
70 Göschenen CH B3
88 Gościcino PL A4
90 Gościęcin PL C1
91 Gościeradow PL C6
88 Gościno PL A1
73 Gosdorf A B5
10 Gosforth GB A2
63 Goslar D B5
89 Goslice PL C5
77 Gospić CRO B5
15 Gosport GB D1
51 Gössäter S D4
71 Gossau CH A4
96 Goßhoflein A D2
64 Gößnitz D C2
104 Gostimë AL D2
104 Gostivar MAK C2
90 Gostkow PL B3
69 Göstling a.d. Ybbs A D5
88 Gostomia PL B2
88 Gostycyn PL B3
65 Gostyń PL B7
90 Gostynin PL A3
90 Goszcz PL B1
88 Goszczanowo PL C1
51 Göta S D3
54 Göteborg S A4
51 Götene S D4
63 Gotha D C5
105 Gotse Delchev BG C5
69 Gottersdorf D C3
63 Göttingen D B4
96 Gottwaldov (Zlin) CZ B3
71 Götzis A A4
17 Gouda NL A4
15 Goudhurst GB C3
18 Gouesnou F B1
105 Gouménissa GR D4
110 Goúra GR B3
27 Gourdon F B5
9 Gourdon GB B5
18 Gourin F B2
20 Gournay-en-Bray F B2
8 Gourock GB C3
21 Goussancourt F B4
31 Gouveia P D3
112 Gouves, *Kriti* GR
21 Gouzeacourt F A4
24 Gouzon F B2
81 Govedari CRO B4
105 Govedartsi BG B5
75 Govérnolo I A5
91 Gowarczów PL B4
12 Gowerton GB B3
64 Goyatz D A4
91 Gózd PL B5
65 Gozdnica PL B5
17 Gozee B C4
26 Gr. Poujeaux F A3
60 Graal-Müritz D A3
68 Grabenstätt D D3
100 Grabovac CRO C2
101 Grabovac YU B5
101 Grabovci YU B4
98 Grabovnik YU B1
60 Grabow D B2
91 Grabow PL B5
90 Grabów Łęczycki PL A2
90 Grabów-nad-Prosną PL B2
71 Grabs CH A4
77 Gračac CRO B5
100 Gračanica BO B3
104 Gračanica, *A. P. Kosovo* YU B3
101 Gračanica, *Srbija* YU B4
24 Graçay F A1
104 Gracen AL C1
73 Grad SL B6
100 Gradac CRO C2
101 Gradac, *Crna Gora* YU C4
101 Gradac, *Srbija* YU C5
100 Gradačac BO B3
98 Gradec CRO C1
105 Gradec MAK C4
32 Gradefes E B1
73 Grades A B4
102 Gradets BG B3
107 Gradets BG A4
105 Gradevo BG C5
26 Gradignan F B3
36 Gradil P C1
98 Gradina CRO C2
103 Grădinaro RO B5
72 Gradisca d'Isonzo I C3
73 Gradišče SL B5
101 Gradište CRO A3
30 Grado E A4
72 Grado I C3
105 Gradsko MAK C3
89 Gradzanowo Kościelne PL C6
55 Grærup Strand DK C1
55 Græsted DK B5
106 Graf-Ignatievo BG A2
68 Grafelfing D C2
69 Grafenau D C4
68 Gräfenberg D B2
73 Grafendorf A A5
64 Gräfenhainichen D B2
69 Grafenschlag A C6
73 Grafenstein A B4
63 Gräfenthal D C6
63 Grafentonna D B5
68 Grafenwöhr D B2
68 Grafing D C2
69 Grafling D C3
68 Grafrath D C2
79 Gragnano I C5
73 Grahovo SL B3
5 Graigue IRL B5
5 Graiguenamanagh IRL B4
15 Grain GB C3
71 Grainau D A6
11 Grainthorpe GB B6
40 Graja de Iniesta E B1
33 Grajera E C3
55 Gram DK C2
102 Gramada BG C3
71 Gramais A A5
27 Gramat F B5
107 Gramatikovo BG A5
96 Gramatneusiedl A C2
61 Grambow D B5
6 Gramisdale GB C1
111 Grammatikón GR A4
109 Grammeni Oxiá GR C3
85 Grammichele I B3
104 Gramsh AL D2
61 Gramzow D B5
49 Gran N A7
44 Granada E B3
34 Granadella E B3
3 Granard IRL C4
30 Grañas E A3
44 Granátula de Calatrava E A3
25 Grancey-le-Château F A5
18 Grand-Champ F C3
20 Grand Couronne F B2
30 Grandas de Salime E A4
19 Grandcamp-Maisy F A4
70 Grandcour CH B1
42 Grândola P A1
21 Grandpré F B5
17 Grandrieu B C4
28 Grandrieu F B2
70 Grandson CH B1
28 Grandvals F B2
20 Grandvilliers F B2
34 Grañén E B2
50 Grangärde S B5
2 Grange IRL B3
10 Grange over Sands GB A3
9 Grangemouth GB B4
34 Granges-de Crouhens F A3
66 Granges-sur-Vologne F C2
50 Grängesberg S B6
60 Gräningen D C3
84 Granitola I B1
108 Granitsa GR B3
42 Granja P A2
34 Granja de Escarpe E B3
32 Granja de Moreruelo E C1
37 Granja de Torrehermosa E C5
56 Gränna S A3
35 Granollers E B5
47 Granön S D9
65 Granowo PL A6
61 Gransee D B4
49 Gransherad N B6
14 Grantham GB B2
7 Grantown-on-Spey GB C5
9 Grantshouse GB C5
19 Granville F B4
46 Granvin N F3
40 Grao de Gandia E C2
40 Grao de Sagunto E B2
63 Grasleben D A6
10 Grasmere GB A2
52 Grasö S B4
80 Grassano I D3
68 Grassau D D3
74 Grasse F C1
11 Grassington GB A4
55 Gråsten DK D2
51 Grästorp S D3
47 Gratangen N B8
106 Gratini GR B3
73 Gratkorn A A5
73 Gratwein A A5
27 Graulhet F C6
34 Graus E A3
33 Grávalos E B5
50 Gravberget N B3
17 Grave NL B5
71 Gravedona I B4
16 Gravelines F B2
70 Gravellona Toce I C3
17 's Gravendeel NL B4
17 's Gravenhage NL A4
16 Gravenpolder NL B3
17 's Gravenzande NL A4
15 Gravesend GB C3
29 Graveson F C3
109 Graviá GR C4
80 Gravina in Púglia I D3
25 Gray F A5
15 Grays GB C3
15 Grayshott GB C2
73 Graz A A5
43 Grazalema E C4
89 Grazawy PL B5
75 Grazzano Visconti I B4
105 Grdelica YU B4
51 Greåker N C1
11 Great Ayton GB A4
15 Great Chesterford GB B3
10 Great Clifton GB A2
15 Great Cornard GB B3
15 Great Dunmow GB C3
10 Great Eccleston GB B3
13 Great Malvern GB A5
15 Great Missenden GB C2
15 Great Shefford GB C1
14 Great Shelford GB B3
12 Great Torrington GB C3
14 Great Yarmouth GB B4
11 Greatham GB A4
51 Grebbested S D2
63 Grebenstein D B4
89 Gręboсin PL B4
68 Greding D B2
55 Gredstedbro DK C1
11 Green Hammerton GB B4
9 Greenhead GB D5
3 Greenisland GB B6
9 Greenlaw GB C5
8 Greenock GB C3
3 Greenore IRL B5
12 Greenway GB B3
17 Grefrath D B6
70 Gréggio I C3
109 Gregolimano GR C4
72 Greifenburg A B3
61 Greiffenberg D B4
61 Greifswald D A4
69 Grein A C5
49 Greipstad N C4
64 Greiz D C2
60 Gremersdorf D A1
54 Grenå DK B3
27 Grenade F C5
26 Grenade-sur-l'Adour F C3
70 Grenchen CH A2
49 Grendi N C4
54 Grenen DK A3
29 Grenoble F A4
11 Grenside GB B4
29 Gréoux-les-Bains F C4
60 Gresenhorst D A3
6 Gress GB B2
70 Gressoney-la-Trinité I C2
70 Gressoney-St.-Jean I C2
67 Greßthal D A6
51 Gressvik N C1
69 Gresten A D6
9 Gretna GB D4
63 Greußen D B5
75 Greve I C6
60 Greven, *Mecklenburg-Vorpommern* D B1
62 Greven, *Nordrhein-Westfalen* D A2
108 Grevená GR A3
62 Grevenbroich D B1
62 Grevenbrück D B3
66 Grevenmacher L B2
60 Grevesmühlen D B2
55 Grevestrand DK C5
57 Grevie S C1
10 Greystoke GB A3
5 Greystones IRL A5
17 Grez-Doiceau B C4
19 Grez-en-Bouère F C5
27 Grèzec F B5
71 Grezzana I C6
101 Grgurevci YU A4
72 Gries A A1
67 Gries D B6
67 Gries F C3
71 Gries in Sellrain A A6
69 Griesbach D C4
67 Griesheim D B4
69 Grieskirchen A C4
73 Griffen A B4
29 Grignan F B3
72 Grignano I C3
72 Grigno I B1
26 Grignols F B3
25 Grignon F C6
25 Grigny F C4
32 Grijota E B2
58 Grijpskerk NL B3
53 Grillby S C3
29 Grimaud F C5
17 Grimbergen B C4
64 Grimma D B2
61 Grimmen D A4
70 Grimmialp CH B2
56 Grimsås S B2
11 Grimsby GB B5
56 Grimslöv S C3
49 Grimstad N C5
56 Grimstorp S B3
70 Grindelwald CH B3
48 Grindheim N C4
55 Grindsted DK C1
38 Griñón E B3
56 Gripenberg S B3
53 Gripsholm S C3
27 Grisolles F C5
52 Grisslehamn S B4
7 Gritley GB B6
105 Grivas GR D4
103 Grivitsa BG C5
109 Grizanon GR B4
10 Grizebeck GB A2
64 Gröbers D B2
73 Gröbming A A3
63 Gröbzig D B6
91 Grochów PL A6
101 Grocka YU B5
72 Grodig A A3
64 Gröditz D B3
89 Gródki PL B6
65 Grodków PL C7
97 Grodziec, *Bielsko-Biala* PL B4
90 Grodziec, *Konin* PL A2
65 Grodziec, *Legnica* PL B5
91 Grodzisk Maz. PL A4
65 Grodzisk Wielkopolski PL A6
62 Groenlo NL A1
12 Groes-goch GB B2
17 Groesbeek NL B5
100 Grohote CRO C1
64 Groitzsch D B2
18 Groix F C2
91 Grójec PL B4
89 Grom PL B6
100 Gromiljck BO C3
60 Grömitz D A1
71 Gromo I C4
63 Gronau, *Niedersachsen* D A4
62 Gronau, *Nordrhein-Westfalen* D A2
67 Grönenbach D D6
46 Grong N D6
57 Grönhögen, *Öland* S C5
63 Groningen D B6
67 Gröningen D B6
58 Groningen NL B3
71 Grono Roveredo CH B4
89 Gronowo PL A5
56 Grönskåra S B4
58 Grootebroek NL C2
58 Grootegast NL B3
74 Gropello Cairoli I A3
103 Gropsani RO B4
49 Grorud N B7
71 Grósio I B5
101 Grošnica YU C5
64 Groß Beeren D A3
63 Groß Berkel D A4
63 Groß Denkte D A5
61 Groß-Dölln D C4
67 Groß-Gerau D B4
60 Groß Gronau D B1
63 Groß Ilsede D A5
64 Groß Kreutz D A2
63 Groß Lafferde D A5
68 Groß Mehring D C2
60 Groß Oesingen D C1
62 Groß Reken D B2
64 Groß Rosenburg D B1
64 Groß Särchen D B4
63 Groß Schneen D B4
61 Groß Schönebeck D C4
96 Groß Schweinbarth A C2
67 Groß Umstadt D B4
60 Groß Warnow D B2
96 Groß Weikersdorf A C2
60 Groß-Welle D B3
60 Groß Wokern D B3
63 Großalmerode D B4
72 Großarl A A3
63 Großbodungen D B5
64 Großbothen D B2
67 Großbotwar D B5
59 Großburgwedel D C6
65 Großchönau D C4
60 Großenbrode D A2
63 Großengottern D B5
64 Großenhain D B3
59 Grossenkneten D C5
63 Großenlüder D C4
60 Großensee D B1
96 Großenzersdorf A C2
23 Grossereix F C6
67 Großerlach D B5
78 Grosseto I A2
69 Großgerungs A C5
69 Großglobnitz A C6
68 Großhabersdorf D B1
59 Großhansdorf D B7
96 Großharras A C2
64 Großhartmannsdorf D C3
70 Grosshöchstetten CH B2
96 Großkrut A C2
63 Großörner D B6
69 Großpertholz A C5
98 Großpetersdorf A A1
64 Großpostwitz D B4
69 Großraming A D5
64 Großräschen D B4
67 Grossrinderfeld D B5
64 Großröhrsdorf D B4
64 Großschirma D C3
96 Großsiegharts A C1
73 Großsölk A A3
98 Großwarasdorf A A1
73 Großwilfersdorf A A6
66 Grostenquin F C2
90 Groszowice PL C1
46 Grotli N E3
83 Grottáglie I A4
80 Grottaminarda I C2
79 Grottammare I A4
78 Grotte di Castro I A2
85 Grotteria I A5
80 Gróttole I D3
58 Grouw NL B2
30 Grove E B2
76 Grožnjan CRO A3
49 Grua N A7
60 Grube D A2
98 Grubisno Polje CRO C2
81 Gruda CRO B5
100 Grude BO C2
107 Grudovo BG A5
89 Grudusk PL B6
91 Grudze PL A3
89 Grudziadz PL B4
50 Grue N B3
102 Gruia RO B3
28 Gruissan F C2
30 Grullos E A4
80 Grumo Appula I C3
51 Grums S C4
69 Grünau i. Almtal A D4
96 Grünbach a. Schneeberg A D1
62 Grünberg D C3
69 Grünburg A D5
67 Gründelhardt D B5
50 Grundforsen S A3
73 Grundlsee A A3
51 Grundsund S D2
63 Grünenplan D B4
64 Grunewald D B3
49 Grungedal N B4
64 Grunow D A4
67 Grünsfeld D B5
67 Grünstadt D B4
68 Grünwald D C2
89 Grunwald PL B6
89 Grupa Graniczna PL B4
104 Grupčin MAK C3
6 Grutness, *Shetland Is.* GB
52 Gruvberget S A2
70 Gruyères CH B2
94 Grybów PL B4
52 Grycksbo S B1
61 Gryfice PL B6
61 Gryfino PL B5
65 Gryfów Śląski PL B5
49 Grymyr N A7
53 Gryt S D2
53 Grytgöl S D1
51 Grythyttan S C5
88 Grzmiaga PL B2
61 Grzybno PL B5
91 Grzybów PL C5
89 Grzywna PL B4
72 Gschnitz A A1
67 Gschwend D C5
70 Gstaad CH B2
70 Gsteig CH B2
44 Guadahortuna E B3
39 Guadalajara E B3
39 Guadalaviar E B5
43 Guadalcanal E A4
43 Guadalcázar E B5
38 Guadalix de la Sierra E B3
44 Guadálmez E A2
38 Guadalupe E C1
38 Guadamur E C2
38 Guadarrama E B2
43 Guadiaro E C4
44 Guadix E B3
83 Guagnano I A4
86 Guagno F B1
44 Guajar-Faragüit E C3
44 Gualchos E C3
76 Gualdo Tadino I C2
75 Gualtien I B5
79 Guarcino I B4
9 Guard Bridge GB B5
31 Guarda P D3
45 Guardamar del Segura E A6
31 Guardão P D2
83 Guardavalle I C3
78 Guardea I A3
80 Guárdia I D2
79 Guárdia Sanframondi I B5
79 Guardiagrele I A5
79 Guardiarégia I B5
45 Guardias Viejas E C4
35 Guardiola de Berga E A4
32 Guardo E B2
37 Guareña E C4
44 Guaro E C2
44 Guarromán E A3
87 Guasila I C2
75 Guastalla I B5
76 Gúbbio I C2
65 Güben D B4
65 Gubin PL B4
101 Guča YU C5
100 Gudavac BO B1
55 Güderup DK D2
51 Gudhem S D4
57 Gudhjem DK D3
66 Güdingen D B3
98 Gudovac CRO C1
46 Gudvangen N F3
66 Guebwiller F D3
44 Guéjar-Sierra E B3
22 Guéméné-Penfao F A3
33 Güeñes E A3
19 Guer F C3
22 Guérande F A2
24 Guéret F B1
24 Guérigny F A3
33 Guernica y Luno E A4
33 Guerricaiz E A4
34 Guesa E A1
26 Guèthary F C2
25 Gueugnon F B4
79 Guglionesi I B5
106 Gugutka BG B3
61 Gühlen Glienicke D B3
36 Guia P B2
19 Guichen F C4
75 Guidizzolo I A5
78 Guidónia I B3
75 Guiglia I B5
21 Guignes F C3
44 Guijo E A2
37 Guijo de Coria E A4
37 Guijo de Granadilla E A4
37 Guijo de Santa Bábera E A5
38 Guijuelo E B1
15 Guildford GB C2
29 Guillaumes F B5
43 Guillena E B3
29 Guillestre F B5
18 Guilvinec F C1
31 Guimarães P C2
36 Guincho P C1
16 Guînes F C1
18 Guingamp F B2
18 Guipavas F B1
103 Guirgita RO B4
38 Guisando E B1
11 Guisborough GB A4
21 Guiscard F B4
18 Guiscriff F B2
21 Guise F B4
35 Guisona E B4
14 Guist GB B3
30 Guitiriz E A3
26 Guîtres F A3
26 Gujan Mestras F B2
55 Guldborg DK D4
77 Gulin CRO C5
56 Gullabo S C4
9 Gullane GB B5
56 Gullaskruv S C4
56 Gullbrandstorp S C1
52 Gulleråsen S A1
49 Gullhaug N B7
51 Gullholmen S D2
56 Gullringen S B4
51 Gullspång S D5
112 Güllük TR B1
49 Gulsvik N A6
107 Gūlūbitsi BG A4
106 Gūlūbovo BG A3
103 Gulyantsi BG C5
32 Gumiel de Hizán E C3
62 Gummersbach D B2
103 Gumoshtnik BG D5
106 Gumoshtnik BG A2
102 Gümzovo BG B3
67 Gundel-Fingen D C3
68 Gundelfingen D C1
67 Gundelsheim D B5
66 Gunderschoffen F C3
100 Gundinci CRO A3
50 Gunnarskog S C3
56 Gunnebo S B5
96 Gunselsdorf A D2
63 Güntersberge D B5
67 Guntersblum D B4
96 Guntersdorf A C2
30 Guntin de Pallarés E B3
96 Guntramsdorf A C2
21 Guny F B4
68 Günzburg D C1
68 Gunzenhausen D B1
103 Gura Padinii RO C5
102 Gura Väii RO B3
33 Guriezo E A3
73 Gurk A B4
106 Gurkovo BG A3
105 Gūrlyano BG B4
34 Gurrea de Gállego E A2
89 Guryevsk R A6
98 Gušće CRO C1
64 Güsen D A1
93 Gusev R C8
102 Guševac YU C3
104 Gusinje YU B1
87 Gúspini I C1
53 Gusselby S C1
98 Güssing A A1
69 Gußwerk A D6
50 Gustav Adolf S B4
53 Gustavsberg S C4
51 Gustavsfors S C3
60 Güstrow D B3
53 Gusum S D2
6 Gutcher, *Shetland Is.* GB
96 Gutenstein A D1
62 Gütersloh D B3
70 Guttannen CH B3
73 Guttaring A B4
64 Guttau D B4
71 Güttingen CH A4
61 Gützkow D B4
14 Guyhirn GB B3
91 Guzów PL A4
89 Gvardeyskoye R A6
89 Gvardieysk R A7
100 Gvozdansko CRO A1
10 Gwalchmai GB B1
88 Gwda Wielka PL B2
2 Gweedore IRL A3
25 Gy F A5
99 Gyál H A4
98 Gyarmat H A2
21 Gye-sur-Seine F C5
98 Gyékényes H B2
48 Gyland N C3
55 Gylling DK C3
97 Gyögyössolymòs H D5
99 Gyoma H B5
98 Gyömöre H A2
99 Gyömrö H A4
99 Gyón H A4
98 Gyöngyfa H C2
97 Gyöngyös H D5
97 Gyöngyöspata H D5
99 Gyönk H B3
98 Györ H A2
98 Györszemere H A2
98 Györszentivan H A2
98 Györvár H B1
70 Gypsera CH B2
52 Gysinge S B2
51 Gyttorp S C5
105 Gyueshevo BG B4
98 Gyulafirátót H A2
98 Gyulaj H B3

H

17 Haacht B C4
68 Haag D C3
69 Haag, *Nieder Östereich* A C5
69 Haag, *Ober Östereich* A C4
62 Haaksbergen NL A1
16 Haamstede NL B3
62 Haan D B2
93 Haapsalu EW A8
68 Haar D C2
17 Haarlem NL A4
47 Haarpajärvi SF E12
26 Habas F C3
66 Habay-la-Neuve B B1
56 Habo S B3
96 Habry CZ B1
70 Habsheim F A2
62 Hachenburg D C2
33 Hacinas E C3
107 Haciumur TR B4
5 Hacketstown IRL B5
10 Hackthorpe GB A3
62 Hadamar D C3
14 Haddenham GB B3
9 Haddington GB C5
55 Haderslev DK C2
15 Hadleigh GB B3
15 Hadlow GB C3
63 Hadmersleben D A6
63 Hadmersleben D B6
96 Hadres A C2
54 Hadsen DK B3
55 Hadsten DK B3
54 Hadsund DK B3
100 Hadžici BO C3
48 Hægebostad N C4
49 Hægeland N C4
60 Haffkrug D A1
98 Haganj CRO C1
56 Hagby S C5
58 Hage D B4
59 Hagen, *Niedersachsen* D B5
62 Hagen, *Nordrhein-Westfalen* D B2
67 Hagenbach D B4
69 Hagenberg A C5
59 Hagenburg D C6
60 Hagenow D B2
26 Hagetmau F C3
50 Hagfors S B4
52 Hagsta S B3
67 Haguenau F C3
68 Hahnbach D B2
62 Hahnstäten D C3
98 Hahót H B1
62 Haiger D C3
67 Haigerloch D C4
62 Hailer D C4
15 Hailsham GB D3
96 Hainburg A C2
96 Hainfeld A C1
64 Hainichen D C3
96 Haitzendorf A C1
102 Hajdučica YU A2
94 Hajdúszoboszló H C4
98 Hajmásker H A3
97 Hajnáčka SQ C5
99 Hajós H B4
51 Håkantorp S D3
47 Hakkas S C10
52 Håksberg S B1
66 Halanzy B B1
96 Halaszi H D3
63 Halberstadt D B6
13 Halberton GB C4
54 Hald DK B2
62 Haldem D A3
51 Halden N C2
63 Haldensleben D A6
17 Haldern D B6
60 Halenbeck D B3
97 Halenkov CZ B4
11 Halesowen GB C3
14 Halesworth GB B4
68 Halfing D D3
97 Halič SQ C5
11 Halifax GB B4
102 Halinga RO B3
57 Häljarp S D1
7 Halkirk GB B5
57 Hallabro S C4
53 Hällabrottet S C1
46 Hålland S E6
48 Hallaskar N A4
53 Hällberga S C2
53 Hällbybrunn S C2
17 Halle B C4
62 Halle, *Nordrhein-Westfalen* D A3
64 Halle, *Sachsen-Anhalt* D B1

48 Husnes N B2
66 Hussigny F B1
62 Hüsten D B3
96 Hustopeče, *Jihomoravský* CZ C2
96 Hustopeče, *Severomoravsky* CZ B3
59 Husum D A6
47 Husum S E9
88 Huta PL C2
91 Huta Zawadzka PL B4
73 Hüttenberg A B4
59 Hüttenbusch D B5
67 Hüttlingen D C6
72 Hüttshlag A A3
70 Huttwil CH A2
17 Huy B C5
49 Hval N A7
51 Hvaler N C2
54 Hvalpsund DK B2
100 Hvar CRO C1
49 Hvarnes N B6
54 Hvidbjerg DK B1
55 Hvide Sande DK C1
49 Hvittingfoss N B7
97 Hybe SQ B5
56 Hycklinge S B4
29 Hyères F C5
29 Hyeres Plage F C5
48 Hylestad N B4
55 Hylke DK C2
57 Hyllstofta S C2
56 Hyltebruk S B2
9 Hyndford Bridge GB C4
8 Hynish GB B1
49 Hynnekleiv N C5
47 Hyrynsalmi SF D14
13 Hythe, *Hampshire* GB C6
15 Hythe, *Kent* GB C4
47 Hyvinkää SF F12

I

102 Iablanita RO B3
103 Ianca RO C5
94 Iaşi RO C7
106 Iasmos GR B3
37 Ibahernando E B5
33 Ibarranguelua E A4
62 Ibbenburen D A2
33 Ibeas E B3
40 Ibi E C2
41 Ibiza E
26 Ibos F C4
107 Ibrice Iskelesi TR C4
107 Ibriktepe TR B4
44 Ibros E A3
11 Ibstock GB C4
62 Iburg D A3
67 Ichenhausen D C6
16 Ichtegem B B3
63 Ichtershausen D C5
33 Iciar E A4
37 Idanha-a-Nova P B3
66 Idar-Oberstein D B3
51 Idd N C2
105 Idha GR C4
111 Idhra GR B4
33 Idiazábal E B4
52 Idkerberget S B1
99 Idos YU C5
46 Idre S F6
73 Idrija SL B4
71 Idro I C5
62 Idstein D C3
101 Idvor YU A5
79 Ielsi I B5
16 Ieper B C2
112 Ierápetra, *Kriti* GR
109 Ierissós GR A5
108 Ieropiyi GR A3
87 Ierzu I C2
76 Iesi I C3
72 Iésolo I C2
46 Ifjord N A13
98 Igal H B2
81 Igalo YU B5
33 Igea E B4
76 Igea Marina I B2
53 Igelfors S D1
67 Igersheim D B5
47 Iggesund S F8
104 Iglarevo YU B2
32 Iglesias E B3
87 Iglésias I C1
72 Igls A A1
107 Iğneada TR B5
108 Igoumenítsa GR B2
34 Igries E A2
35 Igualada E B4
30 Igüeña E B4
25 Iguerande F B4
98 Iharosberény H B2
66 Ihringen D C3
68 Ihrlerstein D C2
47 Iisalmi SF E13
58 IJlst NL B2
17 IJmuiden NL A4
58 IJsselmuiden NL C2
17 IJsselstein NL A5
16 IJzendijke NL B3
47 Ikaalinen SF F11
55 Ikast DK B2
98 Ikervár H A1
105 Ikhtiman BG B5
75 Il Castagno I C5
101 Ilandza YU A5
71 Ilanz CH B4
97 Ilava SQ C4
89 Ilawa PL B5
34 Ilche E B3
13 Ilchester GB C5
63 Ilfeld-Wiegersdorf D B5
12 Ilfracombe GB B3
31 Ilhavo P D2
100 Ilijaš BO C3
111 Iliókastro GR B4
106 Iliokómi GR C2
73 Ilirska Bistrica SL C4
100 Ilijdza BO C3
14 Ilkeston GB B1
11 Ilkley GB B4
39 Illana E B4
30 Illano E A4
30 Illas E A5
26 Illats F B3
35 Ille-sur-Tét F A5
67 Illereichen-Altenstadt D C6
67 Illertissen D C6
38 Illescas E B3
70 Illfurth F A2
20 Illiers-Combray F C2
66 Illingen D B3
66 Illkirch F C3
64 Illmersdorf D B3
96 Illmitz A D2
44 Illora E B3
33 Illueca E C5
47 Ilmajoki SF E11
63 Ilmenau D C5
13 Ilminster GB C5
101 Ilok CRO A4
47 Ilomantsi SF E15
88 Ilowiec PL B2
89 Ilowo PL B6
63 Ilsenburg D B5
67 Ilshofen D B5
73 Ilz A A5
91 Ilza PL B5
8 Imachar GB C2
47 Imatra SF F14
106 Imeron GR C3
90 Imielin PL C3
57 Immeln S C3
67 Immendingen D D4
63 Immenhausen D B4
71 Immenstadt D A5
11 Immingham GB B5
11 Immingham Dock GB B5
76 Ímola I B1
39 Imon E A4
100 Imotski CRO C2
74 Impéria I C3
24 Imphy F B3
75 Impruneta I C6
48 Imsland N B2
71 Imst A A5
4 Inagh IRL B2
46 Inari SF B13
41 Inca, *Mallorca* E
6 Inchnadamph GB B4
9 Inchture GB B4
33 Incinillas E B3
112 Incirliova TR B1
75 Incisa in Val d'Arno I C6
101 Indija YU A5
48 Indre Ålvik N A3
112 İnebolu TR A1
107 Inece TR B5
107 Inecik TR C5
71 Inerthal CH A3
31 Infesta P C2
32 Infiesto E A1
15 Ingatestone GB C3
56 Ingatorp S B4
51 Ingedal N C2
67 Ingelheim D B4
16 Ingelmunster B C3
56 Ingelstad S C3
10 Ingleton GB A3
49 Ingolfsland N B5
68 Ingolstadt D C2
22 Ingrandes, *Maine-et-Loire* F A4
23 Ingrandes, *Vienne* F B5
66 Ingwiller F C3
39 Iniesta E C5
4 Inishannon IRL C3
2 Inishcrone IRL B2
5 Inistiogue IRL B4
13 Inkberrow GB A6
98 Inke H B2
46 Innbygda N F6
8 Innellan GB C3
9 Innerleithen GB C4
8 Innermessan GB D3
70 Innertkirchen CH B3
72 Innervillgraten A B2
5 Innfield IRL A5
46 Innhavet N C7
59 Innien D A6
72 Innsbruck A A1
111 Inói, *Attikí* GR A4
110 Inói, *Ilía* GR B2
91 Inowlódz PL B4
89 Inowroclaw PL C4
70 Ins CH A2
7 Insch GB C6
52 Insjön S B1
88 Ińsko PL B1
45 Instinción E C4
70 Interlaken CH B2
70 Intra I C3
70 Intragna CH B3
71 Introbio I C4
2 Inver IRL B3
7 Inverallochty GB C7
7 Inveran GB C4
4 Inveran IRL A2
8 Inveraray GB B2
9 Inverbervie GB B5
8 Invergarry GB A3
7 Invergordon GB C4
8 Inverie GB A2
9 Inverkeilor GB B5
9 Inverkeithing GB B4
8 Inverlussa GB B2
7 Invermoriston GB C4
7 Inverness GB C4
8 Inversanda GB B2
6 Invershiel GB C3
70 Inveruno I C3
7 Inverurie GB C6
107 Inzovo BG A4
108 Ioánnina GR B2
76 Iolanda di Savoia I B1
82 Ióppolo I C2
112 Íos GR D2
109 Ipáti GR C4
107 Ipsala TR C4
108 Ipsos GR B1
110 Ipsous GR B3
15 Ipswich GB B4
105 Iráklia GR C5
112 Iráklion, *Kriti* GR
73 Irdning A A4
107 Irechekovo BG A4
98 Iregszemcse H B3
87 Irgoli I B2
111 Iria GR B4
101 Irig YU A4
10 Iron Bridge GB C3
66 Irrel D B2
80 Irsina I D3
14 Irthlingborough GB B2
30 Iruela E B4
33 Irun E A5
33 Irurita E A5
33 Irurzun E B5
8 Irvine GB C3
3 Irvinestown GB B4
25 Is-sur-Tille F A5
34 Isaba E A2
44 Isabela E A3
103 Işalnita RO B4
110 Isaris GR B3
99 Isaszeg H A4
103 Isbiceni RO C5
6 Isbister, *Shetland Is.* GB
32 Iscar E C2
71 Ischgl A A5
79 Íschia I C4
78 Ischia di Castro I A2
80 Ischitella I C2
103 Iscroni RO A4
24 Isdes F A2
51 Ise N C2
70 Iselle I B3
70 Iseltwald CH B2
68 Isen D C3
63 Isenbüttel D A5
70 Isenthal CH B3
71 Iseo I C5
70 Isérables CH B2
62 Iserlohn D B2
79 Isérnia I B5
104 Ishm AL C1
19 Isigny F A4
87 Ísili I C2
106 Iskra BG B3
42 Isla-Cristina E B2
33 Islares E A3
103 Islaz RO C5
10 Isle of Whithorn GB A1
68 Ismaning D C2
36 Isna P B3
71 Isny D A5
32 Isoba E A1
74 Isola F B2
79 Isola del Gr. Sasso d'Italia I A4
79 Isola del Liri I B4
84 Isola delle Fémmine I A2
75 Isola delle Scala I A6
83 Ísola di Capo Rizzuto I C4
35 Isona E A4
28 Ispagnac F B2
85 Íspica I C3
17 Isselburg D B6
62 Isselhorst D B3
27 Issigeac F B4
70 Issime I C2
70 Issogne I C2
24 Issoire F C3
66 Issoncourt F C1
24 Issoudun F B2
17 Issum D B6
24 Issy-l'Evêque F B3
44 Istán E C2
95 İstanbul TR F8
97 Istebna PL B4
97 Istenmezeje H C6
78 Istia d'Ombrone I A2
109 Istiaia GR C5
105 Istibanja MAK C4
104 Istok YU B2
107 İstrance TR B6
29 Istres F C3
98 Istvándi H B2
108 Itéa, *Florina* GR A3
110 Itéa, *Fokís* GR A3
108 Itéa, *Grevená* GR A3
109 Itéa, *Kardhítsa* GR B4
110 Itháki GR A1
109 Íti GR C4
34 Itoiz E A1
44 Ítrabo E C3
79 Itri I B4
87 Ittireddu I B1
87 Íttiri I B1
59 Itzehoe D B6
47 Ivalo SF B13
98 Iván H A1
96 Ivančice CZ B2
99 Iváncsa H A3
98 Ivanec CRO B1
104 Ivangrad YU B1
98 Ivanić Grad CRO C1
73 Ivanjci SL B5
101 Ivanjica YU C5
100 Ivanjska BO B2
97 Ivanka p. N. SQ C4
101 Ivankovo CRO A3
94 Ivano-Frankivs'k U B6
96 Ivanovice na Hané CZ B3
98 Ivanska CRO C1
107 Ivaylovgrad BG B4
109 Ívira GR A5
70 Ivrea I C2
95 İvrindi TR G7
25 Ivry-en-Montagne F A4
20 Ivry-la-Bataille F C2
12 Ivybridge GB C4
91 Iwaniska PL C5
16 Iwuy F C3
14 Ixworth GB B3
33 Izarra E B4
90 Izbica Kujawska PL A2
102 Izbisté YU A2
31 Izeda P C4
16 Izegem B C3
25 Izernore F B5
107 Izgrev BG A5
94 Izmail U D8
95 İzmir TR G7
44 Iznájar E B2
44 Iznalloz E B3
44 Iznatoraf E A3
72 Izola SL C3
99 Izsák H B4
105 Izvor BG B4
105 Izvor MAK C3
102 Izvor Makhala BG C3
102 Izvor Makhala BG C3

J

44 Jabalquinto E A3
34 Jabarrella E A2
77 Jablanac CRO B4
100 Jablanica BO C2
65 Jablonec n. Jizerou CZ C5
65 Jablonec n. Nisou CZ C5
96 Jablonica SQ C3
90 Jablonka, *Konin* PL A2
97 Jablonka, *Nowy Sacz* PL B5
91 Jablonna PL A4
65 Jablonne Podještědi CZ C4
89 Jablonowo PL B5
97 Jablúnka CZ B3
101 Jabucje YU B5
43 Jabugo E B3
101 Jabuka, *A. P. Vojvodina* YU B5
101 Jabuka, *Srbija* YU C4
100 Jabukovac CRO A1
102 Jabukovac YU B3
97 Jabunkov CZ B4
34 Jaca E A2
64 Jáchymov CZ C2
46 Jäckvik S C8
59 Jacobidrebber D C5
97 Jacovce SQ C4
59 Jade D B5
52 Jäderfors S B2
52 Jädraås S B2
39 Jadraque E B4
55 Jægerspris DK C4
44 Jaén E B3
100 Jagare BO B2
59 Jagel D A6
69 Jagenbach A C6
99 Jagodnjak CRO C3
67 Jagstheim D B6
67 Jagstzell D B6
96 Jahodna SQ C3
100 Jajce BO B2
98 Ják H A1
99 Jakabszálbs H B4
47 Jakobstad SF E11
100 Jakšic CRO A2
40 Jalance E B1
47 Jalasjärvi SF E11
17 Jalhay B C5
22 Jallais F A4
25 Jallieu F C5
40 Jalón E C2
101 Jalovik YU B4
102 Jalovik Izvor YU C3
17 Jambes B C4
101 Jamena YU B4
44 Jamilena E B3
57 Jämjö S C4
73 Jamnička Kiselica CRO C5
88 Jamno PL A2
66 Jamoigne B B1
47 Jämsä SF F12
47 Jämsänkoski SF F12
57 Jämshög S C3
102 Jamu Mare RO A2
69 Jandelsbrunn D C4
64 Jänickendorf D A3
88 Janikowo PL C4
101 Janja BO B4
104 Janjevo YU B3
81 Janjina CRO B4
91 Janki PL A4
69 Jankov CZ B5
90 Janków PL B1
88 Jankowo Dolne PL C3
99 Jánoshalma H B4
98 Jánosháza H A2
99 Jánoshida H A5
69 Janovice n. Uhlavou CZ B4
90 Janów PL C3
91 Janów Lubelski PL C6
91 Janowiec PL C5
88 Janowiec Wielkopolski PL C3
89 Janowo PL B6
20 Janville F C2
19 Janzé F C4
97 Jarabá SQ C5
65 Jaraczewo PL B7
40 Jarafuel E B1
37 Jaraicejo E B5
37 Jaraiz de la Vera E A5
101 Jarak YU B4
37 Jarandilla E A5
33 Jaray E C4
52 Jarbo S B2
91 Jarczew PL B5
22 Jard-sur-Mer F B3
97 Járdánháza H C6
50 Jaren N B1
20 Jargeau F D3
101 Jarkovac YU A5
52 Järlåsa S C3
61 Jarmen D B4
53 Järna S C3
23 Jarnac F C4
56 Järnforsen S B4
66 Jarny F B1
90 Jarocin PL B1
65 Jaroměr CZ C5
96 Jaroměřice n. Rokytnou CZ B1
96 Jaroslavice CZ C2
94 Jaroslaw PL A5
88 Jaroslawiec PL A2
69 Jarošov n. Nežarkou CZ B6
51 Järpås S D3
46 Järpen S E6
9 Jarrow GB D6
47 Järvenpää SF F12
46 Järvsö S F8
23 Jarzé F A4
99 Jaša Tomić CRO C5
103 Jasen BG C5
77 Jasenak CRO A5
77 Jasenice CRO B5
97 Jasenie SQ C5
100 Jasenovac BO B1
100 Jasenovac CRO A1
101 Jasenovo, *Srbija* YU C4
102 Jasenovo, *Srbija* YU B2
65 Jasień PL B5
102 Jasika YU C2
94 Jaslo PL B4
97 Jásova SQ D4
25 Jasseron F B5
89 Jastarnia PL A4
73 Jastrebarsko CRO C5
88 Jastrowie PL B2
88 Jastrzębia-Góra PL A4
97 Jastrzebie-Zdroj PL B4
99 Jászalsószentgyorgy H A5
99 Jászapáti H A5
99 Jászárokszállás H A4
99 Jászberény H A4
99 Jászdózsa H A5
99 Jászfényszaru H A4
99 Jászjakóhalma H A5
99 Jászkarajenö H A5
99 Jászkisér H A5
99 Jászladány H A5
99 Jásztelek H A5
44 Játar E C3
40 Jativa (Xátive) E C2
97 Jatov SQ C4
61 Jatznick D B4
17 Jauche B C4
21 Jaulgonne F B4
70 Jaun CH B2
29 Jausiers F B5
40 Jávea E C3
60 Jävenitz D C2
23 Javerlhac F C5
34 Javier E A1
100 Javorani BO B2
97 Javorina SQ B6
65 Javornik CZ C7
19 Javron F B5
65 Jawor PL B6
91 Jaworznia PL C4
90 Jaworzno PL C3
65 Jaworzyna Ślaska PL C6
44 Jayena E C3
54 Jebjerg DK B2
9 Jedburgh GB C5
91 Jedlanka PL B6
65 Jedlina Zdrój PL C6
91 Jedlinsk PL B5
91 Jedlnia PL B5
91 Jedlnia Letnisko PL B5
89 Jednorožec PL B7
96 Jedovnice CZ B2
89 Jędrychow PL B5
91 Jędrzejów PL C4
89 Jedwabno PL B6
89 Jeglownik PL A5
27 Jégun F C4
48 Jektevik N B2
101 Jelakci YU C5
102 Jelašnica YU C3
97 Jelenec SQ C4
65 Jelenia Góra PL C5
88 Jelenino PL B2
93 Jelgava LV B8
96 Jelka SQ C3
55 Jelling DK C2
55 Jels DK C2
100 Jelsa CRO C1
48 Jelsa N B3
97 Jelšlava SQ C6
17 Jemeppe B C5
58 Jemgum D B4
96 Jemnice CZ B1
63 Jena D C6
71 Jenaz CH B4
72 Jenbach A A1
69 Jeneč CZ A5
98 Jennersdorf A B1
56 Jenny S B5
60 Jerchel D C2
44 Jeres del Marquesado E B3
43 Jerez de la Frontera E C3
37 Jerez de los Caballeros E C4
108 Jergucat AL B2
40 Jérica E B2
60 Jerichow D C3
102 Jermenovci YU A2
54 Jerslev DK A3
37 Jerte E A5
54 Jerup DK A3
63 Jerxheim D A5
65 Jerzmanice PL B5
90 Jerzmanowice PL C3
89 Jerzwald PL B5
62 Jesberg D C4
73 Jesenice SL B4
69 Jesenice, *Stredočesky* CZ A4
69 Jesenice, *Stredočesky* CZ B5
65 Jesenik CZ C7
97 Jesenké SQ C6
64 Jeserig D A2
64 Jessen D B2
50 Jessheim N B2
64 Jeßnitz D B2
59 Jesteburg D B6
68 Jettingen D C1
17 Jeumont F C4
59 Jevenstedt D A6
59 Jever D B4
96 Jevicko CZ B2
96 Jevišovice CZ C2
49 Jevnaker N A7
77 Jezerane CRO A5
100 Jezero BO B2
89 Jeżewo PL C5
89 Jeziorany PL B6
91 Jeziorna PL A5
91 Jezów PL B3
91 Jezowe PL C6
89 Ježowo PL B4
65 Jičin CZ C5
65 Jičiněves CZ C5
96 Jihlava CZ B1
40 Jijona E C2
65 Jilemnice CZ C5
64 Jilové CZ C4
69 Jilové u. Prahy CZ B5
99 Jimbolia RO C5
44 Jimena E B3
43 Jimena de la Frontera E C4
43 Jimera de Libar E C4
96 Jimramov CZ B2
69 Jince CZ B4
64 Jindřichovice CZ C2
69 Jindřichuv Hradec CZ B5
64 Jirkov CZ C3
69 Jistebnice CZ B5
61 Joachimsthal D C4
36 João da Loura P C2
97 Jobbágyi H D5
72 Jochberg A A2
67 Jockgrim D B4
44 Jódar E B3
17 Jodoigne B C4
47 Joensuu SF E14
66 Jœuf F B1
65 Jogodzin PL B5
64 Johanngeorgenstadt D C2
57 Johannishus S C4
69 Johanniskirchen D C3
56 Johansfors S C4
7 John o'Groats GB B5
9 Johnshaven GB B5
8 Johnstone GB C3
5 Johnstown IRL B4
5 Johnstown Bridge IRL A5
21 Joigny F D4
21 Joinville F C6
96 Jois A D2
47 Jokkmokk S C9
62 Jöllenbeck D A3
53 Jönåker S D2
21 Jonchery-sur-Vesle F B4
49 Jondal, *Buskerud* N B6
48 Jondal, *Hordaland* N A3
56 Jönköping S B3
49 Jønnbu N B6
28 Jonquières F C3
53 Jonsberg S D2
65 Jonsdorf D C4
54 Jonsered S A5
57 Jonstorp S C1
23 Jonzac F C4
35 Jorba E B4
97 Jordanów PL B5
65 Jordanów Śląski PL C6
65 Jordanowo PL A5
53 Jordbro S C4
60 Jördenstorf D B3
50 Jordet N A3
55 Jordøse DK C3
31 Jorjaes P C3
59 Jork D B6
47 Joroinen SF E13
48 Jørpeland N B3
40 Jorquera E B1
101 Jošanička Banja YU C5
100 Jošavka BO B2
77 Josipdol CRO A5
99 Josipovac CRO C3
51 Jössefors S C3
18 Josselin F C3
21 Jouarre F C4
23 Jouè-les-Tours F A5
22 Joué-sur-Erdre F A3
58 Joure NL C2
47 Joutsa SF F13
47 Joutseno SF F14
47 Joutsijärvi SF C13
24 Joux-la-Ville F A3
20 Jouy, *Eure-et-Loir* F C2
66 Jouy, *Moselle* F B2
21 Jouy-le-Châtel F C4
20 Jouy-le-Potier F D2
28 Joyeuse F B3
24 Joze F C3
91 Józefów PL B5
91 Józełow PL A5
74 Juan-les-Pins F C2
59 Jübek D A6
33 Jubera E B4
43 Jubrique al Genalguacil E C4
63 Jüchsen D C5
73 Judenburg A A4
55 Juelsminde DK C3
18 Jugon F B3
73 Jugorje SL C5
27 Juillac F A5
58 Juist D B3
3 Julianstown IRL C5
17 Jülich D C6
25 Juliénas F B4
26 Jullian F C4
19 Jullouville F B4
20 Jumièges F B1
23 Jumilhac-le-Grand F C6
40 Jumilla E C1
34 Juncosa E B3
34 Juneda E B3
51 Jung S D4
67 Jungingen D C5
66 Junglingster L B2
104 Junik YU B2
21 Juniville F B5
31 Junqueira P C3
30 Junquera de Ambia E B3
47 Junsele S E8
33 Junta de la Cerca E B3
33 Junta de Oteo E A3
103 Jupănesti RO A5
96 Jur SQ C3
26 Jurançon F C3
89 Jurata PL A4
77 Jurjevo CRO B4
37 Juromenha P C3
28 Jussac F B1
66 Jussey F D1
21 Jussy F B4
64 Jüterbog D B3
47 Juuka SF E14
47 Juva SF F13
19 Juvigny-le-Terte F B4
19 Juvigny-sous-Andaine F B5
21 Juvincourt F B4
20 Juvisy-sur-Orge F C3
21 Juzennecourt F C5
55 Jyderup DK C4
47 Jyväskylä SF E12

K

46 Kaamanen SF B13
47 Kaaresuvanto SF B11
60 Kaarßen D B2
17 Kaatscheuvel NL B5
47 Kåbdalis S C9
107 Kableshkovo BG A5
104 Kačanik YU B3
101 Kačarevo YU B5
104 Kačikol YU B3
64 Kadań CZ C3
98 Kadarkút H B2
107 Kadiköy TR C4
47 Kåge S D10
57 Kågeröd S D2
67 Kahl D A5
63 Kahla D C6
110 Kaiáfa Spa GR B2
73 Kaibing A A5
73 Kainach A A5
73 Kaindorf A A5
73 Kaindorf a.d. Sulm A B5
108 Kainourion GR C3
62 Kaisersesch D C2
67 Kaiserslautern D B3
68 Kaisheim D C1
47 Kajaani SF D13
98 Kajárpéc H A2
99 Kajdacs H B3
100 Kakanj BO B3
99 Kakasd H B3
111 Kaki Thálassa GR B5
91 Kakolewnica Wschodnia PL B6
65 Kakolewo PL B6
110 Kakóvatos GR B2
99 Kál H A5
108 Kalabáka GR B3
106 Kalabáki GR B2
112 Kalafatis GR D1
47 Kalajoki SF D11
112 Kalamáfka, *Kriti* GR
109 Kalamáki, *Lárisa* GR B4
109 Kalamáki, *Magnisía* GR B5
110 Kalamáki, *Messinía* GR C2
110 Kalamáta GR B3
111 Kálamos, *Attikí* GR A4
108 Kálamos, *Lefkás* GR C2
109 Kalamotó GR A5
109 Kalándra GR B5
110 Kalanistra GR A2
112 Kalatádos GR D1
110 Kalávrita GR A3
60 Kalbe D C2
73 Kalce SL C4
107 Kalchevo BG A4
98 Káld H A2
17 Kaldenkirchen D B6
9 Kalemouth GB C5
102 Kalenic YU C1
108 Kalenji GR B2
110 Kaléntzi GR B2
90 Kalety PL C2
49 Kalhovd N A5
109 Kali GR A4
111 Kalianós GR A5
110 Kalifónio GR B3
112 Kálimnos GR B2
89 Kaliningrad R A6
93 Kaliningrad R C7
93 Kalinkavichy BL D11
98 Kalinovac CRO B2
100 Kalinovik BO C3
97 Kalinovo SQ C5
109 Kalipéfki GR B4
106 Kalirrákhi GR C2
88 Kaliska, *Gdansk* PL A4
89 Kaliska, *Gdansk* PL B4
104 Kalista MAK C2
90 Kalisz PL B2
88 Kalisz Pomorski PL B1
108 Kalitákhi GR A3
108 Kalithéa, *Aitolía kai Acarnanía* GR C3
109 Kalithéa, *Khalkidhikí* GR A5
111 Kalithéa, *Lakonía* GR B3
112 Kalithéa, *Sámos* GR C1
110 Kalithéa, *Zákinthos* GR B1
109 Kalithiro GR B3
112 Kalives, *Kriti* GR
106 Kalives, *Thásos* GR C2
111 Kalivia, *Attikí* GR B4
109 Kalivia, *Évia* GR C5
109 Kalivia, *Lárisa* GR A4
47 Kalix S D11
17 Kalkar D B6
17 Kall D C6
54 Kållered S A5
52 Källfallet S C1
53 Kallhäl S C3
69 Kallham A C4
109 Kallifóni GR B3
57 Kallinge S C4
110 Kallithéa GR C2
104 Kallmet AL C1
50 Kallmora S A5
68 Kallmünz D B2
56 Kalmar S C5
17 Kalmthout B B4
97 Kálna SQ C4
102 Kalna, *Srbija* YU C3
105 Kalna, *Srbija* YU B4
98 Kalnik CRO B1
110 Kaló Neró GR B2
99 Kalocsa H B3
106 Kalofer BG A2
110 Kalogriá GR A2
112 Kaloi-Liménes, *Kriti* GR
105 Kalókastro GR C5
111 Kaloni, *Argolís* GR B4
112 Kaloni, *Tínos* GR D1
103 Kalotina BG D3
110 Kaloúsi GR A2
106 Kaloyanovo BG A2
99 Káloz H B3
72 Kals A A2
73 Kalsdorf A B5
71 Kaltbrunn CH A4
72 Kaltenbach A A1
67 Kaltenhouse F C3
59 Kaltenkirchen D B6
63 Kaltennordheim D C5
55 Kalundborg DK C4
91 Kaluszyn PL A5
55 Kalvehave DK C5
73 Kalwang A A4
97 Kalwaria-Zebrzydowska PL B5
98 Kam H A1
110 Kamára GR B3
112 Kamárai, *Kriti* GR
112 Kamares GR E2
111 Kamári GR A3
109 Kamári, *Magnisía* GR B4
112 Kamári, *Thíra* GR D2
108 Kamaroúla GR C3
112 Kámbos, *Kriti* GR
112 Kámbos, *Pátmos* GR C1
62 Kamen D B2
107 Kamenets BG A4
101 Kamenica YU B4
102 Kamenica YU C2
105 Kamenica YU B3
69 Kamenice n. Lipou CZ B6
64 Kamenický Šenov CZ C4
97 Kameničná SQ D4
97 Kamenin-Most SQ D4
104 Kamenjane MAK C2
69 Kamenny Ujezd CZ C5
107 Kameno BG A5
103 Kamenopole BG C4
100 Kamensko CRO C1
64 Kamenz D B4
8 Kames GB C2
91 Kamień PL B4
91 Kamień PL C6
88 Kamień Kraj. PL B3
61 Kamień Pomorski PL B5
90 Kamienica Polska PL C3
65 Kamieniec Zabk PL C6
65 Kamienna Góra PL C6
90 Kamiensk PL B3
108 Kamili GR C2
108 Kaminia GR B2
109 Kámmena Voúrla GR C4
73 Kammern i. Liesingtal A A4
73 Kamnik SL B4
17 Kamp-Lintfort D B6
55 Kampen D D1
58 Kampen NL C2
91 Kampinos PL A4
110 Kampos GR C3
69 Kamýk n Vltavou CZ B5
72 Kanal SL B3
111 Kanála GR B5
109 Kanália, *Kardhítsa* GR B3
109 Kanália, *Magnisía* GR B4
108 Kanallákion GR B2
105 Kanatlarci MAK C3
112 Kándanos, *Kriti* GR
67 Kandel D B4
70 Kandern D A2
70 Kandersteg CH B2
108 Kandhila, *Aitolía kai Acarnanía* GR C2
110 Kandhila, *Arkadhía* GR B3
111 Kándia GR B3
89 Kandyty PL A6
77 Kanfanar CRO A3
47 Kangasniemi SF F13
61 Kania PL B6
108 Kanine AL A1
100 Kaniža CRO A2
99 Kanjiža CRO B5
112 Kanli Kastéllion, *Kriti* GR
4 Kanturk IRL B3
102 Kaonik YU C2
107 Kapakli TR B5
111 Kapandhriti GR A4
109 Kapanós GR A4
110 Kaparéli GR B3
98 Kapela CRO C1
73 Kapellen A A5
17 Kapellen B B4
111 Kaperéli GR A4
73 Kapfenberg A A5
73 Kapfenstein A B5
107 Kapitan Andreevo BG B4
69 Kaplice CZ C5
97 Kápolna H D6
99 Kapolnásnyék H A3
98 Kaposfö H B2
98 Kaposvár H B2
50 Kapp N B1
66 Kappel D C3
55 Kappeln D D2
53 Kappelskär S C5
71 Kappl A A5
72 Kaprun A A2
111 Kapsáli GR C3
98 Kaptol CRO C2
98 Kapuvár H A2
99 Karacsond H A5
98 Karád H B2
107 Karahidir TR B5
101 Karan YU C4
97 Karancslapujto H C5
112 Karaoua TR B1
46 Karasjok N B12
110 Karátoulas GR B2
111 Karavás GR C3
106 Karavelovo BG A2
109 Karavómilos GR C4
112 Karavostásis GR E2
52 Karbenning S B2
51 Kårberg S D5
46 Kårbole S F7
59 Karby D A6
54 Karby DK B1
53 Karby S C4
94 Karcag H C4
91 Karczew PL A5
91 Karczmiska PL B6
90 Karczów PL C1
65 Karczowiska PL B6
110 Kardamili GR C3
69 Kardašova Rečice CZ B5
112 Kardhámaina GR B2
110 Kardhamás GR B2
109 Kardhítsa GR B3
109 Kardhitsomagoúla GR B3
108 Kareiskákis GR C3
65 Kargowa PL A5
47 Karhula SF F13
110 Kariá, *Argolís* GR B3
109 Kariá, *Lárisa* GR B4
108 Kariá, *Lefkás* GR C2
110 Kariai, *Arkadia* GR B3
46 Karigasniemi SF B12
51 Käringön S D2
109 Kariotissa GR A4
47 Karis Karjaa SF F11
55 Karise DK C5
111 Káristos GR A5
110 Karitaina GR B3
108 Karitsa GR B2
108 Karitsa, *Kardhítsa* GR B3
109 Karitsa, *Lárisa* GR B4
109 Karitsa, *Piería* GR A4
110 Karkalou GR B3
112 Karkinágri GR C1
52 Karlholmsbruk S B3
88 Karlino PL A1
77 Karlobag CRO B5
73 Karlovac CRO C5
112 Karlovásion GR C1
101 Karlovčic YU B5
90 Karlovice CZ C1
64 Karlovy Vary CZ C2
51 Karlsborg, *Skaraborg* S D5
53 Karlsby S D1
63 Karlshafen D B4
57 Karlshamn S C3
59 Karlshöfen D B6
49 Karlshus N B7
51 Karlskoga S C5
57 Karlskrona S C4
67 Karlsruhe D B4
51 Karlstad S C4
67 Karlstadt D B5
96 Karlstetten A C1
69 Karlstift A C5
103 Karlukovo BG C5
98 Karmacs H B2
110 Karnási GR B2
111 Karnezéika GR B4
107 Karnobat BG A4
109 Karoplési GR B3
108 Karousadhes GR B1
60 Karow D B3
65 Karpacz PL C5
112 Kárpathos, *Kárpathos* GR
109 Karpenision GR C3
108 Karperón GR B3
109 Karpokhóri GR B3
112 Karpuzlu, *Aydin* TR B1
107 Karpuzlu, *Edirne* TR C4
55 Karrebaeksminde DK C4
47 Kärsämäki SF E12
88 Karsin PL B3
53 Kårsta, *Stockholm* S C4
53 Kärsta, *Västmanland* S C2
60 Karstadt D B2
99 Kartal H A4
109 Karterés GR A5
72 Kartitsch A B2
88 Kartuzy PL A4
55 Karup DK B2
97 Karviná CZ B4
108 Karvounári GR B2
54 Kås DK A2
96 Kašava CZ B3
69 Kasejovice CZ B4
61 Kasekow D B5
104 Kashnjet AL C1
98 Kašina CRO C1
97 Kasina-Wlk. PL B6
47 Kaskinen SF E10
47 Kaskö SF E10
69 Kašperské Hory CZ B4
109 Kassandra GR A5
60 Kasseedorf D A1
63 Kassel D B4
107 Kastanéai GR B4
105 Kastaneri GR D4
109 Kastaniá, *Imathía* GR A4
109 Kastania, *Kardhítsa* GR B3
110 Kastania, *Korinthía* GR B3
111 Kastaniá, *Lakonía* GR C4
110 Kastaniá, *Messinía* GR C3
108 Kastanófito GR A3
100 Kaštel Stari CRO C1
66 Kastellaun D A3
109 Kastelli GR C4
112 Kastéllion, *Kriti* GR
17 Kasterlee B B4
68 Kastl D B2
56 Kastlösa, *Öland* S C5
60 Kastorf D B1
110 Kastóri GR B3
108 Kastoría GR A3
108 Kastráki, *Aitolía kai Acarnanía* GR C3
112 Kastráki, *Náxos* GR D1
108 Kastráki, *Tríkkala* GR B3
110 Kastri, *Akhaia* GR B3
111 Kastri, *Évia* GR B5
109 Kastri, *Lárisa* GR B4
110 Kastria GR B3
108 Kastritsa GR B2
111 Kástron GR A4
108 Kastsikás GR B2
110 Katákolon GR B2
112 Katápola GR D2
108 Kataráktis GR B3
110 Katastári GR B1
60 Katerbow D C3
109 Kateríni GR A4
3 Katesbridge GB B5
111 Kathenoi GR A4
63 Kathlenburg-Duhm D B5
50 Kåtila S A5
105 Katlanovo MAK C3
110 Káto Akhaía GR A2
111 Kato Alepokhóri GR A4
111 Kato Dhimínion GR A3
110 Káto Figalia GR B2
108 Kato Klinai GR A3
110 Káto Klitoria GR B3
110 Káto Makrinoú GR A2
109 Káto Miliá GR A4
106 Káto Nerokópion GR B1
109 Káto Skholárion GR A5
109 Kato Tithoréa GR C4
109 Kato Vermion GR A4
105 Káto Vrondou GR C5
110 Katokhi GR A2
108 Katoúna, *Aitolía kai Acarnanía* GR C3
108 Katoúna, *Lefkás* GR C2
69 Katovice CZ B4
90 Katowice PL C3
52 Katrineberg S A2
53 Katrineholm S D2
57 Kattarp S C1
112 Kattavia GR B3
50 Kattbo S B5
62 Kattenvenne D A2
56 Kattilstorp S A2
105 Katuntsi BG C5
17 Katwijk aan Zee NL A4
65 Katy Wroclawskie PL B6

28 Le Bleymard F B2
23 Le Boulay F A5
35 Le Boulou F A5
27 Le Bourg F B5
29 Le Bourg-d'Oisans F A5
25 Le Bourget-du-Lac F C5
19 Le Bourgneuf-la-Forêt F B5
28 Le Bousquet d'Orb F C2
25 Le Brassus CH B6
24 Le Breuil F B3
20 Le Breuil-en-Auge F B1
29 Le Brusquet F B5
70 Le Bry CH B2
27 Le Bugue F B4
27 Le Buisson F B4
26 Le Caloy F C3
29 Le Cannet-des-Maures F C5
28 Le Canourgue F B2
28 Le Cap d'Agde F C2
83 le Castella I C4
21 Le Cateau-Cambrésis F A4
28 Le Caylar F C2
28 Le Cayrol F B1
25 Le Celle F A4
70 Le Châble CH B2
28 Le Chambon-Feugerolles F A3
28 Le Chambon-sur-Lignon F A3
22 Le Château F C3
25 Le Châtelard F C6
24 Le Châtelet F B2
21 Le Chatelet-en-Brie F C3
21 Le Chesne F B5
28 Le Cheylard F B3
29 Le Ciotat Plage F C4
18 Le Conquet F B1
25 Le Creusot F B4
22 Le Croisic F A2
16 Le Crotoy F C1
25 Le Deschaux F B5
24 Le Donjon F B3
23 Le Dorat F B6
18 Le Faou F B1
18 Le Faouët F B2
18 Le Folgoet F B1
27 Le Fossat F C5
27 Le Fousseret F C5
29 Le Freney F A5
29 Le Fugeret F B5
21 Le Gault-Soigny F C4
23 Le Gond-Pontouvre F C5
70 Le Grand Bornand F C1
24 Le-Grand-Bourg F B1
19 Le Grand Fougeray F C4
20 Le Grand-Lucé F D1
23 Le Grand Pressigny F B5
28 Le Grau-du-Roi F C3
29 Le Guâ F A4
19 Le Havre F A6
66 Le Hohwald F C3
26 Le Houga F C3
27 Le Lardin F A5
29 Le Lauzet-Ubaye F B5
29 Le Lavandou F C5
23 Le Lion-d'Angers F A4
70 Le Locle CH A1
22 Le Loroux-Bottereau F A3
22 Le Louroux Béconnais F A4
29 Le Luc F C5
23 Le Lude F A5
28 Le Malzieu-Ville F B2
20 Le Mans F D1
27 Le Mas-d'Azil F C5
28 Le Massegros F B2
23 Le May-sur-Evre F A4
24 Le Mayet-de Montagne F B3
20 Le Mèle sur Sarthe F C1
66 Le Ménil, *Vosges* F C2
66 Le Ménil, *Vosges* F D2
21 Le Meriot F C4
20 Le Merlerault F C1
21 Le Mesnil-sur-Oger F C5
25 Le Miroir F B5
28 Le Monastier F B2
29 Le Monêtier-les-Bains F B5
24 Le Mont-Dore F C2
24 Le Montet F B3
26 Le Muret F B3
29 Le Muy F C5
20 Le Neubourg F B1
21 Le Nouvion-en-Thiérache F A4
22 Le Palais F A1
16 Le Parcq F C2
29 Le Péage-de-Roussillon F A3
22 Le Pellerin F A3
35 Le Perthus F A5
25 Le Petit Bornand F C6
24 Le Pin F B3
29 Le Poët F B4
22 Le Poirè-sur-Vie F B3
25 Le Pont CH B6
29 Le Pont-de-Claix F A4
28 Le Pont-de-Montvert F B2
29 Le Pont-du-Fossé F B5
29 Le Pontet F C3
26 Le Porge F B2
16 Le Portel F C1
28 Le Poujol F C2
18 Le Pouldu F C2
22 Le Pouliguen F A2
26 Le Pouyalet F A3
71 Le Prese I B5
28 Le Puy-en-Velay F A2
29 Le Puy-Ste-Réparade F C4
16 Le Quesnoy F C3
20 Le Raincy F C3
18 Le Relecq-Kerhuon F B1
27 Le Rouget F B6
28 Le Rozier F B2
19 Le Sel de Bretagne F C4
25 Le Sentier CH B6
29 Le Teil F B3
19 Le Teilleul F B5
22 Le Temple-de-Bretagne F A3
20 Le Theil F C1
66 Le Thillot F D2
16 Le Touquet-Paris-Plage F C1
29 Le Touvet F A4
20 Le Translay F B2
21 Le Transloy F A3
20 Le Tréport F A2
29 Le Val F C5
18 Le-Val-André F B3
66 Le Val d'Ajol F D2
25 Le Valdahon F A6
22 Le Verdon-sur-Mer F C3
29 Le Vernet F B5
19 Le Vieux Bourg F B4
28 Le Vigan F C2
76 Le Ville I C2
19 Le Vivier-sur-Mer F B4
11 Lea GB B5
9 Leadburn GB C4
11 Leadenham GB B5
9 Leadgate GB D6
9 Leadhills GB C4
14 Leamington GB B1
8 Leanach GB B2
4 Leap IRL C2
15 Leatherhead GB C2
88 Łeba PL A3
66 Lebach D B2
105 Lebane YU B3
17 Lebekke B C4
98 Lébény H A2
30 Leboreiro E B3
88 Lębork PL A3
43 Lebrija E C3
73 Lebring A B5
64 Lebusa D B3
83 Lecce I A5
71 Lecco I C4
34 Lécera E B2
71 Lech A A5
71 Lechbruck D A5
13 Lechlade GB B6
96 Lechovice CZ C2
34 Leciñena E B2
55 Leck D D1
27 Lectoure F C4
33 Lecumberri E A5
89 Łęcze PL A5
90 Łeczyca PL A3
39 Ledaña E C5
13 Ledbury GB A5
15 Lede B C3
69 Ledeč n. Sazavou CZ B6
69 Ledenice CZ C5
31 Ledesma E C4
28 Lédignan F C3
32 Lédigos E B2
6 Ledmore GB B4
96 Lednice CZ C2
97 Lednicke-Rovné SQ B4
88 Ledyczek PL B2
90 Lędziny PL C3
11 Leeds GB B4
11 Leek GB B3
58 Leek NL B3
11 Leeming Bar GB A4
2 Leenaun IRL C2
58 Leens NL B3
59 Leer D B4
17 Leerdam NL B5
59 Leerhafe D B4
59 Leese D C6
59 Leeste D C5
58 Leeuwarden NL B2
60 Leezen D B1
109 Lefkádia GR A4
109 Lefkaditi GR C4
111 Lefkandi GR A4
108 Lefkás GR C2
112 Léfkes GR D1
108 Lefkimi GR B2
38 Leganés E B3
67 Legau D D6
88 Legbąd PL B3
60 Legde D C2
62 Legden D A2
22 Legé F B3
91 Legionowa PL A4
66 Léglise B B1
75 Legnago I A6
71 Legnano I C3
72 Legnaro I C1
65 Legnica PL B6
89 Łegowo PL A4
98 Legrad CRO B1
111 Legrena GR B5
27 Léguevin F C5
33 Legutiano E B4
63 Lehesten D C6
96 Lehnice SQ C3
64 Lehnin D A2
68 Lehrberg D B1
63 Lehre D A5
63 Lehrte D A4
60 Lehsen D B2
73 Leibnitz A B5
14 Leicester GB B1
62 Leichlingen D B2
17 Leiden NL A4
17 Leiderdorp NL A4
17 Leidschendam NL A4
10 Leigh GB B3
15 Leighton Buzzard GB C2
17 Leignon B C5
46 Leikanger, *Sogn og Fjordane* N F3
67 Leimen D B4
111 Leimonas GR C3
63 Leinefde D B5
67 Leingarten D B5
74 Leini I A2
10 Leintwardine GB C3
67 Leipheim D C6
64 Leipzig D B2
36 Leiria P B2
48 Leirvik, *Hordaland* N B2
72 Leisach A B2
64 Leisnig D B2
70 Leissigen CH B2
14 Leiston GB B4
9 Leitholm GB C5
2 Leitrim IRL B3
64 Leitzkau D A1
33 Leiza E A5
106 Lekáni GR B2
90 Łękawa PL B3
97 Łekawica PL B5
33 Lekeitio E A4
98 Lekenik CRO C1
56 Lekeryd S B3
110 Lekhainá GR B2
103 Lekhchevo BG C4
111 Lékheo GR B3
109 Lekhónia GR B5
108 Lékhovon GR A3
65 Lęknica PL B4
50 Leksand S B6
50 Lekvattnet S B3
103 Leleşti RO A4
89 Lelkowo PL A6
90 Lelów PL C3
58 Lelystad NL C2
54 Lem DK B1
69 Lembach A C4
67 Lembach F B3
62 Lembeck D B1
17 Lembeek B C4
66 Lemberg F B3
26 Lembèye F C3
58 Lemelerveld NL C3
62 Lemgo D A3
58 Lemmer NL C2
47 Lempäälä SF F11
28 Lempdes F A2
6 Lemreway GB B2
54 Lemvig DK B1
59 Lemwerder D B5
25 Len F B5
32 Lena E A1
50 Lena N B1
99 Lenauheim RO C5
23 Lencloitre F B5
72 Lend A A3
8 Lendalfoot GB C3
98 Lendava SL B1
76 Lendinara I A1
72 Lendorf A B3
62 Lendringsen D B2
54 Lendum DK A3
64 Lengefeld D C3
96 Lengenfeld A C1
59 Lengerich, *Niedersachsen* D C4
62 Lengerich, *Nordrhein-Westfalen* D A2
72 Lenggries D A1
63 Lenglern D B4
98 Lengyeltóti H B2
56 Lenhovda S C4
70 Lenk CH B2
51 Lennartsfors S C2
8 Lennoxtown GB C3
75 Leno I A5
79 Lenola I B4
102 Lenovac YU C3
16 Lens B C3
16 Lens F C2
29 Lens Lestang F A4
60 Lensahn D A1
112 Lentas, *Kriti* GR
30 Lentellais E B3
59 Lentföhrden D B6
98 Lenti H B1
85 Lentini I B3
70 Lenzburg CH A3
60 Lenzen D B2
71 Lenzerheide CH B4
69 Lenzing A D4
73 Leoben A A5
96 Leobersdorf A D2
72 Leogang A A2
26 Léognan F B3
13 Leominster GB A5
32 León E B1
26 Léon F C2
67 Leonberg D C4
29 Léoncel F B4
69 Leonding A C5
110 Leóndio GR A2
79 Leonessa I A3
85 Leonforte I B3
111 Leonidhion GR B3
109 Leontári GR B4
17 Leopoldsburg B B5
69 Leopoldschlag A C5
96 Leopoldsdorf i.Mfd. A C2
61 Leopoldshagen D B4
103 Leordeni RO B6
42 Lepe E B2
102 Lepenac YU C2
108 Lepenoú GR C3
81 Lepetani YU B5
6 Lephin GB C2
98 Lepoglava CRO B1
47 Leppävirte SF E13
60 Leppin D C2
110 Lépreo GR B2
98 Lepsény H A3
109 Leptokaria GR A4
66 Lepuix F D2
83 Léquile I A5
84 Lercara Friddi I B2
51 Lerdal S D2
24 Leré F A2
75 Lérici I B4
34 Lérida E B3
33 Lerin E B5
26 Lerm-et-Musset F B3
32 Lerma E B3
71 Lermoos A A5
66 Lerouville F C1
54 Lerum S A5
49 Lervik N B7
6 Lerwick, *Shetlands* GB
34 Lés E A3
24 Les-Ancizes-Comps F C2
25 Les Abrets F C5
24 Les Aix-d'Angillon F A2
70 Les Allues F C1
20 Les Andelys F B2
70 Les Arcs, *Savoie* F C1
29 Les Arcs, *Var* F C5
23 Les-Aubiers F B4
29 Les Barraques F B5
21 Les Bézards F D3
70 Les Bois CH A1
20 Les Bordes F D3
35 Les Cabanes de Fitou F A5
35 Les Cabanes-de-Lapalme F A5
35 Les Cabannes F A4
70 Les Contamines-Montjoie F C1
25 Les Déserts F C6
29 Les Deux-Alpes F A5
70 Les Diablerets CH B2
25 Les Echelles F C5
35 Les Escaldes AND A4
22 Les-Essarts F B3
28 Les Estables F B3
27 Les Eyzies-de Tayac F B5
20 Les Fontaines F D2
70 Les Fonteneles F A1
70 Les Gets F B1
20 Les Grandes-Ventes F B2
21 Les Granges F C5
70 Les Haudères CH B2
20 Les Hayons F B2
22 Les Herbiers F B3
25 Les Hôpitaux-Neufs F B6
70 Les Houches F C1
21 Les Islettes F B5
29 Les Lecques F C4
22 Les Lucs-sur-Boulogne F B3
28 Les Mages F B3
25 Les Marches F C5
29 Les Mées F B4
29 Les Menuires F A5
20 Les Mureaux F C2
29 Les Omergues F B4
21 Les Ormes-sur-Voulzie F C4
29 Les Orres F B5
29 Les Pennes Mirabeau F C4
19 Les Pieux F A4
23 Les Ponts-de-Cé F A4
70 Les Ponts-de-Martel CH B1
70 Les Praz F C1
21 Les Riceys F D5
25 Les Roches F C4
18 Les Rosaires F B3
23 Les Rosiers F A4
25 Les Rousses F B6
22 Les Sables-d'Olonne F B3
29 Les Salles F C5
28 Les Ternes F B2
23 Les Trois Moûtiers F A4
28 Les Vans F B3
70 Les Verrières CH B1
28 Les Vignes F B2
33 Lesaca E A5
101 Lešak YU C5
104 Lešani MAK C2
9 Lesbury GB C6
26 Lescar F C3
77 Lešce CRO B5
25 Lescheraines F C6
18 Lesconil F C1
105 Lescovac YU B3
21 Lesdins F B4
98 Lesenceistvánd H B2
106 Lesichovo BG A2
80 Lesina I C2
110 Lesini GR A2
46 Lesjaskog N E4
50 Lesjöfors S C5
94 Lesko PL B5
73 Leskova SL C4
96 Leskovec CZ B3
69 Leskovice CZ B6
108 Leskovik AL A2
9 Leslie GB B4
9 Lesmahagow GB C4
21 Lesmont F C5
65 Leśna PL B5
18 Lesneven F B1
90 Lešnica PL C2
101 Lešnica YU B4
65 Leśniów Wielkoplski PL B5
26 Lesparre-Médoc F A3
28 Lespignan F C2
26 Lesponne F C4
73 Lessach A A3
19 Lessay F A4
56 Lessebo S C4
16 Lessines B C3
23 Lesterps F B5
90 Leszczyny PL C2
65 Leszno PL B6
91 Leszno PL A4
65 Leszno Din PL B5
15 Letchworth GB C2
98 Letenye H B1
79 Letino I B5
62 Letmathe D B2
103 Letnitsa BG C6
96 Letohrad CZ A2
96 Letovice CZ B2
61 Letschin D C5
62 Lette D B2
2 Letterfrack IRL C2
3 Letterkenny IRL B4
2 Lettermacaward IRL B3
12 Letterston GB B3
7 Lettoch GB C5
45 Letur E A4
34 Letux E B2
60 Letzlingen D C2
103 Leu RO B4
83 Léuca I B5
35 Leucate F A6
9 Leuchars GB B5
21 Leuglay F D5
70 Leuk CH B2
70 Leukerbad CH B2
64 Leuna D B2
63 Leutenberg D C6
71 Leuterschach D A5
68 Leutershausen D B1
67 Leutkirch D D6
17 Leuven B C4
16 Leuze, *Hainault* B C3
17 Leuze, *Namur* B C4
111 Levádhia GR A3
108 Levan AL A1
49 Levang N C6
46 Levanger N E5
100 Levanjska Varoš CRO A3
75 Lévanto I B4
75 Levata I A5
9 Leven, *Fife* GB B5
11 Leven, *Humberside* GB B5
83 Leverano I A4
6 Leverburgh GB C2
62 Leverkusen D B2
62 Levern D A3
24 Levet F B2
97 Levice SQ C4
72 Lévico I B1
110 Levidhi GR B3
25 Levier F B6
21 Lévignen F B3
98 Levinovac CRO C2
109 Levkás GR C3
107 Levkimi GR B4
109 Levkóvrisi GR A3
106 Levkoyia GR B1
111 Lévktra GR A4
97 Levoča SQ B6
23 Levroux F B6
103 Levski BG C6
106 Levskigrad BG A2
105 Levunovo BG C5
15 Lewes GB D3
90 Lewin Brzeski PL C1
11 Leyburn GB A4
10 Leyland GB B3
15 Leysdown on Sea GB C3
70 Leysin CH B2
91 Lezajsk PL C6
89 Lęzany PL B7
18 Lézardrieux F B2
27 Lézat-sur-Léze F C5
23 Lezay F B5
104 Lezhë AL C1
28 Lézignan-Corbières F C1
28 Lezignan-la-Cèbe F C2
101 Ležimir YU A4
21 Lézinnes F D5
24 Lezoux F C3
39 Lezuza E D4
27 Lherm F C5
23 Lhommaizé F B5
21 Lhuître F C5
20 Liancourt, *Oise* F B3
21 Liancourt, *Somme* F B3
109 Lianokládhion GR C4
108 Liapádhes GR B1
21 Liart F B5
56 Liatorp S C3
65 Libáň CZ C5
13 Libanus GB B4
64 Libceves CZ C3
64 Liběchov CZ C4
65 Liberec CZ C5
64 Libešice CZ C4
90 Libiaź PL C3
96 Libina CZ B3
64 Libochovice CZ C4
108 Libofshë AL A1
108 Libohovë AL A2
26 Libourne F B3
66 Libramont B B1
104 Librazhd AL C2
45 Librilla E B5
40 Libros E A1
84 Licata I B2
75 Licciana Nardi I B5
79 Licenza I A3
33 Liceros E C3
62 Lich D C3
24 Lichères-près-Aigremont F A3
11 Lichfield GB C4
17 Lichtart B B4
69 Lichtenau A C6
62 Lichtenau D B3
63 Lichtenfels D C6
71 Lichtensteig CH A4
64 Lichtenstein D C2
17 Lichtenvoorde NL B6
16 Lichtervelde B B3
77 Licke Jesenice CRO A5
77 Lički Osik CRO B5
85 Licodia Eubea I B3
103 Licuriciu RO B4
93 Lida BL D9
8 Liddesdale GB B2
97 Lidečko CZ B4
110 Lidhorikion GR A3
56 Lidhult S C2
51 Lidköping S D4
72 Lido I C2
83 Lido Azzurro I A4
76 Lido degli Estensi I B2
76 Lido degli Scacchi I B2
76 Lido del Savio I B2
76 Lido della Nazioni I B2
75 Lido di Camaiore I C5
79 Lido di Casalbordino I A5
78 Lido di Castel Fusano I B3
78 Lido di Cincinnato I B3
76 Lido di Classe I B2
77 Lido di Fermo I C3
79 Lido di Fondi I B4
72 Lido di lésolo I C2
79 Lido di Licola I C5
83 Lido di Metaponto I A3
78 Lido di Óstia I B3
85 Lido di Pláia I B4
83 Lido di Policoro I A3
76 Lido di Pomposa I B2
83 Lido di Scanzano I A3
80 Lido di Siponto I C2
83 Lido di Squillace I C3
76 Lido di Volano I B2
79 Lido Riccio I A5
83 Lido Silvana I A4
89 Lidzbark Warminski PL A6
93 Lidzbark Warmiński PL C7
89 Lidzbart PL B5
69 Liebenau A C5
59 Liebenau D C6
63 Liebenburg D A5
63 Liebenstein D C5
61 Liebenwalde D C4
64 Lieberose D B4
73 Lieboch A B5
17 Liederkerke B C4
17 Liège B C5
47 Lieksa SF E15
62 Lienen D A2
72 Lienz A B2
93 Liepaja LV B7
17 Lier B B4
49 Lier N B7
25 Liernais F A4
24 Liernolles F B3
62 Liesborn D B3
72 Liesing A B2
17 Liessel NL B5
70 Liestal CH A2
45 Liétor E A5
20 Lieurey F B1
16 Liévin F C2
73 Liezen A A4
66 Liffol-le-Grand F C1
3 Lifford IRL B4
19 Liffré F B4
27 Ligardes F B4
73 Ligist A B5
72 Lignano Sabbiadoro I C3
22 Ligne F A3
24 Lignières F B2
66 Ligny-en-Barrois F C1
21 Ligny-le-Châtel F D4
111 Ligourion GR B4
23 Ligueil F A5
97 Likavka SQ B5
50 Likenäs S B4
109 Likhás GR C4
107 Likófos GR B4
110 Likoporiá GR A3
110 Likósoura GR B3
109 Likoúdhi GR B4
110 Likouria GR B3
109 Lilaia GR C4
54 Lild Strand DK A1
96 Lilienfeld A C1
59 Lilienthal D B5
105 Liljakovo BG C5
106 Lilkovo BG B2
51 Lilla Edet S D3
56 Lilla Tjärby S C2
53 Lillån S C1
17 Lille B B4
16 Lille F C3
20 Lillebonne F B1
50 Lillehammer N A1
55 Lillerød DK C5
16 Lillers F C2
49 Lillesand N C5
10 Lilleshall GB C3
50 Lillestrøm N C2
39 Lillo E C3
50 Lima S B4
17 Limal B C4
111 Limáni Yéraka GR C4
97 Limanowa PL B6
3 Limavady GB A5
20 Limay F B2
64 Limbach-Oberfrohna D C2
17 Limbourg B C5
62 Limburg D C3
67 Limburgerhof D B4
50 Limedsforsen S B4
106 Limenária GR C2
109 Liménas GR C5
110 Liméni GR C3
4 Limerick IRL B3
20 Limésy F B1
112 Limin Chersonisou, *Kriti* GR
47 Liminka SF D12
56 Limmared S B2
58 Limmen NL C1
111 Limnes GR B3
109 Limni GR C5
110 Limnista GR A2
23 Limoges F C6
27 Limogne F B5
74 Limone Piemonte I B2
71 Limone s. Garda I C5
24 Limons F C3
20 Limours F C3
27 Limoux F C6
33 Limpias E A3
44 Linares E A3
40 Linares de Mora E A2
38 Linares de Riofrio E B1
34 Linas de Broto E A2
11 Lincoln GB B5
55 Lind DK B1
67 Lindach D C5
10 Lindale GB A3
56 Lindås S C4
71 Lindau D A4
55 Lindelse DK D3
71 Lindenberg, *Bayern* D A4
64 Lindenberg, *Brandenburg* D A4
17 Lindenheuvel NL C5
59 Lindern D C4
57 Linderöd S D2
53 Lindesberg S C1
51 Lindfors S C4
55 Lindholm D D1
55 Lindknud DK C2
62 Lindlar D B2
53 Lindö S D2
54 Lindome S A5
112 Lindos GR A2
31 Lindoso P C2
61 Lindow D C3
56 Lindshammar S B4
60 Lindstedt D C2
69 Líně CZ B4
52 Lingbo S A2
58 Lingen D C4
15 Lingfield GB C2
52 Linghed S B1
108 Lingos GR B2
85 Linguaglossa I B4
88 Linia PL A3
61 Linie PL B5
89 Liniewo PL A4
67 Linkenheim D B4
53 Linköping S D1
9 Linlithgow GB C4
17 Linne NL B5
56 Linneryd S C4
52 Linnes Hammarby S C3
17 Linnich D C6
34 Liñola E B3
56 Linsdal S C5
15 Linslade GB C2
71 Linthal CH B4
14 Linton, *Cambridgeshire* GB B3
15 Linton, *Kent* GB C3
61 Linum D C3
69 Linz A C5
62 Linz D C2
19 Lion-sur-Mer F A5
112 Liónas GR D1
80 Lioni I D2
109 Liópraso GR B3
108 Lipa GR B2
99 Lipar CRO C4
85 Lipari I A3
15 Liphook GB C2
61 Lipiany PL B5
73 Lipica SL C3
98 Lipik CRO C2
88 Lipka PL B3
105 Lipkovo MAK B3
104 Lipljan YU B3
89 Lipniaki R A7
88 Lipnica PL B3
97 Lipnica-Murowana PL B6
96 Lipnik CZ B3
91 Lipnik PL C5
89 Lipno PL C5
109 Lipokhori GR A4
26 Liposthey F B3
94 Lipova RO C4
101 Lipovac CRO A4
98 Lipovljani CRO C1
77 Lipovo Polje CRO B5
89 Lipowina PL A5
62 Lippborg D B3
63 Lippoldsberg D B4
62 Lippstadt D B3
91 Lipsko PL B5
97 Liptovská-Lúžna SQ C5
97 Liptovská Osada SQ C5
97 Liptovská Teplá SQ B5
97 Liptovská-Teplička SQ C6
97 Liptovský Hrádok SQ B5
97 Liptovský-Mikuláš SQ B5
88 Lipusz PL A3
96 Lipuvka CZ B2
107 Lira GR B4
22 Liré F A3
110 Lirkia GR B3
101 Lisa YU C5
3 Lisbellaw GB B4
36 Lisboa P C1
3 Lisburn GB B5
4 Lisdoonvarna IRL A2
96 Lišeň CZ B2
91 Lisia Góra PL C4
90 Lisięcice PL C1
20 Lisieux F B1
12 Liskeard GB C3
27 Lisle-sur-Tarn F C5
5 Lismore IRL B4
105 Lisna YU B4
3 Lisnacree GB B5
3 Lisnaskea GB B4
100 Lišnja BO B2
69 Lišov CZ B5
90 Lisów, *Częstochowa* PL C2
61 Lisów, *Gorzów Wielkopolski* PL C5
91 Lisów, *Radom* PL B4
15 Liss GB C2
17 Lisse NL A4
11 Lissett GB A5
20 Lissy F C3
4 Lissycasey IRL B2
55 List D C1
108 Lista GR B2
57 Listerby S C4
100 Lištica BO C2
4 Listowel IRL B2
26 Listrac-Médoc F A3
97 Liszki PL A5
46 Lit S E7
26 Lit-et-Mixe F B2
103 Lita RO C5
97 Litava SQ C5
14 Litcham GB B3
96 Litenčice CZ B3
110 Lithakiá GR B1
109 Liti GR A4
73 Litija SL B4
97 Litke H C5
48 Litlabø N B2
48 Litlos N A4
109 Litókhoron GR A4
64 Litoměřice CZ C4
96 Litomyšl CZ B2
96 Litovel CZ B3
69 Litschau A C6
6 Little Assynt GB B3
7 Little Ayre GB B5
15 Little Clacton GB C4
6 Little Gruinard GB C3
14 Little Walsingham GB B3
11 Littleborough GB B3
15 Littlehampton GB D2
7 Littlemill, *Highland* GB C5
8 Littlemill, *Strathclyde* GB C3
15 Littlemore GB C1
14 Littleport GB B3
5 Littleton IRL B4
47 Litto SF B10
19 Littry-la-Mine F A5
64 Litvmov CZ C3
98 Litzelsdorf A A1
109 Livadherón GR A3
109 Livádhion GR A4
108 Livadhjë AL B2
111 Livádi, *Sérifos* GR B5
109 Livádi, *Thessaloníki* GR A5
105 Livádia, *Sérrai* GR C5
112 Livádia, *Tílos* GR B2
105 Livadokhóri GR C5
109 Livanátais GR C5
20 Livarot F B1
27 Livernon F B5
81 Liverovici YU B6
10 Liverpool GB B3
71 Livigno I B5
9 Livingston GB C4
100 Livno BO C1
73 Livold SL C4
75 Livorno I C5
74 Livorno Ferraris I A3
29 Livron F B3
21 Livry-sur-Louvercy F B5
66 Lixheim F C3
110 Lixourion GR A1
12 Lizard GB D2
21 Lizy-sur-Ourcq F B4
83 Lizzano I A4
75 Lizzano in Belvedere I B5
104 Ljesane YU B2
101 Ljig YU B5
50 Ljørdal N A3
48 Ljosland N C4
105 Ljubata YU B4
106 Ljuben BG A2
100 Ljubija BO B1
81 Ljubinje BO B5
73 Ljubljana SL B4
73 Ljubno SL B4
108 Ljubojno MAK A3
56 Ljung S B2
56 Ljungby S C2
57 Ljungbyhed S C2
56 Ljungbyholm S C5
53 Ljungsbro S D1
51 Ljungskile S D2
46 Ljusdal S F8
53 Ljusfallshammar S D1
50 Ljusnarsberg S C5
52 Ljusne S A3
98 Ljutomer SL B1
35 Lladurs E A4
35 Llafranch E B6
35 Llagostera E B5
10 Llanaber GB C1
10 Llanaelhaiarn GB C1
12 Llanarth GB A3
10 Llanbedr GB C1
10 Llanbedrog GB C1
10 Llanberis GB B1
13 Llanbister GB A4
7 Llanbryde GB C5
12 Llandeilo GB B4
12 Llandgadog GB B4
12 Llandovery GB A4
13 Llandrindod Wells GB A4
18 Llandudec F B1
10 Llandudno GB B2
12 Llandybie GB B3
12 Llandyssul GB A3
12 Llanelli GB B3
10 Llanerchymedd GB B1
32 Llanes E A2
10 Llanfair Caereinion GB C2
10 Llanfair P.G. GB B1
10 Llanfair Talhairn GB B2
10 Llanfairfechan GB B2
13 Llanfihangel-nant-Melan GB A4
10 Llanfyllin GB C2
10 Llangefni GB B1
10 Llangelynin GB C1
10 Llangoed GB B1
10 Llangollen GB C2
10 Llangurig GB C2
10 Llangynog GB C2
13 Llanharan GB B4
10 Llanidloes GB C2
10 Llanilar GB C1
10 Llanilyfni GB B1
12 Llanon GB A3
10 Llanrhaedr-ym-Mochnant GB C2
12 Llanrhidian GB B3
12 Llanrhystyd GB A3
10 Llanrwst GB B2
35 Llansá E A6
12 Llanstephan GB B3
33 Llanteno E A3
13 Llantrisant GB B4
13 Llantwit-Major GB B4
10 Llanuwchllyn GB C2
13 Llanvihangel Crucorney GB B5
12 Llanwrda GB B4
13 Llanwrtyd Wells GB A4
12 Llanybyther GB A3
34 Lleida-Lérida E B3
37 Llera E C4
43 Llerena E A3
35 Lles E A4
35 Llesúy E A4
35 Llinás E A4
40 Lliria E B2
35 Llivia F A4
96 Lljezd u. Brna CZ B2
33 Llodio E A4
35 Lloret de Mar E B5
40 Llosa de Ranes E B2
41 Lloseta, *Mallorca* E
65 Llowa PL B5
41 Lluchmayor, *Mallorca* E
40 Llutxent E C2
10 Llynclys GB C2
13 Llyswen GB A4
45 Lo Pagán E B6
9 Loanhead GB C4
74 Loano I B3
8 Loans GB C3
34 Loarre E A2
65 Löbau D B4
17 Lobberich D B6
64 Löbejün D B1
63 Lobenstein D C6
57 Löberöd S D2
61 Łobez PL B6
61 Löbnitz D A3
37 Lobón E C4
64 Loburg D A2
88 Łobženica PL B3
70 Locana I C2
70 Locarno CH B3
59 Loccum D C6
7 Loch Loyal Lodge GB B4
8 Lochailort GB B2
8 Lochaline GB B2
71 Lochau A A4
6 Lochboisdale GB C1
6 Lochcarron GB C3
8 Lochearnhead GB B3
17 Lochem NL A6
23 Loches F A5
9 Lochgelly GB B4
8 Lochgilphead GB B2
8 Lochgoilhead GB B3
6 Lochinever GB B3
8 Lochlaggan Hotel GB B3
9 Lochmaben GB C4
6 Lochmaddy GB C1
8 Lochranza GB C2
8 Lochwinnoch GB C3
102 Ločika YU C2
98 Lockenhaus A A1
61 Löcknitz D B5
22 Locmaria F A1
22 Locmariaquer F A2
18 Locminé F C3
81 Locorotondo I D4
18 Locquirec F B2
85 Locri I A5
18 Locronan F B1
18 Loctudy F C1
33 Lodares de Osma E C4
57 Löddeköpinge S D2
14 Loddon GB B4
87 Lode I B2
57 Löderup S D3
28 Lodève F C2
75 Lodi I A4
46 Lødingen N B7
33 Lodosa E B4
51 Lödöse S D3
97 Lodygowice PL B5
90 Łódź PL B3
39 Loeches E B3
46 Loen N F3
17 Loenen NL A6
48 Løfallstrand N A2
72 Lofer A A2
110 Lofos, *Akhaia* GR A3
109 Lófos, *Piería* GR A4
56 Loftahammar S B5
48 Lofthus N A3
11 Loftus GB A5
59 Loga D B4
48 Loga N C3
10 Loggerheads GB C3
71 Lograto I C5
33 Logroño E B4
37 Logrosán E B5
54 Løgstør DK B2
55 Løgumkloster DK C1
55 Lohals DK C3
47 Lohja SF F12
62 Löhlbach D B3
60 Lohmen, *Mecklenburg-Vorpommern* D B3
64 Lohmen, *Sachsen* D C4
62 Löhnberg D C3
59 Lohne D C5
62 Löhne D A3
67 Lohr D B5
62 Lohra D C3
64 Lohsa D B4
75 Loiano I B6
47 Loimaa SF F11
25 Loire F C4
87 Lóiri I B2
19 Loiron F B5
61 Loitz D B4
31 Loivos P C3
31 Loivos do Monte P C3
21 Loivre F B4
44 Loja E B2
55 Løjt Kirkeby DK C2
73 Loka SL B5
97 Lokca SQ B5
50 Løken N C2
17 Lokeren B B3
64 Loket CZ C2
54 Løkken DK A2
46 Lökken N E4
93 Loknya R B12
102 Lokve YU A2
62 Lollar D C3
73 Lölling A B4
103 Lom BG C4
64 Lom CZ C3
46 Lom N F4
97 Lom SQ C5
27 Lombez F C4
74 Lomello I A3
46 Lomen N F4
91 Lomianki PL A4
57 Lomma S D2
64 Lommatzsch D B3
17 Lommel B B5
62 Lommerssum D C1
96 Lomnice CZ B2
69 Lomnice n. Lužnici CZ B5
65 Lomnice-n. Popelkou CZ C5
93 Lomonosov R A11
93 Łomża PL D8
56 Lönashult S C3
71 Lonato I C5
55 Lønborg DK C1
17 Londerzeel B B4
20 Londinières F B2
15 London GB C2
3 Londonderry GB B4
6 Londubh GB C3
14 Long Bennington GB B2
15 Long Crendon GB C1
14 Long Eaton GB B1
15 Long Hanborough GB C1
15 Long Melford GB B3
10 Long Preston GB A3
14 Long Sutton GB B3
110 Longá, *Messinía* GR C2
109 Longá, *Tríkkala* GR B3
110 Longanikos GR B3
72 Longare I C1
34 Longares E B1
72 Longarone I B2
76 Longastrino I B1
13 Longbridge Deveril GB B5
21 Longchamp F C5
66 Longchamps B A1
25 Longchaumois F B5
25 Longeau F A5
25 Longecourt F A5
66 Longeville, *Moselle* F B2
22 Longeville, *Vendée* F B3
66 Longeville-en-Barrois F C1
3 Longford IRL C4
9 Longforgan GB B4
9 Longhorsley GB C6
9 Longhoughton GB C6
85 Longi I A3
109 Longitsi GR C4
66 Longlier B B1
20 Longny-au-Perche F C1
83 Longobucco I B3
110 Lóngos GR A3
23 Longré F B4
31 Longroiva P D3
7 Longside GB C7

9	Longtown	GB	C5
23	Longué	F	A4
20	Longueau	F	B3
66	Longuyon	F	B1
25	Longvic	F	A5
66	Longvilly	B	A1
66	Longwy	F	B1
72	Lonigo	I	C1
59	Löningen	D	C4
91	Łoniów	PL	C5
56	Lönneberga	S	B4
62	Lonneker	NL	A1
25	Lons-le-Saunier	F	B5
57	Lönsboda	S	C3
54	Lønstrup	DK	A2
12	Looe	GB	C3
17	Loon op Zand	NL	B5
16	Loone-Plage	F	C2
96	Loosdorf	A	C1
77	Lopar	CRO	B4
101	Lopare	BO	B3
104	Lopatica	MAK	C3
44	Lopera	E	B2
58	Loppersum	D	B4
58	Loppersum	NL	B3
91	Łopuszno	PL	C4
21	Lor	F	B5
44	Lora de Estepa	E	B2
43	Lora del Rio	E	B4
39	Loranca del Campo	E	B4
45	Lorca	E	B5
67	Lorch	D	A3
50	Lørenfallet	N	B2
49	Lørenskog	N	B7
66	Lorentzweiler	L	B2
30	Lorenzana	E	A3
76	Loreo	I	A2
76	Loreto	I	C3
79	Loreto Aprutino	I	A4
25	Lorette	F	C4
29	Lorgues	F	C5
83	Lorica	I	B3
18	Lorient	F	C2
23	Lorignac	F	C4
99	Lörinci	H	A4
29	Loriol	F	B3
24	Lormes	F	A3
76	Loro Ciuffenna	I	C1
45	Lorqui	E	A5
70	Lorrach	D	A2
20	Lorris	F	D3
59	Lorup	D	C4
91	Łoś	PL	B4
45	Los Alcázares	E	B6
33	Los Arcos	E	B4
33	Los Ausines	E	B3
32	Los Barios de Luna	E	B1
43	Los Barrios	E	C4
43	Los Caños de Meca	E	C3
45	Los Cerricos	E	B4
44	Los Corrales	E	B2
32	Los Corrales de Buelna	E	A2
45	Los Dolores	E	B6
45	Los Gallardos	E	B5
39	Los Hinojosos	E	C4
40	Los Isidros	E	B1
43	Los Molinos, *Badajóz*	E	A3
38	Los Molinos, *Madrid*	E	B2
43	Los Morales	E	B4
38	Los Navalmorales	E	C2
38	Los Navalucillos	E	C2
45	Los Nietos	E	B6
30	Los Nogales	E	B3
43	Los Palacios y Villafranca	E	B4
30	Los Peares	E	B3
33	Los Rábanos	E	C4
38	Los Santos	E	B1
39	Los Santos de la Humosa	E	B3
37	Los Santos de Maimona	E	C4
32	Los Tijos	E	A2
44	Los Villares	E	B3
38	Los Yébenes	E	C3
31	Losacino	E	C4
37	Losar de la Vera	E	A5
69	Losenstein	A	D5
66	Losheim	D	B2
17	Losheimer Graben	D	C6
25	Losne	F	A5
55	Løsning	DK	C2
67	Loßburg	D	C4
62	Losser	NL	A2
7	Lossiemouth	GB	C5
64	Lößnitz	D	C2
96	Loštice	CZ	B2
12	Lostwithiel	GB	C3
50	Løten	N	B2
23	Lothiers	F	B6
7	Lothmore	GB	B5
53	Lotorp	S	D1
62	Lotte	D	A2
52	Lottefors	S	A2
88	Lotyń	PL	B2
87	Lotzorai	I	C2
18	Louargat	F	B2
28	Loubaresse	F	B2
18	Loudéac	F	B3
109	Loudias	GR	A4
23	Loudun	F	A5
19	Loué	F	C5
14	Loughborough	GB	B1
3	Loughbrickland	GB	B5
4	Loughrea	IRL	A3
25	Louhans	F	B5
2	Louisburgh	IRL	C2
110	Loukás	GR	B3
23	Loulay	F	B4
42	Loulé	P	B1
64	Louny	CZ	C3
26	Lourdes	F	C3
36	Loures	P	C1
27	Loures-Barousse	F	C4
36	Louriçal	P	A2
36	Lourinha	P	B1
29	Lourmarin	F	C4
108	Loúros	GR	B2
20	Loury	F	D3
31	Lousa, *Bragança*	P	C3
36	Lousa, *Coimbra*	P	A2
36	Lousa, *Lisboa*	P	C1
30	Lousada	E	B3
31	Lousada	P	C2
110	Lousi	GR	B3
110	Lousiká	GR	A2
11	Louth	GB	B5
110	Loutrá, *Ilía*	GR	B2
111	Loutra, *Kíthnos*	GR	B5
109	Loutrá, *Thessaloníki*	GR	A5
109	Loutrá Aidhipsou	GR	C5
106	Loutrá Eleftherón	GR	C2
110	Loutra Kilinis	GR	B2
110	Loutra Kounoupeli	GR	A2
108	Loutráki, *Aitolía kai Acarnanía*	GR	C3
111	Loutráki, *Korinthía*	GR	B3
109	Loutrakion	GR	A3
111	Loutro Elénis	GR	B3
108	Loutrón	GR	C3
109	Loutropiyi	GR	B4
107	Loutrós, *Évros*	GR	C4
109	Loutros, *Imathía*	GR	A4
19	Louverne	F	B5
26	Louvie-Juzon	F	C3
20	Louviers	F	B2
19	Louvigné-du-Désert	F	B4
20	Louvres	F	B3
72	Lova	I	C2
99	Lovasberény	H	A3
98	Lovászpatona	H	A2
96	Lovčice	SQ	C3
103	Lovech	BG	C5
16	Lovendegem	B	B3
51	Lovene	S	D4
17	Lövenich	D	B6
71	Lóvere	I	C5
57	Lövestad	S	D2
97	Lovinobaňa	SQ	C5
47	Lovisa	SF	F13
81	Loviste	CRO	A4
77	Lovke	CRO	A4
51	Lövnäs	S	C4
98	Lövö	H	A1
64	Lovosice	CZ	C4
77	Lovran	CRO	A4
100	Lovrec	CRO	C1
99	Lovrin	RO	C5
52	Lövstabruk	S	B3
61	Löwenberg	D	C4
67	Löwenstein	D	B5
14	Lowestoft	GB	B4
91	Łowicz	PL	A3
59	Loxstedt	D	B5
73	Lož	SL	C4
25	Lozanne	F	C4
107	Lozarevo	BG	A4
107	Lozen	BG	B4
107	Lozenec	BG	A5
101	Loznica	YU	B4
96	Lozorno	SQ	C3
102	Lozovik	YU	B2
38	Lozoya	E	B3
39	Lozoyuela	E	B3
72	Lozzo di Cadore	I	B2
32	Luanco (Gozón)	E	A1
30	Luarca	E	A4
65	Lubań	PL	B5
90	Lubanów	PL	B3
64	Lubars	D	A2
91	Lubartów	PL	B6
88	Lubasz	PL	C2
89	Lubawa	PL	B5
65	Lubawka	PL	C5
62	Lübbecke	D	A3
64	Lübben	D	B3
64	Lübbenau	D	B3
60	Lübbow	D	C2
6	Lubcroy	GB	C4
61	Lubczyna	PL	B5
60	Lübeck	D	B1
64	Lubenec	CZ	C3
23	Lubersac	F	C6
60	Lübesse	D	B2
33	Lubia	E	C4
31	Lubian	E	B4
61	Lubiatowo	PL	B6
89	Lubichowo	PL	B4
90	Lubien Kujawski	PL	A3
91	Lubienia	PL	B5
88	Lubieszewo	PL	B1
65	Lubin, *Legnica*	PL	B6
65	Lubiń, *Leszno*	PL	B6
61	Lubin, *Szczecin*	PL	B5
65	Lubin, *Zielona Góra*	PL	A4
91	Lublin	PL	B6
94	Lublin	PL	A5
90	Lubliniec	PL	C2
61	Lubmin	D	A4
102	Lubnica	YU	C3
61	Lubniewice	PL	C6
91	Lubochnia	PL	B4
65	Lubomierz, *Jelenia Góra*	PL	B5
97	Lubomierz, *Nowy Secz*	PL	B6
89	Lubomino	PL	A6
65	Luboń	PL	A6
89	Lubowidz	PL	B5
88	Łubowo, *Koszalin*	PL	B2
88	Łubowo, *Poznań*	PL	C3
89	Lubraniec	PL	C4
45	Lubrin	E	B4
90	Lubrza	PL	C1
65	Lubsko	PL	B4
60	Lübtheen	D	B2
88	Lubuczewo	PL	A3
64	Luby	CZ	C2
60	Lübz	D	B3
28	Luc	F	B2
29	Luc-en-D	F	B4
19	Luc-sur-Mer	F	A5
45	Lucainena de las Torres	E	B4
5	Lucan	IRL	A5
101	Lučani	YU	C5
45	Lúcar	E	B4
23	Luçay-le-Mâle	F	A6
75	Lucca	I	C5
44	Lucena, *Córdoba*	E	B2
43	Lucena, *Huelva*	E	B3
40	Lucena del Cid	E	A2
25	Lucenay-l'Évêque	F	A4
24	Lucenay-les-Aix	F	B3
97	Lučenec	SQ	C5
34	Luceni	E	B1
70	Lucens	CH	B1
80	Lucera	I	C2
74	Luceram	F	C2
60	Lüchow	D	C2
38	Luciana	E	D2
76	Lucignano	I	C1
64	Lucka	D	B2
64	Luckau	D	B3
64	Luckenwalde	D	A3
94	Łucków	PL	A5
60	Lückstedt	D	C2
97	Lúčky	SQ	B5
79	Luco dei Marsi	I	B4
22	Luçon	F	B3
97	Ludanice	SQ	C4
11	Ludborough	GB	B5
98	Ludbreg	CRO	B1
62	Lüdenscheid	D	B2
60	Lüderitz	D	C2
21	Ludes	F	B5
11	Ludford Magna	GB	B5
13	Ludgershall	GB	B6
53	Ludgo	S	D3
62	Lüdinghausen	D	B2
10	Ludlow	GB	C3
88	Ludomy	PL	C2
89	Ludushkin	R	A6
57	Ludvigsborg	S	D2
52	Ludvika	S	B1
66	Ludweiler Warndt	D	B2
67	Ludwigsburg	D	C5
64	Ludwigsfelde	D	A3
67	Ludwigshafen	D	B4
60	Ludwigslust	D	B2
63	Ludwigsstadt	D	C6
34	Luesia	E	A1
99	Lug	CRO	C3
93	Luga	R	A11
75	Lugagnano Val d'Arda	I	B4
71	Lugano	CH	B3
64	Lugau	D	C2
78	Lugnola	I	A3
25	Lugny	F	B4
30	Lugo	E	A3
76	Lugo	I	B1
94	Lugoj	RO	D4
32	Lugones	E	A1
70	Lugrin	F	B1
44	Lugros	E	B3
13	Lugwardine	GB	A5
96	Luhačovice	CZ	B3
68	Luhe	D	B3
70	Luino	I	C3
63	Luisenthal	D	C5
44	Lújar	E	C3
102	Luka	YU	B3
96	Luka n. Jihlavou	CZ	B1
101	Lukavac	BO	B3
69	Lukavec	CZ	B6
100	Lukavica	BO	B3
73	Lukovica	SL	B4
103	Lukovit	BG	C5
77	Lukovo	CRO	B4
104	Lukovo	MAK	C2
102	Lukovo	YU	C2
77	Lukovo Šugorje	CRO	B5
91	Łuków	PL	B6
90	Lukowice	PL	C1
49	Luksefjell	N	B6
89	Łukta	PL	B6
87	Lula	I	B2
47	Luleå	S	D11
107	Lüleburgaz	TR	B5
59	Lüllau	D	B6
81	Lumbarda	CRO	B4
34	Lumbier	E	A1
31	Lumbrales	E	D4
33	Lumbreras	E	B4
16	Lumbres	F	C2
17	Lummen	B	C5
34	Lumpiaque	E	B1
52	Lumsheden	S	B2
77	Lun	CRO	B4
34	Luna	E	A2
87	Lunamatrona	I	C1
76	Lunano	I	C2
104	Lunar	AL	C2
28	Lunas	F	C2
103	Lunca Corbului	RO	B5
57	Lund	S	D2
55	Lunde	DK	C1
49	Lunde, *Telemark*	N	B6
59	Lunden	D	A6
50	Lunderseter	N	B3
55	Lunderskov	DK	C2
60	Lüneburg	D	B1
28	Lunel	F	C3
28	Lunel-Viel	F	C3
62	Lünen	D	B2
66	Lunéville	F	C2
70	Lungern	CH	B3
82	Lungro	I	B3
51	Lungsund	S	C5
93	Luninyets	BL	D10
49	Lunner	N	A7
17	Lunteren	NL	A5
69	Lunz a. See	A	D6
87	Luogosanto	I	A2
102	Lupac	RO	A2
88	Łupawa	PL	A3
103	Lupeni	RO	A4
44	Lupioń	E	A3
64	Luppa	D	B2
44	Luque	E	B2
71	Lurago d'Erba	I	C4
87	Lúras	I	B2
24	Lurcy-Lévis	F	B2
70	Lure	F	A1
3	Lurgan	GB	B5
24	Lury-sur-Arnon	F	A2
100	Lušci Palanka	BO	B1
72	Lusévera	I	B3
104	Lushnje	AL	D1
23	Lusignan	F	B5
24	Lusigny	F	B3
21	Lusigny-sur-Barse	F	C5
36	Luso	P	A2
65	Lusówko	PL	A6
8	Luss	GB	B3
26	Lussac, *Gironde*	F	B3
23	Lussac, *Haute-Vienne*	F	B6
23	Lussac-les-Châteaux	F	B5
28	Lussan	F	B3
64	Lußen	D	B3
71	Lustenau	A	A4
65	Luštěnice	CZ	C4
17	Lustin	B	C4
72	Lutago (Luttach)	I	B1
70	Luthern Bad	CH	A2
60	Lütjenburg	D	A1
60	Lütjensee	D	B1
90	Lutomiersk	PL	B3
15	Luton	GB	C2
70	Lutry	CH	B1
89	Lutry	PL	A6
94	Lutsk	U	A6
63	Lutter a. Barenberge	D	B5
66	Lutterbach	F	D3
14	Lutterworth	GB	B1
90	Lututów	PL	B2
64	Lützen	D	B2
60	Lutzow	D	B2
47	Luvozero	R	D15
66	Luxembourg	L	B2
66	Luxeuil-les-Bains	F	D2
26	Luxey	F	B3
36	Luz, *Évora*	P	C3
42	Luz, *Faro*	P	B1
42	Luz, *Faro*	P	B2
34	Luz-St. Sauveur	F	A3
20	Luzarches	F	B3
96	Luže	CZ	B2
27	Luzech	F	B5
70	Luzern	CH	A3
96	Lužice	CZ	C3
88	Luzino	PL	A4
97	Lužjanky	SQ	C4
24	Luzy	F	B3
82	Luzzi	I	B3
94	Lviv	U	B6
88	Lwówek	PL	C2
65	Lwówek Śląski	PL	B5
7	Lybster	GB	B5
61	Lychen	D	B4
57	Lyckeby	S	C4
47	Lycksele	S	D9
15	Lydd	GB	D3
15	Lydden	GB	C4
10	Lydham	GB	C3
13	Lydney	GB	B5
93	Lyepyel	BL	C11
48	Lykling	N	B2
13	Lyme Regis	GB	C5
13	Lymington	GB	C6
15	Lympne	GB	C4
13	Lympstone	GB	C4
13	Lyndhurst	GB	C6
13	Lyneham	GB	B6
49	Lyngdal, *Buskerud*	N	B6
48	Lyngdal, *Vest-Agder*	N	C4
49	Lyngnør	N	C6
12	Lynmouth	GB	B4
46	Lynseidet	N	B10
12	Lynton	GB	B4
25	Lyon	F	C4
20	Lyons la Forêt	F	B2
51	Lyrestad	S	D5
97	Lysá	SQ	B4
65	Lysá n. Labem	CZ	C4
48	Lysebotn	N	B3
51	Lysekil	S	D2
96	Lysice	CZ	B2
89	Lysomice	PL	B4
70	Lyss	CH	A2
55	Lystrup	DK	B3
50	Lysvik	S	B4
10	Lytham St. Annes	GB	B2
106	Lyubenova Makhala	BG	A3
107	Lyubimets	BG	B4
103	Lyuborod	BG	C4
107	Lyulyakovo	BG	A5

M

4	Maam Cross	IRL	A2
17	Maarheeze	NL	B5
47	Maarianhamina	SF	F10
17	Maarssen	NL	A5
2	Maas	IRL	B3
17	Maaseik	B	B5
17	Maasniel	NL	B6
17	Maassluis	NL	B4
17	Maastricht	NL	C5
11	Mablethorpe	GB	B6
25	Mably	F	B4
45	Macael	E	B4
36	Mação	P	B2
26	Macau	F	B3
70	Maccagno	I	B3
78	Maccarese	I	B3
79	Macchiagodena	I	B5
11	Macclesfield	GB	B3
7	Macduff	GB	C6
30	Maceda	E	B3
31	Macedo de Cavaleiros	P	C4
31	Maceira, *Guarda*	P	D3
36	Maceira, *Leiria*	P	B2
73	Macelj	SL	B5
76	Macerata	I	C3
76	Macerata Féltria	I	C2
103	Mäcesu de Jos	RO	C4
21	Machault	F	B5
22	Machecoul	F	A3
89	Mchowo	PL	B6
8	Machrihanish	GB	C2
10	Machynlleth	GB	C2
31	Macieira	P	C2
91	Maciejowice	PL	B5
86	Macinaggio	F	B2
105	Mačkatica	YU	B4
63	Mackenrode	D	B5
73	Mackovci	SL	B6
87	Macomer	I	B1
21	Macon	B	A5
25	Mâcon	F	B4
3	Macosquin	GB	A5
70	Macot	F	C1
38	Macotera	E	B1
4	Macroom	IRL	C3
70	Macugnaga	I	C2
77	Macure	CRO	B5
106	Madan	BG	B2
51	Madängsholm	S	D4
99	Madaras	H	B4
79	Maddaloni	I	B5
17	Made	NL	B4
71	Maderno	I	C5
33	Maderuelo	E	C3
99	Madocsa	H	B3
71	Madonna di Campiglio	I	B5
39	Madrid	E	B3
39	Madridejos	E	C3
38	Madrigal de la Vera	E	B1
38	Madrigal de las Altas Torres	E	A1
32	Madrigalejo, *Burgos*	E	B3
37	Madrigalejo, *Cáceres*	E	B5
33	Madriguera	E	C3
39	Madrigueras	E	C5
37	Madroñera	E	B5
96	Madunice	SQ	C3
18	Mael-Carhaix	F	B2
34	Maella	E	B3
38	Maello	E	B2
10	Maentwrog	GB	C2
12	Maesteg	GB	B4
33	Maestu	E	B4
36	Mafra	P	C1
37	Magacela	E	C5
33	Magallon	E	C5
41	Magalluf, *Mallorca*	E	
38	Magán	E	C3
33	Magaña	E	C4
71	Magasa	I	C5
32	Magaz	E	C2
63	Magdeburg	D	A6
71	Magenta	I	C3
26	Magescq	F	C2
3	Maghera	GB	B5
3	Magherafelt	GB	B5
10	Maghull	GB	B3
91	Magierowa Wola	PL	B5
76	Magione	I	C2
100	Maglaj	BO	B3
103	Maglavit	RO	B4
57	Maglehem	S	D3
79	Magliano de Marsi	I	A4
78	Magliano in Toscana	I	A2
78	Magliano Sabina	I	A3
99	Maglić	CRO	C4
83	Máglie	I	A5
99	Maglód	H	A4
23	Magnac-Bourg	F	C6
23	Magnac Laval	F	B6
66	Magnieres	F	C2
50	Magnor	N	C3
91	Magnuszew	PL	B5
24	Magny-Cours	F	B3
20	Magny-en-Vexin	F	B2
98	Mágocs	H	B3
13	Magor	GB	B5
111	Magoúla	GR	A4
36	Magoute	P	C1
37	Maguilla	E	C5
3	Maguiresbridge	GB	B4
104	Magura	YU	B3
98	Magyarkeszi	H	B3
98	Magyarszék	H	B3
81	Mahala	YU	B6
31	Mahide	E	C4
93	Mahilyow	BL	D12
41	Mahon, *Menorca*	E	
39	Mahora	E	C5
98	Mahovo	CRO	C1
68	Mähring	D	B3
31	Maia	P	C2
39	Maiaelrayo	E	A3
70	Maîche	F	A1
82	Maida	I	C3
13	Maiden Newton	GB	C5
15	Maidenhead	GB	C2
66	Maidières	F	C2
15	Maidstone	GB	C3
71	Maienfeld	CH	A4
20	Maignelay	F	B3
23	Maillezais	F	B4
21	Mailly-le-Camp	F	C5
24	Mailly-le-Château	F	A3
34	Mainar	E	B1
68	Mainbernheim	D	B1
68	Mainburg	D	C2
67	Mainhardt	D	B5
68	Mainleus	D	A2
20	Maintenon	F	C2
67	Mainz	D	A4
36	Maiorca	P	A2
43	Mairena del Alcor	E	B4
68	Maisach	D	C2
72	Maishofen	A	A2
21	Maison-Celle	F	B5
21	Maison-Rouge	F	C4
96	Maißau	A	C1
20	Maisse	F	C3
68	Maitenbeth	D	C3
66	Maizières-le-Vic	F	C2
66	Maizières-les-Moselles	F	B2
38	Majadahonda	E	B3
37	Majadas	E	B5
46	Majavatn	N	D6
96	Majcichov	SQ	C3
91	Majdan Królewski	PL	C5
102	Majdanpek	YU	B2
99	Majs	H	C3
100	Makarska	CRO	C2
110	Makhairádhon	GR	B1
108	Makherás	GR	C3
58	Makkum	NL	B2
97	Maklár	H	D6
94	Makó	H	C4
99	Makó	H	B5
73	Makole	SL	B5
90	Makoszyce	PL	C1
97	Makov	SQ	B4
104	Makovac	YU	B3
105	Makovo	MAK	C3
89	Maków Mazowiecki	PL	C7
97	Maków-Podhal	PL	B5
88	Makowarsko	PL	B3
109	Makrakomi	GR	C4
106	Mákri	GR	C3
109	Makrikhóri	GR	B4
109	Makrikhórion	GR	A4
109	Makrirrákhi	GR	B4
110	Makrisia	GR	B2
112	Makriyialos, *Kriti*	GR	
109	Makriyialos, *Piería*	GR	A4
108	Makrokhórion	GR	A3
99	Mala Bosna	CRO	B4
98	Mala Bukovec	CRO	B1
77	Mala Cista	CRO	C5
77	Mala Kladuša	BO	A5
102	Mala Krsna	YU	B2
97	Malá Lehota	SQ	C4
99	Mala Pijace	CRO	B4
102	Mala Plana	YU	C2
98	Mala Subotica	CRO	B1
96	Malacky	SQ	C3
93	Maladzyechna	BL	C10
44	Málaga	E	C2
38	Malagón	E	C3
39	Malaguilla	E	B3
5	Malahide	IRL	A5
103	Malaia	RO	A4
111	Malakása	GR	A4
108	Malakási	GR	B3
76	Malalbergo	I	B1
110	Malandrinon	GR	A3
90	Malanów	PL	B2
29	Malaucène	F	B4
20	Malaunay	F	B2
72	Malborghetto	I	B3
89	Malbork	PL	A5
66	Malborn	D	B2
28	Malbouzon	F	B2
25	Malbuisson	F	B6
71	Malbun	FL	A4
102	Malča	YU	C3
71	Malcesine	I	C5
61	Malchin	D	B3
69	Malching	D	C4
60	Malchow	D	B3
43	Malcocinado	E	A4
65	Malczyce	PL	B6
103	Măldareşti	RO	A4
16	Maldegem	B	B3
15	Maldon	GB	C3
71	Malé	I	B5
112	Máleme, *Kriti*	GR	
27	Malemort	F	A5
60	Malente	D	A1
56	Malerås	S	C4
112	Máles, *Kriti*	GR	
70	Malesco	I	B3
20	Malesherbes	F	C3
109	Malesina	GR	C5
18	Malestroit	F	C3
85	Maletto	I	B3
106	Malevo	BG	B3
35	Malgrat	E	B5
31	Malhadas	P	C4
99	Mali Idoš	CRO	C4
77	Mali Lošinj	CRO	B4
112	Mália, *Kriti*	GR	
19	Malicorne-sur-Sarthe	F	C5
21	Maligny	F	D4
29	Malijai	F	B5
56	Målilla kyrkby	S	B4
56	Målilla station	S	B4
3	Malin	IRL	A4
2	Malin More	IRL	B3
97	Málinec	SQ	C5
52	Malingsbo	S	C1
90	Maliniec	PL	A2
77	Malinska	CRO	A4
108	Maliq	AL	A2
77	Maljevac	CRO	A5
107	Malkara	TR	C4
89	Malki	PL	B5
106	Malki Iswor	BG	B3
106	Malko Gradishte	BG	B3
107	Malko Târnovo	BG	B5
8	Mallaig	GB	B2
33	Mallén	E	C5
68	Mallersdorf	D	C3
71	Málles Venosta (Mals)	I	B5
55	Malling	DK	B3
72	Mallnitz	A	A3
4	Mallow	IRL	B3
10	Mallwyd	GB	C2
56	Malmbäck	S	B3
47	Malmberget	S	C10
17	Malmédy	B	C5
13	Malmesbury	GB	B5
53	Malmköping	S	C2
57	Malmö	S	D1
51	Malmon	S	D2
53	Malmslätt	S	D1
71	Malnate	I	C3
72	Malo	I	C1
106	Malo Konare	BG	A2
104	Malo Konjari	MAK	C3
16	Malo-les-Bains	F	B2
71	Maloja	CH	B4
65	Malomico	PL	B5
103	Malorad	BG	C4
102	Malošište	YU	C2
46	Måløy	N	F2
37	Malpartida de Cáceres	E	B4
37	Malpartida de la Serena	E	C5
37	Malpartida de Plasencia	E	B4
34	Malpas	E	A3
10	Malpas	GB	B3
36	Malpica	P	B3
30	Malpica, *Coruña*	E	A2
38	Malpica, *Toledo*	E	C2
67	Malsch	D	C4
69	Malšice	CZ	B5
72	Malta	A	B3
24	Maltat	F	B3
11	Maltby	GB	B4
70	Malters	CH	A3
11	Malton	GB	A5
50	Malung	S	B4
50	Malungsfors	S	B4
65	Maluszów	PL	A5
91	Maluszyn	PL	C3
32	Malva	E	C1
71	Malvaglia	CH	B3
36	Malveira	P	C1
13	Malvern Wells	GB	A5
36	Mamarrosa	P	A2
66	Mamer	F	B1
20	Mamers	F	C1
68	Mammendorf	D	C2
85	Mámmola	I	A5
87	Mamoiada	I	B2
104	Mamurras	AL	C1
110	Mána, *Korinthía*	GR	B3
112	Mána, *Síros*	GR	E1
41	Manacor, *Mallorca*	E	
80	Manacore	I	C3
106	Manastir	BG	B2
38	Mancera de Abajo	E	B1
44	Mancha Real	E	B3
11	Manchester	GB	B3
68	Manching	D	C2
37	Manchita	E	C4
78	Manciano	I	A2
66	Mancieulles	F	B1
26	Manclet	F	C4
48	Mandal	N	C4
85	Mandanici	I	B4
87	Mándas	I	C2
109	Mandasiá	GR	B4
83	Mandatoríccio	I	B3
39	Mandayona	E	B4
71	Mandello d'Lario	I	C4
59	Mandelsloh	D	C6
17	Manderfeld	B	C6
66	Manderscheid	D	A2
109	Mandoúdhion	GR	C5
106	Mándra	GR	C2
111	Mándra, *Attikí*	GR	A4
112	Mandrákhi	GR	B2
107	Mandritsa	BG	B4
83	Mandúria	I	A4
29	Mane, *Alpes-de-Haute-Provence*	F	C4
27	Mane, *Haute-Garonne*	F	C4
75	Manérbio	I	A5
33	Mañeru	E	B5
69	Manetin	CZ	B4
80	Manfredónia	I	C2
106	Mángana	GR	C2
112	Manganári	GR	D2
32	Manganeses de la Lampreana	E	C1
32	Manganeses de la Polvorosa	E	B1
112	Manganitis	GR	C1
50	Mangen	N	C2
66	Mangiennes	F	B1
13	Mangotsfield	GB	B5
50	Mångsoodarna	S	A4
31	Mangualde	P	D3
107	Máni	GR	B4
72	Maniago	I	B2
110	Maniáki	GR	B2
111	Manika	GR	A4
43	Manilva	E	C4
97	Maniowy	PL	B6
95	Manisa	TR	G7
40	Manises	E	B2
96	Mank	A	C1
52	Månkarbo	S	B3
35	Manlleu	E	A5
70	Männedorf	CH	A3
96	Mannersdorf a. Leithageb.	A	D2
67	Mannheim	D	B4
15	Manningtree	GB	C4
26	Mano	F	B3
110	Manolás	GR	A2
2	Manorhamilton	IRL	B3
29	Manosque	F	C4
88	Manowo	PL	A2
35	Manresa	E	B4
35	Manresana	E	B4
56	Månsarp	S	B3
63	Mansfeld	D	B6
11	Mansfield	GB	B4
11	Mansfield Woodhouse	GB	B4
32	Mansilla de Burgos	E	B3
32	Mansilla de las Mulas	E	B1
50	Manskog	S	C3
23	Mansle	F	C5
86	Manso	F	B1
46	Manstuen	N	F4
47	Mäntaa	SF	E12
36	Manteigas	P	A3
68	Mantel	D	B3
20	Mantes-la-Jolie	F	B2
20	Mantes-la-Ville	F	C2
23	Manthelan	F	A5
53	Mantorp	S	D1
75	Mántova	I	A5
47	Mäntsälä	SF	F12
40	Manuel	E	B2
25	Manurolle	F	A6
31	Manzanal de Arriba	E	B4
39	Manzanares, *Ciudad Real*	E	C3
38	Manzanares, *Madrid*	E	B3
32	Manzaneda, *Burgos*	E	B3
30	Manzaneda, *León*	E	B4
30	Manzaneda, *Orense*	E	B3
38	Manzaneque	E	C3
40	Manzanera	E	A2
43	Manzanilla	E	B3
24	Manzat	F	C2
78	Manziana	I	A3
25	Manziat	F	B4
101	Maoča	BO	B3
100	Maovice	CRO	C1
104	Maqellarë	AL	C2
38	Maqueda	E	B2
33	Mara	E	C5
44	Maracena	E	B3
32	Maraña	E	A1
39	Maranchón	E	A4
108	Marandokhóri	GR	C2
75	Maranello	I	B5
79	Marano	I	C5
72	Marano Lagunare	I	C3
22	Marans	F	B4
107	Marásia	GR	B4
82	Maratea	I	B2
36	Marateca	P	C2
109	Marathéa	GR	B4
112	Marathókambos	GR	C1
111	Marathón	GR	A4
110	Marathópolis	GR	B2
108	Márathos	GR	B3
12	Marazion	GB	C2
66	Marbach	F	C2
67	Marbach, *Baden-Württemberg*	D	C5
63	Marbach, *Hessen*	D	C4
56	Marbäck	S	B2
50	Marbacka	S	C4
44	Marbella	E	C2
25	Marboz	F	B5
49	Mårbu	N	A5
62	Marburg	D	C3
98	Marcali	H	B2
77	Marcaňa	CRO	B3
75	Marcaria	I	A5
97	Marcelová	SQ	D4
28	Marcenat	F	A1
14	March	GB	B3
39	Marchamalo	E	B3
25	Marchaux	F	A6
17	Marche-en-Famenne	B	C5
96	Marchegg	A	C2
43	Marchena	E	B4
20	Marchenoir	F	D2
26	Marcheprime	F	B3
16	Marchiennes	F	C3
27	Marciac	F	C4
86	Marciana Marina	I	B3
79	Marcianise	I	B5
25	Marcigny	F	B4
33	Marcilla	E	B5
27	Marcillac-la-Croisille	F	A6
28	Marcillac-Vallon	F	B1
24	Marcillat-en-Combraille	F	B2
21	Marcille-sur-Seine	F	C4
25	Marcilly	F	C4
21	Marcilly-le-Hayer	F	C4
88	Marcinkowice	PL	B2
65	Marciszów	PL	C6
16	Marck	F	C1
66	Marckolsheim	F	C3
31	Marco de Canevezes	P	C2
21	Marcoing	F	A4
20	Mardie	F	D3
11	Mareham le Fen	GB	B5
22	Marennes	F	C3
15	Maresfield	GB	D3
16	Maresquel	F	C1
23	Mareuil	F	C5
24	Mareuil-sur-Arnon	F	B2
22	Mareuil-sur-Lay	F	B3
21	Mareuil-sur-Ourcq	F	B4
108	Margarition	GR	B2
15	Margate	GB	C4
26	Margaux	F	A3
21	Margerie-Hancourt	F	C5
29	Margès	F	A4
80	Margherita di Savóia	I	C3
102	Margita	YU	A2
21	Margny	F	B3
74	Margone	I	A2
88	Margonin	PL	C3
66	Margut	B	B1
21	Margut	F	B6
45	Maria	E	B4
73	Maria Gail	A	B3
73	Maria Lankowitz Edelschrott	A	A5
96	Maria Lanzendorf	A	C2
69	Maria Neustift	A	D5
73	Maria Saal	A	B4
54	Mariager	DK	B2
39	Mariana	E	B4
56	Mariannelund	S	B4
84	Marianópoli	I	B2
68	Mariánské Lázně	CZ	B3
72	Mariapfarr	A	A3
96	Mariazell	A	D1
55	Maribo	DK	D4
73	Maribor	SL	B5
53	Marieberg	S	C1
53	Mariedamm	S	D1
53	Mariefred	S	C3
47	Mariehamn	SF	F10
57	Marieholm	S	D2
17	Marienbaum	D	B6
64	Marienberg	D	C3
21	Marienbourg	B	A5
62	Marienheide	D	B2
51	Mariestad	S	D4
46	Marifjöra	N	F3
79	Marigliano	I	C5
29	Marignane	F	C4
25	Marigny, *Jura*	F	B5
19	Marigny, *Manche*	F	A4
21	Marigny le Châtel	F	C4
98	Marija Bistrica	CRO	B1
105	Marikostinovo	BG	C5
30	Marin	E	B2
100	Marina	CRO	C1
109	Marina	GR	A4
79	Marina d. Caritone	I	C5
35	Marina de Cambrils	E	B4
82	Marina di Acquappesa	I	B2
78	Marina di Alberese	I	A2
83	Marina di Amendolara	I	B3
74	Marina di Andora	I	C3
87	Marina di Árbus	I	C1
82	Marina di Camerota	I	B2
86	Marina di Campo	I	B3
75	Marina di Carrara	I	B5
75	Marina di Castagneto Donorático	I	C5
83	Marina di Castellaneta	I	A3
75	Marina di Cécina	I	C5
87	Marina di Gáiro	I	C2
83	Marina di Ginosa	I	A3
85	Marina di Gioiosa Iónica	I	A5
78	Marina di Grosseto	I	A1
75	Marina di Massa	I	B5
83	Marina di Novàglie	I	B5
75	Marina di Pisa	I	C5
85	Marina di Ragusa	I	C3
76	Marina di Ravenna	I	B2
78	Marina di Tarquinia	I	A2
87	Marina di Torre Grande	I	C1
76	Marina Romea	I	B2
43	Marinaleda	E	B5
86	Marine de Sisco	F	B2
84	Marinella	I	B1
75	Marinella di Sarzana	I	B5
84	Marineo	I	B2
20	Marines	F	B2
66	Maring-Noviand	D	B2
24	Maringues	F	C3
36	Marinha das Ondas	P	A2
36	Marinha Grande	P	B2
31	Marinhas	P	C2
78	Marino	I	B3
106	Maritsa	BG	A3
112	Maritsá	GR	A2
93	Mariyampole	LT	C8
38	Marjaliza	E	C3
57	Markaryd	S	C2
108	Markat	AL	B2
97	Markaz	H	D6
71	Markdorf	D	A4
17	Markelo	NL	A6
11	Market Bosworth	GB	C4
14	Market Deeping	GB	B2
10	Market Drayton	GB	C3
14	Market Harborough	GB	B2
11	Market Rasen	GB	B5
11	Market Weighton	GB	B5
3	Markethill	GB	B5
14	Markfield	GB	B1
67	Markgröningen	D	C5
59	Markhausen	D	C4
91	Marki	PL	A5
9	Markinch	GB	B4
64	Märkische Buchholz	D	A3
64	Markkleeberg	D	B2
59	Marklohe	D	C6
58	Marknesse	NL	C2
64	Markneukirchen	D	C2
63	Markoldendorf	D	B4
111	Markópoulon	GR	B4
65	Markosice	PL	B4
102	Markovac	YU	A2
102	Markovac	YU	B2
90	Markowice	PL	C2
64	Markranstädt	D	B2
15	Marks Tey	GB	C3
63	Marksuhl	D	C5
69	Markt	D	C3
73	Markt Allhau	A	A6
68	Markt Bergel	D	B1
68	Markt Erlbach	D	B1
68	Markt Indersdorf	D	C2
68	Markt Rettenbach	D	D1
68	Markt Schwaben	D	C2
69	Markt St. Florian	A	C5
67	Marktbreit	D	B6
67	Marktheidenfeld	D	B5
64	Marktleuthen	D	C2
71	Marktoberdorf	D	A5
68	Marktredwitz	D	A3
99	Markusica	CRO	C3
62	Marl	D	B2
13	Marlborough	GB	B6
21	Marle	F	B4
25	Marlens	F	C6
28	Marlhes	F	A3
25	Marlieux	F	B5
60	Marlow	D	A3
15	Marlow	GB	C2
52	Marma	S	B3
25	Marmagne	F	B4
27	Marmande	F	B4
89	Marmanovo	R	A5
108	Mármara	GR	B2
107	Marmara	TR	C5
107	Marmaracik	TR	B5
107	Marmaraereğlisi	TR	C5
111	Marmári	GR	A5
112	Marmaris	TR	A2
52	Marmaverken	S	A2
42	Marmelete	P	B1
44	Marmolejo	E	A2
66	Marmoutier	F	C3
25	Marnay	F	A5
59	Marne	D	B6
67	Marnheim	D	B4
13	Marnhull	GB	C5
60	Marnitz	D	B2
63	Maroldsweisach	D	C5
20	Marolles-les-Braults	F	C1
20	Maromme	F	B2
71	Marone	I	C5
106	Marónia	GR	C3
99	Maroslele	H	B5
72	Maróstica	I	C1
76	Marotta	I	C3
112	Márpissa	GR	D1
33	Marquina	E	A4
16	Marquion	F	C3
16	Marquise	F	C1
76	Marradi	I	B1
58	Marrum	NL	B2
38	Marrupe	E	B2
66	Mars	F	B1
27	Marsac	F	C6
24	Marsac-en-Livradois	F	C3
75	Marságlia	I	B4
84	Marsala	I	B1
78	Marsciano	I	A3
28	Marseillan	F	C2
29	Marseille	F	C4
20	Marseille en Beauvaisis	F	B2
82	Mársico Nuovo	I	A2
11	Marske by the Sea	GB	A4
21	Marson	F	C5
66	Marspich	F	B2
53	Marsta	S	C3
55	Marstal	DK	D3
54	Marstrand	S	A4
78	Marta	I	A2
83	Martano	I	A5
27	Martel	F	B5
66	Martelange	B	B1
59	Martfeld	D	C6
99	Martfü	H	A5
14	Martham	GB	B4
23	Marthon	F	C5
37	Martiago	E	A4
23	Martigné-Briand	F	A4
19	Martigné-Ferchaud	F	C4
66	Martigny-les-Bains	F	C1
70	Martigny-Ville	CH	B2
29	Martigues	F	C4
26	Martillac	F	B3
42	Martim-Longo	P	B2
11	Martin	GB	B5
97	Martin	SQ	B4
44	Martin de la Jara	E	B2
38	Martin Muñoz de las Posadas	E	A2
71	Martina	CH	B5
81	Martina Franca	I	D4
38	Martinamor	E	B1
21	Martincourt-sur-Meuse	F	B6
71	Martinengo	I	C4
111	Martinon	GR	A4
69	Martinsberg	A	C6
77	Martinšcica	CRO	B4
66	Martinshöhe	D	B3
79	Martinsicuro	I	A4
71	Martinszell	D	A5
87	Mártis	I	B1
98	Martjanci	SL	B1
13	Martock	GB	C5
55	Martofte	DK	C3

48 Nesflaten N B3
49 Nesland N B4
49 Neslandsvatn N C6
21 Nesle F B3
109 Néson GR B4
96 Nesovice CZ B3
71 Nesselwang D A5
71 Nesslau CH A4
58 Nessmersiel D B4
71 Nesso I C4
110 Nestáni GR B3
73 Nestelbach A A5
10 Neston GB B2
108 Nestórion GR A3
48 Nesttun N A2
97 Nesvady SQ D4
9 Nether Howecleuch GB C4
13 Nether Stowey GB B4
48 Netlandsnes N C3
69 Netolice CZ B5
73 Netretić CRO C5
71 Netstal CH A4
15 Nettlebed GB C1
11 Nettleham GB B5
63 Nettlingen D A5
78 Nettuno I B3
64 Netzschkau D C2
63 Neu Buddenstedt D A6
60 Neu Darchau D B1
67 Neu-Isenburg D A4
60 Neu Kaliß D B2
64 Neu Lübbenau D A3
64 Neu Petershain D B4
71 Neu-Ravensburg D A4
67 Neu-Ulm D C6
68 Neualbenreuth D B3
68 Neubau D B3
62 Neubeckum D B3
98 Neuberg A A1
61 Neubrandenburg D B4
59 Neubruchhausen D C5
60 Neubukow D A2
68 Neuburg D C2
70 Neuchâtel CH B1
63 Neudietendorf D C5
96 Neudorf A C2
67 Neudorf D B4
96 Neudorfl A D2
67 Neuenbürg, *Baden-Württemberg* D C4
59 Neuenburg, *Niedersachsen* D B4
68 Neuendettelsau D B1
61 Neuendorf D A4
58 Neuenhaus D C3
70 Neuenkirch CH A3
62 Neuenkirchen D C3
59 Neuenkirchen, *Niedersachsen* D B5
59 Neuenkirchen, *Niedersachsen* D B6
59 Neuenkirchen, *Niedersachsen* D C5
62 Neuenkirchen, *Nordrhein-Westfalen* D A2
62 Neuenrade D B2
67 Neuenstein D B5
59 Neuenwalde D B5
66 Neuerburg D A2
66 Neuf-Brisach F C3
68 Neufahrn D C2
66 Neufchâteau B B1
66 Neufchâteau F C1
21 Neufchâtel F B5
20 Neufchâtel-en-Bray F B2
69 Neufelden A C5
67 Neuffen D C5
21 Neuflize F B5
63 Neugattersleben D B6
64 Neugersdorf D C4
68 Neuhaus, *Bayern* D B2
69 Neuhaus, *Bayern* D C4
59 Neuhaus, *Niedersachsen* D B6
60 Neuhaus, *Niedersachsen* D B1
63 Neuhaus, *Niedersachsen* D B4
63 Neuhaus a Rennweg D C6
63 Neuhaus-Schierschnitz D C6
70 Neuhausen a Rheinfall CH A3
67 Neuhausen ob Eck D D4
68 Neuhof D B1
69 Neuhofen A C5
23 Neuillé F A4
23 Neuillè Pont-Pierre F A5
20 Neuilly-en-Thelle F B3
66 Neuilly-l'Éveque F D1
24 Neuilly-le-Réal F B3
21 Neuilly St. Front F B4
61 Neukalen D B3
63 Neukirchen, *Hessen* D C4
69 Neukirchen, *Ober Östereich* A C4
69 Neukirchen, *Ober Östereich* A D4
55 Neukirchen, *Schleswig-Holstein* D D1
72 Neukirchen-am Großy A A2
69 Neukirchen b. Hl. Blut D B3
17 Neukirchen-Vluyn D B6
60 Neukloster D B2
96 Neulengbach A C1
25 Neulise F C4
81 Neum BO B4
66 Neumagen D B2
64 Neumark D C2
68 Neumarkt D B2
69 Neumarkt a.W. A D4
69 Neumarkt i. Mühlkn A C5
73 Neumarkt i. Steiermark A A4
68 Neumarkt St. Veit D C3
59 Neumünster D A6
68 Neunburg v.W. D B3
24 Neung-sur-Beuvron F A1
70 Neunkirch CH A3
96 Neunkirchen A D2
62 Neunkirchen, *Nordrhein-Westfalen* D C2
66 Neunkirchen, *Saarland* D B3
68 Neuötting D C3
67 Neureut D B4
61 Neuruppin D C3
96 Neusiedl A C2
96 Neusiedl am See A D2
62 Neuß D B1
28 Neussargues-Moissac F A2
67 Neustadt, *Baden-Württemberg* D D4
68 Neustadt, *Bayern* D B1
68 Neustadt, *Bayern* D B2
68 Neustadt, *Bayern* D B3
68 Neustadt, *Bayern* D C2
60 Neustadt, *Brandenburg* D C3
62 Neustadt, *Hessen* D C4
64 Neustadt, *Sachsen* D B4
60 Neustadt, *Schleswig-Holstein* D A1
63 Neustadt, *Thüringen* D C6
67 Neustadt a.d. Weinstraße D B4
59 Neustadt am Rübenberge D C6
63 Neustadt bei Coburg D C6
60 Neustadt-Glewe D B2
71 Neustift im St Tubaital A A6
61 Neustrelitz D B4
98 Neutal A A1
61 Neutrebbin D C5
66 Neuves-Maisons F C2
27 Neuvic, *Corrèze* F A6
27 Neuvic, *Dordogne* F A4
25 Neuville, *Rhône* F C4
20 Neuville, *Seine-Maritime* F B2
20 Neuville-aux-Bois F C3
23 Neuville-de-Poitou F B5
25 Neuville-les-Dames F B4
21 Neuvy-Santour F C4
24 Neuvy-St.Sépulchre F B1
24 Neuvy-sur-Barangeon F A2
62 Neuwied D C2
64 Neuzelle D A4
29 Névache F A5
69 Neveklov CZ B5
93 Nevel R C12
16 Nevele B B3
24 Nevers F B3
100 Nevesinje BO C3
100 Nevest CRO C1
105 Nevestino BG B4
18 Névez F C2
62 Neviges D B2
49 Nevlunghavn N C6
9 New Abbey GB D4
7 New Aberdour GB C6
15 New Alresford GB C1
3 New Buildings GB B4
7 New Byth GB C6
4 New Chapel Cross IRL C1
8 New Cumnock GB C3
7 New Deer GB C6
8 New Galloway GB C3
11 New Holland GB B5
5 New Inn IRL A4
4 New Kildimo IRL B3
11 New Mills GB B4
13 New Milton GB C6
7 New Pitsligo GB C6
12 New Quay GB A3
15 New Romney GB D3
5 New Ross IRL B5
11 New Rossington GB B4
9 New Scone GB B4
11 Newark GB B5
9 Newbiggin-by-the-Sea GB C6
9 Newbigging GB C4
3 Newbliss IRL B4
10 Newborough GB B1
2 Newbridge IRL C3
13 Newbridge on Wye GB A4
9 Newburgh, *Fife* GB B4
7 Newburgh, *Grampian* GB C7
15 Newbury GB C1
10 Newby Bridge GB A3
3 Newcastle GB B6
12 Newcastle Emlyn GB A3
10 Newcastle under Lyme GB B3
9 Newcastle upon Tyne GB C6
4 Newcastle West IRL B2
9 Newcastleton GB C5
13 Newent GB B5
12 Newgale GB B2
13 Newham, *Gloucestershire* GB B5
15 Newham, *London* GB C3
15 Newhaven GB D3
11 Newhaven House GB B4
5 Newinn IRL B4
7 Newmachar GB C6
4 Newmarket IRL B3
6 Newmarket, *Lewis* GB B2
14 Newmarket, *Suffolk* GB B3
4 Newmarket on Fergus IRL B3
3 Newmills IRL B4
8 Newmilns GB C3
15 Newport, *Essex* GB C3
13 Newport, *Gwent* GB B5
15 Newport, *I. of Wight* GB D1
2 Newport, *Mayo* IRL C2
10 Newport, *Shropshire* GB C3
4 Newport, *Tipperary* IRL B3
9 Newport on Tay GB B5
15 Newport Pagnell GB B2
12 Newquay GB C2
3 Newry GB B5
10 Newton, *Lancashire* GB B3
6 Newton, *Western Isles* GB C1
13 Newton Abbot GB C4
11 Newton Aycliffe GB A4
9 Newton Bridge GB B4
12 Newton Ferrers GB C3
8 Newton Mearns GB C3
8 Newton Stewart GB D3
9 Newtongrange GB C4
8 Newtonmore GB A3
4 Newtown IRL B3
13 Newtown, *Hereford & Worcester* GB A5
10 Newtown, *Powys* GB C2
3 Newtown Cunningham IRL B4
3 Newtown Forbes IRL C4
3 Newtown Gore IRL B4
3 Newtown Monasterboice IRL C5
5 Newtown Mount Kennedy IRL A5
9 Newtown St. Boswells GB C5
3 Newtownabbey GB B6
3 Newtownards GB B6
3 Newtownbutler GB B4
3 Newtownhamilton GB B5
3 Newtownstewart GB B4
23 Nexon F C6
12 Neyland GB B3
96 Nezamyslice CZ B3
111 Niáta GR C3
75 Nibbiano I B4
54 Nibe DK B2
104 Nicaj-Shale AL B1
82 Nicastro I C3
76 Niccone I C2
74 Nice F C2
74 Nichelino I B2
96 Nickelsdorf A D3
85 Nicolosi I B4
85 Nicosia I B3
82 Nicótera I C2
62 Nidda D C4
108 Nidri GR C2
89 Nidzica PL B6
43 Niebla E B3
91 Nieborów PL A4
55 Niebüll D D1
61 Niechorze PL A6
88 Niedalino PL A2
63 Nieder Kaufungen D B4
62 Nieder Netphen D C3
67 Nieder-Olm D B4
67 Nieder Ramstadt D B4
62 Nieder-Wöllstadt D C3
72 Niederaudf D A2
63 Niederaula D C4
62 Niederbieber-Segendorf D C2
70 Niederbipp CH A2
62 Niederbreechen D C3
62 Niederfischbach D C2
64 Niedergörsdorf D B2
17 Niederkrüchten D B6
62 Niedermarsberg D B3
62 Niedermendig D C2
72 Niederndorf A A2
63 Niedersachswerfen D B5
67 Niederstetten D B5
71 Niederurnen CH A4
67 Niederwerrn D A6
73 Niederwölz A A4
97 Niedobczyce PL A4
65 Niedoradz PL B5
91 Niedrzwica-Duża PL B6
97 Niedzica PL B6
65 Niegosławice PL B5
62 Nieheim D B4
17 Niel B B4
65 Niemcza PL C6
64 Niemegk D A2
90 Niemodlin PL C1
91 Nienadówka PL C6
62 Nienberge D A2
59 Nienburg, *Niedersachsen* D C6
63 Nienburg, *Sachsen-Anhalt* D B6
60 Nienhagen D C1
97 Niepołomice PL A6
89 Nieporet PL C7
67 Nierstein D B4
65 Niesky D B4
89 Nieszawa PL C4
91 Nietulisko PL C5
22 Nieul-sur-Mer F B3
58 Nieuw-Amsterdam NL C3
58 Nieuw-Buinen NL C3
17 Nieuw-Namen NL B4
58 Nieuw-Schoonebeek NL C3
17 Nieuw-Tonge NL B4
58 Nieuw-Weerdinge NL C3
58 Nieuwe Niedorp NL C1
58 Nieuwe-Pekela NL B3
58 Nieuwe-Schans D B4
17 Nieuwegein NL A5
17 Nieuwendijk NL B4
17 Nieuwerkerk NL B4
17 Nieuwerkerken, *Flandre Orientale* B C3
17 Nieuwerkerken, *Limburg* B C5
58 Nieuwolda NL B3
16 Nieuwpoort B B2
62 Nievenheim D B1
31 Nieves E B2
91 Niewachlów PL C4
88 Niezabyszewo PL A3
105 Nigrita GR D5
44 Nigüelas E C3
45 Nijar E C4
101 Nijemci CRO A4
17 Nijkerk NL A5
17 Nijlen B B4
17 Nijmegen NL B5
17 Nijverdal NL A6
109 Nikaia GR B4
108 Niki GR A3
106 Nikifóros GR B2
101 Nikinci YU B4
106 Nikisiani GR C2
109 Nikitas GR A5
98 Nikitsch A A1
73 Niklasdorf A A5
109 Nikóklia GR A5
106 Nikolaevo BG A3
108 Nikolitsi GR B2
103 Nikopol BG C5
81 Nikšic YU B5
48 Nilsebu N B3
28 Nîmes F C3
106 Nimfaia GR B3
72 Nimis I B3
54 Nimtofte DK B3
77 Nin CRO B5
59 Nindorf D A6
5 Ninemilehouse IRL B4
15 Ninfield GB D3
17 Ninove B C3
109 Niokhóri GR B3
23 Niort F B4
102 Niš YU C2
36 Nisa P B3
85 Niscemi I B3
108 Nisi GR A3
109 Nision GR A4
102 Niška Banja YU C3
91 Nisko PL C6
94 Nisko PL A5
56 Nissafors S B2
108 Nissáki GR B1
28 Nissan-les-Ensérune F C2
49 Nissedal N B5
54 Nissumby DK B1
17 Nistelrode NL B5
15 Niton GB D1
97 Nitra SQ C4
97 Nitrany SQ C4
97 Nitrianske-Pravno SQ C4
97 Nitrianske Rudno SQ C4
24 Nitry F A3
49 Nittedal N A7
68 Nittenau D B3
60 Nitzahn D C3
47 Nivela SF E12
17 Nivelles B C4
66 Nives B B1
89 Nivienskoye R A6
96 Nivnice CZ C3
103 Nivyanin BG C4
97 Nizná Boca SQ C5
74 Nizza Monferrato I B3
99 Njegŭsevo CRO C4
77 Njivice CRO A4
47 Njutånger S F8
20 Noailles F B3
33 Noain E B5
72 Noale I C2
44 Noalejo E B3
3 Nobber IRL C5
39 Noblejas E C3
79 Nocera I C5
82 Nocera Tirinese I B3
76 Nocera Umbra I C2
75 Noceto I B5
64 Nochten D B4
81 Noci I D4
83 Nociglia I A5
54 Nödinge S A5
25 Nods F A6
27 Noé F C5
82 Noépoli I A3
16 Noeux-les-Mines F C2
105 Noevtsi BG B4
38 Noez E C2
37 Nogales E C4
75 Nogara I A6
30 Nogarejas E B4
26 Nogaro F C3
66 Nogent-en-Bassigny F C1
21 Nogent l'Artaud F C4
20 Nogent-le-Roi F C2
20 Nogent-le-Rotrou F C1
20 Nogent-sur-Marne F C3
20 Nogent-sur-Oise F B3
21 Nogent-sur-Seine F C4
21 Nogent-sur-Vernisson F D3
57 Nogersund S C3
97 Nógrád H D5
30 Nogueira de Ramuin E B3
40 Noguera E A1
44 Noguerones E B2
66 Nohfelden D B3
81 Noicáttaro I C4
24 Noirétable F C3
22 Noirmoutier-en-l'Ile F B2
33 Noja E A3
88 Nojewo PL C2
47 Nokia SF F11
54 Nol S A5
79 Nola I C5
25 Nolay F B4
74 Noli I B3
38 Nombela E B2
66 Nomeny F C2
66 Nomexy F C2
111 Nómia GR C4
20 Nonancourt F C2
19 Nonant-le-Pin F B6
75 Nonántola I B6
34 Nonaspe E B3
74 None I B2
23 Nontron F C5
86 Nonza F B2
58 Noord Bergum NL B3
58 Noord Scharwoude NL C1
58 Noordbroek NL B3
58 Noordhorn NL B3
17 Noordwijk NL A4
58 Noordwolde NL C3
47 Noormarkku SF F10
51 Nora S C6
52 Norberg S B1
79 Nórcia I A4
50 Nord-Odat N B2
16 Nordausques F C2
55 Nordborg DK C2
55 Nordby, *Aarhus Amt.* DK C3
55 Nordby, *Ribe Amt.* DK C1
58 Norddeich D B4
58 Norden D B4
59 Nordenham D B5
49 Norderhov N A7
58 Norderney D B4
59 Norderstapel D A6
59 Norderstedt D B7
46 Nordfjordeid N F2
63 Nordgermersleben D A6
63 Nordhalben D C6
63 Nordhausen D B5
63 Nordheim v.d. Rhön D C5
58 Nordhorn D C4
46 Nordli N D6
68 Nördlingen D C1
47 Nordmaling S E9
50 Nordmark S C5
50 Nordre Osen N A2
46 Nordreisa N B10
63 Nordstemmen D A4
62 Nordwalde D A2
17 Nordwijk aan Zee NL A4
17 Nordwijkerhout NL A4
49 Nore N A5
32 Noreña E A1
58 Norg NL B3
48 Norheimsund N A3
57 Norie S C3
79 Norma I B3
14 Norman Cross GB B2
50 Nornäs S A4
50 Norra Finnskoga S B3
50 Norra Ny S B4
56 Norra Vi S B4
56 Norrahammar S B3
52 Norrala S A2
55 Nørre Åby DK C2
55 Nørre Alslev DK D4
54 Nørre Bindslev DK A3
55 Nörre Broby DK C3
55 Nørre Lyndelse DK C3
55 Nørre Nebel DK C1
55 Nørre Snede DK C2
16 Norrent-Fontes F C2
54 Nørresundby DK A2
56 Norrhult S B4
53 Norrköping S D2
52 Norrskedika S B4
52 Norrsundet S B3
52 Norrtälje S C4
54 Nors DK A1
51 Norsbron S C4
53 Norsholm S D1
47 Norsjö S D9
22 Nort-sur-Erdre F A3
63 Nörten-Hardenberg D B4
8 North Ballachulish GB B2
9 North Berwick GB B5
6 North Collafirth, *Shetland Is.* GB
11 North Ferriby GB B5
15 North Hinksey GB C1
11 North Hykeham GB B5
13 North Petherton GB B4
9 North Queensferry GB B4
6 North Roe, *Shetland Is.* GB
11 North Somercotes GB B6
12 North Tawton GB C4
13 North Tidworth GB B6
6 North Tolsta GB B2
14 North Walsham GB B4
11 Northallerton GB A4
12 Northam GB B3
14 Northampton GB B2
63 Northeim D B5
15 Northfleet GB C3
15 Northiam GB D3
13 Northleach GB B6
10 Northop GB B2
7 Northwaa GB A6
10 Northwich GB B3
15 Northwood GB D1
11 Norton GB A5
13 Norton Fitzwarren GB B4
59 Nortorf D A6
14 Norwich GB B4
6 Norwick, *Shetland Is.* GB
36 Nossa Senhora do Cabo P C1
51 Nossebro S D3
51 Nössemark S C2
64 Nossen D B3
79 Notaresco I A4
105 Nótia GR C4
85 Noto I C4
49 Notodden N B6
14 Nottingham GB B1
62 Nottuln D B2
24 Nouan-le-Fuzelier F A2
23 Nouans-les-Fontaines F A6
27 Nougaroulet F C4
21 Nouvion, *Aisne* F B4
16 Nouvion, *Somme* F C1
98 Nova H B1
97 Nová Baňa SQ C4
97 Nová Belá CZ B4
96 Nová Bošáca SQ C3
104 Nova Breznica MAK C3
97 Nová Bystrica SQ B5
69 Nová Bystrice CZ B6
99 Nova Crnja CRO C5
72 Nova Gorica SL C3
100 Nova Gradiška CRO A2
101 Nova Kasaba BO B4
72 Nova Levante (Welschnofen) I B1
106 Nova Nadezhda BG A3
65 Nová Paka CZ C5
101 Nova Pazova YU B5
100 Nova Topola BO A2
101 Nova Varoš YU C4
73 Nova Vas SL C4
97 Nova Ves SQ C4
106 Nova Zagora BG A3
103 Novachene BG C5
103 Novachene BG D4
104 Novaci MAK C3
76 Novafeltria I C2
97 Novăky SQ C4
25 Novalaise F C5
34 Novales E A2
77 Novalja CRO B4
70 Novara I C3
85 Novara di Sicilia I A4
71 Novate Mezzola I B4
96 Nové Dvory CZ B1
69 Nové Hrady CZ C5
96 Nové Mesto SQ C3
65 Nové Mesto n. Metuji CZ C6
96 Nové Město n. Moravě CZ B2
65 Nové Město p. Smrkem CZ C5
69 Nové Mitrovice CZ B4
64 Nové Strašeci CZ C3
97 Nové Zámky SQ C4
66 Novéant F B2
40 Novelda E C2
75 Novellara I B5
72 Noventa di Piave I C2
76 Novento Vicentina I A1
38 Novés E B2
29 Noves F C3
35 Novés de Segre E A4
93 Novgorod R A12
99 Novi Bečej CRO C5
75 Novi di Módena I B5
105 Novi Dojran MAK C4
105 Novi Khan BG B5
99 Novi Kneževac CRO B5
99 Novi Kozarc YU C5
74 Novi Lígure I B3
98 Novi-Marof CRO B1
101 Novi Pazar YU C5
101 Novi Sad YU A4
101 Novi Slankamen YU A5
100 Novi Travnik BO B2
77 Novi Vinodolski CRO A4
77 Novigrad CRO B5
98 Novigrad CRO B1
76 Novigrad Podravski CRO A3
66 Noville B A1
21 Novion-Porcien F B5
104 Novo Brdo YU B3
102 Novo Korito YU C3
73 Novo Mesto SL C5
99 Novo Miloševo YU C5
107 Novo Selo BG B4
100 Novo Selo BO A3
105 Novo Selo MAK C4
104 Novo Selo, *A. P. Kosovo* YU B2
106 Novo selo, *Lovech* BG A2
101 Novo Selo, *Srbija* YU C5
94 Novohrad-Volynskyy U A7
108 Novoselë AL A1
107 Novoselets BG A4
90 Novosolna PL B3
100 Novska CRO A2
97 Nový Bohumin CZ B4
64 Nový Bor CZ C4
65 Nový Bydžov CZ C5
21 Novy-Chevrières F B5
97 Nový-Hrozenkov CZ B4
97 Novy Jočin CZ B3
69 Novy Knin CZ B5
97 Nový Sady SQ C3
97 Nový Tekov SQ C4
103 Novzci RO A4
90 Nowa Cerekwia PL C1
91 Nowa Dęba PL C5
91 Nowa Huta PL C4
88 Nowa Karczma PL A4
65 Nowa Kościoł PL B5
65 Nowa Miasteczko PL B5
65 Nowa Ruda PL C6
91 Nowa Sarzyna PL C6
91 Nowa Słupia PL C5
65 Nowa Sol PL B5
61 Nowa Warpno PL B5
89 Nowa Wieś PL B5
89 Nowa Wieś PL B7
88 Nowa-Wieś Wielka PL C4
89 Nowe PL B4
89 Nowe Kiejkuty PL B7
89 Nowe Miasto PL C6
90 Nowe Miasto PL A1
89 Nowe Miasto Lubawskie PL B5
91 Nowe Miasto nad Pilicą PL B4
90 Nowe-Skalmierzyce PL B1
61 Nowogard PL B6
65 Nowogród Bobrzański PL B5
65 Nowogrodziec PL B5
89 Nowy Dwor Gd. PL A5
91 Nowy-Dwór Mazowiecki PL A4
91 Nowy Korczyn PL C4
91 Nowy Majdan PL C6
94 Nowy Sacz PL B4
97 Nowy Targ PL B6
65 Nowy Tomyśl PL A6
90 Nowy Wachów PL C2
30 Noya E B2
18 Noyal-Pontivy F B3
22 Noyalo F A2
24 Noyant, *Allier* F B3
23 Noyant, *Maine-et-Loire* F A5
16 Noyelles F C1
19 Noyen F C5
23 Noyers, *Cher* F A6
25 Noyers, *Yonne* F A4
29 Noyers-sur-Jabron F B4
21 Noyon F B3
22 Nozay F A3
23 Nuaillé F A4
22 Nuaillé-d'Aunis F B4
32 Nubledo E A1
63 Nudlingen D C5
34 Nuéno E A2
41 Nuestra Señora del Pilar, *Formentera* E
32 Nueva E A2
44 Nueva Carteya E B2
39 Nuevalos E A5
39 Nuevo Seseña E B3
25 Nuits-St.George F A4
16 Nukerke B C3
87 Nule I B2
40 Nules E B2
87 Nulvi I B1
76 Numana I C3
17 Numansdorp NL B4
62 Nümbrecht D C2
64 Nunchritz D B3
11 Nuneaton GB C4
37 Nuñomoral E A4
64 Nunsdorf D A3
17 Nunspeet NL A5
87 Núoro I B2
79 Nuovo Balsorano Vecchio I B4
87 Nurallao I C2
35 Nuria E A5
47 Nurmes SF E14
68 Nürnberg D B2
87 Nurri I C2
67 Nürtingen D C5
70 Nus I C2
50 Nusnäs S B5
67 Nusplingen D C4
101 Nustar CRO A3
99 Nyáregyháza H A4
99 Nyarlörinc H B4
50 Nybergsund N A3
55 Nyborg DK C3
56 Nybro S C4
7 Nybster GB B5
55 Nyby DK D5
56 Nydala S B3
99 Nyergesufalu H A3
50 Nygard N B2
50 Nyhammar S B5
57 Nyhamnsläge S C1
51 Nyhyttan S C5
98 Nyirád H A2
94 Nyírbátor H C5
94 Nyíregyháza H C4
47 Nykarleby SF E11
57 Nyker DK D3
55 Nykøbing, *Falster* DK D4
55 Nykøbing, *Vestsjællands Amt.* DK C4
54 Nykøbing, *Viborg Amt.* DK B1
53 Nyköping S D3
51 Nykroppa S C5
53 Nykvarn S C3
47 Nyland S E8
65 Nymburk CZ C5
53 Nynäshamn S D3
25 Nyon CH B6
29 Nyons F B4
69 Nýřany CZ B4
69 Nýrsko CZ B4
46 Nyrud N B14
90 Nysa PL C1
51 Nysåter S C3
50 Nyskoga S B3
55 Nysted DK D4
49 Nystrand N B6
51 Nysund S C5
98 Nyúl H A2

O

30 O Barco de Valdeorras E B4
14 Oadby GB B1
10 Oakengates GB C3
14 Oakham GB B2
94 Oancea RO D8
48 Oanes N C3
71 Oapolago CH C3
103 Oaria RO B5
100 Obalj BO C3
8 Oban GB B2
73 Obdach A A4
44 Obejo E A2
96 Ober Grafendorf A C1
63 Ober-Kaufungen D B4
62 Ober-Morlen D C3
67 Ober-Roden D B4
63 Ober Seemen D C4
71 Oberammergau D A6
68 Oberasbach D B1
71 Oberau D A6
72 Oberaudorf D A2
66 Oberbronn F C3
66 Oberbruck F D2
70 Oberdießbach CH B2
70 Oberdorf CH A2
63 Oberdorla D B5
72 Oberdrauburg A B2
63 Oberelsbach D C5
68 Obergermaringen D D1
68 Obergünzburg D D1
71 Obergurgl A B6
73 Oberhaag A B5
67 Oberhausen, *Baden-Württemberg* D B4
62 Oberhausen, *Nordrhein-Westfalen* D B1
63 Oberhof D C5
63 Oberkatz D C5
67 Oberkirch, *Baden-Württemberg* D C4
66 Oberkirch, *Rheinland-Pfalz* D B2
62 Oberkirchen D B3
67 Oberkochen D C6
64 Oberkotzau D C1
62 Oberlahnstein D C2
63 Oberlauringen D C5
67 Obermarchtal D C5
63 Obermaßfeld-Grimmenthal D C5
66 Obernai F C3
67 Obernau D B5
69 Obernberg A C4
67 Obernburg D B5
67 Oberndorf D C4
69 Oberndorf b. Salzburg A D3
69 Oberneukirchen A C5
62 Obernkirchen D A4
65 Oberoderwitz D C4
73 Oberort A A5
62 Oberpleis D C2
98 Oberpullendorf A A1
67 Oberried D D3
71 Oberriet CH A4
63 Oberröblingen D B6
64 Oberröslau D C1
67 Oberrot D B5
68 Oberschleißheim D C2
67 Oberseebach F C3
96 Obersiebenbrunn A C2
71 Oberstaufen D A5
71 Oberstdorf D A5
72 Obertilliach A B2
68 Obertraubling D C3
72 Obertraun A A3
68 Obertrubach D B2
69 Obertrum A D4
62 Oberursel D C3
72 Obervellach A B3
63 Obervellmar D B4
68 Oberviechtach D B3
69 Oberwang A D4
98 Oberwart A A1
66 Oberwesel D A3
64 Oberwiesenthal D C3
62 Oberwinter D C2
73 Oberwölz A A4
69 Oberzell D C4
36 Obidos P B1
104 Obilic YU B3
68 Obing D D3
27 Objat F A5
73 Öblarn A A4
91 Oblęgorek PL C4
106 Oborishte BG A2
88 Oborniki PL C2
65 Oborniki Śląskie PL B6
99 Obornjača CRO C4
98 Oborovo CRO C1
101 Obrenovac YU B5
101 Obrež, *A. P. Vojvodino* YU B4
102 Obrež, *Srbija* YU C2
67 Obrigheim D B5
77 Obrovac CRO B5
101 Obrovac YU A4
100 Obrovac Sinjski CRO C1
104 Obršani MAK C3
88 Obrzycko PL C2
101 Obudovac BO B3
107 Obzor BG A5
39 Ocaña E C3
76 Occhiobello I B1
74 Occimiano I A3
100 Očevlja BO B3
34 Ochagavia E A1
8 Ochiltree GB C3
97 Ochotnica-Dolna PL B6
97 Ochotnica-Górna PL B6
67 Ochsenfurt D B6
67 Ochsenhausen D C5
17 Ochten NL B5
62 Ochtendung D C2
62 Ochtrup D A2
52 Ockelbo S B2
54 Öckerö S A4
103 Ocnele Mari RO A5
70 Ocourt CH A2
97 Očová SQ C5
99 Ócsa H A4
99 Öcsöd H B5
19 Octeville F A4
57 Ödåkra S C1
54 Odby DK B1
48 Odda N A3
55 Odder DK C3
51 Ödeborg S D2
42 Odeceixe P B1
91 Odechów PL B5
42 Odeleite P B2
42 Odemira P B1
95 Ödemis TR G8
66 Odenbach D B3
53 Odensbacken S C1
55 Odense DK C3
62 Odenthal D B2
61 Oderberg D C5
72 Oderzo I C2
51 Ödeshög S D5
42 Odiáxere P B1
36 Odivelas, *Lisboa* P C1
42 Odivelas, *Setúbal* P A1
90 Odolanów PL B1
39 Odón E B5
94 Odorhei RO C6
91 Odrowaz PL B4
96 Odry CZ B3
91 Odrzywól PL B4
55 Odsted DK C2
99 Odžaci CRO C4
100 Odžak BO A3
63 Oebisfelde D A5
16 Oedelem B B3
64 Oederan D C3
62 Oeding D B1
17 Oeffelt NL B5
17 Oegstgeest NL A4
36 Oeiras P C1
62 Oelde D B3
64 Oelsnitz D C2
70 Oensingen CH A2
69 Oepping A C4
62 Oer-Erkenschwick D B2
62 Oerlinghausen D B3
66 Oermingen F B3
62 Oesede D A3
63 Oeslau D C6
68 Oettingen D C1
21 Œuilly F B4
62 Oeventrop D B3
71 Offanengo I C4
67 Offenbach D A4
69 Offenberg D C3
67 Offenburg D C3
67 Offendorf F C3
79 Offida I A4
68 Offingen D C1
20 Offranville F B2
31 Ofir P C2
49 Ofte N B5
67 Ofterdingen D C5
71 Ofterschwang D A5
70 Oftringen CH A2
71 Oggiono I C4
44 Ogihares E B3
82 Ogliastro Cilento I A2
82 Ogliastro Marina I A1
13 Ogmore Vale GB B4
48 Ogna N C2
105 Ognyanovo BG C5
105 Ogoste YU B3
102 Ogradena RO B3
90 Ogrodzieniec PL C3
64 Ogrosen D B4
77 Ogulin CRO A5
45 Ohanes E B4
17 Ohey B C5
71 Ohlstadt D A6
60 Ohrdorf D C1
63 Ohrdruf D C5
104 Ohrid MAK C2
67 Öhringen D B5
112 Oía GR D2
31 Oiã P D2
5 Oilgate IRL B5
31 Oimbra E C3
17 Oirschot NL B5
20 Oisemont F B2
20 Oissel F B2
17 Oisterwijk NL B5
110 Oitilon GR C3
91 Ojców PL C3
50 Öje S B4
47 Öjebyn S D10
44 Ojén E C2
89 Ojrzeń PL C6
43 Ojuelos Altos E A4
89 Okalewo PL B5
12 Okehampton GB C3
63 Oker D B5
106 Okhiron GR B1
100 Oklaj CRO C1
96 Okoč SQ D3
98 Okoli CRO C1
97 Okoličné SQ B5
33 Okondo E A3
88 Okonek PL B2
89 Okonin PL B4
107 Okop BG A4
96 Okřisky CZ B1
105 Okruglica YU B4
91 Oksa PL C4
55 Oksbøl DK C1
55 Oksby DK C1
50 Øksna N B2
111 Oktoniá GR A5
100 Okučani CRO A2
33 Olagué E B5
28 Olargues F C1
65 Olawa PL C7
33 Olazagutia E B4
64 Olbernhau D C3
63 Olbersleben D B6
87 Ólbia I B2
55 Ølbylyng DK C5
68 Olching D C2
7 Old Deer GB C6
3 Oldcastle IRL C4
58 Oldeberkoop NL C3
58 Oldeboorn NL B2
17 Oldebroek NL A5
46 Olden N F3
59 Oldenbrok D B5
59 Oldenburg, *Niedersachsen* D B5
60 Oldenburg, *Schleswig-Holstein* D A1
62 Oldenzaal NL A1
46 Olderdalen N B10
58 Oldersum D B4
11 Oldham GB B3
63 Oldisleben D B6
7 Oldmeldrum GB C6
65 Oldrzychowice PL C6
32 Olea E B2
50 Oleby S B4
37 Oledo P B3
70 Oléggio I C3
30 Oleiros E B2
36 Oleiros P B3
17 Olen B B4
48 Olen N B2
35 Olesa de Montserrat E B4
90 Oleśnica PL B1
96 Olešnice CZ B2
90 Olesno PL C2
61 Oleszna PL B5
35 Olette F A5
62 Olfen D B2
71 Olgiate Comasco I C3
71 Olginate I C4
55 Ølgod DK C1
7 Olgrinmore GB B5
42 Olhão P B2
36 Olhavo P B1
42 Olhos de Agua P B1
35 Oliana E A4
38 Olias del Rey E C3
87 Oliena I B2
34 Oliete E C2
109 Olimbiás GR B4
112 Olimbos GR
109 Ólinthos GR A5
33 Olite E B5
40 Oliva E C2
43 Oliva de la Frontera E A3
37 Oliva de Mérida E C4
37 Oliva de Plasencia E A4
83 Olivadi I C3
36 Olival P B2
44 Olivar E C3
43 Olivares E B3
32 Olivares de Duero E C2
39 Olivares de Júcar E C4
31 Oliveira de Azemeis P D2
31 Oliveira de Frades P D2
36 Oliveira do Conde P A3
36 Oliveira do Hospital P A3
37 Olivenza E C3
20 Olivet F D2
71 Olivone CH B3
90 Olkusz PL C3
11 Ollerton GB B4
55 Ollerup DK C3
24 Olliergues F C3
29 Ollioules F C4
70 Ollon CH B2
21 Olloy-sur-Viroin B A5
53 Ölmbrotorp S C1
51 Ölme S C4
39 Olmeda E B4
39 Olmedilla de Alcarcón E C4
32 Olmedilla de Roa E C3
32 Olmedo E C2
87 Olmedo I B1
86 Olmeto F C1
32 Olmillos de Castro E C1
32 Olmos de Ojeda E B2
14 Olney GB B2
40 Olocau del Rey E A2
57 Olofström S C3
103 Ologi RO C6
96 Olomouc CZ B3
22 Olonne-sur-Mer F B3
28 Olonzac F C1
26 Oloron-Ste. Marie F C3
35 Olost E B5
35 Olot E A5
101 Olovo BO B3
62 Olpe D B2
96 Olšany CZ B3
62 Olsberg D B3
66 Olsbrücken D B3
16 Olsene B C3
51 Ölserud S C4
51 Olshammar S D5
64 Olsig D B3
57 Olsker DK D3
17 Olst NL A6
91 Olszanka PL A6

90 Olsztyn, *Częstochowa* PL C3
89 Olsztyn, *Olsztyn* PL B6
89 Olsztynek PL B6
65 Olszyna PL B5
48 Oltedal N C3
70 Olten CH A2
48 Ølve N B2
33 Olvega E C5
63 Olvenstedt D A6
43 Olvera E C4
110 Olympia GR B2
109 Olympiás GR A5
87 Olzai I B2
3 Omagh GB B4
112 Omalós, *Kriti* GR
107 Omarchevo BG A4
13 Ombersley GB A5
70 Omegna I C3
82 Omignano Scalo I A2
100 Omiš CRO C1
77 Omišalj CRO A4
58 Ommen NL C3
109 Omólion GR B4
101 Omoljica YU B5
108 Omorfoklisia GR A3
109 Omvriaki GR B4
17 On B C5
33 Oña E B3
78 Onano I A2
33 Oñate E A4
10 Onchan GB A1
40 Onda E B2
40 Ondara E C3
33 Ondárroa E A4
26 Onesse-et-Laharie F B2
15 Ongar GB C3
29 Ongles F B4
17 Onhaye B C4
40 Onil E C2
32 Onis E A2
16 Onnaing F C3
57 Onnestad S C3
54 Onsala S A5
55 Onsbjerg DK C3
57 Onslunda S D3
58 Onstwedde NL B4
40 Ontur E C1
23 Onzain F A6
32 Onzonilla E B1
16 Oost-en-West-Souburg NL B3
58 Oost-Vlieand NL B2
16 Oostakker B B3
16 Oostburg NL B3
16 Oostende B B2
17 Oosterbeek NL B5
58 Oosterend NL B2
17 Oosterhout NL B4
58 Oosterwolde NL C3
16 Oosterzele B C3
58 Oosthuizen NL C2
16 Oostkamp B B3
17 Oostmalle B B4
16 Oostrozebeke B C3
16 Oostvleteren B C2
17 Oostvoorne NL B4
58 Ootmarsum NL C3
65 Opalenica PL A6
69 Opařany CZ B5
102 Oparic YU C2
77 Opatija CRO A4
90 Opatów, *Częstochowa* PL C2
91 Opatów, *Tarnobrzeg* PL C5
90 Opatówek PL B2
91 Opatowiec PL C4
96 Opava CZ B3
58 Opeinde NL B3
17 Opglabbeerk B C5
16 Ophasselt B C3
73 Opicina I C3
62 Opladen D B1
73 Oplotnica SL B5
58 Opmeer NL C1
93 Opochka R B11
65 Opočno CZ C6
91 Opoczno PL B4
90 Opole PL C1
91 Opole Lubelskie PL B5
90 Oporów PL A3
101 Opovo YU A5
64 Oppach D B4
46 Oppdal N E4
53 Oppeby S D2
49 Oppegård N B7
67 Oppenau D C4
73 Oppenberg A A4
67 Oppenheim D B4
58 Oppenhuizen NL B2
59 Oppenwehe D C5
67 Oppenweiler D C5
80 Oppido Lucano I D2
85 Oppido Mamertina I A4
69 Opponitz A D5
50 Oppstad N B2
77 Oprtalj CRO A3
50 Opsahedan S B4
81 Opuzen CRO A4
72 Ora (Auer) I B1
36 Orada P C3
94 Oradea RO C4
23 Oradour-sur-Glane F C6
23 Oradour-sur-Vayres F C5
104 Orahovac YU B2
98 Orahovica CRO A2
100 Orahovo CRO A2
106 Oraion GR B2
29 Oraison F C4
29 Orange F B3
87 Orani I B2
64 Oranienbaum D B2
61 Oranienburg D C4
4 Oranmore IRL A3
101 Orašac, *Srbija* YU B5
102 Orašac, *Srbija* YU C3
101 Orašje BO A3
102 Orašje YU B3
102 Oraviţa RO A2
97 Oravská Lesná SQ B5
97 Oravská Polhora SQ B5
97 Oravské Veselé SQ B5
97 Oravsky-Podzámok SQ B5
40 Orba E C2
31 Orbacém P C2
55 Ørbæk DK C3
21 Orbais F C4
74 Orbassano I A2
70 Orbe CH B1
20 Orbec F B1
78 Orbetello I A2
78 Orbetello Scalo I A2
52 Örbyhus S D3
45 Orce E B4
45 Orcera E A4
25 Orchamps F A4
70 Orchamps-Vennes F A1
40 Orchete E C2
16 Orchies F C3
29 Orcières F B5
30 Ordes E A2
34 Ordesa E A2
9 Ordhead GB A5
9 Ordie GB A5
59 Ording D A5
35 Ordino AND A4
33 Orduña E B4
52 Ore S A1
39 Orea E B5
81 Orebić CRO B4
53 Örebro S C1
99 Öregcsertő H B4
52 Öregrund S B4
55 Orehoved DK D4
37 Orellana de la Sierra E B5
37 Orellana la Vieja E C5
112 Orén TR B1
109 Oreoi GR C5
107 Orestiás GR B4
109 Orfaná GR B4
14 Orford GB B4
35 Organá E A4
106 Orgáni GR B3
38 Orgaz E C3
25 Orgelet-le-Bourget F B5
49 Ørgenvika N A6
20 Orgères-en-Beauce F C2
34 Orgibet F A3
7 Orgill GB B5
28 Orgnac-l'Aven F B3
29 Orgon F C3
87 Orgósolo I B2
107 Orhaniye TR C4
111 Orhomenós GR B4
45 Oria E B4
83 Oria I A4
21 Origny-Ste Benoite F B4
45 Orihuela E A6
39 Orihuela del Tremedal E B5
108 Orik AL A1
37 Orini GR C5
33 Orio E A4
36 Oriola P C3
83 Oriolo I A3
47 Oripää SF F11
87 Oristano I C1
98 Öriszentpéter H B1
47 Orivesii SF F12
107 Orizare BG A5
105 Orizari MAK C4
106 Orizovo BG A3
51 Ørje N C2
44 Orjiva E C3
46 Orkanger N E4
57 Örkelljunga S C2
99 Örkény H A4
63 Orlamünde D C6
104 Orlane YU B3
104 Orlate YU B2
90 Orle PL A2
20 Orléans F D2
97 Orlova CZ B4
101 Orlovat YU A5
109 Órma GR A3
53 Ormaryd S B3
74 Ormea I B2
47 Ormelet N B7
49 Ormemyr N B6
107 Ormenion GR B4
109 Ormilia GR B5
112 Órmos, *Andros* GR E1
109 Órmos, *Thessaloniki* GR A4
112 Ormos, *Tinos* GR D1
106 Órmos Prinou GR C2
98 Ormož SL B1
14 Ormsby St. Margaret GB B4
10 Ormskirk GB B3
25 Ornans F A6
52 Ornäs S B1
89 Orneta PL A6
55 Ørnhoj DK B1
112 Órnos GR D1
47 Ornsköldvik S E9
103 Orodelu RO B4
101 Orolik CRO B4
99 Orom CRO C4
70 Oron-la-Ville CH B1
91 Orońsko PL B4
70 Oropa I C2
40 Oropesa, *Castellon* E A3
38 Oropesa, *Toledo* E C1
92 Orosei I B2
99 Orosháza H B5
98 Oroszlány H A3
98 Oroszlo H B3
82 Orotelli I B2
33 Orozco E A4
7 Orphir GB B5
48 Orre N C2
56 Orrefors S C4
52 Orresta S C3
50 Orsa S A5
80 Orsara di Púglia I C2
52 Orsay F C3
48 Orscholz D B2
24 Orsennes F B1
56 Orserum S A3
93 Orsha BL C12
82 Orsières CH B2
56 Orsjö S C4
55 Ørslev DK C4
79 Orsogna I A5
82 Orsomarso I B2
102 Orşova RO B3
103 Orsoya BG C4
46 Ørstav N E3
56 Orsted DK B3
53 Örsundsbro S C3
80 Orta Nova I C2
70 Orta san Giulio I C3
78 Orte I A3
69 Ortenburg D C4
96 Orth A C2
26 Orthez F C3
66 Ortho B A1
30 Ortigueira E A3
34 Ortilla E A2
72 Ortisei (St. Ulrich) I B1
57 Örtofta S D2
10 Orton GB A3
79 Ortona I A5
64 Ortrand D B3
100 Orubica CRO A2
54 Ørum DK B2
97 Orune I B3
39 Orusco E B3
36 Orvalho P B3
22 Orvault F A3
78 Orvieto I A3
79 Orvinio I A3
103 Oryakhovo BG C4
90 Orzesze PL C2
24 Orzinuovi I C4
71 Orzivécchi I C4
101 Osaonica YU C5
56 Osbruk S B3
57 Osby S C2
97 Osčadnica SQ B4
64 Oschatz D B3
63 Oschersleben D A6
87 Oschiri I B2
89 Ościsłowo PL C6
59 Osdorf D A7
101 Osečina YU B4
32 Oseja de Sajambre E A1
64 Osek CZ C3
34 Osera E B2
74 Ősi H A3
103 Osica de Sos RO B5
87 Osidda I B2
89 Osie PL B4
91 Osieck PL B5
69 Osieczna PL B6
89 Osiek PL B5
89 Osiek, *Gdansk* PL B4
88 Osiek, *Piła* PL B3
91 Osiek, *Tarnobrzeg* PL C5
97 Osielec PL B5
89 Osielsko PL B4
99 Osijek CRO C3
73 Osilnica SL C4
87 Osilo I B1
76 Ósimo I C3
100 Osinja BO B2
102 Osipaonica YU B2
93 Osjaków PL B2
101 Osječani BO C3
56 Oskarshamn S B5
56 Oskarström S C1
97 Oslany SQ C4
96 Oslavany CZ B2
49 Oslo N B7
107 Osmanli TR B4
53 Ösmo S D3
91 Osmolin PL A3
62 Osnabrück D A3
61 Ośno PL C5
77 Osor CRO B4
32 Osorno E B2
48 Osøyra N A2
74 Ospedaletti I C2
71 Ospitaletto I C5
17 Oss NL B5
109 Ossa GR A5
39 Ossa de Montiel E D4
17 Ossi I B1
49 Ossjøen N A5
26 Ossun F C3
57 Ostanå S C3
51 Ostansjo S C5
52 Ostanvik S A1
46 Østavall S E7
62 Ostbevern D A2
49 Østby N A3
50 Osted DK C4
76 Ostellato I B1
54 Øster Hornum DK B2
53 Øster Hurup DK B3
55 Øster Lindet DK C2
57 Øster Marie DK D4
55 Øster Tørslev DK B3
54 Øster Vrå DK A3
62 Osterath Büderich D B1
60 Osterburg D C2
67 Osterburken D B5
53 Österbybruk S B3
54 Osterbyhavn DK A4
55 Österbymo S B4
52 Österfärnebo S B2
63 Osterfeld D B6
60 Osterhofen D C4
59 Osterholz-Scharmbeck D B5
56 Österkorsberga S B4
54 Østerlid DK A1
52 Österlövsta S B3
69 Ostermiething A C3
53 Osterode D B5
50 Osterronfeld D A6
62 Osterspai D C2
46 Östersund S E7
52 Östervåla S B3
51 Östervallskog S C2
62 Osterwick D A2
53 Osterwieck D B5
62 Osterzell D D1
98 Ostffyasszonyfa H A2
52 Östhammar S B4
66 Ostheim F C3
63 Ostheim v.d. Rhön D C5
67 Osthofen D B4
75 Ostiano I A5
75 Ostiglia I A6
52 Ostmark S B2
33 Ostiz E B5
50 Östmark S B3
16 Ostnor S A5
50 Ostojićevo CRO C5
76 Ostra I C3
76 Östra Amtervik S C4
76 Östra Husby S D2
53 Östra Ljungby S C2
53 Östra Ryd S D2
57 Östraby S D2
67 Ostrach D D5
64 Ostrau D B3
97 Ostrava CZ B4
49 Østre Halsen N B7
104 Ostren i math AL C2
58 Ostrhauderfehn D B4
67 Östringen D B4
64 Ostritz D B4
89 Ostróda PL B5
96 Ostroh CZ C3
97 Ostrołeka PL D7
89 Ostropole PL B5
104 Ostros YU B1
77 Ostrošovac BO B5
100 Ostrov BG C5
64 Ostrov CZ C2
93 Ostrov R B11
96 Ostrov n. Oslavou CZ B2
89 Ostrów Maz. PL D7
90 Ostrów Wielkopolski PL B1
90 Ostrówek PL B2
88 Ostrowiec PL A2
91 Ostrowiec Świętokrzyski PL C5
88 Ostrowice PL C4
90 Ostrowy PL A3
100 Ostrožac BO B3
90 Ostrzeszów PL B1
60 Ostseebad Kühlungsborn D A2
81 Ostuni I D4
97 Osturňa SQ B6
43 Osuna E B4
96 Osvětimany CZ B3
10 Oswestry GB B2
97 Oświecim PL A5
47 Otava SF F13
33 Oteiza E B5
49 Oterbekk N B7
38 Otero de Herreros E B2
30 Otero de Rey E A3
102 Oteteliș RO B4
15 Otford GB D3
63 Othfresen D A5
40 Otinyent E C2
11 Otley GB B4
89 Otloczyn PL C4
65 Otmuchów PL C7
46 Otnes N F5
77 Otočac CRO B5
107 Otok CRO A3
100 Otoka BO B1
83 Otranto I A5
78 Otricoli I A3
96 Otrokovice-Kvitkovice CZ B3
46 Otta N F4
87 Ottana I B2
66 Ottange F B2
79 Ottaviano I C5
57 Ottenby, *Öland* S C5
64 Ottendorf-Okrilla D B3
67 Ottenhöfen D C4
69 Ottenschlag A C6
69 Ottensheim A C5
8 Otter Ferry GB B2
67 Otterbach D B3
51 Otterbäcken S D5
9 Otterburn GB C5
68 Otterfing D D2
17 Otterlo NL A5
59 Otterndorf D B5
59 Ottersburg D B6
67 Ottersweier D C4
55 Otterup DK C3
13 Ottery St. Mary GB C4
17 Ottignies B C4
66 Ottmarsheim F D3
67 Ottobeuren D D6
99 Öttömös H B4
75 Ottone I B4
67 Ottweiler D B3
91 Otwock PL A5
75 Otyn PL B5
71 Ötz A A5
111 Otziás GR B5
24 Ouanne F A3
20 Ouarville F C2
25 Oucques F D2
17 Oud-Beijerland NL B4
17 Oud Gastel NL B4
17 Ouddorp NL B3
58 Oude-Pekela NL B4
17 Oude-Tonge NL B4
58 Oudehaske NL B2
58 Oudemirdum NL C2
16 Oudenaarde B C3
17 Oudenbosch NL B4
16 Oudenburg B B2
17 Ouderkerk NL A2
17 Oudewater NL B4
22 Oudon F A3
4 Oughterard IRL A2
37 Ouguela P B3
19 Ouistreham F A5
47 Oulainen SF D12
21 Oulchy-le-Château F B4
25 Oullins F C4
25 Oulmes F B4
47 Oulu SF D12
14 Oundle GB B2
30 Ourense-Orense E B3
42 Ourique P B1
30 Ourol E A3
24 Ouroux, *Nièvre* F A3
25 Ouroux, *Saône-et-Loire* F B4
7 Ousdale GB B5
35 Oust F A4
36 Outeiro P A2
30 Outes E B2
47 Outokumpu SF E14
14 Outwell GB B3
30 Ouviñaño E A4
20 Ouzouer-le-Marché F D2
20 Ouzouer-sur-Loire F D3
74 Ovada I B3
54 Ovanåker S A1
52 Ovansjo S B2
31 Ovar P D2
107 Ovcharovo BG A4
54 Ove DK B2
59 Oveligönne D B5
62 Ovenstädt D A3
55 Over-jerstal DK C2
13 Over Wallop GB B6
62 Overath Much D C2
7 Overbister GB A6
62 Overdinkel NL A2
46 Överhogdal S E7
47 Överijse B C4
47 Överkalix S C11
54 Overlade DK B2
56 Överlida S B1
17 Overpelt B B5
7 Overscaig Hotel GB B4
14 Overstrand GB B4
8 Overton GB B3
10 Overton, *Clwyd* GB B2
15 Overton, *Hampshire* GB C1
47 Övertorneå S C11
56 Överum S B5
32 Oviedo E A1
74 Oviglio I B3
79 Ovindoli I B4
87 Ovodda I B2
48 Øvre Sirdal N C3
51 Övre Ullerud S C4
42 Övrebygd N C3
94 Ovruch U A8
55 Övrup DK C1
88 Owińska PL C2
50 Oxberg S A5
53 Oxelösund S D3
15 Oxford GB C1
111 Oxilithos GR A5
71 Oy D A5
33 Oyarzun E A5
51 Øyenkilen N C1
50 Øyer N A1
49 Oyfjell N B5
7 Oykel Bridge GB C4
51 Øymark N C2
25 Oyonnax F B5
47 Øyslebø N C4
47 Øystese N A3
59 Oyten D B6
48 Øyuvsbu N B4
33 Ozaeta E B4
31 Ozarów PL C5
91 Ożarów Maz PL A4
73 Ożbalt SL B5
112 Ozbaşi TR B1
57 Özd H C6
97 Ožďany SQ C5
87 Ozieri I B2
89 Ozierki R A6
90 Ozimek PL C2
100 Ozimica BO B3
73 Ozjaz CRO C5
20 Ozoir la Ferrière F C3
98 Ozora H B3
90 Ozorków PL B3
74 Ozzano Monferrato I A3

P

45 Pa Paca E B5
17 Paal B B5
90 Pabianice PL B3
69 Pabneukirchen A C5
91 Pacanów PL C5
84 Paceco I B1
102 Pačejevce YU C2
85 Pachino I C4
99 Pačir CRO C4
73 Pack A A5
31 Paços de Ferreira P C2
69 Pacov CZ B5
98 Pacsa H B2
20 Pacy-sur-Eure F B2
65 Paczków PL C7
47 Padasjoki SF F12
55 Padborg DK D2
9 Paddockhole GB C4
103 Padea RO B4
99 Padej CRO C5
100 Padene CRO B1
62 Paderborn D B3
42 Paderne P B1
10 Padiham GB B3
101 Padina YU A5
101 Padinska Skela YU B5
31 Padornelo P C2
72 Pádova I C1
98 Padragkút H A2
87 Padria I B1
30 Padrón E B2
87 Padru I B2
12 Padstow GB C3
44 Padul E B3
82 Padula I A2
79 Paduli I B5
103 Păduroiu RO B5
74 Paesana I B2
72 Paese I B2
77 Pag CRO B5
79 Pagani I C5
79 Pagánica I A4
79 Pagánico I A2
79 Paglieta I A5
66 Pagny-sur-Moselle F C1
109 Pagóndas GR C5
112 Pagóndhas GR C1
41 Paguera, *Mallorca* E
68 Pahl D D2
111 Paiania GR B4
13 Paignton GB C4
27 Pailhès F C5
22 Paimboeuf F A2
18 Paimpol F B2
18 Paimpont F B3
13 Painswick GB B5
68 Painten D C2
36 Paio Pires P C1
8 Paisley GB C3
47 Pajala S C11
32 Pajares E A1
32 Pajares de los Oteros E B1
90 Pajęczno PL B2
98 Páka H B1
111 Pákia GR C3
88 Pakość PL C4
90 Pakosławice PL C1
77 Pakoštane CRO C5
99 Pákozd H A3
98 Pakrac CRO C2
99 Paks H B3
32 Palacios de Benaber E B3
33 Palacios de la Sierra E C3
32 Palaciós de la Valduerna E B1
31 Palacios de Sanabria E B4
30 Palacios del Sil E B4
38 Palaciosrubios E A1
35 Palafrugell E B6
83 Palagiano I B3
85 Palagonia I B3
75 Paláia I C5
111 Palaia Epidhavros GR B4
106 Palaiokómi GR C1
112 Palaiokhora, *Kriti* GR
109 Palaiokhórion GR A5
109 Palaiovrákha GR C2
108 Pálairos GR C2
10 Palaiseau F C3
109 Palamás, *Fthiótis* GR B4
109 Palamás, *Kardhítsa* GR B4
35 Palamós E B6
93 Palanga LT C7
75 Palanzano I B5
97 Palárikovo SQ C4
30 Palas de Rei E B3
79 Palata I B5
109 Palatitsia GR A4
87 Palau I A2
28 Palavas F C2
33 Palazuelos de la Sierra E B3
84 Palazzo Adriano I B2
76 Palazzo del Pero I C1
80 Palazzo S. Gervásio I D2
85 Palazzolo Acréide I B3
71 Palazzolo sull Oglio I C4
76 Palazzuolo sul Senio I B1
93 Paldiski EW A9
101 Pale BO C3
112 Palékastron, *Kriti* GR
79 Palena I B5
32 Palencia E B2
44 Palenciana E B2
112 Paleópoli GR E1
84 Palermo I A2
84 Palestrate I A2
79 Palestrina I B3
99 Pálfa H B3
73 Palfau A A4
14 Palgrave GB B4
31 Palhaça P D2
36 Palheiros da Tocha P A2
36 Palheiros de Mira P A2
36 Palheiros de Quiaios P A2
108 Paliambela GR B2
99 Palić CRO B4
78 Palidoro I B3
82 Palinuro I A2
108 Paliokastritsa GR B1
110 Paliopanayiá GR C3
108 Paliópirgos, *Aitolía kai Acarnania* GR A2
109 Paliópirgos, *Trikkala* GR B3
107 Paliouri, *Évros* GR B4
109 Palioúri, *Khalkidhikí* GR C5
21 Paliseul B B6
70 Pallanza I C3
41 Pallares E A3
4 Pallas Green (New) IRL B3
35 Pallerols E A4
68 Palling D D3
111 Pallini GR B4
22 Pallnau F B3
79 Palma I B4
36 Palma P C2
41 Palma, *Mallorca* E
43 Palma del Rio E B4
84 Palma di Montechiaro I B2
41 Palma Nova, *Mallorca* E
72 Palmanova I C3
36 Palmela P C2
35 Palmerola E A5
85 Palmi I A4
99 Pálmonostora H B4
74 Palo I B3
80 Palo del Colle I C3
47 Palojcensuu SF B11
45 Palomares E B5
39 Palomares del Campo E C4
37 Palomas E C4
78 Palombara Sabina I A3
45 Palos E B6
43 Palos de la Frontera E B3
99 Palotabozsok H B3
97 Palotás H D5
35 Pals E B6
53 Pålsboda S C1
47 Paltamo SF D13
72 Paluzza I B3
17 Pamel B C4
98 Pamhagen A A1
27 Pamiers F C5
88 Pamietowo PL B3
44 Pampaneira E C3
74 Pamparato I B2
36 Pampilhosa, *Aveiro* P A2
36 Pampilhosa, *Coimbra* P A3
32 Pampliega E B3
33 Pamplona E B5
106 Panagyurishte BG A2
112 Panatólion GR C3
109 Panayia, *Grevená* GR A3
109 Panayia, *Thasos* GR C2
108 Panayia, *Trikkala* GR B3
109 Panayitsa GR A3
101 Pančevo YU B5
105 Pancharevo BG B5
33 Pancorvo E B3
111 Pandánassa GR C3
71 Pandino I C4
54 Pandrup DK A2
64 Panenský-Týnec CZ C3
93 Panevežys LT C9
15 Pangbourne GB C1
25 Panissières F C4
30 Panjon E B2
90 Panki PL C2
20 Pannes F C3
17 Panningen NL B5
98 Pannonhalma H A2
109 Panórama GR A5
112 Panormitis GR B2
112 Pánormos, *Kriti* GR
112 Pánormos, *Tínos* GR D1
64 Panschwitz-Kuckau D B4
60 Pansdorf D B1
66 Pansey F C1
34 Panticosa E A2
38 Pantoja E B3
30 Pantón E B3
82 Páola I B3
98 Pápa H A2
108 Papadátes GR B2
109 Papádes GR C5
111 Papadhianika GR C3
110 Páparis GR B3
89 Paparzyn PL B4
82 Papasidero I B2
98 Papateszér H A2
59 Papenburg D B4
108 Pápingo GR B2
68 Pappenheim D C1
91 Paprotnia PL A4
91 Paprotnia PL A5
84 Parábita I A4
102 Paraćin YU C2
98 Parád H D6
31 Parada, *Bragança* P C4
31 Parada, *Viseu* P D2
43 Paradas E B4
30 Paradaseca E B4
30 Paradela E B3
38 Parades de Rubiales E A1
110 Paradhisia GR B3
32 Paradilla E C3
38 Paradinas de S. Juan E A1
109 Parádisos GR A5
91 Paradyż PL B4
111 Paralia, *Arkadhia* GR B3
109 Paralia, *Lakonía* GR C4
109 Paralia, *Piería* GR A4
111 Paralia, *Voiotía* GR A3
111 Parália Kimis GR A5
109 Parália Skofinas GR A4
110 Paralimnion GR B3
111 Parálion Ástrous GR B3
104 Paralovo YU B3
19 Paramé F B4
108 Paramithiá GR B2
30 Páramo E A4
30 Páramo del Sil E B4
31 Parandaça P C3
106 Paranéstion GR B3
108 Parapótamos GR B2
30 Paravadella E A3
108 Parávrison GR B2
25 Paray-le-Monial F B4
36 Parceiros P B2
25 Parcey F A5
60 Parchim D B3
89 Parciaki PL B7
26 Pardies F C3
96 Pardubice CZ A1
31 Paredes P C2
31 Paredes de Coura P C2
32 Paredes de Nava E B2
39 Paredes de Siguenza E A4
39 Pareja E B4
19 Parennes F B5
83 Parenti I B3
26 Parentis-en-Born F B2
64 Parey D A1
73 Parg CRO C4
108 Párga GR B2
47 Pargas SF F11
21 Pargny-sur-Saulx F C5
20 Parigné-l'Évêque F D1
47 Parikkala SF F14
20 Paris F C3
27 Parisot F B5
47 Parkano SF E11
9 Parkgate GB C4
3 Parkmore GB A5
4 Parknasilla IRL C2
38 Parla E B3
35 Parlabà E A6
75 Parma I B5
96 Parndorf A D2
97 Párnica SQ B5
93 Parnu EW A9
21 Parois F B6
47 Parola SF F12
45 Parolis E A4
109 Paróri GR C4
112 Páros GR D1
38 Parrillas E B1
60 Parsberg D B2
68 Parsdorf D C2
61 Parstein D C5
84 Partanna I B1
23 Parthenay F B4
111 Partheni, *Évia* GR B4
112 Parthéni, *Léros* GR C1
84 Partinico I B2
106 Partizani BG A3
101 Partizani YU B5
97 Partizánske SQ C4
11 Partney GB B6
10 Parton GB A2
56 Påryd S C4
91 Parysów PL B5
90 Parzymiechy PL B2
61 Pasewalk D B4
101 Pasina Voda YU C4
56 Påskallavik S B5
89 Pasłęk PL A5
77 Pašman CRO C5
5 Passage East IRL B5
4 Passage West IRL C3
73 Passail A A5
19 Passais F B5
69 Passau D C4
31 Passegueiro P D2
16 Passendale B C3
76 Passignano sul Trasimeno I C2
76 Passo di Tréia I C3
85 Passopisciaro I B4
61 Passow D B5
79 Pástena I B5
30 Pastoriza E A3
39 Pastrana E B4
71 Pastrengo I C5
89 Pasym PL B6
97 Pásztó H D5
96 Pata SQ C3
102 Pătas RO B3
20 Pataÿ F C2
11 Pateley Bridge GB A4
40 Paterna E B2
43 Paterna de Rivera E C4
43 Paterna del Campo E B3
45 Paterna del Madera E A4
72 Paternion A B3
85 Paternò I B3
80 Paternópoli I D2
69 Patersdorf D B4
58 Paterswolde NL B3
108 Patiópoulo GR B3
112 Patmos GR C1
8 Patna GB C3
88 Patnow PL A3
108 Patos AL A1
110 Pátrai GR A2
4 Patrickswell IRL B3
86 Patrimonio F B2
11 Patrington GB B6
87 Pattada I B2
59 Pattensen, *Niedersachsen* D B7
63 Pattensen, *Niedersachsen* D A4
10 Patterdale GB A3
85 Patti I A3
103 Pătulele RO B3
99 Páty H A3
26 Pau F C3
26 Pauillac F A3
72 Paularo I B3
28 Paulhaguet F A2
28 Paulhan F C2
87 Paulilatino I B1
56 Paulistrom S B4
71 Paullo I C4
64 Pausa D C2
106 Pavel Banya BG A3
74 Pavia I A4
36 Pavia P C2
40 Pavias E B2
20 Pavilly F B1
109 Pavliani GR C4
111 Pávlos GR A4
75 Pavullo nel Frignano I B5
61 Päwesin D C3
97 Pawlowice PL B4
90 Pawonkow PL C2
112 Paxi(Gaios) GR B2
70 Payerne CH B1
42 Paymoyo E B2
108 Páyoi GR B1
27 Payrac F B5
106 Pazardzhik BG A2
77 Pazin CRO A3
35 Paziols F A5
106 Pčelarovo BG B3
98 Pčelić CRO C2
97 Pcim PL B5
105 Pčinja MAK B3
15 Peacehaven GB D3
44 Peal de Becerro E B3
14 Peasenhall GB B4
15 Peasmarsh GB D3
104 Peć YU B2
75 Péccioli I C5
99 Pécel H A4
42 Pechao P B2
68 Pechbrunn D B3
32 Pechón E A2
94 Pecica RO C4
102 Pećinci YU B4
62 Peckelsheim D B4
98 Pécs H B3
98 Pecsvárad H B3
81 Pečurice YU B6
90 Peczniew PL B2
77 Pedaso I C3
72 Pedavena I B1
33 Pedernales E A4
57 Pedersker DK D3
72 Pedescala I C1
103 Pedești RO B4
108 Pedhini GR B2
32 Pedrajas de San Esteban E B2
40 Pedralba E B2
31 Pedralba de la Praderia E B4
38 Pedraza E A3
40 Pedreguer E C3
30 Pedreira E A2
44 Pedrera E B2
44 Pedro Abad E A2
38 Pedro Bernardo E B2
44 Pedro-Martinez E B3
39 Pedro Muñoz E C4
43 Pedroche E A4
36 Pedrógão, *Beja* P A2
37 Pedrógão, *Castelo Branco* P A3
36 Pedrógão, *Leiria* P B2
36 Pedrógão Grande P B2
34 Pedrola E B1
33 Pedrosa E B3
32 Pedrosa del Rey, *León* E B2
32 Pedrosa del Rey, *Valladolid* E C1
32 Pedrosa del Rio Urbel E B3
38 Pedrosillo E A1
38 Pedrosillo de los Aires E B1
89 Pędzewo PL B4
9 Peebles GB C4
10 Peel GB A1
61 Peenemünde D A4
17 Peer B B5
109 Péfki GR B5
110 Péfki GR C4
37 Pega P A3
44 Pegalajar E B3
64 Pegau D B2
73 Peggau A A5
74 Pegli I B3
68 Pegnitz D B2
40 Pego E C2
36 Pegões-Estação P C2
36 Pegões Velhos P C2
9 Pegswood GB C6
105 Pehčevo MAK C4
107 Pehlivanköy TR B4
6 Peinchorran GB C2
63 Peine D A5
71 Pèio I B5
29 Peipan F B4
70 Peisey-Nancroix F C1
68 Peißenberg D D2
68 Peiting D D1
64 Peitz D B4
101 Peka YU B4
38 Pelahustán E B2
110 Peléna GR B3
109 Pelasyia GR C4
61 Pelczyce PL B6
108 Pélekas GR B1
111 Peletá GR B3
69 Pelhřimov CZ B6
29 Pélissanne F C4
109 Pella GR A4
29 Pellafol F B4
75 Pellegrino Parmense I B4
26 Pellegrue F B4
98 Pellérd H B3
76 Pellestrina I A2
23 Pellevoisin F B6
71 Pellizzano I B5
47 Pello SF C11
38 Peloche E C1
103 Pelovo BG C5
89 Pelplin PL B4
29 Pelussin F A3
99 Pély H A5
12 Pembrey GB B3
13 Pembridge GB A5
12 Pembroke GB B3
12 Pembroke Dock GB B3
15 Pembury GB C3
10 Pen-y-groes GB B1
38 Peña de Cabra E B1
35 Peñacerrada E B4
36 Penacova P A2
10 Penaenmawr GB B2
32 Peñafiel E C2
31 Penafiel P C2
32 Peñaflor E B4
44 Peñalsordo E A1
31 Penalva do Castelo P D3
37 Penamacor P A3
32 Penamellera Alta E A2
32 Penamellera Baja E A2
37 Peñaparda E A4
38 Peñaranda de Bracamonte E B1
33 Peñaranda de Duero E C3
34 Peñarroya de Tastavins E C3
37 Peñarroya-Pueblonuevo E C5
44 Peñarrubia E C2
40 Peñarrubla E B3
13 Penarth GB B4
45 Peñas de S. Pedro E A5
32 Peñascosa E A4
32 Peñausende E C1
97 Penc H D5
13 Pencoed GB B4
110 Pendálofos, *Aitolia kai Acarnania* GR A2
107 Pendálofos, *Évros* GR B4
109 Pendayi GR C4
12 Pendeen GB C2
32 Pendueles E A2
31 Penedono P D3
36 Penela P A2
31 Penhas Juntas P C3
36 Peniche P B1
9 Penicuik GB C4
64 Penig D C2
42 Penilhos P B2
41 Peñíscola E A3
11 Penistone GB B4
105 Penkovtsi BG B4
10 Penkridge GB C3
61 Penkun D B5
18 Penmarche F C1
76 Pennabilli I C2
27 Penne F B4
79 Penne I A4
72 Pennes (Pens) I B1
8 Pennyghael GB B1
10 Penrhyndeudraeth GB C1
10 Penrith GB A3
12 Penryn GB C2
108 Pentálofos GR A3
10 Pentraeth GB B1
10 Pentrefoelas GB B2
12 Penzance GB C2
68 Penzberg D D2
68 Penzing D C1
61 Penzlin D B4
29 Péone F B5
102 Peplievac YU C2
107 Péplos GR C4
104 Peqin AL C1
98 Pér H A2
36 Pera Boa P A3
111 Péra Mélana GR B3
47 Perä-Posio SF C13
37 Perafita P C2
109 Peraia, *Péla* GR A3
109 Peraia, *Thessaloniki* GR A4
111 Perakhóra GR A3
111 Perakhórion GR A1
38 Peraleda de la Mata E C1
38 Peraleda de S.Román E C1
40 Perales de Alfambra E A1
39 Perales de Tajuña E B3
33 Peralta E B5
34 Peralta de la Sal E B3
42 Peralva P B2
39 Peralveche E B4
111 Pérama, *Attikí* GR B4
108 Pérama, *Ioánnina* GR B2
112 Pérama, *Kriti* GR
47 Peranka SF D14
81 Perast YU B5
99 Perbál H A3
96 Perchtoldsdorf A C2
19 Percy F B4
87 Perdasdefogu I C2
108 Pérdhika GR B2
111 Pérdhika, *Égina* GR B4
108 Pérdhika, *Kozani* GR A3
34 Perdiguera E B2
94 Perecin U B5
39 Peredes E A4
31 Peredo P C4
42 Pereiro, *Faro* P B2
37 Pereiro, *Guarda* P D3
36 Pereiro, *Santarém* P B2
30 Pereiro de Aguiar E B3
35 Perelada E A6
37 Pereleda de Zaucejo E C5

39 Perelejos de las Truchas E B5
34 Perello E C3
31 Pereña E C4
32 Pereruela E C1
103 Peretu RO B6
87 Pérfugas I B1
69 Perg A C5
71 Pérgine Valsugana I B6
76 Pérgola I C2
85 Pergusa I B3
47 Perho SF E12
71 Peri I C5
99 Periam RO B5
44 Periana E C2
19 Périers F A4
27 Périgueux F A4
75 Perino I B4
103 Perişoru RO B4
109 Peristéra GR A5
110 Peristéri GR B2
108 Perithia GR B1
105 Perithórion GR C5
108 Perivóli, *Grevená* GR B3
108 Perivóli, *Kérkira* GR B2
77 Perjasica CRO A5
99 Perkáta H A3
60 Perleberg D B2
101 Perlez YU A5
108 Përmet AL A2
25 Pernand-Vergelesses F A4
69 Pernarec CZ B4
73 Pernegg a.d. Mur A A5
96 Pernek SQ C3
36 Pernes P B2
29 Pernes-les-Fontaines F C4
106 Pérni GR B2
105 Pernik BG B5
64 Pernink CZ C2
47 Perniö SF F11
96 Pernitz A D1
36 Pero Pinheiro P C1
42 Peroguarda P A1
28 Pérols F C2
25 Peron F B5
21 Péronne F B3
17 Péronnes B C4
32 Perorrubio E C3
74 Perosa Argentina I B2
31 Perozinho P C2
35 Perpignan F A5
12 Perranporth GB C2
25 Perrecy-les-Forges F B4
74 Perrero I B2
24 Perrier F C3
70 Perrignier F B1
18 Perros-Guirec F B2
20 Persan F B3
50 Persberg S C5
69 Persenbeug A C6
13 Pershore GB A5
51 Pershyttan S C6
64 Perštejn CZ C3
57 Perstorp S C2
9 Perth GB B4
72 Pertisau A A1
108 Pertouli GR B3
29 Pertuis F C4
101 Perućac YU C4
76 Perúgia I C2
106 Perushtitsa BG A2
77 Perusic CRO B5
16 Péruwelz B C3
17 Perwez B C4
33 Pesadas de Burgos E B3
32 Pesaguero E A2
76 Pésaro I C2
107 Peşayigit TR C4
71 Pescantina I C5
79 Pescara I A5
79 Pescasseroli I B4
80 Peschici I C3
71 Peschiera d. Garda I C5
75 Péscia I C5
79 Pescina I A4
79 Pesco Sannita I B5
79 Pescocostanzo I B5
80 Pescopagano I D2
104 Peshk AL C2
104 Peshkopi AL C2
106 Peshtera BG A2
25 Pesmes F A5
32 Pesquera de Duero E C2
26 Pessac F B3
107 Pessáni GR B4
104 Peštani MAK C2
103 Peşteana-Jui RO B4
103 Peştişani RO A4
107 Pet Mogili BG A4
108 Péta GR B3
110 Petalidhion GR C2
66 Pétange L B1
98 Peteanec CRO B1
16 Petegem B C3
14 Peterborough GB B2
13 Peterchurch GB A5
9 Peterculter GB A5
7 Peterhead GB C7
9 Peterlee GB D6
15 Petersfield GB D2
61 Petershagen, *Brandenburg* D C4
61 Petershagen, *Brandenburg* D C5
62 Petershagen, *Nordrhein-Westfalen* D A3
68 Petershausen D C2
68 Peterskirchen D C3
4 Peterswell IRL A3
97 Pétervására H C6
83 Petilia Policastro I B3
64 Petkus D B3
99 Petlovac CRO C3
101 Petlovača YU B4
102 Petnic RO B3
99 Petöfiszallás H B4
108 Petoúsi GR B2
41 Petra, *Mallorca* E
109 Pétra, *Pieriá* GR A4
84 Petralia Sottana I B3
109 Petralona GR A5
109 Pétrana GR A3
77 Petrcane CRO B5
40 Petrel E C2
104 Petrelë AL C1
79 Petrella Tifernina I B5
86 Petreto-Bicchisano F C1
105 Petrich BG C5
98 Petrijanec CRO B1
99 Petrijevci CRO C3
98 Petrinja CRO C1
97 Petrkovice CZ B4
93 Petrokrepost R A12
40 Pétrola E C1
83 Petronà I B3
96 Petronell A C2
94 Petroşeni RO D5
107 Petrotá GR B4
109 Petrotó GR B3
106 Petroúsa GR B2
81 Petrovac, *Crna Gora* YU B5
102 Petrovac, *Srbija* YU B2
101 Petrovaradin YU A4
97 Petrovice, *Severomoravsky* CZ B4
69 Petrovice, *Zapadočeský* CZ B4
69 Pettenbach A D5
9 Petterden GB B5
3 Pettigoe IRL B4
68 Petting D D3
15 Petworth GB D2
31 Peubla de Sanabria E B4
69 Peuerbach A C4
32 Peuntenansa E A2
15 Pevensey GB D3
13 Pewsey GB B6
58 Pewsum D B4
24 Peyrat-le-Château F C1
26 Peyrehorade F C2
28 Peyriac-Minervois F C1
29 Peyrins F A4
24 Peyrissac F C1
29 Peyruis F B4
21 Pézarches F C3
28 Pézenas F C2
96 Pezinok SQ C3
39 Pezuela de las Torres E B3
27 Pézuls F B4
68 Pfaffenhausen D C1
67 Pfaffenhofen, *Bayern* D C6
68 Pfaffenhofen, *Bayern* D C2
66 Pfaffenhoffen F C3
70 Pfäffikon CH A3
17 Pfalzdorf D B6
69 Pfarrkirchen D C3
63 Pfarrweisach D C5
109 Pfatikambos GR B4
67 Pfedelbach D B5
68 Pfeffenhausen D C2
70 Pfetterhouse F A2
67 Pforzheim D C4
68 Pfreimd D B3
71 Pfronten D A5
67 Pfullendorf D D5
67 Pfullingen D C5
71 Pfunds A B5
70 Pfungen CH A3
67 Pfungstadt D B4
71 Pfyn CH A3
66 Phalsbourg F C3
17 Philippeville B C4
69 Philippsreut D C4
63 Philippsthal D C4
75 Piacenza I A4
76 Piacenza d'Adige I A1
75 Piádena I A5
86 Piana F B1
74 Piana Crixia I B3
84 Piana degli Albanesi I B2
79 Piana di Caiazzo I B5
78 Piancastagnáio I A2
75 Piandelagotti I B5
79 Pianella, *Abruzzi* I A5
76 Pianella, *Toscan* I C1
75 Pianello Val Tidone I B4
74 Piano I B3
75 Pianoro I B6
86 Pianosa I B3
71 Pians A A5
42 Pias P A2
61 Piasek PL C5
88 Piaśnica Wielka PL A4
91 Piastow PL A4
90 Piątek PL A3
91 Piatkowiec PL C5
103 Piatra RO B5
103 Piatra RO C6
94 Piatra Neamt RO C7
103 Piatra Olt RO B5
75 Piazza al Sérchio I B5
85 Piazza Armerina I B3
71 Piazza Brembana I C4
78 Piazze I A2
72 Piazzola s. Brenta I C1
40 Picassent E B2
76 Piccione I C2
80 Picerno I D2
69 Pichl b. Wels A C4
11 Pickering GB A5
79 Pico I B4
38 Picón E C2
20 Picquigny F B3
13 Piddletrenthide GB C5
88 Piechcin PL C4
89 Piecki PL B7
88 Piecnik PL B2
70 Piedicavallo I C2
86 Piedicroce F B2
79 Piedimonte d'Alife I B5
85 Piedimonte Etneo I B4
70 Piedimulera I B3
79 Piedipaterno sul Nera I A3
38 Piedra Escrita E C2
38 Piedrabuena E C2
32 Piedrafita E A1
30 Piedrafita do Cebreiro E B4
38 Piedrahita E B1
38 Piedralaves E B2
37 Piedras Albas E B4
78 Piegaro I A3
90 Piekary Sl. PL C2
47 Pieksämäki SF E13
68 Pielenhofen D B2
65 Pielgrzymka, *Legnica* PL B5
89 Pieniężno PL A6
66 Piennes F B1
65 Pieńsk PL B5
76 Pienza I C1
35 Piera E B4
89 Pieranie PL C4
39 Pieresteban E C4
7 Pierowall GB A6
23 Pierre-Buffière F C6
29 Pierre-Châtel F B4
25 Pierre-de-Bresse F B5
29 Pierrefeu F C5
28 Pierrefiche F B2
34 Pierrefitte-Nestalas F A2
66 Pierrefitte-sur-Aure F C1
21 Pierrefonds F B3
70 Pierrefontaine F A1
28 Pierrefort F B1
29 Pierrelatte F B3
21 Pierrepont, *Aisne* F B4
66 Pierrepont, *Meurthe-et-Moselle* F B1
72 Piesendorf A A2
96 Piěštany SQ C3
89 Pieszkowo PL A6
65 Pieszyce PL C6
47 Pietarsaari SF E11
68 Pietenfeld D C2
74 Pietra Ligure I B3
80 Pietragalla I D2
76 Pietralunga I C2
79 Pietramelara I B5
84 Pietraperzia I B3
75 Pietrasanta I C5
79 Pietravairano I B5
74 Pieve del Cáiro I A3
71 Pieve di Bono I C5
72 Pieve di Cadore I B2
75 Pieve di Cento I B6
72 Pieve di Soligo I C2
74 Pieve di Teco I B2
76 Pieve S. Stefano I C2
76 Pieve Torina I C3
75 Pievepélago I B5
111 Pigádi GR B3
79 Piglio I B4
74 Pigna I C2
79 Pignataro Maggiore I B5
47 Pihtipudas SF E12
47 Piippola SF D12
17 Pijnacker NL A4
88 Piła PL B2
109 Pilaia GR A5
43 Pilas E B3
106 Pilashevo BG B3
75 Pilastri I B6
65 Piława PL C6
89 Pilawki PL B5
65 Pilchowice, *Jelenia Góra* PL C5
90 Pilchowice, *Katowice* PL C2
108 Pili, *Tríkkala* GR B3
111 Pili, *Voíotía* GR A4
90 Pilica PL C3
109 Pilio GR C5
112 Pilion GR B2
99 Pilis H A4
99 Piliscaba H A3
99 Pilisszántó H A3
99 Pilisvörösvár H A3
26 Pillelardit F C3
10 Pilling GB B3
110 Pilos GR C2
73 Pilštanj SL B5
96 Pilszcz PL A3
13 Pilton GB B5
34 Pina de Ebro E B2
44 Piñar E B3
107 Pinarhisar TR B5
112 Pinarlibelen TR B1
27 Pinas F C4
98 Pincehely H B3
14 Pinchbeck GB B2
91 Pińczów PL C4
33 Pineda de la Sierra E B3
40 Pinedo E B2
107 Pineke TR B5
34 Pinell de Bray E B3
76 Pinerella I B2
74 Pinerolo I B2
79 Pinetamare I C4
79 Pineto I A5
21 Piney F C5
73 Pinggau A A6
36 Pinhal-Novo P C2
31 Pinhão P C3
31 Pinheiro, *Aveiro* P C2
31 Pinheiro, *Aveiro* P D2
36 Pinheiro Grande P B2
31 Pinhel P D3
40 Pinilla E C1
32 Pinilla de Toro E C1
73 Pinkafeld A A6
59 Pinneberg D B6
64 Pinnow D B4
86 Pino F B2
32 Pino del Rio E B2
37 Pinofranqueado E A4
28 Pinols F A2
30 Piñor de Cea E B3
44 Pinos del Valle E C3
44 Pinos-Puente E B3
40 Pinoso E C1
93 Pinsk BL D10
38 Pinto E B3
8 Pinwherry GB C3
72 Pinzano al Tagliamento I B2
31 Pinzio P D3
71 Pinzolo I B5
76 Pióbbico I C2
29 Piolenc F B3
78 Piombino I A1
91 Pionki PL B5
24 Pionsat F B2
103 Piopii Slăviteşti RO C5
76 Pióraco I C2
37 Piornal E A5
74 Piossasco I B2
91 Piotrków PL B6
89 Piotrków-Kujawski PL C4
90 Piotrków Trybunalski PL B3
91 Piotrkowice PL C4
91 Piotrowice PL A5
97 Piotrowice Wielkie PL A4
76 Piove di Sacco I A2
72 Piovene I C1
56 Piperskärr S B5
19 Pipriac F C4
108 Piqeras AL A1
109 Pirá GR C4
72 Piran SL C3
104 Pirane YU B2
106 Pirdop BG A2
19 Piré-sur-Seiche F B4
111 Pireás GR B4
109 Pirgadikia GR A5
109 Pirgetos GR B4
109 Pirgos, *Fthiótis* GR C4
110 Pirgos, *Ilía* GR B2
112 Pirgos, *Kriti* GR
110 Pirgos, *Messinía* GR B2
112 Pírgos, *Sámos* GR C1
109 Pirgos, *Thessaloníki* GR A4
110 Pirgos Dhirou GR C3
22 Piriac-sur-Mer F A2
105 Pirin BG C5
98 Piringsdorf A A1
66 Pirmasens D B3
64 Pirna D C3
102 Pirot YU C3
77 Pirovac CRO C5
108 Pirsóyianni GR A2
109 Piryoi GR A3
75 Pisa I C5
23 Pisany F C4
73 Pisarovina CRO C5
73 Pischelsdforf i. St A A5
82 Pisciotta I A2
69 Pisek CZ B5
112 Piso Meriá GR E1
71 Pisogne I C5
111 Pisónas GR A4
111 Pisses GR B5
26 Pissos F B3
83 Pisticci I A3
75 Pistóia I C5
7 Pitcaple GB C6
47 Piteå S D10
103 Piteşti RO B5
107 Pithion, *Évros* GR B4
109 Pithion, *Lárisa* GR A4
20 Pithiviers F C3
78 Pitigliano I A2
9 Pitlochry GB B4
98 Pitomača CRO C2
44 Pitres E C3
9 Pitscottie GB B5
112 Pitsidhia, *Kriti* GR
9 Pittenweem GB B5
68 Pittersberg D B3
99 Pitvaros H B5
73 Pivka SL C4
99 Pivnice CRO C4
101 Pivski Monastir YU C3
94 Piwniczna PL B4
90 Piwonice PL B2
108 Piyés GR B3
44 Pizarra E C2
71 Pizzano I B5
75 Pizzighettone I A4
82 Pizzo I C3
79 Pizzoli I A4
84 Pizzolungo I A1
35 Plá de Manlleu E B4
35 Plá de Santa Maria E B4
18 Plabennec F B1
33 Placencia E A4
70 Plaffeien CH B2
7 Plaidy GB C6
26 Plaisance, *Gers* F C4
27 Plaisance, *Haute-Garonne* F C5
28 Plaisance, *Tarn* F C1
111 Pláka, *Arkadhía* GR B3
109 Pláka, *Piería* GR A4
108 Plakoti GR B2
106 Plakovo BG A3
34 Plan E A3
29 Plan-d'Orgon F C3
29 Plan-de-Baix F B4
74 Plan du Var F C2
68 Planá CZ B3
69 Planá n. Luznici CZ B5
69 Plaňany CZ A6
70 Planay F C1
25 Planchez F A4
19 Plancoët F B3
21 Plancy F C4
102 Plandište YU A2
69 Plánice CZ B4
73 Planina SL B5
73 Planina SL C4
102 Planinica YU C3
100 Planjane CRO C1
67 Plankstadt D B4
37 Plasencia E A4
37 Plasenzuela E B4
77 Plaški CRO A5
50 Plassen N A3
97 Plášt'ovce SQ C4
69 Plasy CZ B4
88 Plaszczyna PL A3
81 Plat CRO B5
111 Plataiai GR A4
109 Platamón GR B4
87 Platamona Lido I B1
82 Platania I B3
106 Plataniá, *Dráma* GR B2
110 Platánia, *Ilía* GR B2
109 Platania, *Magnisía* GR B5
112 Platanias, *Kriti* GR
111 Platanistós GR A5
110 Platanitis GR A2
109 Plátanos, *Aitolía kai Acarnanía* GR C3
110 Plátanos, *Akhaia* GR A3
110 Plátanos, *Ilía* GR B2
112 Plátanos, *Kriti* GR
108 Plataria GR B2
85 Plati I A5
109 Plati, *Imathía* GR A4
110 Pláti, *Messinía* GR B2
110 Platiána GR B2
101 Platičevo YU B4
112 Platis Yialos GR E2
109 Platistomo GR C4
110 Platithriás GR A1
69 Plattling D C3
60 Plau D B3
60 Plaue, *Brandenburg* D C3
63 Plaue, *Thüringen* D C5
64 Plauen D C2
104 Plav YU B1
77 Plavča CRO A5
96 Plavecký Mikuláš SQ C3
102 Plavisevita RO B3
101 Plavna YU A4
102 Plavna YU B3
100 Plavno CRO B1
65 Plawce PL A7
90 Plawce PL A1
41 Playa d'en Bossa, *Ibiza* E
33 Playa de Ajo E A3
35 Playa de Aro E B6
44 Playa de Calahonda E C2
30 Playa de Doria Vallina E A4
35 Playa de Fanalş E B5
35 Playa de la Canonja E B4
45 Playa de la Torre Vieja E C5
40 Playa de Parais E C2
45 Playa de Perches E B5
32 Playa de Quintes E A1
35 Playa de Rifa E B3
40 Playa de S.Juan E C2
44 Playa de Sta. Amalia E C2
43 Playa de Sta. Catalina E C3
32 Playa de Tenredo E A1
40 Playa del Agua Amarga Ó del Saladar E C2
43 Playa del Negro E C4
45 Playa Negrete E B6
18 Playben F B2
112 Playiá, *Ikaría* GR C1
110 Playia, *Kefallinía* GR A1
27 Pleaux F A6
19 Pleine-Fourgères F B4
68 Pleinfeld D B1
69 Pleinting D C4
19 Plélan-le-Grand F C3
18 Plémet-la-Pierre F B3
33 Plencia E A4
18 Pléneuf-Val-André F B3
103 Pleniţa RO B4
18 Plerin F B3
97 Plešivec SQ C6
73 Plesnik SL B4
64 Plessa D B3
22 Plessé F A3
18 Plestin-les-Grèves F B2
90 Pleszew PL B1
100 Pleternica CRO A2
62 Plettenberg D B2
105 Pletvar MAK C3
18 Pleubian F B2
23 Pleumartin F B5
18 Pleumeur-Bodou F B2
21 Pleurs F C4
103 Pleven BG C5
97 Plevnik-Drienové SQ B4
18 Pleyber-Christ F B2
45 Pliego E B5
97 Pliešovce SQ C5
108 Plikáti GR A2
111 Plitra GR C3
77 Plitvička Jezera CRO B5
77 Plitvički Ljeskovac CRO B5
101 Pljevlja YU C4
87 Ploaghe I B1
100 Ploče CRO C2
67 Plochingen D C5
89 Płock PL C5
16 Ploegsteert B C2
18 Ploëmeur F C2
18 Ploërmel F C3
18 Plœuc-sur-Lie F B3
18 Plogastel St. Germain F C1
18 Plogoff F B1
95 Ploieşti RO D7
66 Plombières-les-Bains F D2
25 Plombières-lès-Dijon F A4
77 Plomin CRO A4
60 Plön D A1
18 Plonéour-Lanvern F C1
89 Płonsk PL C6
103 Plosca RO B6
68 Ploßberg D B3
61 Ploty PL B6
18 Plouagat F B2
18 Plouaret F B2
18 Plouay F C2
19 Ploubalay F B3
18 Ploubazlanec F B2
18 Ploudalmezéau F B1
18 Ploudiry F B1
18 Plouescat F B1
18 Plouézec F B3
18 Plougasnou F B2
18 Plougastel-Daoulas F B1
18 Plougonven F B2
18 Plougonver F B2
18 Plougrescant F B2
18 Plouguenast F B3
18 Plouguerneau F B1
18 Plouguernevel F B2
18 Plouha F B3
18 Plouhinec F B1
18 Plouigneau F B2
18 Ploumanach F B2
18 Plouray F B2
18 Plouzévédé F B1
106 Plovdiv BG A2
18 Plozévet F C1
102 Plugova RO B3
3 Plumbridge GB B4
18 Pluméliau F C3
96 Plumlov CZ B3
93 Plunge LT C7
89 Pluty PL A6
18 Pluvigner F C3
101 Pluzine YU C3
89 Płuznica PL B4
12 Plymouth GB C3
88 Plytnica PL B2
93 Plyusa R A11
69 Plzeň CZ B4
89 Pniewo PL C7
88 Pniewy PL C2
33 Pobes E B4
68 Poběžovice CZ B3
88 Pobiedziska PL C3
61 Pobierowo PL A5
35 Pobla de Segur E A3
38 Poblado de Cijara E C2
69 Počatky CZ B6
36 Poceirão P C2
69 Pochlarn A C6
64 Pockau D C3
69 Pocking, *Bayern* D C4
68 Pöcking, *Bayern* D D2
11 Pocklington GB B5
104 Poda YU B1
105 Podareš MAK C4
103 Podari RO B4
97 Podbiel SQ B5
64 Podbořany CZ C3
97 Podbrezovo SQ C5
73 Podcetrtek SL B5
90 Poddębice PL B2
65 Poděbrady CZ C5
61 Podelzig D C5
31 Podence P C4
26 Podensac F B3
75 Podenzano I B4
103 Podern BG C5
96 Podersdorf a.S. A D2
88 Podgaje PL B2
98 Podgarić CRO C1
100 Podgora CRO C2
98 Podgorač CRO C3
102 Podgorac YU C2
108 Podgori AL A2
104 Podgorica YU B1
73 Podgrad SL C4
97 Podhájska SQ C4
106 Podhokhóri GR C2
100 Podhum BO C1
106 Podkova BG B3
89 Podlejki PL B6
97 Podlužany SQ C4
100 Podnovlje BO B3
96 Podolie SQ C3
77 Podolopac CRO B5
98 Podravska Moslavina CRO C3
98 Podravska Slatina CRO C2
101 Podromanija BO C3
73 Podsused CRO C5
98 Podturen CRO B1
104 Podujevo YU B3
96 Podunajské Biskupice SQ C3
96 Podvin CZ C2
107 Podvis BG A4
97 Podwilk PL B5
16 Poelkapelle B C2
87 Poetto I C2
103 Poganu RO B5
61 Poggendorf D A4
83 Poggiardo I A5
75 Poggibonsi I C6
75 Póggio a Caiano I C6
80 Poggio Imperiale I C2
78 Poggio Mirteto I A3
79 Poggio Moiano I A3
76 Póggio Renatico I B1
75 Póggio Rusco I B6
69 Poggstall A C6
21 Pogny F C5
108 Pogoniani GR A2
65 Pogorzela PL B7
88 Pogorzelice PL A3
104 Pogradec AL D2
89 Pogrodzie PL A5
97 Pohorelá SQ C6
96 Pohorelice CZ B2
97 Pohranice SQ C4
97 Pohronská Polhora SQ C5
103 Poiana Mare RO C4
103 Poiana Seciuri RO B4
36 Poiares P A2
106 Poibrene BG A2
21 Poinchy F D4
28 Pt.-Salomon F A3
74 Poirino I B2
25 Poisson F B4
66 Poissons F C1
20 Poissy F C3
23 Poitiers F B5
20 Poix F B2
21 Poix-Terron F B5
108 Pojan AL A2
90 Pokój PL C1
98 Pokupsko CRO C1
30 Pol E A3
32 Pola de Siero E A1
66 Polaincourt-et-Clairefontaine F D2
38 Polán E C2
65 Polanica Zdrój PL C6
91 Połaniec PL C5
88 Polanów PL A2
102 Polatna YU C2
93 Polatsk BL C11
62 Polch D C2
88 Pólczno PL A3
88 Polczyn-Zdrói PL B2
15 Polegate GB D3
34 Poleñino E B2
76 Polesella I B1
11 Polesworth GB C4
73 Polfing-Brunn A B5
98 Polgárdi H A3
110 Poliani GR B3
106 Polianthos GR B3
108 Poliçan AL A2
61 Police PL B5
91 Polichna Grn. PL C6
96 Polička CZ B2
77 Poličnik CRO B5
83 Policoro I A3
91 Policzna PL B5
109 Polidhéndron GR A4
109 Polidhrosos GR C4
109 Polifiton GR A4
28 Polignac F A2
81 Polignano a Mare I D4
19 Poligné F C4
25 Poligny F B5
105 Polikárpi GR D4
105 Polikastron GR D4
108 Polinéri GR B3
108 Polipótamon GR A3
82 Polistena I C3
108 Polithéa GR B3
109 Politiká GR C5
109 Poliyiros GR A5
84 Polizzi Generosa I B3
77 Poljak CRO B5
98 Poljana CRO C1
102 Poljana YU B2
77 Poljanák CRO B5
73 Poljčane SL B5
100 Polje BO A3
100 Poljice BO B3
102 Poljna YU C2
65 Polkowice PL B6
7 Polla GB B4
82 Polla I A2
32 Pollas E C1
73 Pöllau A A5
63 Polleben D B6
41 Pollença, *Mallorca* E
68 Pollenfeld D C2
62 Pollhagen D A4
25 Polliat F B5
82 Póllica I A2
2 Pollremon IRL C3
28 Polminhac F B1
96 Polná CZ B1
88 Polne PL B2
77 Poloj CRO A5
97 Polomka SQ C5
107 Polos TR B5
103 Polovragi RO A4
12 Polperro GB C3
73 Pöls A A4
61 Polßen D B4
97 Poltár SQ C5
75 Pomarance I C5
26 Pomarez F C3
83 Pomárico I A3
99 Pomáz H A4
36 Pombal P B2
112 Pombia, *Kriti* GR
26 Pomerol F B3
78 Pomézia I B3
89 Pomiechowek PL C6
25 Pommard F A4
107 Pomorie BG A5
79 Pompei I C5
28 Pompignan F C2
76 Pomposa I B2
25 Poncin F B5
105 Pondokerasiá GR C5
109 Pondokómi GR A3
68 Pondorf D C2
21 Pondrôme B A6
30 Ponferrada E B4
32 Ponga E A1
91 Poniatowa PL B6
90 Poniatowice PL B1
65 Poniec PL B6
97 Poniky SQ C5
60 Pönitz D A1
35 Pons E B4
23 Pons F C4
75 Ponsacco I C5
17 Pont-a-Celles B C4
66 Pont-à-Mousson F C2
20 Pont-Audemer F B1
18 Pont-Aven F C2
70 Pont Canavese I C2
20 Pont Couronne F B2
18 Pont-Croix F B1
25 Pont-d'Ain F B5
34 Pont-d'Espagne F A2
19 Pont d'Quilly F B5
35 Pont de Armentera E B4
25 Pont de-Beauvoisin F C5
18 Pont-de-Buis F B1
25 Pont-de-Chéruy F C5
24 Pont de Dore F C3
20 Pont-de-l'Arche F B2
28 Pont-de-Labeaume F B3
35 Pont de Molins E A5
70 Pont-de-Roide F A1
28 Pont-de-Salars F B1
34 Pont de Suert E A3
25 Pont-de-Vaux F B4
24 Pont-du-Château F C3
25 Pont-du-Navoy F B5
29 Pont-en-Royans F A4
19 Pont. Farcy F B4
18 Pont l'Abbé F C1
20 Pont l'Evêque F B1
20 Pont-Remy F A2
70 Pont-S-Martin I C2
18 Pont Scorff F C2
29 Pont-St. Esprit F B3
22 Pont-St. Martin F A3
66 Pont-St. Vincent F C2
20 Pont-Ste-Maxence F B3
16 Pont-sur-Marcq F C3
21 Pont-sur-Yonne F C4
26 Pontacq F C3
25 Pontailler-sur-Saône F A5
36 Pontão P B2
12 Pontardawe GB B4
12 Pontardulais GB B3
24 Pontarion F C1
25 Pontarlier F B6
76 Pontassieve I C1
19 Pontaubault F B4
24 Pontaumur F C2
25 Pontchara-sur-Turdine F C4
25 Pontcharra F C6
22 Pontchâteau F A2
75 Ponte a Elsa I C5
75 Ponte a Moriano I C5
71 Ponte Arche I B5
70 Ponte Brolla CH B3
71 Ponte Cáffaro I C5
31 Ponte de Lima P C2
36 Ponte de Sor P B2
75 Ponte dell'Ólio I B4
72 Ponte di Barbarano I C1
71 Ponte di Legno I B5
74 Ponte di Nava I B2
72 Ponte di Piave I C2
76 Ponte Felcino I C2
72 Ponte Gardena (Waidbruck) I B1
86 Ponte Leccia F B2
72 Ponte nelle Alpi I B2
71 Ponte S. Pietro I C4
76 Ponte San Giovanni I C2
70 Ponte Tresa CH C3
72 Pontebba I B3
80 Pontecagnano I D1
79 Pontecorvo I B4
74 Pontedássio I C3
74 Pontedécimo I B3
75 Pontedera I C5
30 Pontedeume E A2
11 Pontefract GB B4
75 Ponteginori I C5
76 Pontelagoscuro I B1
9 Ponteland GB C6
79 Pontelandolfo I B5
76 Pontelongo I A2
75 Pontenure I B4
26 Pontenx-les-Forges F B2
10 Ponterwyd GB C2
10 Pontesbury GB C3
30 Pontevedra E B2
75 Pontevico I A5
21 Pontfaverger-Moronvillers F B5
24 Pontgibaud F C2
76 Ponticino I C1
21 Pontigny F D4
23 Pontijou F A6
79 Pontínia I B4
74 Pontinvrea I B3
18 Pontivy F B3
23 Pontlevoy F A6
31 Ponto da Barca P C2
20 Pontoise F B3
45 Pontones E A4
26 Pontonx F C3
19 Pontorson F B4
75 Pontrémoli I B4
71 Pontresina CH B4
12 Pontrhydfendigaid GB A4
18 Pontrieux F B2
13 Pontrilas GB B5
19 Pontvallain F C6
13 Pontyclun GB B4
13 Pontypool GB B4
13 Pontypridd GB B4
79 Ponza I C3
32 Poo E A2
13 Poole GB C5
16 Poperinge B C2
106 Popintsi BG A2
103 Popinzăleşti RO B5
79 Pópoli I A4
102 Popovac YU C2
98 Popovača CRO C1
106 Popovitsa BG A3
107 Popovo BG A4
89 Popowo Koscielne PL C7
88 Popowo Kościelne PL C3
17 Poppel B B5
63 Poppenhausen, *Bayern* D C5
63 Poppenhausen, *Hessen* D C4
63 Poppenlauer D C5
76 Poppi I C1
97 Poprad SQ B6
101 Popučke YU B4
31 Pópulo P C3
75 Populónia I D5
44 Porcuna E B2
72 Pordenone I C2
18 Pordic F B3
103 Pordim BG C5
90 Poręba PL C3
76 Poreč CRO A3
47 Pori SF F10
69 Poriči n. Sázavou CZ B5
47 Porjus S C9
93 Porkhov R B11
71 Porlezza I B4
13 Porlock GB B4
68 Pörnbach D C2
22 Pornic F A2
22 Pornichet F A2
102 Porodin YU B2
111 Póros, *Argolís* GR B4
110 Póros, *Kefallinía* GR A1
108 Póros, *Lefkás* GR C2
99 Poroszlo H A5
77 Porozina CRO A4
43 Porquera E C4
29 Porquerolles F C5
70 Porrentruy CH A2
41 Porreres, *Mallorca* E
75 Porretta Terme I B5
30 Porriño E B2
49 Porsgrunn N B6
18 Porspoder F B1
8 Port Askaig GB C1
8 Port Bannatyne GB C2
35 Port Bou E A6
41 Port d'es Torrent, *Ibiza* E
29 Port-de-Bouc F C3
26 Port-de-Lanne F C2
22 Port-des-Barques F C3
10 Port Dinorwic GB B1
8 Port Ellen GB C1
19 Port-en-Bessin F A5
10 Port Erin GB A1
7 Port Erroll GB C7
12 Port Eynon GB B3
8 Port Glasgow GB C3
6 Port Henderson GB C3
12 Port Isaac GB C3
22 Port-Joinville F B2
28 Port-la-Nouvelle F C2
5 Port Laoise IRL A4
10 Port Logan GB A1
18 Port-Louis F C2
18 Port Manech F C2
22 Port Navalo F A2
6 Port of Ness GB B2
8 Port Sonachan GB B2
29 Port-St-Louis F C3
27 Port St. Marie F B4
10 Port St. Mary GB A1
25 Port-sur-Saône F A6
12 Port Talbot GB B4
35 Port Vendres F A6
10 Port William GB A1
78 Port'Ercole I A2
3 Portadown GB B5
3 Portaferry GB B6
37 Portaje E B4
36 Portalegre P B3
34 Portalrubio E C1
109 Portariá, *Khalkidhikí* GR A5
109 Portariá, *Magnisía* GR B4
5 Portarlington IRL A4
19 Portbail F A4
72 Portegrandi I C2
42 Portel P A2
36 Portela P A2
31 Portelo P C4
30 Portemouro E B2
29 Portes F B3
110 Pórtes, *Akhaia* GR B2
111 Pórtes, *Égina* GR B4
27 Portet F C5
26 Portets F B3
37 Portezuelo E B4
3 Portglenone GB B5
7 Portgower GB B5
13 Porth GB B4
13 Porthcawl GB B4
12 Porthleven GB C2
10 Porthmadog GB C1
79 Portici I C5
76 Portico di Romagna I B1
32 Portilla de la Reina E A2
32 Portillo E C2
42 Portimão P B1
36 Portinho da Arrabida P C1
8 Portinnisherrich GB B2
13 Portishead GB B5
7 Portknockie GB C6
7 Portmahomack GB C5
45 Portman E B6
10 Portmeirion GB C1
8 Portnacroish GB B2
6 Portnaguiran GB B2
8 Portnahaven GB C1
86 Porto F B1
31 Porto P C2
36 Porto-Alto P C2
78 Porto Azzurro I A1
109 Porto Carrás GR A5
71 Porto Cerésio I C3
87 Porto Cervo I A2
83 Porto Cesareo I A4
41 Porto Colom, *Mallorca* E
42 Porto Covo P B1
41 Porto Cristo, *Mallorca* E
79 Porto d'Ascoli I A4
42 Porto de Lagos P B1
36 Porto de Mos P B2
36 Porto de Rei P C2
84 Porto Empédocle I B2
76 Porto Garibaldi I B2
110 Pórto Káyio GR C3
111 Porto-Khéli GR B4
74 Porto Maurizio I C3
41 Porto Petro, *Mallorca* E
87 Porto Pino I D1
76 Porto Potenza Picena I C3
111 Porto Rafti GR B5
76 Porto Recanati I C3
87 Porto Rotondo I A2
77 Porto S. Elpidio I C3
77 Porto S. Giórgio I C3
78 Porto Santo Stefano I A2
76 Porto Tolle I B2
87 Porto Tórres I B1
86 Porto-Vecchio F C2
80 Portocannone I C2
86 Portoferráio I B3
75 Portofino I B4
72 Portogruaro I C2
76 Portomaggiore I B1
30 Portomarin E B3
30 Portonovo E B2
85 Portopalo I C4
49 Portør N C6
72 Portoroz SL C3
87 Portoscuso I C1
75 Portovénere I B4
8 Portpatrick GB D2
6 Portree GB C2
3 Portrush GB A5
18 Portsall F B1
73 Pörtschach A B4
7 Portskerra GB B5
8 Portslogan GB D2
15 Portsmouth GB D1
7 Portsoy GB C6
3 Portstewart GB A5
33 Portugalete E A3
4 Portumna IRL A3
38 Porzuna E C2
87 Posada I B2
32 Posada, *Oviedo* E A1
32 Posada, *Oviedo* E A2
32 Posada de Valdeón E A2
43 Posadas E B4
71 Poschiavo CH B5
77 Posedarje CRO B5
112 Posidonia GR E1
47 Posio SF C14
79 Positano I C5
105 Posjane YU B3
72 Possagno I C1
64 Posseck D C2
64 Possendorf D C3
21 Possesse F C5
63 Poßneck D C6
79 Posta I A4
80 Posta Piana I C2
71 Postal (Burgstall) I B6
68 Postbauer D B2
17 Posterholt NL B6
72 Postioma I C2
100 Postira CRO C1
73 Postojna SL C4
64 Postoloprty CZ C3
88 Postomino PL A2
100 Posušje BO C2
106 Potamiá GR C2
112 Potamiais, *Kriti* GR
106 Potamoi GR B2
111 Potamós GR C3
110 Potamoúla GR A2
88 Potęgowo PL A3
80 Potenza I D2
76 Potenza Picena I C3
32 Potes E A2
110 Potidánia GR A3
19 Potigny F B5
101 Potkrajci YU C4
106 Potochnitsa BG B3
100 Potoci BO C2
98 Potok CRO C1
108 Potom AL A2
98 Potony H C2
40 Potries E C2
61 Potsdam D C4
96 Potštát CZ B3

65 Potštejn CZ C6
96 Pottenbrunn A C1
96 Pottendorf A D2
96 Pottenstein A D2
68 Pottenstein D B2
15 Potters Bar GB C2
68 Pöttmes D C2
14 Potton GB B2
73 Pottschach A A5
96 Pöttsching A D2
91 Potworów PL B4
19 Pouancé F C4
24 Pougues-les-Eaux F A3
25 Pouillenay F A4
25 Pouilly F A5
25 Pouilly-en-Auxois F A4
25 Pouilly-sous Charlieu F B4
24 Pouilly-sur-Loire F A2
110 Pouláta GR A1
111 Poulithra GR B3
18 Poullaouen F B2
10 Poulton le Fylde GB B3
112 Pounda GR D1
21 Pourcy F B4
109 Pouri GR B5
109 Pournári GR B4
21 Pourrain F D4
27 Pouy de Touges F C5
27 Pouyastruc F C4
23 Pouzauges F B4
97 Považská Bystrica SQ B4
45 Povedill E A4
77 Povljana CRO B5
42 Póvoa, *Beja* P A2
36 Póvoa, *Santarém* P B2
36 Póvoa da Galega P C1
31 Povoa de Lanhoso P C2
36 Póvoa de Sta. Iria P C1
31 Póvoa de Varzim P C2
36 Póvoa e Meadas P B3
39 Povos E B4
64 Povrly CZ C4
90 Powidz PL A1
38 Poyales del Hoyo E B1
3 Poyntzpass GB B5
96 Poysbrunn A C2
96 Poysdorf A C2
33 Poza de la Sal E B3
32 Pozaldez E C2
34 Pozán de Vero E A3
104 Požaranje YU B3
102 Požarevac YU B2
101 Požega YU C5
20 Pozières F A3
65 Poznań PL A6
44 Pozo Alcón E B4
45 Pozo Cañada E A5
44 Pozo de la Serna E A3
42 Pozo del Camino E B2
32 Pozoantiguo E C1
44 Pozoblanco E A2
45 Pozohondo E A5
40 Pozondón E A1
88 Pozrzadło Wlp. PL B1
39 Pozuel del Campo E B5
38 Pozuelo de Alarcón E B3
38 Pozuelo de Calatrava E D3
37 Pozuelo de Zarzón E A4
32 Pozuelo del Páramo E B1
38 Pozuelos de Calatrava E D2
85 Pozzallo I C3
87 Pozzomaggiore I B1
79 Pozzuoli I C5
76 Pozzuolo I C1
89 Prabuty PL B5
69 Prachatice CZ B4
98 Pračno CRO C1
30 Prada E B3
29 Pradelle F B4
28 Pradelles F B2
35 Prades E B3
35 Prades F A5
90 Pradła PL C3
31 Prado P C2
43 Prado del Rey E C4
33 Pradoluengo E B3
103 Pradu RO B5
55 Præstø DK C5
69 Prag D C4
74 Pragelato I A1
72 Prägraten A A2
69 Praha CZ A5
23 Prahecq F B4
102 Prahovo YU B3
36 Praia P B1
82 Práia a Mare I B2
31 Praia da Granja P C2
42 Praia da Oura P B1
42 Praia da Rocha P B1
36 Praia da Viera P B2
42 Praia da Zambugueira P B1
42 Praia de Carvoeiro P B1
42 Praia de Faro P B1
42 Praia de Melides P A1
31 Praia de Miramar P C2
36 Praia de Troia P C2
36 Praia Grande P C1
75 Pralboino I A5
70 Pralognan F C1
29 Pra Loup F B5
108 Prámanta GR B3
107 Prángi GR B4
101 Pranjani YU B5
100 Prapatnica CRO C1
91 Praseczno PL A4
25 Praslay F A5
112 Prassés, *Kriti* GR
111 Prastós GR B3
90 Praszka PL B2
34 Prat de Compte E C3
35 Prat de Llobregat E B5
75 Prata I C5
72 Prata di Pordenone I C2
64 Pratau D B2
34 Pratdip E B3
79 Pratella I B5
75 Prato I C6
79 Pratola Peligna I A4
79 Pratola Serra I C5
35 Prats-de-Mollo-la-Preste F A5
35 Prats del Rey E B4
70 Pratteln CH A2
25 Prauthoy F A5
89 Pravdinsk R A6
106 Pravets BG A1
30 Pravia E A4
71 Praxmar A A6
27 Prayssac F B5
74 Prazzo I B2
19 Pré-en-Pail F B5
73 Prebold SL B5
25 Précy-sur-Thil F A4
76 Predáppio I B1
72 Predazzo I B1
105 Predejane YU B4
96 Predin CZ B1
73 Preding A B5
73 Predjamski Grad SL C4
73 Predlitz A A3
73 Predmeja SL C3
72 Predoi I A2
74 Predosa I B3
10 Prees GB C3
60 Preetz D A1
22 Préfailles F A2
69 Pregarten A C5
73 Pregrada CRO B5
26 Preignac F B3
73 Preitenegg A B4
77 Preko CRO B5
101 Preljina YU C5
98 Prelog CRO B1
98 Prelošćica CRO C1
96 Přelouč CZ A1
24 Prémery F A3
35 Premiá de Mar E B5
60 Premnitz D C3
21 Prémont F A4
77 Premtura CRO B3
61 Prenzlau D B4
100 Preodac BO B1
96 Přerov CZ B3
60 Prerow D A3
97 Presel'any SQ C4
32 Presencio E B3
105 Preševo YU B3
83 Presicce I B5
24 Presly F A2
94 Přesov SQ B4
23 Pressac F B5
68 Pressath D B2
96 Preßbaum A C2
63 Pressig D C6
10 Prestatyn GB B2
13 Prestbury GB B5
13 Presteigne GB A4
69 Přeštice CZ B4
9 Preston, *Borders* GB C5
13 Preston, *Dorset* GB C5
11 Preston, *Humberside* GB B5
10 Preston, *Lancashire* GB B3
9 Prestonpans GB C5
8 Prestwick GB C3
64 Prettin D B2
79 Preturo I A4
64 Pretzchendorf D C3
64 Pretzsch D B2
23 Preully-sur-Claise F B5
59 Preußisch Ströhen D C5
103 Prevala BG C3
73 Prevalje SL B4
28 Prevenchères F B2
24 Préveranges F B2
108 Préveza GR C2
73 Prezid CRO C4
79 Priano I C5
30 Priaranza del Bierzo E B4
25 Priay F C5
97 Pribeta SQ D4
101 Priboj BO B3
101 Priboj YU C4
97 Příbor CZ B4
69 Příbram CZ B5
97 Pribylina SQ B5
96 Přibyslav CZ B1
39 Priego E B4
44 Priego de Córdoba E B2
68 Prien D D3
64 Priestewitz D B3
96 Prievaly SQ C3
97 Prievidza SQ C4
80 Prigradica CRO B3
99 Prigrevica CRO C4
77 Prijeboj CRO B5
100 Prijedor BO B1
101 Prijepolje YU C4
96 Přikazy CZ B3
107 Prilep BG A4
105 Prilep MAK C3
102 Prilipeti RO B3
100 Priluka BO C1
68 Primda CZ B3
18 Primel-Trégastel F B2
77 Primisje CRO A5
89 Primorsk R A5
100 Primorski Dolac CRO C1
107 Primorsko BG A5
77 Primošten CRO C5
66 Primstal D B2
15 Princes Risborough GB C2
12 Princetown GB C3
78 Principina a Mare I A2
25 Pringy F C6
17 Prinsenbeek NL B4
85 Priolo Gargallo I B4
30 Prior E A2
32 Prioro E B2
64 Přísečnice CZ C3
103 Priseka BG C5
102 Prisjan YU C3
100 Prisoje BO C2
104 Priština YU B3
102 Pristol RO B3
63 Prititz D B6
60 Pritzerbe D C3
60 Pritzier D B2
60 Pritzwalk D B3
29 Privas F B3
79 Priverno I B4
101 Privlaka CRO A3
77 Privlaka CRO B5
77 Prizna CRO B4
104 Prizren YU B2
84 Prizzi I B2
100 Prnjavor BO B2
73 Prnjavor CRO C5
101 Prnjavor YU B4
30 Proaza E A4
105 Probistip MAK B4
60 Probsteierhagen D A1
63 Probstzella D C6
12 Probus GB C3
86 Prócchio I B3
97 Prochot SQ C4
65 Prochowice PL B6
79 Prócida I C5
108 Pródhromos GR C3
106 Prodkrepa BG B3
78 Prodo I A3
111 Pródromos GR A3
36 Proença-a-Nova P B3
37 Proença-a-Velha P A3
109 Profitis GR A5
111 Profitis Ilias GR C4
17 Profondeville B C4
106 Progled BG B2
108 Progonat AL A1
105 Prohor Pčinjski YU B3
109 Prokhoma GR A4
109 Prokópion GR C5
102 Prokuplje YU C2
105 Prómakhoi GR C4
109 Promiri GR B5
86 Propriano F C1
64 Proschim D B4
96 Prosec CZ B2
64 Prösen D B3
107 Prosenik BG A5
111 Prosimna GR B3
106 Proskinitai GR C3
106 Prosotsáni GR B1
96 Prostějov CZ B3
91 Proszowice PL C4
96 Protivanov CZ B2
69 Protivin CZ B5
108 Protopápa GR B2
96 Prottes A C2
61 Prötzel D C4
108 Proussós GR C3
105 Provatás GR C5
21 Provins F C4
100 Prozor BO C2
104 Prrenjas AL C2
9 Prudhoe GB D6
90 Prudnik PL C1
73 Pruggern A A3
17 Prüm D C6
43 Pruna E C4
103 Prundeni RO B5
64 Prunéřov CZ C3
75 Prunetta I B5
24 Pruniers F B2
65 Prusice PL B6
97 Pruské SQ B4
89 Pruszcz Gd. PL A4
91 Pruszków PL A4
71 Prutz A A5
60 Prüzen D B3
97 Pružina SQ B4
61 Pryłęg PL C6
89 Przasnysz PL B6
89 Przebrno PL A5
88 Przechlewo PL B3
89 Przechowo PL B4
91 Przecław PL C5
91 Przedbórz PL B3
90 Przedecz PL A2
65 Przemków PL B5
61 Przemocze PL B5
94 Przemyśl PL B5
65 Przerzeczyn Zdrój PL C6
89 Przewodowo Parcele PL C6
91 Przeworsk PL C6
65 Przewóz PL B4
61 Przybiernów PL B5
89 Przyborowice PL C6
90 Przykona PL B2
88 Przyłęg PL C1
91 Przysucha PL B4
88 Przytóczna PL C1
91 Przytoczno PL B6
91 Przytyk PL B4
89 Przywidz PL A4
105 Psača MAK B4
108 Psáka GR B2
109 Psakhna GR C5
110 Psari, *Korinthía* GR B3
110 Psári, *Messinía* GR B2
110 Psathópirgos GR A2
112 Psili Amos GR B1
93 Pskov R B11
88 Pszczew PL C1
89 Pszczólki PL A4
97 Pszczyna PL B4
97 Pszów PL A4
106 Pteléa GR B2
109 Pteleós GR B4
109 Ptolemaïs GR A3
73 Ptuj SL B5
73 Ptujska gora SL B5
72 Puch A A3
89 Puchalowo PL B6
96 Puchberg a. Schneeberg A D1
96 Puchenstuben A D1
97 Púchov SQ B4
89 Puck PL A4
15 Puckeridge GB C3
40 Puçol E B2
47 Pudasjärvi SF D13
13 Puddletown GB C5
62 Puderbach D C2
11 Pudsey GB B4
34 Puebla de Albortón E B2
38 Puebla de Alcocer E D1
39 Puebla de Beleña E B3
45 Puebla de Don Fadrique E B4
38 Puebla de Don Rodrigo E C2
42 Puebla de Guzmán E B2
37 Puebla de la Calzada E C4
37 Puebla de la Reina E C4
32 Puebla de Lillo E A1
37 Puebla de Obando E B4
37 Puebla de Sancho Pérez E C4
30 Puebla de Trives E B3
40 Puebla de Vallbona E B2
30 Puebla del Brollón E B3
30 Puebla del Caramiñal E B2
43 Puebla del Maestre E A3
40 Puebla-Tornesa E A2
38 Pueblo Nuevo del Bullaque E C2
32 Puente Almunhey E B2
30 Puente Caldelas E B2
30 Puente de Domingo Flórez E B4
45 Puente de Génave E A4
33 Puente de la Reina E B5
34 Puente de Montañana E A3
38 Puente del Congosto E B1
32 Puente Duero E C2
44 Puente-Genil E B2
43 Puente Mayorge E C4
32 Puente-Viesgo E A3
30 Puenteáreas E B2
30 Puentecesures E B2
33 Puentelarra E B3
30 Puentes de Gatin E B3
30 Puento-Ceso E A2
32 Puerta E A2
31 Puertas E C4
41 Puerto Cabrera, *Mallorca* E
41 Puerto de Alcudia, *Mallorca* E
41 Puerto de Andraitx, *Mallorca* E
35 Puerto de la Selva E A6
35 Puerto de Llansá E A6
45 Puerto de Mazarrón E B5
38 Puerto de S. Vicente E C1
37 Puerto de Santa Cruz E B5
41 Puerto de Sóller, *Mallorca* E
38 Puerto del Rey E C1
30 Puerto del Son E B2
39 Puerto-Lápice E C3
45 Puerto Lumbreras E B5
43 Puerto Moral E B3
43 Puerto Real E C3
31 Puerto Seguro E D4
43 Puerto Serrano E C4
44 Puertollano E A2
29 Puget F C5
74 Puget-Théniers F C1
29 Puget-ville F C5
80 Pugnochiuso I C3
35 Puigcerdá E A4
41 Puigpuñent, *Mallorca* E
35 Puigreig E B4
26 Puillon F C3
29 Puimichel F C5
29 Puimoisson F C5
20 Puiseaux F C3
20 Puisieux F A3
28 Puisserguier F C2
35 Puivert F A5
97 Pukanec SQ C4
57 Pukavik S C3
104 Pukë AL B1
77 Pula CRO B3
87 Pula I C2
94 Puławy PL A5
15 Pulborough GB D2
72 Pulfero I B3
38 Pulgar E C2
62 Pulheim D B1
25 Puligny-Montrachet F B4
96 Pulkau A C1
47 Pulkkila SF D12
45 Pulpi E B5
83 Pulsano I A4
64 Pulsnitz D B4
89 Pułtusk PL C7
66 Pulversheim F D3
12 Pumpsaint GB A4
77 Punat CRO A4
76 Punta Marina I B2
41 Punta Prima, *Menorca* E
72 Punta Sabbioni I C2
43 Punta Umbria E B3
47 Puolanka SF D13
96 Purbach a. N.S. A D2
45 Purchena E B4
15 Purfleet GB C3
69 Purgstall A C6
45 Purias E B5
96 Purkersdorf A C2
58 Purmerend NL C1
13 Purton GB B6
44 Purullena E B3
106 Pŭrvomay BG A3
105 Pŭrvornay BG C5
94 Püspökladány H C4
96 Pusté Ulany SQ C3
108 Pustec AL A2
91 Pustelnik PL A5
91 Puszcza Marianska PL B4
65 Puszczykowo PL A6
99 Pusztafoldvár H B5
98 Pusztamagyaród H B1
99 Pusztamonostor H A4
99 Pusztaszabolcs H A3
98 Pusztavám H A3
19 Putanges F B5
91 Putawy PL B5
61 Putbus D A4
81 Putignano I D4
101 Putino YU B4
60 Putlitz D B3
97 Putnok H C6
17 Putte B B4
66 Puttelange F B2
17 Putten NL A5
60 Puttgarden D A2
17 Pütz D C6
87 Putzuldu I B1
24 Puy-Guillaume F C3
27 Puy-l'Evêque F B5
27 Puylaroque F B5
27 Puylaurens F C5
27 Puymirol F B4
23 Puyrolland F B4
10 Pwllheli GB C1
89 Pyatidorozhnoye R A6
47 Pyhäjärvi SF E12
47 Pyhäjoki SF D12
47 Pyhäntä SF D13
47 Pyhäsalmi SF E12
96 Pyhra A C1
26 Pyla-sur-Mer F B2
13 Pyle GB B4
61 Pyrzyce PL B5
69 Pysely CZ B5
90 Pyskowice PL C2
112 Pythagórion GR C1
90 Pyzdry PL A1

Q

108 Qesarakë AL A2
59 Quakenbrück D C4
16 Quaregnon B C3
74 Quargnento I B3
25 Quarré-les-Tombes F A4
40 Quart-de-Poblet E B2
42 Quarteira P B1
87 Quarto S. Élena I C2
17 Quatre Bras B C4
21 Quatre Champs F B5
13 Quedgeley GB B5
63 Quedlinburg D B6
15 Queenborough GB C3
10 Queensferry, *Clwyd* GB B2
9 Queensferry, *Lothian* GB C4
70 Queige F C1
43 Queipo E B3
33 Quel E B4
31 Queljada P C2
59 Quelkhorn D B6
33 Quemada E C3
75 Quercianella I C5
63 Querfurt D B6
39 Quero E C3
72 Quero I C1
44 Quesada E B3
16 Quesnoy-sur-Deûle F C2
22 Questembert F A2
19 Quettehou F A4
62 Quetzen D A4
20 Quevauvillers F B3
36 Quiaois P A2
22 Quiberon F A1
20 Quiberville F B1
59 Quickborn D B6
16 Quiévrain B C3
35 Quillan F A5
20 Quillebeuf F B1
4 Quilty IRL B2
18 Quimper F B1
18 Quimperlé F C2
20 Quincampoix F B2
25 Quincieux F C4
33 Quincoces de Yuso E B3
24 Quincy F A2
21 Quincy-Voisins F C3
19 Quinéville F A4
25 Quingey F A5
29 Quinson F C5
24 Quinssaines F B2
36 Quinta-Grande P C2
32 Quintana del Castillo E B1
32 Quintana del Marco E B1
32 Quintana del Puenta E B2
33 Quintana-Martin Galindez E B3
33 Quintanaortuño E B3
33 Quintanapalla E B3
39 Quintanar de la Orden E C3
33 Quintanar de la Sierra E B3
39 Quintanar del Rey E C5
32 Quintanilla de la Mata E B3
32 Quintanilla de Onésimo E C2
30 Quintanilla de Somoza E B4
33 Quintanilla del Coco E C3
32 Quintas de Valdelucio E B2
31 Quintela P D3
18 Quintin F B3
34 Quinto de Ebro E B2
75 Quinzano d'Oglio I A5
30 Quiroga E B3
38 Quismondo E B2
28 Quissac F C2
75 Quistello I A5

R

69 Raab A C4
96 Raabs A C1
47 Raahe SF D12
17 Raalte NL A6
17 Raamsdonksveer NL B4
77 Rab CRO B4
77 Rabac CRO A4
30 Rábade E A3
98 Rábahidvég H A1
31 Rabanales E C4
98 Rábapatona H A2
98 Rabapordány H A2
27 Rabastens F C5
27 Rabastens-de-Bigorre F C4
97 Rabča SQ B5
97 Rabčiće SQ B5
99 Rabe CRO B5
69 Rabi CZ B4
88 Rabino PL B1
102 Rabisha BG C3
97 Rabka PL B5
102 Rabrovo YU B2
102 Raca YU C2
102 Rača YU B1
83 Rácale I B5
99 Rácalmás H A3
84 Racalmuto I B2
103 Răcarii de Sus RO B4
102 Răcăşdia RO B2
74 Racconigi I B2
21 Rachecourt F C6
89 Raciaz PL C6
97 Racibórz PL A4
96 Račice CZ B2
97 Raciechowice PL B6
101 Račinovci CRO B3
51 Rackeby S D4
99 Ráckeve H A3
91 Raclawice, *Kielce* PL C4
90 Raclawice, *Opole* PL C1
65 Racot PL A6
50 Råda S B4
101 Radalj YU B4
94 Rădăuţi RO C6
97 Radava SQ C4
75 Radda in Chianti I C6
60 Raddingsdorf D B1
85 Raddusa I B3
64 Radeberg D B3
64 Radebeul D B3
64 Radeburg D B3
73 Radeče SL B5
64 Radegast D B2
94 Radekhiv U A6
73 Radenci SL B6
72 Radenthein A B3
103 Rădesti RO A6
62 Radevormwald D B2
105 Radičevo MAK C4
78 Radicofani I A2
75 Radicóndoli I C6
106 Radievo BG A3
101 Radinci YU A4
103 Rădinesti RO B4
64 Radiumbad Brambach D C2
73 Radkersburg A B5
65 Radków PL C6
97 Radlin PL A4
73 Radlje SL B5
73 Radmer a.d. Stube A A4
106 Radnevo BG A3
69 Radnice CZ B4
97 Radobica SQ C4
73 Radoboj CRO B5
73 Radohova Vas SL C4
99 Radojevo YU C5
104 Radokal i Poshtëm AL D2
71 Radolfzell D A3
91 Radom PL B5
89 Radomice PL C5
89 Radomin PL B5
105 Radomir BG B4
103 Radomireşti RO B5
90 Radomsko PL B3
91 Radomyśl Wlk. PL C5
96 Radošina SQ C3
96 Radošovce SQ C3
89 Radostowo PL B6
91 Radoszyce PL B4
65 Radoszyn PL A5
69 Radotin CZ B5
103 Radovanu RO B4
107 Radovets BG B4
105 Radoviš MAK C4
73 Radovljica SL B4
105 Radovnica YU B4
104 Radožda MAK C2
72 Radstadt A A3
55 Rådsted DK D4
13 Radstock GB B5
77 Raduc CRO B5
102 Radujevac YU B3
97 Radziechowy PL B5
89 Radziejów PL C4
91 Radziejowice PL B4
90 Radzionków PL C2
97 Radzovce SQ C5
91 Radzymin PL A5
89 Radzyń Chelm PL B4
91 Radzyń Podlaski PL B6
62 Raesfeld D B1
84 Raffadali I B2
111 Rafina GR A5
13 Raglan GB B5
64 Ragösen D A2
50 Ragsveden S B5
64 Raguhn D B2
46 Ragunda S E8
85 Ragusa I C3
62 Rahden D A3
50 Råholt N B2
79 Raiano I A4
68 Rain D C1
69 Rainbach Mühlkreis A C5
31 Rairiz de Veiga E B3
60 Raisdorf D A1
31 Raiva, *Aveiro* P C2
36 Raiva, *Coimbra* P A2
97 Rajbrot PL B6
97 Rajcza PL B5
97 Rajec SQ B4
96 Rajec Jestrebi CZ B2
97 Rajecké Teplice SQ B4
96 Rajhrad CZ B2
100 Rajič CRO A2
96 Rajka H D3
103 Rakevo BG C4
109 Rákhes GR C4
98 Rakintnica CRO B1
103 Rakita BG C5
105 Rakita BG B4
73 Rakitna SL C4
106 Rakitovo BG B2
51 Rakkestad N C2
107 Raklitsa BG A5
99 Rákóczifalva H A5
99 Rákócziújfalu H A5
65 Rakoniewice PL A6
97 Raková SQ B4
102 Rakova Bara YU B2
77 Rakovica CRO A5
102 Rakovitsa BG C3
69 Rakovník CZ A4
61 Rakow D A4
91 Raków PL C5
93 Rakvere EW A10
101 Ralja YU B5
38 Ramacastañas E B1
85 Ramacca I B3
33 Ramales de la Victoria E A3
66 Rambervillers F C2
20 Rambouillet F C2
66 Rambucourt F C1
57 Ramdala S C4
17 Ramet B C5
73 Ramingstein A A3
30 Ramiranes E B2
70 Ramiswil CH A2
56 Ramkvilla S B3
54 Ramme DK B1
50 Rämmen S B5
52 Ramnäs S C2
49 Ramnes N B7
66 Ramonchamp F D2
10 Rampside GB A2
96 Ramsau A C1
72 Ramsau D A2
62 Ramsbeck D B3
52 Ramsberg S C1
14 Ramsey, *Cambridgeshire* GB B2
10 Ramsey, *I. of Man* GB A1
15 Ramsgate GB C4
5 Ramsgrange IRL B5
46 Ramsjö S E7
66 Ramstein D B3
71 Ranalt A A6
50 Rånåsfoss N B2
17 Rance B C4
76 Ránchio I C2
70 Randa CH B2
48 Randaberg N B2
3 Randalstown GB B5
24 Randan F B3
85 Randazzo I B3
69 Randegg A C5
54 Randers DK B3
67 Randersacker D B5
31 Randin E C3
19 Rânes F B5
8 Ranfurly GB C3
56 Rångedala S B2
64 Rangsdorf D A3
63 Ranis D C6
91 Ranizów PL C5
71 Rankweil A A4
56 Rånnaväg S B2
62 Rannerod D C3
57 Ränneslöv S C2
8 Rannoch Station GB B3
102 Ranovac YU B2
50 Ransäter S C4
62 Ransbach-Baumbach D C2
52 Ransta S C2
20 Rantigny F B3
47 Rantsila SF D12
55 Rantum D D1
47 Ranua SF D13
54 Ranum DK B2
36 Ranvalhal P B1
64 Ranzig D A4
66 Raon-l'Étape F C2
71 Ráossi I C6
75 Rapallo I B4
29 Raphèle F C3
3 Raphoe IRL B4
7 Rapness GB A6
76 Rapolano Terme I C1
80 Rapolla I D2
36 Raposa P B2
97 Rapovce SQ C5
70 Rapperswil CH A3
109 Rapsáni GR B4
34 Rasal E A2
52 Rasbo S C3
38 Rascafria E B3
63 Rasdorf D C4
33 Rasines E A3
101 Raška YU C5
103 Rasovo BG C4
65 Raspenava CZ C5
34 Rasquera E C3
76 Rássina I C1
67 Rastatt D C4
59 Rastede D B5
63 Rastenberg D B6
101 Rastošnica BO B4
103 Rastu RO C4
38 Rasueros E A1
90 Raszków PL B1
102 Rataje YU C2
46 Rätan S E7
73 Ratece SL B3
73 Ratek SL C4
60 Ratekau D B1
4 Rath Luire IRL B3
5 Rathangan IRL A5
5 Rathcoole IRL A5
4 Rathcormack IRL B3
5 Rathdowney IRL B4
5 Rathdrum IRL B5
61 Rathebur D B4
60 Rathenow D C3
3 Rathfriland GB B5
4 Rathkeale IRL B3
3 Rathmelton IRL A4
5 Rathmolyon IRL A5
4 Rathmore IRL B2
5 Rathnew IRL A5
3 Rathowen IRL C4
69 Ratibořské Hory CZ B5
62 Ratingen D B1
97 Ratková SQ C6
104 Ratkovac YU B2
99 Ratkovo CRO C4
97 Ratkovské Bystré SQ C6
68 Rattelsdorf D A1
73 Ratten A A5
9 Rattray GB B4
52 Rättvik S B1
60 Ratzeburg D B1
63 Rätzlingen D A6
21 Raucourt-et-Flaba F B5
50 Raufoss N B1
49 Rauhellern N A4
49 Rauland N B4
28 Raulhac F B1
47 Rauma SF F10
14 Raunds GB B2
72 Rauris A A3
47 Rautalampi SF E13
62 Rauxel D B2
26 Rauzan F B3
94 Rava-Ruska U A5
84 Ravanusa I B2
17 Ravels B B5
56 Rävemåla S C4
10 Ravenglass GB A2
76 Ravenna I B2
61 Ravensbrück D B4
71 Ravensburg D A4
25 Ravières F A4
56 Rävlanda S B1
105 Ravna Banja YU B3
102 Ravna Dubrava YU C3
77 Ravna Gora CRO A4
102 Ravna Reka YU B2
73 Ravne SL B4
102 Ravnište YU C2
101 Ravnje YU B4
81 Ravno BO B4
99 Ravno Selo CRO C4
106 Ravnogor BG B2
91 Rawa Mazowiecka PL B4
65 Rawicz PL B6
10 Rawtenstall GB B3
105 Rayko Daskalovo BG B5
15 Rayleigh GB C3
29 Rayol F C5
27 Razac-sur-l'Isle F A4
77 Ražanac CRO B5
102 Ražanj YU C2
100 Razboj BO A2
105 Razdol BG C5
23 Razes F B6
95 Razgrad BG E7
105 Razlog BG C5
105 Razlovci MAK C4
30 Razo E A2
15 Reading GB C1
27 Réalmont F C6
7 Reay GB B5
21 Rebais F C4
31 Rebordelo P C3
105 Rebrovo BG B5
103 Rebürkovo BG C4
76 Recanati I C3
38 Recas E B3
74 Recco I B4
103 Recea RO B6
4 Recess IRL A2
21 Recey-sur-Ource F D5
31 Recezinhos P C2
67 Rechberghausen D C5
98 Rechnitz A A1
100 Rečiće BO C2
62 Recke D A2
68 Reckendorf D A1
62 Recklinghausen D B2
71 Recoaro Terme I C6
66 Recogne B B1
97 Recsk H D6
61 Recz PL B6
9 Red Dial GB D4
6 Red Point GB C3
89 Reda PL A4
50 Redalen N B1
66 Redange L B1
15 Redbridge GB C3
11 Redcar GB A4
13 Redditch GB A6
103 Redea RO B5
60 Redefin D B2
98 Redics H B1
7 Redland GB A5
60 Redlin D B3
22 Redon F A2
30 Redondela E B2
36 Redondo P C3
45 Redován E A6
12 Redruth GB C2
14 Reedham GB B4
14 Reepham GB B4
17 Rees D B6
11 Reeth GB A4
60 Reetz D B2
56 Reftele S B2
85 Regalbuto I B3
76 Regello I C1
69 Regen D C4
68 Regensburg D B3
68 Regenstauf D B3
85 Réggio di Calábria I A4
75 Réggio nell'Emília I B5
75 Reggiolo I B5
94 Reghin RO C6
33 Régil E A4
64 Regis Breitingen D B2
25 Regny F C4
36 Rego da Leirosa P A2
98 Regöly H B3
31 Régua P C3
30 Regueiro E B2
36 Reguengo, *Portalegre* P B3
36 Reguengo, *Santarém* P B2
36 Reguengos P C3
64 Rehau D C2
59 Rehburg D C6
59 Rehden D C5
60 Rehna D B2
66 Rehon F B1
96 Rehorov Kamenice CZ B1
67 Reichelsheim D B4
67 Reichelshofen D B6
73 Reichenau, *Karnten* A B3
73 Reichenau, *Nieder Östereich* A A5
69 Reichenau i. Mühlkreis A C5
67 Reichenbach, *Baden-Württemberg* D C5
68 Reichenbach, *Bayern* D B3
64 Reichenbach, *Sachsen* D C2
65 Reichenbach, *Sachsen* D B4
67 Reichenberg D B5
73 Reichenfels A A4
63 Reichensachsen D B5
68 Reichertshofen D C2
67 Reicholzheim D B5
66 Reichshoffen F C3
70 Reiden CH A2
31 Reigada P D4
30 Reigada, *Asturias* E A4
30 Reigada, *Galicia* E B3
15 Reigate GB C2
11 Reighton GB A5
25 Reignier F B6
29 Reillanne F C4
21 Reims F B5
70 Reinach, *Argau* CH A3
70 Reinach, *Basel* CH A2
60 Reinbek D B1
61 Reinberg D A4
60 Reinfeld D B1
67 Reinheim D B4
32 Reinosa E B2
67 Reinstetten D C5
60 Reinstorf D B2
50 Reinsvoll N B1
72 Reisach A B3
68 Reisbach D C3
7 Reiss GB B5
72 Reit im Winkl D A2
97 Rejdová SQ C6
102 Rekovac YU C2
40 Relleu E C2
59 Rellingen D B6
53 Relmyra S D1
99 Rém H B4
62 Remagen D C2
20 Rémalard F C1
21 Rembercourt F C6
91 Rembertów PL A5
36 Remedios P B1
59 Remels D B4
66 Remich L B2
25 Remigny F B4
66 Rémilly F B2
66 Remiremont F D2
63 Remlingen D A5
34 Remolinos E B1
28 Remoulins F C3
62 Remscheid D B2
50 Rena N A2
24 Renalson F B3
70 Renan CH A1
19 Renazé F C4
67 Renchen D C4
29 Rencurel F A4
82 Rende I B3
109 Rendina GR B3
59 Rendsburg D A6
32 Renedo E C2
32 Renedo de Valdetuéjar E B1
8 Renfrew GB C3
109 Renginio GR C4
52 Rengsjö S A2
94 Reni MD D8
17 Renkum NL B5
68 Rennertshofen D C2
19 Rennes F B4
35 Rennes-les-Bains F A5
72 Rennweg A A3
55 Rens DK D2
33 Renteria E A5
32 Reocin E A2
98 Répcelak H A2
40 Requena E B1
28 Réquista F B1
60 Rerik D A2
112 Resadiye TR B2
72 Resana I C1
53 Resarö S C4
104 Resen MAK C3
31 Resende P C3
104 Rëshen AL C1
71 Résia (Reschen) I B5
79 Resina I C5
102 Reşiţa RO A2
61 Resko PL B6
101 Resnik YU B5
13 Resolven GB B4
21 Ressons F B3
9 Reston GB C5
84 Resuttano I B3
89 Reszel PL A7
37 Retamal E C4
103 Retevoesti RO A5
21 Rethel F B5
59 Rethem D C6
63 Rethen D A4
112 Réthimnon, *Kriti* GR
17 Retie B B5
19 Rétiers F C4
65 Retków PL B6
31 Retortillo E D4
33 Retortillo E C3
28 Retournac F A3
97 Rétság H D5
73 Rettenegg A A5
38 Retuerta de Bullaque E C2
96 Retz A C1
67 Retzbach D B5
64 Reuden D A2
24 Reuilly F A2
35 Reus E B4
17 Reusel NL B5
68 Reuth D B3
67 Reutlingen D C5
71 Reutte A A5
17 Reuver NL B6
29 Revel, *Alpes-de-Haute-Provence* F B5
27 Revel, *Haute-Garonne* F C6
74 Revello I B2
38 Revenga E B2
25 Reventin-Vaugris F C4
75 Revere I A6
29 Revest F B4
21 Revigny F C5
21 Revin F B5
57 Revingeby S D2
69 Řevnice CZ B5
64 Řevničov CZ C3
71 Revo I B6
97 Revúca SQ C6
89 Rewa PL A4
61 Rewal PL A6
93 Rezekne LV B10
107 Rezovo BG B6
71 Rezzato I C5
75 Rezzoáglio I B4
102 Rgotina YU B3
66 Rhaunen D B3
13 Rhayader GB A4
62 Rheda D B3
58 Rhede, *Niedersachsen* D B4
62 Rhede, *Nordrhein-Westfalen* D B1
17 Rheden NL A6
62 Rheinbach D C1
62 Rheinberg D B1
62 Rheine D A2
70 Rheinfelden CH A2
70 Rheinfelden D A2
62 Rheinkamp D B1
61 Rheinsberg D B3
70 Rhêmes-Notre-Dame I C2
17 Rhenen NL B5
62 Rhens D C2
17 Rheydt D B6
6 Rhiconich GB B4
60 Rhinow D C3
71 Rho I C4
13 Rhoose GB B4

85 Seminara I A4
21 Semoine F C5
98 Šemovci CRO B2
73 Šempeter SL B5
73 Semriach A A5
25 Semur-en-Auxois F A4
34 Sena E B2
32 Sena de Luna E B1
21 Senan F D4
20 Senarpont F B2
29 Sénas F C4
67 Senden, *Bayern* D C6
62 Senden, *Nordrhein-Westfalen* D B2
62 Sendenhorst D B2
31 Sendim P C4
96 Senec SQ C3
17 Seneffe B C4
87 Séneghe I B1
45 Senés E B4
29 Senez F C5
64 Senftenberg D B4
59 Sengwarden D B5
96 Senica SQ C3
96 Senice na Hané CZ B3
76 Senigállia I C3
87 Sénis I C1
82 Senise I A3
77 Senj CRO B4
102 Senje YU C2
102 Senjski Rudnik YU C2
20 Senlis F B3
56 Sennan S C1
25 Sennecey-le-Grand F B4
12 Sennen GB C2
62 Sennestadt D B3
103 Sennik BG D6
87 Sennori I B1
71 Sennwald CH A4
13 Sennybridge GB B4
69 Senohraby CZ B5
97 Senohrad SQ C5
20 Senonches F C2
66 Senones F C3
87 Senorbi I C2
73 Senožeče SL C4
21 Sens F C4
19 Sens-de-Bretagne F B4
99 Senta CRO C5
34 Senterada E A3
73 Sentilj SL B5
73 Šentjur SL B5
35 Seo de Urgel E A4
30 Seoane de Caurel E B3
70 Seon CH A3
70 Sépey CH B2
79 Sepino I B5
88 Sępólno-Krajenskie PL B3
89 Sepopol PL A6
62 Seppenrade D B2
29 Septèmes F C4
106 Septemvri BG A2
20 Septeuil F C2
25 Septmoncel F B5
32 Sepúlveda E C3
72 Sequals I B2
31 Sequeros E D4
17 Seraing B C5
21 Seraucourt le Grand F B4
75 Seravezza I C5
103 Serbaneşti RO B5
35 Serchs E A4
96 Sered SQ C3
99 Seregélyes H A3
71 Seregno I C4
18 Sérent F C3
71 Serfaus A A5
107 Sergen TR B5
71 Seriate I C4
20 Sérifontaine F B2
111 Sérifos GR B5
28 Sérignan F C2
71 Serina I C4
20 Sermaises F C3
21 Sermaize-les-Bains F C5
70 Sermamagny F A1
75 Sérmide I B6
79 Sermoneta I B3
36 Sernache de Bonjardim P B2
31 Sernancelhe P D3
89 Serock PL C7
91 Seroczyn PL A5
45 Serón E B4
33 Serón de Najima E C4
16 Serooskerke NL B3
34 Serós E B3
42 Serpa P B2
82 Serra S. Bruno I C3
76 Serra S. Quirico I C3
80 Serracapriola I C2
32 Serrada E C2
84 Serradifalco I B2
37 Serradilla E B4
31 Serradilla del Arroyo E D4
105 Sérrai GR C5
87 Serramanna I C1
75 Serramazzoni I B5
38 Serranillos E B2
76 Serrapetrona I C3
83 Serrastretta I B3
35 Serrat E B4
76 Serravalle RSM C2
70 Serravalle, *Piemonte* I C3
79 Serravalle, *Umbria* I A4
76 Serravalle di Chienti I C2
74 Serravalle Scrivia I B3
82 Serre I A2
37 Serrejón E B5
87 Serrenti I C2
29 Serres F B4
29 Serrières F A3
83 Sersale I B3
36 Serte P B2
71 Sertig Dörfli CH B4
66 Servance F D2
28 Serverette F B2
109 Sérvia GR A4
28 Servian F C2
28 Serviers F B3
76 Servigliano I C3
101 Servojno YU C4
41 Ses Salines, *Mallorca* E
36 Sesimbra P C1
3 Seskanore GB B4
33 Sesma E B4
79 Sessa Aurunca I B4
75 Sesta Godano I B4
33 Sestao E A4
76 Sestino I C2
72 Sesto (Sexten) I B2
70 Sesto Calende I C3
79 Sesto Campano I B5
75 Sesto Fiorentino I C6
75 Séstola I B5
75 Sestri Levante I B4
74 Sestriere I B1
106 Sestrimo BG A1
87 Sestu I C2
73 Sesvete CRO C6
111 Séta GR A4
35 Setcasas E A5
28 Sète F C2
43 Setenil E C4
47 Setermoen N B9
102 Šetonje YU B2
50 Setskog N C2
17 Setterich D C6
74 Settimo Torinese I A2
10 Settle GB A3
36 Setúbal P C2
68 Seubersdort D B2
87 Seúi I C2
87 Seúlo I C2
25 Seurre F B5
108 Sevaster AL A1
54 Sevel DK B1
12 Seven Sisters GB B4
15 Sevenoaks GB C3
31 Sever do Vouga P D2
28 Séverac-le-Château F B2
71 Séveso I C4
69 Ševětin CZ B5
21 Sevières F C4
21 Sévigny F B5
43 Sevilla E B4
38 Sevilla la Nueva E B2
38 Sevilleja de la Jara E C2
103 Sevlievo BG C6
73 Sevnica SL B5
25 Sevrier F C6
110 Sevros GR B3
58 Sexbierum NL B2
56 Sexdrega S B2
27 Seyches F B4
64 Seyda D B2
29 Seyne F B5
28 Seynes F B3
25 Seyssel F C5
73 Sežana SL C3
21 Sézanne F C4
96 Sezemice CZ A1
69 Sezimovo-Usti CZ B5
31 Sezulfe P C3
79 Sezze I B4
76 Sforzacosta I C3
13 Shaftesbury GB B5
13 Shaldon GB C4
4 Shanagolden IRL B2
15 Shanklin GB D1
10 Shap GB A3
107 Sharkovo BG A4
6 Shawbost GB B2
10 Shawbury GB C3
15 Sheerness GB C3
11 Sheffield GB B4
15 Shefford GB B2
104 Shëmëri AL B2
104 Shëngjin AL C1
108 Shepër AL A2
94 Shepetivka U A7
14 Shepshed GB B1
13 Shepton Mallet GB B5
13 Sherborne GB C5
11 Sherburn GB A5
11 Sherburn in Elmet GB B4
3 Shercock IRL C5
14 Sheringham GB B4
13 Sherston GB B5
6 Shieldaig GB C3
10 Shifnal GB C3
104 Shijak AL C1
9 Shilbottle GB C6
11 Shildon GB A4
5 Shillelagh IRL B5
13 Shillingstone GB C5
93 Shimsk R A12
7 Shinness GB B4
14 Shipdham GB B3
106 Shipka BG A3
106 Shipkovo BG A2
11 Shipley GB B4
15 Shipston on Stour GB B1
102 Shishentsi BG C3
102 Shishentsi BG C3
104 Shkodër AL B1
15 Shoreham-by-Sea GB D2
15 Shotley Gate GB C4
9 Shotts GB C4
10 Shrewsbury GB C3
13 Shrewton GB B6
13 Shrivenham GB B6
2 Shrule IRL C2
107 Shtit BG B4
95 Shumen BG E7
88 Sianów PL A2
108 Siátista GR A3
28 Siauges F A2
93 Šiauliai LT C8
83 Sibari I B3
57 Sibbhult S C3
77 Sibenik CRO C5
100 Sibinj CRO A2
94 Sibiu RO D6
15 Sible Hedingham GB C3
101 Sibnica YU B5
52 Sibo S A2
66 Sibret B B1
11 Sibsey GB B6
103 Siceneşti RO B5
102 Sičevo YU C3
84 Siculiana I B2
101 Šid YU A4
108 Sidari GR B1
58 Siddeburen NL B3
108 Sideras GR A3
85 Siderno I A5
107 Sidhiró GR B4
105 Sidhirókastron GR C5
110 Sidirokastro GR B2
13 Sidmouth GB C4
97 Sidzina PL B5
64 Siebenlehn D B3
91 Siedlce PL A6
93 Siedlce PL D8
62 Siedlinghausen D B3
88 Siedlisko PL B2
62 Siegburg D C2
62 Siegen D C3
68 Siegenburg D C2
98 Sieggraben A A1
96 Sieghartskirchen A C2
62 Sieglar D C2
68 Siegsdorf D D3
61 Siekierki PL C5
64 Sielow D B4
91 Sielpia PL B4
89 Sieluń PL C7
91 Siemień PL B6
75 Siena I C6
91 Sienawa PL C6
65 Sieniawka PL C4
91 Siennica PL A5
90 Sieradz PL B2
88 Sieraków PL C2
88 Sierakowice PL A3
89 Sierakowo PL C4
70 Sierentz F A2
66 Sierk-les-Bains F B2
69 Sierning A C5
90 Sieroty PL C2
89 Sierpc PL C5
37 Sierra de Fuentes E B4
34 Sierra de Luna E A2
30 Sierra de Outes E B2
44 Sierra de Yeguas E B2
70 Sierre CH B2
91 Siestrzen PL A4
34 Sietamo E A2
90 Siewierz PL C3
49 Sigdal N A6
102 Sige YU B2
28 Sigean F C1
46 Sigerfjord N B7
94 Sighetul Marmatiei RO C5
94 Sighişoara RO C6
76 Sigillo I C2
67 Siglingen D B5
67 Sigmaringen D C5
96 Sigmundsherberg A C1
29 Signes F C4
21 Signy-l'Abbaye F B5
21 Signy-le-Petit F B5
23 Sigogne F C4
53 Sigtuna S C3
30 Sigueiro E B2
39 Sigüenza E A4
34 Sigües E A1
47 Siilinjärvi SF E13
111 Sikéa GR C3
47 Sikeå S D10
97 Sikenica SQ C4
50 Sikfors, *Örebo* S C5
109 Siki GR B5
109 Sikiá, *Kardhítsa* GR B4
109 Sikiá, *Khalkidhikí* GR A5
112 Sikinos GR D2
98 Siklós H C3
89 Sikórz PL C5
109 Sikoúrion GR B4
71 Silandro (Schlanders) I B5
87 Silánus I B1
99 Silbaš CRO C4
59 Silbersted D A6
14 Sileby GB B1
45 Siles E A4
95 Silestra BG D7
31 Silgueiros P D3
29 Silhac F B3
87 Silíqua I C1
103 Silistea-Gumeşti RO B6
107 Silivri TR B6
49 Siljan N B6
50 Siljansnäs S B5
55 Silkeborg DK B2
40 Silla E B2
19 Sille-le-Guillaume F B5
30 Silleda E B2
59 Sillenstede D B4
51 Sillerud S C3
72 Sillian A B2
9 Silloth GB D4
88 Silno PL B3
77 Silo CRO A4
35 Sils E B5
11 Silsden GB B4
93 Šilute LT C7
71 Silvaplana CH B4
36 Silvares P A3
56 Silverdalen S B4
14 Silverstone GB B1
42 Silves P B1
79 Silvi Marina I A5
17 Silvolde NL B6
71 Silz A A5
25 Simandre F B4
101 Šimanovci YU B5
109 Simantra GR A5
25 Simard F B5
40 Simat de Valldigna E B2
68 Simbach, *Bayern* D C3
69 Simbach, *Bayern* D C4
82 Simbário I C3
106 Simeonovgrad BG A3
112 Simi GR B2
102 Simian RO B3
102 Simićevo YU B2
105 Simitli BG C5
56 Simlångsdalen S C2
68 Simmelsdorf D B2
17 Simmerath D C6
71 Simmerbg D A4
66 Simmern D B3
67 Simmringen D B5
104 Simnica MAK C2
47 Simo SF D12
97 Šimonovce SQ C6
12 Simonsbath GB B4
53 Simonstorp S D2
99 Simontornya H B3
110 Simópoulon GR B2
110 Simos GR A2
70 Simplon CH B3
57 Simrishamn S D3
94 Sinaia RO D6
76 Sinalunga I C1
108 Sinanaj AL A1
108 Sinarádhes GR B1
40 Sinarcas E B1
54 Sindal DK A3
67 Sindelfingen D C4
109 Sindhos GR A4
87 Sindia I B1
95 Sindirgi TR G8
107 Sinemorets BG A5
42 Sines P B1
41 Siñeu, *Mallorca* E
67 Singen D D4
15 Singleton GB D2
87 Siniscola I B2
100 Sinj CRO C1
38 Sinlabajos E A2
62 Sinn D C3
87 Sínnai I C2
48 Sinnes N C3
99 Sinnicolau Mare RO B5
94 Sînnicolaul Mare RO C4
70 Sins CH A3
67 Sinsheim D B4
36 Sintra P C1
67 Sinzheim D C4
62 Sinzig D C2
98 Siófok H B3
70 Sion CH B2
3 Sion Mills GB B4
27 Siorac-en-Périgord F B4
81 Sipanska Luka CRO B4
100 Šipovo BO B2
67 Sipplingen D D5
48 Sira N C3
85 Siracusa I B4
106 Sirakovo BG B3
94 Siret RO C7
48 Sirevåg N C2
99 Sirig CRO C4
103 Sirineasa RO B5
105 Sirishtnik BG B4
71 Sirmione I C5
97 Sirok H D6
106 Široka lŭka BG B2
76 Sirolo I C3
38 Siruela E D1
98 Sisak CRO C1
39 Sisante E C4
73 Šišljavić CRO C5
70 Sissach CH A2
21 Sissonne F B4
31 Sistelo P C2
29 Sisteron F B4
72 Sistiana I C3
106 Sitagri GR B2
108 Sitarás GR B3
108 Sitariá GR B2
35 Sitges E B4
112 Sitía, *Kriti* GR
109 Sitokhóri GR A5
108 Sitómena GR C3
17 Sittard NL B5
59 Sittensen D B6
15 Sittingbourne GB C3
64 Sitzenroda D B2
99 Sivac CRO C4
100 Siveric CRO C1
109 Siviri GR A5
108 Sivota GR B2
108 Sivros GR C2
29 Six-Fours-la-Plage F C4
4 Sixmilebridge IRL B3
3 Sixmilecross GB B4
70 Sixt F B1
75 Siziano I A4
18 Sizun F B1
101 Sjenica YU C5
73 Sjenicak CRO C5
57 Sjöbo S D2
46 Sjöhoit N E3
50 Sjøli N A2
56 Sjømarken S B1
54 Sjørring DK B1
56 Sjötofta S B2
51 Sjötorp S D4
51 Sjuntorp S D3
55 Skælskør DK C4
55 Skærbæk DK C1
55 Skævinge DK C5
49 Skafsa N B5
54 Skagen DK A3
51 Skagersvik S D5
7 Skail Hotel GB B4
102 Skakevtsi BG C3
91 Skała PL C3
109 Skála, *Fthiótis* GR C5
110 Skála, *Kefallinía* GR A1
111 Skála, *Lakonía* GR C3
112 Skála, *Pátmos* GR C1
109 Skála, *Piería* GR A4
109 Skála Foúrkas GR A5
111 Skála Oropoú GR A4
112 Skaláni, *Kriti* GR
91 Skalbmierz PL C4
49 Skålevik N C5
96 Skalica SQ C3
107 Skalista BG A4
97 Skalité SQ B4
108 Skalitina GR C3
65 Skalka PL B6
53 Skällvik S D2
64 Skalná CZ C2
106 Skaloti GR B2
54 Skals DK B2
55 Skanderborg DK B2
57 Skånes-Fagerhult S C2
48 Skånevik N B2
51 Skänninge S D6
57 Skanör S D1
51 Skåpafors S C3
65 Skąpe PL A5
51 Skara S D4
46 Skarberget N B8
53 Skärblacka S D1
48 Skare N B3
51 Skåre S C4
54 Skärhamn S A4
50 Skarnes N B2
52 Skärplinge S B3
55 Skarrild DK C1
56 Skärstad S B3
89 Skarszewy PL A4
55 Skårup DK C3
91 Skaryszew PL B5
91 Skarżysko Kamienna PL B4
91 Skarzysko Ksiazece PL B4
9 Skateraw, *Grampian* GB A5
9 Skateraw, *Lothian* GB C5
49 Skatøy N C6
51 Skattkärr S C4
50 Skattungbyn S A5
54 Skave DK B1
97 Skawina PL B5
6 Skeabost GB C2
52 Skebobruk S C4
53 Skebokvarn S C2
51 Skedet S D5
50 Skedsmokorset N B2
49 Skedsmorkorset N A8
51 Skee S D2
11 Skegness GB B6
57 Skegrie S D2
101 Skela YU B5
101 Skelani BO C4
47 Skellefteå S D10
47 Skelleftehamn S D10
6 Skellister, *Shetland Is.* GB
10 Skelmersdale GB B3
8 Skelmorlie GB C3
10 Skelton GB A3
54 Skelund DK B3
100 Skender Vakuf BO B2
56 Skene S B1
110 Skepastón GR A3
89 Skępe PL C5
56 Skeppshult S B2
53 Skepptuna S C4
3 Skerries IRL C5
111 Skhimatárion GR A4
49 Ski N B7
110 Skiadhas GR B2
109 Skiathos GR B5
4 Skibbereen IRL C2
46 Skibotn N B10
109 Skidhra GR A4
49 Skien N B6
91 Skierniewice PL B4
56 Skillingaryd S B3
57 Skillinge S D3
50 Skillingmark S C3
110 Skiloundia GR B2
52 Skinnskatteberg S C1
8 Skipness GB C2
11 Skipsea GB B5
11 Skipton GB B3
51 Skiptvet N C2
109 Skiti GR B4
57 Skivarp S D2
54 Skive DK B2
104 Skivjani YU B2
51 Skjærhollen N C2
51 Skjeberg N C2
55 Skjern DK C1
48 Skjold, *Rogaland* N B2
46 Skjolden N F3
97 Sklené SQ C4
97 Sklenov CZ B4
108 Sklithron GR A3
108 Sklivani GR B2
106 Skobelevo BG A3
52 Skoby S B4
108 Skočivir MAK A3
73 Škocjan SL C5
97 Skoczów PL B4
55 Skodborg DK C2
73 Škofja Loka SL B4
73 Škofljica SL C4
52 Skog S A2
51 Skoghall S C4
56 Skogsby, *Öland* S C5
56 Skogstorp, *Halland* S C1
53 Skogstorp, *Södermanland* S C2
88 Skoki PL C3
53 Skokloster S C3
53 Sköldinge S C2
91 Skolimów-Konstancin PL A5
49 Skollenborg N B6
53 Sköllersta S C1
90 Skomlin PL B2
109 Skópelos, *Skópelos* GR B5
112 Skopi, *Kriti* GR
108 Skopiá, *Florina* GR A3
109 Skopiá, *Lárisa* GR B4
104 Skopje MAK C3
108 Skopós GR A3
89 Skórcz PL B4
65 Skoroszów PL B7
65 Skoroszyce PL C7
54 Skørping DK B2
111 Skorponéria GR A4
110 Skortinos GR B3
91 Skórzec PL A6
49 Skotfoss N B6
109 Skotiná GR A4
105 Skotoúsa GR C5
49 Skotselv N B6
50 Skotterud N C3
57 Skottorp S C1
108 Skoulikaría GR B3
110 Skoura GR B3
110 Skourokhóri GR B2
111 Skoúrta GR A4
108 Skourtoú GR C3
110 Skoutari, *Lakonía* GR C3
105 Skoutari, *Sérrai* GR C5
51 Skövde S D4
73 Skrad CRO C4
77 Skradin CRO C5
96 Škrdlovice CZ B1
56 Skreanäs S C1
50 Skreia N B1
57 Skromberga S D1
105 Skrút BG C4
56 Skruv S C4
55 Skrydstrup DK C2
48 Skudeneshavn N B2
49 Skui N B7
51 Skultorp S D4
53 Skultuna S C2
57 Skurup S D2
96 Skuteč CZ B1
52 Skutskär S B3
61 Skwierzyna PL C6
97 Skýcov SQ C4
51 Skyllberg S D5
52 Skyttorp S B3
97 Sl'ažany SQ C4
96 Sládeckovce SQ C3
96 Sládkovicovo SQ C3
55 Slagelse DK C4
58 Slagharen NL C3
9 Slamannan GB C4
3 Slane IRL C5
98 Slanje CRO B1
81 Slano CRO B4
93 Slantsy R A11
64 Slaný CZ C4
96 Slapanice CZ B2
103 Slatina RO B5
102 Slatina YU B3
102 Slatina Nera RO B2
96 Slatiňany CZ B1
96 Slatinice CZ B3
103 Slătioara RO A4
50 Slättberg S A5
103 Slaveşti RO B6
96 Slavičin CZ B3
96 Slavkov CZ C3
96 Slavkov u. Brna CZ B2
101 Slavkovica YU B5
69 Slavonice CZ B6
100 Slavonska Požega CRO A2
100 Slavonski Brod CRO A3
100 Slavonski Kobas CRO A2
97 Slavŏsovce SQ C6
103 Slavotin BG C4
103 Slavyanovo BG C5
65 Slawa PL B6
88 Sława PL B1
90 Sławkow PL C3
88 Sławno PL A2
88 Slawoborze PL B1
11 Sleaford GB B5
11 Sledmere GB A5
16 Sleidinge B B3
11 Sleights GB A5
89 Slemiany PL B5
49 Slemmestad N B7
90 Slesin PL A2
97 Sliač SQ C5
17 Sliedrecht NL B4
6 Sligachan GB C2
2 Sligo IRL B3
17 Slikkerveer NL B4
105 Slišane YU B3
51 Slitu N C2
107 Sliven BG A4
73 Slivnica SL B5
105 Slivnitsa BG B5
88 Śliwice PL B4
58 Slochteren NL B3
56 Slöinge S C1
91 Slomniki PL C4
93 Slonim BL D9
61 Słońsk PL C5
97 Slopnice PL B6
51 Slottsbron S C4
15 Slough GB C2
73 Slovenjgradec SL B5
73 Slovenska Bistrica SL B5
97 Slovenská L'upča SQ C5
64 Słubice PL A4
93 Sluck BL D10
71 Sluderno (Schluderns) I B5
16 Sluis NL B3
16 Sluiskil NL B3
64 Šluknov CZ B4
77 Slunj CRO A5
90 Słupca PL A1
65 Słupiec PL C6
88 Słupsk PL A3
56 Slutarp S A2
56 Smålandsstenar S B2
73 Šmarje SL B5
73 Šmarjeta SL C5
64 Smečno CZ C4
56 Smedby, *Kalmar* S C5
53 Smedby, *Östergötland* S D2
69 Smědec CZ C5
102 Smederevo YU B1
101 Smederevska Palanka YU B5
52 Smedjebacken S B1
91 Smęgorzow PL C5
89 Smetowo PL B4
65 Smidary CZ C5
65 Śmigiel PL A6
110 Smila GR B2
58 Smilde NL C3
106 Smilyan BG B2
65 Smiřice CZ C5
3 Smithborough IRL B4
9 Smithfield GB D5
88 Śmitowo PL B2
108 Smixi GR A3
51 Smögen S D2
88 Smogulec PL B3
105 Smojmirovo MAK C4
109 Smókoron GR B4
80 Smokvica CRO B3
105 Smokvica MAK C4
96 Smolenice SQ C3
106 Smolyan BG B2
103 Smolyanovtsi BG C4
57 Smygehamn S D2
91 Smykow PL B4
11 Snainton GB A5
11 Snaith GB B4
49 Snarum N A6
51 Snavlunda S D5
54 Snedsted DK B1
58 Sneek NL B2
4 Sneem IRL C2
55 Snejbjerg DK B1
14 Snettisham GB B3
100 Šnjegotina BO B2
55 Snøde DK C3
57 Snogebaek DK D4
56 Snöstorp S C1
71 Soave I C6
30 Sober E B3
66 Sobernheim D B3
69 Soběslav CZ B5
91 Sobienie Jeziory PL B5
65 Sobieszów PL C5
65 Sobota PL B5
90 Şobota PL A3
96 Sobotište SQ C3
65 Sobotka CZ C5
90 Sobótka, *Kalisz* PL B1
65 Sobótka, *Wrocław* PL C6
89 Sobowidz PL A4
30 Sobrado, *Coruña* E A2
30 Sobrado, *Lugo* E B3
42 Sobral da Adica P A2
36 Sobral de Monte Argraço P B1
36 Sobreira Formosa P B3
32 Sobrescobio E A1
55 Søby DK D3
72 Soca SL B3
101 Sočanica YU C5
91 Sochaczew PL A4
70 Sochaux F A1
102 Socol RO B2
45 Socovos E A5
39 Socuéllamos E C4
47 Sodankylä SF C13
57 Soderåkra S C5
52 Söderala S A2
52 Söderås S B1
52 Söderbärke S B1
52 Söderfors S B3
52 Söderhamn S A3
53 Söderköping S D2
53 Södertälje S C3
73 Södingberg A A5
50 Södra Finnskoga S B3
51 Södra Ny S C4
51 Södra Råda S C5
57 Södra Sandby S D2
56 Södra Unnaryd S C2
56 Södra Vi S B4
73 Sodražica SL C4
33 Sodupe E A3
31 Soengas P C2
62 Soest D B3
17 Soest NL A5
17 Soestdijk NL A5
17 Soesterberg NL A5
109 Sofádhes GR B4
109 Sofia GR C5
111 Sofikón GR B4
105 Sofiya BG B5
107 Sofular TR B5
59 Sögel D C4
76 Sogliano al Rubicone I C2
46 Sogndalsfjöra N F3
49 Søgne N C4
14 Soham GB B3
66 Sohren D B3
17 Soignies B C4
21 Soissons F B4
20 Soisy F C3
108 Sojnik AL A2
98 Söjtör H B1
112 Söke TR B1
109 Sokhós GR A5
49 Sokna N A6
48 Sokndal N C3
100 Soko BO B3
102 Soko Banja YU C2
101 Sokolac BO C3
105 Sokolarci MAK C4
64 Sokolov CZ C2
91 Sokolów Matopolski PL C6
91 Sokolów Podlaski PL A6
91 Sól PL C6
48 Sola N C2
37 Solana de los Barros E C4
44 Solana del Pino E A2
32 Solares E A3
85 Solarino I B4
87 Solarussa I C1
72 Solbad Hall in Tirol A A1
56 Solberga S B3
49 Solbergelva N B7
97 Solčany SQ C4
73 Solcava SL B4
71 Solda I B5
71 Sölden A B5
89 Solec Kujawski PL B4
29 Soleils F C5
86 Solenzara F C2
44 Solera E B3
34 Solerás E B3
16 Solesmes F C3
83 Soleto I A5
66 Solgne F C2
49 Solheimsstul N A5
48 Solheimsvik N B3
23 Solignac F C6
11 Solihull GB C4
100 Solin CRO C1
62 Solingen D B2
35 Solivella E B4
72 Solkan SL C3
72 Söll A A2
40 Sollana E B2
51 Sollebrunn S D3
47 Sollefteå S E8
96 Sollenau A D2
41 Soller, *Mallorca* E
50 Sollerön S B5
55 Søllested DK D4
29 Solliès-Pont F C5
49 Søllihogda N B7
65 Solnice CZ C6
107 Solnik BG A5
79 Solofra I C5
27 Solomiac F C4
79 Solopaca I B5
33 Solórzano E A3
70 Solothurn CH A2
17 Solre-le-Château F C4
55 Solrød DK C5
35 Solsona E B4
99 Solt H B4
59 Soltau D C6
99 Soltszentimre H B4
99 Soltvadkert H B4
49 Solumsmo N B6
25 Solutre F B4
12 Solva GB B2
52 Solvarbo S B1
57 Sölvesborg S C3
99 Solymár H A3
95 Soma TR G7
16 Somain F C3
99 Somberek H B3
25 Sombernon F A4
99 Sombor CRO C4
17 Sombreffe B C4
17 Someren NL B5
47 Somero SF F11
14 Somersham GB B3
13 Somerton GB B5
30 Somiedo E A4
88 Sominy PL A3
70 Somma Lombardo I C3
74 Sommariva del Bosco I B2
84 Sommatino I B3
66 Sommedieue F B1
17 Sommelsdijk NL B4
51 Sommen S D5
21 Sommepy F B5
63 Sömmerda D B6
61 Sommerfeld D C4
61 Sommersdorf D B5
55 Sommersted DK C2
21 Sommesous F C5
28 Sommières F C3
23 Sommières-du Clain F B5
32 Somo E A3
98 Somogyfajsz H B2
98 Somogyjad H B2
98 Somogysámson H B2
98 Somogysárd H B2
98 Somogyszil H B3
98 Somogyszob H B2
98 Somogyudvarhely H B2
98 Somogyvár H B2
45 Somontin E B4
39 Somosiero E A3
97 Somoskoújifalu SQ C5
103 Somovit BG C5
90 Sompolno PL A2
21 Sompuis F C5
49 Son N B7
17 Son NL B5
41 Son Bou, *Menorca* E
41 Son Severa, *Mallorca* E
70 Sonceboz CH A2
32 Soncillo E B3
71 Soncino I C4
49 Søndeled N C6
55 Sønder Bjert DK C2
55 Sønder Broby DK C3
55 Sønder Felding DK C1
55 Sønder Hygum DK C1
54 Sønder Kongerslev DK B3
55 Sønder Lem DK B1
55 Sønder Omme DK C1
55 Sønderborg DK D2
55 Sønderho DK C1
63 Sondershausen D B5
55 Søndersø DK C3
55 Søndervig DK B1
51 Søndre Enningdal Kappel N D2
50 Søndre Osen N A2
71 Sóndrio I B4
49 Songe N C6
20 Songeons F B2
57 Sönnarslöv S D3
63 Sonneburg D C6
63 Sonnefeld D C6
64 Sonnewalde D B3
79 Sonnino I B4
70 Sonogno CH B3
17 Sonsbeck D B6
38 Sonseca E C3
50 Sønsterud N B3
53 Sonstorp S D1
99 Sonta CRO C4
67 Sontheim D C6
71 Sonthofen D A5
63 Sontra D B4
26 Soorts F C2
33 Sopelana E A4
98 Sopje CRO C2
103 Sopol BG C5
106 Sopot BG A2
89 Sopot PL A4
104 Sopotnica MAK C3
102 Şopotu Nou RO B2
98 Sopron H A1
101 Šor YU B4
79 Sora I B4
75 Soragna I B5
78 Sorano I A2
75 Sorbara I B6
45 Sorbas E B4
8 Sorbie GB D3
24 Sorbier F B3
75 Sórbolo I B5
7 Sordale GB B5
26 Sore F B3
70 Sörenberg CH B3
75 Soresina I A4
27 Sorèze F C6
27 Sorges F A4
87 Sórgono I B2
29 Sorgues F B3
33 Soria E C4
82 Soriano Cálabro I C3
78 Soriano nel Cimino I A3
44 Sorihuela del Guadalimar E A3
8 Sorisdale GB B1
89 Sorkwity PL B7
98 Sormás H B1
8 Sorn GB C3
55 Sorø DK C4
94 Soroki MD B8
112 Soroni GR A2
79 Sorrento I C5
47 Sorsele S D8
50 Sorsjön S A4
87 Sorso I B1
35 Sort E A4
85 Sortino I B4
46 Sortland N B7
50 Sørumsand N C2
53 Sorunda S D3
55 Sörup D D2
46 Sørvika N E5
27 Sos F B4
34 Sos del Rey Católico E A1
105 Sosándra GR D4
57 Sösdala S C2
73 Sošice SL C5
90 Sośnicowice PL C2
90 Sosnowiec PL C3
74 Sospel F C2
73 Šoštanj SL B5
30 Sotelo de Montes E B2
110 Sótena GR A3
38 Sotillo de Adrada E B2
32 Sotillo de la Ribera E C3
101 Sotin CRO A4
47 Sotkamo SF D14
30 Soto de los Infantes E A4
30 Soto del Barco E A4
32 Soto la Marina E A3
32 Sotobañado y Priorato E B2
98 Sótony H A1
37 Sotoserrano E A4
32 Sotresgudo E B2
86 Sotta F C2
20 Sotteville F B2
76 Sottomarina I A2
59 Sottrum D B6
39 Sotuelamos E C4
21 Souain F B5
27 Soual F C6
21 Soucy F C4
112 Soúdha, *Kriti* GR
21 Soudron F C5
24 Souesmes F A2
67 Soufflenheim F C3
107 Souflion GR B4
66 Souilly F B1
22 Soulac-sur-Mer F C3
21 Soulaines-Dhuys F C5
110 Souláriı GR A1
111 Soúli GR B3
110 Soulinári GR C2
67 Soultz, *Bas-Rhin* F C3
66 Soultz, *Haut-Rhin* F D3
17 Soumagne B C5
26 Soumoulou F C3
21 Souppes F C3
26 Souprosse F C3
26 Souquet F C2
19 Sourdeval F B5
36 Soure P A2
35 Sournia F A5
31 Souro Pires P D3
109 Souroti GR A5
109 Soúrpi GR B4
20 Sours F C2
27 Sousceyrac F B6
36 Sousel P C3
26 Soustons F C2
15 South Benfleet GB C3
12 South Brent GB C4
11 South Cave GB B5
6 South Dell GB B2
8 South Feorline GB C2
15 South Godstone GB C2
15 South Hayling GB D2
11 South Kirkby GB B4
12 South Molton GB B4
9 South Shields GB D6
15 South Woodham Ferrers GB C3
14 Southam GB B1
15 Southampton GB D1
15 Southborough GB C3
9 Southdean GB C5
8 Southend GB C2
15 Southend-on-Sea GB C3
14 Southery GB B3
15 Southminster GB C3
10 Southport GB B2
11 Southwell GB B5
15 Southwick GB D2
14 Southwold GB B4
36 Souto P A3
36 Souto da Carpalhosa P B2
9 Soutra Mains GB C5
31 Soutuchao E C3
24 Souvigny F B3
112 Souyia, *Kriti* GR
103 Sovarna RO B3
100 Sovciči BO C2
83 Soverato I C3
82 Soveria Mannelli I B3
57 Sövestad S D2
93 Sovetsk R C7
11 Sowerby GB A4
29 Soyons F B3
107 Sozopol BG A5
17 Spa B C5
96 Špačince SQ C3
85 Spadafora I A4
67 Spaichingen D C4
17 Spakenburg NL A5
14 Spalding GB B2
69 Spálené Poříči CZ B4
68 Spalt D B1
102 Spance YU C2
63 Spangenberg D B4
48 Spangereid N C4
53 Spangsholm S D1
79 Sparanise I B4
54 Sparkær DK B2
13 Sparkford GB B5
53 Sparreholm S C2
85 Spartà I A4
110 Spárti GR B3
108 Spárto GR C3
108 Spartokhóri GR C2
111 Spáta GR B4
110 Spátharis GR B2
8 Spean Bridge GB B3
49 Spedalen N C5
66 Speicher D B2
76 Spello I D2
62 Spenge D A3
11 Spennymoor GB A4
64 Sperenberg D A3
109 Sperkhiás GR C4
85 Sperlinga I B3
79 Sperlonga I B4
111 Spétsai GR B4
8 Spey Bridge GB A3
67 Speyer D B4
18 Spézet F B2
82 Spezzano Albanese I B3
82 Spezzano della Sila I B3
4 Spiddle IRL A2
59 Spiekeroog D B4
67 Spielbach D B6
70 Spiez CH B2
74 Spigno Monferrato I B3
58 Spijk NL B3
17 Spijkenisse NL B4
75 Spilamberto I B6
112 Spili, *Kriti* GR
109 Spiliá, *Lárisa* GR B4
110 Spiliá, *Messinía* GR B2
72 Spilimbergo I B2
11 Spilsby GB B6
80 Spinazzola I D3
66 Spincourt F B1
48 Spind N C3
65 Spindleruv-Mlyn CZ C5
82 Spinoso I A2
98 Špišjc Bukovica CRO C2
97 Spišská Belá SQ B6
97 Spišská Nová Ves SQ C6
97 Spisská Stará Ves SQ B6
97 Spišské Bystré SQ C6

99 Tatárszentgyörgy H A4
97 Tatranská Kotlina SQ B6
97 Tatranská-Lomnica SQ B6
48 Tau N B2
67 Tauberbischofsheim D B5
64 Taucha D B2
68 Taufkirchen D C3
69 Taufkirchen a.d. Pram A C4
18 Taule F B2
29 Taulignan F B3
55 Taulov DK C2
13 Taunton GB B4
67 Taunusstein D A4
93 Taurage LT C8
85 Taurianova I A5
83 Taurisano I B5
34 Tauste E B1
24 Tauves F C2
99 Tavankut CRO B4
70 Tavannes CH A2
75 Tavarnelle val di Pesa I C6
25 Tavaux F A5
83 Taverna I B3
71 Taverne CH B3
76 Tavernelle I C2
71 Tavérnola Bergamasca I C5
20 Taverny F B3
20 Tavers F D2
83 Taviano I B5
42 Tavira P B2
12 Tavistock GB C3
101 Tavnik YU C5
2 Tawnyinah IRL C3
109 Taxiárkhis, *Khalkidhikí* GR A5
109 Taxiárkhis, *Tríkkala* GR B3
8 Taychreggan GB B2
8 Taynuilt GB B2
9 Tayport GB B5
32 Tazones E A1
89 Tczew PL A4
8 Teangue GB A2
79 Teano I B5
104 Tearce MAK B3
44 Teba E C2
10 Tebay GB A3
72 Techendorf A B3
62 Tecklenburg D A2
57 Teckomatorp S D2
94 Tecuci RO D7
112 Teféli, *Kriti* GR
17 Tegelen NL B6
52 Tegelsmora S B3
72 Tegernsee D A1
82 Teggiano I A2
76 Tegoleto I C1
63 Teichel D C6
13 Teignmouth GB C4
30 Teijeiro E A2
19 Teillay F C4
68 Teisendorf D D3
63 Teistungen D B5
103 Teiu RO B6
30 Teixeira E B3
37 Tejada de Tiétar E A5
33 Tejado E C4
38 Tejares E B1
30 Tejera E A4
57 Tejn DK D3
102 Tekija YU B3
107 Tekirdağ TR C5
97 Tekovske-Lužany SQ C4
48 Telavåg N A1
96 Telč CZ B1
79 Telese I B5
10 Telford GB C3
71 Telfs A A6
62 Telgte D B2
103 Telish BG C5
59 Tellingstedt D A6
93 Telšiai LT C8
87 Telti I B2
61 Teltow D C4
39 Tembleque E C3
69 Temelin CZ B5
105 Temelkovo BG B4
110 Teméni GR A3
99 Temerin CRO C4
33 Temiño E B3
87 Témpio Pausánia I B2
10 Temple Sowerby GB A3
5 Templemore IRL B4
4 Templenoe IRL C2
16 Templeuve B C3
61 Templin D B4
3 Tempo GB B4
17 Temse B B4
102 Temska YU C3
58 Ten Boer NL B3
25 Tenay F C5
13 Tenbury Wells GB A5
12 Tenby GB B3
28 Tence F A3
74 Tende F B2
107 Tenevo BG A4
68 Tengling D D3
56 Tenhult S B3
99 Tenja CRO C3
66 Tenneville B A1
52 Tensta S B3
15 Tenterden GB C3
30 Teo E B2
80 Teora I D2
108 Tepelenë AL A2
69 Teplá CZ B3
64 Teplice CZ C3
65 Teplice n. Metuji CZ C6
58 Ter Apel NL C4
58 Ter Apelkanaal NL C4
33 Tera E C4
79 Téramo I A4
17 Terborg NL B6
97 Terchová SQ B5
102 Teregova RO A3
36 Terena P C3
40 Teresa de Cofrentes E B1
69 Terešov CZ B4
98 Terezino Polje CRO C2
21 Tergnier F B4
71 Terlano (Terlan) I B6
80 Terlizzi I C3
37 Termas de Monfortinho P A4
78 Terme di Roselle I A2
79 Terme di Suio I B4
74 Terme di Valdieri I B2
34 Termens E B3
28 Termes F B2
99 Termia Mare RO C5
84 Términi Imerese I B2
79 Terminillo I A3
80 Térmoli I C2
3 Termonfeckin IRL C5
23 Ternay F A4
69 Ternberg A D5
54 Terndrup DK B3
16 Terneuzen NL B3
78 Terni I A3
96 Ternitz A D2
94 Ternopil U B6
108 Térovo GR B2
108 Terpan AL A2
97 Terpes H D6
103 Terpezita RO B4
105 Térpillos GR C4
105 Terpni GR D5
110 Terpsithéa, *Aitolía kai Acarnanía* GR A2
109 Terpsithéa, *Lárisa* GR B4
79 Terracina I B4
87 Terralba I C1
82 Terranova di Pollino I B3
82 Terranova di Sibari I B3
31 Terras do Bouro P C2
84 Terrasini I A2
27 Terrasson-la-Villedieu F A5
33 Terrazos E B3
40 Terriente E A1
14 Terrington St. Clement GB B3
36 Terrugem P C3
87 Tertenia I C2
40 Teruel E A1
47 Tervola SF C12
17 Tervuren B C4
39 Terzaga E B5
100 Tešanj BO B3
97 Tesáske-Mlyňany SQ C4
100 Teslić BO B2
60 Tessin D A3
19 Tessy-sur-Vire F B4
98 Tét H A2
13 Tetbury GB B5
60 Teterow D B3
106 Teteven BG A2
100 Tetovo BO B2
104 Tetovo MAK B2
108 Tetrákomo GR B3
63 Tettau D C6
71 Tettnang D A4
68 Teublitz D B3
64 Teuchern D B2
40 Teulada E C3
87 Teulada I D1
63 Teutschenthal D B6
98 Tevel H B3
9 Teviothead GB C5
13 Tewkesbury GB B5
63 Thale D B6
66 Thalfang D B2
69 Thalgau A D4
64 Thalheim D C2
71 Thalkirch CH B4
71 Thalkirchdorf D A5
68 Thalmässing D B2
70 Thalwil CH A3
15 Thame GB C2
66 Thann F D3
68 Thannhausen D C1
66 Thaon-les-Vosges F C2
64 Tharandt D C3
42 Tharsis E B2
106 Thásos GR C2
15 Thatcham GB C1
15 Thaxted GB C3
70 Thayngen CH A3
5 The Downs IRL A4
15 Theale GB C1
59 Thedinghausen D C6
64 Theeßen D A2
63 Themar D C5
23 Thénezay F B4
27 Thenon F A5
108 Theodorianá GR B3
111 Theológos, *Évia* GR A4
109 Theológos, *Fthiótis* GR C5
106 Theológos, *Thásos* GR C2
108 Theópetra GR B3
74 Théoule F C1
112 Thérma GR C1
109 Thérmi GR A5
111 Thermissia GR B4
110 Thérmon GR A2
16 Therouanne F C2
108 Thesprotikón GR B2
109 Thessaloníki GR A4
14 Thetford GB B3
104 Theth AL B1
17 Theux B C5
28 Thézar F C1
26 Theze F C3
66 Thiaucourt F C1
20 Thiberville F B1
21 Thibie F C5
21 Thiéblemont-Farémont F C5
24 Thiel F B3
64 Thiendorf D B3
72 Thiene I C1
68 Thierhaupten D C1
70 Thierrens CH B1
24 Thiers F C3
68 Thiersheim D A3
64 Thierstein D C2
87 Thiesi I B1
61 Thießow D A4
28 Thiezac F A1
66 Thil F B1
66 Thionville F B2
112 Thira GR D2
10 Thirlspot GB A2
20 Thiron F C2
11 Thirsk GB A4
54 Thisted DK B1
111 Thívai GR A4
47 Thivalkoski SF D14
20 Thivars F C2
23 Thiviers F C5
25 Thizy F B4
17 Tholen NL B4
110 Tholó GR B2
4 Thomas Street IRL A3
5 Thomastown IRL B4
25 Thônes F C6
21 Thonnance-les-Joinville F C6
70 Thonon F B1
29 Thorame-Basse F B5
29 Thorame-Haute F B5
25 Thorens-Glières F C6
21 Thorigny-sur-Oreuse F C4
73 Thörl A A5
11 Thornaby on Tees GB A4
11 Thorne GB B5
14 Thorney GB B2
8 Thornhill, *Central* GB B3
9 Thornhill, *Dumfries & Galloway* GB C4
10 Thornthwaite GB A2
10 Thornton Cleveleys GB B2
11 Thornton-le-Dale GB A5
15 Thorpe-le-Soken GB C4
23 Thouarcé F A4
23 Thouars F B4
110 Thouria GR B3
107 Thóurion GR B4
21 Thourotte F B3
112 Thrapsanon, *Kriti* GR
14 Thrapston GB B2
10 Threlkeld GB A2
11 Threshfield GB A3
7 Thrumster GB B5
28 Thueyts F B3
17 Thuin B C4
35 Thuir F A5
68 Thumau D A2
70 Thun CH B2
67 Thüngen D B5
24 Thuret F C3
25 Thurey F B5
71 Thüringen A A4
25 Thurins F C4
60 Thürkow D B3
5 Thurles IRL B4
14 Thurmaston GB B1
55 Thurø DK C3
9 Thursby GB D4
7 Thurso GB B5
19 Thury Harcourt F B5
71 Thusis CH B4
54 Thyborøn DK B1
55 Thyregod DK C2
40 Tibi E C2
51 Tibro S D5
15 Ticehurst GB C3
107 Ticha BG A4
11 Tickhill GB B4
103 Ticleni RO B4
51 Tidaholm S D4
51 Tidan S D5
56 Tidersrum S B4
32 Tiedra E C1
68 Tiefenbach D B3
71 Tiefencastel CH B4
63 Tiefenort D C5
61 Tiefensee D C4
17 Tiel NL B5
39 Tielmes E B3
16 Tielt B B3
17 Tienen B C4
70 Tiengen D A3
23 Tiercé F A4
33 Tierga E C5
34 Tiermas E A1
52 Tierp S B3
94 Tighina MD C8
8 Tighnabruaich GB C2
70 Tignes F C1
103 Tigveni RO A5
20 Tigy F D3
98 Tihany H B2
77 Tijesno CRO C5
58 Tijnje NL B2
45 Tijola E B4
107 Tikherón GR B4
17 Tilburg NL B5
15 Tilbury GB C3
25 Tilchâtel F A5
26 Tilh F C3
112 Tilissos, *Kriti* GR
107 Tilkipinar TR B5
27 Tillac F C4
53 Tillberga S C2
20 Tille F B3
9 Tillicoultry GB B4
15 Tillingham GB C3
21 Tilloy-et-Bellay F B5
19 Tilly-sur-Seulles F A5
55 Tim DK B1
72 Timau I B3
112 Timbákion, *Kriti* GR
69 Timelkam A D4
109 Timfristós GR C3
94 Timişoara RO D4
56 Timmele S B2
60 Timmendorfer Strand D B1
56 Timmernabben S C5
51 Timmersdala S D4
5 Timolin IRL B5
56 Timsfors S C2
5 Tinahely IRL B5
36 Tinalhas P B3
19 Tinchebray F B5
16 Tincques F C2
30 Tineo E A4
112 Tingáki GR B2
15 Tingewick GB C1
55 Tinglev DK D2
56 Tingsryd S C3
46 Tingvoll N E4
49 Tinnoset N B6
112 Tinos GR D1
12 Tintagel GB C3
103 Tintäreni RO B4
19 Tinténiac F B4
13 Tintern Parva GB B5
66 Tintigny B B1
71 Tione di Trento I B5
4 Tipperary IRL B3
15 Tiptree GB C3
104 Tiranë AL C1
71 Tirano I B5
95 Tire TR G7
72 Tires I B1
95 Tîrgovişte RO D6
103 Tîrgu Cărbuneşti RO B4
103 Tîrgu Jiu RO A4
103 Tîrgu Logreşti RO B4
94 Tîrgu Mureş RO C6
39 Tiriez E D4
40 Tirig E A3
83 Tiriolo I C3
109 Tírnavos GR B4
111 Tirós GR B3
75 Tirrénia I C5
68 Tirschenreuth D B3
55 Tirstrup DK B3
44 Tirteafuera E A2
103 Tishevitsa BG C4
103 Tismana RO A3
96 Tišnov CZ B2
97 Tisovec SQ C5
51 Tisselskog S D3
51 Tistedal N C2
55 Tistrup DK C1
55 Tisvildeleje DK B5
99 Tiszabö H A5
94 Tiszacsege H C4
99 Tiszaderzs H A5
99 Tiszaföldvár H B5
94 Tiszafüred H C4
99 Tiszafüred H A5
99 Tiszaigar H A5
99 Tiszakécske H B5
99 Tiszakürt H B5
99 Tiszanána H A5
99 Tiszaörs H A5
99 Tiszapüspöki H A5
99 Tiszaroff H A5
99 Tiszasüly H A5
99 Tiszaszentimre H A5
99 Tiszasziget H B5
99 Tiszaszölös H A5
99 Tiszatenyö H A5
40 Titaguas E B1
111 Titáni GR B3
101 Titel YU A5
109 Tithoréa GR C4
67 Titisee D D4
80 Tito I D2
105 Titov Veles MAK C3
77 Titova Korenica CRO B5
104 Titova Mitrovica YU B2
101 Titovo Užice YU C4
69 Tittling D C4
68 Tittmoning D C3
17 Titz D B6
81 Tivat YU B5
51 Tived S D5
13 Tiverton GB C4
34 Tivisa E B3
79 Tivoli I B3
99 Tiz Tiszaalpán H B4
55 Tjæreborg DK C1
53 Tjällmo S D1
51 Tjärnö S D2
49 Tjonnefoss N C5
57 Tjörnarp S D2
77 Tkon CRO C5
89 Tłuchowo PL C5
96 Tlumačov CZ B3
91 Tłuszcz PL A5
99 Tóalmas H A4
75 Toano I B5
63 Toba D B5
40 Tobarra E C1
3 Tobermore GB B5
8 Tobermory GB B1
52 Tobo S B3
98 Toboriste CRO C1
27 Tocane-St. Apre F A4
36 Tocha P A2
43 Tocina E B4
51 Töcksfors S C2
78 Todi I A3
11 Todmorden GB B3
70 Todtmoos D A2
67 Todtnau D D3
30 Toén E B3
51 Tofta, *Skaraborg* S D4
49 Tofte N B7
51 Töftedal S D2
55 Toftlund DK C2
68 Töging D C3
47 Toijala SF F11
101 Tojšići BO B3
106 Tokachka BG B3
90 Tokary PL B2
99 Tokod H A3
99 Tököl H A3
95 Tolbukhin BG E7
38 Toledo E C2
76 Tolentino I C3
78 Tolfa I A2
52 Tolfta S B3
56 Tolg S B3
89 Tolkmicko PL A5
57 Tollarp S D2
56 Tollered S B1
15 Tollesbury GB C3
15 Tolleshunt D'Arcy GB C3
55 Tølløse DK C4
72 Tolmezzo I B3
72 Tolmin SL B3
99 Tolna H B3
98 Tolnanémedi H B3
111 Tolón GR B3
33 Tolosa E A4
36 Tolosa P B3
44 Tolox E C2
34 Tolva E A3
80 Tolve I D3
36 Tomar P B2
101 Tomaševac YU A5
100 Tomašica BO B1
96 Tomášikovo SQ C3
94 Tomaszów Lubelski PL A5
91 Tomaszów Mazowiecki PL B4
7 Tomatin GB C4
78 Tomba di Nerone I B3
27 Tombeboeuf F B4
8 Tomdoun GB A2
57 Tomelilla S D2
39 Tomellosa E B4
39 Tomelloso E C3
7 Tomintoul GB C5
90 Tomisławice PL A2
55 Tommerup DK C3
7 Tomnavoulin GB C5
103 Tomşani RO A5
51 Tomter N C1
35 Tona E B5
87 Tonara I B2
15 Tonbridge GB C3
31 Tondela P D2
55 Tønder DK D1
17 Tongeren B C5
7 Tongue GB B4
23 Tonnay-Boutonne F C4
22 Tonnay-Charente F C4
27 Tonneins F B4
21 Tonnerre F D4
59 Tönning D A5
49 Tonsberg N B7
48 Tonstad N C3
3 Toome GB B5
5 Toomyvara IRL B3
4 Toormore IRL C2
45 Topares E B4
38 Topas E A1
103 Topesti RO A3
102 Toplet RO B3
102 Topli Dol YU C3
97 Topol'čany SQ C4
97 Topol'čianky SQ C4
96 Topol'niky SQ D3
101 Topola YU B5
104 Topolčani MAK C3
112 Topólia, *Kriti* GR
94 Topolovatul-Mare RO D4
103 Topoloveni RO B6
107 Topolovgrad BG A4
106 Topolovo BG B2
98 Toponár H B2
65 Toporów PL A5
13 Topsham GB C4
77 Topusko CRO A5
30 Toques E B3
78 Tor Vaiánica I B3
35 Torá E B4
30 Toral E B4
32 Toral de los Guzmanes E B1
13 Torbay GB C4
50 Tørberget N A3
51 Torbjörntorp S D4
71 Torbole I C5
83 Torchiarolo I A5
20 Torcy-le-Petit F B2
99 Torda CRO C5
49 Tørdal N B5
32 Tordehumos E C1
32 Tordesillas E C1
39 Tordesilos E B5
39 Tordesnos E B5
47 Töre S D11
51 Töreboda S D5
55 Toreby DK D4
57 Torekov S C1
80 Torella dei Lombardi I D2
35 Torelló E A5
30 Toreno E B4
22 Torfou F A3
64 Torgau D B3
61 Torgelow D B5
6 Torgyle Bridge GB C4
57 Torhamn S C4
16 Torhout B B3
19 Torigni-sur-Vire F A5
39 Torija E B3
40 Toril E A1
74 Torino I A2
80 Toritto I D3
34 Torla E A2
57 Tormestorp S C2
71 Tórmini I C5
36 Tornada P B1
36 Tornado P B1
37 Tornavacas E A5
54 Tornby DK A2
59 Tornesch D B6
7 Torness GB C4
75 Torniella I C6
79 Tornimparte I A4
55 Torning DK B2
47 Tornio SF D12
99 Tornjoš CRO C4
39 Tornos E B5
32 Toro E C1
99 Törökbalint H A3
94 Törökszentmiklós H C4
99 Törökszentmiklós H A5
109 Toróni GR B5
98 Torony H A1
87 Torpè I B2
9 Torphins GB A5
12 Torpoint GB C3
56 Torpsbruk S B3
46 Torpshammer S E8
13 Torquay GB C4
32 Torquemada E B2
33 Torralba de Burgo E C4
38 Torralba de Calatrava E C3
36 Torrão P C2
79 Torre Annunziata I C5
81 Torre Canne I D4
44 Torre Cardela E B3
36 Torre das Vargens P B3
35 Torre de Capdella E A3
36 Torre de Coelheiros P C3
31 Torre de D. Chama P C3
44 Torre de Juan Abad E A3
43 Torre de la Higuera E B3
37 Torre de Miguel Sesmero E C4
31 Torre de Moncorvo P C3
37 Torre de Sta. Maria E B4
30 Torre del Bierzo E B4
39 Torre del Burgo E B3
44 Torre del Campo E B3
34 Torre del Español E B3
79 Torre del Greco I C5
75 Torre del Lago Puccini I C5
44 Torre del Mar E C2
83 Torre dell'Orso I A5
85 Torre di Faro I A4
31 Torre do Terranho P D3
34 Torre los Negros E C1
82 Torre Orsáia I A2
45 Torre-Pacheco E B6
74 Torre Péllice I B2
83 Torre Santa Susanna I A4
33 Torreblacos E C4
40 Torreblanca E A3
44 Torreblascopedro E A3
39 Torrebuceit E C4
38 Torrecaballeros E A2
44 Torrecampo E A2
39 Torrecilla E B4
38 Torrecilla de la Jara E C2
38 Torrecilla de la Orden E A1
32 Torrecilla del Pinar E C2
33 Torrecilla en Cameros E B4
37 Torrecillas de la Tiesa E B5
35 Torredembarra E B4
44 Torredonjimeno E B3
34 Torregrosa E B3
31 Torreira P D2
39 Torrejón de Ardoz E B3
38 Torrejón de Velasco E B3
39 Torrejón del Rey E B3
37 Torrejon el Rubio E B4
37 Torrejoncillo E B4
39 Torrelaguna E B3
33 Torrelapaja E C5
32 Torrelavega E A2
32 Torrelobatón E C1
38 Torrelodones E B3
80 Torremaggiore I C2
40 Torremanzanas E C2
37 Torremayor E C4
37 Torremegia E C4
82 Torremezzo di Falconara I B3
37 Torremocha E B4
44 Torremolinos E C2
76 Torrenieri I C1
40 Torrenostra E A3
78 Torrenova I B3
40 Torrente E B2
44 Torrenueva, *Ciudad Real* E A3
44 Torrenueva, *Granada* E C3
37 Torreorgaz E B4
44 Torreperogil E A3
44 Torres E B3
44 Torres-Cabrera E B2
39 Torres de la Alameda E B3
36 Torres Novas P B2
36 Torres Vedras P B1
32 Torresandino E C3
55 Tørreso DK C3
45 Torrevieja E B6
71 Torri d. Benaco I C5
83 Torricella I A4
6 Torridon GB C3
74 Torriglia I B4
38 Torrijos E C2
7 Torrish GB B5
76 Torrita di Siena I C1
36 Torroal P C2
7 Torroboll GB C4
35 Torroella de Montgri E A6
44 Torrox E C3
51 Torrskog S C3
52 Torsåker S B2
57 Torsås S C4
50 Torsby S B4
53 Torshälla S C2
57 Torskors S C4
54 Torslanda S A4
54 Torslev DK A2
54 Torsminde DK B1
99 Törtel H A4
9 Torthorwald GB C4
38 Tórtoles E B1
32 Tórtoles del Esgueva E C2
74 Tortona I B3
82 Tórtora I B2
79 Tortoreto Lido I A4
85 Tortorici I A3
34 Tortosa E C3
36 Tortozendo P A3
39 Tortuera E B5
39 Tortuero E B3
89 Toruń PL B4
54 Torup DK A2
56 Torup S C2
10 Torver GB A2
44 Torviscón E C3
65 Torzym PL A5
71 Toscolano I C5
93 Tosno R A12
35 Tossa de Mar E B5
26 Tosse F C2
51 Tøsse S D3
79 Tossicia I A4
59 Tostedt D B6
99 Tószeg H A5
90 Toszek PL C2
45 Totana E B5
56 Totebo S B5
20 Tôtes F B2
99 Tótkomlós H B5
15 Totland GB D1
48 Tøtlandsvik N B3
13 Totnes GB C4
98 Tótszerdahely H B1
13 Totton GB C6
31 Touça P C3
24 Toucy F A3
74 Touët F C2
66 Toul F C1
29 Toulon F C5
24 Toulon-sur-Allier F B3
25 Toulon-sur-Arroux F B4
27 Toulouse F C5
77 Touni CRO A5
16 Tourcoing F C3
19 Tourlaville F A4
110 Tourlis GR A2
16 Tournai B C3
21 Tournan-en-Brie F C3
27 Tournay F C4
21 Tournes F B5
27 Tournon-d'Agenais F B4
23 Tournon-St. Martin F B5
29 Tournon-sur-Rhône F A3
25 Tournus F B4
30 Touro E B2
31 Touro P D3
20 Tourouvre F C1
23 Tourriers F C5
23 Tours F A5
21 Tours-sur-Marne F B5
29 Tourves F C4
20 Toury F C2
27 Toutens F C5
31 Touvedo P C2
22 Touvois F B3
69 Toužim CZ A3
96 Tovačov CZ B3
101 Tovariševo YU A4
101 Tovarnik CRO A4
49 Tovdal N C5
102 Tovrljane YU C2
11 Tow Law GB A4
14 Towcester GB B1
9 Town Yetholm GB C5
106 Toxótai GR B2
97 Tplička SQ B4
30 Trabada E A3
30 Trabadelo E B4
31 Trabanca E C4
31 Trabanca P C4
31 Trabazos E C4
90 Trąbczyn PL A1
66 Traben-Trarbach D B3
84 Trabia I B2
73 Traboch A A4
21 Tracy-le-Mont F B3
71 Tradate I C3
56 Trädet S B2
36 Trafaria P C1
39 Tragacete E B5
109 Tragána GR C5
110 Traganon GR B2
108 Tragjas AL A1
69 Tragwein A C5
103 Traian RO C6
33 Traibuenas E B5
40 Traiguera E A3
21 Trainel F C4
96 Traisen A C1
96 Traiskirchen A C2
96 Traismauer A C1
68 Traitsching D B3
111 Trakhiá GR B4
53 Träkvista S C3
4 Tralee IRL B2
34 Tramacastilla E A2
36 Tramagal P B2
87 Tramariglio I B1
87 Tramatza I B1
70 Tramelan CH A2
72 Tramonti di Sopra I B2
5 Tramore IRL B4
74 Trana I A2
56 Tranås, *Jönköping* S A3
57 Tranås, *Kristianstad* S D2
31 Trancoso P D3
55 Tranebjerg DK C3
55 Tranekær DK D3
56 Tranemo S B2
9 Tranent GB C5
56 Trånghalla S B3
50 Trängslet S A4
80 Trani I C3
51 Trankil S C2
109 Tranóvalton GR A3
29 Trans-en-Provence F C5
50 Transtrand S A4
84 Trápani I A1
20 Trappes F C2
56 Traryd S C2
79 Trasacco I B4
43 Trasierra E A3
54 Träslövsläge S A5
31 Trasmiras E B3
32 Traspinedo E C2
73 Trata SL B4
71 Trauchgau D A5
69 Traun A C5
68 Traunstein D D3
68 Traureut D D3
51 Trävad S D4
60 Travemünde D B1
75 Traversétolo I B5
30 Traviesta E A2
100 Travnik BO B2
75 Travo I B4
10 Trawsfynydd GB C2
73 Trbovlje SL B5
101 Trbušani YU C5
24 Tréban F B3
96 Třebařov CZ B2
64 Trebbin D A3
60 Trebel D C2
64 Třebenice CZ C3
104 Trebenište MAK C2
18 Trébeurden F B2
96 Třebíč CZ B1
81 Trebinje BO B5
83 Trebisacce I B3
64 Trebitz D B2
73 Trebnje SL C4
69 Třeboň CZ B5
96 Třebovice CZ B2
64 Trebsen D B2
43 Trebujena E C3
85 Trecastagni I B4
70 Trecate I C3
76 Trecenta I A1
13 Tredegar GB B4
76 Tredózio I B1
73 Treffen A B3
25 Treffort F B5
63 Treffurt D B5
10 Trefriw GB B2
12 Tregaron GB A4
18 Trégastel F B2
71 Tregnago I C6
18 Tréguier F B2
18 Trégunc F C2
13 Treherbert GB B4
76 Tréia I C3
70 Treib CH B3
24 Treignac F C1
24 Treignat F B2
62 Trëis D C2
56 Trekanten S C5
105 Treklyano BG B4
23 Trélazé F A4
12 Trelech GB B3
27 Trélissac F A4
57 Trelleborg S D2
21 Trélon F A5
21 Trelou-sur-Marne F B4
20 Tremblay F C2
36 Tremés P B2
71 Tremezzo I C4
69 Třemošna CZ B4
34 Tremp E A3
97 Trenčianska Mitlice SQ C4
97 Trenčianska Turná SQ C4
97 Trenčianske Teplá SQ C4
97 Trenčianske Teplice SQ C4
97 Trenčín SQ C4
63 Trendelburg D B4
48 Trengereid N A2
26 Trensacq F B3
61 Trent D A4
71 Trento I B6
13 Treorchy GB B4
104 Trepča YU B2
83 Trepuzzi I A5
71 Trescore Balneário I C4
71 Tresenda I B5
76 Tresigallo I B1
99 Trešnjevac CRO C4
102 Trešnjevica YU C2
87 Tresnurághes I B1
33 Trespaderne E B3
96 Třešť CZ B1
76 Tréstina I C2
13 Tretower GB B4
29 Trets F C4
68 Treuchtlingen D C1
64 Treuen D C2
64 Treuenbrietzen D A2
49 Treungen N B5
44 Trevelez E C3
79 Trevi I A3
79 Trevi nel Lazio I B4
33 Treviana E B3
71 Treviglio I C4
78 Trevignano Romano I A3
72 Treviso I C2
25 Trévoux F C4
62 Treysa D C4
24 Trézelles F B3
71 Trezzo I C4
105 Trgoviste YU B4
96 Trhová Kamenice CZ B1
96 Trhové Myto SQ D3
69 Trhové Sviny CZ C5
30 Triacastela E B3
22 Triaize F B3
112 Triánta GR A2
21 Triaucourt F C6
67 Triberg D C4
61 Tribsees D A3
80 Tricárico I D3
83 Tricase I B5
72 Tricésimo I B3
27 Trie F C4
73 Trieben A A4
64 Triebes D C2
20 Triel F C3
61 Triepkendorf D B4
66 Trier D B2
72 Trieste I C3
66 Trieux F B1
108 Trifos GR C3
80 Triggiano I C3
60 Triglitz D B3
22 Trignac F A2
43 Trigueros E B3
32 Trigueros del Valle E C2
101 Trijebine YU C4
110 Trikala, *Korinthía* GR B3
109 Trikeri GR B5
109 Trikkala GR A4
109 Tríkkala, *Tríkkala* GR B3
100 Trilj CRO C1
3 Trillick GB B4
109 Trilofon GR A4
21 Trilport F C3
3 Trim IRL C5
11 Trimdon GB A4
15 Trimley GB C4
8 Trinafour GB B3
42 Trindade, *Beja* P B2
31 Trindade, *Bragança* P C3
97 Trinec CZ B4
15 Tring GB C2
87 Trinità d'Agultu I B1
80 Trinitápoli I C3
74 Trino I A3
31 Trinta P D3
74 Triora I C2
110 Tripi GR B3
110 Tripolis GR B3
79 Triponzo I A3
110 Tripótama GR B2
63 Triptis D C6
34 Triste E A2
60 Trittau D B1
79 Trivento I B5
70 Trivero I C3
82 Trivigno I A2
100 Trnava CRO A3
96 Trnava SQ C3
102 Trnjane YU C2
96 Trnovec SQ C3
100 Trnovo BO C3
19 Troarn F A5
67 Trochtelfingen D C5
52 Trödje S B3
55 Trœnse DK C3
31 Trofa P C2
73 Trofaiach A A5
46 Trofors N D6
100 Trogir CRO C1
51 Trøgstad N C2
80 Tróia I C2
85 Troina I B3
62 Troisdorf D C2
21 Troissy F B4
66 Troisvierges L A2
73 Trojane SL B4
91 Trojanów PL B5
55 Troldhede DK C1
51 Trollhätan S D3
74 Tromello I A3
49 Tromøy N C5
46 Tromsø N B9
31 Tronco P C3
46 Trondheim N E5
24 Tronget F B3
54 Trönninge, *Halland* S A5
56 Trönninge, *Halland* S C1
52 Trönö S A2
66 Tronville-en-Barrois F C1
74 Tronzano-Vercellese I A3
20 Trôo F D1
8 Troon GB C3
110 Trópaia GR B2
82 Tropea I C2
104 Tropojë AL B2
89 Tropy PL B5
53 Trosa S D3
21 Trosly F B3
68 Trossenfurt D B1
67 Trossingen D C4
68 Trostberg D C3
19 Trouville F A6
13 Trowbridge GB B5
106 Troyan BG A2
107 Troyanovo BG A5
21 Troyes F C5
81 Trpanj CRO A4
104 Trpezi YU B2
99 Trpinja CRO C3
96 Třsice CZ B3
97 Trstená SQ B5
100 Trstenci BO A2
104 Trstenik, *A. P. Kosovo* YU B2
102 Trstenik, *Srbija* YU C2
81 Trsteno CRO B4
96 Trstice SQ C3
96 Trstin SQ C3
32 Trubia E A1
30 Truchas E B4
105 Trudovets BG B5
37 Trujillanos E C4
37 Trujillo E B5
6 Trumpan GB C2
105 Trŭn BG B4
71 Trun CH B3
19 Trun F B6
103 Trunchovitsa BG C6
12 Truro GB C2
63 Trusetal D C5
103 Trüstenik BG C5
54 Trustrup DK B3
65 Trutnov CZ C5
106 Tryavna BG A3
91 Tryńcza PL C6
53 Tryserum S D2
50 Trysil N A3
88 Tryszczyn PL B3
91 Trzciana PL C5
88 Trzcianka PL B2
65 Trzciel PL A5
61 Trzcińsko Zdrój PL C5
61 Trzebiatów PL A6
88 Trzebielino PL A3
65 Trzebień PL B5
91 Trzebieszów PL B6
61 Trzebież PL B5
90 Trzebinia-Siersza PL C3
65 Trzebnica PL B7
65 Trzebnice PL B6
73 Trzec SL B5
89 Trzeciewiec PL B4
88 Trzemeszno PL C3
61 Trzemeszno-Lubuskie PL C6
73 Tržič SL B4
108 Tsamandas GR B2
109 Tsangarádha GR B5
109 Tsaritsáni GR B4
71 Tschagguns A A4
64 Tschernitz D B4
108 Tsepélovo GR B2
110 Tséria GR C3
108 Tsotilion GR A3
108 Tsouka, *Evritanía* GR C3
109 Tsoúka, *Fthiótis* GR C4
108 Tsoukaládes GR C2
105 Tsŭrkva BG B5
105 Tsŭrvaritsa BG B4
97 Ttzemeśnia PL B6
31 Tua P C3
2 Tuam IRL C3
4 Tuamgraney IRL B3
2 Tubbercurry IRL B3
58 Tubbergen NL C3
33 Tubilla E C3
67 Tübingen D C5
17 Tubize B C4
69 Tučapy CZ B5
100 Tučepi CRO C2
35 Tuchan F A5
64 Tucheim D A2
60 Tüchen D B3
64 Tuchlovice CZ C3
88 Tuchola PL B3
88 Tuchomie PL A3
88 Tuczno PL B2
49 Tuddal N B5
33 Tudela E B5
32 Tudelo de Duero E C2
10 Tudweiliog GB C1
103 Tufeni din Vale RO B5
20 Tuffé F C1
64 Tuhaň CZ C4
97 Tuhár SQ C5
6 Tuirnaig GB C3
93 Tukums LV B8
94 Tul'chyn U B8
87 Tula I B1
104 Tulare YU B3
94 Tulcea RO D8
29 Tulette F B3
90 Tuliszków PL A2
4 Tulla IRL B3
5 Tullamore IRL A4
27 Tulle F A5
53 Tullinge S C3
29 Tullins F A4
96 Tulln A C2
5 Tullow IRL B5
3 Tullyhogue GB B5
106 Tulovo BG A3
90 Tulowice PL C1
2 Tulsk IRL C3
53 Tumba S C3
9 Tummel Bridge GB B4
51 Tun S D3
56 Tuna, *Kalmar* S B5
52 Tuna, *Uppsala* S B4
52 Tuna Hästberg S B1
15 Tunbridge Wells GB C3
42 Tunes P B1
53 Tungelsta S C4
56 Tunnerstad S A3
76 Tuoro sul Trasimeno I C2
89 Tupadly PL C4
105 Tupale YU B3
101 Tupanari BO B3
65 Tuplice PL B4
99 Tura H A4
77 Turanj CRO C5
97 Turany SQ B5
100 Turbe BO B2
71 Turbenthal CH A3

103 Turburea RO B4
32 Turcia E B1
36 Turcifal P B1
103 Turcineşti RO A4
66 Turckheim F C3
94 Turda RO C5
38 Turégano E A3
90 Turek PL A2
95 Turgovishte BG E7
112 Turgut TR A1
95 Turgutlu TR G7
81 Turi I D4
102 Turija YU B2
40 Turis E B2
98 Türje H B2
94 Turka U B5
99 Túrkeve H A5
107 Türkgücü TR B5
67 Turkheim, *Baden-Württemberg* D C5
68 Türkheim, *Bayern* D C1
47 Turku SF F11
39 Turleque E C3
73 Turnau A A5
8 Turnberry GB C3
17 Turnhout B B4
62 Türnich D C1
96 Türnitz A D1
65 Turnov CZ C5
95 Tŭrnovo BG E6
103 Turnu Măgurele RO C5
44 Turón E C3
65 Turoszów PL C4
36 Turquel P B1
87 Turri I C1
7 Turriff GB C6
45 Turrilla E A4
83 Tursi I A3
70 Turtmann CH B2
97 Turzovka SQ B4
84 Tusa I B3
78 Tuscánia I A2
73 Tušilovic CRO C5
90 Tuszyn PL B3
11 Tutbury GB C4
101 Tutnjevac BO B3
61 Tutow D B4
67 Tuttlingen D D4
103 Tutuleşti RO B5
68 Tutzing D D2
47 Tuusniemi SF E14
11 Tuxford GB B5
31 Tuy E B2
106 Tŭzha BG A3
104 Tuzi YU B1
101 Tuzla BO B3
56 Tvaåker S B1
49 Tvedestrand N C5
54 Tversted DK A3
51 Tveta S C3
57 Tving S C4
97 Tvrdošovce SQ C4
106 Tvŭrditsa BG A3
90 Twardawa PL C2
90 Twardogóra PL B1
7 Twatt GB A5
9 Tweedshaws GB C4
59 Tweelbake D B5
17 Twello NL A6
14 Twenty GB B2
59 Twistringen D C5
12 Two Bridges GB C4
15 Twyford GB C1
13 Twyning GB A5
88 Tychówko PL B2
88 Tychowo PL B2
90 Tychy PL C3
14 Tydd St. Giles GB B3
50 Tyfors S B5
57 Tygelsjö S D1
46 Tyin N F4
54 Tylstrup DK A2
97 Tymbark PL B6
69 Týn n. Vltavou CZ B5
8 Tyndrum GB B3
96 Tynec n. Labem CZ A1
9 Tynemouth GB C6
50 Tyngsjö Kapell S B4
65 Tyniste n Orlici CZ C6
46 Tynset N E5
5 Tyrellspass IRL A4
53 Tyresö S C4
57 Tyringe S C2
49 Tyristrand N A7
48 Tysnes N A2
48 Tysse N A2
48 Tyssedal N A3
53 Tystberga S D3
48 Tysvær N B2
12 Tywardreath GB C3
10 Tywyn GB C1
112 Tzermiádhon, *Kriti* GR
58 Tzummarum NL B2

U

101 Ub YU B5
17 Ubbergen NL B5
55 Ubby DK C4
44 Ubeda E A3
73 Ubelbach A A5
67 Uberach D B4
66 Uberach F C3
71 Überlingen D A4
33 Ubidea E A4
80 Ubli CRO B3
104 Ubli YU B1
43 Ubrique E C4
67 Ubstadt-Weiher D B4
33 Ucero E C3
28 Uchaud F C3
25 Uchizy F B4
59 Uchte D C5
66 Uckange F B2
62 Uckerath D C2
15 Uckfield GB D3
39 Uclés E C4
85 Ucria I A3
103 Uda RO B5
103 Uda-Clococlov RO C5
77 Udbina CRO B5
56 Uddebo S B2
50 Uddeholm S B4
51 Uddevalla S D2
50 Uddheden S C3
17 Uden NL B5
63 Uder D B5
97 Udiča SQ B4
72 Udine I B3
105 Udovo MAK C4
99 Udvar H C3
61 Ueckermünde D B5
68 Uehlfeld D B1
58 Uelsen D C3
60 Uelzen D C1
59 Uetersen D B6
60 Uetze D C1
68 Uffenheim D B1
83 Ugento I B5
83 Uggiano la Chiesa I A5
44 Ugijar E C3
70 Ugine F C1
101 Uglejevik BO B4
100 Ugljane CRO C1
98 Ugod H A2
101 Ugrinovci YU B5
103 Ugŭrchin BG C5
96 Uherské Hradiště CZ B3
96 Uherský Brod CZ B3
67 Uhingen D C5
69 Uhlířské-Janovice CZ B6
69 Uhřiněves CZ A5
64 Uhyst D B4
6 Uig, *Skye* GB C2
6 Uig, *Western Isles* GB B1
58 Uitgeest NL C1
17 Uithoorn NL A4
58 Uithuizen NL B3
58 Uithuizermeeden NL B3
16 Uitkerke B B3
90 Ujazd, *Opole* PL C2
91 Ujazd, *Piotrków* PL B3
96 Ujezd CZ B3
99 Ujhartyán H A4
98 Ujpetre H C3
88 Ujście PL B2
99 Ujsolt H B4
99 Újszász H A5
33 Ujué E B5
93 Ukmerge LT C9
56 Ukna S A5
112 Ula TR A1
91 Ulan PL B6
91 Ulanów PL C6
107 Ulas TR B5
7 Ulbster GB B5
11 Ulceby Cross GB B6
81 Ulcinj YU C6
55 Uldum DK C2
49 Ulefoss N B6
45 Uleila del Campo E B4
55 Ulfborg DK B1
17 Ulft NL B6
98 Uljanik CRO C2
102 Uljma YU A2
6 Ullapool GB C3
56 Ullared S B1
48 Ullatun N B3
41 Ulldecona E A3
34 Ulldemolins E B3
48 Ullensvang N A3
55 Ullerslev DK C3
55 Ullerup DK D2
51 Ullervad S D4
99 Üllö H A4
50 Ullvi, *Kopparberg* S B6
53 Ullvi, *Västmanland* S C2
67 Ulm D C5
36 Ulme P B2
62 Ulmen-Meiserich D C1
100 Ulog BO C3
56 Ulricehamn S B2
69 Ulrichsberg A C4
96 Ulrichskirchen A C2
62 Ulrichstein D C4
53 Ulrika S D1
58 Ulrum NL B3
46 Ulsberg N E5
6 Ulsta, *Shetland Is.* GB
54 Ulsted DK A3
55 Ulstrup, *Vestsjællands Amt.* DK C3
54 Ulstrup, *Viborg Amt.* DK B2
17 Ulvenhout NL B4
10 Ulverston GB A2
46 Ulvik N F3
29 Ulzio (Oulx) I A5
72 Umag SL C3
76 Umbértide I C2
83 Umbriático I B3
101 Umčari YU B5
47 Umeå S E10
71 Umhausen A A5
101 Umka YU B5
62 Ummelm D B3
112 Umurlu TR B1
6 Unapool GB B3
34 Uncastillo E A1
51 Undenäs S D5
69 Úněšov CZ B4
69 Ungenach A C4
103 Ungheni RO B5
36 Unhais da Serra P A3
69 Unhošt CZ A5
88 Unichowo PL A3
96 Uničov CZ B3
90 Uniejów PL B2
88 Unieście PL A2
89 Unislaw PL B4
62 Unkel D C2
72 Unken A A2
62 Unna D B2
32 Unquera E A2
67 Unter Reichenbach D C4
67 Unter-Schönmattenwag D B4
67 Unter Schwarzach D D5
68 Unter Steinbach D B1
69 Unterach A D4
70 Unterägeri CH A3
71 Unterammergau D A6
68 Unterbaar D C1
68 Unterhaching D C2
70 Unteriberg CH A3
67 Unterkochen D C6
60 Unterlüß D C1
67 Untermünkheim D B5
67 Untermunstertal D D3
70 Unterschächen CH B3
68 Unterschwaningen D B1
96 Untersiebenbrunn A C2
63 Untersiemau D C5
69 Unterweißenbach A C5
68 Unterwössen D D3
68 Unterzell D B3
13 Upavon GB B6
9 Uphall GB C4
65 Úpice CZ C6
3 Upper Ballinderry GB B5
13 Upper Chapel GB A4
11 Upper Tean GB C4
5 Upperchurch IRL B3
51 Upphärad S D3
14 Uppingham GB B2
53 Upplands-Väsby S C3
52 Uppsala S C3
10 Upton, *Cheshire* GB B3
13 Upton, *Dorset* GB C5
13 Upton upon Severn GB A5
35 Ur F A4
104 Ur'e Shtrenjtë AL B1
67 Urach D C5
87 Uras I C1
65 Uraz PL B6
76 Urbánia I C2
76 Urbino I C2
24 Urçay F B2
38 Urda E C3
33 Urdax E A5
30 Urdilde E B2
34 Urdos F A2
108 Ure Vajgurorë AL A1
26 Urepel F C2
58 Urk NL C2
98 Úrkut H A2
95 Urla TR G7
5 Urlingford IRL B4
10 Urmston GB B3
71 Urnäsch CH A4
104 Uroševac YU B3
102 Urovika YU B3
45 Urracal E B4
34 Urries E A1
33 Urroz E B5
26 Urrugne F C2
68 Ursensollen D B2
56 Urshult S C3
67 Urspringen D B5
91 Ursus PL A4
89 Urszulewo PL C5
20 Ury F C3
95 Urziceni RO D7
87 Urzulei I B2
37 Usagre E C4
101 Ušće YU C5
61 Usedom D B4
66 Useldange L B1
87 Uséllus I C1
62 Usingen D C3
87 Usini I B1
13 Usk GB B5
48 Uskedal N B2
107 Üsküp TR B5
63 Uslar D B4
58 Usquert NL B3
87 Ussássai I C2
35 Ussat-les-Bains F A4
23 Ussé F A5
74 Usséglio I A2
28 Ussel, *Cantal* F A1
24 Ussel, *Corrèze* F C2
62 Usseln D B3
23 Usson-du Poitou F B5
28 Usson-en-Forez F A2
35 Usson-les-Bains F A5
46 Ustaoset N F4
26 Ustaritz F C2
64 Uštěk CZ C4
70 Uster CH A3
97 Ústi CZ B3
64 Ústí n. Labem CZ C4
96 Usti n Orlici CZ B2
101 Ustibar BO C4
101 Ustikolina BO C3
101 Ustipračă BO C4
88 Ustka PL A2
107 Ustrem BG A4
97 Ustroń PL B4
88 Ustronie Morskie PL A1
33 Usurbil E A4
99 Uszód H B3
48 Utåker N B2
34 Utebo E B2
69 Utery CZ B3
40 Utiel E B1
48 Utne N A3
17 Utrecht NL A5
43 Utrera E B4
34 Utrillas E C2
46 Utsjoki SF B13
48 Utstein kloster N B2
72 Uttendorf A A2
67 Uttenweiler D C5
55 Utterslev DK D4
68 Utting D C2
11 Uttoxeter GB C4
48 Utvik, *Rogaland* N B2
47 Uusikaarlepyy SF E11
47 Uusikaupunki SF F10
69 Uvaly CZ A5
49 Uvdal N A5
101 Uzdin YU A5
89 Uzdowo PL B6
18 Uzel F B3
24 Uzerche F C1
28 Uzès F B3
94 Uzhhorod U B5
94 Uzhok U B5
71 Uznach CH A3
108 Uznove AL A2
106 Uzundzhovo BG B3
107 Uzunköprü TR B4

V

57 Vä S D3
47 Vaajakoski SF E12
47 Vaasa SF E10
17 Vaasen NL A5
28 Vabre F C1
97 Vác H D5
63 Vacha D C4
99 Váchartyán H A4
56 Väckelsång S C3
52 Vad S B1
75 Vada I C5
103 Vădastra RO C5
52 Väddö S C4
51 Väderstad S D5
46 Vadheim N F2
38 Vadillo de la Sierra E B1
39 Vadillos E B4
48 Vadla N B3
75 Vado I B6
74 Vado Ligure I B3
53 Vadsbro S D2
46 Vadsø N A14
51 Vadstena S D5
54 Vadum DK A2
71 Vaduz FL A4
55 Væggerløse DK D4
105 Vafiokhóri GR C4
49 Vafos N C6
98 Vág H A2
108 Vagalat AL B2
56 Vaggeryd S B3
75 Vaǵlia I C6
80 Váglio Basilicata I D2
66 Vagney F C2
53 Vagnhärad S D3
31 Vagos P D2
112 Vái, *Kriti* GR
111 Váia GR B4
75 Vaiano I C6
103 Vaideeni RO A4
19 Vaiges F B5
67 Vaihingen D C4
25 Vaillant F A5
21 Vailly F B4
24 Vailly-sur Sauldre F A2
79 Vairano Scalo I B5
29 Vaison-la-Romaine F B4
25 Vaîte F A5
51 Väjern S D2
98 Vajszló H C3
105 Vakarel BG B5
105 Vaksevo BG B4
30 Val E B2
29 Val d'Esquières F C5
70 Val-d'Isère F C1
30 Val de San Lorenzo E B4
38 Val de Santo Domingo E B2
25 Val Suzon F A4
29 Val-Thorens F A5
36 Valada P B2
31 Valadares P C2
36 Valado P B1
102 Valakonje YU C2
23 Valance F C5
105 Valandovo MAK C4
109 Valanidha GR B4
97 Valaska SQ C5
97 Valaská Belá SQ C4
97 Valaská Dubová SQ B5
97 Valašská Polanka CZ B3
97 Valašske Klobouky CZ B4
97 Valašské Meziříčí CZ B3
51 Vålberg S C4
52 Valbo S B3
31 Valbom P C2
71 Valbondione I B4
29 Valbonnais F B4
32 Valbuena de Duero E C2
71 Valdagno I C6
39 Valdaracete E B3
93 Valday R A13
34 Valdealgorfa E C2
38 Valdecaballeros E C1
39 Valdecabras E B4
38 Valdecarros E B1
39 Valdeconcha E B4
43 Valdeflores E B3
32 Valdefresno E B1
39 Valdeganga E C5
38 Valdelacasa E B1
38 Valdelacasa de Tajo E C1
43 Valdelarco E B3
38 Valdelosa E A1
34 Valdeltormo E C3
38 Valdemanco de Esteras E D2
53 Valdemarsvik S D2
38 Valdemorillo E B2
38 Valdemoro E B3
39 Valdemoro Sierra E B5
37 Valdeobispo E A4
39 Valdeolivas E B4
44 Valdepeñas E A3
44 Valdepeñas de Jaēn E B3
32 Valdepiélago E B1
32 Valdepolo E B1
32 Valderas E B1
84 Valdérice I A1
34 Valderrobres E C3
32 Valderrueda E B2
32 Valdestillas E C2
32 Valdeteja E B1
37 Valdetorres E C4
39 Valdetorres de Jarama E B3
38 Valdeverdeja E C1
32 Valdevimbre E B1
74 Valdieri I B2
39 Valdilecha E B3
72 Valdobbiádene I C2
33 Valdocondes E C3
30 Valdoviño E A2
71 Valé CH B4
42 Vale de Açor, *Beja* P B2
36 Vale de Açor, *Portalegre* P B3
42 Vale de Agua P B1
31 Vale de Cambra P D2
36 Vale de Prazeres P A3
36 Vale de Reis P C2
42 Vale de Rosa P B2
36 Vale de Santarém P B2
42 Vale de Vargo P B2
36 Vale do Peso P B3
94 Valea lui Mihai RO C5
103 Valea Ursului RO B5
31 Valega P D2
75 Valéggio sul Mincio I A5
36 Valeiro P C2
31 Valença do Minho P B2
23 Valençay F A6
29 Valence, *Drôme* F B3
27 Valence, *Tarn-et-Garonne* F B4
28 Valence-d'Albigeois F B1
27 Valence-sur-Baise F C4
40 Valencia E B2
37 Valencia de Alcántara E B3
32 Valencia de Don Juan E B1
37 Valencia de las Torres E C4
42 Valencia de Mombuey P A2
43 Valencia del Ventoso E A3
16 Valenciennes F C3
29 Valensole F C4
78 Valentano I A2
70 Valentigney F A1
27 Valentine F C4
74 Valenza I A3
44 Valenzuela E B2
38 Valenzuela de Calatrava E D3
50 Våler, *Hedmark* N B2
49 Våler, *Østfold* N B7
39 Valera de Abajo E C4
39 Valera de Arriba E C4
110 Valeriános GR A1
48 Valestrand N B2
48 Valevåg N B2
76 Valfabbrica I C2
28 Valflaunes F C2
93 Valga EW B10
28 Valgorge F B3
70 Valgrisenche I C2
85 Valguarnera Caropepe I B3
36 Valhelhas P A3
110 Valimi GR A3
110 Valira GR B2
102 Văliug RO A3
101 Valjevo YU B4
17 Valkenburg NL C5
17 Valkenswaard NL B5
99 Valkó H A4
40 Vall d'Alba E A2
40 Vall de Uxo E B2
53 Valla, *Södermanland* S C2
40 Vallada E C2
30 Vallado E A4
32 Valladolid E C2
57 Vallåkra S D1
80 Vallata I C2
74 Vallauris F C2
56 Vallberga S C2
46 Valldal N E3
41 Valldemosa, *Mallorca* E
48 Valle N B4
79 Valle Castellana I A4
44 Valle de Abdalagis E C2
32 Valle de Cabuérniga E A2
37 Valle de la Serena E C5
37 Valle de Matamoros E C4
37 Valle de Santa Ana E C4
70 Valle Mosso I C3
84 Valledolmo I B2
87 Valledórie I B1
25 Valleiry F B5
32 Vallelado E C2
84 Vallelunga Pratameno I B2
62 Vallendar D C2
53 Vallentuna S C4
50 Vallerås S B4
28 Valleraugue F B2
87 Vallermosa I C1
22 Vallet F A3
10 Valley GB B1
35 Vallfogona E B4
71 Valli d. Pasúbio I C6
82 Vallo della Lucánia I A2
29 Valloire F A5
76 Vallombrosa I C1
28 Vallon-Pont-d'Arc F B3
25 Vallorbe CH B6
29 Vallouise F B5
35 Valls E B4
50 Vallset N B2
52 Vallvik S A3
34 Valmadrid E B2
29 Valmeinier F A5
38 Valmojado E B2
20 Valmont F B1
79 Valmontone I B3
70 Valmorel F C1
21 Valmy F B5
52 Valö S B4
19 Valognes F A4
36 Valonga P A2
44 Válor E C3
32 Valoria la Buena E C2
31 Valpaços P C3
70 Valpelline I C2
75 Valpiana I D5
98 Valpovo CRO C3
28 Valras-Plage F C2
29 Valréas F B3
28 Vals-les-Bains F B3
110 Valsamáta GR A1
70 Valsavarenche I C2
55 Vålse DK D4
37 Valsequillo E C5
25 Valsonne F C4
72 Valstagna I C1
39 Valtablado del Rio E B4
110 Valtesiniko GR B3
110 Valtétsi GR B3
96 Valtice CZ C2
32 Valtiendas E C3
33 Valtierra E B5
47 Valtimo SF E14
109 Váltoi GR A4
76 Valtopina I C2
71 Valtorta I C4
107 Váltos GR B4
70 Valtournenche I C2
37 Valverde de Burguillos E C4
37 Valverde de la Vera E A5
32 Valverde de la Virgen E B1
37 Valverde de Leganés E C4
43 Valverde de Llerena E A4
37 Valverde de Mérida E C4
43 Valverde del Camino E B3
37 Valverde del Fresno E A4
39 Valverde del Júcar E C4
65 Vamberk CZ C6
55 Vamdrup DK C2
50 Våmhus S A5
47 Vammala SF F11
112 Vámos, *Kriti* GR
99 Vamosgyörk H A4
97 Vámosmikola H D4
94 Vámospercs H C4
96 Vámosszabadi H D3
105 Vamvakófiton GR C5
110 Vamvakou, *Lakonía* GR B3
109 Vamvakoú, *Lárisa* GR B4
21 Vanault-les-Dames F C5
55 Vandel DK C2
66 Vandières F C2
24 Vandnesse F B3
72 Vandóies (Vintl) I B1
51 Vänersborg S D3
50 Vangsås N B2
47 Vännäs S E9
47 Vännäsby S E9
22 Vannes F A2
52 Vannsätter S A2
50 Vansbro S B5
48 Vanse N C3
57 Vanstad S D2
97 Vanyarc H D5
27 Vaour F B5
71 Vaprio d'Adda I C4
104 Vaqarr AL C1
42 Vaqueiros P B2
51 Vara S D3
29 Varacieux F A4
22 Varades F A3
29 Varages F C4
48 Varaldsøy N A2
70 Varallo Sésia I C3
75 Varano de Melegari I B5
98 Varaždin CRO B1
98 Varaždinske Mučna CRO B1
98 Varazdinske Toplice CRO B1
74 Varazze I B3
54 Varberg S A5
110 Várda GR A2
55 Varde DK C1
46 Vardø N A15
59 Varel D B5
111 Vareléi GR A5
48 Vårenes N B2
20 Varengeville F B1
71 Varenna I B4
21 Varennes-en-Argonne F B6
25 Varennes-le-Grand F B4
24 Varennes-lès-Nevers F A3
25 Varennes-St. Sauveur F B5
24 Varennes-sur-Allier F B3
100 Vareš BO B3
70 Varese I C3
75 Varese Ligure I B4
56 Vårgårda S A1
32 Vargas E A3
36 Vargas P B2
51 Vargon S D3
48 Varhaug N C2
112 Vári GR E1
112 Varídi GR E1
74 Varigotti I B3
27 Varilhes F C5
97 Varin SQ B4
51 Väring S D4
31 Váriz P C4
47 Varkaus SF E13
111 Várkiza GR B4
51 Värmlands Bro S C4
51 Värmskog S C3
95 Varna BG E7
101 Varna YU B4
56 Värnamo S B3
51 Varnhem S D4
64 Varnsdorf CZ C4
54 Värö S A5
100 Varoška Rijeka CRO A1
98 Városlöd H A2
98 Várpalota H A3
21 Varreddes F B3
29 Vars F B5
75 Varsi I B4
17 Varsseveld NL B6
53 Vårsta S C3
110 Vartholomion GR B2
56 Vartofta S A2
107 Varvara BG A5
109 Varvára GR A5
102 Varvarin YU C2
110 Varvásaina GR B2
51 Vårvik S C3
98 Várvölgy H B2
75 Varzi I B4
31 Varzjelas P D2
70 Varzo I B3
24 Varzy F A3
50 Väsa S A5
99 Vasad H A4
110 Vasarás GR B3
94 Vásárosnamény H B5
51 Väse S C4
101 Vašica YU A4
106 Vasil Levski BG A3
110 Vasiláki GR B2
109 Vasiliká, *Khalkidhikí* GR A5
111 Vasilikón GR A4
110 Vasilikón, *Akhaia* GR A2
108 Vasilikón, *Ioánnina* GR A2
110 Vasilikón, *Messinía* GR B2
110 Vasilikós GR B1
99 Vaskút H B4
94 Vaslui RO C7
29 Vassieux-en-Vercors F B4
108 Vassiki GR C2
109 Vassilika GR C5
56 Vassmolösa S C5
19 Vassy F B5
50 Västanvik S B5
50 Väster Myckeläng S A5
53 Västerås S C2
52 Västerby S B1
52 Västerfärnebo S C2
53 Västerhaninge S C4
53 Vastermo S C2
56 Västervik S B5
79 Vasto I A5
51 Västra Ämtervik S C4
56 Västra-Bodarne S B1
57 Västra Karup S C1
98 Vasvár H A1
98 Vaszar H A2
98 Vát H A1
24 Vatan F A1
109 Vaterón GR A3
112 Vathi, *Astipália* GR C2
105 Váthi, *Kilkís* GR C4
111 Vathi, *Voíotía* GR A4
110 Váthia GR C3
109 Vathilakkon GR A4
109 Vathilakkos GR A3
112 Vathis GR B2
105 Vathitopos GR C5
49 Vatnås N B6
52 Vätö S C4
108 Vatokhórion GR A3
108 Vátos GR C2
94 Vatra Dornei RO C6
21 Vatry F C5
52 Vattholma S B3
71 Vättis CH B4
21 Vauchassis F C4
66 Vaucouleurs F C1
21 Vaudoy F C4
25 Vaugneray F C4
48 Vaulen N C2
29 Vaulnaveys-le-Haut F A4
70 Vaulruz CH B1
21 Vaulx Vraucourt F A3
24 Vaumas F B3
23 Vausseroux F B4
29 Vauvenargues F C4
28 Vauvert F C3
66 Vauvillers F D2
109 Vávdhos GR A5
93 Vawkavysk BL D9
53 Vaxholm S C4
56 Växjö S C3
57 Våxtorp S C2
111 Váyia GR A4
27 Vayrac F B5
97 Važec SQ B5
57 Veberöd S D2
63 Vechelde D A5
59 Vechta D C5
38 Vecinos E B1
53 Veckholm S C3
99 Vecsés H A4
48 Vedavågen N B2
56 Veddige S B1
55 Vedersø DK B1
71 Vedeseta I C4
53 Vedevåg S C1
30 Vedra E B2
51 Vedum S D3
58 Veendam NL B3
17 Veenendaal NL A5
58 Veenwouden NL B2
32 Vega E A1
30 Vega de Espinareda E B4
32 Vega de Infanzones E B1
32 Vega de Liébana E A2
32 Vega de Pas E A3
30 Vega de Valcarce E B4
32 Vega de Valdetronco E C1
30 Vegadeo E A3
32 Vegamian E B1
30 Vegarienza E B4
49 Vegårshei N C5
37 Vegas de Coria E A4
37 Vegas de Domingo Rey E A4
32 Vegas del Condado E B1
56 Vegby S B2
49 Veggli N A6
17 Veghel NL B5
83 Véglie I A4
39 Veguillas E B3
49 Vegusdal N C5
49 Veikåker N A6
63 Veilsdorf D C5
56 Veinge S C2
73 Veitsch A A5
67 Veitshöchheim D B5
57 Vejbystrand S C1
55 Vejen DK C2
43 Vejer de la Frontera E C4
55 Vejle DK C2
64 Vejprty CZ C3
96 Vel'ká Mača SQ C3
97 Vel'ká Maňa SQ C4
96 Vel'ké Čanikovce SQ C3
96 Vel'ké Leváre SQ C3
97 Vel'ké Rovné SQ B4
97 Vel'ké Uherce SQ C4
96 Vel'ké Zálužie SQ C3
96 Vel'ke' Kostol'any SQ C3
97 Vel'ký Blh. SQ C6
97 Vel'ký Cetin SQ C4
97 Vel'ký Krtiš SQ C5
80 Vela Luka CRO B3
38 Velada E B2
51 Velanda S D3
111 Velanidia GR C4
108 Velaóra GR B3
38 Velayos E B2
62 Velbert D B1
68 Velburg D B2
73 Velden A B4
68 Velden, *Bayern* D B2
68 Velden, *Bayern* D C3
17 Veldhoven NL B5
45 Velefique E B4
62 Velen D B1
99 Velence H A3
73 Velenje SL B5
98 Velesevec CRO C1
69 Velešin CZ C5
104 Velešta MAK C2
109 Velestinon GR B4
45 Velez Blanco E B4
44 Vélez de Benaudalla E C3
44 Vélez-Málaga E C2
45 Vélez Rubio E B4
77 Veli Lošinj CRO B4
98 Velika CRO C2
110 Velika GR B2
104 Velika YU B1
102 Velika Drenova YU C2
98 Velika Gorica CRO C1
98 Velika Grdevac CRO C2
102 Velika Greda YU A2
100 Velika Ilova BO B2
77 Velika Kladusa BO A5
100 Velika Kopanica CRO A3
101 Velika Krsna YU B5
104 Velika Krusa YU B2
98 Velika Mučna YU B1
101 Velika Obarska BO B4
98 Velika Pisanica CRO C2
102 Velika Plana, *Srbija* YU B2
102 Velika Plana, *Srbija* YU C2
102 Velika Vrbica YU B3
98 Velika Zdenci CRO C2
102 Velike Bonjince YU C3
73 Velike Lašče SL C4
102 Veliki Gaj YU A2
102 Veliki Izvor YU C3
102 Veliki Popović YU B2
102 Veliki Šiljegavac YU C2
93 Velikiye Luki R B12
101 Veliko Gradište YU B5
102 Veliko Laole YU B2
102 Veliko Selo YU B2
102 Veliko Središte YU A2
73 Veliko Trgovišće CRO B5
32 Velilla E B2
39 Velilla de S. Antonio E B3
110 Velimákhi GR B2
107 Velimeşe TR B5
106 Velingrad BG A1
104 Velipojë AL C1
77 Veljun CRO A5
96 Velká CZ C3
96 Velká Bites CZ B2
69 Velka Dobra CZ A5
68 Velka Hled'scbe CZ B3
96 Velká Losenice CZ B1
97 Velká Polom CZ B4
96 Velké Bystřice CZ B3
96 Velké Heraltice CZ B3
97 Velké Karlovice CZ B4
96 Velké Losiny CZ A3
96 Velké Meziříčí CZ B2
96 Velké Nemčice CZ B2
96 Velké Pavlovice CZ C2
69 Velky Bor CZ B4
96 Velky Ujezd CZ B3
73 Vellach A B4
60 Vellahn D B1
67 Vellberg D B5
78 Velletri I B3
57 Vellinge S D1
39 Vellisca E B4
32 Velliza E C2
111 Véllon GR B3
111 Vélos GR A5
17 Velp NL A5
63 Velpke D A5
17 Velsen NL A4
61 Velten D C4
64 Veltrusy CZ C4
64 Velvary CZ C4
109 Velvendós GR A4
54 Vemb DK B1
49 Veme N A7
99 Véménd H B3
55 Vemmedrup DK C5
56 Vena S B4
86 Venaco F B2
79 Venafro I B5
25 Venarey-les-Laumes F A4
74 Venaria Reale I A2
74 Venasca I B2
101 Venčane YU B5
74 Vence F C2
36 Venda Nova, *Coimbra* P A2
36 Venda Nova, *Leiria* P B2
28 Vendargues F C2
36 Vendas Novas P C2
26 Vendays Montalivet F A2
52 Vendel S B3
21 Vendeuvre-sur-Barse F C5
16 Vendin-le-Vieil F C2
23 Vendœuvres F B6
20 Vendôme F D2
97 Vendryně CZ B4
107 Venets BG A4
72 Venézia I C2
32 Venialbo E C1
50 Venjan S B4
17 Venlo NL B6
106 Venna GR B3
49 Vennesla N C4
80 Venosa I D2
17 Venraij NL B5
17 Venray NL B5
71 Vent A B5
34 Venta de Arraco E A2
44 Venta de los Santos E A3
40 Venta del Moro E B1
38 Venta del Obispo E B1
30 Ventanueva E A4
33 Ventas de Cervera E C5
44 Ventas de Huelma E B3
44 Ventas de Zafarraya E C2
29 Ventavon F B4
74 Ventimíglia I C2
15 Ventor GB D1
33 Ventosa de la Sierra E C4
33 Ventosilla E C4
93 Ventspils LV B7
75 Venturina I C5
86 Venzolasca F B2
72 Venzone I B3
98 Vép H A1
45 Vera E B5
42 Vera Cruz P A2
33 Vera de Bidasoa E A5
33 Vera de Moncayo E C5
70 Verbania I C3
21 Verberie F B3
82 Verbicaro I B2
70 Verbier CH B2
70 Vercel F A1
74 Vercelli I A3
29 Vercheny F B4
29 Verclause F B4
46 Verdalsøra N E5
59 Verden D C6
109 Verdhikoúsa GR B3
23 Verdille F C4
35 Verdú E B4
66 Verdun, *Meuse* F B1
27 Verdun, *Tarn-et-Garonne* F C5
25 Verdun-sur-le-Doubs F B5
99 Veresegyház H A4
27 Verfeil F C5
110 Vérga GR B3
75 Vergato I B6
40 Vergel E C3
70 Vergeletto CH B3
35 Verges E A6
70 Vergiate I C3
27 Vergt F A4
93 Verhnjadvinsk BL C10
29 Vérignon F C5
31 Verín E C3
67 Veringenstadt D C5
62 Verl D B3
21 Vermand F B4
36 Vermelha P B1
24 Vermenton F A3
23 Vern-d'Anjou F A4
71 Vernago (Vernagt) I B5
74 Vernante I B2
23 Vernantes F A5
97 Vernár SQ C6
75 Vernasca I B4
70 Vernayaz CH B2
64 Verneřice CZ C4
27 Vernet F C5
24 Vernet-la-Varenne F C3
35 Vernet-les-Bains F A5
21 Verneuil F B4
20 Verneuil-sur-Avre F C1
75 Vérnio I B6
83 Vérnole I A5
20 Vernon F B2
29 Vernoux-en-Vivarais F B3
97 Verőce H D5
109 Véroia GR A4
75 Verolanuova I A5
79 Veroli I B4
21 Véron F C4
71 Verona I C6
97 Verpelét H D6
70 Verrès I C2
23 Verrières F B5
25 Verry-sous-Salmaise F A4
20 Versailles F C3
71 Versam CH B4
99 Verseg H A4
62 Versmold D A3
25 Versoix CH B6
27 Verteillac F A4
99 Vértesacsa H A3
98 Vértesszölös H A3
24 Vertolaye F C3
22 Vertou F A3
21 Vertus F C5
17 Verviers B C5
21 Vervins F B4
13 Verwood GB C6
105 Véryi GR D5
109 Veryina GR A4
73 Veržej SL B6
74 Verzuolo I B2
21 Verzy F B5
86 Vescovato F B2
98 Vése H B2
96 Veseli CZ C3
69 Veselí n. Lužnici CZ B5
107 Veselie BG A5
25 Vésenaz CH B6
74 Vésime I B3
20 Vesly F B2
25 Vesoul F A6
74 Vespolate I A3
56 Vessigebro S C1
48 Vestbygd, *Vest-Agder* N C3
71 Vestenanova I C6
55 Vester Nebel DK C2
55 Vester Vedsted DK C1
54 Vesterøhavn DK A3
54 Vestervig DK B1
49 Vestfossen N B6
50 Vestmarka N C2
71 Vestone I C5
98 Veszprém H A2
56 Vetlanda S B4
98 Vetovo CRO C2
78 Vetralla I A3
25 Vetraz F B6
106 Vetren BG A2
106 Vetren, *Stara Zagora* BG A3
69 Větřni CZ C5
96 Vetrny Jenikov CZ B1
70 Vétroz CH B2
64 Vetschau D B4
75 Vetto I B5
78 Vetulónia I A1
20 Veules-les-Roses F B1
20 Veulettes-sur-Mer F B1
49 Veum N B5
16 Veurne B B2
104 Vevčani MAK C2
96 Veverskä Bityška CZ B2
70 Vevey CH B1
108 Vévi GR A3
70 Vex CH B2
29 Veynes F B4
24 Veyre-Monton F C3
25 Veyrier F C6
24 Vézelay F A3
66 Vézelise F C2
28 Vézenobres F B3
28 Vézins F B1
71 Vezza di Óglio I B5
86 Vezzani F B2
71 Vezzano I B6
75 Vezzano sul Cróstolo I B5
42 Via Gloria P B2
75 Viadana I B5
33 Viana E B4
36 Viana Alentejo P C2
30 Viana del Bollo E B3
31 Viana do Castelo P C2
66 Vianden L B2
17 Vianen NL B5
75 Viaréggio I C5
82 Vibo Valéntia I C3
54 Viborg DK B2
20 Vibraye F C1
26 Vic-en-Bigorre F C4
27 Vic-Fézensac F C4

W